Beginnings & Beyond

FOURTH EDITION

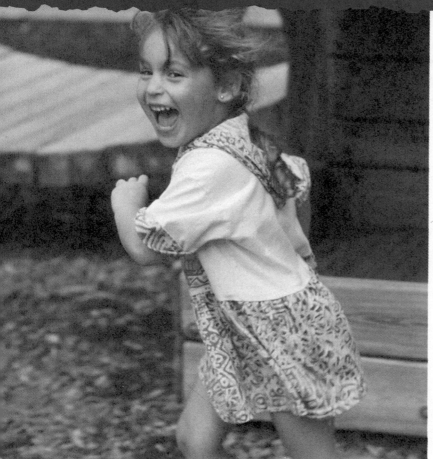

Ann Miles Gordon
Executive Director
National Association of
  Episcopal Schools
New York, New York

Kathryn Williams Browne
Cañada College
Redwood City, California
DeAnza College
Cupertino, California

Guest Editors
James L. Hymes, Jr.
Louise Derman-Sparks
Douglas R. Powell
Jim Greenman
Elizabeth Jones
Jerlean Daniel

Contributors
Karen McLaughlin
Connecticut College
New London, Connecticut
and
Gay Spitz
Salinas, California

Delmar Publishers

I(T)P™

Albany • Bonn • Boston • Cincinnati • Detroit • London • Madrid • Melbourne
Mexico City • New York • Pacific Grove • Paris • San Francisco • Singapore • Tokyo
Toronto • Washington

NOTICE TO THE READER

Dedication

For my mother, Evelyn Kearney Lacock, Eileen Allen, and Jay Thorp.
May I always reflect your influence with grace and affection.—*AMG*

This one's for Marty.—*KWB*

COPYRIGHT © 1995
By Delmar Publishers
a division of International Thomson Publishing Inc.
The ITP logo is a Trademark under license
Printed in the United States of America.

For more information, contact:

Delmar Publishers
3 Columbia Circle, Box 15015
Albany, New York 12212-5015

International Thomson Publishing Europe
Berkshire House 168–173
High Holborn
London WC1V7AA
England

Thomas Nelson Australia
102 Dodds Street
South Melbourne, 3205
Victoria, Australia

Nelson Canada
1120 Birchmount Road
Scarborough, Ontario
Canada M1K 5G4

International Thomson Editores
Campos Eliseos 385, Piso 7
Col Polanco
11560 Mexico D F Mexico

International Thomson Publishing GmbH
Königswinterer Strasse 418
53227 Bonn
Germany

International Thomson Publishing Asia
221 Henderson Road
#05–10 Henderson Building
Singapore 0315

International Thomson Publishing–Japan
Hirakawacho Kyowa Building, 3F
2-2-1 Hirakawacho
Chiyoda-ku, Toyko 102
Japan

All rights reserved. No part of this work covered by the copyright hereon may be reproduced or used in any form or by any means—graphic, electronic, or mechanical, including photocopying, recording, taping, or information storage and retrieval systems—without the written permission of the publisher.

1 2 3 4 5 6 7 8 10 XXX 01 00 99 98 97 96 95

Library of Congress Cataloging-in-Publication Data

Gordon, Ann Miles.
    Beginnings & beyond : foundations in early childhood education / Ann Gordon, Kathryn Williams Browne : contributor, Karen McLaughlin . . . [et al.].—4th ed.
        p.   cm.
    Includes bibliographical references and index.
    ISBN 0-8273-7271-X
    1. Early childhood education. 2. Early childhood education—Curricula. 3. Child development. I. Browne, Kathryn Williams. II. Title.
    LB1139.23.G67   1995
    372.21—dc20   95-18928
                                                              CIP

Delmar Staff
Administrative Editor: Jay Whitney
Associate Editor: Erin J. O'Connor
Art & Design Coordinator: Tim Conners
Production Manager: Karen Leet

Contents

Preface

As classroom teachers we have often used Pat Hutchin's wordless book *Changes! Changes!* (MacMillan, 1971). While revising the fourth edition of *Beginnings and Beyond: Foundations in Early Childhood Education,* we were reminded of that delightful book and felt a kinship with its message. The two characters in the story are called upon to rearrange their original building, which was made of blocks, several times over. They form a new version when circumstances dictate that it is time for a change. The original purpose remains the same, as does the substance; only the structure is altered. So it is with this edition of *Beginnings and Beyond.*

What changes and what stays the same are decided by people and circumstances. As early childhood educators, active in the field and involved in teaching, we have our own ideas of what we want to keep and what we want to change. So do the people who have to used the book previously as well as those who have not yet adopted *Beginnings and Beyond* for their classes. Changes, therefore, come from what we hear and learn is current and useful for teaching about young children.

New users as well as old friends will appreciate that we maintain our original purpose: "to promote the competence and effectiveness of new teachers through a presentation of basic knowledge, skills, attitudes, and philosophies . . . based on the premise that new teachers must have opportunities to learn fundamental skills as they begin their teaching experience." That remains our primary commitment.

Changes have occurred with each of the Guest Editorials and Focus Boxes. New contributors bring diverse opinions and perspective to the students' learning, and we hope these voices from other early childhood educators provoke discussion and reflection.

Why change? If a book is serving a useful purpose, why do we alter it? As authors, we are aware that the moment the book is in print, there is something else to add, new data to include, or an issue that has suddenly become national news. Each edition provides us with the opportunity to make necessary updates, but more than that, reflects the vitality, life, and energy of the field of early childhood education.

Why some changes and not others? Each change is weighed carefully. We walk that fine line between raising issues that a beginning teacher should be familiar with and an in-depth discourse on a given subject. That is a tension that will always be present in a text that serves the purposes of *Beginnings and Beyond.* Some of the changes obviously reflect our own biases as teacher educators.

Why not add more curriculum to all the chapters? Why not take out all the curriculum? Since *Beginnings and Beyond* is used in a variety of introductory courses, it is designed to meet the requirements for the majority of those classes. Some instructors want and need more on curriculum areas; others require less since a separate curriculum course is available for their students. Again, we strike a middle ground. As teachers, it is natural for us to use curriculum examples and activities to demonstrate a point about how children learn and how teachers teach. We are heartened by the creative use many instructors make of this book in the wide variety of courses for which it is used.

Chapters 1 and 15 serve as bookends for the text, reflecting the continuum from past to future. We believe that you should begin to teach about early childhood by placing it in its historical context so that students will have a perspective about the field of education and the depth of history underlying the early childhood movement. The last chapter raises today's critical issues, the ones students will read about in today's newspapers, and repeats the same themes of early childhood cited in the first chapter.

Like the building blocks in *Changes! Changes!*, a revision allows us to expand and modify *Beginnings and Beyond* to meet the challenges of educating today's student for the twenty-first century. It is a world that requires changes: changing your opinion, changing your mind, changing attitudes, and perhaps even changing the course you are now on. We hope the changes we have made and the issues we have raised will help you transform tomorrow's teachers into competent and caring early childhood professionals.

NEW FEATURES OF THE FOURTH EDITION

As we prepare to enter a new millennium, we are aware of a changing and shifting world and its influence on our life in the United States. Some of the changes in this revision of *Beginnings and Beyond* reflect this time of flux in ways which are important to early childhood educators. A thorough assessment of each chapter has also resulted in the addition of several pedagogical devices to make the material more accessible to the student. The most significant changes and additions to this edition are:

- A feature entitled "Our Diverse World" will highlight the chapter content throughout the text which relates to cultural diversity, antibias curriculum, and children with special needs. A footnote at the bottom of the page provides additional information that will enrich the student's understanding of the diversity of the children they will teach. Demographics and statistics found in many parts of the text, but particularly in Chapter 15, dramatize the need to train teachers who are culturally sensitive to children and their families whose beliefs and values may differ from their own. By highlighting this material, we enhance the multicultural focus begun in previous editions and emphasize the need to help students learn that the children they teach will have to interact in new and different ways with others in a world grown small. Additional material on issues of equity and diversity are found throughout the book.

- The addition, particularly in Chapter 4, of the impact of the Russian psychologist, Lev Vygotsky, as a pioneer in seeing children in a larger social and cultural context than other theorists is an important new feature. Students will learn how his work influences our understanding of children's language, play, and social creative development and how Vygotsky's theory helps us look at the cultural diversity issues of such great importance today.

- Another challenge to our preconceived notion of how children learn are the early childhood programs in Reggio Emilia, Italy. We include more information on this world-renowned approach in the chapters dealing with curriculum planning, the role of the teacher and the way in which children learn. Students will have a greater understanding of the influence of the Reggio Emilia schools on the programs and philosophy of early childhood education in the 1990s.

- The new Focus Box contributors add strength to the chapters by speaking more directly to issues related to the chapter content. Topics bring additional information, such as working with children with AIDS, portfolio assessment, children and technology, and multicultural perceptions. There is now a Focus Box in every chapter.

● The look of a book is important. The graphics must catch the student's interest, expand their knowledge, and bring the world of early childhood into the readers' experience. The addition of full-color photographs is a great enhancement to this edition.

● The last chapter, "Issues and Trends in Early Childhood Education," has been modified to reflect social and political realities of the day, with particular emphasis on demographics and changing populations.

ABOUT THE AUTHORS

Ann Gordon has been in the field of early childhood for more than 30 years as a teacher of young children, a teacher of parents, and a teacher of college students. She has taught in laboratory schools, church-related centers, and private and public preschool and kindergarten programs. While at Stanford, Ann was at the Bing Nursery School for 11 years and a Lecturer in the Psychology Department. For ten years she also served as an adjunct faculty member in four different colleges, teaching the full gamut of early childhood courses. Today, Ann is the executive director of the National Association of Episcopal Schools, where her commitment and interest in education stretches the full age range from infancy through high school. More than 1,100 early

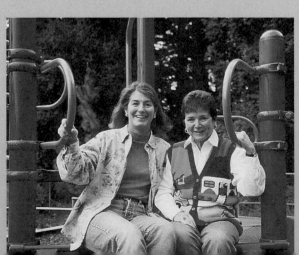

childhood programs are a part of her network. Ann is the mother of two grown children.

Kathryn Williams Browne, most recently a lecturer in the Early Childhood Education Department of Canada College, has been a teacher of young children for 20 years and a teacher of college students and parents for 15 years. Her work with children includes nursery school, parent cooperatives, full-day child care, pre-kindergarten and bilingual preschools, and kindergarten and first grade. Kate's background in child development research led her to choose early childhood education, for to truly understand child development one needs to *be* with children. While a Head Teacher at Bing Nursery School and Lecturer with Stanford University, Kate developed a professional relationship with Ann, which blossomed into work in teacher- and parent-education. Additionally *Beginnings and Beyond* now has the flavor of a current parent; Kate's two children are in elementary school. The balance of career and family, of work *with* children and *for* children, and of the special challenges of early childhood as a professional field give this edition a unique flavor.

Ann and Kate are co-authors of "Guiding Young Children In a Diverse Society." (Allyn & Bacon, 1996).

ACKNOWLEDGMENTS

Photographs communicate an immediacy about children and their environments. There are a wide variety of settings and age groups represented from all over the country. For this truly representative sample, we thank M. Barbee Pleasant of Hampton Va.; Michael Eanes of the American Montessori Society; and Dr. Sergio Spaggieri of Reggio Emilia, Italy.

Reviewers who have participated in this revision are Cleona R. Bazzy, Walla Walla College, College Place, Washington and Karen L. Peterson, Ph.D., Washington State University, Vancouver, Washington. We are grateful for their timely and candid evaluations and their constructive suggestions.

Unsolicited reviews, especially from students, are particularly helpful as well as enjoyable. Elaine Lang, of Belleville Area College in Red Bud, Ill., wrote that her students took exception with the order in which the ten essentials of successful teaching were listed (Chapter 5) and, after some lively discussion, suggested changes. We agreed that the students' perceptions and rationale were compelling and have altered the list accordingly. We are grateful to her students for helping us remember that as teachers we are always learners and that from our students we are taught!

We are beholden to Guest Editors James L. Hymes, Jr., Louise Derman-Sparks, Douglas R. Powell, Jim Greenman, Elizabeth Jones, and Jerlean Daniel for sharing their insights and vision and adding new voices to the text. Focus Box contributors Mary Stuart Gile, Monica Bassett, Gretchen Buchenholz, Laura E. Berk, Miriam Silver, Janet Gonzales-Mena, Elizabeth Crary, Yvonne Ricketts, Rebecca New, Gayle Mendez, Edgar Klugman, Paula J. Carreiro, Bernadette Caruso-Davis, and Cary A. Buzzelli earn our everlasting thanks for saying yes to an abbreviated deadline and for coming through with contributions that add depth to this edition.

A special word of thanks goes to our good friend and long-time colleague, Karen McLaughlin of Connecticut College, whose research of new material and contributions to Our Diverse World has been invaluable. We are particularly grateful for her insightful observations and questions, which have made this book stronger. Our long association with Delmar publishers has now weathered four revisions. We have been particularly appreciative of a team approach for this edition. Johnny Ross merits praise for keeping a cool head, a warm fax, and a ready wit. The Gordon and Browne households continue to be places from which we thankfully draw support and encouragement.

Delmar Publishers' Online Services
To access Delmar on the World Wide Web, point your browser to:
http://www.delmar.com/delmar.html
To access through Gopher: gopher://gopher.delmar.com
(Delmar Online is part of "thomson.com", and Internet site with information on more
than 30 publishers of the International Thomson Publishing organization.)
For more information on our products and services:
email: info@delmar.com
or call 800-347-7707

GUEST EDITORIAL
Childcare, Then and Now:
An Interview with Dr. James Hymes, Jr.

Q: Dr. Hymes, you have been active in the child-care field for over 50 years. When you started at the Kaiser Shipyard Center in the 1940s, how many children did you start out with?

Dr. Hymes: Our main concern, and we were scared to death, was that we couldn't get enough children. It was hard because the notion of turning a child over to somebody made many of these people think of the county orphanage. For example, on opening day we fully expected from 300 to 500 children and had the whole staff of both centers working, and 37 children showed up! Our main commitment was we were going to serve these children and their families. That was where they got their name, the Child Service Centers. Unfortunately, the children didn't show up! The big problem was how we were going to persuade people to send their children to the Kaiser Shipyard Center. We invited every master in town, everyone related to a church, every doctor in town, and every person heading up a team of workers to tour the Center. Finally, we reached a maximum of over 1000 children.

Q: How did you hire the teachers, and how might that reflect in terms of today's teachers?

Dr. Hymes: Well, Lois Meeks Stolz was the overall boss, and I was the Manager of the two centers. Between us, we pretty much knew every training center in the country and often knew individuals doing the training, so we learned one useful trick: if you are going to send a telegram, always send it two-paged. Instead of struggling to get a message in ten words, we sent out these long telegrams to every effective place in the country. About a year later, I had an occasion to visit many of them, and these telegrams would be up on the bulletin board, almost like a piece of art!

Another thing to understand, and this is one of the difficult things about teaching today, Lois spoke with Edgar Kaiser, the son of Henry Kaiser and the one who really ran the Center, and he asked what we were going to pay these people. She quoted him a salary and he said, "You can't do that. If you bring college educated people in and pay them those [low] salaries, in 24 hours every one of my head of a branch here in the yard will steal them from you. You have to pay them good salaries." I was always impressed by the fact that it was the industrialist who said that you have to pay people good salaries if you want to keep them. That idea has been long lost.

Q: We know that salaries are an issue and a problem. So many people feel that they can't stay in the field because they don't get paid properly.

Dr. Hymes: My experience with this kind of thing has persuaded me, although I've become a great minority, that there is no big future in industrially sponsored centers. The number of centers has grown very slowly and the reason why is that the industry soon discovers that if it is to be a good program, it has to be expensive.

Q: So holding up what Kaiser did during the Second World War for that extreme patriotic measure is not a good analogy to make about child care today?

Dr. Hymes: I really don't think it is. It was an emergency and war time, and when the war ended, Kaiser left Portland, Ore., because there

1

was nothing there for them. But there was a great need for child care after Kaiser left. In this country there are many other examples where a factory has closed or an industry has been wiped out and the workers are still there and need the care. If a company would give them support in the community it would be good. The one industry in peacetime is hospitals. Another example is flight attendants; some airlines have their own company-sponsored child-care centers.

Q: So what can we take from the War experience?

Dr. Hymes: I think I have learned no end of things, but one has to make generalizations: (1) To me this is the great tragedy, we are held to the notion that you must be trained to be a teacher and that you must be a college graduate who majors in child development. Teachers with that same background and 3 to 4 years of experience get paid the same as new recruits. Today I am troubled by the fact that nobody is paid enough to make this their field. (2) The other thing is that training as such is a giant step forward, but it is not enough to be a head teacher. In many cases a paraprofessional becomes the Head. The original child development associate (CDA) was to bring up the floor, not lower the ceiling.

Q: What is the future for children and teachers?

Dr. Hymes: The only constructive future I can see is that we have public school groups for 3- and 4-year-olds that will operate the necessary hours of the day. So many people work 12 months a year with weekends off. My reason for saying it is I don't know any other ways in which one can guarantee decent salaries and good requirements and so forth. Because of my wife, I have become involved in the progressive education movement. One of my roles is to say, in effect, you've got to

improve the public schools. I know if they take on 4-year-olds and do what they have done with 5-year-olds, it is a real dilemma and no good solution. Except, I think the only kind of solution is that get can get better when there is public support; then you have hope.

Just let me make one other point: one other possible help in the situation and it would have to merge with some of the other things, there is no reason that women or men or workers in general have to work as many hours a week as they do. There is no reason that we can't have a 30- or 24-hour workweek. I don't really see much movement in this area, but I think that the technology of it has to move at some point. If we can move toward a shorter workweek, then maybe it can be related to better teachers and better salaries.

Q: You talk about getting good training. When you are a product of laboratory school training, you are getting the kind of grounding in the field that helps with quality. What do ECE teachers need to know?

Dr. Hymes: I think you need to know what a good school is like. You can learn when you work in a school that is bad; I did. But I think you need a breath; you need a school experience which may not be real, but is ideal. And you also need reality. I think it is so important for young people who are studying to know some of the real obstacles. And the kind of training that makes them feel as if they are really skilled in understanding kids and know what they are trying to do.

Dr. James Hymes, Jr., is a noted leader in the field of early childhood education, former president of N.A.E.Y.C., author of Living History Interviews *(Hacienda Press, Carmel, CA) and* The Year in Review *(NAEYC, 1979–).*

QUESTIONS FOR THOUGHT

What distinguishes early childhood education from other levels of education?

Why is it important to know about the history of early childhood education?

What other fields have influenced the development of the early childhood philosophy? What has been their impact?

Why are the roots of psychology and early childhood education so intertwined?

What have been the basic themes in early education throughout history?

How do current events—political, social, and economic—affect the direction of education?

CHAPTER 1

History of Early Childhood Education

INTRODUCTION TO THE FIELD

Early childhood education has a rich and exciting history. The story of its development is the chronicle of people who took bold steps toward improving children's lives. Critical events have had a hand in shaping the history of early childhood education. As the images of the child change through the centuries, so, too, does the education of the young child and the educators themselves. For example, a national campaign such as the 1960s' "War on Poverty" can bring a nation together to support a program such as Head Start. A new model is forged through necessity and innovation, thus changing what we know about children and their care and education. Across the globe and through the centuries, the education of children has evolved.

Why History?

Most early childhood students and many educators know little about the origins of their chosen profession. The names of Rousseau, Froebel, Montessori, and Dewey may not seem to have much significance at this time (although many teachers are familiar with some of their techniques), but knowing something about the roots of this profession is important.

First of all, there is a sense of *support* that comes from knowing that history. Contemporary education has its roots in the past; finding a suitable beginning point for that past helps provide an educator with perspective. New insights blend with ideas from past traditions, as the history of early childhood education is truly a history of rediscovery.

Think about this, then: the "education" of the 21st century actually stems from children's schooling thousands of years ago. Socrates, Plato, and Aristotle are a part of the philosophical foundation on which this field is built. Even in ancient Greece and Rome, schools were established where literature, the arts, and science were taught.

Knowing that early childhood *philosophy* has deep roots can be an *inspiration* and helps teachers develop *professional expression*. As early childhood educators, we must learn to express our ideas, finding our own voice. Professionalism in educa-

tion "relates to doing things well, at the right time, and for the right reason" (Spodek, 1988). The past as well as the present and future must be considered when developing sound educational programs for young children. The *tenets* expressed by past educators help develop better methods of teaching. Looking at history gives an overview of how various ages looked at children and their learning, based on the religious, political, and economic pressures of the time. Reviewing the professional record demonstrates how the needs of society affect education. Perhaps some of the mistakes of the past can be avoided if history is remembered.

Drawing upon knowledge of the past creates *an awareness and understanding* of changes in education. Into the fabric of early childhood education are woven many threads of influence that are responsible for current philosophies. By understanding and telling the story of the past, we are better equipped to interpret our own history, to have a sense of mission and purpose. Gile's *Focus* article illustrates why "doing history" is a good idea for early childhood educators. And Spodek tells us

> When we [become] early childhood educators, each of us accepts as our own, either deliberately or implicitly, the mission that is central to our field: We are committed to enhancing the education, development, and well-being of young children. Our saga helps renew our sense of identity and commitment to our profession (Spodek in Bauch, 1988).

In this chapter, the people, the ideas, and the circumstances that have influenced early childhood are introduced by examining historical forces that have affected educational trends. It is important to note that the historical resources available are dominated by works from Europe and America, and schools of the past were overwhelmingly created for boys and men. However, educational programs that included girls and the role of people of color in the early childhood movement are documented whenever such resources are available.[1] Educational changes of a more recent nature follow. The impact of other disciplines, such as medicine and psychology, and the recurrent themes of early childhood education are also explored.

Defining the Terms

The term early **childhood education** refers to group settings deliberately intended to effect developmental changes in children from birth to the age of entering first grade. More recent definitions include the elementary years as well. For our purposes, we shall define early childhood as from infancy through third grade. In terms of a child's life, that is roughly from birth to eight years of age. In school terms, it includes group settings for infants through the primary years of elementary school, grades one through three. In programmatic terms, the education of young children includes formal and informal group settings regardless of their initial purpose. For instance, after-school programs for kindergarten and first-graders are included, as are their formal academic sessions.

Early childhood educators thus build bridges between a child's two worlds, school (or group experience) and home. It is during these years that the foundation for future learning is set; these are the building block years, during which a child learns to walk, talk, establish an identity, print, and count. In later years, that same child builds on these skills to be able to climb mountains, speak a foreign language, learn to express and negotiate, learn cursive writing, and understand multiplication.

INFLUENCES FROM ABROAD

When did early childhood education first begin? *A Timeline for Early Childhood Education* can be found in Appendix A. It is impossible to pinpoint the origins of humankind, since there are few records from millions of years ago. Some preparation for adult life was done informally, mostly through imitation. As language developed, communication took place. Children learned dances, rituals, and ceremonies, and both boys and girls were taught skills or their respective roles in the tribe. Ancient historical documents seem to indicate that child-rearing practices were somewhat crude; De Mause (1974) even suggests that

the further one goes back in history, the more likely the case of abandonment and brutality.

In Ancient Times

The definition of childhood has varied greatly throughout history. For example, in ancient times children were considered adults by age seven. A society's definition of childhood influences how it educates its children.

Many of our own beliefs are founded on those developed in Greece and Rome. Greek education—and virtually all classical European schooling—was provided for the boys of wealthy families, while girls and working-class children received training for domestic work or a trade.[2] Education began by age 6 or 7, although Plato and Aristotle both spoke of the need to educate the younger child. Some ancient Romans felt that education should begin at home as soon as a child began to talk, and highlighted the use of rewards and ineffectiveness of corporal punishment. (Hewes & Hartman, 1974).

Through medieval times (approximately the fifth through the thirteenth centuries), childhood hardly lasted beyond infancy. This period was largely an era of ignorance. Faced with the fall of the Roman Empire and the beginning of lawlessness and anarchy, people left villages and towns for the safety of a local baron or king, and schools ceased to exist. Few members of the ruling class could read or write their names, and the monastery schools were for priests and religious instruction only. The education of children was fairly simple before the fifteenth century; there was no educational system, and the way of life was uncomplicated as well. The church control of school in the medieval period meant that education projected a view of children as basically evil in their natural state. The value of education was in preparation for an afterlife. Children learned mostly through their parents or by apprenticeship outside the family. The child was expected and encouraged to move into adulthood as fast as possible.

OUR DIVERSE WORLD OUR DIVERSE WORLD OUR DIVERSE WORLD OUR DIVERSE WORLD OUR DIVERSE WORLD

[1]Early childhood professionals need to keep in mind the heavy influence of Western European thought in the philosophy that dictates our teaching practice; especially when working with children from families of non-Western European cultures.

[2]Keep in mind of how much of the research and history in our field has a race, class, and gender bias (i.e. the tendency to be based on the experiences of and research on White, middle-upper class males).

Survival was the primary goal in life. Since the common religious belief was that people were naturally evil, children had to be directed, punished, and corrected constantly.

What little learning occurred during the Dark Ages came through the policies of Charlemagne of France, who proclaimed that the nobility should know their letters, and from a few monastery schools that maintained libraries. A new social class in the form of craft guilds began to grow as apprenticeships expanded. Although education was sparse, the seeds of learning were planted, including the introduction of the concepts of equality and brotherhood, a continuing concern of educators today.

The Renaissance and the Reformation

With the Renaissance (late 1300s and early 1400s) and the Reformation (14th through 16th centuries), society gradually became more enlightened. Society's notion of childhood as abandonment or ambivalence was giving way to the sense that childhood was a legitimate period of life. Several political, social, economic, and religious movements combined. The first humanist educators began to advocate a basic education for all children, including girls and the poor. The call for a *universal education* and *literacy* are two fundamental effects of this period on education as we know it today. Concern for the common man was on the rise, as skilled craftsmen formed a kind of middle class. By the 1500s, schools that taught subjects such as reading, writing, arithmetic, and bookkeeping were fairly common throughout Europe.

The German school system had its beginnings established at this time and would continue to influence education in all parts of Europe. People changed the way they looked at children and their education. Towns grew and expanded, and there was an opportunity to move to new lands. Living conditions improved and infant mortality waned. Children were living longer. The acquisition of knowledge and skills at an earlier age became important. If educated, children could be expected to help their family improve its situation. Parents found they needed help in teaching their children.

Into Modern Times

Comenius

John Amos Comenius (1592–1670), a Czech educator, wrote the first picture books for children. Called *Orbis Pictus (The World of Pictures, 1658)*, it was a guide for teachers that included training of the senses and the study of nature. Comenius fostered the belief that education should follow the natural order of things. His ideas included the "school of the mother's lap," where children's development follows a timetable of its own and their education should reflect that fact. He felt teachers must observe and work with this natural order, the timetable, to ensure successful learning. This idea was later reflected in Montessori's sensitive periods and Piaget's stages of development. Today it is recognized as the issue of **school readiness**.

Comenius also stressed a basic concept that is now taken for granted: learning by doing. He encouraged parents to let their children play with other children of the same age. He also reflected the growing social reform that would educate the poor as well as the rich. In summary, probably the three most significant contributions of Comenius are *books with illustrations*, an emphasis on *education with the senses*, and the *social reform* of education.

Locke

An English philosopher of the 1600s, John Locke (1632–1714) is considered to be the founder of modern educational philosophy. He based his theory of education on the scientific method and the study of the mind and learning. Locke theorized the concept of **tabula rasa**, the belief that the child is born neutral, rather than evil, and is a "clean slate" upon which the experiences of parents, society, education, and the world are written. He based his theory on the scientific method, and approached a child as a doctor would examine a patient. He was one of the first European educators to discuss the idea of individual differences gleaned from observing one child rather than simply teaching a group. Education needed to take the individual learner into account.

The purpose of education, he claimed, is to make man a reasoning creature (Cubberly, 1920).

Cornix cornicatur,	à à	A a
The *Crow* crieth.		
Agnus balat,	b è è è	B b
The *Lamb* blaiteth.		
Cicàda stridet,	cì cì	C c
The *Grasshopper* chirpeth.		
Upupa dicit,	du du	D d
The *Whooppoo* saith.		
Infans ejulat,	è è è	E e
The *Infant* crieth.		
Ventus flat,	fi fi	F f
The *Wind* bloweth.		
Anser gingrit,	ga ga	G g
The *Goose* gagleth.		
Os halat,	hà'h hà'h	H h
The *Mouth* breatheth out.		
Mus mintrit,	ì ì ì	I i
The *Mouse* chirpeth.		
Anas tetrinnit,	kha, kha	K k
The *Duck* quaketh.		
Lupus ululat,	lu ulu	L
The *Wolf* howleth.		
	[mum	
Ursus murmurat,	mum-	M m
The *Bear* grumbleth.		

FIGURE 1.1 *Orbis Pictus*, by John Comenius, is considered the first picture book written for children.

For beginners, a knowledge of the Bible and business was enough. Locke suggested that such instruction should be pleasant, with playful activities as well as drills. Locke's influence on education was not felt strongly at the time. Later, however, his best ideas were popularized by Rousseau, such as the notion that the teacher must work through the senses to help children reach understanding. Today, teachers still emphasize a sensory approach to learning.

In summary, Locke's contribution is felt most in our acceptance of *individual differences*, in *giving children reasons* as the basis for helping children to learn, and in his theory of a "clean slate" that points to the effect of the environment on learning.

Rousseau

After Comenius, new thoughts were everywhere in Europe. Locke offered some educational challenges, and Darwin brought a change to science. The time was ripe for new ideas about childhood. Jean Jacques Rousseau (1712–1778), a writer and philosopher of the middle 1700s, brought forth the idea that children were not inherently evil, but naturally good. He is best known for his book *Emile* in which he raised a hypothetical child to adulthood. He reasoned that education should reflect this goodness and allow spontaneous interests and activities of the children. Soon, children

FIGURE 1.2 Hampton Institute.

were actively involved in their own education. Each child was considered unique and valuable. While he was not an educator, Rousseau offered insights that were valuable. He suggested that school atmosphere should be less restrained and more flexible to meet the needs of the children. He insisted on using concrete teaching materials, leaving the abstract and symbolism for later years. His call to *naturalism* transformed education in such a way that led educators to eventually focus more on the early years. Pestalozzi, Froebel, and Montessori were greatly influenced by him. The theories of developmental stages, such as of Jean Piaget and Arnold Gesell (see chapter 4), support Rousseau's idea of natural development. In Europe, his ideas had a ripple effect that sent waves across the Atlantic Ocean.

Rousseau's ideas are still followed today in early childhood classes. Free play is based on Rousseau's belief in children's inherent goodness and ability to choose what they need to learn. Environments that stress autonomy and self-regulation have their roots in Rousseau's philosophy. Using concrete rather than abstract materials for young

children is still one of the cornerstones of developmentally appropriate curriculum in the early years.

Pestalozzi

Johann Heinrich Pestalozzi (1746–1827) was a Swiss educator whose theories on education and caring have formed the basis of many common teaching practices of early childhood education. Like Rousseau, he used nature study as part of the curriculum and believed that good education meant the development of the senses. Rather than simply glorify nature, however, Pestalozzi became more pragmatic, including principles on how to teach basic skills and the idea of "caring" as well as "educating" the child. Pestalozzi stressed the idea of the **integrated curriculum** which would develop the whole child. He wanted education to be of the hand, the head, and the heart of the child. Teachers were to guide self-activity through intuition, exercise, and the senses. Along with intellectual content, he proposed that practical skills be taught in the schools. He differed from Rousseau in that he proposed teaching children in groups rather than using a tutor with an individual child. Pestalozzi's work *How Gertrude Teaches Her Children* and *Book for Mothers* detailed some procedures for mothers to use at home with their children. Probably his greatest contribution is the blending of Rousseau's strong romantic ideals with his own egalitarian attitude that built skills and independence in a school atmosphere that paralleled that of a firm and loving home.

Froebel

Friedrich Wilhelm Froebel (1782–1852) is one of the major contributors to early childhood education, particularly in his organization of educational thought and ideas about learning, curriculum, and teacher training. He is known to us as the "father of the kindergarten," not only for giving it a name, but for devoting his life to the development of a system of education for young children. The German word **kindergarten** means "children's garden," and that is what Froebel felt best expressed what he wanted for children under six years of age. Since his own childhood had been unhappy, he resolved that early education should be pleasant. He advocated the radical thought that children should be able to play, to have toys, and to be with trained teachers, so he started the first training school. Early childhood historian Dorothy Hewes (1993) notes:

> "Froebel started his kindergarten in 1836, for children aged about two to six, after he had studied with Pestalozzi in Switzerland and had read the philosophy promoted by Comenius two hundred years earlier. His system was centered around self-activity and the development of children's self-esteem and self-confidence. In his *Education of Man*, he wrote that 'Play is the highest phase of child development—the representation of the inner necessity and impulse. He had the radical idea that both men and women should teach young children and that they should be friendly facilitators rather than stern disciplinarians."

Over one hundred years ago, Froebel's kindergartens included blocks, pets, and fingerplays, Figure 1.3. Froebel observed children and came to understand how they learned and what they liked to do. He developed the first educational toys, which he termed "gifts."

FIGURE 1.3   Finger plays, which are common activities in today's early childhood programs, were also a part of Froebel's kindergarten programs. (From Wiggins and Smith, 1895.)

> When the children are just making friends with the teacher and with each other, it is very interesting and profitable for them to formulate their mite of knowledge into a sentence, each one holding his ball high in the air with the right hand, and saying:
> My ball is red like a cherry.
> My ball is yellow like a lemon.
> My ball is blue like the sky.
> My ball is orange like a marigold.
> My ball is green like the grass.
> My ball is violet like a plum.

Angeline Brooks (1886), a teacher in an American Froebelian kindergarten in the late 1800s, described the gifts this way:

> "Froebel regarded the whole of life as a school, and the whole world as a school-room for the education of the [human] race. The external things of nature he regarded as a means to making the race acquainted with the invisible things of the minds, as God's *gifts* for use in accomplishing the purpose of this temporal life. Regarding the child as the race in

A Letter to Students in Early Childhood Education

Mary Stuart Gile, Ed.D

Welcome to the world of young children, childhood and to this profession, early child care and education. This is a dynamic, complex and diverse profession focusing on young children, yet rich in historical perspectives and ideologies.

As students beginning professional studies with intentions of teaching beyond the 21st century, the fact that early childhood education has a history may come as a surprise. But for the moment, imagine yourself a time traveller for our history is indeed a tapestry of fascinating stories and events spanning the centuries, linking and affirming people committed to the importance of children to our society. To understand our history is to know the how, when, where and why of all that we value and practice in early childhood education today.

A brief journey back in time to meet the men and women whose vision and energy helped to shape our profession reveals stories of passion, struggle and dedication. Their efforts on behalf of children, particularly in education and social reform, were bold and often contrary to popular belief.

The legacies of Rousseau, Pestalozzi, Froebel, Montessori, the McMillans, Dewey and others seem remote today, yet our roots, traditions and pedagogy are intricately connected to their teachings and beliefs. History sensitizes us to their importance and helps us to understand and relate them to current realities. The whole child philosophy and programs such as Headstart, nursery schools, kindergartens, teacher development, parent education and developmentally appropriate practices are all extensions of their insights and initiatives.

We study history in early childhood education because it is our foundation; it salutes our successes, reminds us of our vulnerabilities and helps us to better understand the human condition as it affects children, childhood and our profession.

History challenges and inspires. It is the bond that connects the wisdom and experience of the past, with the energy and commitment of the present. It can also be the catalyst that combined with your optimism and vision may enable our profession to grow and to create in the new millennium, a world where childhood is honored and where children and those who nurture and educate them come first. Again, welcome.

Dr. Mary Stuart Gile is a Professor and Department Head of Early Education at the New Hampshire Technical Institute of Concord, New Hampshire.

miniature, he selected a few objects which should epitomize the world of matter in its most salient attributes, and arranged them in an order which should assist the child's development at successive stages of growth."

Some of his theories about children and their education later influenced Montessori and were reflected in the educational materials she developed.

Every day, teachers in centers and homes across the country practice the Froebelian belief that a child's first educational experiences should be a garden: full of pleasant discoveries and delightful adventure, where the adults' role is to plant ideas and materials for children to use as they grow at their own pace.

Montessori   *Founder*

At the turn of the century, Maria Montessori (1870–1952) became the first female physician in Italy. She worked in the slums of Rome with poor children and with mentally retarded children. Sensing that what they lacked was proper motivation and environment, she opened a preschool, Casa di Bambini, in 1907. Montessori designed materials, classrooms, and a teaching procedure that proved her point to the astonishment of people all over Europe and America.

Before her, no one with medical or psychiatric training had articulated so clearly the needs of the growing child. Her medical background added credibility to her findings and helped her ideas gain recognition in this country. The Montessori concept is both a philosophy of child development and a plan for guiding growth, believing that education begins at birth and the early years are of the utmost importance. During this time, children pass through "sensitive periods," in which their curiosity makes them ready for acquiring certain skills and knowledge. Through her enlightenment, child-sized furniture and materials are now used in classrooms. By focusing on the *sequential steps of learning*, Montessori developed a set of learning materials still used widely today. One of her most valuable contributions was a theory of how children learn. She believed that any task could be reduced to a series of small steps. By using this process, children could learn to sweep a floor, dress themselves, or multiply numbers.

FIGURE 1.4   Maria Montessori designed materials, classrooms, and learning methods for young children. (Photo courtesy of American Montessori Society, New York, NY.)

Montessori materials are graded in difficulty and emphasize her interest in self-help skills. To foster this, she developed frames with buttons and laces so children could learn to be responsible for themselves when dressing. The layout of the room and the distribution and presentation of materials furthered this concept. Montessori placed great emphasis on the environment—the "prepared environment," as she called it. A sense of order, a place for everything, and a clear rationale are hallmarks of the Montessori influence.

Her procedures as well as her materials contain **self-correcting** features. Nesting cylinders, for example, fit together only one way and are to be used that way. Montessori supported earlier educational ideas of sensory development; she felt that cognitive abilities stem from sensory discrimination. Thus, most of her equipment was **tactile** and enhanced the senses as well as the mind. In the Montessori method, the role of the teacher is primarily one of observer and facilitator. Teachers demonstrate proper use of materials and communicate as needed, avoiding any acts that might cause a child to become dependent on them for help or approval. At the same time, Montessori saw the goal of education as the formation of the child and development of character. After Montessori was introduced in the United States in 1909, her methods received poor reception and were often misunderstood. Chattin-McNichols (1993) notes that "adaptation of her methods in a variety of ways, a focus on academics by demanding middle class parents, and a flood of 'trainers' and authors eager to capitalize on Montessori contributed to a rapid downfall of Montessori schools in the U.S. by 1925 or so." A second American Montessori movement began in the late 1950s and early 1960s. Differences between Europeans and Americans generated the American Montessori Society, founded by Dr. Nancy McCormick Rambusch. According to Chattin-McNichols (1993):

> "Today with a much wider range of children than ever before, the majority of Montessori schools are private preschools and child care centers, serving 3- to 6-year-old children. But there are many which also serve elementary students, and a small (but growing) number of programs for infants, toddlers, and middle-school students. . . . The word *Montessori*, however, remains in the public domain, so that Montessori in the name of a school or teacher education program does not guarantee any adherence to Montessori's original ideas."

(See Chapter 2 for more information on Montessori programs.)

Rudolf Steiner

Rudolf Steiner (1861–1925) was a German educator whose method of education is known today as the Waldorf School of Education. This system has influenced mainstream education in Europe and its international reputation is being felt in American early childhood programs today. Steiner theorized that childhood is a phase of life important in its own right. It has three periods: that of the "will" (0–7 years), the "heart" or feelings (7–14 years), and the "head" or a fusion of the spirit and the body (14 years on). Early childhood is the period of "willing," and the environment must be carefully planned to protect and nurture the child.

As did Froebel and Montessori, Steiner emphasized the whole child and believed that different areas of development and learning were connected into a kind of unity. The role of the teacher is that of a mother-figure, and her goal is to allow the child's innate self-motivation to predominate. The teacher is to understand the temperament of each child, and to go with it; thus, play has a large place in Waldorf classrooms.

Self-discipline will emerge from the child's natural willingness to learn and initiate, and the classroom needs to support this self-regulation process. Yet, while the child's inner life is deeply valued by Steiner, experiences in early childhood must be carefully selected. For instance, fairy stories help children acquire time-honored wisdom; modern Waldorf followers insist television be eliminated. For Steiner, the people with whom the child interacts are of central importance. Waldorf Schools are discussed later in this chapter and in Chapter 2.

AMERICAN INFLUENCES

Colonial Days

The American educational system began in the Colonies. When thinking of Colonial America, people often envision the one-room schoolhouse. Indeed, this was the mainstay of education in the New England Colonies. Although home teaching of the Bible was not uncommon, children were sent to school primarily for religious reasons. Everyone needed to be able to read the Bible, the Puritan fathers reasoned. All children were sent to study, though historically boys were educated before girls.[1] Not only the Bible was used in school, however; new materials like the New England Primer and the Horn Book were also used.

Early life in the New England colonies was difficult, and estimates run as high as 60–70 per-

OUR DIVERSE WORLD OUR DIVERSE WORLD OUR DIVERSE WORLD OUR DIVERSE WORLD OUR DIVERSE WORLD

[1]Provide reminders of the strides that have been made in American society in providing equal educational experiences for both boys and girls—the challenge continues.

FIGURE 1.5 The history of early childhood education includes contributions from many ethnic groups. San Francisco's Golden Gate Kindergarten Association provided nursery education for the city's various neighborhoods from the turn of the century to the present.

cent of children under four dying in colonial towns during the "starving season." Discipline was harsh and children were expected to obey immediately and without question. Parents may have loved their children, but Puritan families showed little overt affection. Children were important as economic tools, and they worked the land and were apprenticed into trades early.

In the South, it was a different story. Plantation owners imported tutors from England or opened small private schools to teach just their sons to read and write.[1] While the reasons were different, the results were similar: a very high percentage of adult readers. From these came the leaders of the American Revolution and the new nation.

The Revolutionary War brought the establishment of both the Union and religious freedom. By affirming fundamental principles of democratic liberty, the Founding Fathers paved the way for a system of free, common, public school systems, the first the world had seen (Cubberly, 1920). However, after the Revolutionary War, there were no sig-

nificant advances in education until the late 1800s. Leaders like Thomas Jefferson felt that knowledge ought to be available to all, but that opinion was not widely shared. Most of the post-Revolutionary period focused on growing crops and pioneering the frontier, not teaching and educating children. Even by the 1820s, education for the common man was not readily available. Industrialization in both the North and South did little to encourage reading and writing skills. Manual labor and machine-operating skills were more important. While public schools were accepted in principle, in reality no tax basis was established to support them.

Children in Enslavement

The first African Americans were not slaves but indentured servants, whose debts repaid by their labor would buy them their freedom. However, by 1620 Africans were being brought to the New World as slaves. In many states, children of slaves were not seen as human beings but rather as property of the owner. During the Revolutionary War, many Americans turned against slavery because of the principles of the natural rights of the individual, as embodied in the Declaration of Independence and the U.S. Constitution. By the early 1800s, most northern owners had freed their slaves, although living conditions for them were generally poor.

Because of the high economic value of children, there was a certain level of care given to pregnant women and babies. Osborn (1991) tells of a nursery on a South Carolina plantation (around 1850) in which

> infants and small children were left in a small cabin while the mothers worked in the fields nearby. An older woman was left in charge and assisted by several girls 8–10 years of age. The infants, for the most part, lay on the cabin floor or the porch—and once or twice daily, the mother would come in from the field to nurse the baby. Children of toddler age played on the porch or in the yard and, at times, the older girls might lead the group in singing and dancing.

Prior to the Civil War, education was severely limited for African Americans. Formal schools

OUR DIVERSE WORLD OUR DIVERSE WORLD OUR DIVERSE WORLD OUR DIVERSE WORLD OUR DIVERSE WORLD

[1]Provide reminders of the strides that have been made in American society in providing equal educational experiences for both boys and girls—the challenge continues.

were scarce, and most education came through the establishment of "Sabbath schools."[1] As part of religious instruction, slaves were often provided literary training. However, many plantation owners found these schools threatening, and banned them. Another facility then developed, that of the clandestine, or midnight school. Because of its necessary secretive existence, few records are available, although it is reasonable to conclude that the curriculum was similar to that of the prohibited Sabbath schools.

After the Civil War, private and public schools were opened for African Americans. Major colleges and universities were founded by the end of the 1800s, and many former slaves and graduates established schools for younger children. Of integrated schools, Osborn (1991) reports

> Generally, however, if the schools accepted Blacks at all, it was on a strictly quota basis . . . Blacks were often excluded from kindergartens. Thus, as the early childhood education movement began to grow and expand in the years following the Civil War, it grew along separate color lines.

Hampton Institute of Virginia established a laboratory kindergarten for African Americans in 1873, and by 1893 the Institute offered a kindergarten training school and courses in child care.[2] The graduates of Hampton Institute became the teachers at the laboratory school because, in the words of its principal "[the] students know the children and the influences surrounding them. . . . Their people are proud to see them teaching. They furnish what has always been a missing link between me and the parents" (Pleasant, 1992).

John Dewey

real Influence American

By the end of the 1800s, however, a nationwide reform movement had begun. In education, the *Progressive Movement*, as it was called, got its direction primarily through one individual, John Dewey (1858–1952).

Dewey was the first real American influence on American education. Raised in Vermont, he be-

came a professor of philosophy at both the University of Chicago and Columbia University. In the years that followed, Dewey would be responsible for one of the greatest impacts on American education of all time.

Dewey believed that children were valuable and that childhood was an important part of their lives. Like Froebel, he felt that education should be integrated with life and should provide a training ground for cooperative living. As did Pestalozzi and Rousseau, Dewey felt that schools should focus on the nature of the child. Until this time, children were considered of little consequence. Childhood was rushed. Children as young as seven were a regular part of the work force—on the farms, in the mines, and in the factories. Dewey's beliefs about children and learning are summarized in Figure 1.6.

A new kind of school emerged from these ideals. Even the buildings began to take on a different look. Movable furniture replaced rows of benches. Children's projects, some still under construction, were found everywhere. The curriculum of the school began to focus on all of the basics, not just a few of the academics. If a group of six-year-olds decided to make a woodworking table, they would first have to learn to read in order to understand the directions. After calculating the cost, they would purchase the materials. In building the table, geometry, physics, and math were learned along the way. This was a group effort that encouraged children to work together in teams and so school became a society in miniature. Children's social skills were developed along with reading, science, and math. The teacher's role in the process was one of ongoing support, involvement, and encouragement.

The contribution of John Dewey to American education cannot be underestimated. As described in Figure 1.6, Dewey's ideas are part of today's classrooms in several ways. His child-oriented schools are a model of child care centers and family child care homes, as learning and living are inseparable. As the following sections on kindergarten and nursery schools illustrate, John Dewey had a vision that is still alive today.

OUR DIVERSE WORLD OUR DIVERSE WORLD OUR DIVERSE WORLD OUR DIVERSE WORLD OUR DIVERSE WORLD

[1]See footnote on page 13. Although great strides have been made in providing public education for all children in America, remember inequities based on color, linguistic ability, and social class continue to exist.

[2]Hampton Institute understood the importance of honoring diversity far ahead of the times.

KINDERGARTEN

The word *kindergarten*—which is German for "children's garden"—is a delightful term. It brings to mind the image of young seedlings on the verge of blossoming. The similarity between caring for young plants and young children is not accidental. Froebel, the man who coined the word *kindergarten*, meant for that association to be made. As a flower opens from a bud, so too does a child go through a natural unfolding process. This idea—and ideal—are part of the kindergarten story.

The first kindergarten was a German school started by Froebel in 1837. Over a dozen years later, in 1856, Margaretha Schurz, a student of Froebel, opened the first kindergarten in the United States. It was for German-speaking children and held in her home in Wisconsin. Schurz inspired Elizabeth Peabody (1804–1894) of Bos-

ton, who opened the first English-speaking kindergarten there in 1860. Peabody, in turn, after studying kindergartens in Germany, influenced William Harris, superintendent of schools in St. Louis, Missouri. In 1873, Harris allowed Susan Blow (1843–1916) to open the first kindergarten in the United States that was associated with the public schools. By the 1880s kindergarten teachers such as Eudora Hailmann were hard at work inventing wooden beads, paper weaving mats, and songbooks to use with active 5-year-old children (Hewes, 1993).

Looking at the kindergarten in historical perspective, it is interesting to trace the various purposes of this specialized educational experience. During the initial period in this country (1856–1890), Froebel's philosophy (see section on "Froebel" earlier in this chapter) remained the mainstay of kindergarten education. At the same time, kin-

My Pedagogic Creed—John Dewey	What It Means Today
1. ". . . I believe that only true education comes through the stimulation of the child's powers by the demands of the social situations in which he finds himself."	This tells us that children learn to manage themselves in groups, to make and share friendships, to solve problems, and to cooperate.
2. ". . . The child's own instinct and powers furnish the material and give the starting point for all education."	We need to create a place that is child-centered, a place that values the skills and interests of each child and each group.
3. ". . . I believe that education, therefore, is a process of living and not a preparation for future living."	Prepare the child for what is to come by enriching and interpreting the present to him. Find educational implications in everyday experiences.
4. ". . I believe that . . . the school life should grow gradually out of the home life . . . it is the business of the school to deepen and extend . . . the child's sense of the values bound up in his home life."	This sets the rationale for a relationship between teachers and parents. Values established and created in the home should be enhanced by teaching in the schools.
5. ". . . I believe, finally, that the teacher is engaged, not simply in the training of individuals, but in the formation of a proper social life. I believe that every teacher should realize the dignity of his calling."	This says that the work teachers do is important and valuable. They teach more than academic content; they teach how to live.

FIGURE 1.6   John Dewey expressed his ideas about education in an important document titled *My Pedagogic Creed* (Washington, D.C.: The Progressive Education Association, 1897).

dergartens began to become an instrument of social reform; since these included a "day care" function, they were called charity kindergartens.

Moreover by early 1900, the voices of dissent were being heard. Traditional kindergarten ideas had come under the scrutiny of G. Stanley Hall and others, who were interested in a scientific approach to education, and of Dewey, who also advocated a community-like (rather than garden-style) classroom. A classic clash of ideals developed between followers of Froebel (conservatives) and those of Dewey's new educational viewpoint (progressives). Support for the latter came from those who saw kindergartens as a social service. Many of the kindergartens started in the late 1800s were established by churches and other agencies that worked with the poor. It was an era of rising social conscience, and the reasons for helping the less fortunate were not unlike the rationale that led to the creation of Head Start and Follow-Through sixty years later.

Critics of Froebel took exception to his seemingly rigid approach. The emphasis in a Froebelian kindergarten was on teacher-directed learning.

Dewey's followers preferred a more child-centered approach, with teachers serving as facilitators of children's learning. It is the same tension that exists today between the "back to basics" movement and the supporters of open education. The progressives found fault with the "gifts" of Froebel's curriculum. Those who followed Dewey believed that "real objects and real situations within the child's own social setting" should be used (Read and Patterson, 1980). Froebel was viewed as too structured and too symbolic; Dewey was perceived as child-oriented and child-involved. Even the processes they employed were different. Froebel believed in the unfolding of the child's mind and learning, whereas Dewey stressed the child's "potential developed through social interaction" (Broman, 1978).

The debate raged on. The progressives succeeded in influencing the content of kindergarten programs, retaining some of Froebel's basic concepts. "The reform of kindergarten education continued through the 1920s and 1930s leading to the creation of the modern American kindergarten . . ." (Spodek, 1972).

FIGURE 1.7　John Dewey's lab school involved children in activities of a practical, real-life nature, such as weaving small rugs to use in the classroom. (Special thanks to Sheila Roper of MacClintock Photo Collection, Special Collections, Morris Library, Southern Illinois University at Carbondale.)

Founder Naec

Patty Smith Hill

Patty Smith Hill (1868–1946) of Teacher's College, Columbia University, was an outstanding innovator of the time and one of the Progressive Movement's most able leaders. It was she who wrote the song "Happy Birthday" and founded the National Association for Nursery Education (NANE). Now the largest association of early childhood educators, it is known today as the National Association for the Education of Young Children (NAEYC). Trained originally in the Froebelian tradition, she worked closely with G. Stanley Hall and later with John Dewey. Thus, her philosophy and classroom teaching was a blended one. She believed strongly in basing curricula and programs on the nature and needs of the children, and she was one of the major education experimenters of her day. She was

> . . . guided by principles of democracy and respect for individuals. She argued for freedom and initiative for children, as well as a curriculum relevant to children's lives. It was she who originated large-muscle equipment and materials suitable for climbing and construction, a departure from the prescribed small-muscle activities of the Froebelians. Patty Hill also urged unification of kindergarten and first grade work, but her objective was not to start 5 year olds on first grade work, we today might readily assume. Rather, emphasis was on giving six year olds the opportunity for independent, creative activities before embarking on the three R's.
>
> (Cohen and Randolph, 1977)

These ideas became the backbone of kindergarten practice. Moreover, Hill did not work for kindergarten alone. In fact, during the 1920s Hill rekindled Froebel's early ideas to promote nursery schools for children too young to attend kindergarten. Regardless of controversy within, kindergartens were still on the fringes of the educational establishments as a whole. However, when the 1960s highlighted the problems of the poor and their failure in schools and society, kindergarten and the early years were brought back into the spotlight. Today, the kindergarten is found in some

form in nearly every country of the world. While the content of the program and the length of the day vary widely in the United States, kindergarten is available in every one of the United States.

The stability of both the Froebelian and the Dewey kindergartens has been challenged in the latter part of this century, as the "basic skills" curriculum is moved down to the kindergarten classroom. The problems in this shift from developmentally appropriate practices to more academic material is not new. Educators have been discussing various curriculum content and teaching approaches for years. Chapter 2 will discuss the issue of programs, as we continue to decide "how the best ideas of the past can be integrated with the best practices of today and transformed into the best programs for the future (Himitz in Bauch, 1988).

Nursery Schools

Establishment in America

Early childhood educators took Dewey's philosophy to heart. Their schools reflected the principles of a **child-centered approach**, active learning, and social cooperation. By the 1920s and 1930s, early childhood education had reached a professional status in the United States. Nursery schools and day nurseries went beyond custodial health care. They fostered the child's total development. The children were enrolled from middle- and upper-class homes as well as from working families. However, until the 1960s, nursery schools served few poor families.[1]

Parent education was acknowledged as a vital function of the school and led to the establishment of **parent cooperative schools**. Brook Farm, a utopian cooperative community in the 1840s, had "the equivalent of an on-site child care center 'for the use of parents doing industrial work' or for mothers to use 'as a kindly relief to themselves when fatigued by the care of children'" (Hewes, 1993). The first of these parent participation schools was developed in 1915 at the University of Chicago. A group of faculty wives started the Chicago Cooperative Nursery School.

OUR DIVERSE WORLD OUR DIVERSE WORLD OUR DIVERSE WORLD OUR DIVERSE WORLD OUR DIVERSE WORLD

[1] A challenge in our profession is to create funding mechanisms to provide an early childhood education experience for all children and families-regardless of income.

Susan Blow 1st Founder Kindergarden U.S.A

Research centers and child development laboratories were started in many colleges and universities from about 1915 to 1930. These schools followed one of two basic models. One model, patterned after the first psychological laboratory in Leipzig, Germany, in 1879, was formed to train psychologists in the systematic training of child study. This model adopted a scientific approach to the study of human beings, as the field of psychology itself attempted to become more like the biological sciences. The second approach, like the Butler School of Hampton Institute and later at Spellman College, was established primarily for training teachers. The latter model took its influence almost exclusively from educational leaders. However, the nursery school laboratory schools attempted a multidisciplinary approach, blending the voices from psychology and education with those of home economics, nursing, social work, and medicine. These laboratory schools were active in expanding the knowledge of how important a child's early years are.

Lucy Sprague Mitchell

Early childhood education in the United States grew out of John Dewey's progressive movement largely because of Lucy Sprague Mitchell (1878–1967) and her contemporaries. Raised in an environment of educational and social reform, Mitchell developed the idea of schools as community centers as well as places for children to learn to think. As Greenberg (1987) explained, she gathered together, in a democratic, cooperative venture, many talented people to brainstorm, mastermind, and sponsor:

● A remarkable Bureau of Educational Experiments

● A school to implement and experiment with these principles

● A laboratory to record and analyze how and why they function as she knew they did (and as we know they do!)

● A teachers' college to promote them

● A workshop for writers of children's literature (a new genre—a number of currently famous authors of juvenile books attended) and

● A bulletin to disseminate it all, as well as disseminating what a plethora of progressive educators were up to elsewhere, *beginning in 1916*!

By establishing Bank Street College of Education (and its laboratory school), Lucy Sprague Mitchell emphasized the link between theory and practice, namely, that the education of young children and the study of how children learn are intrinsically tied together.

Abigail Eliot

The nursery school movement was pioneered by Abigail Eliot (1892–1992). A graduate of Radcliffe College and Harvard University, she was the director of the Ruggles Street Nursery School and Training Center, which opened in Boston in 1922. Eliot had worked with the McMillan sisters in the slums of London. A social worker by training, she became interested in children and their relationships with their parents. Eliot had a lively and clear view of what good schools for children could be. She is generally credited with bringing the nursery school movement to the United States. As she put it (Hymes, 1979) "Margaret McMillan invented the name [nursery school]. She was a genius and a true pioneer . . . the difference wasn't age, although we did not take babies under Two as the day nurseries did. The big difference—the *new* idea—was program. I had visited many day nurseries in Boston as a social worker. I can remember them even now: dull green walls, no light colors, nothing pretty—spotlessly clean places, with rows of white-faced listless little children sitting, doing nothing. In the new nursery school, the children were active, alive, choosing." Thus did early childhood education include from its beginnings a partnership between parents and teachers.

Midcentury Developments

Bertrand Russell

British scholar Bertrand Russell (1872–1970) first published his views of education in the book *On Education, Especially in Early Childhood.* Critical of education, this internationally known philosopher was skeptical of both the traditional strict methods and the more romantic notions,

FIGURE 1.8   American nursery schools, from the turn of the century through the present day, have included time for the group to be together. (Photo from Golden Gate Kindergarten Association, San Francisco, Calif.)

preferring a model of the child as morally neutral, such as did John Locke (hence, the clean slate). His primary school at Beacon Hill, England, was quite open, being noncompetitive and free of punishments, and giving the choice of classes and even some of the instruction over to the children themselves. As to early education, Russell states

> I think the arguments in favour of the nursery school are quite overwhelming—not only for children whose parents are poor, ignorant, and overworked, but for all children, or at the very least, for all children who live in towns. I believe that the children at Miss Margaret McMillan's nursery school in Deptford get something better than any children of well-to-do parents can at the present obtain . . . To begin with, early childhood is of immeasurable importance both medically and psychologically.
>
> (Russell, 1926)

Russell's focus on the education of both character and intellect drew from Rousseau, Montessori, the McMillan sisters, and modern, more scientific, psychology of the day. Surprisingly, his works even stimulated B.F. Skinner's interest in education and child-rearing.

The Depression

It was during the Depression, World War II, and the postwar years that the American public focused more sharply than ever before on the needs of young children. These were times when the general public became aware of the importance of early childhood. Government-funded nursery schools later became the Works Progress Administration (WPA) nursery schools, which hired unemployed teachers. Government support from 1941 (Lanham Act War Nurseries) continued until 1946 when the Lanham Act schools were turned over to the states or closed.

Kaiser Child Care Centers

Excellent sample of workplace childcare

During World War II, funds were provided to deal with the common situation of mothers working in war-related industries. Further support came from industry during World War II. An excellent model for child care operated from 1943 to 1945 in Portland, Oregon. It was the Kaiser Child Care Centers. Kaiser became the world's largest such center and functioned "round the clock" all year long. A number of services were made available on site. An infirmary was located nearby for both mothers and children. Hot meals were made available for mothers to take home when they picked up their children. Lois Meek Stolz was the director of the centers, and James L. Hymes, Jr., the manager. Edith Dowley, who was one of the teachers, describes in detail the environment and experiences of this remarkable project:

> Each center was built around a large, octagonally shaped courtyard with four wading pools where children could play away from the hazards of traffic. The courtyard itself was grass-covered, with a

hard-surfaced area designed for wheel toys that extended around the perimeter. Covered porches equipped with jungle gyms, climbing boxes, slides, and large, hollow blocks connected the interior rooms to the grassy areas. . . . Between and opposite every two playrooms were smaller rooms for teachers' meetings, special play, or story times. . . . Window seats, low enough for the children to sit on, were built so that the children could curl up on them and watch the ships, cars, trucks, and cranes in the busy shipyard below, where their parents were working.

Stolz and Hymes describe the centers this way:

> . . . The centers were to have three distinctive qualities. One, they were to be located not out in the community but right at the entrance to the two shipyards, convenient to mothers on their way to and from work. They were to be industry-based, not neighborhood-centered. Two, the centers were to be operated by the shipyards, not by the public schools and not by community agencies. They were to be industrial child care centers, with the cost borne by the Kaiser company and by parents using the service. Three, they were to be large centers, big enough to meet the need. In the original plan each center was to serve a thousand preschool children on three shifts.
>
> (Hymes, 1978)

These centers served 3,811 different children. As Hymes points out, they provided 249,268 child care days. They had freed 1,931,827 woman work-hours. Once the war ended, though, the workers left. Child care was no longer needed, and the centers closed. The model they provide for child care remains exemplary.

The "Free School" Movement

A.S. Neill (1883–1973) was the most famous proponent of the "free/natural school" movement of the midcentury. His book, *Summerhill*, describes 40 years of that educational program, of which he was headmaster. Neill claimed that most education was defective because it arose from the model of original sin. Assuming children were inherently evil caused educators to force children into doing what was contrary to their nature. Neill shared Rousseau's belief in noninterference, as he states: "I believe that a child is innately wise and realistic. If left to himself without adult suggestion

of any kind, he will develop as far as he is capable of developing." (Neill, 1960)

Neill's belief in freedom was practiced in his school, where children governed themselves and worked towards equal rights with adults. The benefits from such liberties were touted as highly therapeutic and natural, an escape from repression and guilt. Several influences are clear in these educational programs—Rousseau's belief in the child's innate goodness, Freud's idea of the dangerous effects of guilt, and some of the social idealism of Dewey and the Progressives.

Head Start

After the war, few innovations took place until a small piece of metal made its worldwide debut. Sputnik, the Soviet satellite, was successfully launched in 1957 and caused an upheaval in educational circles. Two questions were uppermost in the minds of most Americans: Why weren't we first in space? What is wrong with our schools? The emphasis in education quickly settled on engineering, science, and math in the hope of catching up with Russian technology.

The civil rights struggle in the early 1960s soon followed. In pointing out the plight of the poor, education was highlighted as a major stumbling block toward equality of all people. It was time to act, and Project Head Start was conceived as education's place to fight the "war on poverty." The same goals of Froebel and Montessori formed the basis of Head Start: helping disadvantaged preschool children.

Project Head Start began in 1965 as a demonstration program aimed at providing educational, social, medical, dental, nutritional, and mental health services to preschool children from a diverse population of low-income families. Initially, Head Start was devised as an eight-week summer program serving 500,000 children. In 1972, it was transformed into a predominantly part-day, full-year program. Over the years, Head Start has provided comprehensive developmental services to more than ten million children and their families. Head Start currently services approximately 20 percent of eligible low-income children (Murphy and Waxler, 1989).

This was an exciting time—a national recognition of the needs of young children and a hope for a better quality of life. Three major points included in the Head Start program are noteworthy:

- *Compensatory education*—programs that compensate for inadequate early life experiences.

- *Parental involvement*—inclusion of parents in planning, teaching, and decision making.

- *Community control*—local support and participation.

These three objectives combined to reinforce the goals of the program in real and concrete ways. Head Start was an attempt to make amends, to compensate poor children by preparing them for school and educational experiences. Parents, by being required to participate at all levels, were educated along with their children. The purpose of the community-based governing boards was to allow the program to reflect local values and concerns. Concurrently, underprivileged, poor people were being encouraged to take part in solving some of their own problems.

The spirit of Head Start was infectious. As a result of community interest in Head Start, there was a burst of enthusiasm for many programs for the young child. Because of Head Start's publicity, there has been an expanding enrollment in nursery school, kindergarten, and day care programs. Thanks to Head Start, there is national attention to the need for providing good care and educational experiences for young children. The Head Start program is alive and well today, and is nationally recognized as an effective means of providing comprehensive services to children and families, serving as a model for the development of the ABC Child Care Act of 1990. We will discuss it further in Chapter 2.

INTERDISCIPLINARY INFLUENCES

Several professions enrich the heritage of early childhood. This diversity was apparent from the beginning; the first nursery schools drew from six different professions: social work, home economics, nursing, psychology, education, and medicine. Three of the most consistent and influential of those disciplines were medicine, education, and child psychology.

Medicine

The medical field has contributed to the study of child growth through the work of several physicians. These doctors became interested in child development and extended their knowledge to the areas of child rearing and education.

Maria Montessori

Maria Montessori (1870–1952) was the first woman in Italy ever granted a medical degree. She began studying children's diseases, and through her work with mentally defective children found education more appealing. Her philosophy is discussed earlier in this chapter, and will be part of Chapter 2 on educational programs.

Sigmund Freud

Sigmund Freud (1856–1939) made important contributions to all modern thinking. The father of personality theory, he drastically changed how we look at childhood. Freud reinforced two specific ideas: (1) a person is influenced by his early life in fundamental and dramatic ways, and (2) early experiences shape the way people live and behave as adults. Thus, psychoanalytic theory is mostly about personality development and emotional problems. Freud's work set into motion one of the three major strands of psychological theory that influence the developmental and learning theories of early childhood today. Although the impact of psychoanalysis on child psychology is not as great as it was 25 years ago, it still contributes significantly to the study of early childhood. Though he was not involved directly in education, Dr. Freud influenced its development. Dr. Freud and psychoanalytic theory influenced education greatly. Chapter 4 will enlarge on the theory and its application in early childhood education.

Arnold Gesell

Arnold Gesell (1880–1961) was a physician who was concerned with growth from a medical point of view. Gesell began studying child development when he was a student of G. Stanley Hall, an early advocate of child study. He later established the Clinic of Child Development at Yale University, where the data he collected with his colleagues became the recognized norms of how children grow and develop. He was also instrumental in encouraging Abigail Eliot to study with the McMillan sisters in England, and influenced Edna Noble White to open the Merrill-Palmer School.

Gesell's greatest contribution was in the area of child growth. He saw maturation as an innate and powerful force in development. "The total plan of growth," he said, "is beyond your control. It is too complex and mysterious to be altogether entrusted to human hands. So nature takes over most of the task, and simply invites your assistance" (Gesell, Ames, and Ilg, 1977). This belief became known in psychological circles as the maturation theory, and will be discussed at length in Chapter 4.

Through the Gesell Institute, guides were published using this theory. With such experts as Dr. Frances Ilg and Dr. Louise Bates Ames, Gesell authored articles that realistically portrayed the child's growth from birth to adolescence. These guides have sharp critics regarding their overuse and inappropriate application to children of cultures other than those studied.[1] Still, the "ages and stages" material is used widely as a yardstick of normal development.

Benjamin Spock

Spock's book, *Baby and Child Care*, was a mainstay for parents in the 1940s and 1950s. In a detailed "how-to" format Dr. Spock (1903–) preached a common-sense approach that helped shape the childhood of many of today's adults. He suggested that mothers use the playpen less and allow children freedom to explore the world firsthand. To that end, he asked parents to "child proof" their homes—a radical thought at the time. The word *permissiveness*, as it relates to child rearing, became associated with Dr. Spock's methods.

Dr. Spock has become an outspoken advocate for causes that extend his ideas. He is an active critic of those forces, be they economic, social, or political, that destroy people's healthy development. In his own words:

> I'll summarize my thoughts this way: Child care and home care, if well done, can be more creative, make a greater contribution to the world, bring more pleasure to family members, than 9 out of 10 outside jobs. It is only our mixed-up, materialistic values that make so many of us think the other way around.
>
> (Spock, 1976)

T. Berry Brazelton   *parental leave*

Dr. Brazelton (1918–) is a well-known pediatrician who supports and understands the development of infants and toddlers. His pediatric guide to parents deals with both physical and emotional growth. His writings speak to the parents' side of child raising, such as setting limits, or listening to what children say and observing what they do. Brazelton (1974) discusses the two-year-old and sharing this way:

> Understanding such concepts as fair and unfair, of giving and receiving and the process of sharing, all demands a kind of self-awareness. If a child is not sure of his own limits and of his own strengths, he cannot afford to allow his toys, equivalent to parts of himself, to be passed out to someone else, trusting that they will come back. At the same time, the ability to do so is evidence of an awareness of behavior in others comparable to his own and denotes the beginning of an awareness of non-self.

More recently Dr. Brazelton has advocated a national parental leave standard and is involved in organizing a federal lobbying group known as "Parent Action."

Education

Early childhood is one part of the larger professional field known as education. This includes elementary, secondary, and college or postsecondary schools. Along with John Dewey and Abi-

OUR DIVERSE WORLD   OUR DIVERSE WORLD   OUR DIVERSE WORLD   OUR DIVERSE WORLD   OUR DIVERSE WORLD

[1]This is another reminder of the importance of being able to notice the socio-cultural bias in the research in our field, keeping the information that is supportive to sound practice, and to expand or disregard what does not support good practice with children in a multicultural society.

gail Eliot, several other influences from this field bear attention.

The McMillan Sisters

In the first three decades of this century, these two sisters pioneered in early education. Nursery schools in Britain and America probably were developed because of the drive and dedication of the McMillan sisters.

Both women had broad international backgrounds. They grew up in North America and Scotland. Margaret studied music and language in Europe. She was well read in philosophy, politics, and medicine. Rachel studied to become a health inspector in England.

Health studies of 1908–1910 showed that 80 percent of children were born in good health, but that by the time they entered school, only 20 percent could be classified that way. Noticing the deplorable conditions for children under five, the McMillan sisters began a crusade for the slum children in England. Their concern extended beyond education to medical and dental care for young children. In 1910 they set up a clinic in Deptford, a London slum area, which became an open-air nursery a year later. The McMillans called it a "nurture school." Later, a training college nearby was named for Rachel. With no private financial resources, these two women faced tremendous hardships in keeping their school open. It is to their credit that Deptford still exists today.

The McMillan theory of fresh air, sleep, and bathing proved successful. "When over seven hundred children between one and five died of measles, there was not one fatal case at Deptford School" (Deasey, 1978). From the school's inception, a primary function was to research the effects of poverty on children.

Of the two sisters, Margaret had the greatest influence at the school at Deptford. Abigail Eliot writes of her:

> Miss McMillan invented the name [nursery school]. She paid great attention to health: a daily inspection, the outdoor program, play, good food—what she called "nurture." But she saw that an educational problem was also involved and she set to work to establish her own method of educa-

FIGURE 1.9 Margaret McMillan, along with her sister Rachel, developed the "open-air" nursery school and training schools in England. (Reproduced from *Margaret McMillan: Framework and Expansion of Nursery Education* by Dr. Elizabeth Bradburn with permission of the National Christian Education Council.)

> tion for young children. This was why she called it a "school."

> (Hymes, 1978)

Susan Isaacs

Susan Isaacs (1885–1948) was an educator of the early 20th century whose influence on nursery and progressive schools of the day was substantial. In 1929 she published *The Nursery Years*, which emphasized a different point of view than that of the behaviorist psychologists of the times. She interpreted Freudian theory for teachers and provided guidance for how schools could apply this new knowledge of the unconscious to the education of children. She proposed

> the opportunity for free unhindered imaginative play not only as a means to discover the world but also as a way to reach the psychic equilibrium, in working

through wishes, fears, and fantasies so as to integrate them into a living personality (Biber, 1984).

The teacher's role was different than that of a therapist, she asserted, in that teachers were "to attract mainly the forces of love, to be the good but regulating parent, to give opportunity to express aggression but in modified form, and not to attract herself to the negative explosive reactions of hatred and oppression" (Biber, 1984).

Isaacs' influence is felt today in schools whose philosophy emphasizes the child's point of view and the notion of play as the child's work.

The Progressive Education Movement

As indicated earlier in the sections on John Dewey and Patty Smith Hill, it is the Progressive Movement of the late 1800s and first half of the 20th century that changed the course of education in both elementary and nursery schools in America. Coinciding with the political Progressivism in this country, this philosophy emphasized a child-centered approach that had advocates from a more scientific viewpoint, such as G. Stanley Hall and John Dewey, and those of a psychoanalytic bent, such as Susan Isaacs and Patty Smith Hill.

Some of the major features of the educational progressive philosophy were:

1. Recognizing individual needs and individual differences in children.

2. Teachers [must be] more attentive to the needs of children.

3. Children learn best when they are highly motivated and have a genuine interest in the material.

4. Learning via rote memory is useless to children.

5. The teacher should be aware of the child's total development—social, physical, intellectual, and emotional.

6. Children learn best when they have direct contact with the material. (Osborn, 1980)

These beliefs were instrumental in changing the old traditional schools from a strict and subject-based curriculum to one that centered on children's interests as the foundation for curriculum development. While Dewey and others did not reject the teaching of basic skills, the shift was away from such subject matter education. Therefore, it is no surprise that progressive education had many critics among those interested in schooling for academic preparation. Still, most early childhood centers can thank the progressives for much of their philosophy and techniques for developing curriculum for their children today.

The Waldorf School

The first Waldorf School was established in Stuttgart, Germany, in 1919, by Rudolf Steiner, who is described earlier in this chapter. Patterned after his educational philosophy and personal beliefs, it was based on the premise that education's aim is to help all people find their right place in life and thus fulfill their destiny. There is close personal attention to the child's developing temperament and self-directed activity is valued. Children must be protected as they develop, so the teacher and parents must adhere to specific actions to protect the child from the noise of the modern world and technology.

Steiner agreed with Froebel and others that education should begin where the learner is. Whatever the child brings to the educational experience is to be worked with, not against. The curriculum of Waldorf schools is, therefore, both interdisciplinary and multisensory, with an emphasis on the arts, on tales of wisdom, and the concepts of community and respect for a person's individual needs. Often a teacher stays with the same group of children for eight years.

While this movement is essentially an elementary and secondary one, it is noteworthy as one of the largest nonsectarian, independent school movements in the world. Waldorf has more than 640 schools, 1087 kindergartens, 300 curative (special needs) centers, and 60 teacher education institutes worldwide; moreover, it is the model of choice for the changing Soviet and Eastern European school systems (Canniff, 1990). It is one of the fastest growing movements in America today. With its foundations in Froebelian tradition, and elements of Montessori and progressive education, the Waldorf school has a contribution to make to our knowledge of children and educational practices.

The Child Study Movement

A survey of education influences is incomplete without mentioning the child study movement in the 1920s and 1930s. It was through the child study movement that education and psychology began to have a common focus on children. Besides the Gesell Institute, many research centers and child development laboratories were established at colleges and universities around the country. Their inception reflects the interest of several disciplines in the growth of the young child. Schools of psychology looked for children to observe and study; schools of education wanted demonstration schools for their teachers-in-training and for student-teacher placement. Schools of home economics wanted their students to have first-hand experiences with children. These on-campus schools provided a place to gather information about child development and child psychology.

This period of educational experiment and child study led to an impressive collection of normative data by which we still measure ranges of ordinary development. Broman (1978) sums up the influence of the movement this way:

> From the beginning of the child study movement in the 1920s . . . early childhood was not a major emphasis in education until after the War on Poverty and the establishment of Head Start in 1965. The child study movement, however, was the impetus that began the search for the most appropriate means of educating young children.

The British Infant School

Developed by Robert Owen in the early nineteenth century, the British infant schools had a strong commitment to social reform (Spodek, 1985). In England, the term *infant school* refers to the kindergarten and primary grades. Then in 1967, the Plowden Report proposed a series of reforms for the schools. These changes paralleled those of American early childhood education. As a result, many American teachers in both the preschool and primary grades adapted the British infant school approach to their own classrooms.

Three aspects of this open school style that received the most attention were:

1. **Vertical, or family, groupings.** Children from five to eight years of age are placed in the same classroom. Several teachers may combine their classes and work together in teaching teams. Children may be taught by the same teachers for two or three years.

2. **Integrated day.** The classroom is organized into various centers, for math, science, and the arts. The teacher moves from one child or center to another as needed. Play is often the central activity, with an emphasis on follow-through with children's ideas and interests as they arise.

3. **Underlying concept.** There is a fundamental belief that the process of thinking takes precedence over the accumulation of facts. Learning how to think rather than stockpiling data is encouraged. How to identify and solve problems is valued more than having a finished product. Teachers focus on the child's current learning rather than on the future.

Just as Owen's ideas took hold in America in the nineteenth century, so, too, did the twentieth-century version of the infant school fire the imaginations of teachers in the United States. Their tenets of open education are developmentally appropriate for both preschool and primary schools (Bredekamp, 1988).

Reggio Emilia

In the last part of this century, yet another educator and educational system have influenced early childhood thinking. Loris Malaguzzi (1920–1994) developed his theory of early childhood education from his work with infants, toddlers, and preschoolers while working as the founder and director of the Department of Education in the town of Reggio Emilia, Italy. His philosophy includes creating "an amiable school" (Malaguzzi, 1993) that welcomes families and the community and invites relationships among teachers, children, and parents to intensify and deepen in order to strengthen a child's sense of identity.

Reggio Emilia has attracted the attention and interest of American educators because of its respect for children's work and creativity, its project approach, and its total community support. Reggio Emilia serves as a model of exemplary early childhood practices. This high-quality program is also discussed in Chapters 2, 9, 11, and 14.

Psychology

The roots of early childhood education are wonderfully diverse, but one tap root is especially deep: the connection with the field of psychology. In this century particularly, the study of people and their behavior is linked with the study of children and their growth.

Initially, child development was mostly confined to the study of trends and descriptions of changes. Then the scope and definition of child development began to change. Developmental psychologists now study the processes associated with those changes. Specifically, child development focuses on language acquisition, the effect of early experiences on intellectual development, and the process of attachment to others. Such is the world of early childhood—it is no wonder that we are so closely tied to the world of psychology.

There is no one theory or name that encompasses all of developmental psychology. Indeed, there are many. The major theories, their creators, and their influence on early education will be discussed in depth in Chapter 4.

THEMES IN EARLY CHILDHOOD EDUCATION

When we review the colorful and rich history of early childhood education, three major themes

FIGURE 1.10   Childhood is a special time of life.

emerge. These same themes reappear and are reflected in the ensuing thought and theory of each age.

Ethic of Social Reform

The first theme is that of the ethic of social reform. Early childhood education programs often have had the expectation that schooling for the young will lead to social change and improvement. Montessori, the McMillans, Patty Smith Hill, Abigail Eliot, and Head Start all tried to improve children's health and physical well-being by attending first to the physical and social welfare aspects of children's lives. The ABC Act of 1990, spawned by the tireless work of Marian Wright Edelmen and the Children's Defense Fund, received much of its impetus from the impoverished state of so many children in America. Educators today still assert that tired, undernourished children are not ready to learn or to be educated. Social reform can go a step further, such as with Head Start, improving the whole family situation and involving the community in its efforts.

Importance of Childhood

The second theme is the importance and uniqueness of childhood. In fact, the entire notion of the importance of childhood rests on the concept of the child as a special part of human existence and, therefore, a valuable part of the life cycle. Before 1700 or so, Western society showed little concern for children. Infanticide was persistent, if not actually accepted. Once families and society began to value children, life changed dramatically for the young. The saying "As the twig is bent, so grows the tree" could apply to all children and their early childhood learning experiences as well as to an individual child. When people accepted the importance of childhood, they began to take responsibility for a quality life for children. From Comenius, Rousseau, and Froebel of earlier centuries to Neill, Russell, and the Child Study Movement of more recent times, society has begun to provide for the health and physical welfare of children and come to understand the necessity to care for their minds.

Modern early childhood teachers believe the early years form the foundation for later development, physically, intellectually, socially, and emotionally. Children need special attention during these years. Childhood is fundamentally different from adulthood; it needs to be understood and respected as such. Children's styles of learning, of letting the child "learn by doing" and "learn by discovery" are part of the essential respect for children and childhood. Public recognition of that need has created a wealth of programs for the young not dreamed of at any other time in history.

Transmitting Values

The third recurrent theme in our educational heritage is that of transmitting values. What children should ultimately *do* and *be* is at the core of all childrearing practices, whether in the home or the school. Values—be they social, cultural, moral, or religious—have been the essence of education for centuries. For example, the Puritan fathers valued hard work and Biblical theology. Therefore, schools of their time taught children to read in order to learn the Bible. Rousseau and Froebel valued the child. The works of Montessori, Dewey, and Steiner reflected a belief in the worth and dignity of childhood. They transmitted these values into the educational practices we have inherited. Finally, the initiators of Head Start (see Chapter 2) and the Anti-bias Curriculum (see Chapter 9) realized the child's self-worth would be enhanced by valuing one's culture or origin. An awareness and an appreciation of ethnic heritage is becoming an integral part of the early childhood curriculum.[1]

Since the early 1900s, the group of early childhood educators has begun to develop a sense of professionalism, in the realm of identity as well as mission and purpose. Professional organizations such as the National Association for the Education of Young Children (NAEYC) and the Association for Childhood Education International (ACEI) have been advocating for the concerns of children, families, and educators for the better part of a century. Both groups have worked to develop standards for working with children. These efforts have resulted in important improvements in the status of children in group care, and have begun to establish appropriate practices (NAEYC's Academy standards will be discussed in Chapters 9 and 10), pay, and working standards for teachers (Quality-Compensation-Affordability studies will be discussed in Chapter 15), and a Code of Ethics for early childhood educators (Code of Ethical Conduct will be discussed in Chapter 5).

Teaching children to live in a democratic society has always been valued in the United States. In the curriculum from kindergarten through college, this belief is reflected as we educate our children for citizenship.[2] It is how we define these values and how we teach them that are the critical issues in education.

These three themes have been at the center of early education for centuries. Occasionally, one theme dominates, as it did in the 1960s when the desire for social reform led to the creation of Head Start. At other times they seem indistinguishable from one another. Together, they have shaped the direction of early childhood education as we know it today. As we learn more about children, society, and ourselves, the 1990s will be a time to reconsider and redefine our aims and directions. It is a formidable challenge—and a worthy one.

INTEGRATING HISTORY WITH THEORY

The history of early childhood education is like a tapestry—woven of many influences. A broad field such as medicine is a thread in this cloth, as is the passion of a Patty Smith Hill or a Lucy Sprague Mitchell. The history forms the theory on which we base our teaching, and every child, every class, every experience translates our history into educational practice and makes another thread in this grand cloth.[2]

Events of history have had a hand in shaping early childhood education. Forces such as war (which produced the Kaiser Shipyards project),

[1] Informed early childhood educators really are leading the way in educational practice in terms of *celebrating* the diversity of the families!

[2 and 3] See footnote on page 30. The early childhood profession provides the opportunity for one to be an agent for social change—to actually translate the values of democracy into practice.

political movements (such as progressivism), and the state of the economy (which brought the War on Poverty and Head Start) bring about change and development in how children are cared for in this country. The ingredients that early childhood considers essential today—that care and education are inseparable, that teaching practices are developmentally appropriate, and that adequate funding is critical for success (Smith, 1989)—all stem from historical events and people.

Several fields of study and a number of professions have added to our knowledge of children and, therefore, have affected educational theory. From the professions of education, medicine, and psychology, early childhood education has developed a theory of what is best for children. The medical model offered a view of childhood that is both maturational and environmental. Psychology confirmed this blending of nature and nurture and offered observational study as a basis for educational practice. As a result, early childhood theory includes both an attention to physical growth and developmental stages and a respect for personal experience in learning. The field of education brought to early childhood theory the components of a holistic approach to child and family, variable grouping of children and activities, and a sensitivity to the social and reform possibilities of educating our young. These influences will be described at length in Chapter 4.

The individuals who created our history have had a profound effect on early childhood theory. Their strong and passionate beliefs have captured our imaginations and fueled our commitment to enhancing the well-being of children. What John Dewey, Lucy Sprague Mitchell, and Susan Isaacs all had in common was a drive to extend themselves on behalf of young children. Thus, early childhood theory has a *personal* component, an emotional investment that gives each early childhood teacher and caregiver a sense of belonging to a larger cause. The work that has gone before goes on through us and extends beyond us—to children of all ages and any era.

From this blending of professional discoveries and personal commitment comes a challenge. Early childhood history calls on teachers to learn from the past and to know the theories on which the profession is based. These theories must be continually tested in the classroom and refined as they apply

to children every day. In this way, the profession stays relevant and legitimate. Finally, early childhood education history affirms the value of being connected with others and remaining steadfastly committed to the common cause of young children (see Chapter 5 and Appendix B). As the NAEYC Code of Ethics states:

> I will know about, abide by, and advocate for laws and regulations that enhance the quality of life for young children.
>
> I will support the rights of children to live and learn in environments that are responsive to their developmental needs.
>
> I will improve my competencies in providing for children's needs.
>
> I will appreciate each child's uniqueness, thus enhancing the child's self-respect.
>
> (NAEYC, 1988)

S U M M A R Y

This chapter traces the roots of early childhood education from ancient times. Knowing this history gives teachers a sense of support and inspiration. An historical overview offers insights that illuminate present program and societal needs and prevent future mistakes. It helps us appreciate the legacy left by others.

Early childhood education involves children from infancy through the primary years. The term itself offers its own professional challenges:

EARLY:	How do YOUNG children grow and learn best?
CHILDHOOD:	How do CHILDREN think, feel, learn?
EDUCATION:	How can children LEARN and be TAUGHT?

These questions have been addressed by educators in Europe and America throughout history. Their answers have influenced educational philosophy and practice and, in turn, have been affected by the social and political forces of the day. The most notable modern developments in this country have been the advent of nursery schools and kindergartens, the Kaiser Child Care Center in

World War II as a day care model, and Head Start.

Early childhood education itself is an interdisciplinary field. Important contributions have come from medicine, education, and psychology.

Certain themes emerge in early childhood education with a study of its history. The ethic of social reform, the importance of childhood, and the transmission of values have been at the core of this field throughout history.

The contributions of many pioneers leave us dreams for the young children of our society. This can give meaning to our lives as teachers as we continue to create a climate for the child who will make history tomorrow.

R E V I E W   Q U E S T I O N S

1. Identify and describe five key people who influenced the field of early childhood education. With whom would you like to have studied or worked? Why?

2. Match the name with the appropriate phrase. Put them in the order that best matches your own theory of early childhood education. State your reasons.

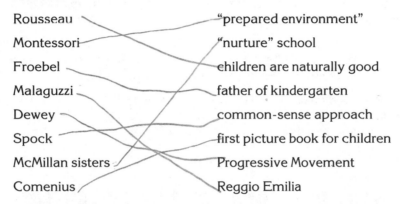

Rousseau — "prepared environment"

Montessori — "nurture" school

Froebel — children are naturally good

Malaguzzi — father of kindergarten

Dewey — common-sense approach

Spock — first picture book for children

McMillan sisters — Progressive Movement

Comenius — Reggio Emilia

3. Define early childhood education in your own words. Include age ranges and what you believe to be its purpose. Contrast this to the text definition and defend your position.

4. Name three institutions or living persons who are influencing the history of early childhood today. Describe your reactions to each, and how they have influenced your educational philosophy.

5. Maria Montessori made several contributions to education. What are some of her theories and how did she adapt them for classroom use? How are Montessori materials or teaching methods used in your classroom?

6. "Who Said It?" Match the historic figures with their quotations:

"If we wish him [the child] to make great progress in the pursuit of wisdom, we must direct his faculties towards it in infancy... when memory is tenacious."   Rousseau

"Since everything that comes into the human mind enters through the gates of sense, man's first reason is a   Montessori reason of sense-experience... To substitute books for these... teaches us to believe much and know little."

"Play is the purest, most spiritual activity of man... It gives, therefore, joy, freedom, contentment..."   Comenius

"There exists only one real biological manifestation: the living individual; and toward single individuals, one by one observed, education must direct itself."   Steiner

"What is of the very greatest importance is what kind of men we are, what impressions the child receives through us."   Froebel

L E A R N I N G   A C T I V I T I E S

1. Find out when and by whom the school or center in which you are student teaching was started. What were some of the social, economic, and political issues of those times? How might they have affected the philosophy of the school?

2. Write your own pedagogic creed. List five of what you consider to be the most important beliefs you hold about educating young children. How do you see those beliefs expressed in school today?

3. Make a list of the values you think are important to teach children. In an adjoining column, add the ways in which you would help children learn those values. In other words, list the materials and curriculum you would use.

B I B L I O G R A P H Y

Archambault, R.D. (Ed.). *John Dewey on Education: Selected Writings*. Chicago, IL: University of Chicago Press, 1964.

Aries, Phillipe. *Centuries of Childhood*. New York: Knopf, 1962.

Bain, Winifred E. *75 Years of Concern for Children*. Washington, DC: Association for Childhood Education International, 1967.

Bauch, Jerold P. (Ed.). *Early Childhood Education in the Schools*. Washington, DC: National Education Association, 1988.

Biber, Barbara. *Early Education and Psychological Development*. New Haven, CT: Yale University Press, 1984.

Bradburn, Elizabeth. *Margaret McMillan: Framework and Expansion of Nursery Education. Surrey*, England: Denholmouse Press, 1976.

Bradburn, Elizabeth. *Margaret McMillan: Portrait of a Pioneer*. London & New York: Routledge, 1989.

Brooks, Angeline. *Four Active Workers*. Springfield, MA: Milton Bradley Co., 1886.

Caniff, Diane I. "Why the 'Waldorf' Movement Is Thriving in Eastern Europe." *Education Week*, Volume X, Number 13, November 28, 1990.

Chattin-McNichols. "Montessori in the U.S.—Then and Now." In *Beginnings and*

Beyond, ed. A. Gordon and K.W. Browne. Albany, NY: Delmar Publishers, 1993 (3rd Ed.).

Cleverley, John, and Phillips, D.C. *Visions of Childhood: Influential Models from Locke to Spock*. New York: Teachers College, 1986 (Revised Ed.).

De Mause, L. *The History of Childhood*. New York: The Psychohistory Press, 1974.

Dowley, Edith. "Early Childhood Education in the Shipyards." In *Beginnings and Beyond*, ed. A. Gordon and K.W. Browne. Albany, NY: Delmar Publishers, 1993 (3rd Ed.).

Elkind, David. "The Child Yesterday, Today, and Tomorrow." *Young Children*. Washington, DC.: NAEYC, Volume 42, Number 4, May, 1987.

Froebel, Friedrich. *The Education of Man*, translated by M.W. Hailman. New York: D. Appelton, 1887.

Hewes, Dorothy. "On Doing History." in *Beginnings and Beyond*, ed. A. Gordon and K.W. Browne. Albany, NY: Delmar Publishers, 1993 (3rd Ed.).

Hymes, James L., Jr. *Living History Interviews*. Carmel, CA: Hacienda Press, 1978–79 (Books 1–3).

Lall, Geeta R., and Lall, Bernard M. *Comparative Early Childhood Education*. Springfield, IL: Charles C. Thomas, 1983.

Malaguzzi, Loris, "For an Education Based on Relationships." *Young Children*, November 1993.

McMillan, Margaret. *The Nursery School*. London & Toronto: J.M. Dent & Sons. New York: E.P. Dutton & Co., 1919.

Montessori, Maria. *The Montessori Method*, translated by Anne E. George. Cambridge, MA, 1967.

Murphy, Clennie H., and Waxler, Trellis. "Head Start: a Brief Review and Preview." *The Journal of Negro Education*. Vol. 58, No. 1, Winter 1989.

Neill, A.S. *Summerhill: a Radical Approach to Child Rearing*. New York: Hart Publishing Co., 1960.

New, Rebecca. "Excellent Early Childhood Education: A City in Italy Has It." *Young Children*, September, 1990.

Osborn, D. Keith. *Early Childhood Education in Historical Perspective*. Athens, GA: Education Associates, 1991 (3rd Ed.).

Pleasant, Mae Barbee Boone. *Hampton University: Our Home by the Sea*. Virginia Beach, VA: Donning Co., 1992.

Russell, Bertrand. *On Education, Especially in Early Childhood*. London, Unwin paperbacks, 1926 & 1976.

Smith, Marilyn M. "Excellence and Equity for America's Children." *Tennessee's Children*, Spring, 1989.

Spodek, Bernard, Saracho, Olivia, N., and Peters, Donald L. (Eds.). *Professionalism and the Early Childhood Practitioner*. New York: Teacher College, 1988.

Steiner, Rudolf. *The Essentials of Education*. London: Anthroposophical Publishing Company, 1926.

Suransky, Valerie Poklakov. *The Erosion of Childhood*. Chicago: University of Chicago Press, 1982.

Weber, Evelyn. *Ideas Influencing Early Childhood Education: a Theoretical Analysis*. New York: Teachers College, 1984.

Wiggins & Smith. *Froebel's Gifts*. Boston: Houghton Mifflin Co., 1895.

CHAPTER 2

Types of Programs

QUESTIONS FOR THOUGHT

What are some of the different types of early childhood programs?

What are the indicators of quality in group programs for young children?

What is the range of early childhood education, and which programs correspond to the various age levels?

What is unique about caring for infants and toddlers?

What are the major issues facing kindergartens today?

Around which programs are there controversies—and why?

How does the role of the teacher differ in each of the early childhood settings?

What criteria affect programs in early childhood?

How does Head Start differ from other early childhood programs?

How do infant/toddler programs differ from preschool programs, and how do they differ from one another?

DIVERSITY OF PROGRAMS

From the types available to the numbers of children who attend these schools, the name of the game in early childhood programs is diversity. Early childhood programs abound; every community has some type of schooling for the young child. The range can encompass a morning nursery school for toddlers, an infant-parent stimulation program, or a full child care service for three-to-six-year-olds. Some programs run for only a half-day; others are open from 6:00 A.M. until 7:00 P.M. Still other centers accept children on a drop-in basis, or for 24-hour care, such as hospitals. Churches, school districts, community-action groups, parents, governments, private social agencies, and businesses may run schools.

Schools exist to serve a number of needs, which often overlap. Some of these are:

1. caring for children while parents work

2. enrichment programs for children

3. educational programs for parent and child

4. an activity arena for children

5. academic instruction

Programs generally reflect the needs of society as a whole. Millions of mothers of children under six are in the labor force as never before. Early childhood schools provide a wide range of services for children from infancy through eight years of age to meet some of that need. According to the U.S. Census Bureau (1995), enrollment in early childhood programs has more than doubled since 1973, so that by 1993 68 percent of all preschool children were participating in some type of organized, out-of-home group program (National Center for Education Statistics, 1993).

In the human life cycle, early childhood is a period of maximum dependency. The various programs available reflect this in a number of ways. The teacher-child ratio varies in relation to the child's age; infants, at the higher end of the dependency scale, require more teachers per child in a classroom than do five-year-olds. The program itself reflects the age group it serves. The size of the group, the length of the program, and the equipment used relate to the enrolled children's capabilities and needs. Even the daily schedule mirrors the dependent relationship between the child and the teacher. Bathrooming, snack and meal routines, as well as clothing needs, call for longer periods of time in a toddler group than in a class of four-year-olds.

Diversity is apparent, too, in the philosophy expressed by the specific program. Some schools, such as Montessori programs, follow a very clear, precise outline based on a philosophical approach developed by Maria Montessori at the turn of the century. Other schools are more eclectic; they draw from a number of theories, choosing those methods and ideas that best suit their needs.

Indicators of Quality ✷

Early childhood programs vary greatly in their educational goals and practices, their methods of instruction, and even in the kind of social "mood" or atmosphere they create. Yet, varied as they are, most early childhood programs share some common principles. The quality of these programs is based on three essential factors: (1) the teacher/child ratio, that is, the number of children cared for by each staff member; (2) the total size of the group or class; and (3) the education, experience, and training of the staff. The importance of these three factors cannot be underestimated and they underline each of the principles that follow.

The NAEYC has established a list of criteria for high-quality early childhood programs, based on a consensus of thousands of early childhood professionals. The following ten indicators serve as a standard of excellence for any group program for young children. After each one is a reference to the chapter(s) in the text where the topic is more fully developed.

1. *Interactions between children and staff* provide opportunities for children to develop an under-

OUR DIVERSE WORLD OUR DIVERSE WORLD OUR DIVERSE WORLD OUR DIVERSE WORLD OUR DIVERSE WORLD OUR DIVERSE WORLD

[1]In observing programs for young children, consider the influences on the teachers' philosophy and practice—in many cases it is eclectic, a little bit of this and a little bit of that." It is another indication of how practice is influenced by life in a democratic and multicultural society.

standing of self and others and are character-ized by warmth, personal respect, individuali-ty, positive support, and responsiveness. (Chapters 3, 5, 7, and 14)

2. *The curriculum* encourages children to be ac-tively involved in the learning process, to expe-rience a variety of developmentally appropri-ate activities and materials, and to pursue their own interests in the context of life in the com-munity and the world. (Chapters 11, 12, 13 and 14).

3. *Communication with families* is based on the concept that families are the principal influ-ence in children's lives. Parents are well-in-formed about and welcome as observers and contributors to the program. (Chapter 8)

4. *The program is staffed by adults who are trained in child development and early education* and who recognize and provide for children's needs since the quality and competence of the staff are the most important determinants of the quality of an early childhood program. (Chapters 3, 5 and 15).

5. *The staffing structure of the program is organized* to assure that the needs of individual children are met, and to maintain positive interactions and constructive activity among the children and staff. (Chapters 3, 5).

6. The quality of the early childhood experience for children is affected by the efficiency and sta-bility of the program's administration. *Effective administration* includes good communication, positive community relationships, fiscal stabili-ty, and attention to the needs and working con-ditions of staff members. (Chapters 10, 15).

7. *The indoor and outdoor physical environments* should be designed to promote involvement in the daily activities and easy, constructive inter-actions among adults and children. (Chapter 10)

8. *The health and safety of children and adults* are protected and enhanced. Good programs act to prevent illness and accidents, are prepared to deal with emergencies should they occur, and also educate children concerning safe and healthy practices. (Chapter 9)

9. *Children are provided with adequate nutrition* and are taught good eating habits. (Chapter 9)

10. *Ongoing and systematic evaluation* is essential to improving and maintaining the quality of an early childhood program. Evaluation should fo-cus on the program's effectiveness in meeting the needs of children and parents. (Chapters 2, 10)

(Bredekamp in Willer, 1990)

These are the ten essential components on which a program is judged for accreditation through NAEYC's Academy of Early Childhood Programs.

THE CORE OF EARLY CHILDHOOD EDUCATION

What do programs for the young child look like? How are the similarities and differences ex-pressed in school settings? What marks a program as unique? The answers to these questions can be found by looking at some of the most common programs in early childhood education.

The Traditional Nursery School

At the core of early education is what is labeled **traditional nursery school:** a place for 2-1/2-to-five-year-olds designed for educational experi-ences. This includes nursery schools, the variations of day care centers and their sister programs, labo-ratory schools, and parent cooperatives.

The philosophy of these schools is best de-scribed by Katherine Read in her now classic book, *The Nursery School: A Human Relationships Laboratory.* First published over 45 years ago, this book serves as an encyclopedia of the traditional nursery school, its methods, and its philosophy.

The idea of a school as a place of human ac-tivity mirrors the thoughts of Dewey, Piaget, Erik-son, and others. Read develops this philosophy fully, with an educational model that emphasizes the human needs, growth patterns, and relation-ships in a young child's life. Developmentally, a traditional nursery school focuses on social com-petence and emotional well-being. The curricu-lum encourages self-expression through language, creativity, intellectual skill, and physical activity.

The basic underlying belief is the importance of interpersonal connections children make with themselves, each other, and adults.

In theory, the objectives of traditional nursery schools are prescribed. The schools have some general characteristics in common, like the daily schedule (see Figure 2.1). The schedule reflects the values of the school. For example, large blocks of time are devoted to free play, a time when children are free to initiate their own activities and become deeply involved without interruptions, emphasizing the importance of play. In this way, children learn to make their own choices, select their own playmates, and work on their interests and issues at their own rate. A dominant belief is that children learn best in an atmosphere free from excessive restraint and direction.

A typical daily schedule also indicates an awareness of the developing child's characteristics and needs. Programs attend to the physical and health needs (toileting, snacks, fresh air). There is a balance of activities (indoors and out, free choice, and teacher-directed times). Closer inspection of the environment reveals a wide variety of activities (large- and small-muscle games, intellectual choices, creative arts, social play opportunities).

Then, too, there is the clear acknowledgment of change and the time it takes children to make and adjust to changes. Children must have plenty of time for arrival and departure from school, greetings, cleanup, and transition times between activities. The amount of time given to any one part of the day's activities directly reflects the values the school endorses.

There are also aspects of the traditional model that are not immediately evident by looking at a daily schedule. The role of the teacher and methods of teaching are important. Nursery schools assume that young children need individual attention and should have personal, warm relationships with important adults (see Figure 2.2). Therefore, the groups of children are generally small, often fewer than 20 in a class. The teacher-child ratio is low, as few as six to ten children for each teacher. Teachers learn about children's development and needs by observation and direct interaction, rather than from formalized testing. They work with children individually and in small groups (perhaps three or four) and often teach through conversation and materials. Always, the teacher encourages the children to express themselves, their feelings, and their thinking. Such rapport between teacher and pupil fosters self-confidence, security, and belonging. Proponents of the traditional nursery school believe that these feelings promote positive self-image, healthy relationships, and an encouraging learning environment.

There are several programs within the traditional preschool framework. Three important variations on the theme are: child care centers, laboratory schools, and parent cooperative nursery schools.

Child Care Centers

Some of the first nursery schools in England operated from 8:00 A.M. until 4:00 or 5:00 P.M. It was only later in America that the nursery school evolved into a part- or half-day program. Child care, then, is not a modern phenomenon. Child care center patterns differ from those of half-day nursery schools. By definition, a child care center is a place for children who need care for a greater portion of the day. The school schedule is extended to fit the hours of working parents. The program roughly models what ordinarily happens in the routines of a child's day at home. Therefore, the adults who work in a child care center have somewhat different responsibilities and training. Child care centers are for infants and toddlers, as well as for the 2-1/2-to-five-year-old range. In this section, the focus is on those centers for the nursery school age range.

Child care has a number of unique qualities.

Scheduling. Compare the nursery school schedule to the child care schedule (see Figure 2.3). The

9:00	Children arrive at school
9:00–9:45	Free play (indoors)
9:45	Cleanup
10:00	Singing time (large group)
10:15–10:30	Toileting/snack time (small groups)
10:30–11:30	Free play (outdoors)
11:30	Cleanup
11:45	Story time
12:00	Children leave for home

FIGURE 2.1 A sample schedule for traditional half-day nursery schools is the core of early education programs.

FIGURE 2.2 Individual attention and warm relationships—essential components in every program.

morning starts slowly. Children arrive early since their parent(s) must go to work. The center will usually supply breakfast; midmorning and midafternoon snacks supplement a noon lunch. A nap period for one to two hours for all the children gives a needed rest and balances their active, social day with quiet, solitary time. The program also includes extended experiences outside the school—field trips, library story hour, or swimming lessons—since children spend the major portion of their waking hours on-site. As the day draws to a close, children gather together quietly, with less energy and activity.

Licensing. There are no national standards or policies regarding licensing of child care facilities in the United States. Many local and state governments, however, do require licensing of child care centers and family day care homes. Nor is there one central licensing agency. Depending upon the state, a license may be issued by the Department

of Health, Department of Education, or Department of Social Welfare. Certification of child care workers is again left to local options.

Early childhood professional groups are calling for increased standardization of licensing procedures to ensure that children are receiving the best possible care in safe and healthy environments. The primary concern is to establish effective licensing policies that are reinforced and will ensure that all programs will provide adequate care to meet the basic developmental needs of children. Standardized licensing regulations will protect children at all economic levels. All children will be treated equally whether they attend a family day care home in Houston, a Head Start classroom in Jacksonville, a child care center in Harlem, or a public school extended day program in Sacramento. The same minimum standards will apply to adult: child ratios, suitable safety precautions, health and nutrition needs, and the amount of training and preparation required of caregivers.

7:00–8:30	Arrival/breakfast; limited indoor play
8:30	Large group meeting
8:45–9:45	Free play (inside)
9:45	Cleanup/toileting
10:00	Snack time (small groups)
10:15–11:30	Free play (outside)
11:30	Cleanup/handwashing
12:00	Lunch
12:30	Toothbrushing/toileting
1:00–2:00	Nap time
2:00–3:00	Free play (outside)
3:00	Group time
3:15	Snack time (small groups)
3:30–5:00	Inside and outside free play/ library hour
5:00	Cleanup
5:15–5:30	Departure

FIGURE 2.3 A typical full-day care schedule. Most child-care programs combine education and caring for basic needs.

The need for standards arises out of recent changes in early childhood. The number of children in out-of-home care settings has increased. Many are infants and toddlers, a younger population than previously served. Children are spending longer hours in child care, and there are more programs sponsored by a variety of agencies such as churches, public schools, and private for-profit firms. With this diverse mix, a common set of standards for licensing is imperative to ensure the best possible care for all children who need these services. (See Chapters 3, 9, 10, and 15 for further discussion of licensing, regulations, and standards for early childhood programs.)

While professionalization of centers is worthwhile, implementation is controversial and costly. The question arises as to which agency should rightfully evaluate licensing and enforce the policies and procedures established by law. Many see it as a natural extension of the state Department of Education. Others argue equally for the Department of Social Welfare or Board of Health.

Until government and professionals can agree on implementation, enforcement, and funding, licensing of child care facilities and personnel will remain an unsolved issue.

Staffing. What does child care mean for teachers? First, they must be aware of and trained to deal with the parenting side of teaching. The children may need more nurturing, clearer consistency in limits, and established routines. At the same time, they need individual flexibility and understanding and regular private time with caring adults.

Parents' needs also may be greater and require more of the teachers' time. Teachers should communicate with and support parents effectively. Parents want to trust their children's teachers and be relaxed with them. Teachers in a child care center find it valuable to take the time to be good listeners and clear communicators to parents about their child; this builds the trust and support that is so vital when working with young children. Child care parents may require extra effort; they have full-time jobs as well as child-rearing responsibilities draining their energies. It takes a strong team effort on the part of the teacher and the parent to make sure the lines of communication stay open.

The teaching staff undoubtedly has staggered schedules, perhaps a morning and an afternoon shift. Administration of this type of program is therefore more complex. An effort must be made to ensure that all teachers get together on a regular basis to share the mutual information and details about the children in their care. Both shifts must be aware of what happens when they are not on-site in order to run the program consistently.

Need for Child Care

Child care in the United States used to be primarily **custodial,** providing basic health and physical care. But times have changed. Full day care is an American way of life, providing enriched programs for total development. Thousands of families rely on child care centers. The Children's Defense Fund (1990) chronicles the growth of such programs: In 1970 only three out of ten preschool children had mothers who worked outside the home. Today that number has reached over fifty percent. By 2000, that figure will rise to nearly seven in ten preschoolers with mothers in the workforce. According to the Children's Defense Fund, in 1994 60 percent of mothers with children under 6 years of age were employed. That is a 50 percent increase in the past 20 years. When more than half the new mothers in the U.S. are in the workplace, a reality of family life is established.

The rising divorce rate, single-parent families, the women's movement, and the economy have all contributed to a greater need than ever for child care.

Further data from the National Center for Educational Statistics (1993) tell another part of the story. Over 75 percent of preschool children whose mothers are employed are in an early childhood setting; 50 percent of the children whose mothers are not employed also attend a program. The same study showed that almost twice as many preschool children participate in a center-based program as in home-based care. There is no doubt about the desire for parents to have child care options for their families.

Good, affordable, accessible child care that will meet the increasing needs of American families is one of today's most critical issues. The distinction between day care (stressing the protective, custodial services) and early education (emphasizing schooling) has appropriately blurred. Today, child care professionals recognize the concept of child care inherent in all programs for young children and the concept of education as an integral part of caring for young children.

This desire to link child care services with educating the young child is best expressed by the trend toward labeling many early childhood programs "child care" rather than the traditional "day care." This term implies that child care is a permanent part of American life, including both teaching and nurturing functions. It removes some of the stigma previously attached to day care as primarily a babysitting, custodial function. The one exception to this terminology seems to be family day care. Although many family day care providers are trained and provide quality programs, the label "day care" persists. It appears that the words "family day care" are appropriate in this case because they serve to distinguish a type of child care program from regular, ongoing family child-rearing. See also Chapter 15.

Child Care Issues

Millions of children are in child care settings every day. The questions and concerns, the issues and the controversies no long center around the question of whether or not child care should exist. Instead, they have turned to questions concerning the effects on children who spend so much of their early years in group care and the quality of that care.

The issue is complex and related to economic trends as well as social forces. Families need and want child care. Child care exists as a response to the trend toward working mothers. It is a solution to economic and social pressures, not a cause.

The impact of child care on children, families, and the community is not yet fully understood. Most research shows that child care has either positive effects or no effects on intelligence and little impact on children's attachment to parents. (See "What Is Good Quality Infant/Toddler Care?", found later in this chapter, for more information on infant attachment.) There is some question that child care may increase the rate of aggressiveness in elementary school, yet the same children were seen by teachers as more curious and more intelligent (Bee, 1995). Ongoing research can help answer the critical questions regarding the effect of child care on a child's development and ages of greatest vulnerability, on parent-child relationships, and on the quality of child care.

The focus of the child care issues centers on a few core problems that threaten the *quality* of child care throughout the country. A few statistics highlight the issues:

- The annual turnover rate for child care staff in 1991–1992 was 26 percent, compared to 5.6 percent for public school teachers and 916 percent for businesses (Children's Defense Fund, 1994).

- More than two-thirds of the states do not require preservice training for child-care teachers (Morgan et al, 1993).

- A United States Department of Education survey revealed that the *child/staff ratios* in child care centers rose from 6.8 children per staff in 1976 to 8.5 in 1990 (U.S. Department of Education).

- The same survey showed an increase in *group size* from an average of 13.5 children per group in 1976 to 15.7 in 1990 (U.S. Department of Education).

Each of the four indicators of quality programs for young children is being undermined. Low salaries contribute to high staff turnover. The quality of child care is jeopardized when increasingly more children are being served by fewer adults.

Fees for parents have remained relatively unchanged over the last 15 years, however. Child care costs for families, according to the U.S. Bureau of Census, seem unevenly distributed. Higher income families spent 7 percent of their monthly income on child care while families below poverty level pay nearly 21 percent of their monthly income (Education Week, 1992). Obtaining affordable child care for those for whom it is a financial burden is a major concern that must be resolved.

In spite of these threats to quality child care, there are a few encouraging signs. A U.S. Department of Education study (1990), for instance, notes that the number of licensed child care centers tripled between 1976 and 1990 and that early childhood providers significantly increased their levels of education and training.

The National Academy of Early Childhood Programs reports that as of January 1995, 3713 early childhood programs have been accredited and that 7488 are in the process of self-study. Eighty-five percent of those who begin the self-study go on to be accredited.

The Child Care and Development Block Grant Act was passed by Congress in 1990, the most comprehensive child care bill to date. A landmark piece of legislation, this bill includes a program of direct aid to lower income parents through child care certificates that can be used to purchase services from child care providers. It will surely be tested in the courts since it allows parents vouchers to pay for child care in church-based centers. The bill further provides for expansion of Head Start services to full-day and full-year care, for before-school and after-school care programs, and an "earned income tax credit" for low income families. Improving the standards for child care and incentives for businesses to provide child care are also included in this legislation.

Where are the children who are in child care? What types of settings do parents commonly choose? A 30-year pattern has been dramatically altered: in the early 1960s only one out of every three preschool children of a working mother was enrolled in a child-care center. In 1990 that number was one in every three children attending a center (Willer, 1990).

The issues can be reduced to their core: how to expand affordable quality child care and at the same time address the lack of salary compensation and benefits so urgently due the early childhood professionals who subsidize the enterprise. Chapter 15 discusses the issue of child care in greater depth.

Work in child care is long, intense, and coupled with undesirable wages. This creates high staff turnover and low morale. Full-time child care is expensive. Sometimes it is too costly for poorly paid or underemployed parents to pay for quality child care. Occasionally, a center will cut corners to keep tuition reasonable, but the results of these shortcuts are usually detrimental to children.

Family Child Care

This type of service cares for children in ways reminiscent of an extended family grouping. The child care provider takes in small numbers of children in the family residence. The group size can range from two to twelve, but most homes keep a low adult:child ratio, enrolling fewer than six children. It is one of the most popular child care options.

The home setting, sometimes right within the child's own neighborhood, offers a more intimate, flexible, convenient, and possibly less expensive service for working parents. The children in a family child care home can range from infants to school-age children who are cared for after regular school hours.

Advantages. Family child care has many advantages. It is especially good for children who do well in small groups or whose parents prefer them in a family-style setting. This is especially appropriate care for infants and toddlers. Family child care homes often schedule flexible hours to meet the needs of parents who work. The wide age range can be advantageous as well. Consistency and stability from a single caregiver throughout the child's early years and a family grouping of children provide a home-like atmosphere that is especially appropriate for infants and toddlers.

Family child care providers own and operate their own small business in their homes. Providing child care is a way for women who want to remain at home with their children to contribute to the family income. Meeting the requirements for licensing, fulfilling all the administrative tasks of a

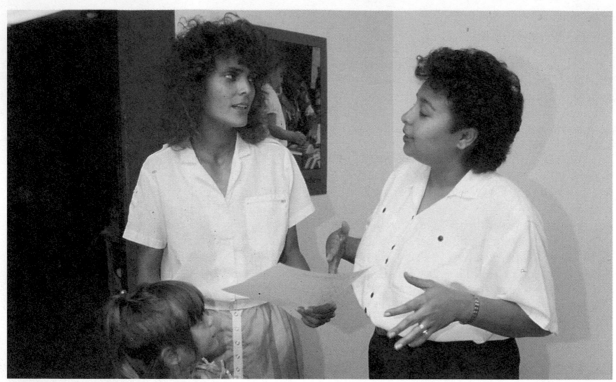

FIGURE 2.4 The family child-care provider runs a small business in her home. She is flexible enough to adapt to changing work schedules and children's needs.

business and an educational program, and keeping current with the local, state, and federal tax requirements are part of the professionalism required for this type of child care arrangement.

Disadvantages. Family child care has its disadvantages, too. Many homes are unregulated; that is, they are not under any sponsorship or agency that enforces quality care, and many are exempt from state licensing.

Accountability to a licensing agency and training in child development are the two major factors affecting the quality of family child care programs. According to the Child Care Action Campaign of New York, there are at least 1.5 million family child care providers, only 20 percent of which are regulated (Rubenstein, 1993). Training on an annual basis is mandated for family child care providers in only 19 states (Children's Defense Fund, 1994). Another study by the Families and Work Institute (CHIRA, 1994) found poor quality and care in the family child care homes they investigated, exemplified by the fact that 41

percent of the providers said they did not plan activities for the children in their care. The study did, however, identify six criteria found in good family child care settings: the providers enjoyed their work and considered it important, and they had training in child development, planned children's learning activities, charged higher fees, were better educated, and were regulated in some way.

Family child care providers can feel isolated from others in the child care field. A hopeful sign, however, is that more articles on family child care are being included in professional publications and early childhood conferences and workshops are now including issues related to the family child care provider. The National Association for Family Day Care, a network of family child care providers, has been established and publishes a quarterly publication of interest to its members.

This type of care could be a star in the galaxy of child care options. Small and personalized, it offers parents an appealing choice of home-based care. It is obvious, though, that further regulation of standards, availability of training for providers, and an awareness of the advantages of family child care need to be addressed. For those who need child care, this should be a viable alternative; for those who want to work at home, this type of career should be given serious consideration.

Children in the Workplace

Employer-Sponsored Child Care*

Employer-sponsored child care refers to child care facilities on or near the job site and supported by the business or industry. Hospitals, factories, colleges, and military bases often provide this service.

The role of industry and business in group child care has an outstanding, if brief, history. The most notable example in this country is the Kaiser Shipyard Centers during World War II. When child care was equated with a national cause—winning the war— government and industry joined forces to provide quality child care in industrial settings. Recently this model has been examined as one way businesses can support working parents' efforts to find quality child care.

The number of women working outside the home and the increase in single-parent families encourage us to look at the workplace as a logical solution for child care needs. Employers who have implemented child care claim that the benefits are increased employee morale, as well as an aid in recruitment and retention of employees. For parents, there is the added appeal of having their children close by and being part of their educational process.

Studies now show that child care can be cost effective in business terms, and more businesses are realizing that involvement in employee child care issues can have a positive effect on profits. Satisfied parents equal satisfied employees. More than 80 research studies show that companies who have addressed the needs of parents have reduced turnover and absenteeism and increased productivity (Hymowitz, 1991). It is interesting to note that seven of every ten employer-supported child care centers are operated by hospitals (Child Care Information Exchange, 1991).

Industry has begun to respond to the need to create a supportive structure for women who combine work and family. Child care is rapidly becoming a corporate issue and is the fringe benefit for the nineties. Of the 5000 businesses that have taken action on this issue, 1300 have on-site or near-site child care centers. Other benefits may include the option for one or more of the following: parental leave, flexible hours, corporate group discounts at local centers or family child care homes, resource and referral services, pretax salary reductions for child care, vouchers to purchase child care, reserved spaces in specific child care settings supported by the company. Companies located near each other may collaborate on the costs of these benefits. Recently, the inclusion of day care for elderly relatives has been incorporated into the flexible benefits plan. A few companies exceed the benefits discussed here. Apple Computer Inc. not only offers on-site child care, but gives $500 to new babies born to its employ-

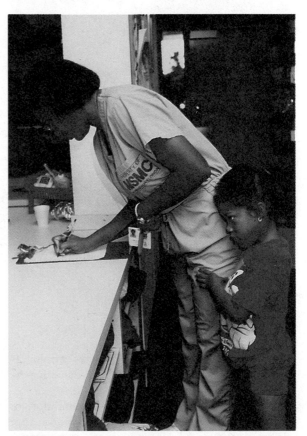

FIGURE 2.5 More and more corporations and businesses, including hospitals, help parents by offering on-the-job child-care facilities.

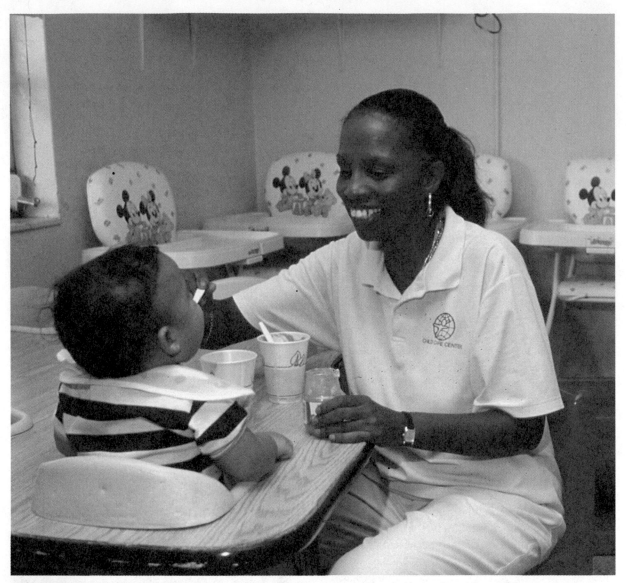

FIGURE 2.6 Routines, such as feeding, provide a balance to an active and busy day at the child-care center.

ees and up to $3000 to assist with adoptions (Education Week, 1989).

While there are signs of growth, employer-supported child care still reaches less than one percent of all employees (Neugebauer, 1991). A recent survey of the International Foundation of Employee Benefit Plans, however, found that while only 29 percent of businesses surveyed offer child care resources now, 74 percent said they would do so by 2000 (Education Week, 1991).

Workplace Schools

A recent spinoff of employer-supported child care has emerged in an unusual collaboration between businesses and public school districts. In Florida and Minnesota, kindergartens have been established in rent-free corporate space while the school district supplies the staff and materials. Children ride to work with their parents, attend school, and stay on for a child care program until their parents are ready to go home. This innovative program, which is open to employees of other local businesses, hopes to include first and other elementary grades in the future and is a way for businesses to become more sensitive to families. It is a movement that bears watching.

Laboratory Schools *UCR RCC*

The college and university laboratory schools were among the first preschools established in the United States. They usually focus on teacher training, research, and innovative education. These schools serve as standards for model programs in early childhood education. They add to our knowledge of children, child development, and teaching methods. An important part of education in the United States, they are often supported or subsidized by the college.

As part of the child study movement, laboratory schools gathered information previously unknown about children and child development. Early ones include Hampton Institute in 1873, the University of Chicago, founded by John Dewey in 1896, Bank Street School in 1919, begun by Harriet Johnson, and the laboratory nursery school at Columbia Teacher's College, started in 1921 by Patty Smith Hill. In the late 1920s, Vassar, Smith, and Mills colleges all opened laboratory schools. Shortly after World War II, the Bing Nursery School at Stanford University opened. Much more recently, community-college campuses have followed the lead of these pioneers. Campus child care centers have begun to combine child care services with the laboratory function of teacher training in one setting. The types and roles of the schools vary, depending on the educational philosophy and needs of the college and its students.

Regardless of their specific purposes, laboratory schools enlarge our understanding of children. They are often excellent places for beginning teachers to learn ways of teaching children. They encourage the joining of psychology, medicine, and other related fields to early education, and they serve as professional models for the public at large for what is good in child care and education.

The isolation of college campuses sometimes restricts the number and type of children who enroll. The program itself is tailored to meet the needs of student teachers who, under the guidance of skilled people, do much of the teaching. College

FIGURE 2.7 Child care around the world: These cribs in a Russian child-care center are ready for the toddlers' nap time. Why do you think the pillows are arranged this way? How is this different from child-care centers in the United States?

calendars may be unable to accommodate the needs of children for full-time and year-round care. In addition, teachers trained in a laboratory school atmosphere will have to adjust to the realities of subsequent school settings.

Parent Cooperatives

Parent cooperatives are those schools organized and run by parents. This type of early childhood setting offers a unique opportunity for parents to be involved in the education of their child. The very first parent cooperative, the Chicago Cooperative Nursery School, was started in 1915 by faculty wives at the University of Chicago.

Parent cooperative schools may offer half-day or full-day child care programs and are usually nonprofit organizations. They are similar to other nursery schools, with two notable exceptions. First, parents organize and maintain the school: they hire the teachers, buy supplies and equipment, recruit members, raise funds, influence school philosophy, and manage the budget. Traditionally, parents or their substitutes were required to participate in the classroom on a regular basis. In light of current family work patterns and the unavailability of many parents, this requirement has been modified in most programs. More professional teachers are hired, or other parents who are available are paid to substitute for parents who cannot work at the center.

Cooperative schools work well for many reasons. Popular with young families, they have low operating costs, the appeal of being with parents in similar circumstances, and the mutual support that is generated among members of a co-op. Friendships grow among parents who share child rearing as participants in their own and in their child's education. But what a co-op does not cost in dollars, it may cost in time. By their very nature, cooperatives can exclude working parents unless another adult is able to substitute for them in classroom participation. Maintenance is very much the parents' responsibility; they must regularly schedule work parties to refurbish the facility.

Depending upon the size of the school, parents hire one or more professional teachers. These teachers must be able to work well with adults, have curriculum-building skills, and model good guidance and discipline techniques. Since many parent cooperatives require a weekly or monthly parent meeting, the teaching staff must also be competent in parent education. Child development and child-rearing topics are part of almost any cooperative nursery school discussion and require a practiced teacher to lead. The role of the teacher in this setting, then, is two-fold: to provide for a sound educational experience for young children and to guide and direct parents in their own learning.

Church-Based Programs

Church-related schools are those owned or operated by an individual congregation or other recognized church organization. They are considered part of that congregation's community service or outreach and represent the church's intentional ministry to families. Two-thirds of church-based programs are owned and operated by the local church; the remaining third are operated by other parties who rent space from the church but are not an integral part of the church's program (Neugebauer, 1991). Many different denominations house a variety of educational and child care programs.

Throughout this nation's history, churches have demonstrated their concern for the welfare of children and their families. It was the churches that established many of the early schools, advocating the education of children. At the turn of the century, church day nurseries and settlement houses cared for children of immigrants and poor working mothers. Later, hospitals and orphanages were founded, and churches spoke out for children's rights and the creation of child labor laws. In each era, depending on social and economic conditions, the churches have responded to the needs of children.

Role in Child Care

It is no surprise, then, to find that churches are deeply involved in child care today; there are over 20,000 child care programs housed in churches through the country and more than 75 percent operate on a full-day basis, supporting the claim that churches are the largest single provider of child care in the United States (Neugebauer, 1991 and Lindner et al, 1983).

Church-housed programs are broad-based. Toddler groups, full- and part-time nursery classes, all-day care, and after-school care are typical. Some churches sponsor programs for children with special needs and children of migrant farm workers. They serve the community-at-large and rarely restrict participation to their own congregations or denominations.

Religious or spiritual development is not the explicit aim of the majority of programs for preschoolers. Churches are committed to caring for children of working parents, providing a warm and loving environment to help children develop positive self-esteem (Lindner et al., 1983). The teaching of religious values to children in this age group is not common practice in most child care settings. The policy will vary, however, with each individual setting.

Church support of child care programs is primarily in the use of space. Known as "benign landlords" (Lindner et al., 1983), churches typically offer free or reduced-cost rent and may subsidize utilities, maintenance services, repairs, and some insurance. The church's nonprofit tax-exempt sta-

OUR DIVERSE WORLD OUR DIVERSE WORLD OUR DIVERSE WORLD OUR DIVERSE WORLD OUR DIVERSE WORLD

[1]Churches and Synagogues have been forerunners in providing comprehensive early care and education to the underserved populations of children and families in the United States, adding to the diversity of program options for all families.

FIGURE 2.8 There are similarities among all programs, but the relationship among parents, children, and caregiver is the universal consideration.

tus is usually applied to child care programs that exist as part of the congregation's ministry. Programs housed in churches, however, suffer the same indignities of other child care professionals in low wages and poor or nonexistant benefits.

Common problems that arise in church-housed settings include sharing space with other church programs; frequent changes in leadership in the church's governing body; unclear policies and procedures regarding decision-making groups within the church; and inappropriate church governance structures regulating the operation of the child care program.

Academic Church Schools

For those parents who seek alternative education in a religious context, church schools fill the need. Many denominations serve children from early childhood through senior high. The relationship with the individual church organizations and the academic philosophy will vary from setting to setting.

Church and State Controversy

Two issues that cause controversy regarding church-housed programs are licensing and government funding. The landmark federal Child Care and Development Block grant passed by Congress in 1990, presently allows for parents to use the funds in programs that they choose, even those that are religiously based. This is sure to be tested in the courts at the first opportunity. Supporters of this issue cite parents' right to choose their own child care and the fact that nine of the ten organizations with the most child care centers in the country are religious organizations (Neugebauer, 1991). Those who oppose use of public funds in any church-housed center argue that the First Amendment prohibits such use of government monies.

Becoming A Nanny

Monica M. Bassett*

Nanny education originated in England in the last century. It evolved into nursery nurse training, which takes 2 years and leads to a national examination and certification. The concept of a trained American nanny began to take hold in the 1980s. Increasing numbers of working parents in the United States who wanted their children cared for at home created a demand for skilled in-home caregivers and a new career alternative in the early childhood field. In response, nanny training programs were established in community colleges, vocational/technical schools, and private career schools.

Colleges provide most of the nanny education now available in this country. By 1994 there were about ninety college-based programs. Colleges typically offer a 1-year certificate program with the option to complete a second year for an associate degree. Programs include early childhood courses required of all students preparing for careers in early child care and education, with additional courses to develop the special skills needed in the home situation. Nanny professionalism and interpersonal skills are commonly areas of specialized study to enable nannies to build effective relationships with parents while promoting the physical, social, emotional, and intellectual well-being of the children in their care.

*Monica Bassett has trained nannies and is the author of Infant and Child Care Skills, *a manual for nannies and other caregivers (Bassett, 1995).*

Most religious groups support the need for regulations and abide by licensing procedures even if their state exempts them. One out of every four programs accredited by NAEYC's Academy of Early Childhood Programs is housed in a church (Neugebauer, 1991).

Early childhood professionals, joined by many church leaders, are deeply concerned that exemption from even the most minimal standards not only undermines the national effort to create uniform standards for child care but threatens the safety and welfare of children.

For-Profit Child Care

Sometimes called "proprietary child care," the for-profit establishments comprise over half of all child care centers. A number of national chains of child care centers developed rapidly over the last decade, with anywhere from 100 to 1000 centers under their control. Yet 80 percent of the for-profit child care centers are owned by individuals who operate one center (Neugebauer, 1991).

For-profit centers offer a variety of programs to meet parents' needs. Infant and toddler programs, preschools, kindergartens, before-school and after-school care, as well as summer sessions accommodate working parents. Originally criticized for minimal wage salaries, lack of benefits, and a less educated staff (Miesels & Sternberg, 1989), the quality of for-profit centers seems to reflect as wide a range as all other types of child care (Neugebauer, 1991). A small study conducted in one state concluded that for-profit and nonprofit child care did not differ significantly in general quality of programs, but where differences did occur, the nonprofits were often superior. The nonprofit centers had better ratios of teachers to children, more screening and referral services, better group management, and their environments were more child-centered (Kagan & Newton, 1989). Many for-profit owners are providing on-site child care in industrial parks or focusing on employer-based child care.

Nanny Movement

The Nanny movement has gained attention over the past decade as a child care option for those who can afford it, accounting for five percent of the child care market. Nannies are trained in two-year programs and generally live in the child's home. *Au pairs*, who, like nannies, are usually from Europe, spend a year with a family who sponsors their stay in the United States. Other household tasks may or may not be part of the job description of these child care providers. The focus box by Monica Bassett tells the story.

Other Schools

To serve the scope of human needs today, some early childhood programs focus on caring for children in a very specific context. Many high schools now have on-campus child care programs. Some serve as laboratory facilities to introduce adolescents to child care principles and practices before they become parents.

Others are part of a growing trend to provide support services to teenage parents. Young mothers are encouraged to complete their high school education by returning to campus with their young children. In addition to their regular academic classes, parents are required to participate in parent education classes where they discuss child-rearing policies and parenting concerns. They also spend time in the children's classroom, applying their skills under the supervision of professional child care workers.

The aim of this program is to help meet the long-term needs of adolescent parents by providing educational skills necessary to secure a job. At the same time, valuable support and training for parenthood helps teenagers deal with the reality of the young children in their lives.

Hospitals also provide group settings for children who are confined for a period of time.[1] Schools for children with special needs address the needs of specific disabilities, offering a combina-

OUR DIVERSE WORLD OUR DIVERSE WORLD OUR DIVERSE WORLD OUR DIVERSE WORLD OUR DIVERSE WORLD

[1]In the study of child development one needs to be aware of the full range of development and not focus on only typically developing children. Many programs are attempting to integrate 75% typically developing children along with 25% children having been recognized as having a special need.

tion of educational, medical, and therapeutic services. Children who attend these schools may or may not be mainstreamed part-time into other school settings.

Homeless Children

The plight of homeless children raises questions about program needs for this new and tragic phenomenon. Families with children now represent more than one-third of the homeless population (Children's Defense Fund, 1994). These children attend schools closest to the shelter in which they stay for a brief time, then change schools when their parents move to another shelter. Many times these are children who already experience problems and failures in school. State and federal legislation is now being enacted to ensure full and equal educational opportunities for homeless children.

SCHOOLS WITH A MESSAGE

Head Start

Beginnings

In 1965, the federal government created its third (see WPA nursery schools and the Lanham Act in Chapter 1) and largest publicly funded education program for young children ever (Greenberg, 1990). Head Start began as part of this country's social action against the war on poverty and the implications of the program were clear: if underprivileged, disadvantaged, poverty-stricken children could be exposed to a program that enhanced their schooling, their intellectual functions might increase, and these gains would help break the poverty cycle.

In over a quarter of a century, Head Start has served more than 13 million children from the ages of two to five, and their families (young children 1994). The success of Head Start can be attributed to its guiding objectives and principles, most notably expressed through:

- *Its comprehensive nature:* The child was seen as a whole, requiring medical, dental, and nutritional assessment, as well as intellectual growth. Extensive health, education, and social services were offered to children and their families. Today, Head Start is "the leading health care system for low-income children in the country" (Greenberg, 1990), providing health and medical screening and treatment for thousands of youngsters.

- *Parent participation and involvement:* Head Start redefined the role of parents by expecting parents to serve as active participants. Head Start parents were involved in the program at all levels: in the classroom as teacher aides, on governing boards making decisions about the program, and as bus drivers and cooks. A 1990 survey taken by the National Head Start Association notes the success of that approach in its finding that 36 percent of the staff were parents of current or former Head Start students (U.S. Department of Health and Human Services, 1990).

- *Services to families:* Many of the comprehensive services offered to children were extended to parents as well in order to assist them in their fight against poverty. Paid jobs in the program, on-the-job training, continuing education and training to prepare for other jobs, and health care are some of the support services families received. Parent education took on new meaning for low-income families with children in Head Start.

- *Community collaboration:* Interest and support from the local community helped Head Start respond to the needs of the children and families it served. Public schools, churches, libraries, service clubs, and local industry and businesses were included as partners in this war on poverty. These contacts throughout the community supported the underlying concepts of Head Start. Fostering responsible attitudes toward society and providing opportunities for the poor to work with members of the community in solving problems was a fundamental Head Start goal.

[1]Advocate for consistent and quality care and education all children whether their challenge is economic, social, or physical.

- *Multicultural/multiracial education:* Since its inception, Head Start has sought to provide a curriculum that reflects the culture, language, and values of the children in the program. Head Start efforts in this regard have been the models for other early childhood programs.

- *Inclusion of children with special needs:* Since 1972, Head Start has pioneered the inclusion of children with disabilities in its classrooms. Head Start has the distinction of being the first and largest federally funded program for children with special needs (Greenberg, 1990).

- *Ecology of the family:* Head Start programs looked at children within the context of the family in which they lived and viewed the family in the context of the neighborhood and community. This concept of taking so many forces that work against low-income families and viewing them as interrelated was a key factor in Head Start's success (See also "Ecology of the Family," Chapter 15).

The success of Head Start led to the creation of three specific programs that furthered the goals of Head Start: Parent and Child Centers, which served infants and toddlers and their families; the Child and Family Resource Programs, which provided family support services; and the Child Development Associate credential, which provided early childhood training and education for Head Start teachers.

These objectives could apply to any good nursery or kindergarten class. They take on an added dimension, though, when viewed as part of the total effort of Project Head Start, which was designed to be comprehensive enough to ensure appropriate programs for children and flexible enough to meet individual needs within the family and community.

Head Start Today

Head Start has had a rocky history, its contributions notwithstanding. Struggling against budget cuts and controversy over its effectiveness,

Head Start serves only 36 percent of those eligible (Children's Defense Fund, 1994).

A national panel of early childhood experts, federal officials, and Head Start administrators formed an Advisory Committee on Head Start Quality and Expansion prior to Head Start's reauthorization by Congress in 1994. While noting Head Start's effective combination of parent involvement in education and health and social services, the panel criticized the uneven quality and management of some Head Start centers. When passed, the bill supported the panel's recommendations for improving the quality of and expanding existing services, as well as for refocusing on the needs of today's families (Cohen, 1994a). The key components of the bill are:

- Improve staff recruitment, training, and compensation

- Improve local management practices, policies, and training

- Promote full-day and full-year services

- Develop model programs for infants and toddlers

- Respond to needs of families, especially those whose primary language is not English

- Develop family resource programs for family-support centers, community-based child-abuse prevention, and temporary child care and crisis nurseries

- Provide continuity and coordination between Head Start and elementary schools

- Promote community collaboration (Cohen, 1993a)

Two significant small grant programs are included in the reauthorization. One creates a group to explore ways to serve children from birth to 3 years of age, and the other is a transition grant that fosters Head Start–type services into elementary grades. Stressing accountability, the bill also allows the withdrawal of funds from programs

OUR DIVERSE WORLD OUR DIVERSE WORLD OUR DIVERSE WORLD OUR DIVERSE WORLD OUR DIVERSE WORLD

1 and 2. See footnote on p. 47. Head Start created a model for providing services that are *inclusive* (i.e. race, ethnicity, languistic, and physical ability) of all children. Quality early childhood programs are moving from a dominant culture centered approach to a more diverse approach.

which did not improve quality within a year's time. It is the first time that a Head Start center's past performance has been factored into its funding (Cohen, 1994b).

The recommendations and subsequent funding indicate the high esteem in which Head Start is held throughout the country. The original vision of Head Start has been improved and expanded for the 1990s as a model that challenges the effects of poverty and promotes physically and mentally healthy families. Head Start has a formidable challenge ahead as it protects the high quality of its original charter while expanding and increasing services.

Evaluating Head Start's Effectiveness

Two studies have helped highlight Head Start's impact over the years. One, the Consortium for Longitudinal Studies, pooled data from a number of smaller studies in the hopes that clear trends regarding early intervention could be identified. Brown (1985) notes two significant findings: 1) that Head Start children were less likely to be placed in special education classes, and 2) that early intervention programs were associated with a significant increase in IQ and school achievement.

The second study was not of a Head Start program but had an enormous impact on policy makers and government officials and affected Head Start funding in significant ways: The Perry Preschool Project.

The High/Scope Perry Preschool Study

This study presented the most convincing evidence to date of the effectiveness of early intervention programs for disadvantaged children. Begun in the 1960s, it is the first longitudinal study to measure the effects of preschool education and to track the children from preschool years through age 27.

One hundred twenty-three African American children from poor families, with IQs ranging from 60 to 90, were randomly assigned to two groups. The first group were placed in high-quality early childhood programs at age three; the other group did not attend preschool. The results

showed great differences between the children who had the advantage of a high-quality program and those who did not. Disadvantaged children who attended preschool significantly outperformed those who did not.

The latest round of data cite the most dramatic benefits to date. The children attending the preschool program were better educated, spent fewer than half as many years in special education programs, had higher earnings, were less likely to receive welfare, and were five times less likely to be arrested (Scheinhart and Weikart, 1993). Gender differences were also noted: preschool program females had a significantly higher rate of graduation than did the females who did not attend preschool, whereas, in comparison, preschool program males completed slightly less schooling than their counterparts (Cohen, 1993b).

Not only does this study underscore the need for high-quality preschool programs for children who live in poverty, but it demonstrates the potential impact that Head Start has on the country's future.

It is the first study of its kind to suggest the economic impact of early intervention. Because most of the children in the high-quality early childhood program required less remedial education, had better earning prospects, and were less costly to the welfare and justice systems, early intervention in education was shown to be cost-effective. The estimated value gained over the lifetime of the students in the preschool program "may be more than seven times the cost of one year's operation of the program." (Berrueta-Clement, et al., 1984). That assessment still holds true today. (See High/Scope section on following pages.)

The High/Scope Perry Preschool Study reinforces the focus of Head Start's vision for the future and has served the early childhood community well by demonstrating that high-quality programs for young children can have a permanent and significant impact on children at risk.

Follow-Through

In 1968, in order to build on the gains children developed in Head Start, Follow-Through provided funds for programs for children in

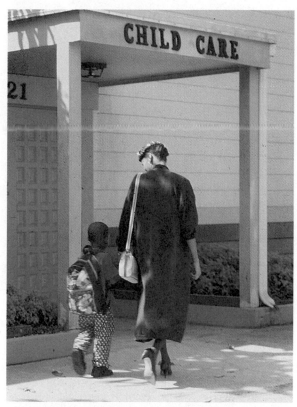

FIGURE 2.9 The need for quality child care has increased as thousands of mothers enter the work force.

kindergarten through third grade. Using many different educational models and approaches, Follow-Through was the beginning of a collective effort to see that the impact of Head Start was not lost and that gains could be strengthened by developmentally appropriate curriculum as well as health and social services up to age 8. It is a unique model which calls for the collaboration between Head Start and public school leadership. Whereas there are relatively few programs in the country today, the transition grant in Head Start's recent reauthorization calls for a continuation of the effort.

High/Scope

Under the leadership of David Weikart, the High/Scope Foundation has become a major source of applied educational research and practical work with teachers. Chief among their accomplishments are the Perry Preschool Project (described earlier) and a cognitively oriented approach to teaching and

curriculum, using Piagetian theory.

High/Scope curriculum stresses active learning through a variety of learning centers with plenty of materials and developmentally appropriate activities. Active problem solving is encouraged as children plan what they will do each day, carry out their plan, and review what they have done. Teachers use small groups to encourage, question, support, and extend children's learning while emphasizing their communication skills.

There is a balance between child-initiated experiences and teacher-planned instructional activities. Teachers use observational techniques to focus on children and to understand children's play.

Children with special needs are integrated readily into High/Scope programs and with a curriculum developed especially for K–3 grades, High/Scope extends its active learning philosophy into the early elementary school years.

High/Scope's approach to children's learning is deeply rooted in Piagetian theory and supports Vygotsky's theory of social interaction and cognition: children learn when interacting with the people and materials in their environment. Core elements of the High/Scope philosophy are shared by the schools of Reggio Emilia. Both philosophies stress the importance of children constructing their knowledge from activities that interest them; team teaching is an important concept, to allow the children access to adult support; and the process of planning, acting, recording, and reassessing is one that both approaches use to foster critical thinking skills.

Open Schools

Open education—sometimes called open schools or informal education—is a term used to describe child-centered learning environments often associated with the British infant schools (see discussion of this type of school in Chapter 1, as well as references to Summerhill, Waldorf, and Bertrand Russell). It is based on the belief that children learn and grow at different rates, that they are eager and curious about learning, and that they learn best when they are able to pursue their own interests. Open school philosophy uses play as the principal means for learning. Not only do children learn from each other as they play in a mixed-age group, they grow through a rich and varied learning environment.

If this description sounds vaguely familiar, it should since it applies to many typical nursery schools and kindergartens. The philosophy has a familiar ring to it. Didn't John Dewey speak of self-initiated learning, social cooperation, active education, and respect for the individual? And before him, Comenius, Rousseau, Pestalozzi, and Froebel all promoted similar concepts. In some ways, open education is the Progressive Movement revisited.

The British infant school movement aided the revival of open education in the United States in the 1970s and today many schools still pattern themselves after the British model. The open school has come to mean an approach, a philosophy, that is practiced in many types of early childhood settings—nursery schools, child care centers, and elementary schools.

The open school is not without criticism, much of which centers around the lack of formal instruction. The deemphasis in direct instruction of reading and writing is questioned. Supporters of open schools counter that the child-centered approach in fact leads to a high motivation to read and write.

Open education allows for a child to respond individually and personally to the experience. The freedom of choice, the development of problem-solving skills, the respect for initiative, are based on the strong belief that allowing children this kind of involvement reflects back to them their worth and dignity. For that reason alone, open classrooms continue to exemplify the best in humanistic education.

The Schools of Reggio Emilia

Respect for children's investigative powers and for their ability to think, plan, criticize, collaborate, and learn from all they do is the hallmark of the Reggio Emilia approach and is a good example of an open education approach to learning. This collection of schools, with separate programs for infants to three-year-olds and three- to six-year-olds, has commanded worldwide attention for its philosophy and practices. "Nowhere else in the world," states Gardner (Edwards, Gandini, and Forman, 1993), "is there such a seamless and symbiotic relationship between a school's progressive philosophy and its practices."

Influenced by Dewey's progressive education movement, the philosophies and practices of Reggio Emilia owe a great deal as well to Piaget's constructivist theory, Vygotsky's belief in social discourse as a method of learning, and Gardner's own theory of multiple intelligences (see Chapters 1, 4, and 13). Therefore, children are actively engaged in long-term projects which they initiate, design, and carry out with the support of the teacher. Art is the primary medium for learning.

Some of the key components of the Reggio Emilia approach are: a materials-rich environment which is aesthetically appealing; a community-based attitude involving the entire city; a family support system; and a commitment to process. These elements are manifested in the program through astonishingly beautiful school settings, replete with the work of children and evidence of their projects elegantly displayed throughout; by support realized through a large portion of the city's budget; through small groups of children who stay together for a 3-year period with the same teacher; and through intentionally bringing the children's culture into school life.

The teacher's role is unique: two co-equal teachers work with a class of twenty-five children. There is no head teacher or director of the school. The teachers are supported by a *pedigogista*, a person trained in early childhood education, who meets with the teachers weekly. Also on the staff of every school is an *atelierista*, a person trained in the arts and who teaches techniques and skills the children learn for their projects.

Process is highly respected as the way to plan and work together. Teachers and children, co-collaborators, listen to one another, and many points of view are encouraged. Debate and discussion are key elements in the process of deciding what project to do and how to go about it. The attitude that a child is a natural researcher as well as an able learner and communicator has molded the organization and structure of the schools. The schools of Reggio Emilia are worth knowing about just for the strong and powerful view they hold of the child and the concept of teacher and student learning from one another.

Montessori

In Chapter 1, the person who started this important movement, Maria Montessori, was discussed in relation to the history of early childhood. What follows here is an explanation of the Montessori method as a program for young children.

Maria Montessori began working with slum children in the early 1900s in Rome, Italy. Her school, the Casa di Bambini, was open to children from the ages of 2-1/2 to 7 years. Montessori's approach to learning has had a continuing influence in education since those early years. Of her work, three features stand out: (1) adapting school work to the individual rather than molding the child to fit the curriculum; (2) insisting on freedom for children in selection of materials and choice of activities; and (3) training of the senses and practical life issues.

The Program

Montessori schools are diverse and the use of the name *Montessori* does not guarantee adherence to the theory and philosophy of the original program. One common misunderstanding is that all schools with the Montessori name are the same. There are many variations and types of Montessori schools throughout the United States, reflecting an infinite variety of interpretations of the Montessori method. Within the Montessori movement itself, there are at least two factions claiming to be the voice of the true Montessori approach to education.

While the most common form of Montessori program is one where 3–5 year olds are grouped together, there are a growing number of schools for 6–9 year olds and even 9–12 year olds. New teacher education programs now prepare Montessori teachers to work with infants and toddlers as well as high schoolers.

The most striking feature of the Montessori classroom is its materials. Many are made of wood and designed to stress the philosophy of learning through the senses. Color, texture, and quality of craftsmanship of the materials appeal to the hand as well as the eye; they demand to be touched. "Smooth" and "oval" take on new meaning as a child runs a finger around Montessori-designed puzzle shapes.

Montessori materials have other unique characteristics besides their tactile appeal. They are self-correcting—that is, they fit together or work in only one way so that children will know immediately whether or not they are successful. Montessori curriculum presents the materials in a sequence, from simplest to most difficult. Many of the learning tasks have a series of steps and must be learned in a prescribed order. Whether sponging a table clean or using the number rods, the child is taught the precise order in which to use the materials. Montessori developed curriculum materials and tasks that related to real life. "Practical life" activities range from cleaning tasks (hands, tables) to clothing tasks (lacing, buttoning, or tying garment closures).

In a Montessori classroom, children work by themselves at their own pace. They are free to choose the materials with which they want to "work"—the word used to describe their activity. Children must accomplish one task before starting another, one including the replacing of the materials on the shelf for someone else to use.

The prepared environment in a Montessori program has child-sized furniture and equipment—one of Froebel's ideas that Montessori used. Materials are set out on low shelves, in an orderly fashion, to encourage children's independent use. Only one set of any materials—their shape, form, and the way they are presented for children to use—are the vehicles for learning.

The teacher in the Montessori setting has a prescribed role, one of observing the children. Teachers become familiar with skills and developmental levels, then match the children to the appropriate material or task. There is little teacher intervention beyond giving clear directions for how to use the materials. Group instruction is not common; learning is an individual experience.

The Controversy

Some controversy surrounds the Montessori method, its schools, its training. Four limitations of the Montessori philosophy most frequently cited are:

- *Lack of social interaction among children and between teachers and children.* Notably, the absence of dramatic play equipment that would foster peer interchange. This is the area in which there is the largest single disagreement between Montessori and traditional schools (Chattin-McNichols, 1992).

● *Lack of self-expression.* In some schools, children are still discouraged from exploring and experimenting with materials in their own way. Creative arts are not part of the pure Montessori method. No vehicle is provided for self-expression through fantasy, imagination, or creative play.

● *Lack of stimulation for language development.* Since children are encouraged to work alone and teachers interact with them in fairly structured ways, many opportunities for verbal exchange are lost. Again, creative arts and dramatic play provide options, if they are available.

● *Lack of gross-motor equipment or emphasis.* Only fine-motor skills are emphasized in most of the Montessori materials. Outdoor play is not an integrated part of the Montessori curriculum.

Research, while not extensive, does show that children from Montessori programs perform as well as children from other types of preschool programs in most areas, such as school readiness and intelligence (Chattin-McNichols, 1992). Continued research is needed to answer more fully the questions concerning the effect of a Montessori school experience.

Many changes have taken place in Montessori practices over the years and today's best Montessori programs are those that are true to philosophical traditions of the Montessori method but constantly make small changes and adjustments. Many Montessori schools are adding curriculum areas of art, dramatic play, and gross-motor development, and computers. There is also greater teacher flexibility to promote social interaction.

For years, Montessori has been separated from the mainstream of American education. Today that is changing, with over 100 public school districts offering Montessori programs in their elementary schools and with the increased interaction between Montessorians and other early childhood professionals.

Maria Montessori has found her way into nearly every early education program in existence today. Whether labeled so or not, much of the material and equipment as well as many of the teach-

ing techniques in use today originated with this dynamic woman nearly one hundred years ago.

She is firmly established in early childhood history of the past and of the future. The Montessori method should be weighed in light of contemporary knowledge and be tailored to meet the needs of vigorous, eager, often needy children of the 1990s.

EXTENDING THE AGE RANGE

Infant/Toddler Programs

There has been a dramatic rise in recent years in the demand for and availability of group care for infants and toddlers. The early 1970s produced a great deal of research concerning the infant/toddler, enhancing public awareness of the potential of children this age. Greater resources and information became available, creating an awareness of the implications for programs that focus specifically on the infant or toddler. Research by Brazelton, White, Honig, Caldwell, Keister, and others has informed us where and how and why we can offer enrichment and learning opportunities to the youngest of children. And we know that this can take place in group care settings under professional guidance.

The trend toward group care for infants and toddlers was affected by the rising number of women in the work force who combine child rearing and careers and by the increasing single-parent families where the parent must work.

Gonzalez-Mena and Eyer (1993) define the infant/toddler age group: Infancy is from babyhood until the child learns to walk. Then he or she is called a toddler until almost three years old.

Infant/toddler centers fall into several categories. They may be full day care centers or they may be part-time. They may be more educational, with parent involvement programs, than centers for group care. Most are a combination of physical care coupled with intellectual stimulation and parent development.

Parent relationships are an important part of any program for young children, but especially so when babies and toddlers are involved. The general intention of these centers is to provide care that is supplemental to family life and that supports the child's family structure. In order to do that, the caregiver at an infant/toddler center involves the parents in the everyday decisions about the care of their child, provides them with information about the child's day, and strengthens the child's sense of belonging to that particular family.

Philosophy of Infant/Toddler Care

Research has enlarged the understanding of the growth process of babies. Piaget defined this time as the sensorimotor stage, and Erikson states that trust and autonomy are the critical lessons to be learned at this age (see Chapter 4). Through these insights, we have come to view the infant more and more as an involved person, one who experiences a wide range of intellectual and emotional abilities. The prevalent philosophy of quality infant/toddler programs recognizes the "personhood" of the baby (Honig, 1981). This means that the infant/toddler is treated with the same consideration as any child. Although they may appear to be helpless beings, babies are in fact persons with feelings, rights, and an individual nature.

This philosophy implies that taking care of infants or toddlers is not just a case of thrusting bottles in their mouths when they are hungry or putting them in a playpen to amuse themselves. The caregiver in a quality infant/toddler center understands that feeding, diapering, and playing are, in fact, the curriculum of this age group. Caregiving routines are at the heart of the infant/toddler program. The challenge for the caregiver is to find ways to use these daily routines to interact, develop trust and security, and provide educational opportunities. In many cases, the caregiver's (or educarer's) role extends to helping parents use these same common occurrences to promote the optimum development of their child.

Magda Gerber has been a pioneer in infant care. She coined the term educaring to describe the relationship between an infant and an adult. Gerber's philosophy is based on a respect for babies and the use of responsive and reciprocal interactions where both baby and caregiver learn about each other. Communicating through caregiving routines (diapering, feeding) in one-to-one intense and focused interactions is a foundation of Gerber's approach to caring for infants and tod-

dlers (Gerber, 1979). Observing, listening, and reading babies' cues are key elements in educaring.

Differences from Preschool

Infant and toddler education differs from preschool education in several important ways. These differences stem from the very nature of infants and toddlers and their needs. According to Cataldo (1983) infant and toddler education is "more intense...more physical...more personal" than working with preschoolers. Infant/toddler education owes its overall philosophy to the traditional tenets of early childhood education; these basic principles are extended to meet the specific requirements of this more vulnerable age group.

In infant and toddler programs as compared with preschool programs, there is a need for:

- more one-to-one physical care
- immediate response from adults
- more follow-up to experiences and activities
- use of ordinary routines as learning opportunities
- skills that go beyond teaching: mothering, being a playmate
- intentional rather than discovery learning
- keener attunement to interpreting need and distress signals in young children

The distinction between programs for infants and those for toddlers is also important to note. Just as a scaled-down version of preschool is not a toddler program, neither is a scaled-down version of a good day for toddlers an appropriate model for infants. The mobility of the toddler, for instance, requires different amounts of space and time in the schedule than are required for infants. Babies sleep more their first year of life; their rhythm of eating, sleeping, and playing must be met. Babies thrive when someone responds to their smiles and developing skills. Common routines such as diapering create the curriculum as caregivers talk with the babies about what they are doing and what is happening to them. Caregivers get babies to focus on themselves in a gentle, extensively personal involvement. Good programs for babies recognize their capacities and the extent of their awareness of themselves and others in their environment.

Routines again become the focus of the toddler day but in a somewhat different way. Mealtimes and toileting provide daily opportunities for toddlers to explore and to express their emerging sense of self. Handwashing—even eating—becomes a time to fill, to taste, to dump, to pick up. Again, the curriculum emerges from a developmental need toddlers have of "Me! Mine!" To foster that independence, that wanting to "do it myself," routines that allow for experimentation, mistakes, and messes make a good toddler curriculum.

Good programs for infants and toddlers, then, are distinctly arranged for them and are not simply modified versions of what works well in a program for three-year-olds.

What Is Good Quality Infant/Toddler Care?

. . . Infants and toddlers need attention to their physical and psychological needs; a relationship with someone they can trust; respect; a safe, healthy, and developmentally appropriate environment; chances to interact with other infants and toddlers; and freedom to explore using all their senses.

(Gonzales-Mena and Eyer, 1989)

The high level of adult dependency, the rapid growth changes from birth to age three, and the interrelationship among developmental areas (see Chapter 3) call for certain elements to insure highquality infant and toddler programs. Honig (1985) calling infant/toddler caregiving "the scarcest commodity in the world of child care," lists key elements for quality programs:

● the quality of the caregiver

● the stability of the staff

● the expensive staff:infant or staff:toddler ratio of at least 1 to 4

● the need for a rich language experience integrated into daily routines

● the need to build a prosocial curriculum that

FIGURE 2.10 An environment in an Italian infant/toddler center—places to crawl safely, toys to push and pull, and a setting to foster social interaction. *(Courtesy of the city of Reggio Emilia, Italy.)*

promotes children to care for and about one another

● the necessity for caregivers to devote individual attention for both learning and caregiving, balancing between the group and the individual child

● the need to support and renew staff so they in turn will be supportive to parents and serve as appropriate resources

● the need to promote a sense of choice and control to young children throughout the curriculum and routines of caregiving

● the critical need for ongoing training for caregivers

Issues

There are many important issues surrounding quality infant/toddler care. First, good care costs money. The factors that combine to make a quality program—low teacher:child ratio, small groups, individual attention—raise the costs to make infant/toddler care one of the most expensive child care programs. Second, critics of child care—any child care—raise even greater fears about the negative effects on family life and the harmful aspects of group care for the very young. Ignoring the statistics, they do not seem to realize that the question is hardly one of whether or not

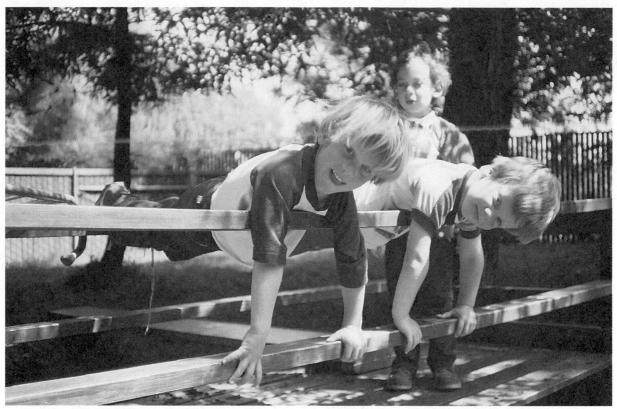

FIGURE 2.11 The kindergartners' day is enhanced with a field trip to a farm. A full day requires curriculum which fits the needs and interests of the five- to-six-year-old.

child care should exist. The need for child care for young children is well documented.

According to the Children's Defense Fund (1994), the availability of child care lags behind the need: By 1995 more than three-quarters of all school-age children and two-thirds of all preschool children had mothers in the labor force. That means 15 million children under the age of six in some kind of child care service.

The most critical question is in regard to infant attachment. It is an accepted conclusion today that children who first enter child care situations at the age of 18 months to two years or older show no loss of attachment to their parents. Some studies (Belsky and Braungart, 1991) concerning children who are placed in child care outside the home before the age of one, however, have raised questions about the higher level of insecurity attachment shown as opposed to infants who were raised at home. Berk (1994), who suggests that this small number of children is at risk for attach-

ment insecurity because of poor quality day care, calls for high quality day care and parent education in infant emotional development.

The task for the early childhood professional seems clear. Learn what the issues are, defend policies that reflect high standards, and be prepared to further influence group care for infants and toddlers that is of the highest quality.

Kindergarten ✳

Kindergarten programs are universally available throughout the United States and have a significant impact in early education. They are found in elementary public and private schools, churches, and as part of preschool child care centers. Thirty years ago only 47 percent of five-year-olds were enrolled in kindergarten (Spodek, 1986). Today that number has doubled (National Center for Education Statistics, 1990), which means that almost all children attend kindergarten before entering elementary school. All states now have publicly supported kindergarten, but attendance is mandatory in only 22 of them.

Length of Day

The length of kindergarten programs is a prime example of the diversity and division in this critical area of early childhood education. Children attend kindergarten programs that operate for:

- half day, every day

- full school day, every day

- full school day, alternate days

- half day, followed by child care/extended day program

- full school day, followed by child care/extended day program

The debate in many school boards focuses on whether or not to offer a five-day-a-week full-day kindergarten. Only a few states fund full-day programs. Too often the arguments regarding the costs of such programs overshadow a more basic question: What is the best and most appropriate kindergarten program and curricula, regardless of the length of day? Five areas that need to be considered in response to this question and the debate on length of day are:

1. *The purpose of the kindergarten program.* What are the goals and how will kindergarten serve the whole of the child's development? How will the program foster the goals in appropriate programming and adapt to the needs of children? The purpose of a full day, every day does not have to mean more academics that will be measured by more testing. It can mean developing a curriculum that is aimed at a wide range of developmental levels, yet that can be individualized, a curriculum that fits the growing and changing five-to-six year old. The goal should begin with the child and build the program to fit the child's needs, skills, and developing abilities.

2. *The effects of a full day on children.* Many children have already been in a child care setting for up to ten hours a day and have shown they thrive in programs that are suited to their ages,

developmental styles, and needs. There is no question that most children can handle a full-day kindergarten program, providing it is adapted to their age, interests, and abilities.

3. *The needs and concerns of parents.* Some parents may want a full-day program because they work and need a safe and nurturing place for their children. Others who do not work outside the home may want to keep their children with them a while longer. Parents clearly need to have a choice about the type of program that best suits their family.

4. *The effect on teachers.* If a full-day kindergarten means that a teacher's class is extended for a longer period of time, that provides an opportunity to improve the quality of the program by individualizing the curriculum and better serving the children and their families who are enrolled. Half-day kindergartens, however, are many times staffed by teachers who have two separate classes of 20–25 students, one in the morning and one in the afternoon. The negative effects on planning, continuity, parent relationships, individualizing curriculum are obvious, not to mention teacher burnout.

5. *The concerns of the administration.* The cost effectiveness of extending a kindergarten program all day will undoubtedly require more staff, more supplies and equipment, and greater food service costs. The policymakers in any school setting must take these into account along with the other issues, but one would hope they would not be limited by them.

6. *The nature and quality of the extended-day program.* Often, in programs where children are in half-day kindergarten, the quality of the extended-care part of their day is not equal to their school experience. In many extended-day programs, the staff is untrained, has a high turnover rate, and does not reflect the same program goals for the kindergartener.

7. *Research findings.* Gullo and Clements (1984) measured academic achievement and social behavior of children enrolled in half-day (every day) and full-day (alternate day) kindergartens and found no significant differences. Further research (Gullo, Bersani, Clements, and Bay-

less, 1986) suggests that five-year-olds benefit socially, emotionally, and academically in full-day programs.

School Entry Age

Every state establishes an arbitrary date by which children must be a certain age in order to enter kindergarten. In the United States, compulsory age for kindergarten ranges from five to eight. Lowering and raising the age for beginning school is debated periodically; currently, the trend is to move the date later into the year in the hopes of enrolling more "mature" kindergarteners. It has long been noted that the youngest children in kindergarten have more academic problems than do their peers, are more likely to be labeled slow learners, and asked to repeat the year. The "birthdate effect," as it is sometimes called (Peck et al, 1988), has led to a number of questionable practices regarding kindergarten entrance: parents hold children out for one year and enroll them when they are six, teachers retain many children each year in kindergarten, and administrators have created an array of kindergarten-substitute programs called trendy names such as "developmental," "extra-year," or "transitional" kindergartens. By the time they finally reach kindergarten, children are now in class with late four-year-olds, fives, and sixes—a vast developmental span under one roof.

An "alarmingly" high rate of children failing kindergarten (Peck et al, 1988) has given rise to a number of these questionable solutions. Yet research shows that children who are held back a year may perform less well academically in the future and that kindergarteners who are retained, show harmful effects on their social and emotional development as well as their self-esteem. Children from minorities and from poor homes are more likely to be held back a year than others (Meisels, 1991). Further, research shows that kindergarten retention does nothing to boost subsequent academic achievement, that there is social stigma for children who repeat a year, and curricular expectations will be geared to the fastest learners (Shepard & Smith, 1988).

Studies of kindergarten alternatives show that by third grade, no differences in math or reading scores were found between those attending a "de-

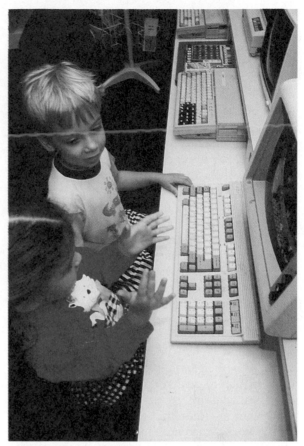

FIGURE 2.12 After-school programs provide opportunities to make new friends and try new skills.

velopmental/transitional" kindergarten and those enrolled in a traditional kindergarten (Meisels, 1991). The "holdout phenomenon" of giving the potential kindergartner an extra year does not seem to be justified in the long run considering that many of the child's needs will not be addressed and that, as older children in a kindergarten class, they may become bored and less motivated.

Curriculum: Developmental or Academic? ✳

Critical issues such as school-entry age and length of school day are deeply interrelated to kindergarten curriculum issues. At the present, kindergarten programs range from relatively traditional classes to highly structured, academically oriented classes. Over the last 20 years, the push to teach separate skills, such as reading, writing, and math, has created more and more academically focused kindergartens where worksheets and teacher-directed lessons are the norm. This movement has caused deep concern in the early childhood field since most of these programs seem inconsistent with the developmental and learning styles of five- and six-year-olds and are viewed as preparation for advancement to first grade rather than as high quality programs aimed at the development of the whole child.

It is clear that the "children's garden" as Froebel pictured this experience to be, has wandered far from its child development roots. Curriculum trends in kindergarten, where play is not respected as a vehicle for learning, where reading is taught as a separate skill, and where attempts are made to accelerate children's learning are at odds with kindergarten history. Revisit Chapter 1 and read again about Froebel, Dewey, Piaget, Patty Smith Hill, Susan Blow, and other pioneers and their approach to learning. Educating the whole child is very much in evidence in their work, as is their basic connection to child development theory and research. Historically developed curriculum, based on interaction and involvement of children in their own learning, with methods and materials to match the child's age level is at the core of developmentally appropriate curriculum. The current system of frequently labeling children "immature," "slow," or "not ready" means the program is not ready for the children; yet we know that young children are ready to learn and grow. It is time to fix the program, not the children.

Differences in teacher training have led to some of the problems associated with kindergarten. Most kindergarten teachers are trained in education schools with methods more appropriate to elementary school teaching. They receive little or no training in early childhood philosophy or child development theory. Qualified teachers are the core of any educational reform and kindergarten teachers must be educated and credentialed in early childhood education (Peck et al, 1989).

For further discussion on the negative effects of early academics, see Chapter 3 for developmen-

tal ranges and Word Pictures for appropriate expectations. In Chapter 10, the related questions of standardized testing and screening are discussed. In Chapters 11 and 15, related issues are explored.

Before-School and After-School Programs

Before-school and **after-school programs** are designed for children after they finish their regular academic day. This type of care is usually available for children in kindergarten through third grade. Some family day care homes provide this service, as do individual programs designed specifically for the five-through-eight-year-old.

Generally, by the time children reach the age of eight or nine, they stay at home or engage in extracurricular activities at school or in the community. Younger children need adult supervision and access to appropriate materials and activities when they finish their school day. There is a critical need for safe, recreational programs for children of this age. It has been estimated that between two and six million children are left alone to take care of themselves before and after school. According to the U.S. Census Bureau (Cohen, 1994c), about 8 percent of school-age children of employed mothers were "self-care" children, a term which replaces "latchkey." Only four percent of all schools operate an after-school program to serve the needs of these children.

What happens to these children after school? For the kindergartener, school may be over at noon. From 1:30 to 3:00 P.M., first-, second-, and third-graders are released from their school day. Too often these children are sent home with a house key around their necks or in their pockets. They are instructed to look after themselves and possibly a younger sibling until the parent (or parents) comes home from work. These "latchkey" **children,** as they were known, are a young and vulnerable population. The early childhood community has embraced their obvious need for good after-school programs.

The essentials of before-school and after-school care reflect the needs of the parents, teach-

OUR DIVERSE WORLD OUR DIVERSE WORLD OUR DIVERSE WORLD OUR DIVERSE WORLD OUR DIVERSE WORLD

1 and 2. If programs are to be based on democratic/inclusive values, then perhaps school readiness should be considered in terms of schools being ready for all children.

ers, and children involved. Flexible hours, reasonable tuition rates, and clear lines of communication are of primary importance to parents. To ensure continual care, scheduling must take into consideration the elementary school calendar. Holidays, conference times, and minimum-day schedules of schools must be considered. Opportunities to extend the after-school program can originate from the use of community resources such as library story hours, swimming facilities, and parks.

Before-school and after-school care is not intended to be an extension of a regular school day. Ideally, the program should supplement and support the regular school program. Many are called "enrichment programs" to distinguish them from the child's academic school day.

The teaching staff is usually different from the regular school faculty and should be specially trained in how to operate extended programs for young children. They must know how to create a homey, relaxed, and accepting atmosphere in an environment that supports large blocks of time for free play, where children can be self-directed and self-paced, where there are many opportunities for creative expression, where cooperation is emphasized and competition is limited, and where children may form small groups or find private spaces and places to play.

A national study of before- and after-school programs compiled in 1991 offers the first nationwide picture of these programs: approximately 1.7 million children in kindergarten through grade 8 were enrolled in nearly 50,000 before- and/or after-school programs in the United States in 1991; 84 percent of those were licensed or regulated by a state agency; and the three most common program locations were child care centers (35 percent), public schools (28 percent), and religious institutions (14 percent). Less than 20 percent of the programs have access to necessary space, and 27 percent report that they do not have access to a playground or a park on at least a weekly basis (USDE, 1993). The study concludes that training and retaining staff is a critical issue if continuity and quality of program are to be maintained.

Programs for school-age children need their own permanent space to support the type of long-term group projects that children of this age enjoy. Some programs may offer homework assistance, but care must be taken not to simply extend an already structured day with more restrictions.

Children need the safety, the creative opportunity, and the emotionally supportive relationships that before-school and after-school care can provide. These programs are natural extensions of responsible child care and are essential services to children and their families.

CRITERIA AFFECTING PROGRAMS

There are many factors that determine exactly what type of program will best serve the young child. Some of these variables emerged through the descriptions of the many kinds of settings available for children today. Programs in early childhood are defined by

● Age of the children served

● Philosophy or theoretical approach taken

● Goals the program hopes to meet

● Purpose for which it was established

● Requirements of sponsoring agency

● Quality and training of teaching staff

● Shape, size, and location of physical environment

● Cultural, ethnic, economic, and social makeup of community

● Financial stability

Programs in early childhood settings are defined by these elements, and each factor was taken into consideration regarding its impact on the program desired. Any given program is a combination of these ingredients.

MIXED-AGE GROUPINGS

One factor that may cut across program considerations is that of placing children of several age levels, generally separated by a year, into the same classroom. In these classes, younger children learn from older children and older children learn by teaching younger children. This practice is often referred to as family, heterogeneous, vertical, or ungraded grouping (Katz et al, 1990) and, while not a new idea, is emerging as an area of considerable interest to early childhood educators.

While reminiscent of the British Infant Schools' open classroom model, mixed-age groupings have been a practice in Montessori programs, in the schools of Reggio Emilia, and in one-room schoolhouses for many years. Advocates of mixed-age groups point to a number of developmental advantages when children interact with peers above and below their age levels:

- The child's own developmental level and pace are accommodated, allowing children to advance as they are ready

- Age and competition are de-emphasized, as co-operative learning is enhanced

- Caring and helping behaviors toward younger children and a sense of responsibility toward one another are fostered

- Diverse learning styles and multiple intelligences are appreciated

- A variety and number of different models for learning and for friendships are available

- Children grow in independence in their work and in socialization

The academic and social advantages of mixed-age grouping cannot take place without a variety of activities from which children may freely choose and the opportunity for small groups of children to work together. Teachers must be intentional about encouraging children to work with others who have skills and knowledge they do not yet possess. Other considerations are the optimal age range, the proportion of older to younger children, the amount of time spent in mixed-age groups, and the implementation of a project-oriented curriculum (Katz, 1990).

It is easy to see how mixed-age groupings reflect the principles of Dewey, Piaget, Gardner, and Vygotsky, whose "zone of proximal development" is made more available through the interactions of peers as well as adults. The practice of mixed-age grouping has much to commend it and must be seriously addressed as an issue in programs for young children.

S U M M A R Y

Educational facilities for young children reach a broad population. They serve children from infancy through elementary-school age. There is an array of programs available, which varies for philosophical reasons as well as because of ages of children enrolled. Early childhood teachers have a wide range of programs from which to choose—as do parents.

The traditional nursery school and its sister programs of child care, laboratory schools, and parent cooperatives form the core of early childhood programs. Many different agencies and people sponsor early childhood programs, including employers, churches, universities, hospitals. Some are located in family homes as a business. The intervention models of the 1960s and 1970s—Head Start and Follow-Through—are variations on the theme. They are specific attempts to provide early education and intervention to children caught in poverty's cycle. Other schools, such as Montessori or High/Scope, are based on clearly stated principles with outlined procedures for teachers and children.

In reflecting the needs of society, it is no wonder that extended day programs have been created. Not only are children being cared for in group situations before and after school hours, they are being placed in the group settings at an earlier age. Infant/toddler programs are quite common and before-school and after-school care is a service that meets the demands for good, safe, and challenging programs for children who need care on either side of their school day.

As varied as they are, there is also a certain similarity among all programs for young children. Consideration must be given to a number of factors when reviewing the needs of young children and their families. Some of these elements are the ages of the children the program will serve, the qualifications and experience of the teaching staff, the funding base and financial support available, and the goals of the program to meet the needs of all children and their families. With so many choices, those who desire child care will find options that suit their specific needs.

R E V I E W   Q U E S T I O N S

1. What are the three most important factors that determine the quality of an early childhood program?

2. Match the type of program with the appropriate description:

   Montessori   Key experiences
   Infant/toddler   Staggered staff schedules
   All day child care   Comprehensive programs
   Church-based   Teacher training
   Head Start   In home
   Employer-supported   Prepared environment
   Proprietary   Benign landlord
   High/Scope   For profit
   Laboratory schools   Educaring
   Family child care   Fringe benefit

3. Why are some early childhood progams called "intervention" schools?

4. Are there differences between preschool and kindergarten programs? Between infant and toddler programs? What are they? Should there be a difference? Why?

5. What are some of the criteria that affect all children's programs?

6. What has been the unique contribution of the Perry Preschool Project and how do you see this affecting legislation, program development in early childhood, and the early childhood profession?

7. What is the controversy regarding for-profit child care centers? Are you for or against the idea of child care centers making a profit? Why?

8. Describe the influence of Piaget, Gardner, and Vygotsky on three types of early childhood programs.

L E A R N I N G   A C T I V I T I E S

1. Choose one program and describe how you would operate that type of class. Include the daily schedule, number and skill level of teachers, types of parent contacts, and the activities for children.

2. Visit a family child care home. Look at the home as if you were a prospective parent. What did you like most? Least? Is the home licensed? If so, for how many children? After talking with the family child care provider, what do you think are the disadvantages of this type of program? What do you think are possible solutions to these problems?

3. What role would children's social skills play in these settings?

   Traditional nursery school

   Montessori

   Kindergarten

   Infant/toddler

4. What are the licensing regulations for child care in your area? Describe the steps necessary in your town to open a

   ● nursery school.
   ● child care center.
   ● family child care home.

5. Which government agencies are involved in the licensing procedure?

6. Visit a Head Start program and a local kindergarten. Compare their programs in terms of appropriate or inappropriate curriculum. What are the major concerns of the teaching staff in each type of setting? What are the controversies about each of these programs in your community?

B I B L I O G R A P H Y

Bee, Helen. *The Developing Child.* Cambridge, Mass.: Harper Collins, 1995.

Belsky, J. and Braungart, J.M. "Are Insecure-Avoidant Infants with Extensive Day-Care Experience Less Stressed By and More Independent in the Strange Situation?" *Child Development,* 62, 567–571, 1991.

Berk, Laura E. *Infants and Children.* Boston: Allyn and Bacon, 1994.

Berrueta-Clement, J.R.; Schweinhart, L.J.; Barnett, W.S.; Epstein, A.S.; and Weikart, D.P. *Changed Lives: The Effects of the Perry Preschool Program on Youths Through 19.* Ypsilanti, Mich.: High/Scope Press, 1984.

Bredekamp, Sue. "An Overview of NAEYC's Criteria for High Quality Early Childhood Programs." In Willer (Ed.). *Reaching the Full Cost of Quality.* Washington, D.C.: National Association for the Education of Young Children, 1990.

Brown, Bernard. "Head Start—How Research Changed Public Policy." *Young Children,* July 1985, pp. 9–13.

Cataldo, Christine Z. *Infant and Toddler Programs.* Reading, Mass.: Addison-Wesley, 1983.

Chattin-McNichols, John. *The Montessori Controversy.* Albany, NY: Delmar Publishers, 1992.

Child Care Information Exchange, November 1986, pp. 7–8.

Children's Defense Fund. *The State of America's Children,* 1991. Washington, DC: 1991, 1994, 1995.

Chira, Susan. "Broad Study Says Home-Based Day Care, Even if by Relatives, Often Fails Children." *New York Times,* Friday, April 8, 1994.

Cohen, Deborah L. "Stress Head Start Quality, But Spotlight 0–3, Panel Says." *Education Week,* November 10, 1993a, p. 20.

——————. "Head Start Measure Appears to be on Congressional Fast Track." *Education Week,* April 27, 1994a, p. 14.

——————. "Bill to Authorize Head Start is Introduced." *Education Week,* February 16, 1994b, p. 21.

——————. "Study Ties Mother's Schedule, 'Latchkey' Status." *Education Week,* May 25, 1994c, p. 12.

——————. *"Perry Preschool Graduates Show Dramatic New Social Gains at 27."* Education Week, April 21, 1993b, p. 1.

"Creating A 21st Century Head Start." Public Policy Report. *Young Children,* March, 1994.

Education Week. "Dimensions." Child Care Costs. September 23, 1992, p. 3.

Education Week. "Dimensions." Employee-Benefit Plans. September 11, 1991, p. 3.

Education Week. "Early Years." December 6, 1989, p. 6.

Edwards, Carolyn, Gandini, Lella, and Forman, George. *The Hundred Languages of Children: The Reggio Emilia Approach to Early Childhood Education.* Norwood, N.J.: Ablex, 1993.

Gerber, Magda. "Respecting Infants: The Loczy Model of Infant Care." In *Supporting the Growth of Infants, Toddlers, and Parents,* ed. E. Jones. Pasadena, CA: Pacific Oaks, 1979.

Goffin, Stacie G. and Stegelin, Dolores A., Eds., *Changing Kindergartens.* Washington, D.C.: NAEYC, 1992.

Gold, Deborah, L. "Church Day Care Wins Exemption from State Law." *Education Week,* May 25, 1988, p. 1.

Gonzalez-Mena, Janet, and Eyer, Dianne W. *Infants, Toddlers, and Caregivers.* Mountain View, CA: Mayfield Publishing Co., 1993.

Greenburg, Polly. "Before the Beginning: A Participant's View." *Young Children*, September, 1990, pp. 41–52.

Gullo, D.F. and Clements, D.H. "The effects of kindergarten schedule on achievement, classroom behavior, and attendance." *Journal of Educational Research*, 78, 1984, pp. 51–56.

Gullo, D.F., Bersani, C., Clements, D.H., and Bayless, K.M. "A comparative study of all-day, alternate-day, and half-day kindergarten schedules: Effects on achievement and classroom social behaviors." *Journal of Research in Childhood Education*, 1, 1986, pp. 87–94.

Honig, Alice S. "High Quality Infant/Toddler Care: Issues and Dilemmas." *Young Children*, November 1985, pp. 40–46.

Hymowitz, Carol. "Managing." "Offering Family Benefits Pays Off, Study Finds." The *Wall Street Journal* Europe, June 19, 1991.

Kagan, Sharon Lynn, and Newton, James W. "For-Profit and Nonprofit Child Care: Similarities and Differences." Public Policy Report. *Young Children*, November, 1989, pp. 4–10.

Katz, Lillian G., Evangelou, Demetra, and Hartman, Jeanette Allison. *The Case for Mixed-Age Groupings in Early Education*. Washington, D.C.: National Association for the Education of Young Children, 1990.

Lindner, Eileen; Mattis, Mary C.; and Rogers, June. *When Churches Mind the Children*. Ypsilanti, Mich.: High/Scope Press, 1983.

Meisels, Samuel J., and Sternberg, L. Steven. "Quality Sacrificed in Proprietary Child Care." *Education Week*, June, 1989, p. 36.

Morgan, G., Azer, S., Costley, J., Genser, A., Goodman, I., Lombardi, J., and McGimsey, B. *Making a Career of It: The State of the States Report on Career Development in Early Care and Education*. Boston, Mass: The Center for Career Development in Early Care and Education at Wheelock College, 1993.

National Association for the Education of Young Children. *Accreditation Criteria and Procedures of the National Academy of Early Childhood Programs*. Washington, D.C.: 1984.

National Center for Education Statistics. *Digest of Education Statistics: 1990*. Washington, D.C.: U.S. Government Printing Office, no date.

National Center for Education Statistics. *Profile of Preschool Children's Child Care and Early Education Program Participation*. Washington, D.C.: United States Government Printing Office, 1993.

Neugebauer, Roger. "How's Business: Status Report #7 on For-Profit Child Care." *Child Care Information Exchange*, January/February, 1991, pp. 46–50.

——————. "Status Report #2 on Employer Child Care." *Child Care Information Exchange*, July/August, 1991, pp. 5–9.

——————. "Churches That Care: Status Report #2 on Church-Housed Child Care." *Child Care Information Exchange*, September/October, 1991, pp. 41–45.

New York Times Editorial "Mothers With Babies—and Jobs." June 19, 1988, p. 26.

Peck, Johanne T., McCaig, Ginny, and Sapp, Mary Ellen. *Kindergarten Policies— What is Best for Children?* Washington, D.C.: National Association for the Education of Young Children, 1988.

Rubenstein, Carin. "Child Care Choices: At Home in Someone Else's House." *New York Times*, Thursday, April 1, 1993, p. C2.

Schweinhart, Lawrence J., and Weikart, David P. "Success by Empowerment: The High/Scope Perry Preschool Study Through Age 27." *Young Children*, November 1993, pp. 54–58.

Shepard, Lorrie A., and Smith, Mary Lee. "Escalating Kindergarten Curriculum."

ERIC Digest, Urbana, IL, no date.

Spodek, Bernard (Ed.). *Today's Kindergarten*. New York: Teacher's College Press, 1986.

United States Bureau of Census. "Who's Minding the Kids? Child Care Arrangements, 1986–87," Series P-70, No. 20. Washington, D.C.: U.S. Government Printing Office.

United States Census Bureau. *How We're Changing. Demographic State of the Nation*, 1995.

United States Department of Education. "A Profile of Child Care Settings: Early Education and Care in 1990." Washington, D.C.: U.S. Government Printing Office, 1990.

United States Department of Education. *National Study of Before and After School Programs*. Washington, D.C.: U.S. Government Printing Office, 1993.

United States Department of Health and Human Services. "Project Head Start Statistical Fact Sheet." Washington, D.C.: U.S. Government Printing Office, 1990.

Whitebrook, M., D. Phillips, and Howes, C. *The National Child Care Staffing Study Revisited*. Oakland, Calif.: Child Care Employee Project, 1993.

Willer, Barbara, ed. *Reaching the Full Cost of Quality in Early Childhood Programs*. Washington, D.C.: National Association for the Education of Young Children, 1990.

Willer, B., Hofferth, S., Kisker, E., Divine-Hawkins, P., Farquhar, E., and Glantz, B. *The Demand and Supply of Child Care in 1990*. Washington, D.C.: National Association for the Education of Young Children, 1991.

GUEST EDITORIAL

Who is the Child?

Louise Derman-Sparks

Alive Walker's advice to "Keep in mind always the present you are constructing; It should be the future you want" speaks to the essence of our mission as educators.[1] Early childhood educators and parents share a profound responsibility for helping children lay a strong foundation for productive and ethical existence in a complex, diverse nation and world. Integral to this work is understanding how children develop as individuals, as members of groups and of a society.

Learning how young children develop their identity and attitudes toward others is a key component of our professional education. A growing body of research tells us that infants as early as 6 months of age begin to notice human differences. By 18 months they begin to identify who is like them and to develop preferences. By four they begin to internalize socially prevailing beliefs, positive and negative, about their own and others group identities. Considerable research also reveals the serious damage that prejudice has on young children's budding awareness and feelings about themselves and others. It appears that we have a sensitive period between ages 6 months and 9 years when we can most effectively work to nurture healthy self and group identity and prevent or reduce prejudice.

To thrive, even to survive in the 21st century, children need environments in which they are "free to publicly affirm their own racial, ethnic, cultural, gender identification; able to transcend their own cultural borders and reach beyond them; and free to participate in action to make our society more democratic and free."[2] Our knowledge about children's development suggests that quality caregiving and education environments must include:

● Fostering of individual development within a child's own cultural group,

● Supporting every child's learning and experiencing the value of diversity, and

● Exposing every child to experiences that counteract bias and stereotypes.[3]

Becoming an excellent teacher requires learning how to effectively infuse these three dimensions in all aspects of early childhood education. Some adults prefer to deny that young children notice differences or that they are aware of and hurt by the various forms of prejudice prevalent in our society. This usually reflects the adult's own discomfort with these issues. However, avoidance doesn't give children the guidance and support they need. Becoming an effective professional challenges us to face and change the myths and stereotypes based on gender, race, ethnicity, class, disabilities, different family formats that we have learned. By so doing we free ourselves to teach children the most current wisdom the field of early childhood offers. Then we can truly build the future we want in the present we are creating.

Dr. Louise Derman Sparks is a faculty member of Pacific Oaks College, the author of the well-known Anti-Bias Curriculum (NAEYC, 1989), and an advocate for diversity in education.

[1]Walker, Alice. (1989). *The Temple of My Familiar.* New York: Harcourt Brace Jovanovich, 236.
[2]Dr. James Banks. California Association for Young Children Conference, 3/12/95, Long Beach
[3]From: Phillips, C.B. (1991) *Essentials for Child Development Associates Working with Young Children.* Council for Early Childhood Professional Recognition, Washington, D.C.

QUESTIONS FOR THOUGHT

What is the age range for early childhood?

What are some of the basic characteristics of each age?

How does the development of one area of growth affect other areas?

What are the implications for teaching children of varying levels of development?

What are some cautions to take when interpreting age-level characteristic charts? How are they useful?

Who is the whole child?

Who are special-needs children?

What are some of the common types of disabilities found in preschoolers?

What is an inclusive classroom?

How do teachers confront bias about children with special needs?

CHAPTER 3

Defining the Young Child

FIGURE 3.1 Children: alike, yet different.

DEFINING THE CHILD

Children—who are they? When entering a class room, questions arise in teachers' minds about the youngsters they see:

● What do children say?

● What can children do?

● What do children think?

● How do children feel?

Glancing around the room brings an awareness of the group as a whole. Individuals blur among a number of children, all the same size and same age. At this point, they are hardly more than a list of names with ages attached. Quickly, however, a teacher becomes conscious of a single child

here and there. In this assortment of small people, different sizes, shapes, and colors emerge.[1]

Through the Teacher's Eyes

Physical Impressions

Teachers usually begin to define children by their physical characteristics. Initially, their differences are most obvious by the way they look.

Eric is a tall blond. He is much larger than his just-three age would indicate. He has long slender fingers and arms to match. His movements are fluid; he lopes across the room toward the easel.

Lamar's short stocky build and constant swagger lend the impression that he is a pretty tough character. His coffee-and-cream complexion, soft, curly hair, and smile offset that image.

Natalie at four is a study in perpetual motion. Green eyes flashing, arms and legs waving, she ignores the bulk of her diaper as she propels herself down the slide. There is little indication that the mild case of spina bifida she has inhibits her motor activities. It certainly hasn't affected her daring.

Nothing will heighten an awareness of the individuality of each child more than working in the classroom. Teachers quickly learn what makes each child special. By watching and observing children, teachers accumulate a great deal of detailed information. Adults learn what children really look like as children move their bodies, change expressions, and assume a posture. A teacher can sense whether Sonja is happy, hurt, or hurried by the way she moves and how she looks. Rodrigo's face mirrors his distress or his delight. The observant teacher learns to read children for evidence of their social, emotional, physical, and intellectual growth. Children quite naturally express these characteristics with their whole body; each child's response is unique.

Children's Behaviors

Children's behaviors are so individual; they show their own personal responses to life. They re-

 OUR DIVERSE WORLD OUR DIVERSE WORLD OUR DIVERSE WORLD OUR DIVERSE WORLD OUR DIVERSE WORLD

[1]Quality early childhood programs can provide the opportunity to celebrate OUR DIVERSE WORLD!

late to people in ways that express their original nature. Dina has an ability to get her peers to wait on her; Sean trails the teachers for constant companionship. Their responses to the classroom environment are also singular. Ginny becomes overstimulated and loses control; Clark stands and watches other children for long periods of time before he joins in. Teachers become aware of individual differences in the skill level of children. They notice that of the five children at the art table, for instance, only one of them is holding scissors correctly and cutting paper.

How Children Are Alike

The similarities of the many children in a class are striking. The more they are different, the more they are the same. There seems to be a natural discrepancy here. Teachers can see the differences—wide differences—yet there are common characteristics within the age group itself. Six toddlers working on an art project exhibit six different personal styles, yet typically, they all become distracted and leave their projects half finished. Observation of children—how they look and how they act—helps the teacher see each child as an individual. When many children in a classroom are observed, behaviors common to that age become clear. There is enough standard behavior appropriate to certain age levels that allows for some generalizations about children's behavior.

Caldwell (1993) cites three universal characteristics that unite children of the world. Each child is like every other child in that (1) they all have the same needs, the most important of which are food, shelter, and care, (2) they all go through the same developmental stages, and (3) they all have the same developmental goals, although the timing and the cultural designations will differ.

Descriptions of these common characteristics date back to a classic collection of research by Gesell and Ilg. See both Chapters 1 and 4 for related discussions. See Figures 3.5–3.11 for a series of "word pictures" depicting these age-level characteristics from infancy through age seven. In

looking at individual children or a group, these descriptions are helpful in understanding the nature of the child and normal growth.

Why Children Differ

Watching and working with children exposes how very different each child is. What makes children differ so, especially when they have so many features in common? Megan gives the tire swing a big push. Ariel shrieks with delight, but Hans bursts into tears and screams to get off. What accounts for the wide range of behaviors evident when you observe any group of children?[1]

Genetic Makeup. This certainly accounts for some of the differences. Each child is a unique combination of genes that "contributes to the emergence and nature of every human trait from the color of the eyes . . . to the individual's ultimate intelligence and creativity" (Gardner, 1982). This also influences a child's hair color, height, body shape, and rate of growth (Bee, 1995).

Environment. The effects of the world on inherited genes also play a role. The number and kinds of experiences children have affect how they develop. The attitudes with which children are raised, their culture, their socioeconomic status, the kinds of caregiving they experience, and their community combine in countless ways to affect growth. In Chapter 15, this is more thoroughly discussed as the "ecology of the family." Good, nutritious food, adequate play space, interested and stimulating adults, the quality of life in the neighborhood, and family stability and relationships affect individual development. Whether a child lives in the South Bronx or Beverly Hills, environmental factors interact with genes to create a single, individual person.

The small child who stands at the classroom door is the sum total of the physical, intellectual, social, and emotional factors of home and heredity. What nature provides, the world shapes and bends. Using intelligence as an example, Gardner (1982) states the interdependency of environment

OUR DIVERSE WORLD OUR DIVERSE WORLD OUR DIVERSE WORLD OUR DIVERSE WORLD OUR DIVERSE WORLD

[1]In considering Developmentally Appropriate Practice think of both the universal and individual characteristics of children. Be aware of observing and honoring (not judging) children's individual characteristics.

and genetics this way: "The limit of intelligence is fixed by genetics, but the actual intelligence achieved reflects the diverse environments."

There are four other factors concerning the developmental scheme of things that account for individual differences.

Children Grow and Develop at Different Rates. Each child has an inner mechanism for monitoring growth. It is a timetable that varies from child to child. It means that each child is ready to learn at a given time, which may or may not coincide with the rest of the group. This readiness factor must be respected.

Development Is Predictable and Follows a Sequence. Even as the rate varies, the sequence remains the same for all children, even those who are disabled (Chandler, 1994). Physical development tends to be from the head downward (notice how large a newborn baby's head is in relation to the rest of its body) and from the center outward (a young child gains control over arm movements before mastering finger control).

A review of maturational theory (Chapter 4) and physical growth and development (Chapter 12) might be helpful. Periods of rapid growth and activity are followed by periods of calmness and consolidation. Behavioral swings at the half-year mark are common in many children. The pleasant, well-balanced three-year-old may become shy and begin to stutter at three-and-one-half. The age at which this occurs is not as important as the sequence in which it happens. The important thing to remember is that children will exhibit markedly different behaviors in the period of one short year. Teachers prepare for these times and appreciate them as a normal course of events for the growing child.

Sex and Race Differences. Girls and boys differ in both the rate and the pattern of growth. This is especially true in adolescence. African American and Asian children seem to have a more rapid tempo of growth than do white children, and children

FIGURE 3.2 In our diverse world teachers should be sensitive to the influence of sex, race, and individual patterns of development.

who are raised at poverty level or below develop more slowly than others (Bee, 1995).[1]

Implications for Teaching

The differences in children's development must be accounted for when planning a program for a group. Teachers take all these factors into consideration as they meet the needs of the individual child while addressing the concerns and interests of the total group.

Program Planning. Teachers generally begin by planning individual and group activities according to the age level of the class they teach, knowing that certain behavior patterns exist. Planning begins around the known similarities, the developmental tasks and age-appropriate behavior common to that group of children, including planning for children with special needs.[2] Goals are set for the children based on these general characteristics. As the school year progresses, teachers observe individuals and the group and change the developmental goals as needed. Individual differences in children are incorporated into the planning; activities selected allow for a variety of responses from children at different stages of de-

OUR DIVERSE WORLD OUR DIVERSE WORLD OUR DIVERSE WORLD OUR DIVERSE WORLD OUR DIVERSE WORLD

[1]See footnote 1. on page 69 ("*In considering Developmentally Appropriate Practice…*") and be reminded of the importance of noticing and knowing, but not judging, children's individual differences.

[2]Planning for children with special needs always begins by looking at typical development.

velopment. A pasting activity encourages creativity in the most adept three-year-old and still allows the less-skilled two-year-old to explore the feel of the paste on fingers and hands. The activity may need to be modified to make it more accessible or appropriate for children with special needs.[1] Programs are planned to meet the needs and challenges of the whole group.

Grouping of children by rigid age levels seems contrary to our understanding of individual rates of growth, readiness factors, and wide ranges of abilities. It is a convenient, though **arbitrary,** system of teaching children. The implication for teachers is clear: plan for the age level with the understanding and appreciation of the variations in development even within a one-year span. Know the child; know what to expect and what development has taken place. Look at the stages of growth for the age level just below and just above the one in which you teach.

Teachers' Response. The key word for teachers is *acceptance*. Teachers must not only accept the differences in children, they must plan for them. In doing so, they show respect for the individuality of each child in the class. Accepting the way children reveal themselves fosters the uniqueness that makes each one a special person.

See Chapter 5, The Teacher's Role, for specific suggestions on how teachers plan to accommodate the individuality of children, particularly the sections Self-awareness; Attitudes and Biases; Ten Essentials to Successful Teaching; and A Student Teacher's Guidelines for Beginning. The curriculum chapters, 11 through 15, demonstrate other examples of planning for a wide range of skills. It might be useful, too, to read Chapter 9, Creating Environments, particularly the self-help environment and the anti-bias curriculum.

Through Children's Eyes

Another way to define children is to look at them from their own point of view. What does it mean to look at the world through children's eyes?

What is a child's perspective on the world?

Adults carry into the classroom a great many perceptions about children. Having the advantage of many more years of experience, they tend to forget how much they know! The child they see is sometimes blurred through a great many filters. These filters are attitudes, concepts, experiences, and prejudices.[2] What looks mundane to an adult, such as a trip on the subway, fills children with the joy and wonder of discovery.

To view a classroom through the eyes of a child, one must set aside the filtered lenses of the grown-up world. The young child in the classroom is of the here and now and likes what is familiar and known. The preschooler takes pleasure in common, everyday experiences, learns by doing, and uses all five senses. Children this age are interested in dabbling in a great many things, yet when given time and opportunity to explore something that catches their eye, they are capable of a great depth of learning, as the children of Reggio Emilia demonstrate. (See Chapters 1, 9, 11, and 13 for further examples.)

The teacher learns to look through children's eyes—what interests them, what they avoid, who their friends are, how they respond in a variety of situations, and how they learn. When Kitty must play it safe with a friend who is less timid than she or Jacques puts together facts in ways that make sense to him, the teacher recognizes these as expressions of individuality.

Adults find that by looking at the world through the eyes of a child, they gain a different and valuable perspective as teacher.

DEVELOPMENTAL RANGES

Each developmental phase has characteristic traits. In the following pages some of the classic normative data collected by Gesell is combined with theories of Piaget, Elkind, and Erikson (see Chapter 4) to demonstrate what children have in common at various ages. Despite the wide range of individual differences at all ages, there are some characteristics children share that are worth keep-

OUR DIVERSE WORLD OUR DIVERSE WORLD OUR DIVERSE WORLD OUR DIVERSE WORLD OUR DIVERSE WORLD

[1]Planning for children with special needs always begins by looking at typical development.
[2]Individual judgments may be based on these "filters." Keep developing an awareness of yourself and your particular "filters."

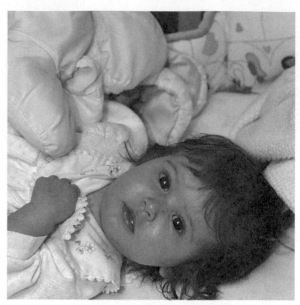

FIGURE 3.3 Adults see children through many filters. What is it like to look through children's eyes?

ing in mind. These common behaviors help teachers prescribe programs and plan activities and curricula. They lend perspective.

Most classes are labeled "the two's," "the three's," and so on. Schools enroll children according to a chronological order based on whether a birthday falls before or after an arbitrary deadline. Yet most child development texts no longer use the narrow one-year age span when setting out behavior characteristics. Larger, more inclusive groupings of Infant, Toddler, Preschooler, and so on are common. The reason for this is that children's growth patterns and individual differences can be so great that a narrow definition of behaviors would lead to inaccurate assessment of a child's development. For this reason, age-level charts can be misunderstood unless used with discretion.

The Value of Word Pictures for Teachers

In Behavior and Guidance

One consideration is what use teachers will make of the charts. It is important to know what range of behaviors occur and to be able to recognize them as normal patterns of growth, whether teaching children with special needs or children whose

growth is typical.[1] That helps to define and interpret the child's action in light of what is considered typical. Guidance and discipline are based on an awareness of the expected behaviors common to a given age range. Many so called "problem behaviors" are normal behaviors of the age in which they occur. This does not imply a passive approach; teachers and parents do not ignore undesirable behavior because the child is "going through a stage." Instead adults seek to guide and direct children in ways that enhance their overall growth. Four-year-olds test limits and are resistant to controls. The wise teacher accepts the testing of power and individuality, yet still maintains necessary limits to behavior.

Word pictures of a child, taken from age-level charts, help teachers know what to expect and when to expect it. By using the charts as a reference, teachers lessen the risk of expecting too much or too little of children at any given age. If, for instance, four-year-olds typically "tell tall tales," teachers' responses to their stories reflect that awareness. The fun of making up a story and the use of imagination are acknowledged, but there is not a concern that the child is lying. Age-level characteristics give a frame of reference with which to handle daily situations and a basis for planning appropriate guidance measures.

OUR DIVERSE WORLD OUR DIVERSE WORLD OUR DIVERSE WORLD OUR DIVERSE WORLD OUR DIVERSE WORLD

[1]Children are more alike than they are different.

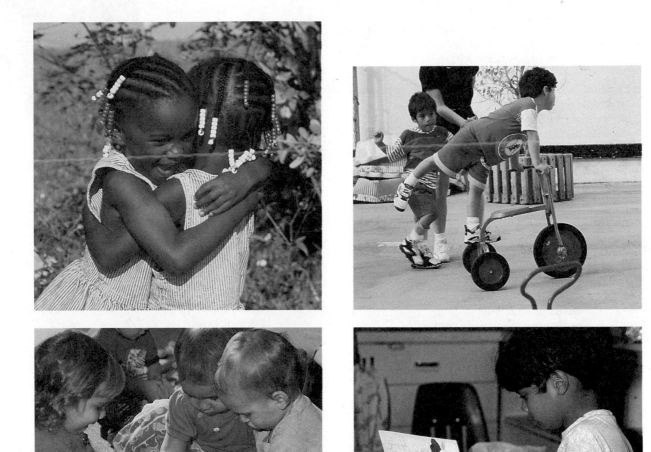

FIGURE 3.4 There is a wide range of individual differences in the way children grow and develop.

In Curriculum

The expression "hurried child," so aptly used by David Elkind in his book of the same name in the early 1980s, has come to mean a disregard for activities and curriculum geared to a child's appropriate developmental level. Instead, children are forced to sit and pay attention far longer than their bodies or minds can tolerate; attempts are made to teach reading and writing before children are developmentally prepared; and curriculum for fours, fives, and sixes include content best suited for later years. The following charts can be invaluable in helping early childhood professionals plan appropriate curriculum and activities for young children. Word pictures can be used to tailor curriculum planning to an individual child or a particular class or group on the basis of known developmental standards. See also The Importance of Childhood, Chapter 15.

Guidelines

Use the charts with care. A profile of the whole child is helpful, but avoid the tendency to overclassify. Look and listen to the children in the classroom in order to interpret theory. Balance your impressions with classroom experience of real

INFANTS

SOCIAL-EMOTIONAL

0-1 month: cries to express emotions; bonding begins
4-10 weeks: social smiles
2 months: begins social games
3 months: distinguishes familiar faces;
　　　　　turns head toward human voice;
　　　　　smiles in response to a smile;
　　　　　kicks, smiles, waves in response;
　　　　　cries when left alone;
　　　　　recognizes parent
4 months: genuine laugh;
　　　　　smiles when spoken to;
　　　　　loves attention
5 months to 1 year: stranger anxiety
6 months: distinguishes between voices;
　　　　　smiles, babbles at strangers;
　　　　　develops attachment;
　　　　　begins to play imitation games;
　　　　　plays peek-a-boo;
　　　　　sensitive to parental moods
8 months: laughs out loud
9 months: screams to get own way

Play is activity only for present moment.
Fears unfamiliar: people, places, things.
Beginning sense of separate self.

LANGUAGE

0-1 month: turns head in response to voices;
　　　　　cries to express needs
6-8 weeks: coos
Gestures to communicate:
　pushes objects away, squirms,
　reaches out to people, pouts,
　smacks lips, shrieks, points
2 months: voluntary vocal sounds
3 months: babbles
6-12 months: imitation sound games
Responds to variety of sounds.
Makes vowel sounds.
Acquires receptive language.
Cries to communicate
12 months: first words

PHYSICAL/MOTOR

By 1 year: grows 10 to 12 inches, triples birth weight,
　　　　　lengthens by 40%, doubles brain size,
　　　　　grows full head of hair
Bounces in crib
Uses whole-body motions
4 months: sees, grasps objects
5 months: examines fingers;
　　　　　sits when propped
6 months: rolls over;
　　　　　discovers feet;
　　　　　teething begins
7 months: crawls
8 months: sits up unaided;
　　　　　pulls to standing position;
　　　　　pincer grasp established
9 months: creeps
10 months: feeds self with spoon
11 months: stands alone; cruises
12 months: first steps
Late infancy: can move hands in rotation to turn knobs
Newborn motor activity is mostly reflexes.

INTELLECTUAL-COGNITIVE

0-1 month: responds to mother's voice:
　　　　　senses function, especially pain, touch
10 weeks: memory is evident
4 months: smiles of recognition
7-10 months: solves simple problems (knocks over
　　　　　box to get toy)
8 months: begins to believe in permanence of objects;
　　　　　follows a simple instruction
8-12 months: intentionality in acts
11 months: begins trial-error experimentation
12 months: plays drop/retrieve games, pat-a-cake
Explores with hands and fingers
Smiles, vocalizes at image in mirror

FIGURE 3.5　Around 8 months, the infant sits up unaided.

TODDLERS

SOCIAL-EMOTIONAL

Almost totally egocentric
Likes to be noticed; loves an audience
Lacks inhibitions
Insists on own way
Likes doing things by self
Assertive, independent
Adapts easily
Plays by self in playpen
Refers to self by name
Laughs loudly at peek-a-boo
Cries when left alone
Curious
Relates to adults better than children
Active, eager
Talks mostly to self
Usually friendly
Strong sense of ownership

LANGUAGE

Some two-word phrases
Enjoys vocalizing to self
Babbles in own jargon
Uses "eh-eh" or "uh-uh" with gestures
Names closest relatives
Repeats adults' words
Points to communicate needs, wants
Shakes head "no" to respond
Responds to directions to fetch, point
Obeys verbal requests
Answers "What's that?"
Understands simple phrases
Uses 5 to 50 words

PHYSICAL/MOTOR

Awkward coordination; chubby body
Tottering stance
Creeps when in a hurry
Walks with increasing confidence
Walks with feet wide apart, arms out, head forward
Finds it difficult to turn corners
Goes up and down stairs holding on

Backs into chair to sit down
Can squat for long periods of time
Motor-minded: constant motion
Loves to pull/push objects
Runs with stiff, flat gait
Uses whole-arm movements
Carry and dump becomes a favorite activity
Scribbles
Turns pages two or three at a time
Zips/unzips large zipper
Likes holding objects in both hands

INTELLECTUAL-COGNITIVE

Points to objects in a book
Matches similar objects
Fits round block in round hole
Loves opposites: up/down, yes/no
Imitates simple tasks
Interest shifts quickly
Short attention span
Follows one direction
Gives up easily, but easily engaged
Conclusions are important: close doors, shut books
Thinks with feet; action-oriented
Builds tower of three to four small blocks

FIGURE 3.6 The toddler loves to play peekaboo.

TWO-YEAR OLDS

SOCIAL-EMOTIONAL

Self-centered
Unable to share, possessive
Clings to familiar; resistant to change
Ritualistic; insists on routines
Dependent
Likes one adult at a time
Quits readily; easily frustrated
Goes to extremes
Impulsive; shifts activities suddenly
Easily distracted
Pushes, shoves
Finicky, fussy eater, some food jags
Refers to self by given name
Treats people as inanimate objects
Dawdles; slow-geared
Plays parallel
Watches others
Likes people
Excited about own capabilities

LANGUAGE

Uses two- or three-word sentences
Telegraphic sentences: "Throw ball"
Has difficulty in pronunciation
"Mine" most prominent pronoun
Spontaneous language; rhythmic, repetitive
Constant talking; interested in sound
Sings phrases of songs, not on pitch
Can't articulate feelings
Frustrated when not understood
May stutter
Asks "Whassat?" about pictures
Can match words with objects
Repeats words and phrases
Uses 50 to 300 words

PHYSICAL/MOTOR

Uses whole-body action
Pushes, pulls, pokes
Climbs into things
Leans forward while running
Climbs stairs one by one
Dependent on adults for dressing
Can help undress
Has reached one-half potential height
Bladder/bowel control begins
Feeds self
Thumb-forefinger opposition complete
Grasps cup with two hands
Awkward with small objects
Lugs, tumbles, topples; unsteady
Alternates hands; preference developing
Can rotate to fit objects
Expresses emotions bodily
Sensory-oriented
Cuts last teeth
Has difficulty relaxing

INTELLECTUAL-COGNITIVE

Investigates with touch and taste
Intrigued by water, washing
Likes to fill, empty things
Has limited attention span
Lives in present
Only understands familiar concepts
Colors and numbers are meaningless
Needs own name used
Likes simple make-believe
Does one thing at a time
Remembers orders of routines
Recalls where toys are left
Knows, points to: arms, nose, mouth, feet, eyes
Names familiar objects in books

FIGURE 3.7   The two-year old watches others.

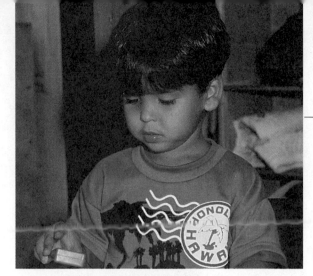

THREE-YEAR OLDS

PHYSICAL/MOTOR

Well-balanced body lines
Walks erect; nimble on feet
Gallops in wide, high steps
Alternates feet in stair climbing
Suddenly starts, stops
Turns corners rapidly
Swings arms when walking
Jumps up and down with ease
Uses toilet alone
Loses baby fat
Achieves bladder control
Rides a tricycle
Puts on, takes off wraps with help
Unbuttons buttons
Has some finger control with small objects
Grasps with thumb and index finger
Holds cup in one hand
Pours easily from small pitcher
Washes hands unassisted
Can carry liquids
Has activity with drive and purpose
Can balance on one foot

SOCIAL-EMOTIONAL

Highly imitative of adults
Wants to please adults; conforms
Responds to verbal suggestions
Easily prompted, redirected
Can be bargained with, reasoned with
Begins to share, take turns, wait
Avid "me-too"er
Exuberant, talkative, humorous
Has imaginary companions
Has nightmares, animal phobias
Plays consciously, cooperatively with others
Plays spontaneously in groups
Dramatizes play
Goes after desires; fights for them
Asserts independence often
Often stymied, frustrated, jealous
Sympathizes
Strong sex-role stereotypes

INTELLECTUAL-COGNITIVE

Estimates "how many"
Enjoys making simple choices
Alert, excited, curious
Asks "why?" constantly
Understands "It's time to. . ."
Understands "Let's pretend. . ."
Enjoys guessing games, riddles
Has lively imagination
Often names block buildings
Has short attention span
Carries out two to four directions in sequence
Often colors pages one color
Can't combine two activities
Names and matches simple colors
Has number concepts of one and two
Sees vague cause/effect relationships
Can recognize simple melodies
Distinguishes between night and day
Understands size/shape comparison

LANGUAGE

Talkative with or without a listener
Can listen in order to learn
Likes new words
Increases use of pronouns, prepositions
Uses "s" to indicate plural nouns
Uses "ed" to indicate past tense
Uses sentences of three or more words
Says "Is that all right?" a lot
Talks about nonpresent situations
Puts words into action
Moves and talks at the same time
Substitutes letters in speech: "w" for "r"
Intrigued by whispering
Uses 300 to 1,000 words

FIGURE 3.8 The three-year old is refining finger movement

FOUR-YEAR OLDS

SOCIAL-EMOTIONAL

Mood changes rapidly
Tries out feelings of power
Dominates; is bossy, boastful, belligerent
Assertive, argumentative
Shows off; is cocky, noisy
Can fight own battles
Hits, grabs, insists on desires
Explosive, destructive
Easily over-stimulated; excitable
Impatient, intolerant in large groups
Cooperates in groups of two or three
Develops "special" friends but shifts loyalties often
In-group develops; excludes others
Resistant; tests limits
Exaggerates, tells tall tales
Alibis frequently
Teases, outwits; has terrific humor
May have scary dreams
Tattles frequently
Has food jags, food strikes

LANGUAGE

Has more words than knowledge
A great talker, questioner
Likes words, plays with them
Has high interest in poetry
Able to talk to solve conflicts
Responds to verbal directions
Enjoys taking turns to sing along
Interested in dramatizing songs, stories
Exaggerates, practices words
Uses voice control, pitch, rhythm
Asks "when?" "why?" "how?"
Joins sentences together
Loves being read to

PHYSICAL/MOTOR

Longer, leaner body build
Vigorous, dynamic, acrobatic
Active until exhausted
"Works," builds, drives, pilots
Can jump own height and land upright
Hops, skips
Throws large ball, kicks accurately
Hops and stands on one foot
Jumps over objects
Walks on a straight line
Races up and down stairs
Turns somersaults
Walks backward toe-heel
Accurate, rash body movements
Copies a cross, square
Can draw a stick figure
Holds paint brush in adult manner, pencil in fisted grasp
Can lace shoes
Dresses self except back buttons, ties
Has sureness and control in finger activities
Alternates feet going down stairs

INTELLECTUAL-COGNITIVE

Does some naming and representation in art
Gives art products personal value
Can work for a goal
Questions constantly
Interested in how things work
Interested in life-death concepts
Has an extended attention span
Can do two things at once
Dramatic play is closer to reality
Judges which of two objects is larger
Has concept of three; can name more
Has accurate sense of time
Full of ideas
Begins to generalize; often faulty
Likes a variety of materials
Calls people names
Has dynamic intellectual drive
Has imaginary playmates
Recognizes several printed words

FIGURE 3.9 Special friends is part of being four.

FIVE-YEAR OLDS

SOCIAL-EMOTIONAL

Poised, self-confident, self-contained
Sensitive to ridicule
Has to be right; persistent
Has sense of self-identity
May get silly, high, wild
Enjoys pointless riddles, jokes
Enjoys group play, competitive games
Aware of rules, defines them for others
Chooses own friends; is sociable
Gets involved with group decisions
Insists on fair play
Likes adult companionship
Accepts, respects authority
Asks permission
Remains calm in emergencies

LANGUAGE

Uses big words and complete sentences
Can define some words
Spells out simple words
Takes turn in conversation
Has clear ideas and articulates them
Uses words to give, receive information
Insists "I already know that"
Asks questions to learn answers
Makes up songs
Enjoys dictating stories
Uses 1,500 words
Tells a familiar story
Defines simple words
Answers telephone, takes a message
Thinks out loud

PHYSICAL/MOTOR

Completely coordinated
Has adultlike posture
Has tremendous physical drive
Likes to use fine-motor skills
Learns how to tie bow knot
Has accuracy, skill with simple tools

Draws a recognizable person
Dresses self completely
Cuts on a line with scissors
Begins to color within the lines
Catches ball from three feet away
Skips using alternate feet
Enjoys jumping, running, doing stunts
Rides a two-wheeler
Balances on a balance beam
Jumps rope
Runs lightly on toes
Likes to dance; is graceful, rhythmic
Sometimes roughhouses, fights

INTELLECTUAL-COGNITIVE

Curious about everything
Wants to know "how?" "why?"
Likes to display new knowledge, skills
Somewhat conscious of ignorance
Attention span increases noticeably
Knows tomorrow, yesterday
Can count 10 objects, rote counts to 20
Sorts objects by single characteristic
Knows name, address, town
Makes a plan, follows it, centers on task
Sorts objects by color, shape
Concepts of smallest, less than, one-half
May tell time accurately, on the hour
Knows what a calendar is used for

FIGURE 3.10 Five-year olds may get silly, high, and wild.

SIX- AND SEVEN-YEAR OLDS

SOCIAL-EMOTIONAL

Six-year-old
Likes to work, yet often does so in spurts
Does not show persistence
Tends to be a know-it-all
Free with opinions and advice
Brings home evidence of good schoolwork
Observes family rules
Gender-role stereotypes are rigid
Friends easily gained, easily lost
Finding a place with peers
Tests and measures self against peers
Makes social connections through play
Friends are of same sex
Believes in rules except for self
Active, outgoing
Own activities, pleasure take precedence
Charming
Proud of accomplishments

Seven-year-old
More serious
Sensitive to others' reactions
Eager for home responsibilities
Tractable and polite at home
Complaining, pensive
Shame is common emotion
Leaves rather than face criticism, ridicule, disapproval
Complains of unfair treatment, not being liked
Shows politeness and consideration for adults
Enjoys solitary activities
First peer pressure: needs to be "in"
Wants to be one of the gang
Relates physical competence to self-concept
Impatient

LANGUAGE

Six- and seven-year-olds
Enjoy putting language skill to paper
Talk *with* adults rather than *to* them
Chatter incessantly
Dominate conversations
Speech irregularities still common
Learning to print/write
Acquisition of new words tapers off
Bilingual capacities nearly complete if English is second language
Ability to learn new language still present

PHYSICAL/MOTOR DEVELOPMENT

Six- and seven-year-olds
Growth has slowed
Basic skills developed; need refinement
Need active play to let off steam
Like to test limits of own bodies
Enjoy acrobatics
Value physical competence
Work at self-imposed tasks
Need daily legitimate channels for high energy
Learn to ride two-wheelers
Enjoy challenges in balancing—skating, skiing
Motor development is tool for socializing
Bones growing and solidifying
Boisterous, enjoy stunts
Like to roughhouse but may get hurt
Susceptible to fatigue
Visual acuity reaches normal
Hungry at short intervals
Insatiable taste for sweets, especially after school
Oral: Chews pencils, fingernails, hair
Moves with speed

INTELLECTUAL-COGNITIVE

Six- and seven-year-olds
Work in spurts, not persistent
Letter and word reversal common
Learn to read
Can consider others' point of view
Use logic, systematic thinking
Can plan ahead
Enjoy collecting: sorting, classifying
Beginning math skills
Can sequence events and retell stories
Concepts of winning/losing are difficult
Like games with simple rules
May cheat or change rules
Appetite for "real" knowledge
Want "real" things: watches and cameras that work
Sift and sort information
Can conceptualize situations

FIGURE 3.11 An important milestone, learning to read.

children. Interpretation of the charts must not focus on what the child *cannot* do. Instead, use them to get a perspective on the wide range of developmental norms a child exhibits over several of the chronological age groupings. Always look at the word picture for the group just below and just above the age level of the children you are assessing. Those children will undoubtedly exhibit some of the developmental behaviors appropriate to all three groups you check.

There are several things to keep in mind for the age-level charts to be a valuable teaching tool. It is very important to realize that these norms of development refer to average or typical behavior. They cannot be applied to an individual child too literally. If you were to look at a class of six-year-olds using the profiles, for instance, you would find that probably half of the children would fit the majority of the description. Some of them would not yet have reached this level of develop-

ment and some would have already gone through this stage. Shawna might well fit the general description of the six-year-old at a physical level. Her language and intellectual levels may be closer to a seven-year-old, while her social skills may be typical of many four-year-olds. There may very well be characteristics that Shawna will *never* exhibit. It won't work to use the chart as a measuring stick, comparing one child to another, since children develop at their own rates and in their own ways.

Remember that children probably go through most of the stages described, and in the same sequence. But they will do so in ways that reflect their own rate of growth and their own background. Use these characteristics not to pit children against each other to see who is developing faster, but to compare the child to himself. Looking at Dwayne, it helps to know where he is in relation to most two-year-olds, but more important, where he is now, six months from now, a year from now, and what he was like a year ago. A clear picture of his rate of growth emerges. His recent change of behavior, for instance, might be attributed to the 2-1/2-year-old stage of disequilibrium, even though Dwayne is chronologically two years, nine months. See also Child Development and Cultural Diversity in Chapter 4.

The word picture on the infant to one-year-old is deliberately vague on the ages when some developmental characteristics might appear. The rapid rate of growth combined with individual growth patterns make it difficult to predict with any surety when Garth will indeed sit up by himself unaided, but he is likely to accomplish that task within one or two months on either side of the average age cited.

Word Pictures

Four basic developmental areas are included in the word pictures:

● *Physical/Motor Development.* Includes gross motor, fine motor, and perceptual motor.

● *Language Development.* Includes children's utterances, pronunciation, vocabulary, sentence length, and the ability to express ideas, needs, and feelings. It includes receptive language (do they understand what they hear?) and verbal levels (what do they say?)

● *Intellectual Development.* This generally means the ability to perceive and think. Includes curiosity, memory, attention span, general knowledge, problem solving, analytical thinking, beginning reading, computing skills, and other cognitive processes.

● *Social-Emotional Development.* Includes a child's relationship with himself and others, self-concept, self-esteem, and the ability to express feelings.

The following word pictures are designed to help classroom teachers. Characteristics listed are:

● behaviors most common to the age group

● those that have implications for children in group settings

● those that suggest guidance and disciplinary measures

● those that have implications for planning developmentally appropriate curriculum

In Chapter 4, students will come to appreciate the importance of research and significant theories from which these word pictures are drawn.

THE WHOLE CHILD

The concept of "the whole child" is based on the accepted principle that all areas of human growth and development are interrelated. It is only for the purpose of studying one area or another in depth that such categories are created. The four developmental areas labeled in the preceding Word Pictures help focus on certain aspects of a child's normal development. In reality, all areas of growth are "intertwined and mutually supportive" (Allen and Marotz, 1994).

Each Child Is Unique

There are several reasons to consolidate different developmental areas into one person. The first is the uniqueness of the children. Each one is a sum total of a multitude of parts and, as such, is different from anyone else. Individual natures and learning styles affect the way teachers will teach two children of the same age in the same class.

Growth Is Interrelated

One area of development affects the other. A child with a hearing loss is likely to have language delay as well; thus, the physical development affects the language part of growth.[1] The child who has trouble making friends (social) is likely to exhibit his unhappiness (emotional) in the school yard (physical) and in the math period (intellectual). The interdependence of the areas of development have some positive aspects as well. The child who has a good breakfast and starts the school day with parent interest is ready to tackle new puzzles and new relationships. The kindergartener who masters using scissors is ready to try printing: the fine-motor skills enhance the cognitive task of learning the alphabet.

One way for new teachers to look at this concept of development is to plot the relationships visually. Think of each area of development as a circle. There are four of them: physical-motor, language, intellectual, and social-emotional. Try to connect them so that they intersect one another, as shown in Figure 3.12.

Think how each area might affect or interact with the others. Can physical development affect how children feel about themselves? Of course; children who appreciate their body and its power feel confident in what they can do. How do intellectual skills interact with language development? When children have mastered their primary language, they can then clarify some of their thought processes. The emphasis on the circularity of the child's growth and development is a primary concept.

OUR DIVERSE WORLD OUR DIVERSE WORLD OUR DIVERSE WORLD OUR DIVERSE WORLD OUR DIVERSE WORLD

[1]Be aware of the full range of child development. Remember to keep working with the whole child, continuing to notice how children are all the same *and* how each child is unique.

Normal physical development, for instance, depends on meeting not only the child's physical (adequate nutrition) needs but psychological (nurturing caregivers/parents) and social (adequate play/exploration) needs as well. Social development is aided by the ability to communicate verbally; a well-developed attention span helps the child develop fine motor skills; relating to others is more successful if intellectual problem-solving skills are already mature.

Three-year-olds frequently pose the question, "Why?" as part of their intellectual curiosity. A teacher matches that understanding with the age-level characteristic of "listening in order to learn" and knows that the child understands some explanations. Thus, intellectual and language development areas influence one another.

Two-year-old Gabe, who has difficulty relaxing, responds better at naptime if allowed to cling to a familiar object or toy. Motor and emotional growth interact with each other in this case.

Valuing Wholeness

The whole-child approach is seen from a medical point of view as well. **Holistic** medicine is basically an attempt to view health care from a "wellness" rather than illness perspective. From this comes the idea of preventive medicine, which attempts to maintain the body in a healthy state, rather than wait for treatment until infection or disease has invaded.

This has a great deal to do with educating children. It is an attitude that begins with a belief in the "wellness" of children, their innate goodness and trustworthiness. A two-year-old who says, "No!" exhibits signs of "wellness" and is to be accepted as behaving normally. Young children wiggle and squirm during naptime. The deadly quiet of 25 kindergartners in a room may indicate anxiety and concern rather than accomplishment. In other words, rather than viewing behavior as "wrong," it is important to notice and value whether what a child is doing is a sign of "wellness."

The concept of the whole child strongly sug-

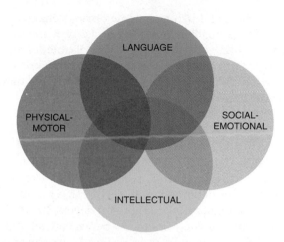

FIGURE 3.12 How areas of growth are interrelated: each area of growth is affected by and influences every other area of development.

gests the uniqueness of the person. Although they are often discussed separately, the areas of development (social, emotional, physical, and intellectual) cannot be isolated from one another. They each make a valuable contribution to the total child.

CHILDREN WITH SPECIAL NEEDS

Two types of children come under the category of children with special needs. Children who are disabled and children who are gifted extend the definition of "Who is the child?".[1] They are discussed separately in this section.

Children Who Are Disabled

More and more of the children in early childhood classrooms have a disabling condition. Five-year-old Pete, blind from birth, has been in nursery school for three years. Chrissy, a multi-handicapped four-year-old, has her daily program in a special school supplemented by attending the child care center three afternoons each week. Travis is a child with **Down syndrome,** and this is his first experience in a school not restricted to *atypical* children.

OUR DIVERSE WORLD OUR DIVERSE WORLD OUR DIVERSE WORLD OUR DIVERSE WORLD OUR DIVERSE WORLD

[1]Our picture of what to consider while thinking about diversity continues to expand—race, gender, ethnicity, social class, physical and cognitive ability . . .

These children have some obvious characteristics that qualify them for special-needs status. Other children with less apparent disabilities also fall into this category. The term **special needs** includes a great many conditions that may or may not be noticeable.

Allen and Schwartz (1996) suggests three conditions under which a child is considered disabled. To be so designated, a child's normal growth and development is (1) delayed; (2) distorted, atypical, or abnormal; or (3) severely or negatively affected. This definition includes the physical, mental, emotional, and social areas of development.

Approximately 15 to 20 percent of all children in the United States will exhibit some form of atypical development and need special services (Bee, 1995). These are children who did not develop according to normal standards. They exhibit a wide range of atypical disorders ranging from short-term behavior problems to long-term physical, mental, and emotional disabilities.[1]

There are a variety of disabilities that may be encountered by teachers of young children:

● *Speech and language:* hard of hearing, deafness, stuttering, articulation problems, cleft palate, chronic voice disorders, learning disabilities

● *Physical-motor:* visual impairment, blindness, perceptual motor deficits, hearing impairments, deafness, orthopedic disabilities such as cerebral palsy, spina bifida, loss of limbs, muscular dystrophy

● *Intellectual:* mental retardation, brain injury, brain dysfunction, dyslexia, learning disabilities

● *Social-emotional:* self-destructive behavior, severe withdrawal, dangerous aggression toward self and others, noncommunicativeness, moodiness, tantrums, attention-deficit hyperactivity disorder, severe anxiety, depression, phobias, psychosis, autism

● *Health impairments:* severe asthma, epilepsy, hemophilia, congenital heart defects, severe anemia, malnutrition, diabetes, tuberculosis, cystic fibrosis, Down syndrome, sickle-cell anemia, Tay-Sachs disease, AIDS (Wolery and Wilbers, 1994)

● *Specific learning disabilities:* difficulties with language use and acquisition, spoken and written language affected, perceptual handicaps, brain injury, minimal brain dysfunction, dyslexia, developmental aphasia (Baron, 1995)

These disorders may range from mild to severe, and children will exhibit a wide variety of abilities and needs, even if they are diagnosed with the same condition. For further information concerning a specific one, the student will want to consult a special education textbook.

In the course of normal development, any one area of a child's growth is affected by the development of the whole child. This is true for children who are disabled also; the disability may have led to problems in other areas of growth. A child with a profound hearing loss is often delayed in speech production or language abilities and suffers social isolation due to the inability to hear and speak with peers. A child with a speech impairment or cleft palate may have the intellectual capacity to put simple puzzles together but may not yet have the language to engage verbally in songs and fingerplays.

Some disabilities are in and of themselves multihandicapping, affecting several growth areas. Typically, a child with Down syndrome may have congenital heart defects, mental retardation, eye abnormalities, or poor physical coordination. Children who have cerebral palsy, a central nervous system disorder, often have other disabling conditions such as mental retardation, epilepsy, and hearing, visual, and speech problems (Kiernan et al., n.d.).

Learning Disabilities

Children with learning disabilities (LD) are found in almost every classroom—they have no discernable disabling condition but nevertheless are having problems with one or more basic skills or learning. These children may have, among other

[1]More and more early care and education programs are reflecting diversity by creating groups of children exhibiting a wide range of developmental abilities.

things, poor memory skills, difficulty in following directions, eye-hand coordination problems, and trouble discriminating between letters, numbers, and sounds. This keeps them from storing, processing, and producing information (Kelly, 1988). Dyslexia, the most common specific learning disability, occurs when children have difficulty in learning to read. They may reverse letters (such as *d* and *b*) or words (such as *was* and *saw*), although many children do this who are not dyslexic. A child with a learning disability may have a strength in one area, such as math, and yet have a disability in another area, such as language. A learning disability does not mean that a child is retarded.

As we learned earlier in this chapter, growth is interrelated and each area of growth is influenced by and influences other areas of growth. It will come as no surprise to discover that learning disorders are usually not a singular dysfunction. Children who exhibit problems with reading and writing will often have difficulties with spatial relationships and body coordination. Observations of these behaviors can give teachers some of the first warning signs of learning disorders.

There is continuing controversy on how to define and identify these children; a broad use of the term is commonplace, sometimes in order to qualify for special education funding. While some experts consider minimal brain damage to be the cause of learning disabilities, there is not consensus yet on why children have these problems.

According to Bee (1995), a child with a learning disorder develops normally in other respects and has no obvious brain damage, but the task of reading seems to highlight several areas of difficulty: problems of visual perception, inability to integrate visual and auditory information, impaired memory, problems with language, and difficulty distinguishing the separate sounds in words. This wide range of symptoms, the number of potential causes, and the varying degrees to which children exhibit the symptoms makes learning disorders difficult to diagnose.

Attention-Deficit Disorder

Do you remember a classmate who could never sit still—one who was constantly on the move, talked excessively, and disrupted classroom activities? You may have also seen a preschool counterpart in the form of a child who couldn't finish a puzzle, take a nap, or wait for a turn. These children are typical of children with a condition known as attention-deficit hyperactivity disorder (ADHD), which affects up to 5 percent of children uner 18 years of age (Wallis, 1994).

This disorder, previously called hyperactivity, was renamed by the American Psychiatric Association in 1987. When it exists without the hyperactive components it is called attention-deficit disorder, or ADD. ADHD is commonly thought to appear more often in boys; however, according to Hallowell and Ratty (1994), girls may go undiagnosed because they may not exhibit the hyperactive behavior.

As with learning disabilities, experts do not agree on the cause of this emotional disorder, but it does not appear to be caused by brain damage (Bee, 1995).

Children with ADHD are difficult to manage, both at home and in the classroom. They are prone to restlessness, anxiety, short attention spans, and impulsiveness. Hyperactive children have difficulty remaining seated, they are in constant motion, do not listen well, may talk excessively, are easily distracted, and have difficulty with social relationships. This constellation of behaviors may apply at some level to many children, but teachers must be cautious about labeling the normally active, somewhat disruptive child as hyperactive. The child with ADHD exhibits these behaviors in extreme, usually before age 7.

Medication with a drug, Ritalin, is a common treatment for children with ADHD, but since its effects are short term and its side effects can be serious, it is controversial as a remedy. Research does not support a popular theory that eliminating food additives, preservatives, and refined sugar from the child's diet will alter behavior significantly (Kelly, 1988). There is no easy solution for dealing with children who are hyperactive; further research into the cause of this disability and development of safe effective treatments is clearly called for.

Effective guidance strategies for children with ADHD include:

● Regular and consistent routines: "Remember, Sitara, we always wash hands before snacks."

- Consistent rules: "That's right, Ethan. Walk inside and run outside."

- Realistic expectations: "I know it is hard for you to wait a long time. Why don't you go over to the other cabinet and see if the pencils you want are in there?"

- Eye contact when giving directions and clear and simple explanations: "Look at me, Toby, so I know that you are listening. Good. Now let's go over the assignment together."

- Allowing time for transition and giving a plan for the next step: "In 3 minutes it will be time to get ready to go home. When the other children begin to leave, I want you to get your coat and come back here to sit with us."

- Selecting jobs in which the children can be successful: "Connie, please pass the napkins out to this table today."

- Recognition of accomplishments: "Good work, Connie. You gave everyone a red napkin and then sat down with one for yourself."

Role of Parents and Teachers

Parents are usually the first to notice that their child is not developing according to the norms. They may ask the child's teacher to watch for signs of deafness, lack of necessary motor skills, or language imperfections. Since early diagnosis and intervention are important, teachers should take these requests seriously and should begin to assess the child's overall skills.[1] With the parents, they can then plan appropriate follow-through. This may include a consultation with a physician for further developmental screening and testing. If both parents and teachers feel there is a potential problem, the task is to help identify it and secure the services needed.

The teacher's role is to observe the child and provide current information, to support the parents through their concern, to find appropriate resources for them (such as social service agencies, public health offices, private and public schools), to assist with future placement for child care, and to be available for consultation with others who are working in the best interests of the child. The early childhood professional is not an expert in diagnosing learning disabilities but can be effective in helping parents secure proper referrals and treatment.

Public Recognition

Attention to the problems of people with disabilities in our society has reached national proportion only recently. Since the mid-1960s there has been significant public recognition of and the advent of public funding for the educational programs for disabled persons. Prior to that, public—and private—attitudes seemed to be ones of shame and segregation. Past generations hid disabled adults and children in their homes or secluded them in institutions. Slowly, reform took place. Keeping special populations out of sight gave way to providing separate opportunities for them. Schools, classes, and recreational programs were started exclusively for people with special needs. Public consciousness is now sufficient to understand that many disabled people can lead useful and productive lives, and that all people with special needs are not retarded. The current practice of integrating children with disabilities into ongoing programs in schools—the mainstream of American life—is not only more humane, but practical as well.[2]

Over the years a small number of schools had routinely accepted children with special needs. The idea gained national attention in 1972 when Head Start required that a minimum of 10 percent of its enrollment be reserved for children with disabilities. Head Start led the way toward large-scale inclusion. In 1975, Public Law 94-142, the Education for All Handicapped Children Act, passed. This so-called "Bill of Rights for the Handicapped" guarantees free public education to disabled persons from three to 21 years of age. An individualized program for each person is manda-

OUR DIVERSE WORLD OUR DIVERSE WORLD OUR DIVERSE WORLD OUR DIVERSE WORLD OUR DIVERSE WORLD

[1] Early childhood professionals need to be skilled at carefully observing and documenting the growth and development of individual children.

[2] See footnote 1 on page 47 . . . "Many programs are attempting to include 75% typically developing children along with 25% children having been recognized as having a special need."

tory, to be worked out in concert with the child's parents. Early childhood educators are fulfilling the requirements of that legislation. Public school systems faced with providing preschool programs for children with disabilities are turning to private preschools to fill the need when their own services are unavailable or inadequate.

The success of P.L. 94-142 means that thousands of children who are disabled who would have been denied any educational opportunities a decade ago are now in school. Further, they are being integrated in schools with their nondisabled peers.

P.L. 99-457, the Education of the Handicapped Amendments Act of 1986, has an even more profound impact for early childhood educators. Sections of this law provide funding for children who were not included in the previous law: infants, toddlers, and three-to-five-year-olds. Before P.L. 99-457 was passed, only six states offered any services to infants with special needs at birth. The states were given a five-year period which ended in the 1991–92 school year to establish early intervention programs or lose their early childhood federal funding.

Since the initial law in 1975, parents of children with special needs have been part of the development of their child's Individualized Education Plan (IEP). This role has been strengthened recently to include a more family-centered approach. The family's strengths and needs are taken into account as specific services are arranged for the child, providing a more supportive atmosphere in which the child's unique needs will be met.

The preschool programs are essentially an extension of P.L. 94-142 services, which provide for the least restrictive environments for educating disabled children. The infant/toddler amendment is new, however. Another critical aspect of this law is that it allows for the inclusion of "developmentally delayed" youngsters and leaves local agencies the opportunity to include the "at risk" child in that definition. The vague definitions give local agencies the opportunity to define disabling conditions in terms of local needs.

In 1990 Congress reauthorized P.L. 94-142 and renamed it the Individuals with Disabilities Education Act (IDEA) (P.L. 101-576). Two new categories, autism and traumatic brain injury, were included, and children from birth to age 5

years were now eligible to receive services.

The importance of this legislation cannot be underestimated by those in and entering the field of early childhood. Clearly, the integration and transition of disabled children in early childhood programs will require knowledgeable teachers. Early childhood educators of the 1990s would be wise to avail themselves of special education courses now in order to meet this challenge. Many states now require such course work before certification; others will surely follow in order to fulfill these mandates.

Many programs may be affected by another piece of legislation, P.L. 101-336, the American with Disabilities Act (ADA), which was passed in 1990. This civil rights act makes it unlawful to discriminate against people with disabilities because of their disability and requires that people with disabilities have equal access to public and private services, as well as reasonable accommodations. This law may have an impact on hiring practices in early childhood centers and family child care homes and may require adaptations to facilities and work environments to make them more accessible to individuals with disabilities. While not specifically an education law, ADA is another step toward respecting the dignity and worth of all individuals.

Inclusion of Children with Special Needs

Allen and Schwartz (1996) differentiate between the terms *inclusion* and *mainstreaming*. In the past, children with special needs were integrated into classrooms only after they had met certain standards and expectations. Often they were assigned to separate special education classes. When ready, they were mainstreamed into classrooms with typically developing children. Inclusion means that a child with a disability is a full-time member of a regular classroom, a more natural environment, with children who do, as well as those who do not, have special needs.

More than a word definition is at stake, however. Allen and Schwartz (1996) go on to point out that inclusion is about belonging, having worth, and having choices. An inclusive classroom is about "accepting and valuing human diversity and providing support so that all children and families can participate in the program of their choice."

Placement in the classroom is not all there is

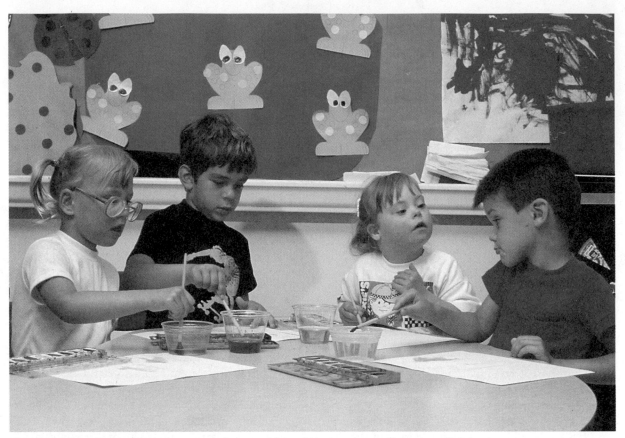

FIGURE 3.13 The inclusive classroom fosters children's interactions with one another.

to inclusion. Planning and care must be given to ensure that

● Teachers foster interactions between children who are disabled and children who are not disabled that promote healthy social relationships.

● Teachers recognize that every child with special needs has strengths as well as deficits and build upon those strengths.

● Teachers receive training and guidance in the critical task of working with children who have special needs and are *developmentally disabled* in their classes.

● Teachers work with parents to plan and implement the child's individualized program.

● Children with disabilities are actively involved and accepted in the total program.

● Children with special needs are helped to take advantage of, to the fullest extent of their capabilities, all the activities the school has to offer.

● Children's individual disabilities are addressed and taken into consideration in program planning and that procedures and curriculum are adapted to fit the children with special needs.

Inclusion is an important concept for all children. For the children without disabilities it is an opportunity to learn to accept differences in people.[1] In the early education center much of the curriculum is directed toward fostering the child's

 OUR DIVERSE WORLD OUR DIVERSE WORLD OUR DIVERSE WORLD OUR DIVERSE WORLD OUR DIVERSE WORLD

[1]One needs to see creating diverse learning situations as a benefit to everyone—everyone has something to learn. It is not a one way street—those born with more privilege are not simply helping "others" (i.e. in an inclusive classroom of 3 year olds, the "special needs child" having had numerous hospitalizations may easily separate from a parent, while the "typically developing" child may still be clinging to his mother's leg at the doorway and gain support from the "special needs child").

self-esteem and self-worth. Teaching is dedicated to helping youngsters see themselves and others as important and valuable. Inclusion presents an opportunity to extend that principle to the full range of human characteristics.

For the child with disabilities, the large numbers of typically developing children who serve as age-appropriate behavior models is important. Many children have not had an opportunity to hear the language of their normal peer group. They may not know how to play with another child or how to communicate in socially acceptable ways. In the inclusive classroom, with sensitive and knowledgeable teachers, children with disabilities are helped to realize their potential as growing and learning children.

Teachers are a key factor in the successful integration of children with disabilities. Their attitude is critical; they must be committed to teaching all children, regardless of their intelligence or skill levels, with equal caring and concern.

Legislation makes strong demands on parents to be intimately involved with their child's program. Parent involvement greatly improves the child's chances for success (Allen and Marotz, 1994). Teachers and parents work together on a planned, consistent set of expectations. The child's confidence is reinforced at home and at school for the same achievements. Parents of children with disabilities find support from other parents since they share common child-rearing concerns.[1] Teachers learn a great deal about disabilities from the parents of the children who have special needs. This helps them become more effective teachers and aware of the special needs of the child.

Fortunately, the preschool teacher rarely needs to face the task of inclusiveness alone. Almost every early childhood center has access to a team of professionals who can provide the child, the family, and the teaching staff with effective therapeutic activities. Their combined knowledge helps teachers understand the specific disability and plan an appropriate curriculum for each child. Together, teachers, clinicians, and parents work out a well-rounded program. This is called **an interdisciplinary approach** to teaching.

In 1993 NAEYC endorsed a Position on Inclusion, written by the Division of Early Childhood of the Council for Exceptional Children. This statement, which follows offers guidelines for implementation.

(Reprinted with permission from NAEYC)
Position on Inclusion

Division for Early Childhood (DEC) of the Council for Exceptional Children

Adopted April 1993
(Endorsed by NAEYC November 1993)

Inclusion, as a value, supports the right of all children, regardless of their diverse abilities, to participate actively in natural settings within their communities. A natural setting is one in which the child would spend time had he or she not had a disability. Such settings include but are not limited to home and family, play groups, child care, nursery schools, Head Start programs, kindergartens, and neighborhood school classrooms.

DEC believes in and supports full and successful access to health, social service, education, and other supports and services for young children and their families that promote full participation in community life. DEC values the diversity of families and supports a family-guided process for determining services that are based on the needs and preferences of individual families and children.

To implement inclusive practices, DEC supports (a) the continued development, evaluation, and dissemination of full inclusion supports, services, and systems **so that the options for inclusion are of high quality;** (b) the development of preservice and inservice training programs that prepare families, administrators, and service providers to develop and work within inclusive settings; (c) collaboration among all key stakeholders to implement flexible fiscal and administrative procedures in support of inclusion; (d) research that contributes to our knowledge of state-of-the-art services; and (e) the restructuring and unification of social, education, health, and intervention supports and services to make them more responsive to the needs of all children.

OUR DIVERSE WORLD OUR DIVERSE WORLD OUR DIVERSE WORLD OUR DIVERSE WORLD OUR DIVERSE WORLD

[1]See footnote 1. on previous page (p.88) "It is not a one way street—those born with more privilege helping others . . ."

[2]This information provides another opportunity to examine the impact of bias in thinking about children (i.e. Do the existing instruments for identifying giftedness identify only particular strengths for a particular segment of the population?).

Cody House

by Gretchen Buchenholz

Executive Director, Association to Benefit Children, New York

Mikey has AIDS. He has learned to ride a tricycle with breathtaking abandon. He is able to eat his Cheerios with a spoon. He pulls off his own shoes and socks often. He's full of himself and full of joy. There's enough warmth in him to melt the hardest heart, enough radiance to light up the darkest hour, and enough life in him each day of his life for a whole lifetime.

Mikey attends Cody House, a preschool program on New York City's East Side. It is one of six programs under the auspices of the Association to Benefit Children (ABC). There, his sunny classroom is further brightened by red, yellow, and blue mats and the smiles of the sickest children in the world. There is a secret garden out back, a beautiful and serene oasis. Doves and hollyhocks are painted on the garden wall. Each dove flies skyward. Some carry the name of a child who has died—Wilfredo 9/15/91, Tenay 6/30/91, Sean 4/9/94, Franklin 9/24/94, James 1/29/94, Laurie 10/17/92, Lisa 12/23/93, and Jacqueline 1/30/95. Others wait. Eric is there splashing in the pool. Laughter rings out from Tunisha, who's playing.

Cody House is warm and nurturing and provides the close attention and special therapies essential for optimizing the mental, physical, emotional, social, and spiritual development of each child. Because Cody House serves children with life-threatening illnesses, the program is specifically designed for managing children's medical needs while simultaneously meeting their educational, social, and emotional needs. Children who require daily infusions are given their treatments during the school day by medically trained staff members. Along with the debilitating emotional and physical stresses of the disease itself, families of young children with terminal illness frequently have their lives disrupted by medical treatments. Hospitalizations make it difficult for families to maintain the relatively stable routine so critical to the emotional health of any young child. Children who would have been faced with these routine but disruptive overnight hospital stays in sterile and frightening settings are now able to receive that same treatment in the stimulating, more "normal" environment of the classroom. Lives are normalized; life spans are increased.

Cody House makes family support services an integral part of the educational program. It provides the array of services necessary to meet each family member's needs and includes educational, medical, pediatric, nutritional, rehabilitative, psychological, and language therapy services. ABC has created with Cody House a safe haven and place of hope for many families who face the devastating combination of terminal illness and poverty. Cody House is a place where parents will find sustenance and where children will find quiet tenderness, the time to wash a doll's hair, put jelly on toast.

ABC's other preschools are for homeless, handicapped, and medically fragile children as well as children from the neighborhoods in which they are located. In bringing together vulnerable children with normally developing kids, each child's experience makes its own unique contribution to the collective experience of all. Children are more alike than different because they care about the same things. They care about transforming Play-Doh into snakes and birthday cakes, singing silly songs, and rolling in the sweet grass. All children need to be part of the mainstream of life. At ABC they are. They're known and loved for their strengths, not for their limitations. And everyone gains infinitely in patience and tenderness and understanding. When children are allowed to learn and play and laugh together, respect and an appreciation for diversity become a part of their lives forever.

Children Who Are Gifted

The child who is gifted demonstrates an intellectual and creative potential superior to that of most children in the same age range and may exhibit an exceptional in-depth knowledge or skill of one or more specific area (Bee, 1995, and Lupkowski and Lupkowski, 1985). Traditionally, children have been identified as gifted if they score between 130–150 on standard IQ tests. Today, more and more programs for gifted children are open to those who exhibit exceptional talent in other than just intellectual superiority—children who are gifted in music, art, and physical skills. Today's definition must include children with disabilities as well, since a child may be hearing-impaired and gifted or learning-disabled and gifted. Children who are gifted come from all social, economic, and cultural groups; however, there is increasing concern that children from low-income populations, children who are ethnically and culturally in the minority, children who have disabilities, and children who are bilingual are underrepresented in the gifted category.[2]

Early childhood teachers should be aware of some traits children who are gifted display so they can recognize potentially gifted children in their care.

In intellectual and academic areas, gifted children have long attention spans, learn rapidly, have good memories and advanced vocabularies. They ask a lot of questions and are able to express their ideas easily. Independent and imaginative, gifted children may be bored by normal activities.

Socially, the gifted child is sought after by peers yet may be uneasy about relationships with other children. Planning and organizing skills are evident in their artwork and other creative endeavors. The gifted child is content to be alone, spending time in purposeful activity. Their use of humor is more advanced than children the same age; originality is typically characteristic of the gifted.

One of the most fascinating studies of gifted children—in fact, the study that is the cornerstone of the gifted child movement—is the Terman Study of the Gifted, which began at Stanford University in 1921. Lewis M. Terman, who developed the Stanford-Binet intelligence test, picked 1,500 California public school children who had scores ranging between 135 and 200 on the test.

This longitudinal study is now in its seventh decade; many of the participants are in their seventies and eighties. It is the longest psychological study ever conducted. This body of work has provided the most complete information to date on gifted children, spanning the grade school years through retirement. Its initial purpose was to dispel the perception, common at that time, that bright children grow into maladjusted and eccentric misfits.

Instead, the study found that the exceptionally bright child is, in later life, more successful, better educated, better satisfied, healthier, more socially adept and popular with peers, better adjusted, and a more productive member of society than the average American. It must be noted that the families from which these exceptional children came were middle class, advantaged, and with an enriched environment.

A recent study by the Sid W. Richardson Foundation highlights a common concern about gifted programs and the exclusion of children from backgrounds other than those cited in the Terman study. The Richardson study calls for opening programs for the gifted to a larger group of "able learners" (Olson, 1985), dropping labels such as "gifted" and "talented," promoting students on the basis of their mastering a subject or skill, and looking for eligible students among populations "excluded from opportunity by ethnic or economic circumstances" (Olson, 1985). Other reports similarly call for making nontraditional students a priority in programs for gifted children.

The current definition of "gifted" limits programs to those children who are intellectually exceptional. There is a call among other gifted-education experts to enlarge the definition to include, for example, children who are gifted in music, art, and physical skills as well as children who have handicaps, bringing to mind Gardner's multiple intelligences (Gardner, 1983). The seven different kinds of knowing that Gardner lists (see p. 389) foster a more open, inclusive approach to the definition of "gifted."

Gifted children, once identified, need to be challenged. In some cases the children may be advanced to an older group, moving on to kindergarten or first grade. A more common approach in early childhood has been in the area of curriculum enrichment. In this way the child remains with age-level peers in order to develop social skills. Some schools segregate gifted children by placing them in special classes exclusively for those identified as being gifted.

The Role of the Early Childhood Educator

Early childhood teachers are well prepared to work with children at their own pace—a key factor in teaching children who have disabilities and children who are gifted, and an underlying principle of early childhood education. The good early childhood teacher is familiar with and endorses an individualized approach to learning, emphasizes discovery learning through self-direction and independence, and accepts and appreciates the unique and individual differences in all children. These are qualities and beliefs that work well with all children, including any who have disabilities.

With Children Who Are Gifted

The teacher's role with the gifted preschool child is that of providing challenge and stimulation. Curriculum areas are developed in more complex ways. The gifted child is ready to learn in greater depth; the teachers provide added materials and activities that will help the children probe the extent of their interests. The nongifted children in the same classroom benefit from this enrichment; each responds according to his or her abilities. Teachers of children who have special gifts and talents can meet their unique needs in a regular school setting at the same time they provide a rich curriculum for the nongifted student.

Parents of the gifted child will need support and encouragement as well as guidance in dealing with their child's exceptionality. Together, teachers and parents can explore what will best suit each individual child so that this giftedness may be nurtured and challenged at home and at school.

With Children Who Have Special Needs

Integrating children with special needs into classroom settings can pose problems if teachers are not aware of how to deal with children who represent both ends of the broad spectrum of normal development. Individual attention is a necessity; so is a climate that supports self-help, interdependence, and responsibility. In kindergarten and early elementary grades, it is important to foster cooperative learning so that students of mixed abilities work together and each finds an appropriate pace at which to work within the team. Successful inclusion requires more planning and preparation on the part of the teaching staff to see that the needs of all the children are being met. Teachers are called on to facilitate and support peer interaction between the children with special needs and those without disabilities on a more frequent and consistent basis. The average early childhood teacher can learn from special education courses, from the parents of special-needs children, and from medical specialists how to adapt teaching strategies for an integrated program. Knowing how to work with parents of special needs children, especially in the area of communication, is a critical factor for teachers. It is also important to keep in mind that most early childhood professionals are not trained diagnosticians but can assist parents in identifying potential problems as they observe children in the classroom setting.

With Bias and Stereotypes

Vincent is a husky 5-year-old boy whose physical skills match those of his classmates. When he was born Vincent was diagnosed with spina bifida, a spinal cord injury, which left him with no bladder or bowel control. As a result, he wears diapers. Noah watched Vincent changing his diapers and later refused to let Vincent join him at the art table. Noah taunted: "I don't like him. He's a baby. He's not like us big guys. He wears diapers. He can't sit here. I'm not gonna play with no babies." Vincent looked both surprised and hurt (Gordon and Browne, 1996).

One of the greatest needs a child with disabilities has is to be accepted (Chandler, 1994). Rejection by their nondisabled peers may occur. Young children are known for their forthrightness in commenting on and asking questions about what confuses and frightens them. They may be anxious about what another child's disability means to them. While this is a common reaction and age-appropriate, we cannot allow an individual to be rejected on the basis of a disability. Derman-Sparks' (1989) suggestions follow, along with examples of supportive and sensitive teacher interactions (Gordon and Browne, 1996).

● The rejection must be handled immediately, with support and assurance given to the child who was rejected that this type of behavior will not be permitted.

Example: The teacher put her arm around Vincent, and said, "Noah, what you said about Vincent is very hurtful. Tell me more about what you meant." Noah began to deny that he said anything, then admitted that Vincent looked funny in diapers because he was so big. The teacher asked Vincent if he would like to tell Noah why he wore diapers. Vincent agreed and responded, "When I was born there was something wrong with my spine so I don't feel it when I have to go to the bathroom. I wear diapers so that I don't wet my pants." "Does it hurt?" asked Noah. "No way," answered Vincent. "I just have to remember to change so I don't get a rash." The teacher then said to Noah, "It's okay for you to ask questions about why Vincent wears diapers, but you can't tell him he can't sit at the table with you. In our class, everybody gets to play and work together."

● It is important to help children recognize how they are different and how they are alike.

Example: "Noah, both you and Vincent have to go to the bathroom during the day. Your body tells you when it is time to go and since Vincent's doesn't, he has to wear protection. You are both good at drawing dinosaurs, too."

● Children need to have their fears about disabilities taken seriously and to have adults understand their concerns.

Example: Noah was approached by the teacher in a way that allowed him to admit part of his concern. The teacher understood his unstated fear, "Noah, what happened to Vincent took place before he was born. It can't happen to you."

● Questions must be answered promptly, truthfully, and simply. Use the children's own natural curiosity and let the child with disabilities answer for himself whenever possible.

Example: Before leaving the art table, the teacher spoke to Noah, "Are there any more questions you have for Vincent?"

All children benefit when adults are willing to confront bias and deal with children's prejudice and misconceptions. This example could have been about girls rejecting boys or one child being rejected because of skin color. When we provide opportunities for children to interact with people who look and act differently than they do, we actively foster acceptance and respect for the individual. See Derman-Sparks' Guest Editorial at the beginning of this section for further insights. Gretchen Buchenholz' Focus Box on p. 00 is an example of confronting prejudice with a group of children who are often treated unfairly because of their disability. More gender diversity issues are found in Chapter 15.

CULTURAL, RACIAL, AND ETHNIC CONSIDERATIONS

The answer to "Who is the young child?" takes on a powerful new meaning as the last decade of this century comes to a close. A multicultural explosion has swept across the nation, filling early childhood programs with children from many different cultural backgrounds. A dramatic shift in demographics is of importance to the early childhood professional if the needs of individual children are to be served. Some indicators of the population changes are:[1]

● Enrollment in public schools increased between 1985 and 1991 by just over 4 percent, yet the

[1]Early childhood educators need to move from an ethnocentric orientation (based on their own and/or the dominant culture experience), and move toward a more multicultural approach.
Examintion is needed of terms such as *minority* and *majority*.

number of students with little or no English language skills increased 50 percent (Gray, 1993)

● Over 127 languages and dialects are spoken by students in the Washington, D.C. school system (Gray, 1993)

● One out of six children in California public schools is born outside the United States, and one-third of them speak a language other than English at home (Gray, 1993)

● By 2010, Hispanics, who can be of any race, will become the largest minority population (Gray, 1993)

For a teacher of young children, these statistics have some important implications. There will be more students in the classroom who are culturally and linguistically different. Unless teachers are informed and educated to these differences, they may misinterpret a child's abilities, learning, and needs. Too often, language barriers between a teacher and a child lead to the conclusion that the child is a slow learner or has a disability.

Working with parents will become more challenging to a teacher's ingenuity and communication skills. Many parents are unfamiliar with school culture in the United States and the expectations schools have about parent involvement and participation. Some parents are illiterate in their own language. An informed and supportive teacher can help parents help their children succeed under these circumstances. (See Chapter 8, Needs of Immigrant Parents).

A lack of understanding about the culture, history, beliefs, and values of the children is harmful to their self-concept (see Anti-Bias and other references in this book). When there are no assessment tools or instructional materials that are in the language of the children or depict their native heritage, they are placed at a distinct disadvantage. Minorities have argued for years that testing instruments that determine IQ and placement in special programs for children who are gifted and talented are biased because they are not written in the predominant culture of the child being tested. As a result, minority children are underrepresented in programs for children who are gifted. Yet they are overrepresented in programs for children with disabilities, a fact that some relate to a lack of sensitivity to a child's cultural and linguistic heritage.

Cultural Sensitivity

Cultural and linguistic sensitivity means that each child's heritage is honored, that it is understood as unique from other cultures, and that it is respected. It means that teachers must become familiar with the cultural norms of the children in their classes and build bridges for children and their families into the more dominant culture.

The following are some examples of four different cultural groups and some of the values and beliefs of their culture. These cultural factors should be addressed as teachers work with parents and children toward a partnership in education.[1] Be careful not to overgeneralize about families from the following examples. There is a tendency to stereotype if we believe that *all* Asians, Hispanics, Native Americans, and African-Americans are represented by such an overview. The culturally sensitive teacher will get to know each of the families as a separate entity and become familiar with their individual expressions of culture and heritage.

Asians

● Teachers are accorded great respect (Yee, in Ramirez, 1988)

● Father is head of household, decisions should include him (Yee, in Ramirez, 1988)

● The structure and use of first and last names among Asian subgroups vary (Morrow, 1969)

● Child represents the family's good name for the future; family may have difficulty accepting a child's disability and see it as a disgrace to the family name (Yee, in Ramirez, 1988)

Hispanics

● Children are highly valued (Valero-Figueira in Ramirez, 1988)

● Others accorded great respect are clergy, teachers and community leaders (Valero-Figueira in Ramirez, 1988)

● Children work best in cooperative situations (Beacher, Castillo, and Cruz in Charlesworth, 1996)

● Sensitive to authority figures and their feelings about them (Beacher, Castillo, and Cruz in Charlesworth, 1996)

Native Americans

- Family encourages independent decision-making by children

- Being recognized as a part of peer group is more important for child than individual recognition

- Extended family members, especially grandmothers, are involved with children and their education

- Value cooperation and sharing

- Respect the dignity of the individual

- Wisdom of the elders is held in high esteem

- Strong oral tradition, especially storytelling (Walker in Ramirez, 1989)

African-Americans

- Parents are highly motivated for their children to achieve

- Children have high degree of stimulation from the creative arts

- Children tend to be active

- Are expressive in music, dance, and drama

- Raised with an emphasis on feelings and intense interpersonal relationships

- Learn from people rather than objects (Hale-Benson, 1989)

Each of these cultural factors has implications for teaching and forming relationships with people from varying backgrounds and cultures. The teacher of the future will be called upon to integrate these insights into curriculum planning as well as home and school relationships. (See also "Attitudes and Biases" in Chapter 5).

S U M M A R Y

The child in early childhood programs ranges from the dependent infant to the outgoing eight-year-old. In those few short years teachers witness tremendous physical, intellectual, social, and emotional gains.

The child learns to crawl, walk, run, climb, throw a ball, write with a pencil, use scissors, hold a spoon, and manipulate toys. Both large and small muscles are called into play throughout each stage of development.

Language development is equally impressive. The nonverbal infant becomes fluent, sometimes in more than one language. Intellectual gains coincide as children become able to express thoughts, solve problems, and exhibit growth in their reasoning powers.

Socially, the child learns to relate to family members, schoolmates, teachers, and other adults. Every range of human emotion is developed during these early years as children learn appropriate ways to express and release their feelings.

Teachers notice that children share many common characteristics at the same time they display wide individual differences. Profile charts—word pictures—describing normal development help teachers understand when a particular behavior is likely to occur. With advance notice, then, teachers can plan activities and curricula that appeal to children at every age level; disciplinary and guidance measures can match the child's specific level of development.

Yet it is obvious that growth and development do not proceed normally for all children. Two groups of children have special needs within the early childhood classroom. Children with disabilities who are mainstreamed require particular attention to their individual disabilities, and teachers need special skills to help them include children who are handicapped and nonhandicapped. Gifted children also require attention; their exceptional abilities must be challenged and stimulated within the regular early childhood program.

The changing demographics that bring more and more culturally and linguistically diverse children into early childhood settings require that teachers become familiar with the specific cultural norms represented in America today. This will call for new teaching strategies, culturally appropriate curriculum, and special efforts to work with parents from a multicultural perspective.

R E V I E W   Q U E S T I O N S

1. Match the word picture to the age group in which it belongs:

Observes family rules	toddlers
Plays peekaboo	fives
Has dynamic intellectual drive	sixes and sevens
Is intrigued by whispering	infants
Needs to be "in"	twos
"Mine" most prominent pronoun	fours
Backs into chair to sit down	sixes
May get silly, high, wild	threes
Can balance on one foot	threes
Letter, word reversal common	fours
Mood changes rapidly	sevens

2. Name one way children are alike and one way they differ from one another. Describe the curriculum planning implications for the teacher of these differing children.

3. One area of development affects another. List two ways that social or emotional problems can affect other areas of growth.

4. What are some of the reasons for using the concept of the whole child in early education?

5. What are some of the advantages of including children with special needs? What are some of the difficulties that must be overcome for successful integration of special-needs children?

6. Why is it important for teachers to know about attention-deficit hyperactivity disorder (ADHD)?

7. How important is it to know and understand the culture of children we teach?

8. How are inclusion and mainstreaming different?

L E A R N I N G   A C T I V I T I E S

1. Select two children who are approximately the same age. Compare their physical and social development. How are they alike? How are they different? What do you think accounts for these differences?

2. Review the cultural factors noted for Asian, Hispanic, Native American, and African American children. Suggest a teaching strategy that would be appropriate in response to each of the characteristics.

3. Look at the word picture for a three-year-old. Compare it with a three-year-old you know. What behavior do you see that falls within the range of the chart? What is different? Are there cultural differences?

4. Observe a class of special-needs children in an inclusive classroom. What would you do to foster interactions between the children who are disabled and children who are not? What verbalizations are used about a child's handicapping condition and do the nondisabled children seem to understand how their friends are similar to them as well as different? Do you think inclusion is a good idea? Why or why not?

5. Using the Word Pictures, how would you design an appropriate art activity for children who are 18 months old? What kind of playground experience would you provide for a three-year-old? How would you schedule a day for a six-year-old you were babysitting? Justify your answers by citing specific developmental references.

B I B L I O G R A P H Y

Allen, K. Eileen, and Marotz, Lynn. *Developmental Profiles: Birth to Eight.* Albany, N.Y.: Delmar Publishers, 1994.

Allen, K. Eileen, and Schwartz, Ilene. *The Exceptional Child: Inclusion in Early Childhood Education.* Albany, N.Y.: Delmar Publishers, 1996.

Ames, Louise B., and Ilg, Frances L. *Your One-Year-Old.* New York: Dell, 1983.

——————. *Your Two-Year-Old.* New York: Dell, 1976.

——————. *Your Three-Year-Old.* New York: Dell, 1976.

——————. *Your Four-Year-Old.* New York: Dell, 1976.

——————. *Your Five-Year-Old.* New York: Dell, 1979.

——————. *Your Six-Year-Old.* New York: Dell, 1979.

Bailey, Donald B. Jr., and Wolery, Mark. *Teaching Infants and Preschoolers with Disabilities.* New York: Merrill, 1992.

Baron, Robert A. *Psychology.* Boston: Allyn and Bacon, 1995.

Bee, Helen. *The Developing Child.* Cambridge, Mass.: Harper Collins, 1995.

Caldwell, Bettye M. "One World of Children." In *Beginnings and Beyond: Foundations in Early Childhood Education,* ed. A. Gordon and K.W. Browne. Albany, N.Y.: Delmar Publishers, 1993 (3rd Ed.).

Chandler, Phyllis A. *A Place for Me.* Washington, D.C.: National Association for the Education of Young Children, 1994.

Charlesworth, Rosalind. *Understanding Child Development.* Albany, NY: Delmar Publishers, 1996.

Derman-Sparks, Louise, and the ABC Task Force. *Anti-Bias Curriculum: Tools for Empowering Young Children.* Washington, D.C.: National Association for the Education of Young Children, 1989.

Elkind, David. *The Hurried Child: Growing Up Too Fast, Too Soon.* Reading, Mass.: Addison-Wesley, 1989. (Rev)

Froschl, Merle, Colon, Linda, Rubin, Ellen, and Sprung, Barbara. *Including All Of Us: An Early Childhood Curriculum About Disability.* New York: Educational Equity Concepts, Inc., 1984.

Gardner, Howard. *Developmental Psychology.* Boston: Little, Brown and Co., 1982.

——————. *Frames of Mind: The Theory of Multiple Intelligences.* New York: Basic Books, 1983.

Gordon, Ann, Miles and Browne, Kathryn Williams. *Guiding Young Children in a Diverse Society.* Boston: Allyn and Bacon, 1996.

Gray, Paul. "Teach Your Children Well." *Time,* special issue, Fall, 1993; pp. 69–71.

Hale-Benson, Janice. *Black Children: Their Roots, Culture and Learning Styles.* Baltimore, Md.: The Johns Hopkins University Press, 1986.

——————. "Designing Instruction for Black Children." *Education Week,* April 12, 1989, p. 26.

Hallowell, E., and Ratty, J. *Driven to Distraction.* New York: Pantheon Books, 1994.

Kelly, Evelyn B. "Learning Disabilities: A New Horizon of Perception." *The World and I,* August, 1988, pp. 314–321. The Washington Times Corp.

Kiernan, Shari, et al. *Mainstreaming Preschoolers: Children with Orthopedic Handicaps.* Washington, D.C.: U.S. Department of Health, Education, and Welfare, n.d.

Lupkowski, Ann, and Lupkowski, Elizabeth. "Meeting the Needs of Gifted Preschoolers." *Children Today,* March/April, 1985, pp. 10–14.

Morrow, Robert D. "What's in a Name? In Particular, A Southeast Asian Name?" *Young Children,* September, 1989, pp. 20–23.

Olson, Lynn. "Programs for Gifted Students Fragmented, Inadequate, Study Says." *Education Week,* January 16, 1985, p. 5.

Ramirez, Bruce A. "Culturally and Linguistically Diverse Children." *Teaching Exceptional Children,* Summer, 1988, pp. 45–51.

Soto, Lourdes Diaz. "Understanding Bilingual/Bicultural Young Children." *Young Children,* January, 1991, pp. 30–36.

Valero-Figueira, Eda. "Hispanic Children." In Ramirez, Bruce, "Culturally and Linguistically Diverse Children," *Teaching Exceptional Children,* Summer, 1988, pp. 45–51.

Walker, Jaqueline L. "Young American Indian Children." In Ramirez, Bruce, "Culturally and Linguistically Diverse Children," *Teaching Exceptional Children,* Summer, 1988, pp. 45–51.

Wallis, Claudia. "Life in Overdrive." *Time,* July 18, 1994, pp. 43–50.

Wolery, Mark, and Wilbers, Jan S. (Eds.). *Including Children with Special Needs in Early Childhood Programs.* Washington, D.C.: Research Monograph of the National Association for the Education of Young Children, 1994.

Wood, Chip. *Yardsticks.* Greenfield, Mass.: Northeast Foundation for Children, 1994.

Woolfolk, Anita E. *Educational Psychology.* Boston: Allyn and Bacon, 1993.

Yee, Leland Y. "Asian Children." In Ramirez, Bruce, "Culturally and Linguistically Diverse Children," *Teaching Exceptional Children,* Summer, 1988, pp. 45–51.

CHAPTER 4

Developmental and Learning Theories

INTRODUCTION

Early childhood education draws from several fields of study. The connection with the field of psychology is particularly strong. Much of what we know about children today comes from child development and child psychology research. As educators, we apply those findings in the classroom. Our knowledge base comes directly from psychological studies.

● How do children develop?

● What do they learn, and in what order?

● What do people need in order to be ready to learn?

● What affects learning?

● Do all people develop in the same ways?

● What are the similarities and differences in growth and development?

To begin to answer these questions, we need some way to look for information and then choose and organize the facts so that we can understand what we see. In other words, we need a **theory.** Psychologists and educators have been doing just that for years, and in the twentieth century a great deal has been discovered about these issues. Theories are especially useful in providing a broad and consistent view of the complexity of human development. They allow us to make educated guesses (called **hypotheses**) about children's behavior and development. Since these theories are based on experience, their validity can be checked by teachers as they observe children everyday. Thus, the basic quest for sound theories about development and knowledge, for systematic statements about behavior and development, has given educators much to consider in bringing forth their own ideas about children.

A key question that is central to all developmental and learning theories is about the source of influence. Are the changes we see in children over time due to internal or external influences? Do children change because of innate, biological, or genetic patterns built into the human being, or are they shaped by the environment and experiences (such as parents, materials, TV, school, and so on) of life? This argument is often referred to as the **nature/nurture controversy,** also known as the

problem of heredity versus environment. As you will remember from Chapter 1, this issue has been discussed for centuries. On the "nature" side, Rousseau argued that the child is born with natural, or innate, goodness. John Locke, however, asserted that it was "nurture" that mattered. He contended that children entered the world with a **tabula rasa,** or clean slate, upon which all experience and learning was then written. Today, most psychologists and educators agree that the patterns of development and learning are complex and not so simply explained. Modern theories are not set in such black-and-white terms but rather focus on variations that emphasize one or the other.

Initially, the study of child development was mostly confined to the study of trends and descriptions of age changes. As this century has progressed, the scope and definition of child development have changed radically. Developmental psychologists now study how psychological processes begin, change, and develop. Specifically, child development focuses on language acquisition, various early effects on later intellectual development, and the process of attachment to others. Early childhood teachers should know how children develop and how they learn. Knowing how children develop is critical in making the daily decisions about curriculum, the classroom setting, and children. To be effective with children, teachers need a thoughtful philosophy and approach that is based on what we know about how children develop and what works to help them learn and understand. The teacher who is well-versed in theory has invaluable tools to work with parents, advise the family of the range of typical behavior, and talk to parents about concerns that are beyond the norms. Therefore, it is important to have a background in both developmental psychology and learning theories.

There is no one set of principles that encompasses all developmental and learning theories. We have chosen three theories that are commonly accepted as major components of the child development field. A fourth focuses on the sociocultural influences in children's lives. A fifth comes from a medical model and outlines developmental norms of growth and behavior. A sixth does not always appear in child psychology texts but highlights some of the processes of working with children. The six theories we will outline are commonly known as (1) psychodynamic theory, (2) behaviorist theory, (3) cognitive theory, (4) sociocultural theory, (5) maturation theory, and (6) humanistic theory.

Since the field of child development is broad, encompassing a wide variety of opinion and fact, not all the experts agree, or even think alike. Indeed, there are differences among them about how children grow, think, and learn, and what motivates them. Each theory describes children and their processes in a different way. The teacher thus has a diversity of thought on which to establish a professional philosophy.

PSYCHODYNAMIC THEORY

Psychodynamic theory is about personality development and emotional problems. **Psychodynamic**, or psychoanalytic, **theories** look at development in terms of internal drives which are often **unconscious**, or hidden from our awareness. These motives are the underlying forces that influence human thinking and behavior and provide the foundation for universal stages of development. In psychoanalytic terms, children's behavior can be interpreted by knowing the various stages and tasks within those stages.

Sigmund Freud

Freud began his career as a medical doctor, and became interested in the irrational side of hu-

man behavior as he treated "hysterics." His technique, asking people to recline on a couch and talk about everything, was ridiculed by the medical establishment as the "talking cure." Then, as patients revealed their thoughts, fantasies, and problems, he began to see patterns. One of his basic ideas is that of childhood sexuality. To Freud, development occurred in psychosexual stages, each characterized by a particular part of the body (see Figure 4.1). In each stage, the sensual satisfaction associated with each body part is linked to major challenges of that age. Clearly, each stage also has its own conflicts between child and parent, and how the child experiences those conflicts will determine basic personality and behavior patterns.

Dr. Sigmund Freud first put forth this theory, and his ideas were expanded upon by Anna Freud (his daughter), Carl Jung, Karen Horney, and others. Although Freud's interest was abnormal adult behavior and its causes, his conclusions have a major effect on our conception of childhood and its place in the life span.

To Freud, the personality was the most important aspect of development, more central to human growth than language, perception, or cognition. He thought that the personality developed in a fixed pattern of stages that emerged as the body matured naturally. But even though the sequence of the stages might be firm, how children were treated while going through those stages determined whether they developed healthy or ab-

Stage	Age	Description/Major Area
Oral	Birth-Two	Mouth (sucking, biting) source of pleasure Eating and teething
Anal	Two-Three	Bowel movements source of pleasure Toilet learning
Phallic	Three-Six	Genitals source of pleasure Sex role identification and conscience development
Latency	Six-Twelve	Sexual forces dormant Energy put into schoolwork and sports
Genital	Twelve-Eighteen	Genital Stimulation and satisfaction from relationships

FIGURE 4.1 Freud's psychoanalytic theory of childhood sexuality. Freud's stage theory contends that each stage has its own area of pleasure and crisis between the child and parent or society.

normal personalities. In particular, the mother-child relationship was important in each stage. Thus, the interaction between the child's wishes and needs and how these were treated (by the mother or other adults) was a focal point for proper development.

All psychoanalytic explanations of human development emphasize the critical importance of relationships with people and the sequence, or stages, of personality development. The psychoanalyst Erik Erikson expanded and refined Freud's theory of development. It is Erikson whose ideas have most affected early childhood education.

Erik Erikson

Erik Homberg Erikson is perhaps the most influential psychoanalyst alive today, certainly a key figure in the study of children and development. His interest in children and education has been a lifelong one, including a teaching background in progressive and Montessori schools in Europe. After clinical training in psychoanalysis, he remained interested in the connections between psychotherapy and education. Erikson became the first child analyst in the Boston area. He continues to work in various universities in this country, without any formal degree of his own.

Erikson's Theory of Human Development

Erikson's theory of human development, like those of Freud and Piaget, states that life is a series of stages through which each person passes, with each stage growing from the previous ones. He proposes eight stages of psychosocial development, each representing a critical period for the development of an important quality or virtue. Positive growth allows the individual to integrate his or her physical and biological development with the challenges that the social institutions and culture present. Each stage is characterized by a pair of basic emotional states. *Balance* is the key word in Erikson's framework: the forming of a balance between a child's wishes and the demands of the environment, of a mentally healthy dose of each emotion, is the base for personality strength.

In other words, every growing organism passes through certain developmental stages. A stage is a period during which certain changes take place. What one achieves in each stage is based on the developments of the previous stages, and each stage presents the organisms with certain kinds of problems to be solved. When children succeed, they go on to attack new problems and grow through solving them.

Everyone has certain biological, social, and psychological needs that must be satisfied in order to grow in a healthy manner. Medicine has

Stage	Description	Challenge
Stage One	The newborn	Trust vs. mistrust
Stage Two	Toddlers	Autonomy vs. shame and doubt
Stage Three	Childhood	Initiative vs. guilt
Stage Four	School	Competence (or Industry) vs. inferiority
Stage Five	Adolescence	Search for identity vs. Role confusion
Stage Six	Young adulthood	Intimacy (love and friendship) vs. Isolation (loneliness)
Stage Seven	Grown-ups	Generativity (caring for the next generation) vs. Stagnation
Stage Eight	Old age	Integrity vs. Despair

FIGURE 4.2 Erikson's theory of psychosocial development centers on basic crises that people face from birth to old age. This stage theory of development proposes that these conflicts are part of the life process and that successful handling of these issues can give a person the "ego strength" to face life positively. (Adapted from Hubley and Hubley, 1976.)

learned much about physical needs—diet, rest, exercise. There are also basic intellectual, social, and emotional needs that must be met for an organism to be healthy. Psychology, such as Eriksonian theory, can speak to these needs. Whether these needs are met or unfulfilled will affect development.

Stage 1: Trust vs. Mistrust (Birth to One Year)

Erikson's first stage is roughly the first year of life and parallels Freud's oral-sensory stage. Attitudes important to development are the capacity to trust—or mistrust—inner and outer experiences. By providing consistent care, parents help an infant develop a basic sense of trust in self and an ability to trust other people. They give affection and emotional security as well as provide for physical needs. Inconsistent or inadequate care prevents the infant from trusting the world. In extreme cases, as shown by Spitz's classic studies on infant deprivation (Spitz, 1946), lack of care can actually lead to infant death. A less extreme case might form isolation or distrust of others. Recent studies suggest a strong hereditary element in this disorder rather than environmental (see J.K. Myers et al., 1984, Archives of General Psychiatry, 41, 259–

267). Given a solid base in early trust, though, the infant develops the virtue, or strength, of hope.

When working with infants and toddlers, teachers must take special care to provide a predictable environment and consistent caregiving. Babies are totally dependent on adults to meet their needs; they are particularly vulnerable to difficulties because they have few skills for coping with discomfort and stress. It is critical, therefore, that they be cared for by warm, positive adults who are sensitive and respond affectionately to an infant's needs as soon as they arise. In this way, the very young develop the trust in the world that will support their growth into the next stage.

Stage 2: Autonomy vs. Doubt (Two to Three Years)

The second stage, corresponding to the second and third years of life, parallels the muscular-anal period in Freudian theory. The child learns to manage and control impulses, and to use both motor and mental skills. To help a child develop a healthy balance between autonomy and shame, parents should consider how to handle their toddlers' toilet training and growing curiosity to explore. Restrictive or compulsive parents may give the child a feeling of shame and doubt, causing a

FIGURE 4.3   An Eriksonian crisis in a young child's life. The child who has successfully mastered the first of Erikson's psychosocial conflicts will then be able to cope with future challenges. In this instance, the child who takes initiative (grabbing a toy) also can feel guilt (returning it).

sense of insecurity. Successful growth in this stage gives a child the strength of will.

When teaching children of this age, adults help children feel ready to explore their world through a full range of activities that employ their senses. Play is encouraged, with plenty of "yes" in the environment. Budding curiosity means high energy, so the daily schedule should include plenty of time for active movement and flexibility to deal with fluctuating energy and mood. Toileting is a learned behavior just as eating, dressing, painting, and singing are; a relaxed attitude about this area helps the child gain mastery without shame. Allowing for plenty of "two steps forward, one back" acknowledges the child's natural doubts and the balancing that happens in this stage.

Stage 3: Initiative vs. Guilt (Three to Five or Six Years)

The third stage of Eriksonian theory corresponds to the preschool and kindergarten years and parallels Freud's genital stage of development. Out of a sense of autonomy grows a sense of initiative. The child is ready to plan and carry out thoughts and ideas. The parent can encourage the child's natural curiosity to plan and execute activities that are constructive and cooperative. An overly restrictive parent may raise a child with an excessive sense of guilt and inhibition. On the other hand, parents or teachers giving no restraints signal to the child no clear idea of what is socially acceptable and what is not. The key strength that grows out of this stage is purpose.

Teaching children of this age is both exhilarating and exasperating. The child who takes initiative is ready to meet the world head-on and wants to do it "all by myself," which may include both putting on a jacket and hitting someone who has said something unkind. The environment that can respond to a child's interests, both in theme and at the moment, will be interesting and successful. At the same time, teachers must be prepared with a small set of logical limits (or "rules") and the means to follow through kindly and firmly when those limits are tested. Socializing at this age is the very point of the emotional states of initiative and guilt; children must have enough freedom to develop their own ways to deal with one another

and still develop a sense of fairness and conscience.

Stage 4: Industry vs. Inferiority (Six to 12 years)

Erikson's fourth stage, beginning with the primary school years and ending with puberty, parallels Freud's latency period. The major theme in this stage is mastery of life, primarily by adapting to laws of society and things. For most children, this means finding a place in one's own school, be it in a classroom, on a soccer field, or at a club meeting. Children are ready to apply themselves to skills and tasks and to receive systematic instruction in the culture. They also need to handle the "tools of the tribe" (Erikson, 1963), and to experience both achievement and disappointment. In the United States, these tools include pencils, reading and arithmetic books, and computers, as well as balls and bats. The danger for the child lies in feeling inadequate and inferior to such tasks. A parent or teacher who overemphasizes children's mistakes could make them despair of ever learning, for instance, the multiplication tables or cursive handwriting. At the same time, adults must encourage children to work toward mastery. Parents must not let their children restrict their own horizons by doing only what they already know. Particularly in social situations, it is essential for children to learn to do things *with* others, as difficult and unfair as this may sometimes be.

Applying Erikson's Theory to Work with Children

How can teachers apply Erikson's theory of psychosocial development to young children? First, Erikson has a clear message about the importance of play. Second, the theory helps shape guidelines for the role of adults in children's lives.

Early childhood teachers have long held that play is a critical part of children's total development. Most schools for children under six have periods of time allotted for play called "choice time" or "free play." Erikson supports these ideas explicitly by stating that the sense of autonomy and of

FIGURE 4.4   In Erikson's theory the adult serves as a social mediator for the child.

initiative are developed mainly through social and fantasy play. He suggests that child's play is "the infantile form of the human ability to deal with experiences by creating model situations and to master reality by experiment and planning. . . . To 'play it out' in play is the most natural self-healing measure childhood affords" (Erikson, 1964).

The adult, from a psychoanalytic point of view, is primarily an emotional base and a social mediator for the child. That is, the adult is the interpreter of feelings, actions, reasons, and solutions. The adult helps children understand situations and motives so that they can solve their own problems. The adult looks at each child's emotional makeup and monitors the progress through developmental crises. Since the infant must learn to trust the world, the parent needs to be responsive and satisfy the basic needs of food, warmth, and love. In a toddler's world, the teacher and parent must allow the child, in Erikson's words:

> . . . to experience over and over again that he is a person who is permitted to make choices. He has to have the right to choose, for example, whether

to sit or whether to stand, whether to approach a visitor or to lean against his mother's knee . . . whether to use the toilet or to wet his pants. At the same time he must learn some of the boundaries of self-determination. He inevitably finds that there are some walls he cannot climb, that there are objects out of reach, that, above all, there are innumerable commands enforced by powerful adults.

> (Erikson, 1969)

In preschool and kindergarten, a teacher allows children to take initiative and does not interfere with the results of those actions. At the same time, teachers and parents provide clear limits so that the children can learn what behaviors are unacceptable to society.

The issues of early childhood, from Erikson's theory, are really our own issues. Since the remnants of these crises stay with us all our lives, teachers must be aware of their own processes to fully appreciate the struggles of children.

BEHAVIORIST THEORY

Behaviorism is the most pragmatic and functional of the modern psychological ideologies. Behaviorist theories describe both development and learning. Developed during the 1920s and continually modified today, behaviorism is "the most distinctively American contribution to psychology" (Suransky, 1982). There are countless developmental psychologists and researchers who have defined and expanded upon this idea, several of whom are mentioned later in this chapter. To summarize the behaviorist theory, we have chosen four theorists: John Watson, Edward Thorndike, B.F. Skinner, and Albert Bandura.

The Behaviorists

What is known today as "behaviorism" begins with the notion that a child is born with a "clean slate," a *tabula rasa* in John Locke's words, on which events are written throughout life. The conditions of those events cause all important human behavior.

John B. Watson was an American theorist who studied the experiments of Russian scientist Ivan

Pavlov. He then translated those ideas of conditioning into human terms. In the first quarter of this century, Watson made sweeping claims about the powers of this classical conditioning. He declared that he could shape a person's entire life by controlling exactly the events of an infant's first year. One of his ideas was to strictly discourage emotional ties between parents and children, though he later modified this. Nonetheless, he gave scientific validity to the idea that teachers should set conditions for learning and reward proper responses.

Edward L. Thorndike also studied the conditions of learning. After working with animals and their problem-solving abilities, he decided that people took an active part in their learning. He set forth the famous "stimulus-response" technique. A stimulus will recall a response in a person; this forms learned habits. Therefore, it is wise to pay close attention to the consequences of behavior and to the various kinds of reinforcement.

B.F. Skinner took the idea of "tabula rasa" one step further. He created the doctrine of the "empty organism." That is, a person is like a vessel to be filled by carefully designed experiences. All behavior is under the control of one or more aspects of the environment. Furthermore, Skinner maintained that there is no behavior that cannot be modified.

Behaviorists often insist that only what can actually be observed will be accepted as fact. Only behavior can be treated, they say, not feelings or internal states. This contrasts to the psychodynamic approach, which insists that behavior is just an indirect clue to the "real" self, that of inner feelings and thoughts.

Skinner's ideas probably stirred up more controversy, and caused more emotional response, than those of any other psychologist of our time. Some people might argue that Skinnerian concepts tend to depersonalize the learning process and treat people as puppets. Others say that behaviorist psychology has made us develop new ways to help people learn and cope effectively with the world.

Albert Bandura has developed another type of learning theory, called social learning. As behaviorists began to accept that what people said about their feelings and internal state was valid data, they looked at how children became socialized. Social-ization is the process of learning to conform to social rules. Social-learning theorists watch how children learn these rules and use them in groups. They study the patterns of reinforcement and reward in socially appropriate and unacceptable behavior.

According to Bandura:

> Children acquire most of their social concepts—the rules by which they live—from models whom they observe in the course of daily life, particularly parents, caregivers, teachers, and peers. Social learning theory [suggests] the models most likely to be imitated are individuals who are nurturant—warm, rewarding, and affectionate. Attachment also affects the process: the most significant or influential models are people to whom the child is emotionally tied.
>
> (Fong & Resnick, 1986)

From this arose a new concept known as **modeling**. This is what used to be known as learning and teaching by example. For instance, children who see their parents smoking will likely smoke themselves. Any behavior can be learned by watching it, from language (listening to others talk) to fighting (watching violence on television).

Theory of Behaviorism and Learning

What is behavior, or learning, theory all about? Many texts have been written on this set of principles; every child development text of the day cites behavior and social-learning concepts. Most early education texts will make mention of the system of positive reinforcement; that is, how to praise children so that they are likely to repeat the desired behavior.

Learning takes place when an organism interacts with the environment. Through experience, behavior is modified, or changed. In the behaviorist's eyes, three types of learning occur: (1) classical conditioning; (2) operant conditioning; and (3) observational learning or modeling. The first two are based on the idea that learning is mostly the development of habit. What people learn is a series of associations, forming a connection between a stimulus and response that did not exist before. The third is based on a social approach. Figure 4.5 summarizes these three types of behaviorist learning processes.

	Classical Conditioning	Operant Conditioning	Social Learning
Kind of behavior	Reflexive	Voluntary	Voluntary
Type of learning	Learning through association	Learning through reinforcement	Learning through observation and imitation
Role of learner	Passive	Active or passive	Active

FIGURE 4.5 Behaviorist learning processes. Classical conditioning, operant conditioning, and social learning are three ways to develop learned behavior. Each describes how certain kinds of behavior will be learned and what role the learner will take in the process.

Classical Conditioning

Classical conditioning can be explained by reviewing Pavlov's original experiments. A dog normally salivates at the sight of food, but not when he hears a bell. By pairing the sound of a bell with the sight of food, the dog "learns" to salivate when he hears the bell, whether or not food is nearby. Thus, the dog has been conditioned to salivate (give the response) for both the food (unconditioned stimulus) and the bell (conditioned stimulus).

Operant Conditioning

Operant conditioning is slightly different from classical conditioning in that it focuses on the response rather than the stimulus. In operant conditioning, the process that makes it more likely that a behavior will reoccur is called **reinforcement** (Skinner, 1953). A stimulus that increases the likelihood of repeated behavior is called a reinforcer. Most people are likely to increase what gives them pleasure (be it food or attention), and decrease what gives them displeasure (such as punishment, pain, or the withdrawal of food or attention). The behaviorist tries to influence the organism by controlling these kinds of reinforcement.

For example, you would like Claire to begin to use a spoon instead of her hands to eat. Before conditioning, you talk to her whenever she eats. During the conditioning period, you can give attention (a *positive reinforcer*), each time she picks up a spoon during feeding times, and ignore her when she uses her hands. Afterward, she is more likely to use a spoon, and less often her hands. This is an example of a positive reinforcer, something that increases the likelihood of the desired response.

The reinforcers can be both positive and negative. A negative reinforcer is removal of an unpleasant stimulus as a result of some particular behavior. Circle time is Jimmy's favorite activity at school. Yet he has difficulty controlling his behavior and consistently disrupts the group. Before conditioning, he is told that if he talks to his neighbors and shouts responses at the teacher, he will be asked to leave the circle. During the conditioning period, Jimmy is praised whenever he pays attention, sings songs, and does not bother those around him (positive reinforcement). When he begins to shout, he is told to leave and return when he can sing without shouting (negative reinforcement). A negative reinforcer is used to stop children from behaving in a particular way by arranging for them to end a mildly adversive situation immediately [in this case, the boy having to leave the group] by improving their behavior. Jimmy, by controlling his own behavior, could end his isolation from the group.

A negative reinforcer is different than punishment. **Punishment** is an unpleasant event that makes the behavior *less* likely to be repeated; that is, if Jimmy was spanked everytime he shouted, then his shouting would be the punished behavior and it is likely he would begin to shout less. However, when leaving the group is the reinforcer for shouting, he tries to stop shouting in order to increase the likelihood of being able to stay, and not being taken away from the group. **Negative rein-**

FIGURE 4.6   A shared smile is a simple and powerful reinforcement.

forcement thus increases the likelihood of the desired behavior being repeated (staying in the group) and removes attention from the less desirable behavior (the shouting).

Reinforcement, both positive and negative, is a powerful tool. It is important for adults to realize that it can be misused. It is wise to be careful, particularly in the case of negative reinforcement. An adult may not be gentle with a negative reinforcer when angry with a child's inappropriate behavior. Educators and parents should be aware of the possibilities and check their own responses.

Modeling

The third kind of conditioning is called "observational learning" or "modeling." Social behavior is particularly noteworthy to early childhood professionals, as most work with children in groups and thus witness social behavior constantly. Any behavior that involves more than one person can be considered social. One of the most negative social behaviors is aggression. It is this type that Albert Bandura researched, finding that much of it is learned by watching others.

Aggression is a complex issue, involving various definitions and behaviors. To illustrate social-learning theory, Bandura and others interpret ag-

gression to mean behavior intended to inflict harm or discomfort to another person or object. Bandura showed a short film of aggressive behavior to young children. The original mid-1960s studies are summarized below:

> Each child in Bandura's experiment viewed one of three films. In all three films, a man hit, kicked, and verbally abused an inflated Bobo doll in ways that young children are unlikely to do spontaneously. The films differed in what happened to the model after the aggressive sequence. In one film the model was lavishly rewarded with praise and foods that appealed to preschoolers, such as candy and caramel popcorn. In another film the model was punished in a dramatic way, including severe scolding and a spanking. The third film simply ended after the model's aggressive behavior, with no consequences following the aggression. After viewing one film, each child in the experiment was allowed to play in a room with a Bobo doll, all the toys used in the aggressive film, and a variety of other toys.

> (McClinton and Meier, 1978)

The results are most impressive, especially to those working with young children. The level of aggression was directly related to what the children saw as the consequences in the film. When offered prizes, they imitated almost exactly what their model had done. Also, children appeared more likely to attack another child after viewing the attacks on the Bobo doll in film. Further studies have shown that children's level of aggression is higher right after viewing the film, but less so when shown it again six months later (McClinton and Meier, 1978). Regardless of the controversy that may surround any study of children's aggression, or the effects of watching filmed violence on youngsters, the social-learning theory deserves serious consideration. The effect of television watching on children is extremely important and will be discussed in Chapter 15.

Applying Behaviorist Theory to Work with Children

Behaviorist theories make a strong case for how the environment influences our behavior. A teacher, a parent, any adult who works closely with children, can use this knowledge to arrange the environment in such a way that positive learning is enhanced. Thus, early childhood educators pay close attention to how to arrange furniture, materials, and the daily schedule. The way teachers interact with children is critical to changing their behavior.

Adults are powerful reinforcers and models for children. A learning situation is comprised of many cues; it is up to adults to know what those cues are and how to control them. Teachers who use behavior modification techniques know both what children are to do and how they will be reinforced for their behavior. The issues of using this kind of control, and the ethics involved, are of deep concern to everyone. The extremes of behaviorist theory suggest programmed instruction and interaction that many early educators reject. Each teacher and program must consider the impact of this theory and how to apply it to classroom and client. Chapter 7, which deals with behavior management and discipline issues, has examples of this theory as it applies to behavior modification techniques.

The implications of behaviorist theory for teachers are far reaching. What children learn is shaped by the circumstances surrounding the learning. Experiences that are enjoyable are reinforcing. From the peek-a-boo game with an infant to a seven-year-old's first ride on a skateboard, an experience is more likely to be repeated and learned if it is pleasant. Social learning is particularly powerful in the lives of young children. Adults must be mindful of their own behavior, and that it is a source of learning. Watching children as young as two years old play "family" or "school" will convince the most skeptical critic that any behavior is learnable and can become part of children's behavioral repertoire.

COGNITIVE THEORY

Adult: What does it mean to be alive?
Child: It means you can move about, play—that you can do all kinds of things.
Adult: Is a mountain alive?
Child: Yes, because it has grown by itself.
Adult: Is a cloud alive?
Child: Yes, because it sends water.
Adult: Is wind alive?
Child: Yes, because it pushes things.
(Peters and Willis, 1978)

How can we tell what children are thinking? How do children learn to think, and what do they think about? Once we begin to ask these questions, we enter the realm of knowledge about how people "know" and "think," and how they learn to do it. The focus of cognitive theory is the structure and development of human thought processes and how those processes affect the way a person understands and perceives the world. Piaget's theory of cognition forms a cornerstone of early childhood educational concepts about children; the works of Gardner and Sternberg (see Chapter 13) in intelligence enrich our knowledge of intellectual development and how to translate theory into educational practice.

Jean Piaget

Jean Jacques Piaget (1896–1980) was one of the most exciting research theorists in child development. A major force in child psychology, he studied both thought processes and how they change with age. Jean Piaget's ideas serve as our guide to the cognitive theory because of the thoroughness of his work. He had great influence on child psychology, theories of learning, intellectual development, even philosophy. He became the foremost expert on the development of knowledge from birth to adulthood.

How did Piaget find out about such matters? A short review of his life and ideas reveals a staggering volume of work and a wide scope of interests. Born at the turn of the century, Piaget built on his childhood curiosity in science and philosophy by working with Dr. Simon at the Binet Laboratory (Simon and Binet devised the first intelligence test). While recording children's abilities to answer questions correctly, he became fascinated with children's incorrect responses. He noticed that children tended to give similar kinds of wrong answers, and that they made different kinds of mistakes at different ages.

Thus, Jean Piaget launched into a lifelong study of intelligence. He believed that children think in fundamentally different ways from adults. He also developed a new method for studying thought processes. Rather than using a standardized test, he adapted the psychiatric method of question and response. Called the "methode clinique," it lets people's answers guide the questions. Therefore, it focuses on the child's own natural ways of thinking. This method is discussed in detail in Chapter 6.

Piaget then began studying children's thought processes. With his wife, one of his former students, he observed his children. He also began to look closely at how actively children engage in their own development. He studied the development of logic and looked at children's understanding of scientific and mathematical principles. In his final works, he returned to his original interest, that of the study of knowledge itself. Prolific his entire life, Jean Piaget has given us a complex theory of intelligence and child development that will influence us for some time. He has recorded, in a systematic way, how children learn, when they learn, and what they learn.

Piaget's Theory of Cognitive Development

What are the concepts of cognitive theory? Detailing all Piaget's ideas is impossible. What follows are several tenets that explain the nature of intelligence and its functions.

Piaget's theory relies on both maturational and environmental factors. It is called maturational because it sets out a sequence of cognitive (thinking) stages that are governed by heredity. For example, heredity affects our learning by (1) how the body is structured biologically, and (2) automatic, or instinctive, behavior, such as an infant's sucking at birth. It is an environmental theory because what experiences children have will directly influence how they develop.

Thinking and learning is a process of interaction between a person and the environment. Piaget also sets out that all species inherit a basic tendency to organize their lives and adapt to the world around them. This is known as a **constructivist** theory; that is, children actively construct knowledge on an ongoing basis. Based on both innate cognitive structures and experience, they are developing—and constantly revising—their own

FIGURE 4.7   In Piagetian theory, the processes of assimilation, accommodation, and equilibrium are basic to how all people organize their thoughts and, therefore, to all cognitive development.

Assimilation: Taking new information and organizing it in such a way that it fits with what the person already knows.

Example: Juanita sees an airplane while walking outdoors with her father. She knows that birds fly. So, never having seen this flying thing before, she calls it a "bird (pájaro)." This is what we call *assimilation*. She is taking in this new information and making it fit into what she already knows. Children assimilate what they are taught into their own worlds when they play. This happens when children play "taking turns" or "school" and "house" with their dolls and toy figures. Another way to see assimilation at work is during carpentry, as children hammer and nail triangles and squares after being shown shape books and puzzles by their teacher.

Accommodation: Taking new information and changing what is already thought to fit the new information.

Example: Aaron is at the grocery store with his mother and newborn baby. He calls the woman in line ahead of them "pregnant" although she is simply overweight. After being corrected, he asks the next person he sees, "Are you pregnant or just fat?" This is what we call *accommodation*. Having learned that all people with large bellies aren't pregnant, he changes his knowledge base to include this new information. Children accommodate to the world as they are taught to use a spoon, the toilet, a computer.

Equilibration: A mental process to achieve a mental balance, whereby a person takes new information and continually attempts to make sense of the experiences and perceptions.

Example: Colby, age 7, gets two glasses from the cupboard for his friend Ajit and himself. After putting apple juice into his short, wide glass he decides he'd rather have milk, so he pours it into Ajit's tall, thin glass. "Look, now I have more than you!" says his friend. This puzzles Colby, who is distressed (in "disequilibrium"): how could it be more when he just poured it out of his glass? He thinks about the inconsistency (and repours the juice several times back and forth) and begins to get the notion that pouring liquid into different containers does not change its amount (the conservation of liquids). "No, it isn't," he says, "It's just a different shape!" Thus, Colby learns to make sense of it in a new way and achieves equilibrium in his thinking. Children do this whenever they get new information that asks them to change the actual schemas, making new ones to fit new experiences.

Stage	Age	What Happens
Sensorimotor	Birth to 1½ to 2	Initial use of inherent reflexes (sucking, crying)—at birth. Out of sight, out of mind, at the beginning; object permanence is learned by experience by around one year. Movements from accidental and random to more deliberate and intentional—throughout stage. Learns to coordinate perceptual and motor functions (such as seeing object and then grabbing it). Learns relationship between means and ends (pushes aside barrier to get a toy). Beginning forms of symbolic behavior (opens and closes mouth when doing same to a jar).
Preoperational	2 to 6-7	Gradual acquisition of language (new words, like "yummed it up," or "my ponytail was keeping me in bothers"). Symbolic (play doll as baby, stick as sword). Egocentric (not aware of another point of view, only one's own). Physical characteristics, such as size, judged by appearance only (a ball of playdough *looks* bigger when made into a long roll, so therefore it *is* bigger). "Conservation" develops slowly; ability to reverse operations is not understood (the milk cannot be visualized as being poured back into the first glass). Inability to think of the whole and its parts at the same time (given a set of blue and red wooden beads, the child will say that the blue beads will make a longer necklace than the wooden beads).
Concrete operational	6 to 12	Begins to "conserve" (can see that quantity, size, length, volume, remain the same no matter how they are arranged). Can handle several ideas at the same time (given an array of objects of various colors and shapes, can find all the "red, square, small ones"). Starts to remove contradictions (can understand and follow rules, and make up own). Can understand other points of view, although needs to be in real situations, rather than abstract ones.

FIGURE 4.8 In their early childhood, children will pass through the sensorimotor and preoperational stages and enter the stage of concrete operations.

knowledge. In doing so, an organism "figures out" what the world is all about, and then works toward surviving in that world. Regardless of their age, all people develop schemas, or mental concepts, as a general way of thinking about, or interacting with, ideas and objects in the environment. For instance, the infant learns about the world first through sensorimotor schemas such as sucking and grasping. Young children learn perceptual schemas and then more abstract ones such as morality schemas that help determine how to act in different situations. Throughout, we use three basic processes to think: these are known as the adaptive processes of assimilation and accommodation, and the balancing process of equilibration. Figure 4.7 demonstrates how these work.

Piaget theorized that thinking develops along certain lines. This coincides with his idea that people tend to organize themselves, and the stages of thinking are the psychological structures that go along with trying to adapt to the environment. Such a series of stages goes beyond individual differences in thinking styles. It focuses on internal structures rather than on external conditions as behavioral theory does. Piaget identified four major stages of cognitive development:

Sensorimotor stage	zero to two years
Preoperational stage	1-1/2 to six or seven years
Concrete operational	six to 12 years
Formal operational stage	12 years to adulthood

Beebop puts cookies in the jar and leaves.

Someone sneaks in and replaces cookies with a pencil.

COOKIES

COOKIES

What will Beebop think is in the jar?

Pencil

Cookies

3-year old

7-year old

FIGURE 4.9 Children have different ways in which they mentally represent the same things. The older child recognizes that, although the contents of the box are only one thing out in the world, they can be represented in people's heads in more than one way—a possibility that escapes the younger child. (Special thanks to John Flavell for the example and the research.)

Each person of normal intelligence will go through these stages in this order, although the rate will change depending on the individual and his or her experiences. Figure 4.8 details the stages of early childhood.

Jean Piaget's theories revolutionized our thinking about children's thinking, and challenged psychologists and educators to focus less on *what* children know than *the ways they come to know*. But was Piaget right? Researchers have been exploring and debating the ideas of cognitive theory for many years, often engaging in what Piaget himself called "the American question"; that is, can you speed up the rate in which children pass through these intellectual stages of development. Certainly there are problems with the theory. The most obvious criticism is that some skills of more advanced stages are present in some form in an earlier stage. Therefore, "he seems to have been wrong about just how *early* many cognitive skills develop. . . . A second blow to the notion of completely separated stages comes from research on

expertise." (Bee, 1995). Children who know a lot about some subject or some set of materials seem to be able to use more advanced-stage thinking in those areas.

Now, developmental psychologists believe that Piaget's theory of distinct stages is not correct. Rather, "he is essentially on target about sequences; that is, cognitive development is made up of a large number of apparently *vertical sequences* . . . [so that] children seem to learn the basic rules or strategies in the same order." (Bee, 1995). Furthermore, research on the brain (Ellison, 1990) supports Piaget's theories; brain maturation, as reflected in the development of neurons called myelination, seems to follow a sequence that parallels the various thinking stages of development. Figure 4.9 illustrates some of the research results from one of America's outstanding cognitive psychologists, Dr. John Flavell.

What we do know is that children progress from one stage to the next, changing their thinking depending on their level of maturation and experience with the environment. Certain physical skills, such as fine-motor coordination, determine how much a child is capable of doing. Certain environmental factors, such as the kinds of experiences the world and adults provide, influence the rate of growth. Yet throughout the process, children take in new knowledge and decide how it fits with what they already know. As new information comes in, the child learns and grows.

Applying Cognitive Theory to Work with Children

What can teachers learn from this complicated theory? Piaget's writings do not apply directly to classroom methods or subject matter per se, and therefore careful interpretation is required. In fact, he never claimed to be an educator. However, Piaget's theories provide a framework, or philosophy, about children's thinking. Piagetian theory has some implications for both environment and interactions. Gardner's theory of multiple intelligences is discussed in Chapter 13.

Materials

Children need many objects to explore, so that they can later incorporate these into their symbolic thinking. Such materials need to be balanced among open-ended ones (such as sand and water activities, basic art and construction materials), guided ones (cooking with recipes, conducting experiments, classification and seriated materials), and self-correcting ones (puzzles, matching games, such as some of the Montessori materials). It is important to remember that young children need to be involved with concrete objects and to explore and use them in their own ways, which include both sensorimotor and beginning symbolic play.

Scheduling

Children need lots of time to explore their own reality, especially through the use of play. A Piagetian classroom would have large periods of time for children to "act out" their own ideas. Also, there should be time scheduled for imitation of adult-given ideas (songs, fingerplays, and stories).

Teachers

Children need teachers who understand and agree with a developmental point of view. The teacher who knows the stages and levels of thinking of the children will be one who can guide that class into new and challenging opportunities to learn and grow.

What are the implications for early childhood teachers and parents? In working with children under five, we must remember that, because they do not understand mental representations very well, they will have trouble recognizing that another person may view or interpret things differently than they do. This "egocentric" viewpoint is both natural and normal, but must be factored into teachers' thoughts as they work with children. For instance, to a 6- or 7-year-old you may be able to ask "How would you feel if you were in that situation?," whereas for a younger child the question is incomprehensible. For the same reason, the younger child may have trouble distinguishing how things seem or appear from how they really are. As Flavell puts it,

> For them, if something *seems* dangerous (the menacing-looking shadow in their unlit bedroom), it *is* dangerous, and if it *seems* nondangerous (the friendly acting stranger), it *is* nondangerous. We often think of young children as naive, credulous, gullible, trusting, and the like. Their inadequate understanding that things may not be as they appear might be partly responsible for this impression. (Flavell, 1989)

To encourage thinking and learning, teachers should refrain from telling children exactly how to solve a problem. Rather, the teacher should ask questions that encourage children to observe and pay attention to their own ideas. Teachers:

● Use or create situations that are personally meaningful to children.

● Provide opportunities for them to make decisions.

● Provide opportunities for them to exchange viewpoints with their peers (Williams & Kamii, 1986).

Vygotsky's Sociocultural Theory*

Laura E. Berk

The ideas of the Soviet developmental psychologist Lev Vygotsky, who early in this century forged an innovative theory granting great importance to social and cultural experience in children's development, have gained increasing visibility over the past decade. In Vygotsky's *sociocultural theory*, cooperative dialogues with more knowledgeable members of society are necessary for children to acquire the ways of thinking that make up a community's culture. Also, language plays a crucial role in the formation of the child's mind because it is our primary way of communicating, serves as the major means by which social experience is mentally represented, and is an indispensable tool for thought.

According to Vygotsky, the aspects of reality a child is ready to master lie within the *zone of proximal (or potential) development*—a range of tasks that the child cannot yet do alone but can accomplish with help from others. When a child discusses a challenging task with a mentor, that person offers spoken directions and strategies. Then children incorporate the language of those dialogues into their self-directed speech and use it to guide independent efforts. Listen closely to young children and you will hear them talk aloud to themselves as they play, explore, and solve problems. Recent research shows that this *private speech* is a vital bridge between social experience and inner thought and helps children learn.

Vygotsky's ideas are stimulating new ways to educate children that emphasize discussion and joint problem-solving. Adult guidance that creates a *scaffold* for children by sensitively adjusting to their momentary progress is essential for cognitive development. Cooperative learning, in which small groups of peers at varying levels of competence work toward a common goal, also fosters more advanced thinking. In a Vygotskian classroom, learning is highly interactive and simultaneously considers where children are and what they are capable of becoming.

*From Berk, Laura E. Infants, Children, and Adolescents. *Boston: Allyn and Bacon, 1996 (2nd Ed.) and Berk, Laura E. "Why Children Talk to Themselves." * Scientific American *271(5), November 1994, pp. 78–83. Dr. Berk is Professor of Psychology at Illinois State University, consulting editor for* Young Children *and author of child development texts.*

Awareness

Perhaps more important is the awareness on the part of all adults that all children have the capability to reason and be thinkers if they are given appropriate materials for their stage of development. Teachers must remember that young children:

1. Think differently than adults.

2. Need many materials to explore and describe.

3. Think in a concrete manner and often cannot think out things in their heads.

4. Come to conclusions and decisions based on what they see, rather than on what is sensible and logical.

5. Need challenging questions, and the time to make their own decisions and find their own answers.

The thoughts and ideas of Jean Piaget are impressive, both in quantity and quality. The collective works of this man are extremely complex, often difficult to understand. Yet they have given us a valuable blueprint. Clearly, Jean Piaget has provided unique and important insights into the development of intelligence and children.

> It is Piaget's genius for empathy with children, together with true intellectual genius, that has made him the outstanding child psychologist in the world today and one destined to stand beside Freud with respect to his contributions to psychology, education, and related disciplines. Just as Freud's discoveries of unconscious motivation, infantile sexuality, and the stages of psychosexual growth changed our ways of thinking about human personality, so Piaget's discoveries of children's implicit philosophies, the construction of reality by the infant, and the stages of mental development have altered our ways of thinking about human intelligence.
>
> (Elkind, 1977)

SOCIOCULTURAL THEORY

In the last decade, one theory (and theorist) has received renewed attention. The sociocultural theory of development of Lev Vygotsky focuses on the child as a whole and incorporates ideas of culture and values into child development, particularly the ideas of the development of language and self-identity. Although his theory was developed in the 1920s, it did not receive attention in the United States until his seminal work, *The Mind in Society*, was translated into English in 1978. Since that time, many developmental psychologists, sociologists, and educators have noticed the implications it has for our thinking about children and culture.

Lev Vygotsky

Born in 1896 in Byelorussia, Vygotsky graduated from Moscow University with a degree in literature in 1917. For the next 6 years he taught literature and psychology and directed adult theater as well as founding a literary journal. In 1924 he began work at the Institute of Psychology in Moscow, where he focused on the problems of educational practice, particularly those of handicapped children. Towards that end, he gathered a group of young scientists during the late 1920s and early 1930s to look closer at psychology and mental abnormality, including medical connections. His roots lie with experimental psychology, American philosopher William James, and contemporaries Pavlov and Watson (see Behaviorist theory section of this chapter). A scholar with interests in art and creativity as well as philosophy, psychology, and politics, Vygotsky died in 1934 of tuberculosis.

Vygotsky's Sociocultural Theory

Vygotsky's work is considered a **sociocultural** theory because it focuses on how values, beliefs, skills, and traditions are transmitted to the next generation. Like Erikson, Vygotsky believed in the connection between culture and development, particularly the interpersonal connection between the child and other important people. Like the Humanists (see later in this chapter), he considered the child as a whole, taking a humanistic, more qualitative approach to studying children. And while he understood the primary behaviorists of his day, he differed from them in that he emphasized family, social interaction, and play as primary influences in children's lives, rather than the stimulus-response and schedules of reinforcement that were becoming so popular in his day.

Vygotsky believed that the child was embedded in the family and culture of his community and that much of a child's development was culturally specific. Rather than moving through certain stages or sequences (as Piaget proposed), children's mastery and interaction differ from culture to culture. Adults, Vygotsky noted, teach socially valued skills at a very early age; children's learning is, therefore, quite influenced by what their social world values. One way he explained this was by his theory of the **zone of proximal development**. If meaningful learning happens in a social context, the learning is interpersonal and dynamic and depends on who and how much a child's experiences interact with others. This zone has an upper and lower limit. Tasks in the zone are too difficult for a child to learn alone, so he needs the assistance of another who has mastered the task. The lower limit of the zone is where the child has reached working and problem-solving independently. The upper limit is the level of mastery the child can reach with assistance from another skilled person.

Who can be part of a child's zone of proximal development, sharing experiences and developing a cooperative dialogue with the child? Initially, of course, it is the family. For instance, a young girl is carried even as a toddler to the open market with her mother. There she watches and is guided towards learning how to touch cloth, smell herbs, taste food, and weigh and compare amounts. Is it any wonder she learns advanced math skills and the language of bargaining early on?

The reciprocal relationships in the child's zone of proximal development can also include the teacher. Think about your role, for example, in helping a child in your program learn problem-solving skills in completing a puzzle, putting on mittens, or resolving a conflict. Finally, other children—older ones who have more expertise or peers who may have superior skills or simply offers of help—can be part of a child's learning in this sociocultural theory. Vygotsky's theory dictates that learning is active and constructed, as did Piaget; unlike Piaget, however, he includes the element of *interaction*; unlike Piaget, Vygotsky believed that interaction and direct teaching are critical aspects of a child's cognitive development.

Further, sociocultural theory challenges Piagetian ideas of language and thought. Vygotsky believed that language, even in its earliest forms, was socially based. Rather than egocentric or immature, children's speech and language development during the years of three to seven is merged and tied to what children are thinking. During these transitions years, the child talks aloud to herself; after awhile, this "self-talk" becomes internalized so that the child can act without talking aloud. Vygotsky contended that children speak to themselves for self-guidance and self-direction and that this private speech helps children think about their behavior and plan for action. With age, **private speech** (once called "egocentric speech"), which goes from out loud to whispers to lip movement, is critical to a child's self-regulation.

Applying Sociocultural Theory to Work with Children

Sociocultural theory has several implications for the classroom teacher. First, teachers work to understand and incorporate a *child's family and culture* into their teaching.[1] This lends credence to the notion of multicultural education, as noted throughout this text in the "Our Diverse World" ideas.

Second, since learning is considered essentially an interpersonal and dynamic process, teachers must develop comfortable and cooperative *relationships* with their children. The teacher and learner adjust to one another; teachers use what they know about children to guide their teaching and plan their curriculum. Sociocultural theory supports both the "emergent curriculum" (see Chapter 11) and the idea of spontaneous, teachable moments such as are advocated by proponents of an anti-bias curriculum (see Chapters 9, 12, 13, and 14). Further, Vygotsky's theory supports the importance of the teacher-child relation-

[1]Vygotsky understood the importance of individual diversity nearly 75 years ago.

ship, a cornerstone of this text (see Chapter 5) and of Developmentally Appropriate Practices (see Chapters 1, 2, and 11). Not all learning is spontaneous, nor is it enough to simply provide interesting objects and expect children to learn all there is to know. Children need adults to mediate, to not only ask questions but also to analyze where the child is with the questions that are asked. In this way, adults help children learn; when a task is mastered so that the child can do it independently, the adults see the shift from the upper to the lower limit of the zone and can offer a new challenge to enter.

Third, teachers pay close attention to the *psychological "tools"* used to learn.[1] These include those of the culture, such as how in the United States children are taught to tie a string around their finger whereas in Russia they tie a knot in their handkerchief. They also include the universal tools of drawing, of language, and of mathematics. Lower mental functions such as using the senses take little effort to do, but the higher mental functions need the help of a person who knows the tools of the society in order to learn.

In regard, teachers realize that there is much value in *play*. It is in play that the child can practice operating the symbols and tools of the culture. Vygotsky (1978) puts it this way:

> Action in the imaginative sphere, in an imaginary situation, the creation of voluntary intentions, the formation of real-life plans and volitional motives—all appear in play and make it the highest level of preschool development. The child moves forward essentially through play activity. Only in this sense can play be considered a leading activity that determines the child's development.

For instance, children might build a structure with blocks; the teacher encourages them to draw the building and then map the entire block corner as a village or neighborhood. The adult serves an important role as an intellectual mediator, continually shifting to another set of symbols in order to give the child a different way of looking at the same thing.

In a Vygotskian classroom there will be activity and an awareness of individual differences. A teacher with this perspective will likely have planned activities that encourage assisted and cooperative learning. Moreover, these classrooms will work best with multi-aged grouping, or at least with plenty of opportunity for older "buddies" or siblings younger and older to be present. Laura E. Berk's Focus Box on p. 116 offers more insight into Vygotsky's theory.

MATURATION THEORY

Arnold Gesell

As noted in Chapter 1, Arnold Gesell was a physician intrigued with the notion that children's internal clock seemed to govern their growth and behavior. In the 1950s, he established norms for both physical-motor growth and the behaviors that accompany that development. The Gesell Institute, which fosters the work of Dr. Louise Bates Ames and others, continues to provide guidelines for how children mature from birth to puberty. The word pictures in Chapter 3 are an excellent example of the information maturational theory and research have provided.

Theory of Maturation

Maturation, by definition, is the process of physical and mental growth that is determined by heredity. The maturation sequence takes place in relatively stable and orderly ways. Maturation theory holds that much growth is genetically determined from conception. This theory differs from behaviorism, which asserts that growth is determined by environmental conditions and experiences, and cognitive theory, which states that growth and behavior are a reflection of both maturation and learning.

Maturation and growth are interrelated and occur together. Maturation describes the *quality* of growth; that is, while a child grows in inches and pounds, the nature (or quality) of that growth changes. Maturation is qualitative, describing the way a baby moves into walking, rather than simply

OUR DIVERSE WORLD OUR DIVERSE WORLD OUR DIVERSE WORLD OUR DIVERSE WORLD OUR DIVERSE WORLD

[1]Sociocultural theory recommends that teachers learn the culture of the children they teach.

the age at which the baby took the first step. Growth is *what* happens; maturation is *how* it happens.

Studies have established that the maturation sequence is the same for all children, regardless of culture, country of origin, or learning environment. But there are two vital points to remember:

● Although maturation determines the sequence of development, the precise age is *approximate*. The sequence of developmental stages may be universal, but the rate at which a child moves through the stages varies tremendously.

● Growth is *uneven*. Children grow in spurts. Motor development may be slow in some stages, fast in others. For instance, a baby may gain an ounce a day for two months, then only half a pound in an entire month. Usually there is a growth spurt at puberty, with some children at 13 nearly their adult height, others not yet five feet tall. This unpredictability brings, again, much individual variation.

FIGURE 4.10 Young children need materials and time to explore the world on their own. (Courtesy of American Montessori Society.)

Applying Maturation Theory to Work with Children

Maturation theory is most useful in describing children's growth and typical behavior. In Chapter 3, these normative data are used to develop Word Pictures that describe common characteristics of children at different ages. Such charts will help adults understand behavior better and will keep them from expecting too much or too little. Teachers can use developmental norms to understand typical growth by remembering that there is great individual variation and uneven growth. Further, maturation theory has inspired excellent developmental norms that help parents, teachers, and physicians alike determine whether a child's growth is within the normal range.

HUMANISTIC THEORY

The Humanists

As the field of psychology began to develop, various schools of thought arose. By the middle of this century, two "camps" dominated the Ameri-

can psychological circles. The first, known as psychodynamic, included the Freudians and is best known to us through the works of Erik Erikson. The second, called behaviorism, began with Watson and Thorndike, and was later expanded by Skinner and Bandura.

In 1954, Abraham Maslow published a book that articulated another set of ideas. He called it the Third Force (or Humanistic Psychology), which focused on what motivated people to be well, successful, and mentally healthy.

This theory has a place in early childhood education because it attempts to explain how people are motivated. Specifically, humanistic theory is centered on people's needs, goals, and successes. This was a change from the study of mental illness, as in psychotherapy, or the study of animal behavior, in the case of much behaviorist research. Instead, Dr. Maslow studied exceptionally mature and successful people. Others, such as Carl Rogers, Fritz Perls, Alan Watts, and Erich Fromm added to what was known about healthy personalities. The humanists developed a comprehensive theory of human behavior based on mental health.

Maslow's Theory of Human Needs

Maslow's theory of self-actualization is a set of ideas about what people need in order to become and stay healthy. He asserts that every human being is motivated by a number of basic needs, regardless of age, sex, race, culture, or geographic location. According to Maslow (1962), a basic need is something:

● Whose absence breeds illness.

● Whose presence prevents illness.

● Whose restoration cures illness.

● Preferred by the deprived person over other satisfactions, under certain conditions (such as very complex, free-choice instances).

● Found to be inactive, at a low ebb, or functionally absent in the healthy person.

These needs, not to be denied, form a theory of human motivation. It is a hierarchy, or pyramid, because there is a certain way these needs are interrelated, and because the most critical needs form the foundation from which the other needs can be met.

Applying Humanistic Theory to Work with Children

The basic needs are sometimes called "deficiency needs" because they are critical for a person's survival, and a deficiency can cause a person to die. Until those are met, no other significant growth can take place. How well a teacher knows that a hungry child will ignore a lesson, or simply be unable to concentrate. A tired child often pushes aside other learning materials and experiences until rested. The child who is deprived of basic physiological needs may be able to think of those needs only; in fact, "such a man can fairly be said to live by bread alone" (Maslow, 1954). The humanists would strongly advocate a school breakfast or lunch program, and support regular rest and naptimes in programs with long hours.

Once the physiological needs are satisfied, the need for safety and security will emerge. Maslow points at insecure and neurotic people as examples of what happens when these needs are left unfulfilled. These people act as if a disaster is about to occur, as if a spanking is on the way. Given an unpredictable home or school, a child cannot find any sense of consistency, and so is preoccupied with worrying and anxiety. Maslow would advise teachers to give freedom within limits, rather than either total neglect or permissiveness.

The growth needs begin to emerge when the basic needs have been met. Higher needs are dependent on those primary ones. They are what we strive for in order to become more satisfied and healthy people.

The need for *love and belonging* is often expressed directly and clearly by the young children in our care. A lack of love and sense of belonging stifles growth. In order to learn to give love later in life, one has to learn about love by receiving it as a child. This means learning early about the responsibilities of giving as well as receiving love.

The *need for esteem* can be divided into two categories: self-respect and esteem from others. "Self-esteem includes such needs as a desire for confidence, competence, mastery, adequacy, achievement, independence, and freedom. Respect from others includes such concepts as prestige, recognition, acceptance, attention, status, reputation, and appreciation." (Goble, 1970)

Self-actualization is what gives a person satisfaction in life. From the desire to know and understand the world and people around us comes a renewal of self-knowledge. For the early childhood educator, these needs are expressed in the enthusiasm, curiosity, and natural "drive" to learn and try. In meeting these needs, a person finds meaning for life, an eagerness to live, and a willingness to do so. Figure 4.11 describes both basic and growth needs in detail.

Children must have their physical and basic emotional needs met before these requirements of higher cognitive learning can be fulfilled. Moreover, the child who seems stuck in a particular "needs area" will likely stay there until that basic need is satisfied. A hungry, insecure, or hurt child is a poor learner. Teachers must continually advocate better physical and social conditions for all children.

Maslow's theory has important implications for child care. Children's basic needs are teachers' first concern: Teachers must ensure that children are properly clothed, fed, and rested as well as safe and secure. Only then are they ready to address curriculum and skill development.

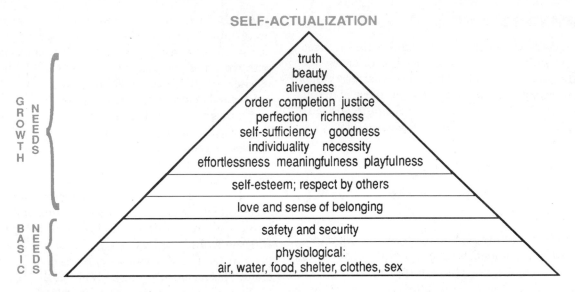

SELF-ACTUALIZATION

truth
beauty
aliveness
order completion justice
perfection richness
self-sufficiency goodness
individuality necessity
effortlessness meaningfulness playfulness

self-esteem; respect by others

love and sense of belonging

safety and security

physiological:
air, water, food, shelter, clothes, sex

GROWTH NEEDS

BASIC NEEDS

FIGURE 4.11 Abraham Maslow studied healthy personalities and found that what people need for growth is universal. One tenet of humanistic psychology is the hierarchy of basic and growth needs. (Adapted from Abraham Maslow, 1954.)

OTHER THEORETICAL VIEWPOINTS FOR EDUCATORS

To complete our discussion of psychology and early education, the contributions of several other aspects are noteworthy. All have added to our knowledge about how people think and learn, how personality and social attitudes develop, and how early attachment and learning affect the developing child. The number of excellent researchers who have contributed to the knowledge of early childhood development far exceeds the space we have here. We include these viewpoints to emphasize the vital links between psychology, developmental research, and education.

Attachment

A key concept in the development of the self and the study of social relationships is that of **attachment**, a term used particularly in the works of John Bowlby and Mary Ainsworth, and a concept used in Burton White's descriptive work and Magda Gerber's RIE programs for infants and toddlers. Attachment is the emotional connection, an "affectional bond" in Bowlby's terms, between two people. The child or adult who is attached to

another uses that person as a "safe base" from which to venture out into the world, a source of comfort when distressed or stressed, and a support for encouragement. **Attachment behaviors**, therefore, are anything that allows a person to get and stay attached. These include smiling, eye contact, talking, touching, even clinging and crying.

Bowlby's theory includes the idea that infants are preprogrammed to form attachments to adults, thus ensuring their survival, and research does show that human and animal babies do indeed send signals to their mothers very early on (Waters & Deane, 1982). In fact, the human infant's early signals include crying and gazing, both of which are powerful to adults, and a kind of rhythmic sucking that appears to keep the mother engaged. Soon after appears the social smile, which is a thrill for parents and a boost in communication skills for the baby.

The nature of children's attachment has been researched extensively by Mary Ainsworth and colleagues. Developmentally, children develop an initial bond, then proceed to develop real mutuality—that is, to learn and practice almost a "dance" between themselves and their favored loved one. She found that, although virtually all infants develop attachments, including to multiple care-

	Exploratory Behavior before Separation	Behavior during Separation	Reunion Behavior	Behavior with Stranger
Secure	Separates to explore toys; shares play with mother; friendly toward stranger when mother is present, touches "home base" periodically.	May cry; play is subdued for a while; usually recovers and is able to play.	If distressed during separation, contact ends distress; if not distressed, greets mother warmly; initiates interaction.	Somewhat friendly; may play with stranger after initial distress reaction.
Anxious/ambivalent (resistant)	Has difficulty separating to explore toys even when mother is present; wary of novel situations and people; stays close to mother and away from stranger.	Very distressed; hysterical crying does not quickly diminish.	Seeks comfort and rejects it; continues to cry or fuss; may be passive—no greeting made.	Wary of stranger; rejects stranger's offers to play.
Anxious/avoidant	Readily separates to explore toys; does not share play with parent; shows little preference for parent versus stranger.	Does not show distress; continues to play; interacts with the stranger.	Ignores mother—turns or moves away; avoidance is more extreme at the second reunion.	No avoidance of stranger.

SOURCE: Compiled from Ainsworth, M. D. S., & Wittig, B. A. (1969). Attachment and exploratory behavior of one-year-olds in a strange situation. In B. M. Foss (Ed.), Determinants of infant behavior (Vol. 4). London: Methuen.

FIGURE 4.12 Patterns of attachment in 12- to 18-month-olds in Ainsworth's "Strange Situation" show how critical the interpersonal environment is for young children. (From *Understanding Children* by Judith Schickendanz by permission of Mayfield Publishing Company. Copyright © 1993 by Mayfield Publishing Company.)

givers, they differ in how secure they are in those attachments. Furthermore, attachment can be measured in the infant and toddler, as seen in children's response to a stranger both in and out of the parent's presence. Figure 4.12 illustrates these patterns of attachment. Researchers have found that a majority of American infants tested in the stranger situation demonstrated secure attachment. Still, when attachment fails, children are placed at tremendous risk.

For instance, this two-part dance requires both infant and parent (or caregiver) to have the skill to connect. Premature infants often lack these skills at first, as their systems are underdeveloped and they often are separated in the first weeks or months, causing parents to report them as quite unresponsive. Some parents of blind infants, who cannot engage in gazing, may wonder if they are being rejected by their babies. Failure of attachment can come from the parent, too. Parents who themselves did not have secure attachments as

children may not know the needed behaviors. Abusing parents are not doing their part to encourage bonding. Other neglectful conditions, such as depression, abject poverty, and other stresses, increase the likelihood that there will be a failure of attachment. Intervention can help unattached persons, teaching specific interactive techniques with ongoing supports such as crisis hotlines and personal counseling.

Also, parents and researchers have asked careful questions about full-day child care, particularly for infants, wondering if such care undermines children's attachment to their parents. The debate, reaching its height in the latter half of the 1980s, has spurred research into both parent-child attachment and child care programs. Whether concerns about infant child care prove valid or not, as of this date we can conclude that children are not at any higher risk in high-quality child care. This highlights the need for such programs, as will be addressed further in chapters 9, 10, and 15.

Sex Differences

Are girls and boys different? What are these differences, and how do they occur? More importantly, what differences are caused by "nature" and which ones from "nurture"? Should we treat our girls and boys the same or differently? The realities and the myths surrounding sex differences and their effect on behavior from infancy to adulthood is the subject of interest, controversy, and research. The work of Eleanor Maccoby and others has provided both hard data and an open forum for discussions about how people grow and the complex interaction between heredity and environment that makes child development so fascinating.

The child's emerging sense of self has several elements, including an awareness of a separate self and in comparison to others (as discussed in chapter 14). One aspect of self is gender identity. Children generally acquire the ability to label themselves and others correctly by age 2 or 3; they develop gender stability (staying the same sex throughout life) by age 4 and gender constancy (keeping the same gender regardless of appearance) by about 5 or 6.

As they grow, children begin to develop ideas about gender roles, what girls/women and boys/men do. Sex-typed behavior begins to appear at 2 or 3, when children tend to choose same-sex playmates and sex-typed toy preferences. Research indicates that there are no significant differences between girls and boys in intelligence or reasoning behavior. Some cognitive functioning and personality differences do exist, but overall the differences are small and there is no overall pattern (Bee, 1995; Fagot & Kronsberg, 1982; Matthews, 1979; Maccoby, 1980; Maccoby & Jacklin, 1974; Tavris & Offir, 1977)

So, why are there these sex differences in behavior? Theorists of several different schools of thought have tried to explain the patterns. Freud's explanation is based on the concept of identification, whereby the child learns to imitate the same-sex parent and acquires the appropriate role. Behaviorists emphasize the role of reinforcement and modeling, and parents do appear to treat boys and girls in systematically different ways. A cognitive-developmental model, by Kohlberg, theorizes that children imitate same-sex models after they develop gender constancy. Current theorists now propose a "schema" model (see "Cognitive theory" for definition); that is, children develop theories about the world from an early age, especially in the preoperational stage, and therefore develop general rules about what girls and boys do as soon as they figure out that there is a difference. The application of such rules would be particularly strong in the preschool and early elementary years, until a child develops an ability to see beyond appearance, and can think in more abstract ways to deeper characteristics and broader categories.

Researchers have found two characteristics of boys—better spatial ability and greater aggressiveness—but have been unable to demonstrate a clear biological connection. Since girls and boys are treated differently by parents and teachers, and are presented with sex stereotypes in the mass media and children's books, they clearly receive different messages. Adults who work with children are thus well-advised to pay careful attention to the messages they give children.[1]

In the environments we prepare for them, the materials they use, and the examples we model, children create their own ideas and learn behavior that works for them in the world. Socialization, then, probably accounts for most of the sex-typed behavior we see in children.

Moral Development

People used to assume that young children needed to be taught exactly what was "right" and "wrong" and that was enough. In the last 20 years, research has shown that moral development is a more complex process with both a cognitive and an emotional side to it. Several theorists and researchers have proposed how to think about children's moral development. Jean Piaget, Lawrence Kohlberg, Nancy Eisenberg, and Carol Gilligan are discussed here.

Piaget investigated children's moral reasoning by presenting children with pairs of stories and

OUR DIVERSE WORLD OUR DIVERSE WORLD OUR DIVERSE WORLD OUR DIVERSE WORLD OUR DIVERSE WORLD

[1]Working with young children and their families invites early childhood educators to carefully examine their own upbringing, values, beliefs, and biases.

I. **Preconventional morality**
Stage 1: Punishment and obedience orientation
  Might makes right; obey authority to avoid punishment
Stage 2: Individualism and relativist orientation
  Look out for number one; be nice to others so they will be nice to you

II. **Conventional morality**
Stage 3: Mutual interpersonal expectations
  "Good girl, nice boy"; approval more important than any reward
Stage 4: Social system and conscience
  "Law and order"; contributing to society's good is important

III. **Postconventional**
Stage 5: Social contract
  Rules are to benefit all, by mutual agreement; may be changed same way; the greatest good for the greatest
Stage 6: Universal ethical principles
  Values established by individual reflection, may contradict other laws

FIGURE 4.13 Kohlberg's Stages of Moral Development. Fairly broad cross-cultural data and extensive American research indicate a persuasive universality and a strong sequence of stage development in children's moral development.

asking them which child was "naughtier." From this, he discovered that children under six base their judgment on the amount of damage done, not the child's intentions. By middle childhood, children are beginning to take intent into account, so that one can begin to see a shift in moral reasoning towards the end of the early childhood period from objective judgments, based on physical results and concrete amounts, to more subjective considerations (such as the purpose of the perpetrator or psychological factors). The connections to children's cognitive stage of development is interesting, and adults might consider that a child's protests over wrongdoing ("I didn't mean to do it!") may very well signal a new level of reasoning, with the realization that one's intentions *do* matter.

Lawrence Kohlberg is best known as a theorist in social development, addressing educational practice and gender constancy as well. Building on Piagetian dimensions, Kohlberg's theory of moral development involves both social growth and intellectual reasoning. People move from stage to stage as a result of their own reasoning power and they see for themselves the contradictions in their own beliefs. As with Erikson and Piaget, Kohlberg's stages are hierarchical—a person moves forward one by one, and no stage can be skipped. On the basis of children's responses to moral dilemmas similar to those of Piaget, Kohlberg identified three levels of moral development, as illustrated in Figure 4.13. For early childhood educators, research shows that preconventional reasoning (stages 1 and 2) is dominant into elementary school.

Most of the stories, or dilemmas, that Piaget and Kohlberg used were about stealing, lying, disobeying rules, and the like. More recently, researcher and theorist Nancy Eisenberg has explored the kinds of reasoning children use to justify good (**prosocial**) behavior. She asks children what they would do in situations with a moral dilemma. One of her stories involves a child on the way to a friend's birthday party. The child encounters someone who has fallen and is hurt. What should the child do, help the hurt child and miss cake and ice cream, or leave the child and go on to the party?

Such questions brought to light several levels of prosocial reasoning. In the early childhood years, children seem to be engaged in level 1 (*hedonistic reasoning*) in which the individual's own needs are put first. In the case mentioned above, the child would leave the hurt person and go to the party ("I won't help because I have to go to the party."). As children move through middle childhood, they tend to move to level 2, in which the needs of another begin to be considered and increase in importance. Answers to the story would begin to shift toward including others ("I'd help because they'd help me next time."). Eisenberg's stages roughly parallel Kohlberg's and help broaden these concepts without contradicting the fundamental arguments.

Carol Gilligan, however, challenges Kohlberg's strong emphasis on justice and fairness and his omission of caring for others. In her book *In a Different Voice* (1982), Gilligan points out that mostly males were studied for such work, and that, since girls and boys are socialized differently, their moral judgments will be quite different. For instance, boys may be raised with the idea that justice and fairness are the key moral basis, whereas girls may be taught that caring and responsibility to others are central.[1] Dr. Cary A. Buzzelli (1992) has also worked extensively on young children's moral understanding and has applied recent research to children's development of peer relationships. (See the Focus Box in Chapter 14.) While this claim has yet to be fully researched, it is an important thought to keep in mind, particularly when teaching and raising young children.

USING DEVELOPMENTAL AND LEARNING THEORIES

As teachers, it is important to think about what you believe about children, development, and learning. This chapter gives much food for thought in this regard, and students are often overwhelmed. Two critical questions arise: (1) Why do contradictions exist among the theories and (2) How can I decide which is the "right" one? To answer the first question, it is important to remember that each theory addresses a particular aspect of development, not every question about all of development. For instance, psychodynamic theory focuses on the development of personality, behaviorist on the conditions of learning, cognitive on how children think and learn, maturation on how development progresses, and humanist on the conditions for overall health. Each has its avid proponents with a body of research that supports it. Since every theory has its own focus and advocates, each viewpoint is rather subjective and

somewhat narrow. In other words, no one theory tells us everything . . . and that is the answer to the second question. Thoughtful teachers develop their own viewpoints. Begin to decide what you believe about children, learning, and education. Try to avoid the pitfall of taking sides. Instead, integrate theory into your teaching practices by comparing the major developmental and learning theories with your own daily experiences with young children.

Similarities Among the Theories

All six theories we have discussed attempt to explain how children grow, more in the socioemotional and cognitive areas than in the physical and motor areas. Maturation theory is the only one of the five that includes physical growth and motor development. In other words, these theories do not try to explain the workings of the body as much as the mind and heart. In general, the theories do not dictate curriculum for the classroom, though behaviorism does recommend teaching/learning techniques. Both Piagetian and Vygotsky's theories support important programmatic elements of good early childhood education, such as the "whole language" approach to literacy (see Chapter 13), the creative collaboration of Reggio Emilia (see Chapters 1, 9, and 14), and Gardner's recommendations for intellectual development in the schools (see Chapter 13). Each theory posits that learning follows an orderly, if not always smooth, path from birth to adulthood. They all see later learning as growing from previous experiences. They all agree that learning must be real, rewarding, and, except in extreme cases, connected to an important person or people in early life. Figure 4.14 summarizes the five major theories and principal theorists.

Differences Among the Theories

More obvious are the differences among the various theories. All five have a particular focus,

[1]These characteristics may not be *gender specific* (i.e. "only girls do this and only boys do that"), but be *gender related* (i.e. "many girls often. . . . and some boys may do the same"). What is important to remember in our diverse world is that one way is *not necessarily better* than another way, just *different*.

Theory	Major Theorists	Important Facts
Psychosocial	Erik Erikson	Maturational emphasis Stage theory of social and emotional development Crises at each level Teacher: Emotional base, social mediator
Behaviorist	John Watson Edward Thorndike B.F. Skinner Albert Bandura	Environmental emphasis Stimulus-response Conditioning (classical and operant) Reinforcement (positive and negative) Modeling Teacher: Arranger of environment and reinforcer of behavior
Cognitive	Jean Piaget	Maturational and environmental emphasis Assimilation and accommodation Stage theory of cognitive development Teacher: Provider of materials and time and supporter of children's unique ways of thinking
Sociocultural	Lev Vygotsky	Zone of proximal development Private speech Collaborative/assisted learning
Maturation	Arnold Gesell	Emphasis on heredity Normative data Teacher: Guider of behavior based on what is typical and normal
Humanist	Abraham Maslow Erich Fromm Fritz Perls Carl Rogers	Environmental emphasis Mental health model Hierarchy of human needs Teacher: Provider of basic and growth needs
Others	Mary Ainsworth John Bowlby Nancy Eisenberg Carol Gilligan Lawrence Kohlberg Eleanor Maccoby Nel Noddings	Attachment and categories research Attachment theory Expands moral development to prosocial Questions categories of moral development Moral, cognitive, and sex-role development Sex differences research Intuition theory and research

FIGURE 4.14   Each of the major theories of development or learning describes children and their growth in a different way.

but not the same one. In developmental terms, Erikson covers the psychosocial area. The behaviorists and Piagetians tend to concentrate on cognitive growth. Maturational theory rests on physical-motor development, although theorists have derived behavior in other areas as well. Gesell's maturation theory concentrates on the larger behaviors that heredity dictates. Maslow builds a framework including physiological, affective, and intellectual needs. Three of the five are developmental theories; that is, they describe changes in children as the result of a combination of growth (controlled mostly by maturation and heredity) and interaction with the environment. Maslow's theory of self-actualization is less developmental than descriptive of overall human needs, though it is clear that in early childhood the basic needs predominate over higher ones that occur later in life.

Behaviorist theory emphasizes changes that occur in the environment. Cognitive and psychosocial ideas are stage theories, explaining growth as a series of steps through which all children pass, regardless of environment. Behaviorists spell out how the children learn no matter what age or stage they may have achieved, while the two stage theorists claim that what and how a child learns is tied to a stage of development. Humanists tend to look at learning as paralleling the child's internal affective state, rather than a stage of growth or external environmental conditions.

Most early childhood educators are eclectic in their theoretical biases. That is, they have developed their own philosophies of education based on a little of each theory, as summarized in Figure 4.14. Each teacher has an obligation to develop a clear set of ideas of how children grow and learn. We are fortunate to have choices. Most educators agree on some basic tenets based, in part, on theories of development and learning.

1. Children's basic physiological needs and their needs for physical and psychological safety must be met satisfactorily before they can experience and respond to "growth motives." [Maslow]

2. Children develop unevenly and not in a linear fashion as they grow toward psychosocial maturity and psychological well-being. A wide variety of factors in children's lives, as well as the manner in which they interpret their own experiences, will have a bearing on the pattern and

Developmental Research Tells Us:	Teachers Can:
1. Growth occurs in a sequence.	Think about the steps children will take when planning projects. Know the sequence of growth in their children's age group.
2. Children in any age group will behave similarly in certain ways.	Plan for activities in relation to age range of children. Know the characteristics of their children's age group.
3. Children grow through certain stages.	Know the stages of growth in their class. Identify to family any behavior inconsistent with general stages of development.
4. Growth occurs in four interrelated areas.	Understand that a person's work in one area can help in another. Plan for language growth, while children use their bodies.
5. Intellectual growth: Children learn through their senses. Children learn by doing; adults learn in abstract ways, while children need concrete learning. Cognitive growth occurs in four areas: perception (visual, auditory, etc.) language memory	Have activities in looking, smelling, tasting, hearing, and touching. Realize that talking is abstract; have children touch, manipulate, act out what they are to do. Provide materials and activities in matching, finding same/different, putting a picture with a sound, taste, or with a symbol. Provide opportunities to find and label things, talk with grown-ups, friends, tell what it "looks like," "smells like," etc. Know that by three, a child can often remember 2–3 directions.

FIGURE 4.15 Developmental research tests theories of growth and learning to find out about children and childhood.

Developmental Research Tells Us:	Teachers Can:
	Know that memory is helped by seeing, holding objects and people.
reasoning	Recognize that it is just beginning, so children judge on what they *see,* rather than what they reason they should see.
	Be sure adult explanations aid in understanding reasons.
	Practice finding "answers" to open-ended questions such as "How can you tell when you are tired?"
6. Social growth: The world *is* only from the child's viewpoint. Seeing is believing.	Expect that children will know their ideas only. Be aware that the rights of others are minimal to them. Remember that if they cannot see the situation, they may not be able to talk about it.
Group play is developing.	Provide free-play sessions, with places to play socially. Understand that group play in structured situations is hard, because of "self" orientation.
Independence increases as competence grows.	Know that children test to see how far they can go. Realize that children will vary from independent to dependent (both among the group, and within one child).
People are born not knowing when it is safe to go on. Adult attention is very important.	Understand that children will need to learn by trial and error. Know the children individually. Be with the child, not just with the group.
Young children are not born with internal mechanism that says "slow down."	Move into a situation before children lose control.
7. Emotional growth: Self-image is developing.	Watch for what each person's self-image is becoming. Give praise to enhance good feelings about oneself. Know that giving children responsibilities helps self-image. Talk to children at eye level. Children learn by example. Model appropriate behavior by doing yourself what you want the children to do.
8. Physical growth: Muscle development is not complete. Muscles cannot stay still for long. Large muscles are better developed than small ones.	Not expect perfection, in either small- or large-muscle activity. Plan short times for children to sit. Give lots of chances to move about, be gentle with expectations for hand work.
Hand preference is being established.	Watch to see how children decide their handedness. Let children trade hands in their play.
A skill must be done several times before it is internalized.	Have available materials to be used often. Plan projects to use the same skill over and over.
Bowel and bladder control is not completely internalized.	Be understanding of "accidents." If possible, have toilet facilities available always, and keep them attractive.

FIGURE 4.15 Continued.

rate of progress toward greater social and emotional maturity. [Erikson, Vygotsky, the behaviorists, maturationists]

3. Developmental crises that occur in the normal process of growing up may offer maximum opportunities for psychological growth, but these crises are also full of possibilities for regression or even negative adaptation. [Erikson]

4. Children strive for mastery over their own private inner worlds as well as for mastery of the world outside of them. [Erikson, Piaget]

5. The child's interactions with significant persons in his life play a major part in his development. [Erikson, the behaviorists, Vygotsky, and Maslow]

Developmental Research Conclusions

Results

Research, and the information it yields, must serve the needs of the practitioner in order to be useful. Teachers can combine researchers' systematic data with personal observations and experiences, including the significance of relationships, language and thinking, biological factors, and special needs (see also Chapters 6, 10, and 12–14). To keep in mind the real child underneath all these theories, teachers apply developmental research to their own classroom settings. Figure 4.15 consolidates what developmental research has found and how it can be put into practical use with young children.

Moreover, it is important for both teachers and parents to know something about the latest research in order to be current about issues critical to children's development. For instance, are there critical periods in child growth? Is there a special time for the development of attachment, or of certain intellectual skills, or other matters? Research has revealed that animals such as ducks will become attached to any quacking or moving object approximately 15 hours after hatching. Therefore, that time is a critical period for ducks to develop "following" behavior.

Are there parallels in child development? It is harder to find such precise periods in human development, but many psychologists hold that looser, broader sensitive periods may exist. The period from 6–12 months may be a sensitive period for the formation of attachment to parents, and the period from 18–60 months may be one for motor skills.

However, other psychologists argue that children are more resilient and flexible than that, and such periods are not all that crucial. Jerome Kagan and many psychotherapists, for instance, assert that there is a potential for *plasticity* (change or growth) throughout the life span. Abused children, for instance, can recover if their environment is improved and if they have the support (therapy, remedial education, and so on) to make those changes.

We suggest that there are good reasons and research to support both positions. The entire period of early childhood is considered a kind of sensitive or critical one by many in this field. At the same time, programs such as Head Start believe in the worthiness of enrichment and intervention. Teachers use research and theory to help them make appropriate decisions in their teaching.

Decision Making in Teaching

Knowledge of child development can help teachers in the many decisions they must make daily concerning their classrooms, the curriculum, and, most important, the children. Consistent and effective teachers have a solid foundation in learning and developmental theory. Instead of basing a decision on whim or the heat of the moment, the thoughtful teacher can use theory along with sharp observation skills to set realistic goals for each child.

Consider, for instance, how useful child development information is in the following circumstances:

15-month-old Kenya and Peter are crying and fussy this morning. The teacher pauses, then realizes that neither has been outdoors yet or eaten a snack. Scheduling regular times for active movement keeps children comfortable; knowing children's physical developmental needs (maturation theory) will help these children.

Mario and Therese, both in wheelchairs, joined the first grade class last month, but their parents report that neither wants to come to school. The teacher, recognizing their need to feel part of the class and their classmates' need to get acquainted with newcomers (sociocultural theory), pairs children in a project to design and build wheel toys for pets. By knowing the children's need for competence (Erikson) and level of cognitive thinking (Piaget), she encourages these six-year-olds toward greater mutual understanding and social skills.

Preschoolers Jared and Panya have been arguing about who has brought the "best" toy to child care. Knowing of their egocentrism (Piaget), the teacher realizes that both are right, but that they may be unable to see this themselves. By praising each child's toy in their presence, the teacher uses herself as a model (behavioral social learning theory) and as an example of how to behave appropriately (sociocultural theory), as she demonstrates how the two children—and their toys—can play together.

Finally, the teacher well versed in child development theory can offer this information to parents. Parents can share the intimate, in-depth view of their children while teachers offer their perspective regarding learning and growth. Together, parents and teachers can make decisions about the child on the basis of concrete, truthful information.

Conditions for Learning

Teachers also look for the best conditions for learning. Caring for children means providing for total growth, in the best possible environment. Developmental theory helps define conditions which enhance learning and from which positive learning environments are created. Research on all theories extends the knowledge of children and learning.

Coupled with practical application, both theory and research have helped all to recognize that:

1. *Learning must be real.* We teach about the children's bodies, their families, their neighborhoods, and their school. We start with who children are and expand this to include the world, in their terms. We give them the words, the ideas, the ways to question and figure things out for themselves.

2. *Learning must be rewarding.* Practice makes better, but only if it is all right to practice, to stumble, and try again. We include the time to do all this, by providing an atmosphere of acceptance and of immediate feedback as to what was accomplished (even what boundary was just overstepped). Also, practice can make a good experience even better, as it reminds children in their terms of what they can do.

3. *Learning must build on children's lives.* We help connect the family to the child and the teacher. We realize that children learn about culture from family and knowledgeable members of the community, such as teachers, librarians, grocers, and the like. We know important family events and help the family support happenings at school. For children learning goes on wherever they may be, awake and asleep. Parents can learn to value learning and help it happen for their child.

4. *Learning needs a good stage.* Healthy bodies make for alert minds, so good education means caring for children's health. This includes physical health, and emotional and mental health, too. Psychological safety and well-being are theoretical terms for the insight, availability, and awareness teachers bring to their classrooms. On the lookout for each child's successes, we prevent distractions in the way furniture is arranged, how noisy it is, how many strangers are around. Mental health is both emotional and intellectual. We try to have a variety of materials and experiences, and a flexible schedule, when someone is pursuing an idea, building a project, finishing a disagreement. As long as we care for children, we will have our hands full. With the theoretical underpinnings presented here, we have the tools with which to make our own way into the world of children and of early childhood education.

CHILD DEVELOPMENT AND CULTURAL DIVERSITY

In many ways, each child is like every other. Certain universals hold for all children, and know-

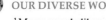

OUR DIVERSE WORLD OUR DIVERSE WORLD OUR DIVERSE WORLD OUR DIVERSE WORLD OUR DIVERSE WORLD

[1]Many people liken our multicultural society to a *tossed salad* (with many unique contributions to a unified whole); rather than thinking of our society as a *melting pot* (in which all of the ingredients blend into one.)

ing them, teachers can apply child development and learning theories. There are limits on such application, however, because some differences among children exist as a result of cultural commonalities and each child's uniqueness.[1] Caldwell (1983) outlines these three areas so that teachers can make child development useful without overgeneralizing:

First, all children have the same needs and rights, go through the same developmental stages, and have the same developmental goals. Cross-cultural research on Piagetian theory has demonstrated that the stages of development are invariant and hold true world-wide, although the ages vary between cultures and among individuals.

Second, children are like each other in some ways; for example, there are similarities within cultural groups. Certain cultural and social expectations will bring about commonalities in how soon youngsters use writing tools or in ways of self-expression. This means that, while all two-year-olds are in the process of developing language, the actual rate of vocabulary increase will differ according to how important language expression is to the cultural and familial groups. What certain children have in common may be broad—from patterns of socializing to cognitive style—but is culture-bound. Teachers without appropriate knowledge of their students' cultures run a risk of misapplying developmental theories and norms.

Third, each child is like no other in many respects. What is unique comes from genetic make-up, temperament, energy level, sensory sensitivity, interests, and motivation, to name several. Child development and learning theories have limits. They can foster a global outlook about children in general, but these theories must be viewed in light of both cultural diversity and a respect for individuality. With the theoretical underpinnings presented here, teachers have the tools with which to make their own way into the world of children and of early childhood education.

S U M M A R Y

The twentieth century has been called "the century of the child." Developmental and learning theories of this century form the cornerstone of our knowledge about children. What we know about how children grow, learn, and adapt to the world around them is critical in our quest for greater understanding of the people we serve. Our field is greater for the contributions of several schools of study. Erikson's theory of psychosocial development gives us insight into children's feelings and how their emotional and social lives affect their learning. The behaviorists, a distinctively American group of psychologists, demonstrate how much we can learn of human affairs by applying the methods of science. Piaget, a "giant in the nursery school" (Elkind, 1977), opens our eyes to a stage theory of growth and shows us how active children are in their own learning. Vygotsky reminds us of how values, beliefs, skills, and traditions are transmitted to the next generation within a "zone of promixal development" based on relationships with other people. Gesell offers us developmental norms. Maslow, a humanistic psychologist, establishes a hierarchy of needs, reminding us that the basic physical and psychological needs must be met before higher learning can take place.

In learning about these theories, we are more able to formulate our own philosophy of education. By tracing our roots to these learning theories, we show our willingness to make a commitment to children. What we know about growth and development helps us fight for our most important resource—our children.

R E V I E W   Q U E S T I O N S

1. Match the theorist with the appropriate description:

   B.F. Skinner   Sex differences
   Abraham Maslow   Attachment
   Jean Piaget   Social learning
   Albert Bandura   Zone of proximal development
   Mary Ainsworth   Psychosocial development
   Eleanor Maccoby   Behaviorism
   Erik Erikson   Developmental norms
   Arnold Gesell   Cognitive theory
   Lev Vgotsky   Self-actualization

2. Describe Piaget's four stages of cognitive development and their implications for early childhood education.

3. Name at least three psychologists who have contributed to the knowledge of development. Describe your reaction to each.

4. Given five theories of learning and development, which one would most likely advocate large blocks of free play? An early academic program? Open-ended questioning by teachers? Regular early mealtime?

L E A R N I N G   A C T I V I T I E S

1. You are a teacher in a large urban child care center. Your children arrive by 7:00, and usually stay until after 5:00 each day. What would you do first thing in the morning? Use Maslow's hierarchy of needs to justify your answer.

2. What do you think of cartoons? From a social learning perspective, what kind of television would you have your daughter watch?

3. You are a teacher in a middle-class suburban preschool. What do you know about your group's needs and developmental stage? What does their cultural background tell you about what to teach? How will you find out about what each child is ready to learn?

4. Observe children in a child care center as they say goodbye to their parents. What can this tell you about their attachment levels? What can teachers do to support attachment and also help children separate?

B I B L I O G R A P H Y

General Texts

Bee, Helen. *The Developing Child.* New York: Harper Collins, 1995.

Berger, Kathleen S. *The Developing Person.* 4th ed. New York: Worth Publishers, 1995.

Fong, Bernadine, and Resnick, Miriam. *The Child: Development Through Adolescence.* Palo Alto, CA: Mayfield, 1986.

Gardner, Howard. *Developmental Psychology.* Boston: Little, Brown and Co., 1982.

McClinton, Barbara S., and Meier, Blanche G. *Beginnings: Psychology of Early Childhood.* St. Louis: C.V. Mosby Co., 1978.

Schickedanz, Hansen, and Forsyth. *Understanding Children.* Mountain View, CA; Mayfield Publishing Co., 1993.

Psychodynamic Theory

Erikson, E.H. "A Healthy Personality for Every Child." In Mussen, Paul H.; Conger, John J.; and Kagan, Jerome (eds.), *Child Development and Personality*, 3rd ed. New York: Harper and Row, 1969.

—————. *Childhood and Society*, 2nd ed. New York: W.W. Norton and Co., 1963.

—————. "Toys and Reasons." In Haworth, M.R. (ed.), *Child Psychotherapy: Practice and Theory.* New York: Basic Books, 1964.

Freud, Sigmund. *A General Introduction to Psychoanalysis.* New York: Washington Square Press, 1968.

Hubley, John, and Hubley, Faith. *Everyone Rides the Carousel.* Santa Monica, Calif.: Pyramid Films, 1976.

Behaviorist Theory

Carpenter, Findley. *The Skinner Primer.* New York: The Free Press, 1974.

Krumboltz, John, and Krumboltz, Helen. *Changing Children's Behavior.* Englewood Cliffs, N.J.: Prentice-Hall, 1972.

Skinner, *Science and Human Behavior.* New York: MacMillan Co., 1953.

Cognitive Theory

Dasen, Pierre R. (ed.) *Piagetian Psychology: Cross-Cultural Contributions.* New York: Gardner Press, Inc. (div. of John Wiley), 1977.

Demetriow, Andreas (ed.) *The Neo-Piagetian Theories of Cognitive Development: Toward and Integration.* New York: Elsevier Science Publishing Co., Inc., 1988.

Elkind, David. "Giant in the Nursery School—Jean Piaget." In Hetherington, E.M., and Parke, R.D. (eds.), *Contemporary Readings in Psychology.* New York: McGraw-Hill, 1977.

Elkind, D. and Flavell, J. (eds.) *Essays in Honor of Jean Piaget.* New York: Oxford University Press, 1969.

Ellison, Launa. "What Does the Brain Have to Do with Learning?" *Holistic Education Review*, Fall, 1990.

Labinowicz, Ed. *The Piaget Primer: Thinking, Learning, Teaching.* Menlo Park, CA: Addison-Wesley, 1980, pp. 41–46.

Sociocultural Theory

Badrava, E. "Vygotsky's theory." Paper presented at seminar, New Orleans, La.: National Association for the Education of Young Children, November, 1992.

Berk, Laura E., *Infants, Children and Adolescents*. Boston: Allyn and Bacon, 1996 (2nd Ed.) and Berk, Laura E. "Why Children Talk to Themselves," *Scientific American* 271(5), November 1994, pp. 78–83.

Frauenglass, M.H., and Diaz, R.M. "Self-Regulatory Functions of Children's Private Speech; A Critical Analysis of Recent Challenges to Vygotsky's Theory." *Developmental Psychology*, 21, 1985, pp. 357–364.

Lipman, M. "Squaring Soviet Pedagogical Theory with American Practice." *Education Digest* Vol. 48, October, 1991, pp. 72–76.

Rogoff, B. *Appreciation in Thinking: Cognitive Development in a Social Context*. New York: Oxford University Press, 1990.

Vygotsky, L.S. *Mind in Society: The Development of Higher Psychological Processes*. Cambridge, Mass.: Harvard University Press, 1978.

——————. *Thinking and Speech* (N. Minick, translator). New York: Plenum Press, 1987.

Maturation Theory

Ames, Louise B., et al., *The Gesell Institute's Child from One to Six, The Gesell Institute's Child from Five to Ten.*, and *The Infant in Today's Culture*. New York: Harper & Row, 1979+.

Humanist Theory

Goble, Frank G. *The Third Force: The Psychology of Abraham Maslow*. New York: Grossman Publishers, 1970.

Maslow, Abraham H. *Motivation and Personality*. New York: Harper & Row, 1954.

Other Educational Theories

General

Caldwell, Bettye. "Child Development and Global Diversity." Future 8 OMEP World Assembly, Geneva, Switzerland, August 1983.

Moyer, Joan. "Child Development as a Base for Decision Making." *Childhood Education*, May–June 1986.

Murphy, Lois B., and Leeper, Ethel M. "Conditions for Learning." Washington, D.C.: U.S. Department of Health, Education, and Welfare, 1973.

Attachment

Ainsworth, Mary. "The Development of Infant-Mother Attachment." In Caldwell, Bettye, ed. *Review of Child Development Research* (Vol. III). Chicago: University of Chicago Press, 1973.

Bowlby, John. *Attachment and Loss* (Vol. I & II). New York: Basic Books, 1969, 1973.

Waters, E., and Deane, K.E. "Infant-mother attachment: theories, models, recent data, and some tasks for comparative developmental analysis." In L.W. Hoffman et al., eds. *Parenting: Its Causes and Consequences*. Hillsdale, NJ: Lawrence Erlebaum, 1982.

Sex Differences

Bee, Helen, ed. *Social Issues in Developmental Psychology.* New York. Harper & Row, 1978.

Maccoby, E.E., and Jacklin, C.N. *The Development of Sex Differences.* Stanford, CA: Stanford University Press, 1974.

Matthews, W.S. *He and She: How Children Develop Their Sex Role Identity.* Englewood Cliffs, NJ: Prentice-Hall, 1979.

Tavris, C., and Offir, C. *The Longest War: Sex Differences in Perspective.* New York: Harcourt Brace Jovanovich, 1977.

Moral Development

Buzzelli, Cary A. "Young Children's Moral Understanding: Learning About Right and Wrong." *Young Children*, September, 1992, pp. 47–53.

Eisenberg, Nancy, et al. "Prosocial Development in Middle Childhood: a Longitudinal Study." In *Developmental Psychology*, 23, 712–718.

Gilligan, Carol. *In a Different Voice.* Cambridge, MA: Harvard University Press, 1982.

Kohlberg, Lawrence. *The Philosophy of Moral Development.* New York: Harper & Row, 1981.

Wadsworth, Barry J. *Piaget's Theory of Cognitive and Affective Development.* 93rd ed. New York: Longman, Inc.

GUEST EDITORIAL

Who Are the Teachers of the Young Child?

Douglas R. Powell

The usual response to this question is to think of the millions of early childhood educators who devote a good portion of their lives to helping young children get off to a good start. The number of early childhood teachers has grown in leaps and bounds in the past two decades because our society has increasingly recognized the long-term benefits of high-quality programs of early childhood education and care.

Professional early childhood educators are not the only teachers of young children. Parents represent another huge group of adults who have powerful effects on young children. Parents may not think of themselves as teachers of their young child, yet the impact of families on children's development cannot be overlooked. Findings from longitudinal research indicate that the quality of the home environment in the early years is a good predictor of academic achievement and school success many years later.

The field of early childhood education has long recognized the need for staff in early childhood programs to work closely with parents. A persistent theme in the field is that goals for children are best achieved when the important adults in a child's life agree on and are consistent about the way they deal with children. A related theme is that parent-teacher cooperation helps ease children's separation from home and entry into an early childhood program. Meaningful collaborations between parents and early childhood programs also are expected to strengthen parents' skills and confidence in managing relations with major institutions in their child's life, including schools.

The standards for professional practice in early childhood programs developed by the National Association for the Education of Young Children include staff-parent interaction as a component of a high-quality program. For example, parents are to be well informed about the program and welcome at all times as observers and contributors. Frequent and respectful communications between program staff and parents are central to good work with children.

What does it take to establish and maintain solid relations with parents? A good starting point is to understand and respect parents. Parenthood is a developmental process with stages that present unique tasks for parents. When children are of preschool age, for instance, a developmental task before parents is to figure out what type of authority to maintain over the child and how to handle relations with other authority figures in the child's everwidening social world. What might be the role of teachers in helping parents with this task? Understanding and respect also require an appreciation of the parent's point of view, including family circumstances and demands in a parent's daily life. Taking the perspective of another is the key to good relationships.

Partnerships with parents require an understanding of the special roles of families and early childhood programs in a child's life. Because family and program contribute in unique ways to a child's development, a complementary rather than competitive arrangement should be possible. The special nature of the child's interests, views, and needs must be considered, too. This means the topic or focus of a teacher's discussions with parents will be different from parent to parent because each child and family bring unique agendas and issues to a program.

Communication with parents flows best when it is frequent and not limited to problems. It is important to share information that will benefit the child, to listen to each other, and to work toward a mutual understanding of how best to support a child's development. Early childhood teachers need to include a family's interests and culture in a program. Good programs are extensions of families.

Teachers benefit when they are open to the professional and personal growth that comes from meaningful relationships with families. Asking the question, "How will I change and grow from my work with parents?" is an approach to partnerships that acknowledges the resourcefulness of parents and the dynamic nature of relationships. To be sure, programs and staff stand to gain in significant ways when respect and equality prevail in relationships with parents. Neither teacher nor parent can "go it alone" in this increasingly complex society. Our challenge is to work collaboratively to create the best possible environments for young children.

Douglas R. Powell is Chair of the Department of Child Development and Family Studies at Purdue University and has written extensively on parent relationships and support.

QUESTIONS FOR THOUGHT

What makes the teacher's role complex?

What qualifications does a good teacher possess?

What is team teaching in early childhood?

What are the essentials for successful teaching?

How does my own personal development relate to my growth as a teacher?

What is a professional code of ethics and why should we have one?

What are some of the common problems associated with beginning teaching, and how can I avoid them?

What does it mean to be a member of the teaching profession?

How can teachers be culturally competent?

WHO ARE THE TEACHERS OF THE YOUNG CHILD?

Margarita had always wanted to be an early childhood teacher. Right after high school she went to a community college and earned her AA degree. Shortly after her first child was born, she became a licensed family child care provider and cares for infants and toddlers in her own home. It is important to Margarita that she feels she is making a contribution to the family's well-being as well as enjoying a satisfying career. She plans to pursue her BA degree in the evenings when her children are older.

Paul spent several years teaching in a school for emotionally disturbed children. He has been a lead teacher for four-year-olds at the child care center for two years, gaining experience with children whose developmental patterns are typical. Paul wants to remain a teacher but is concerned about the salary levels. He has given himself one more year before he will make a decision.

Kendra's four children were in parent cooperative nursery schools, where she enjoyed the companionship of so many other parents of young children. After a few years of teaching elementary school, she is now Director of a parent co-op and teaches children from ages 2 to 5. She particularly enjoys leading weekly parent discussion groups.

Elva was the most sought after parent-aide in the school after she began helping out when her two boys were ages 4 and 5. This success stimulated her to get an AA degree in early childhood education, then a Bachelor's degree in child development. She is now a kindergarten teacher in a bilingual program.

While all of these people had different motivations, they all were drawn to the early childhood classroom. They may teach in different settings, have different educational backgrounds and skills, yet they do share common everyday experiences of the teacher of young children. They plan, observe, listen, help, learn, play, console, discipline, confer, comfort, and teach the children and adults who make up their particular world of early childhood.

Comparison to Teaching in Other Educational Settings

The nature of teaching in the early years is unlike that of other age groups. At first glance, the differences in teaching preschool and older children may outweigh any similarities. There are some common elements, however, that link the two. Early childhood teachers teach what other teachers teach. The curriculum in the early years is rich in math, science, social studies, history, language, art, and geography, as it is in any other grade. Early childhood teachers and their elementary and high school counterparts share many of the frustrations of the teaching profession—long hours, low pay, and a people-intensive workplace. They also share the joy of teaching—the opportunity to influence children's lives and the satisfaction of meeting the daily challenges that teaching children provides. Figure 5.1 highlights the similarities and differences between early childhood teachers and others.

THE TEACHER'S ROLE

Definitions

Over the years the teacher's role in the early childhood classroom has been defined in many ways. The number and variety of tasks teachers perform are innumerable. According to Spodek (1972), the teacher is part lecturer, storyteller, traffic director, conflict mediator, psychological diagnostician, custodian, and file clerk. Stanton (Beyeer, 1968), a pioneer early childhood teacher, adds plumber, carpenter, poet, and musician to the list, as well as degrees and training in psychology, medicine, and sociology. "Now, at 83, she's ready!" says Stanton.

This diversity is exactly what makes teaching in the early years so appealing. The multiple roles a teacher plays add challenge to the job. Nor are these descriptions exhaustive; the list could include adult educator, parent resource, faculty member, chief purchasing agent, nurse, program planner, staff supervisor, business manager, treasurer, personnel director, employee, and employer. (The role of the teacher in relationship to parents and programs as a whole will be further discussed in Chapters 8 and 10, respectively.)

Two prominent early childhood teacher educators reinforce the value of having teachers who have a theoretical and historical grounding. Jones (1994) tells us that teachers, like young children,

Elements of Teaching and Learning	Early Childhood Settings	Elementary and High School Settings
How teaching and learning takes place	Through teacher/child interactions and concrete use of materials	Through lectures and demonstrations that are teacher dominated
	Guides children toward discovery	Teaches subject matter
Play opportunities	Primary learning medium is play	Usually just at recess
Opportunity for child to make choices	Many choices throughout the day both inside and out	Few options—students do same activity most of the day
Classroom environment	Abundant floor space, many activity centers, variety of materials	Rows of desks and tables
Daily schedule	Large blocks of time for unlimited exploration of materials and for play	45-minute to 1-hour periods on subject matter
Small group interactions	Majority of teaching	Much less frequent
Outdoor activity	Teachers involved as intensively as they are in the classroom	Others usually supervise play yard—little direct teacher interaction
Parent relationships	Frequent, if not daily, contact	May see them once a year
Working with other adults	Often works with aide, assistant teachers, and parents	Usually teaches alone
Educational materials	Toys, games, natural materials, blocks	Textbooks and worksheets
Evaluating students	Observational and anecdotal assessments	Grades, tests, and report cards
	Emphasis on growth of whole child	Standardized academic assessment
Age range of students	May have 2-2 1/2 year age span or greater	Usually same age
Art, music and physical education	Available throughout the day as an ongoing part of curriculum	Restricted to a special class, time, or teacher
Teacher training	Strong child development foundation	Emphasis on subject matter

FIGURE 5.1 The nature of teaching in the early years is unlike that of other age groups.

are constructivists. The complexity and unpredictability of teaching, she says, call for on-the-spot decisions, and those decisions are based on developmental and learning theory and constructed from the teacher's own experience and practice. Spodek (1994) calls for teachers to know the history and traditions of the field along with theory but alos stresses the need to know "the cultural, social and political contexts in which early childhood education functions."

Teaching is defined as those daily "acts of creation" (Phillips, 1994) and are constructed from the teacher's own repertoire of skills, knowledge, and training, added to what he or she observes about children and her interactions with their families. The teacher as a collaborator with others—children, parents, and other teachers—is a significant part of the teacher's role definition in the schools of Reggio Emilia, Italy, as well (see Chapter 11), and reinforce the notion underlying many definitions that teachers are, first and foremost, lifelong learners.

Perhaps the job would seem more manageable and less overwhelming to the new teacher if some of the responsibilities were categorized. What teachers do with children is not all there is to teaching. Much of the work takes place outside the classroom. It is helpful to look at the teacher's role in another way. What are the things a teacher does with children? What are the things a teacher does after the children go home? How does the teacher interact with other adults in the early childhood setting?

In the Classroom

Interacting with Children

It is no secret that most teachers find their greatest satisfaction and challenges in the first role—who and what they are with children. The teacher-child interactions, the spur-of-the-moment crisis, the intense activity, the on-the-spot decisions, the loving and nurturing, go far in making one "feel" like a real teacher. Helping Rhonda get a good grip on the hammer, soothing Josh and Benno after they bump heads, and talking with Alexa about her drawing are at the heart of teaching young children. These encounters are enjoyable and provide moments for interactive teaching opportunities. These times help establish good relationships with the children. It is during these spontaneous, anything-can-happen-and-probably-will times that teachers display their craftsmanship. The real art of teaching comes on the floor of the classroom. All teaching skills are called upon in short order. Responses are automatic and sometimes unplanned. Teachers intuitively call upon their knowledge base, their experience, and their proven techniques. Almost unconsciously, they reach back in their minds for all those things they know about children. Throughout the school day they apply that combination of knowledge and know-how.

> The creative genius of a teacher is in the ability to find ways to interact with each child according to that child's needs, to stretch an attention span, motivate a child to persist at a task, or provide opportunity to experiment with materials, actively and autonomously.
>
> (Honig, 1979)

Managing the Classroom

A teacher spends a lot of time being a classroom manager. Being a successful manager is a little like being a successful juggler. Both require the ability to think about and react to more than three things at once. With a simple gesture, a significant look, or merely moving nearby, the teacher maintains the ongoing activity.

Anticipating a clash between Nathan and Julie, the teacher Miriam intervenes, redirects them, and moves away. At the same time she has kept a watchful eye on Bobby at the bathroom sink. Passing close to Francie, she touches the child's shoulder in brief acknowledgment, smiling down as Francie struggles with the doll's dress. Miguel and Lea run up to her, grab her by the skirt and hand, and pull her toward the science display. They need to ask her something about the snake...NOW! Jake, the handyman, has come into the classroom wanting to know exactly which of the climbers needs repair. Sarah, the parent volunteer, waves to her; it's time to check on the corn bread baking in the kitchen. Quickly, the teacher files a mental note of the names of the children who accompany Sarah to the kitchen. As she reaches for a copy of *Ranger Rick* (the one with the great snake pictures in it), she observes Angie and her father entering the

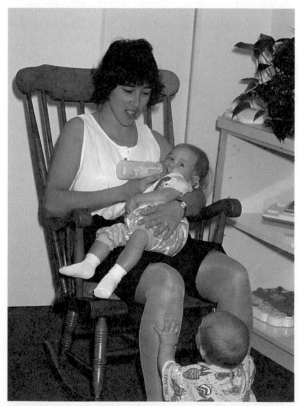

FIGURE 5.2   Teachers model learning, listening, and loving.

room. They both look upset. Telling Miguel and Lea she will return, the teacher walks over to greet the latecomers. As she moves past Doug, the student teacher, she comments on how well his language game is going and suggests he continue for another five minutes. Glancing at the clock, she realizes it is almost cleanup time. Her assistant, Chuck, watches her. She looks his way, and a nonverbal signal passes between them. Without a word, they both understand that snacks will be a little late today. Angie's father begins to explain their delay as the teacher bends down to invite the child to come and look at the new snake cage with her.

In this setting, the teacher has a major role in supervising a number of people. Aides and volunteers, student teachers, and visitors add to the richness of a program. But it is the teacher who coordinates and supervises their various functions. From the description, it is clear that the teacher's role as a supervisor and manager includes being:

● caretaker for a safe environment

● observer of and listener to children

● on-the-spot teacher trainer for students, aides, and volunteers

● on-site supervisor for student teachers

● a liaison and communicator with parents

Setting the Tone

Teachers, obviously, are at the center of activity. Directly or indirectly they control much of the action. Since teachers are responsible for what occurs in the classroom, they must have a finger on its pulse at all times. As part of the juggling act, the teacher takes that pulse while moving around the class or yard. But something else happens. Throughout the day, from the moment of arrival, the teacher puts into effect another vital element. The teacher sets the tone, creating an atmosphere in which teachers and children will work and play. The skill with which it is done can make the critical difference between a classroom that is alive and supportive and one that is chaotic or apathetic. Be-

cause personality has such impact in the early childhood setting, the teacher creates more than an environmental mood, does more than provide the setting and the learning activities.

The teacher establishes what will be the **emotional framework.** This is done with body movements, by the tone of voice, facial expressions or lack of them, and nonverbal as well as verbal gestures. The way the children respond reflects this tone.

This interaction between the atmosphere the teacher creates and the child's behavior sets the tone. Young children are very sensitive to adult moods and attitudes. The teacher who is upset or angry invites the children to react with their own tense brand of activity. A teacher who exudes calm and confidence, strength and support, will inspire a more relaxed, comfortable atmosphere in which children can learn and grow. If the teacher is punitive and harsh, the tone of the classroom will reflect that. On the other hand, if teachers act on their beliefs that children deserve respect and are intelligent, capable human beings, they will create an entirely different climate. And the children will respond in kind.

Normal behavior for the young child includes tantrums, crying, resistance, curiosity, impatience, emotional swings, noise, and self-centeredness. This is the time to achieve a sense of their own separate self. They need a place to work through the developmental stages that their needs and nature indicate. The atmosphere that a teacher creates is a key element in that process.

The way teachers handle fights, react to tears, the words they use, and the voices raised communicate a direct message to the child. The understanding, the soothing, the warmth, the acceptance, create a climate where children feel safe, secure, and guided. This requires teachers who respect childhood, the individuality of children, their growing patterns, their emerging feelings, and their special capacity to learn. Today we would also stress the need for teachers to become culturally competent: to accept and understand cultural differences, having a working knowledge of the cultural backgrounds of the children in the class, and appreciate that this may be the children's first experience outside their own culture.[1] The end re-

OUR DIVERSE WORLD OUR DIVERSE WORLD OUR DIVERSE WORLD OUR DIVERSE WORLD OUR DIVERSE WORLD
[1]Emotional support is evident when children see that their family culture is valued.

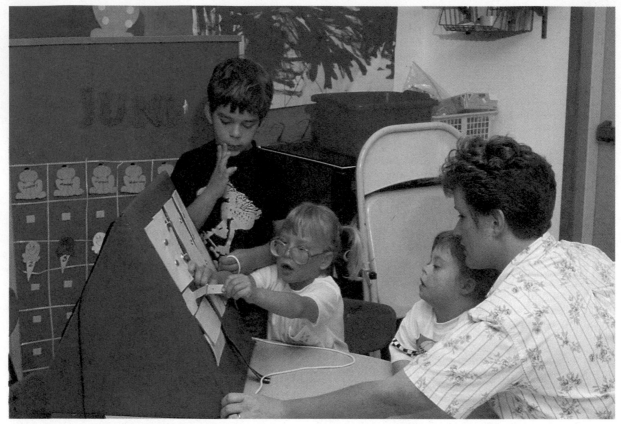

FIGURE 5.3   The teacher determines the quality of the child's school experience by providing a supportive atmosphere in which children can learn.

sult is that preschoolers will thrive in an atmosphere influenced by teachers who understand this time of tension and growth in their lives.

Planning and Evaluating Curriculum

As teachers move through the school day interacting with children, managing the classroom, sensing the tone, they consciously or unconsciously evaluate what is happening:

● The relay race outdoors produced more tears than cheers; most of the children were interested in participating when the game started but drifted away. Why?

● The Cuisenaire rods were never touched today. How can we make this a more inviting activity?

● The toddlers are beginning to participate fully in the "Eensy Weensy Spider" fingerplay. What might they like to learn next?

The teacher notes where and how children played, the quality of their interactions, and possible "next steps" in curriculum. These notes are then discussed with other staff members at the end of the day or in weekly planning sessions.

Effective ways to develop curriculum planning are discussed in Chapter 11. It is important to note here, in discussing the role of the teacher, that the process has its roots in what the teacher sees happening in the classroom as children play and learn. It is constructivist theory in action: teachers watching and observing children in order to give meaning and support to their learning. Early childhood teachers use their observation skills, collect data as they work with children, and build curriculum around their knowledge of actual classroom practice and behavior.

Outside the Classroom

There are some after-hours tasks that are a part of any total teaching effort. There are quite a few of these responsibilities that may be taken for granted. This part of the job may not be as gratifying as working directly with children, yet teachers must understand why it is important.

A good classroom is often dependent on how teachers spend their time away from the children. Many of the tasks that give added strength and depth to a teacher's curriculum are those which, out of necessity, must be accomplished after hours. The two most obvious jobs that fall into this category are record keeping and meetings.

Record Keeping

Preschool teachers keep records on a variety of subjects; the type and kind will vary from school to school. The philosophy of the school, the number of children, the background of the teaching staff, and the purpose for the records will determine the amount the teachers will write. In schools that rely on government funding, record keeping is not optional. The children's progress, the teacher's performance, the program itself, must be evaluated on a regular basis. The data collected will be used to justify the continuation of the program; thus, the paperwork becomes critical to survival. Laboratory schools, teacher training centers, and other programs consider periodic developmental reports on the children as a natural part of teaching; they guide the teacher in more objective ways than casual observations.

While report writing and record keeping may be considered time-consuming, they are essential to any good early childhood program. The ultimate reason for collecting data is to give a more complete and up-to-date picture of each child. Recorded observations, notes, and similar data collected over a 6-month period, for instance, may show that Abraham is not participating in any strenuous physical activity and studiously avoids activities that involve balancing and climbing. This information could lead to a medical evaluation

and diagnosis of possible perceptual motor problems.[1] Once teachers understand the importance and value of ongoing records, they set about the task readily.

Children's progress reports demonstrate a school's commitment to good child development practices. Teachers see them as a means for parent education and information. Curriculum plans and learning activities sprout from such reports and records. It wasn't until such data was collected for entry into first grade that the kindergarten teachers realized most of the children were not sufficiently skilled with the scissors. They were able to plan curriculum experiences around this need and provide an opportunity for the classes to learn a necessary task.

Teachers also find that the social-emotional growth recorded periodically provides information from which insight and interpretation can develop. It may be just a brief note taken on the run, a thoughtful anecdote written at length after class, or a checklist of the child's favorite activities. All of these serve to give teachers a greater understanding of the role they play. If maintaining reports after school hours supports that role, they accept the job willingly.

Meetings

Meetings are probably the most time-consuming of all out-of-class jobs. The teacher may need to communicate with the other people who are involved in the lives of the children, directly or indirectly. Parents, other teachers, baby-sitters, doctors, and social workers are some of the people with whom a teacher may want to confer. Teachers attend many different kinds of meetings. Figure 5.5 lists the most common.

Other Responsibilities

Some of a teacher's after-hours activities are intended to fortify and vitalize the classroom. Therefore, teachers:

● *Organize and collect materials* for use in class. They

[1]Early childhood teachers are in a unique position to support early identification, prevention, and treatment of developmental problems.

might collect space shuttle books from the library, find out if the bagel factory will allow field trips, or cut 18 pumpkin shapes while watching television. Teachers are also responsible for maintaining an orderly classroom. They might add pictures to the bulletin board, obtain new books and records, or replenish curriculum materials.

- *Purchase materials and equipment* that cannot be ordered. They know that the kitchen needs new mixing bowls, the supply room is low on red construction paper, and someone has to pick up fabric for pillow covers.

- *Make phone calls.* This is a quick and efficient way of keeping in touch. Teachers may call parents to check on children who are sick or absent. For children with special needs, teachers may need to contact doctors, therapists, and other specialists.

- *Attend professional conferences and workshops* and visit and observe other school settings. This type of ongoing professional education helps teachers keep abreast of the field.

- *Attend in-service training events* or study for an

advanced degree in an area related to early childhood education.

These duties are a part of the job of teaching young children but many will be shared with other teachers on the team or at the school. Though time-consuming, these responsibilities add to the creativity and care that teachers express for their classes.

THE TEACHER AS A PERSON

Personal Qualities

A teacher's personality has influence and impact. When a teacher exhibits a sense of trust, security, and support, the children echo those feelings and behaviors. Children learn to trust by being trusted; they learn respect by being respected. Children learn to understand others by being understood themselves. They learn responsibility by being treated as responsible human beings. The personal qualities of their teachers should include traits that foster those learnings.

Good teachers should have dedication, compassion, insight, flexibility, patience, energy, and

FIGURE 5.4 Planning and preparation ensure good classroom organization. Teachers need a variety of resources to help them plan their program.

self-confidence. Teachers should also be happy people who can laugh and use their sense of humor wisely. Liking children is part of wanting to work with them; teachers then feel that the job they are doing is important. Teachers need to be fair-minded, showing concern for all, regardless of color or creed. Physical and mental well-being are important, as is a demonstrated sense of responsibility and reliability. Teachers who can be both warm and loving, yet firm when expressing disapproval, have good teaching qualities.

Today, the well-rounded teacher, while maintaining a professional commitment, has other interests as well. Good teachers have an involvement with the world outside the walls of the child care center. They want to help children understand some of the real-life issues and concerns. They know that their interest in the world at large transmits itself to children.

Quality teachers personalize teaching, integrating their individuality into their work in appropriate ways. By exposing the human qualities they possess, teachers strengthen the bond between themselves and the children.

This basic description is a framework, a checklist of personal attributes, a place to begin to look at the human side of teaching. Men and women who are able to nurture and comfort children treat them as real persons and value them as children. Expressing this takes practice so that teachers do not intrude on children's well-being. Teachers do not have to sentimentalize childhood or tolerate misbehavior because it is "cute." Children deserve teachers who understand their nature and respect the limits of behavior.

> . . . The best teachers are the ones who are struggling to become more than they are, on any given day, and who demonstrate to their students that this quest to learn and to grow, to accept failure and go on to new challenges, is what life is all about.
>
> (LeShan, 1985)

Self-Awareness

To be the best teacher possible, understanding and accepting oneself is vital. **Self-awareness** will make a difference in the way teachers relate to children. Each teacher must ask, "Who and what and why am I? And how does knowing this bring some meaning into my life? How does it affect my life as a teacher?"

Teachers may also begin to realize something about themselves. They know how and why chil-

Staff Meetings	*Professional Meetings*
Held usually once a week for individual teaching teams. Purpose is to plan curriculum, set goals, and discuss children's progress. Faculty meetings for all school personnel may be held less frequently.	Attendance at workshops, seminars, in-service training. Local, state, and national conferences are sponsored by the National Association for the Education of Young Children, Association for Childhood Education International, and Child Care Coordinating Council.
Parent–Teacher Conferences	*Student–Teacher Conferences*
May be offered on a scheduled basis or they may be called by either parents or teachers as needed. Each school defines its own policy as to the number and frequency of parent contacts.	In schools used as training sites, teachers arrange time with individual students assigned to their classes.
Parent Education Meetings	*Home Visits*
Many schools offer evening programs for parents. Teacher attendance may or may not be required.	May or may not be optional. Some schools schedule them before opening day. Otherwise teachers must arrange them on their own time.

FIGURE 5.5 Teachers attend many different types of meetings, which help them create better programs, learn more about children, and learn how to become better teachers.

dren learn as they do, but they may not know about themselves as learners. Teachers communicate an authentic appreciation of learning when they have a sense of it in their own lives. Teachers might well ask themselves: "Do I see myself as a learner? Where does my learning take place? How? What happens to me when something is hard or when I make a mistake? Do I learn from other teachers? Do I learn from children?" Teachers' recognition of themselves as learning, growing persons gives an added degree of sincerity to teaching.

Asking—and then answering—these questions helps teachers gain insights into their own behavior as adults alone and as adults who work with children. In perceiving themselves as learners, for instance, they might see a similarity between their own learning style and that of some of the children in the class. Pausing to look at their own behavior when faced with a difficult task or in handling a mistake helps teachers remember what children experience each day. Opening themselves up to the possibility of learning from students stretches teachers' capacity to grow into relationships with children based on mutual respect and trust. This is especially important when teachers do not share the same cultural background or have no experience with a particular disability.[1] Opening themselves to learning from other teachers creates a foundation for mutual support, collegiality, professional mind-stretching, and deepening of friendships. The first step is self-awareness; the second step is self-acceptance. Adults who work with young children weave these insights into what they are learning about children. They also adopt these insights into their relationships with parents and other staff members. When teachers take the time to look at their own style of behavior and how it affects others, they place themselves on a par with children as learning, growing people.

Self-knowledge—examining values and personal qualities—takes courage and a willingness to risk oneself. Children, other teachers, and parents will respond. Accepting oneself is where to begin in accepting children.

FIGURE 5.6 A positive self-concept and a willingness to be open to new experiences are hallmarks of a good teacher of young children.

Attitudes and Biases

Knowingly as well as unintentionally, a teacher's values and attitudes weave their way into relationships with children, parents, and other staff members. This can be both positive and negative. One way it can be harmful is in the area of prejudice. Personal beliefs concerning race, culture, gender, handicaps, and economic status may negatively affect our teaching in ways of which we are not aware.[2] Facing prejudices about children based on long-held beliefs may be one of the most difficult things for a teacher to do. Personal histories are filled with biases. Most teachers will not have lived through the significant and powerful experience of adapting to a new culture, or learning a new language, or surviving on food stamps and aid to dependent children, or living in a wheelchair; therefore, they may be uncomfortable with people who are labeled "different" because they have faced these issues.

Teachers have opinions, born of their own experiences of what is "good" or "naughty" behavior (at least what their family thinks is such). They also feel strongly about how parents should treat their children. Children who are messy, who have

 OUR DIVERSE WORLD OUR DIVERSE WORLD OUR DIVERSE WORLD OUR DIVERSE WORLD OUR DIVERSE WORLD

[1] A teacher's life-long learning includes self-awareness and the ability to learn from others.

[2] Patricia Ramsey in her book, TEACHING AND LEARNING IN A DIVERSE WORLD (1987) provides a format for the start of a thorough self-investigation of individual attitudes and biases.

odors, whose clothes are too big or too small, who eat strange food, who don't do what girls or boys are supposed to do, bother some teachers. Some of these biases can be resolved, but only if a teacher takes the time to examine personal beliefs and biases.

Anti-Bias Movement

There is a great deal of emphasis today on what is termed the "anti-bias approach" to teaching young children. (See sections in Chapter 9, Chapter 11, and Chapter 15 for further discussion as well as Louise Derman Sparks's Guest Editorial). This concern stems from several issues: (1) significant changes in the ethnic makeup in the United States, especially in the last decade; (2) widespread racial and ethnic prejudice still prevalent in this country (Armstrong, 1991); and (3) concern on the part of early childhood educators of the harm being done to children's self-identity and self-esteem. This important movement promotes the concept that all children are born equal and are worthy of our respect; it challenges teachers to examine beliefs, attitudes, and actions that might deny any child that unconditional respect. Some teachers may be forced into further soul searching and reflection before they can untangle their anxiety and attitudes about their prejudices. Our feelings show in our contacts with children, and we do not want those feelings to damage their self-acceptance or self-appreciation. The question is not one of liking or disliking any child, it is one of teacher understanding and acceptance. By achieving that level of acceptance, teachers are better able to accept all the children with whom they work, regardless of their "likeability."

The anti-bias approach affords teachers a tremendous opportunity to: confront their own anxieties and biases; work with parents of various religious and ethnic minority groups, and learn some of their cultural norms and practices; work with parents of children with disabilities and learn more about how to improve the child's school experience; enrich the curriculum; represent accurately the broad ethnic makeup of this nation; influence the development of attitudes and values of young children toward the reality of the human condition; prevent irreparable harm to children's

FIGURE 5.7 Teachers' values and attitudes are reflected in the way they work with children.

concept of themselves; and promote greater global understanding.

As a way to begin, teachers might ask themselves a few questions:

● Do I truly foster a respect for the value of those who are somehow different from me? How?

● Do I examine my biases and look at ways I can change my own attitudes? When? How?

● Do I show a preference for children who most closely fit my own ethnic, cultural, and religious background? When? How?

● Do I somehow pass along my biases to the children I teach? When? How? With whom?

● Do I truly enjoy differences in human beings? When? With whom?

Kuster (1994) suggests five critical issues for teachers who work with children and families who speak languages other than English. First and foremost, fluency in the child's language is critical to effective communication and to maximizing the child's learning experiences. A second concern is to focus on the family's competency and learn to value the family's childrearing practices. A third point stresses a teacher's ability to preserve and enhance families' culture by learning and valuing their own first. Using the Latino culture's strong sense of family bonds, Kuster's fourth point promotes the use of multi-age grouping of children to foster social responsibility. The last is to confront one's own personal attitudes and biases.[1]

Teacher Burnout

Teacher burnout is an occupational hazard of substantial proportion and often results when a teacher is faced with a demanding work load, uncertain or inadequate rewards, and other pressures that damage work effectiveness. At its most extreme, teacher burnout can drive a good professional out of the field altogether, a common situation in early childhood settings and one that creates *one of the highest occupational turnover rates in the nation.*

Burnout, according to Dresden and Myers (1989), "does not result from what we do or when we do it so much as it comes from *a sense of not being able to make a visible impact* . . . on children . . . parents . . . (other) teachers . . . in the working setting . . . or in society." This results in low morale, stress, and disillusionment in a profession where staff quality is the most important single factor in program quality. A school climate where open communication, trust, satisfying interpersonal relations, and clarity of roles and responsibilities exist helps create a positive atmosphere where burnout is less likely to occur (Jorde-Bloom, 1988). In such a climate, where teachers can meet children's needs and program goals can be more effectively addressed, feelings of job satisfaction and productivity will prevail.

Recent research suggests a number of characteristics that produce healthy, happy, and positive school climates:

- friendly, supportive, and trusting staff relationships;
- emphasis on personal and professional growth;
- leadership with clear expectations that encourages and supports staff;
- clearly defined roles and policies;
- fairness and equity regarding promotions, raises, and other rewards;

- staff involved in decision-making;
- agreement among staff on goals and objectives;
- emphasis on efficiency and good planning;
- an equipped and cared-for physical environment to work in; and
- the ability to adapt to change (Jorde-Bloom, 1988).

It is the responsibility of every teacher on the staff to work together to create the kind of climate that enhances success and satisfaction in the workplace. Elsewhere in this text (Chapter 10, Evaluations, and Chapter 15, Issues and Trends) are related discussions.

BECOMING A TEACHER

A Collaborative Effort

The heart of teaching is, of course, what happens when you begin to work in a classroom every day. The teaching role is not restricted to working with children, though. Numerous adults must be met, tolerated, worked with, and included in the total teaching picture. Some of these people may be:

- other professional teachers, aides, and student teachers
- volunteers
- program directors and administrators
- school support personnel: clerical and janitorial staffs, food service workers, bus drivers
- parents
- consultants and specialists

The majority of these interactions will be with other teachers, and these relationships are among the most important a teacher can have.

The beginning teacher may join a team of teachers or may teach in a small class alone. This will depend on many factors, including the age level of the children, licensing or accrediting requirements, the size of the classroom, and the

OUR DIVERSE WORLD OUR DIVERSE WORLD OUR DIVERSE WORLD OUR DIVERSE WORLD OUR DIVERSE WORLD

[1]Teachers may need to learn new skills to effectively enhance a child's sense of self.

school's philosophy and practices. With infant programs, for instance, there is a higher ratio of adults per child (NAEYC suggests as optimal a ratio of 1 to 4), so it is more likely there will be several teachers in one classroom. Together they will shape, direct, and participate in that program as a team of teachers. The team approach is common in many nursery schools and child care centers where larger groups of children attend. Kindergarten, first, and second grade teachers generally teach alone in self-contained classrooms, sometimes with an aide. In extended day, after-school programs, high school and college students may make up the rest of the team.

Most teams of teachers are comprised of people with varying skills, experience, and training. A typical group will have a lead or head teacher—someone who is trained in child development or early childhood education. Assistants with less experience and training add support. Student teachers, interns, and volunteers may round out the group. A resource teacher—someone who specializes in art, music, or physical development, for instance—may also be available on a part-time basis.

Many state regulations mandate a minimum number of adults in the early childhood setting, and this minimum varies with the ages of the children. The prescribed ratio of adult to children changes as the children mature and become able to function in more independent ways.

There are many reasons why teaching in teams is such an integral part of so many early childhood programs. The advantages are numerous:

● *Variety of Adult Role Models.* Teachers who are male, female, disabled, young, middle-aged, older, varying in ethnic backgrounds bring equally diverse attitudes, approaches to children, interests, skills, and knowledge to share, teaching children to accept differences in people as they watch adults interact with others on the teaching team.[1]

● *Support for Children.* The absence of one teacher is not as disruptive when the children can count on other familiar faces. This enables children to learn to trust the teaching environment, since

someone they know is always there.

● *Collegiality.* Teachers can find friendship and support from one another as they share planning, problems, and achievements and grow in admiration and respect for one another.

● *Lightened Workload.* There is a sharing of all the teaching tasks, from curriculum planning and clean up to parent conferencing and record keeping.

● *Enriched Program.* Talents and resources of the team are used to best advantage so that team members will teach to their strengths, adding richness to the program.

Most of the disadvantages of team teaching stem from communication problems among team members. The following ten guidelines to successful teaching are particularly useful for team situations. Teachers new to the team teaching process will want to discuss them with other team members.

Good teachers are "complicated human beings with strengths and weaknesses, talents and limitations, good days and bad days" (LeShan, 1985). They work at becoming good teachers by developing skills in interpersonal relationships with other adults, just as they promote good social relationships between the young children they teach.

Communication problems and conflicts arise in every teaching situation. The following guidelines will help teachers promote good working relationships. These guidelines focus on working with others in the school setting; parent-teacher relationships are discussed in Chapter 8.

Ten Essentials of Successful Teaching

Ten essential attributes of successful teaching are:

1. professionalism
2. a satisfying role
3. flexibility
4. open and frequent communication

OUR DIVERSE WORLD OUR DIVERSE WORLD OUR DIVERSE WORLD OUR DIVERSE WORLD OUR DIVERSE WORLD

[1]The early childhood educator needs to remember to create a DIVERSE WORLD in the professional community; as well as in the community of children and their families.

5. self-awareness

6. mutual respect and acceptance

7. team spirit and empathy

8. a willingness to share the spotlight

9. clearly defined roles

10. evaluation

Each of these attributes is discussed in the following paragraphs.

Professionalism

Professional attitudes and behavior contribute to successful teaching. Teachers should relate to one another as peers, colleagues, and professionals, and keep personal grievances out of the classroom. There is no place in the early childhood setting for petty gossip, ill will, or exclusive cliques. Through written personnel policies, most schools have established appropriate procedures through which teachers may address certain issues. The professional approach, however, is to first attempt to work out personal differences with the other person on a one-to-one basis.

Teachers should ask themselves: Do I behave in a professional manner? Can I keep confidences without being told to do so? Do I try to meet with those with whom I have differences in an attempt to work them out? Do I complain publicly about another member of the staff?

A Satisfying Role

To teach successfully, each person must have a satisfying role to play. That means each person must be appreciated for the special something he or she brings to the classroom and the school. Beginning teachers might want to ask themselves: Is there a place in my school (or on my team) that is uniquely mine? How do my special talents and experiences contribute to the success of this program? These questions would make for a good staff meeting discussion so that all teachers could

FIGURE 5.8 Members of a teaching team need frequent communication with one another.

reflect on their special capabilities and share them with one another.

Flexibility

Just as it is important to change with and adapt to the varying needs of children, so is it crucial to respond to the needs of other staff members with a give-and-take approach. Flexibility involves a willingness to offer and accept negotiation and compromise in order to preserve the effectiveness of the whole staff's effort. Teachers should ask themselves: Do I demonstrate a willingness to change with the changing needs of my coworkers, or do I adhere rigidly to preset plans or attitudes? Am I open to new ideas proposed by others? Do I help children become comfortable with flexibility and change?

Open and Frequent Communication

The ability and opportunity to communicate honestly and openly thoughts, concerns, and feelings to others are perhaps the most important fac-

tors in promoting good interpersonal relationships. Communication takes many forms: verbal and nonverbal, written and spoken, even body language.

Teachers must seek out opportunities for formal and informal communication with others on the staff. This may mean taking advantage of the faculty lounge during lunch hour or arriving five minutes early to catch someone before children arrive. For those who work on teaching teams, set-up and clean-up times can be used to discuss issues, modify strategies, and resolve misunderstandings.

The three basic reasons for developing successful communication links with others on the teaching staff are:

1. *to share information*—about children and their families ("Sheila's grandmother died yesterday"), about changes in the schedule ("The dentist is unable to visit today; who wants to conduct group time?"), and about child development strategies ("Remember, we are all going to observe Leah's gross motor skills this week").

2. *to contribute new ideas*—teachers encourage one another to keep teaching fresh and alive when

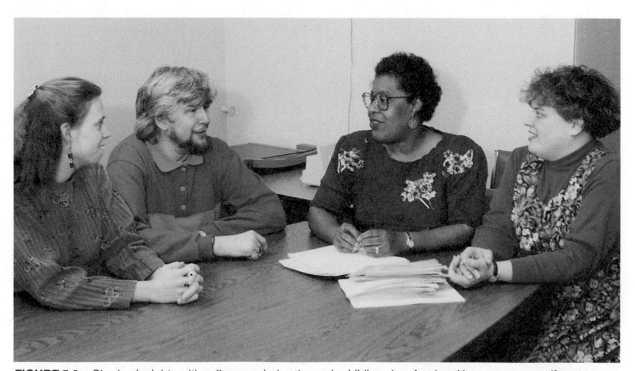

FIGURE 5.9 Sharing insights with colleagues helps the early childhood professional become more self-aware.

they share a recent article of interest, reports from a conference they attended, or a successful art activity.

3. *to solve problems*—accepting differences in opinions, approaches, personality, and style among people is part of the challenge of working closely with others. Open communication is an on-going process where people have honest and frequent discussion of their differences, respecting each other's feelings and integrity, and working together for mutually agreeable solutions.

Self-Awareness

Previously in this chapter, self-awareness as a qualification for a good early childhood teacher was discussed. The focus was primarily on the teacher's self-awareness in relationships with children. In this discussion, the focus is on the teacher's adult relationships. Beginning teachers may feel uncomfortable or inadequate in their relationships with others on the staff; once they know more about themselves and accept who they are, teachers can apply this self-awareness to their relationships with fellow workers.

To promote self-knowledge that contributes to success as a member of a faculty or teaching team, teachers might ask themselves: What are my strengths and weaknesses as a teacher and how do they complement or conflict with others in this school? Do I prefer to follow or lead, to plan programs or carry out the plans developed by others? In what teaching situations do I feel uncomfortable, and why? What have I done lately that caused me to learn more about myself?

Mutual Respect and Acceptance

Appreciating and accepting the individuality of other team members is as important to the success of the program as is appreciating and accepting the individuality of each child. The climate of trust and the nonthreatening atmosphere gained through mutual respect allow each staff member to contribute openly and innovatively to the program. To develop that appreciation for one another, teachers should ask themselves: What do I have in common with my coworkers? Are their teaching philosophies different from mine and, if so, in what way? What are their social and cultural values? What are their previous experiences with young children? What do I want them to respect and accept about me?

Team Spirit and Empathy

A sense of being a team does not happen by accident, but by conscious effort. Every member of the staff must be committed to working together on a daily basis as well as to the long-term goals of the specific program, and to being empathetic to the feelings and needs of coworkers.

To develop staff relationships that enhance a team spirit, teachers should ask themselves: How can I show support to my coworkers? What can I do to promote and sustain high morale among my fellow teachers? Where and how can I offer help to another staff member?

A Willingness to Share the Spotlight

Tension among staff members can arise from a sense of competition. Teachers must be willing to admit that others are just as dedicated to children and deserving of their affections as they are. There must be a feeling of shared success when things work well, as there is a shared responsibility when problems arise. Teachers should ask themselves: How do I feel when another teacher is praised by a parent in front of me? How do I feel when a child prefers another teacher to me? Am I able to acknowledge my coworkers achievements?

Clearly Defined Roles

A clear understanding of the roles and responsibilities a teacher has is essential for the teacher's own sense of well-being and for the smooth functioning of the program. A written job description helps teachers understand the scope of their own position as well as those of staff members. Clearly defined teacher roles also serve as a guard against legal and ethical problems, especially if children are injured at school. Teachers should ask themselves: Is my job description clearly written so I know the extent of my responsibilities? Do

I fulfill my obligations or are there areas where I am lax that might prove harmful to a child?

Evaluation

Evaluations are part of the privilege of claiming membership in the teaching profession. No teacher can become truly successful unless provisions are made for ongoing evaluations which provide a clear picture that confirms strengths and pinpoints areas for growth. (Evaluations are more thoroughly discussed in Chapter 10). Teachers should ask themselves: Do I accept evaluations as an essential part of teaching? Am I responsive to the suggestions made in my evaluations? When I evaluate others, am I fair and do I share my observations in a supportive way?

THE TEACHER AS A PROFESSIONAL

Attitudes and Background

There is a body of knowledge, an educational foundation, that is assumed of anyone entering the early childhood profession. There are also some basic teaching skills that are necessary. These include methods and techniques appropriate for teaching the very young child. Yet there is more if one is to be called a true professional

Being a member of the teaching profession goes beyond an accumulation of methods, coursework, and teaching experiences. Being a professional teacher suggests an attitude about teaching. It is not simply an eight-hour-a-day job, or an occupation chosen lightly. Teachers are called to the profession when they believe they can indeed make a difference in the lives of the children. While that may at first sound *altruistic*, it reflects a dedication to teaching that exceeds the desire for a job or a steady paycheck.

There are professional expectations, starting with having a common background with others in the field. This includes studying child development and human behavior, family relations, parent education and development, and curriculum planning. Some practical teaching experience under the guidance of a master teacher is assumed, as

FIGURE 5.10 Professional attitudes and behavior are crucial. Teachers and administrators work together in solving problems as colleagues and co-workers.

is a familiarity with observation and recording techniques. This foundation of knowledge and experience provides the framework for professional development. Teachers gradually acquire further skills on the job. They learn to juggle three or four interactions with children at once and develop the skill of stopping an argument by a mere look or a quick gesture. Thus, the process of becoming a professional teacher is an orderly progression along a continuum of development. Miriam Silver's Focus Box on p. 157 cites an example of formalized teaching and certification requirements in the state where she lives and teaches. Your state may have different regulations or none at all; only half the states offer a specialized certification for early childhood professionals (Bredekamp, 1992). Professional expectations mandated by the states provide some degree of professionalization of early childhood teachers.

This progression of teaching skills has been described by Lilian Katz (1977) as consisting of four distinct stages of teacher development, ranging from Survival to Maturity. The beginning teacher often feels inadequate and ill-prepared during the first year of teaching (Survival) but soon begins to focus on individual children and specific behavior problems (Consolidation). By the third or fourth year (Renewal) the teacher is ready to explore new ideas and resources and, within another year or two, has come to terms with teaching and searches for insights and perspectives (Maturity). At each stage, teachers need differing degrees of on-site support (mentoring), with increased exposure to professional conferences and organizations.

Professional Development

Developing a Professional Code of Ethics

As teachers mature, they turn their attention to issues and concerns outside themselves. Many of these issues, whether they are called so or not, are related to ethical conflicts and moral principles. Teachers are, after all, human beings, and that entails genuine conflict about behavior. Doing what is right becomes difficult at times; knowing what is right may be elusive. Even identifying what is right—an ethical conflict—may not be obvious.

Every day, situations arise with parents, other teachers, and administrators that require teachers to make some hard choices. Some cases are clearly ethical dilemmas: suspected child abuse by a parent or teacher, talking about children and their families outside of school, or the firing of a staff member without due cause. Others, some of which are common occurrences, may not seem as obvious. Some everyday examples are:

When Parents:

● Ask you to advance their child into the next class against your advice

● Want you to use discipline practices common to their family and culture but at odds with your own sense of what children need[1]

● Attempt to gossip with you about another staff member

When Another Teacher:

● Suggests a private staff meeting outside of school with a select group of teachers

● Refuses to take a turn cleaning out the animal cages

● Regularly is absent from staff meetings

● Disagrees with the school's educational philoso-

phy and continues to teach in ways that differ from the approved methods in that setting

● Goes to the school administrator with a complaint about a staff team member

When the Administrator:

● Insists on adding one more child to an already overenrolled class

● Makes personnel decisions based on friendship, not performance

● Backs a parent who complains about a teacher without hearing the teacher's side of the story

Surveys in the journal *Young Children* have identified some of the ethical issues of most concern to early childhood educators: (1) discussing a child or family outside of school; (2) implementing policies that are not good for children; (3) letting children do an activity that may not be worthwhile or appropriate; (4) knowing that a program is in violation of state regulations; and (5) dealing with conflicting requests from divorced or separated parents (Feeney and Sisko, 1986).

Teachers may find it helpful to discuss their ethical concerns with colleagues. Some schools provide in-service programs for the staff where these issues are raised. Other schools have a code of ethics for their employees to follow.

These are ethical problems that occur daily in any teacher's life. They are not problems of an abstract or impersonal nature. Just what are ethics? Essentially, they are the moral guidelines by which we govern our own behavior and that of society. "Ethics is nothing more than systematic critical reflection about our obligations," says philosopher Kenneth Kipnis (1987).

We can strictly define ethics as "the system or code of morals of a particular philosopher, religion, group, or profession." This definition suggests that a personal code of ethics can be supported by a professional code of ethics. A code of ethics is a set of statements that helps us deal with the temptations inherent in our occupations. It helps us act in terms of what is right rather than what is expedient (Katz and Ward, 1978).

OUR DIVERSE WORLD OUR DIVERSE WORLD OUR DIVERSE WORLD OUR DIVERSE WORLD OUR DIVERSE WORLD

[1]Teachers will need to become aware of child-rearing practices from many cultures.

Certification

Miriam Silver

State governments recognize professionals by conferring certification. Certification is granted to those whose accomplishments adhere to a set of standards. Standards for teacher certification are usually developed by State Departments of Education. This means that there is no uniform standard for certification in the nation. Each state sets its own requirements.

The certification requirements are important because they often drive the course work offered in degree-granting institutions. For example, in New Jersey the State Department of Education has decided that *all* teachers need the same knowledge base and skills, regardless of what grade they teach. There is, therefore, one certification for all teachers from pre-kindergarten to 8th grade! Colleges have dropped programs in early childhood education because no separate certification exists.

Professional early childhood educators believe that teachers of young children require a different set of skills and knowledge than do elementary and middle school teachers. Teaching children in the early years is a specialization and must have its own set of requirements which reflect that specialization. Early childhood advocates in New Jersey have been working to educate the members of the State Department of Education about the differences between teachers of young children and those who teach older children.

Only when the state authorizes a separate certification will early childhood programs be reinstated in the state colleges. When a special certification exists, one can concentrate on developing the special teaching skills necessary for working with young children. An ideal goal for the early childhood profession would be for *all* states to recognize this field by offering a separate early childhood certification.

Dr. Miriam Silver is an Associate Professor at Montclair State University, Upper Montclair, New Jersey in the family/child studies division of the Home Economics department.

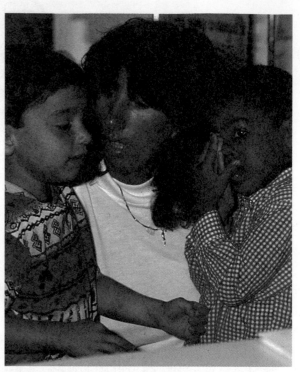

FIGURE 5.11 Ethical questions arise daily. This child has been taught to hit back if anyone hits him. What does the teacher say to him? How should this situation be handled?

Why might the early childhood profession need such a code? A primary reason is that the choices teachers make should be based not simply on personal values and preferences but "on values, judgments, and ethical commitments shared by the professional society or association of which they are a member" (Katz and Ward, 1978).

A code of ethics provides collective wisdom and advice from a broad base in the profession. It states the principles by which each individual can measure and govern professional behavior. It says that a group or association has recognized the moral dimensions of its work. It provides teachers with a known, defined core of professional values—those basic commitments that any early childhood educator should consider inviolate. This protects teachers and administrators from having to make hard ethical decisions on the spur of the moment, possibly on the basis of personal bias. An established professional code supports the teacher's choice by saying, "It isn't that *I* won't act this way: *No early childhood educator* should act this way" (Kipnis, 1987).

The National Association for the Education of Young Children has adopted a Code of Ethical Conduct which "offers guidelines for responsible behavior and sets forth a common basis for resolving the principal ethical dilemmas encountered in early childhood education" (Feeney and Kipnis, NAEYC, 1990). Four sections of the Code outline the major areas of the professional relationship: (1) working with children; (2) working with families; (3) relationships with colleagues; and (4) responsibilities to the community and society. The Statement of Commitment may be found in Appendix B at the back of this text.

A basic list of core values has emerged from this work, values "that are deeply rooted in the history of our field" (Feeney and Kipnis, 1990). Core values form the basis of agreement in the profession about standards of ethical behavior. They are:

● Appreciating childhood as a unique and valuable stage of the human life cycle

● Basing our work with children on knowledge of child development

- Appreciating and supporting the close ties between the child and family

- Recognizing that children are best understood in the context of family, culture, and society

- Respecting the dignity, worth, and uniqueness of each individual (child, family member, and colleague)

- Helping children and adults achieve their full potential in the context of relationships that are based on trust, respect, and positive regard

(Feeney and Kipnis, 1990)

Continuing Education

Creative and stimulating classes are the product of teachers who continue to learn more about how to teach. After the initial stage of teaching, many teachers begin to seek new challenges and new ways to improve the quality of their teaching. Usually, this leads to some form of continuing education, such as participation in workshops, courses, or seminars. If time to pursue continuing education is not built into a teacher's schedule, there may be other options:

- In-service training programs may be brought into the school setting. Resource people can be invited to lead the staff in discussions about children's behavior, parent relationships, assessment charts, or science curriculum.

- Various members of the teaching staff can develop a program of their own, offering their expertise to fellow faculty at an in-service meeting.

- A computer specialist, art resource teacher, or multicultural expert can be invited to visit the classrooms, instructing children and providing staff with some useful ideas and plans.

- A family therapist can be invited to speak at a staff meeting about strategies for supporting families in crisis.

- A library for teachers, stocked with professional books, journals (such as *Young Children*), and newspapers (such as *Education Week*) can provide a teacher with the means to keep up with current trends and practices and to improve teaching skills in the classroom.

- Parents who are professionals in a variety of fields can be utilized whenever possible to enrich the knowledge and skills of the staff.

Direct Services to Children and Families

Teacher in early childhood program
Director of child care facility
Family day care provider
Nanny or au pair
Foster parent
Social worker/adoption agent
Pediatric nurse/school nurse
Family therapist/parent educator
Pediatrician

Community Involvement

State/local licensing worker
Legislative advocate
Child care law specialist
ECE environmental consultant
Interior designer for children's spaces
Government planning agent on
    children's issues
Consultant in bilingual education
Nutrition specialist for children

Indirect Services to Children and Families

Curriculum specialist
Instructional specialist—computers
Child development researcher
Early childhood education specialist
Program consultant
Consumer advocate

Other Options

Communications consultant
Script writer/editor
Freelance writer
Children's book author
Children's photographer
Microcomputer specialist/program
    consultant

FIGURE 5.12   There are many challenges in a variety of careers awaiting the early childhood professional. (Adapted from "Career Options in Early Childhood Education" by Dianne Widmeyer Eyer. In *Beginnings & Beyond: Foundations in Early Childhood Education*, Delmar, 1993. Third edition, pp. 170.)

Setting Professional Goals

As teachers raise their sights beyond "How will I survive?" to "Where am I going?", they begin to set goals for themselves and their teaching career. They develop both long- and short-term objectives for themselves, establishing a framework for professional growth.

The goals that are set will vary with individual teachers. For Jim, this could mean developing a brand new curriculum for his class of two-year-olds. Susan might choose to work toward having greater parent support in her classroom. Thea and Frank might decide to develop a workshop on sensorimotor skills. Stephanie wonders about using her skills with children and computers to go into business for herself. Cassie would like to create a calendar of parent meetings and events for the school year. Whether in the area of children's programs, administration, staff relations, or their own professional development, teachers can learn, grow, and change. (See Chapter 10 for evaluation and goal-setting techniques.)

Professional Affiliations

Teachers who are beginning to perceive themselves as professionals may choose to join one of the professional organizations related to the early childhood field. One of the largest, the National Association for the Education of Young Children (NAEYC), has local and state affiliate groups through which one can become a member. NAEYC offers a range of services to its members, including conferences and publications such as the journal, *Young Children*. The Association for Childhood Education International (ACEI) has a similar function, whereas the Society for Research in Child Development (SRCD) focuses on child psychology, research, and development.

Career Options

The need for quality programs for young children has never been greater and the demand for early childhood specialists will continue, fostered

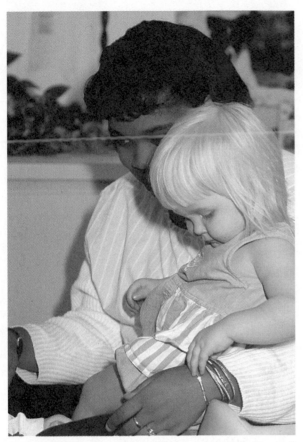

FIGURE 5.13 The beginning teacher invests herself emotionally as well as physically.

by national attention to the issues of children and families. If you are considering a career in early childhood, the options are many and varied. See Figure 5.12 for an overview of some of the possibilities that exist in this profession.

THE BEGINNING TEACHER

Beginning teachers of young children cannot expect to successfully blend all of the many facets of a teacher—personal, team, and professional identity—at once. Certainly, teaching young children carries with it the obligation to understand and accept the many roles and responsibilities associated with the title of "teacher." However, beginning teachers must also be committed to the time and energy needed to *become* that total teacher.

Beginning teaching can be a great deal of fun as well as a unique learning experience. Textbook theories come alive as children naturally demonstrate child development concepts. New teachers expect to learn about individual child growth and development; many are surprised to discover that they also learn how children function in groups and with adults.

Planning and executing activities that fit the needs and abilities of the child are another part of the beginning teacher's role. They provide an opportunity to test curriculum ideas, to see what happens when child meets materials. Working with an experienced teacher who models highly polished skills is an important part of the new teacher's experience. Identification with a number of professionals can help the beginner find a teaching identity, and a team teaching situation can be especially supportive.

Yet we know that first-time teaching is not always fun. It is a time for intensive self-searching and self-revelations. Many teachers' own school experiences loom before them and undermine their confidence. Planning lessons takes long hours. There may still be doubts about being a teacher at all. It is uncomfortable to feel judged and criticized by others. This is a time of anxiety for most beginning teachers. But remember, even the poised, confident, and always-does-the-right-thing master teacher was once a beginner.

The Student Teacher

Many teacher training programs require a formal period of supervised work with young children in either the college's child development center or in early childhood programs throughout the community. For students in such a program, practice teaching may be the first hands-on opportunity to work with children.

Beginnings for student teachers are just as important as they are for young children. A child's first days of school are planned very carefully, likewise, there are some strategies for easing the transition from student to student teacher. The following guidelines will help to make the first days of student teaching a satisfying and positive experience.

Before School Starts

- Contact the teacher and meet before school begins. Find out what time school begins, where the classroom is located, what the age group is, the size and make-up of the class, the daily schedule and what hours you are expected to be on site. Ask if there are children with special needs, and if there are cultural considerations of which you should be aware. Find out what is expected of you the first few days. Be sure to meet the other administrative staff of the school.

- Visit the classroom to which you are assigned to become acquainted with its layout. Tour the yard as well. Find out where the janitor's room, the kitchen, nurse's office, and storeroom are located.

- Share with the master teacher any special skills or talents you may have; let the teacher help you utilize these skills in new ways with young children. Let the teacher know about any other experiences with children: babysitting or camp counseling. Be sure to let the teacher know of any course requirements you must meet by this experience.

- Together, you, the master teacher, and your college instructor in student teaching, will set goals and expectations for your student teaching experience. This will define more concretely what you would like to get out of the time you spend in the classroom, whether it is gaining experience with a group of children or learning to lead a group time by the end of the semester. By establishing common goals, the master teacher will be able to help guide a course so that these goals will be realized. An evaluation process related to those goals should be agreed upon so that you will learn whether you have met the expectations of the teacher, the school, and the program.

Getting Started

After the first few days of teaching, routines will become familiar, you will know most of the children's names, and your presence in the classroom will have become standard procedure. Once a level of comfort is reached, some of the more challenging aspects of working with young chil-

FIGURE 5.14   Good teachers know when to help children learn new skills.

dren can be addressed. The following guidelines will help ease the first week's anxieties.

Student Behavior

Dress Appropriately. Wear clothing that is comfortable, appropriate to the season, and easily covered by a smock or apron. Sturdy, waterproof shoes are good for outdoor activities.

Be Prompt. Arrive on schedule and always inform the master teacher if you will be late or absent.

Know Where Things Are. Find out where important equipment and materials are stored.

Use Professional Ethics. Avoid discussing children and families by name outside the school setting.

Interacting With Children

Move in Slowly. Sit back and watch to see what children are doing and if you are needed before getting involved.

Maintain Your Role as Teacher. Avoid playing adult-centered games with children or entertaining them so that you become the focus of their play. Keep their attention focused on each other or the activities.

Give Children Time. Allow plenty of time for children to do as much as they can possibly do without help.

Help Children Wait. Be alert to times when children may have to wait until the next activity or to move to another room. Have songs and fingerplays memorized or a short book ready to read.

Be Alert to the Whole Group. Know where the children and other teachers are and what they are doing even when they are not in the immediate area.

Never Leave Children Unsupervised. Notify the teacher in charge if you must leave the area, and work out arrangements that will provide full coverage of all the activities.

Maintain the Environment. Keep the room and yard in order as the day moves along, involving children in the clean-up process.

Use Your Voice and Tone Effectively. Go over to a child, bend down, and speak quietly, but distinctly, rather than shout from across the room or yard.

Never Shove or Use Force. Avoid picking up children to get them where they are supposed to go. Learn to use verbalizations, not force or strength, to get children to cooperate.

Relating to Other Adults

Never Interfere When Another Teacher is Solving a Problem. Unless specifically invited to join in, allow other teachers the courtesy of dealing with the situation alone.

Ask Questions. Be sure to ask for help when needed. You are there to learn, so you may feel free to question teachers as to why and how they handle various situations.

Maintain Communication. Keep other staff members informed of significant events and problems that occur. Parents' questions and concerns should be redirected to the teaching staff.

FIGURE 5.15 Through experience, teachers learn how to handle large groups of children. Learning to develop story time and reading skills is an ongoing process.

Consult Your Master Teacher. Work together on selecting and evaluating age-appropriate activities that will fit in with the established curriculum goals.

Keep these guidelines in mind to avoid some of the common pitfalls of the beginning teacher, but remember they are only guidelines. Students must add their own experiences, insights, and interpretations. With the support of the teaching staff, confidence will grow, together with an understanding of what it means to be a total teacher. Further discussion related to guidance and discipline will be found in Chapter 7.

THE WHOLE TEACHER

At some point teachers emerge with their own point of view about teaching, based on self-knowledge of what calls them to teaching, why they teach the way they do, and what they know of the children they teach. This integration of knowledge and training, experience and life, is referred to by several names. Some say "real" teachers. Others refer to the "total" teacher. A common phrase is the "whole" teacher. Any one of these terms is an apt reflection of the relationship between how teachers view children and how they see themselves. There is a meshing of the emotional, physical, intellectual, and social aspects of each human being, adult or child.

Something happens when this blending occurs. During the first few years in the classroom, teachers consolidate their various official functions—merging their teacher training and experience with their personal style and nature. To discover and define the role of a teacher means to develop a personal teaching style. This is the sum of one's response to teaching, and it is unique to each teacher. When it happens, a beginning teacher becomes aware of "feeling" like a teacher. The strengths and convictions one has as a person blend with those one has as a teacher; they become inseparable. What teachers do and what teachers are become woven together. And in adding the personal teacher to the professional teacher, the sum becomes greater than two, allowing the whole teacher the freedom to grow in insight and understanding.

S U M M A R Y

Teachers of young children share with other teachers a variety of subject matter. The curriculum in the early childhood school is rich in math, science, language, social studies, geography, and the like. The format for these learning experiences is a "hands-on" approach. Teachers set out materials, equipment, and activities that invite children's interest and interaction.

In some areas the early childhood teacher differs from others in the field of education. Team teaching, teacher-child interactions, small-group emphasis, and adult relationships are more common in the early years than in other types of schools.

The teaching role is not restricted to working just with children. Teachers must learn to interact with numerous adults—primarily parents, other teachers, and administrators. Teaching roles will vary, depending on whether or not you teach alone or on a team. Team teaching is common in many early childhood programs and has many advantages. By keeping in mind ten essentials for successful teaching, all early childhood teachers can assure themselves of optimal working conditions in their setting.

Early childhood teachers have multiple roles. They supervise and manage the classroom, interact with children and a number of adults, and they set the emotional tone. Much of what they do occurs away from children. There are meetings to attend, reports to write, parent conferences to hold, and materials to purchase. These after-hours duties add to the depth of classroom experiences the teacher provides for the children.

Ethical situations arise frequently, calling on the teacher or administrator to make difficult choices about children and their lives. A professional code of ethics sets out standards of behavior based on core values and commitments all early childhood professionals share. It can support decisions individuals have to make in the best interests of children.

The student teacher gains valuable experience working directly with children under the supervision of a mature teacher. Some of the initial anxieties are overcome by following general guidelines for student teaching. Further help comes from looking at some common problems and ways to avoid them.

As they grow and gain confidence, teachers pass through several stages of professional development and search for ways to be more effectively challenged. As they integrate teaching style and personality, they become whole teachers.

R E V I E W   Q U E S T I O N S

1. What do you think are the five most important qualifications a teacher of young children should have? Why? Which do you possess? Which are most difficult for you?

2. How does a teacher 'set the tone' for a classroom? How does being culturally competent fit in?

3. Give several reasons why team teaching is important in the early years.

4. List some of the common problems associated with student teaching. How can you avoid them?

5. Why is self-awareness important?

6. What does having a code of ethics mean to a teacher?

7. You will note many similarities if you review the Ten Essentials of Successful Teaching and the characteristics of a good school climate found in the teacher burnout section. Why do you think these are interrelated?

L E A R N I N G   A C T I V I T I E S

1. Draw a picture of the first classroom you remember. Place furniture in it and note where your friends sat, where you sat, where the teacher sat. Down one side of the paper write one-word descriptions of what you felt when you were in that classroom.

2. Survey a classroom where you teach or observe. How many different cultures are represented? How does the teacher deal with the cultural diversity?

3. Have you ever had a teacher who was "different"? Describe the person. What did you like most about that teacher? What did you like least? Would you hire that teacher? Why?

4. Write your own code of ethics.

5. Read the ethical situations posed in the section Professional Development. Think about how you would solve them. Discuss your answers with a member of your class, a teacher, and a parent.

6. Observe a teacher working in a team situation and one who works alone in a classroom. What seem to be the advantages of each? Disadvantages? Which would you prefer for your first year of teaching? Why? Your third year? Your seventh year?

7. Do you disagree with any core values listed in the section Ten Essentials of Successful Teaching? What are they? How would you change them? Discuss your response with another teacher, another student, your class instructor.

8. In small groups, discuss the popular images of teachers as reflected in current movies and literature. Is there consensus of the portrait of teachers today? Where do early childhood professionals fit into the picture? Are issues raised about teachers being addressed anywhere? Where? How? By whom? What would you conclude about your role as a member of the teaching profession?

9. What would you add to Figure 5.1 based on your observation of early childhood programs and teachers?

B I B L I O G R A P H Y

Armstrong, L.S. "Census Confirms Remarkable Shifts in Ethnic Makeup." *Education Week*, March 20,1991.

Berk, Laura E. *Infants and Children*. Boston: Allyn and Bacon, 1994.

Beyer, Evelyn. *Teaching Young Children*, New York: Western Publishing, 1968.

Bredekamp, Sue. "Composing a Profession." *Young Children*, January, 1992, pp. 52–54.

Derman-Sparks, Louise. *Anti-Bias Curriculum: Tools for Empowering Young Children*. Washington, D.C. NAEYC, 1989.

—————. "Understanding Diversity." *Scholastic Pre-K Today*, November/December, 1990.

Dresden, Janna, and Myers, Barbara Kimes. "Early Childhood Professionals: Toward Self-Definition." *Young Children*, January, 1989.

Eyer, Dianne. "Career Options in Early Childhood Education." In *Beginnings and Beyond: Foundations in Early Childhood Education*. Albany, NY: Delmar Publishers, 1989.

Feeney, Stephanie, and Kipnis, Kenneth. *Code of Ethical Conduct and Statement of Commitment*. Washington, D.C.: NAEYC, 1990.

—————. "Professional Ethics in Early Childhood Education." *Young Children*, March 1985, pp. 54-58.

Feeney, Stephanie, and Sisko, Lynda. "Professional Ethics in Early Childhood Education: Survey Results." *Young Children*, November 1986, pp. 15–20.

Honig, Alice. *Parent Involvement in Early Childhood Education*. Washington, D.C.: National Association for the Education of Young Children, 1979.

Jones, Elizabeth. "Breaking the Ice: Confronting Status Differences among Professionals." In *The Early Childhood Career Lattice: Perspectives on Professional Development*, ed. Julienne Johnson and Janet B. McCracken. Washington, D.C.: National Association for the Education of Young Children, 1994.

Jorde-Bloom, Paula. *A Great Place to Work*. Washington, D.C.: NAEYC, 1988.

—————. "Teachers Need 'TLC' Too." *Young Children*, September, 1988.

Katz, Lilian G. *Talks With Teachers*. Washington, D.C.: National Association for the Education of Young Children, 1977.

Katz, Lilian G., and Ward, Evangeline H. *Ethical Behavior in Early Childhood Education*. Washington, D.C.: National Association for the Education of Young Children, 1978.

Kipnis, Kenneth. "How to Discuss Professional Ethics." *Young Children*, May 1987, pp. 26–30.

Kuster, Cecelia Alvarado "Language and Cultural Competence." In *The Early Childhood Career Lattice: Perspectives on Professional Development*, ed.

Julienne Johnson and Janet B. McCracken. Washington, D.C.: National Association for the Education of Young Children, 1994.

LeShan, Eda. *When Your Child Drives You Crazy*. New York: St. Martin's Press, 1985.

Phillips, Carol Brunson. "What Every Early Childhood Professional Should Know." In *The Early Childhood Career Lattice: Perspectives on Professional Development*, ed. Julienne Johnson and Janet B. McCracken, Washington, D.C.: National Association for the Education of Young Children, 1994.

Spodek, Bernard. *Teaching in the Early Years*. Englewood Cliffs, N.J.: Prentice-Hall, 1972.

——————. "The Knowledge Base for Baccalaureate Early Childhood Teacher Education Programs." In *The Early Childhood Career Lattice: Perspectives on Professional Development*, ed. Julienne Johnson and Janet B. McCracken. Washington, D.C.: National Association for the Education of Young Children, 1994.

CHAPTER 6

Observation: Learning to Read the Child

QUESTIONS FOR THOUGHT

Why is observing children an important teaching tool?

How do observations help us understand people and their behavior?

What is the difference between fact and inference?

How can observations be used to compare individual behavior and general developmental growth?

What are some of the ways to record observations?

What are the guidelines to follow when observing and recording behavior?

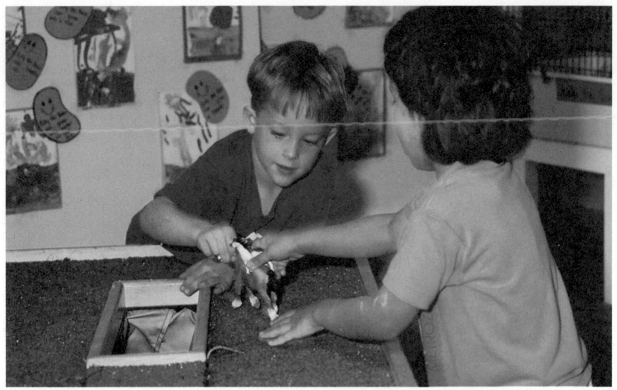

FIGURE 6.1   These two children are seen playing together for the first time. What can teachers learn by observing them about their use of materials? The way they make friends? How they solve problems?

INTRODUCTION

Children are fascinating. They are charming, needful, busy, creative, unpredictable, and emotional. At school, at home, in the grocery store, and in the park, children demonstrate a variety of behaviors. There is the happy child pumping hard on the swing. The angry, defiant child grabs a book or toy and runs away. The studious child works seriously on a puzzle.

These pictures of children flash through the mind, caught for an instant as if by a camera. These minipictures of children working, playing, and living together can be very useful to teachers.[1] Good observational skills can help teachers capture those moments in a child's life. Memory leaves just the impression. The written word is an opportunity to check impressions and opinions against the facts.

What Is Observation?

Teachers learn to make mental notes of the important details in each interaction:

That's the first time I've seen Karen playing with Bryce. They are laughing together as they build with blocks.

For five minutes now, Teddy has been standing on the fringes of the sand area where the toddler group is playing. He has ignored the children's smiles and refused the teacher's invitation to join in the play.

Antonio stops climbing each time he reaches the top of the climbing frame. He looks quickly around and if he catches a teacher's eye, he scrambles down and runs away.

Through their behavior, these three children reveal much about their personalities. The teach-

OUR DIVERSE WORLD OUR DIVERSE WORLD OUR DIVERSE WORLD OUR DIVERSE WORLD OUR DIVERSE WORLD

[1]A skilled observer, with an awareness of our diverse world, is reminded of the ways in which all children are the same, as well as the characteristics which make each child unique.

FIGURE 6.2 Observing children closely reveals their feelings and needs.

er's responsibility is to notice all the clues and put them together in meaningful ways. The teacher sees the obvious clues as well as the more subtle ones. The way observations are put together with other pertinent information becomes critical. The first child, Karen, has been looking for a special friend. Now that she has learned some ways to approach other children that don't frighten and overwhelm them, children want to play with her. Teddy's parents divorced two weeks ago. It appears he is just beginning to feel some of that pain and has become withdrawn at school. At home, Antonio is expected to do things right the first time. At school, he generally attempts only what he knows he can do without making a mistake.

These simple observations, made in the midst of a busy morning at school, give vital information about each child's abilities, needs, and concerns. It is a more developed picture. Children are complex human beings who respond in many ways. Teachers can observe these responses and use their skills to help each child grow and learn.

Observation is more than ordinary looking. It takes energy and concentration to become an accurate observer. Teachers must train themselves to record what they see on a regular basis. They need to discipline themselves to distinguish between detail and trivia as well as learn to spot biases that might invalidate the observation.[1] Once acquired, objective observation techniques help give a scientific and professional character to the role of early childhood education.

Seeing Children Through Observation

Play is the work of childhood. It is the way children express themselves and how they show

OUR DIVERSE WORLD OUR DIVERSE WORLD OUR DIVERSE WORLD OUR DIVERSE WORLD OUR DIVERSE WORLD
[1]Early childhood educators are invited to study and learn about themselves as they learn about children.

what they are really like. By observing play, teachers can see children as they are and as they see themselves. Much of what children do gives clues to their inner beings.

The stage is set; the action begins as soon as the first child enters the room. Here, teachers can see children in action and watch for important behavior. All that is needed is to be alert to the clues and make note of them:

> Allison, normally a cocky, competent three-year-old, wavers in her confidence as she enters school. She knows her best friend, Andy, will be absent today.

> Charlie, full of bravado on the first grade playground, refuses to perform a simple coloring task. He tells the teacher, "I can't do it. I don't know how."

Developing sound observational skills enables teachers to better meet the social, emotional, and intellectual needs of each child.

What are children telling us about themselves? Which actions are most important to note? The teacher makes a point to observe children at critical moments. An alert teacher will notice the way a child enters school each morning. Tina always clings to her blanket after her Dad leaves her at school. Lasauna bounces in each day ready to play the moment she walks in the door. David says good-bye to his grandmother, then circles the room, hugging each adult before settling into an activity. These children show the observant teacher something about their needs. A good observer will continue to watch, taking note of these early morning scenes. One can interpret these behaviors later, seeing how they apply to each child and how behavior changes over time.

Another important behavior to watch is how children use their bodies. The basic routines of eating, napping, toileting, and dressing show how they take care of themselves. Whether Chris learns how to put his jacket on by himself indicates his skills in other areas requiring initiative and self-sufficiency. It also shows whether or not children are developing an awareness of themselves as separate, independent beings.

Seeing children in relation to other people is a third area to notice. Teachers see whom children choose as playmates and whom they avoid. They can tell what children will look for in friends. The observant teacher will also make note of the adults in each child's life. Who does the child seek for comfort? For questions? Who takes care of the child outside of school? Who picks the child up from school each day?

Finally, in selecting play materials and equipment, children show what they like to do, how well they use the environment, and what they avoid. Teachers observe whether or not a child picks materials that are challenging. Bethany starts each morning in the art area, then plays with puzzles before taking care of the animals. Conor prefers the blocks and dramatic play areas and lately has been spending more time in the cooking corner. Observing children at play and at work can tell us how they learn and what methods they use to gain information.

Why Observe?

To Improve Your Teaching

Classrooms are very busy places, especially for teachers, who plan many activities and share in hundreds of interactions everyday. It is difficult to monitor our behavior while we are in the midst of working with children, and time-consuming to reflect on that behavior afterwards. Yet we know that teachers who are most effective are those who are thorough in their preparation and systematic in evaluating their own work. It takes a certain level of awareness—of self, of the children, and of the environment—to monitor our own progress. This includes carefully checking what is happening, looking for feedback, and then acting upon it. Teachers can do this by asking others to observe them, or by observing themselves at work with the children in their care.

Observing children helps teachers become *more objective* about the children in their care. When making observational notes, teachers look first at what the child is doing. This is different from looking at how a child ought to be doing something. The teacher becomes like a camera, recording what is seen without immediately judging it. This **objectivity** can balance the intense, personal side of teaching.

Poor Observation	Analysis and Comments
A. Julio walked over to the coat rack and dropped his sweater on the floor. He is shy (1) of teachers, so he didn't ask anyone to help him pick it up. He walked over to Cynthia because she's his best friend (2). He wasn't nice (3) to the other children when he started being pushy and bossy (4). He wanted their attention (5), so he nagged (6) them into leaving the table and going to the blocks like four-year-old boys do (7).	(1) Inference of a general characteristic. (2) Inference of child's emotion. (3) Observer's opinion. (4) Inference with no physical evidence stated. (5) Opinion of child's motivation. (6) Observer's inference. (7) Overgeneralization; stereotyping.

Good Observation	Analysis and Comments
B. Emilio pulled out a puzzle from the rack with his right hand, then carried it with both hands to the table nearby. Using both hands, he methodically took each piece out of the frame and set it to his left. Sara, who had been seated across from Emilio with some table toys in front of her, reached out and pushed all the puzzle pieces onto the floor. Emilio's face reddened as his eyes stared directly at Sara with his mouth in a taut line. His hands turned to fists, his brow furrowed, and he yelled at Sara in a forced tone, "Stop it! I hate you!"	Emilio was clearly *angry* as demonstrated in his facial expressions, hand gestures, and body movements. What is more, the way a child speaks is as revealing as what a child says when one wants to determine what a child is feeling. Muscular tension is another clue to the child's emotions. But the physical attitude of the child is not enough; one must also consider the context. Just seeing a child sitting in a chair with a red face, one doesn't know if he is embarrassed, angry, feverish, or overstimulated. We need to know the events that led to this conclusion. Then we can correctly assess the entire situation. By attempting to rid ourselves of some of these biases, we begin to see the child more clearly.

FIGURE 6.3   Two observations. Example A contains numerous biases, which are underlined in the left column and explained in the right column. Example B has clear descriptions and is relatively free of biases.

Teachers are influenced in their work by their own early childhood experiences.[1] They have notions about how children learn, play, grow, or behave because of the way they were raised and trained. Moreover, when teachers are in the thick of activity, they see only a narrow picture. To pull back, take some notes, and make an observation gives the teacher a chance to see the larger scene.

Teams of teachers help each other gain perspective on the class, an individual, a time of the day. Observations can be a means of validating one teacher's point of view. By checking out an opinion or idea through systematic observation, teachers get a sense of direction in their planning.

Additionally, all teachers develop ideas and impressions about children when they spend time with them. Some children seem shy, some helpful, some affectionate, aggressive, cooperative, stubborn, and so on. These opinions influence the way teachers behave and interact with children. The child thought to be aggressive, for instance, is more likely to be blamed for starting the quarrel when one occurs nearby. It is no accident that the children teachers consider more polite are the ones who are often given special considerations. The problem stems from teacher biases, and these can be misleading. Assumptions made about a child often stereotype the child (or the group) rather than illuminate it. This gives both teachers and children a narrow view of themselves and others.[2] In the Focus Box in this chapter Gonzalez-Mena offers a multicultural perspective of observation of children.

Cohen and Stern (1978) suggest that to become a careful observer is to become in part a scientist. A good observer makes a clear distinction

1and 2See footnote on page 68. Patricia Ramsey's book, TEACHING AND LEARNING IN A DIVERSE WORLD (1987) provides a format for the start of a thorough self-investigation of individual attitudes and biases.

between fact and **inference,** between real behavior and an impression or conclusion drawn from it. Being aware of the difference between what actually happens and one's opinion and conclusions about those events is critical to good teaching. Refer to Figure 6.3 for an illustration of these differences. By separating what happens from what you *think* about it or how you *feel* about it, you are able to distinguish between fact and inference. That does not mean teachers have to become aloof; their eyes can reflect both warmth and a measure of objectivity at the same time. The picture of the child from a teacher's view is often based on one or two events, not necessarily repeated or typical of the child. Thus, it is not a true picture of the child at all.

No one can be free from bias, nor is that the point.[1] The impressions and influences made can provide valuable insights into children. The important first step in observation, though, is to separate what children *do* from what teachers think or feel about it. This can only be done with an awareness of one's own biases. Knowing personal influences and prejudices, coupled with observation and recording skills, prepares teachers to focus on actual behaviors.

To Link Theory with Practice

Observations are a link between theory and practice. All teachers gain from making this connection. New teachers can see the pages of a textbook come alive as they watch a group of children. They can match what they see with what they read. By putting together psychology and medical research with in-class experiences, teachers gain a deeper understanding of the nature of children.

Early childhood education is the one level of teaching that systematically bases its teaching upon child development. If we are to develop programs that work for young children—what they can do, how they think and communicate, and what they feel—we need to be able to apply sound child development knowledge to the classroom. Further, we can use what researchers have learned to understand the individual children in our care.

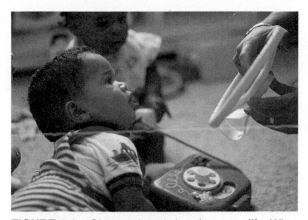

FIGURE 6.4 Observations bring theory to life. What can these babies do with objects? Is the environment safe? Challenging? How does observing answer these questions?

To Help Parents

Parents benefit from observations. A collection of notes about an individual child can be used in parent conferences. The teacher shares fresh, meaningful examples that demonstrate the child's growth and abilities. The child's teachers also gain a perspective when the notes are accumulated and discussed with parents. Problems become more clear and plans can be made to work together. Results can be further tested through continuing observation.

To Use as an Assessment Tool

Notes, time samplings, and running records serve as an informal way to assess children's skills and capabilities. Observation can be used as a tool for teachers to check the accuracy of their own impressions. Comparing notes with other teachers, with parents, or with anyone familiar with the classroom or the child in question refines a teacher's own objective observation skills. The results lead directly into curriculum planning for the class. Teachers observe the room arrangement and use of space. Does the traffic flow easily or are children stuck in play areas and can't get out? Many classroom problems can be solved if teachers will take time to make observations. They can observe

[1]See footnote on page 172.

what happens in the block corner at cleanup time. Who always cleans up? Who avoids it? Or they look at play patterns and find out who children play with or who plays alone. Observations can clarify which children are having problems and give teachers a sense of when and where the trouble starts.

More frequently teachers are called upon to set specific goals for the children in their classes and for the overall class performance. They justify what they do and why and document children's progress. In this way teachers are accountable to their clients: the children, the parents, and the public. Learning to assess children's skills and behavior and to document it is becoming increasingly important to the early childhood educator. Formal assessment techniques such as screening are described in Chapter 10.

To Wonder Why and Solve a Problem

In the spirit of being a kind of scientist, teachers can become researchers in their own classrooms. A scientist, like a child, sees something and wonders why. This curiosity leads to thinking about the various components of a problem and looking at the parts as well as the whole. Next comes the "head-scratching" part—a time of reflection, developing hunches or intuitions about the problem, and generating alternatives. The teacher is then ready to try out an alternative, known in scientific terms as testing the hypothesis. Finally, the teacher gets results, which feeds back into rethinking the problem or celebrating the solution.

There are many ways the teacher can become a researcher. Certainly, systematic observation of children is one way to look at problems and situations. Without extensive training, teachers can engage in this kind of scientific thinking in their daily work. This kind of "action research" is easily adaptable to teaching.

To Communicate with Children

Observation of children's play is a way to encourage teachers to become interested observers/researchers. When teachers get more focused and interested in children's play, they improve their teaching with a heightened awareness of their own work and of the intricacies of children. At the same time, teachers can model the importance of writing. Furthermore, teachers support children in this process by *noticing* them.

See what happens when a teacher begins to write while children are playing:

> Some of the children pay immediate attention. "What are you writing about?" asks four-year-old Nina as I sit down at the edge of the block area. "I'm writing about children playing," I explain. "You're writing about what I'm doing?" Nina asks. "Yes, I am." She's pleased. She goes back to building a careful enclosure with the long blocks.
>
> (Jones & Carter, 1991).

In classrooms, the teacher can be the scribe, a kind of "literate helper" (Jones & Carter, 1991) who helps children become aware of the power of language, the written word, and their own self-importance. Observation helps keep most of the attention child-centered rather than teacher-directed, and increases children's and adult's communication.

UNDERSTANDING WHAT WE OBSERVE

The goal of observing children is to understand them better. Teachers, students, and parents collect a great deal of information by watching children. Observational data helps adults know children in several significant ways.

Children as Individuals

How do children spend their time at school? What activities are difficult? Who is the child's best friend? By watching individual children, teachers help them learn at their own pace, at their own rate of development, in their own time. By watching carefully, they find out each child's learning style. When teachers know how each child functions, they can choose activities and materials to match interests and skills. This is called **individualized curriculum:** tailoring what is taught to what a child is ready and willing to learn.

This kind of curriculum gives children educational experiences that offer **connected knowledge;** that is, a curriculum that is real and relevant to the individual child and is a part of **develop-**

mentally appropriate practices (see Chapters 1, 2, 9, and 11). It is also part of a program for children with special needs; in these cases an **individualized education plan (I.E.P.)** is developed jointly by teachers, education specialists, and parents to better serve the child.

Observing helps a teacher spot a child's strengths and areas of difficulty. Once these are known, teachers plan intervention measures, helping to make the school experience successful for the child. The following example shows how individualizing the curriculum can bring about changes in behavior that help children succeed.

The teachers were concerned about Jody, age 4-1/2, who had minimal fine-motor skills. She used scissors in a "hedge-clippers" fashion and had an awkward grip when using a pencil. Jody also found it difficult to fit puzzle pieces together. She avoided all areas that required the use of those skills: art, table toys, woodworking, and cooking. A check with her parents revealed two important facts: Jody had trouble handling table utensils and couldn't button her sweater. They said there was no provision at home for her to pursue any fine-motor activities. Knowing of Jody's interest in airplanes, the teachers used that to draw Jody into areas of the curriculum she didn't ordinarily pursue. Small airplanes were added to the block corner and airplane stencils were placed near the art table. A large mural of an airport was hung on the fence and children were invited to paint on it. One day children cut airplane pictures out of magazines and used them on a collage. Simple airplane puzzles were placed on the puzzle table. Felt shapes and small plastic airplanes in the water table helped draw Jody toward activities requiring fine-motor skills. Jody's parents supplied her with a special art box at home, full of crayons, scissors, pens, water colors, and stencils. As her fine-motor skills increased and refined, Jody became a more confident and happier child. By the end of three months she was a regular participant in all areas of the school and seemed to be enjoying her newfound interest in art materials.

Children in General

When recording behavior, teachers see growth patterns emerge. These trends reflect the nature of human development. Both Jean Piaget and Erik Erikson used this technique to learn how children think and develop socially and emotionally. Gesell studied large numbers of children to get developmental **norms** of physical growth. Parten and Dawes watched hundreds of preschoolers and arrived at the definitive description of children's play patterns and quarreling behavior. For today's early childhood educator, observing children can provide the answer to these questions:

- What might you expect when a two-year-old pours juice?

- How will the second grade class respond to a field trip?

- What will children do when their parents leave them at school the first day?

- What is the difference between the attention span at storytime of a two-year-old and a five-year-old?

- What kind of social play is typical for the four-year-old?

- How does an infant move from crawling to walking upright?

Observation gives a feeling for group behavior as well as a developmental yardstick to compare individuals within the group. Teachers determine age-appropriate expectations from this. It is important, for example, to know that most children cannot tie their own shoes at four, but can be expected to pull them on by themselves. A general understanding aids in planning thoughtful and challenging curriculum. Teachers in a class of three-year-olds, for instance, know that many children are ready for eight- to 10-piece puzzles, but that the 20-piece jigsaw will most likely be dumped on the table and quickly abandoned.

Finally, knowledge of children in general gives teachers a solid foundation upon which to base decisions about individuals. From observing many children comes an awareness of each child's progression along the developmental scale. Experienced teachers of toddlers will not put out watercolor sets, while the second-grade teacher will do so routinely. Teachers learn that it is typical of four- and five-year-olds to exclude others from their play because they will have seen it happen countless times. The 3-1/2-year-old who is sure she is "too little" to use the toilet won't convince the knowledgeable teacher who knows that this is developmentally appropriate behavior! Decisions about single children come from watching and knowing many children. This understanding is a valuable asset when talking to parents.[1]

Developmental Relationships

Observing brings about an understanding of the various developmental areas and how they are related. Development is at once specific and integrated. Children's behavior is a mix of several distinct developmental areas and, at the same time, an integrated whole whose parts influence each other. Reference to the *whole child* implies a consideration of how development works in unison.

When observing children, one must focus on these different developmental areas. What are the language abilities of three-year-olds? What social skills do preschool children acquire? Which self-help skills can children learn before six? How does fine-motor development interact with intellectual growth? Does gross-motor skill effect successful cognitive learning? How does self-concept relate to all of the other areas?

Observing these separately brings a specific definition to the term "growth." Teachers see how the pieces fit together. When teachers have an understanding of children's thought processes, they can see why children have difficulty with the concept of dual-identity, for instance. When given a set of blocks in various sizes, colors, and shapes, a four-year-old will have no difficulty finding the red ones or square ones, but may be puzzled when asked to find those that are both red and square. No wonder that same child has difficulty understanding that someone can be their best friend and like someone else at the same time.

Practiced observation will show that a child's skills are multiple and varied and have only limited connection to age. Derek has the physical coordination of a 4-1/2-year-old, language skills of a six-year-old, and the social skills of a two-year-old—all bound up in a body that just turned three. A brief picture such as this "whole child" can be helpful to both parents and teachers.

Influences on Behavior

Careful observation in the classroom and on the playground benefits an understanding of child growth and behavior. This includes an understanding of the influences and dynamics of that behavior.

Boaz has a hard time when he enters child care each morning, yet he is competent and says he likes school. Close observation reveals that his favorite areas are climbing outdoor games and the sandbox. Boaz feels least successful in the construction and creative arts areas, the primary choices indoors, where his school day begins.

Mari, on the other hand, starts the day happily but cries frequently throughout the day. Is there a pattern to her outbursts? Watch what happens to Mari when free play is over and group time begins. She falls apart readily when it is time to move outdoors to play, time to have snacks, time to nap, and so on.

Environmental influences have an impact on both these children. The classroom arrangement and daily schedule influence children's behavior, because children are directly affected by the restraints imposed by their activities and their time. Boaz feels unsure of himself in those activities that are offered as he starts his day. Seeing only these choices as he enters the room causes him discomfort, which he shows by crying and clinging to his dad. By adding something he enjoys, such as a sand table indoors, the teacher changes the physical environment to be more appealing and positive. Boaz's difficulties in saying goodbye disappear as he finds he can be successful and comfortable at the beginning of his day.

The cause of Mari's problem is more difficult to detect. The physical environment seems to interest and appeal to her. Upon closer observation, her crying and disruptive behavior appear to happen just at the point of change, regardless of the activities before or afterwards. It is the *time* aspect of the environment that causes difficulty for her. The teacher makes a special effort to signal upcoming transitions and to involve her in bringing them about. Telling Mari "Five more minutes until naptime" or "After you wash your hands, go to the

 OUR DIVERSE WORLD OUR DIVERSE WORLD OUR DIVERSE WORLD OUR DIVERSE WORLD OUR DIVERSE WORLD

[1]Keen observers of young children come to realize that there is wide spectrum of ways in which children develop with numerous ways in which parents support this growth—not good ways and bad ways, but many different ways.

FIGURE 6.5   Understanding the child is the goal of observation. By noticing how children interact with each other and the materials, the teacher's own knowledge of growth and behavior is enriched.

snack table" gives her the clues she needs to anticipate the process of change. Asking her to announce cleanup time to the class lets her be in control of that transition.

Adult behavior affects and influences children. Annika has days of intense activity and involvement with materials; on other days she appears sluggish and disinterested. After a week of observation, teachers find a direct correlation with the presence of a student teacher. On the days the student is in the classroom, Annika calls out to him to see her artwork and watch her various accomplishments. It is on the days that the student is absent that Annika's activity level falls. Once a pattern is noticed, the teacher acts upon these observations. In this case, the teacher and the student teacher work together to encourage Annika's daily involvement in school. The student teacher offers Annika ideas for activities she could demonstrate to him the following day. When he is absent, the teacher tries some of his activities that Annika especially enjoys.

Children also influence one another in powerful ways. Anyone who has worked with toddlers knows how attractive a toy becomes to a child once another has it. The six-year-old who suddenly dislikes school may be feeling left out of a friendship group. Teachers need to carefully observe the social dynamics of the class as they seek to understand individual children.

Understanding of Self

Observing children can be a key to understanding ourselves. People who develop observational skills notice human behavior more accurately. They become skilled at seeing small but important facets of human personality. They learn to differentiate between what is fact and what is inference. This increases an awareness of self as teacher and how one's biases affect the perceptions of children.[1]

 OUR DIVERSE WORLD OUR DIVERSE WORLD OUR DIVERSE WORLD OUR DIVERSE WORLD OUR DIVERSE WORLD

[1]In the field of early childhood education, one is reminded over and over again of the image of learning as a two way, not a one way, street. One teaches children *and* learns from children and families.

Understanding What We Observe:
A Multicultural Perspective

Janet Gonzalez-Mena

When we observe young children, what we see is influenced by our culture. Even though we are objective, culture colors our description.

For example, I watch a two-year-old scream "mine" and fend off a boy trying to grab the blanket she's holding. She is obviously protecting "her security blanket." What I see reveals my culture, because the "her" implies ownership and "security blanket" gives special meaning to the piece of cloth. My choice of words relates to my cultural perspective on property rights as I watch a girl "stand up for herself."

Through a different pair of cultural eyes, this scene might not make the same kind of sense. Suppose I didn't believe in private property nor have the concept that an object could provide security. I might focus on the "selfishness" of this child. The way I understand the situation can affect the words I choose to describe it.

When I see a child shouting at another child in anger, I know he is just "expressing his feelings." I come from a culture in which individuality and self-expression are important. Someone from a culture that puts little focus on the individual may see self-expression in a different light. That person might describe the scene from the view of what the boy is doing to the harmony of the group.

If I observe children fingering rice at a "sensory table," I see their behavior differently from the person who thinks they are playing with food, especially if that person regards rice as sacred.

The observers see the same behavior but think of it in very different terms, thus affecting their description.

Janet Gonzalez-Mena, of Napa Valley College, is co-author of Infants, Toddlers, and Caregivers *(Mayfield, 1993) and author of* Multicultural Issues in Child Care *(Mayfield, 1993)*

The values and benefits of observation are long-lasting. Only by practicing observations—what it takes to look, to see, to become more sensitive—will teachers be able to record children's behavior fully and vividly, capturing the unique qualities, culture and personality of each child. The Focus Box by Janet Gonzales-Mena gives a multicultural perspective to observing children. According to Dr. Edith Dowley, observation of children can be made at three levels. First, report exactly what the child *does*. Second, express how the child seems to *feel* about what happened. Last, include your own impressions and *interpretations*. The challenge of observation is high, but the benefits are well worth the effort.

RECORDING OBSERVATIONS

Once teachers and students understand why observing is important, they must then learn how to record what they see. While children are constantly under the teacher's eyes, so much happens so fast that critical events are lost in the daily routine of classrooms. Systematic observations aid in recording events and help teachers make sense of them.

In recording what you observe, you need to learn how to look and to learn the language of recording. The previous section ("What Is Observation?") helps by pointing out what to look for, and the concluding section of this chapter ("How to Observe and Record") will give you some of the "nuts and bolts" of observing. *Learning to look,* however, requires a certain willingness to become aware and to do more than simply watch. While it is true that teachers rarely have the luxury of observing uninterrupted for long periods of time, they can often plan shorter segments. Practice by paying attention to the content of children's play during free periods—theirs and yours.

Next, try your hand at jotting some notes about that play. It is easy to get discouraged, espe-

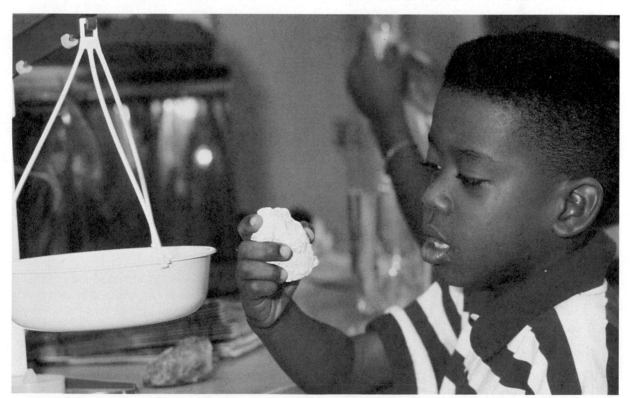

FIGURE 6.6   Teachers balance observing with interacting. When a child asks a question, the teacher is available but not intrusive so that the child's play is uninterrupted and the teacher can resume observation.

cially if you are unaccustomed to writing. The *language of recording* gets easier as you practice finding synonyms for common words. For instance, children are active creatures—how many ways do they run? They may gallop, dart, whirl, saunter, skip, hop. Or think of the various ways children talk to you: they shriek, whisper, whine, shout, demand, whimper, lisp, roar. Once you have a certain mastery of the language (and be sure to record what you see in the language that comes easiest to you), describing the important nuances of children's behavior will become easier. For an example of such descriptions, see Figure 14.7 about children's feelings.

Common Elements of Observations

The key ingredients in all types of observations used in recording children's behavior are (1) defining and describing the behaviors and (2) repeating the observation in terms of several factors such as time, number of children, or activities. All observational systems have certain elements in common:

Focus

● What do you want to know?

● Whom/what do you want to observe? Child? Teacher? Environment? Group?

● What aspects of behavior do you want to know about? Motor skills? Social development? Problem-solving?

● What is your purpose?
Study the environment?
Observe the daily schedule?
Evaluate a child's skills?
Deal with negative behavior?
Analyze transitions?
Do research?
Conference with parents?
Train teachers?

System

● What will you do?

● How will you define the terms?

● How will you record the information you need?

● How detailed will your record be?

● Will you need units of measure? What kind?

● For how long will you record?

Tools

● What will you need for your observations?

● How will you record what you want to know? Video or tape recorder? Camera? Pencil? Chart?

Environment

● Where will you watch? Classroom? Yard? Home?

● What restraints are inherent in the setting?

Using these building blocks of observational systems, teachers seek a method that yields a collection of observable data that helps them focus more clearly on a child or situation. Four major methods of observing and two additional information-gathering techniques will be discussed. They are:

1. Narratives (diary descriptions, running records, specimen descriptions, anecdotal notes)

2. Time sampling

3. Event sampling

4. Modified child study techniques (Checklists, rating scales, shadow study)

5. Experimental procedures

6. The clinical method

Types of Observations

Narratives

At once the most valuable and most difficult of records, narratives are attempts to record nearly everything that happens. In the case of a young child, this means all that the child does, says, gestures, seems to feel, and appears to think about. Narratives maintain a running record of the excitement and tension of the interaction while remaining an accurate, objective account of the events and behavior. Narratives are an attempt to actually recreate the scene by recording it in thor-

The Child Alone

Unoccupied Behavior. SH slowly walks from the classroom to the outside play area, looking up each time one of the children swishes by. SH stops when reaching the table and benches and begins pulling the string on the sweatshirt. Still standing, SH looks around the yard for a minute, then wanders slowly over to the seesaw. Leaning against it, SH touches the seesaw gingerly, then trails both hands over it while looking out into the yard. (*Interpretive comments*: This unoccupied behavior is probably due to two reasons: SH is overweight and has limited language skills compared to the other children. Pulling at the sweatshirt string is something to do to pass the time, since the overweight body is awkward and not especially skillful.)

Onlooker Behavior. J is standing next to the slide watching her classmates using this piece of equipment. She looks up and says, "Hi." Her eyes open wider as she watches the children go down the slide. P calls to J to join them but J shakes her head "no." (*Interpretive comments*: J is interested in the slide but is reluctant to use it. She has a concerned look on her face when the others slide down; it seems too much of a challenge for J.)

Solitary Play. L comes running onto the yard holding two paintbrushes and a bucket filled with water. He stops about 3 feet away from a group of children playing with cars, trucks, and buses in the sandbox and sits down. He drops the brushes into the bucket and laughs when the water splashes his face. He begins swishing the water around with the brushes and then starts wiggling his fingers in it. (*Interpretive comments*: L is very energetic and seems to thoroughly enjoy his outside playtime with water. He adds creative touches to this pleasurable experience.)

FIGURE 6.7 The narrative form of observation gives a rich sample of children's behavior; even though it risks teacher bias, it still records valuable information. (Courtesy Laura Hutton, Foothill College, Calif.)

ough and vivid language. Observers put into words what they see, hear, and know about an event or a person. The result is a full and dynamic report.

Narratives are the oldest and often most informative kind of report. Historically, as Arnold Gesell reported, they were used to set basic developmental norms. They are a standard technique in anthropology and the biological sciences. Irwin and Bushnell (1980) provide a detailed historical background that traces the narrative back to Pestalozzi (1700s) and Darwin (1800s). Jean Piaget watched and recorded in minute detail his own children's growth. His observations resulted in a full report on children's thought processes and development of intelligence. **"Baby biographies,"** narratives written by parents, were some of the first methods used in child study and reached their peak of popularity in the early 1900s.

Diary descriptions are one form of narrative. Just as the term implies, they are, in diary form, consecutive records of everything children do and say and how they do it. The process is a natural one. In the classroom this means describing every action observed within a given time period. It might be a five-minute period during free play to watch and record what one child does. The child who is a loner, the child who wanders, and the

child who is aggressive are prime candidates for a diary description. Another way to use this type of **running record** is to watch an area of the yard or room, then record who is there and how they are using the materials.

A more common form of the narrative is a modified version of a running record, or a **specimen description** as it is often called in research terms. The procedure is to take on-the-spot notes of a specific child each day. This task lends itself easily to most early childhood settings. The teachers carry with them a small notebook and pencil, tucked in a pocket. They jot down whatever seems important or noteworthy during the day. They may focus on one specimen at a time:

- A part of the environment—how is the science area being used?

- A particular time of day—what happens right after naps?

- A specific child—how often is Lucy hitting out at other children?

This system may be even less structured with all the teachers taking "on-the-hoof" notes as daily incidents occur. These notes then become a rich source of information for report writing and parent conferences.

Another form of narrative is a log or journal A page is set aside for each child in the class. At some point, teachers write in details about each child. Since this is time-consuming and needs to be done without interruption, it helps to write immediately after school is over. Sometimes teaching teams organize themselves to enable one member of the staff to observe and record in the journal during class time. The important point is that each child's general behavior is recorded either while it is happening or soon afterward.

The challenging part of this recording technique, the narrative, is to have enough detail so the reader will be able to picture whole situations later. Using language as a descriptive tool requires a large vocabulary and skillful recorder. Whatever notes the teachers use, however brief, need to be both clear and accurate.

At the same time teachers are recording in a graphic way, they need to be aware of the personal biases that can influence observations. When we look at children, what we see is in part a result of our personal experiences, the theories we hold, and the assumptions we make.[1] Teaching is an intensely personal activity, and what the children look like, do, and say may arouse strong feelings and reactions. Figure 6.3 compares two observations to illustrate this point. By becoming aware of our biases and assumptions, we can become more accurate and objective in our work as teachers. Figure 6.7 is an example of the narrative type of observation.

Narratives are an observational technique with roots in psychology, anthropology, and biology. They can follow several formats and are an attempt to record all that happens as it happens. There are many advantages to this type of observation. Narratives are rich in information, provide detailed behavioral accounts, and are relatively easy to record. With a minimum of equipment and training, teachers can learn to take notes on what children do and say. To write down everything is impossible, so some selection is necessary. These judgment calls can warp the narrative. Also, observations of this kind require large amounts of time—just what teachers who are involved with a

group of children lack. The main disadvantages of narratives, then, are the time they can take, the language and the vocabulary that must be used, and the biases the recorder may have. Even though the narrative remains one of the most widely used and effective methods of observing young children today, many teachers prefer more structured procedures because of these problems. These more definite, more precise techniques still involve some personal interpretation, but the area of individual judgment is diminished. The observational techniques discussed in the following sections also tend to be less time-consuming than the narrative.

Time Sampling

This method collects information other than that which a narrative provides. It is less descriptive, more specific, and requires different observational skills. A time sample is an observation of what happens within a given period of time. Developed as an observational strategy in laboratory schools in the 1920s, time sampling was used to collect data on large numbers of children and to get a sense of normative behaviors for particular age groups or sexes.

Time sampling appears to have originated with research in child development. It has been used to record autonomy, dependency, task persistence, aggression, and social involvement. Time sampling has also been used to study dependent, independent, and solitary play patterns and to record nervous habits of schoolchildren, such as nail biting and hair twisting (Prescott, 1973, and Irwin and Bushnell, 1980). The definitive study using time sampling is Mildred Parten's observation in the 1930s of children's play. The codes developed in this study have become classic play patterns: parallel, associative, and cooperative play. These codes are used throughout this text (see Chapters 3, 11, and 14), as well as in the professional field to describe the interactions of children.

In a time sample, behavior is recorded at regular time intervals. To use this method, one needs

OUR DIVERSE WORLD OUR DIVERSE WORLD OUR DIVERSE WORLD OUR DIVERSE WORLD OUR DIVERSE WORLD

[1]It is a given we all have biases. It is not realistic to think one can be "bias-free." The goal is to be conscious of the bias we bring to our work and not let our individual bias dictate our observations and interactions with children from diverse backgrounds.

Child	9:00			9:05			9:10			9:20			9:25			9:30			Total
	P	A	C	P	A	C	P	A	C	P	A	C	P	A	C	P	A	C	
Jamal																			
Marty																			
Dahlia																			
Keith																			
Rosa																			
Cameron																			
Hannah																			

PLAY WITH OTHERS
P = Parallel
A = Associative
C = Cooperative

Time Unit

FIGURE 6.8 Time sampling of play with others involves defining the behavior and making a coding sheet to tally observations.

to sample what occurs fairly frequently. It makes sense to choose those behaviors that might occur, say, at least once every 10 minutes. Figure 6.8 demonstrates a time-sampling procedure.

Time sampling has its own advantages and disadvantages. The process itself helps teachers define exactly what it is they want to observe. Certainly it helps focus on specific behaviors and how often they occur. Time sampling is ideal for collecting information about the group as a whole. Finally, by defining behaviors clearly and developing a category and coding system, the problem of observer bias is reduced.

Yet by diminishing this bias one also eliminates some of the richness and quality of information. It is difficult to get the whole picture when one divides it into artificial time units and with only a few categories. The key is to decide what it is teachers want to know, then choose the observational method that best suits those needs. When narratives or time samplings won't suffice, perhaps an event sampling will.

Event Sampling

This is one of the more intriguing techniques. With this method, the observer defines an event, devises a system for describing and coding it, then waits for it to happen. As soon as it does, the recorder moves into action. Thus, the behavior is recorded as it occurs naturally.

The events that are chosen can be quite interesting and diverse. Consider Helen C. Dawes' classic analysis of preschool children's quarrels. Whenever a quarrel began, the observer recorded it. She recorded how long the quarrel lasted, what was happening when it started, what behaviors happened during the quarrel (including what was done and said), what the outcome was, and what happened afterwards. Her format for recording included duration (X number of seconds), a narrative for the situation, verbal or motor activity, and checklists for the quarrel behavior, outcome, and aftereffects (Irwin & Bushnell, 1980).

Other researchers have studied dominance

Event Sampling Guidelines				
1. Define the behavior to be observed. 2. Decide what information you want to know. 3. Make a simple recording sheet.			*Children's accidents: spills, knock-overs, falls. Child(ren) involved, time, place, cause, results. To watch in early morning:*	
Time	Children	Place	Cause	Outcome
8:50	Shelley, Mike	playdough	M steps on S toes	S cries, runs to Tchr
9:33	Tasauna, Yuki	blocks	T runs through, knocks over Y tower	Y hits T, both cry
9:56	Spencer	yard	S turns trike too sharp, falls off	S cries, wants mom
10:28	Lorena, Shelley	doll corner	L bumps table spills pitcher S has just set there	S cries, runs to Tchr
Total 8:45-10:30 AM = 4				

and emotions. Teachers can use event sampling to look at these and other behaviors such as bossiness, avoidance of teacher requests, or withdrawal. Figure 6.9 is an example of an event sampling.

Like time sampling, event sampling looks at a particular behavior or occurrence. But the unit is the event rather than a prescribed time interval. Here again the behavior must be clearly defined and the recording sheet easy to use. Unlike with time sampling, the event to be recorded may occur a number of times during the observation.

For these reasons, event sampling is a favorite of classroom teachers. They can go about the business of teaching children until the event occurs. Then they can record the event quickly and efficiently. By prescribing the context within which the event occurs, some of the quality often lost in time sampling is regained. The only disadvantage is that the richness of detail of the narrative descriptions is missing.

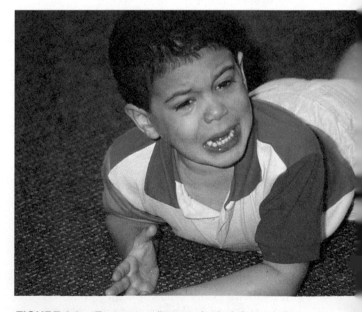

FIGURE 6.9 Event sampling can be helpful in determining how frequently a specific event takes place. For instance, sampling the number and types of accidents for a given child or time frame helps teachers see what is happening in class.

Observer _____   Date _____   Time _____

Learning Center	Anna	Charlie	Leticia	Neroko	Mat	Josie	Totals
Indoors							
Science Area					1		1
Dramatic Play	1	1	1			1	4
Art	1		1	1			3
Blocks		1					1
Manipulatives			1	1	1		3
Easels			1				1
Music			1		1		2
Outdoors							
Water/Sand/Mud		1	1			1	3
Blocks				1	1		2
Wheel Toys		1			1		2
Climbers	1		1			1	3
Woodworking				1			1
Ball Games	1						1
Animal Care	1	1				1	3
Totals	5	5	6	5	5	4	

FIGURE 6.10 An activity checklist. With data collected for a week, teachers have a broad picture of how children spend their time at school and what activities interest them.

Modified Child Study Techniques

Since observation is the key method of studying young children in their natural settings, it makes good sense to develop many kinds of observational skills. Each can be tailored to fit the individual child, the particular group, the kind of staff, and the specific problem. Teachers who live in complex, creative classrooms have questions arise that need fast answers. Modified child study techniques can define the scope of the problem fairly quickly. Some of the techniques are: checklist systems, rating scales, shadow studies, and modified processes that reach both the group and the individuals in it.

Checklists contain a great deal of information that can be recorded rapidly. A carefully planned checklist can tell a lot about one child or the entire class. The data is collected in a short space of time, usually about a week. Figure 6.10 is an example of an activity checklist. With data collected for a week, teachers have a broad picture of how these children spend their time and what activities interest them.

If, however, teachers want to assess children's motor skills, a yes/no list is preferable. Figure 6.11 illustrates the use of such a chart.

Checklists can vary in length and complexity depending on their functions. To develop one, teachers first determine the purpose of the observation. Next they define what the children will do to demonstrate the behavior being observed. Finally comes designing the actual checklist, one

Motor Skills Observation (ages 2-4) Child_____ Date_____ Observer_____ Age_____		
Eating:	Yes	No
1. Holds glass with one hand		
2. Pours from pitcher		
3. Spills little from spoon		
4. Selects food with pincer grasp		
Dressing:		
1. Unbuttons		
2. Puts shoes on		
3. Uses both hands together (such as holding jacket		
with one hand while zipping with the other)		
Fine Motor:		
1. Uses pincer grasp with pencil, brushes		
2. Draws straight line		
3. Copies circles		
4. Cuts at least 2″ in line		
5. Makes designs and crude letters		
6. Builds tower of 6-9 blocks		
7. Turns pages singly		
Gross Motor:		
1. Descends/ascends steps with alternate feet		
2. Stands on one foot, unsupported		
3. Hops on two feet		
4. Catches ball, arms straight, elbows in front of body		
5. Operates tricycle		

FIGURE 6.11   A yes/no checklist gives specific information about an individual child's skills.

that is easy to use and simple to set aside when other duties must take precedence.

Although they are easy to record, checklists lack the richness of the more descriptive narrative. For instance, by looking at the checklist in Figure 6.10 teachers will know which activities children have chosen, but they will not gain a sense of how they played in each area, the time spent there, or whether and with whom they interacted. The advantage of checklists is that they can tally broad areas of information, and teachers can create one with relative ease. Checklists are often used in evaluation. Chapter 10 contains several examples.

Rating scales are like checklists, planned in advance to record something specific. They extend checklists by adding some quality to what is observed. The advantage is that more information is

gathered. A potential problem is added, since the observers' opinions are now required and could hamper objectivity.

Rating scales differ from checklists in several ways. Instead of simply recording where children are playing, the rating scales require the teacher to decide how they are playing. What is the extent of their involvement and the frequency or degree of their play? A rating scale may use word phrases ("always," "sometimes," "never") or a numerical key (1 through 5).

Developing a rating scale is simple, though a good scale can be difficult to make. The full range of behavior teachers will observe cannot always be easily reduced to discrete measurements. However, after deciding what to observe, teachers then determine what the children will do to demonstrate the action. To measure attention at group times, a scale might include the categories in Figure 6.12. Each teacher's rating scale could include a series of checkmarks that record each group time for a period of two weeks. The staff pools information by comparing notes. The result is a detailed description of (1) each child's behavior as each teacher sees it; (2) the group's overall attention level; and (3) an interesting cross-teacher comparison.

The shadow study is a third type of modified technique. It is similar to the diary description and focuses on one child at a time. An in-depth approach, the shadow study gives a detailed picture.

Each teacher attempts to observe and record regularly the behavior of one particular child. Then after a week or so the notes are compared. Although the notes may be random, it is preferable to give them some form and organization. Divide a sheet of paper in half lengthwise, with one column for the environment and the other column for details about the child's behavior or response. This will make it easy to glance at 15-minute intervals to collect the data. Figure 6.13 illustrates this process.

The data in a shadow study is descriptive. In this, it shares the advantages of narratives. One of its disadvantages is that teachers may let other matters go while focusing on one child. Also, the shadow study can be quite time-consuming. Still, one interesting side effect often noted is how the behavior of the child being studied improves while being observed. The disruptive behavior seems to diminish or appear less intense. It would appear that in the act of focusing on the child, teacher attention has somehow helped to alter the behavior. Somehow the child feels the impact of all this positive, caring attention and responds to it.

Modified child study techniques are particularly useful because they are tailored to fit the specific needs and interests of the teachers. Teachers know what it is they want to observe and can develop a method of recording that matches their needs and the time available during school. Devising a new technique is neither easy nor quick. It takes hard work and dedicated teachers committed to improving their observational skills to record accurately what they see.

Additional Information-Gathering Techniques

Two additional strategies are used to obtain information about a child. Because they involve some adult intervention, they do not consist strictly of observing and recording naturally occurring behavior. Still, they are very helpful techniques for teachers to understand and use.

Experimental Procedures

Experimental procedures are those in which adult researchers closely control a situation and its variables. Researchers create a situation in which they can (1) observe a particular behavior, (2) make a hypothesis, or guess, about that behavior, and (3) test the hypothesis by conducting the experiment.

For instance, an experimenter might wish to observe fine-motor behavior in seven-year-olds to test the hypothesis that these children can significantly improve their fine-motor skills in sewing if given specific instructions. Two groups of children are tested. One group is given an embroidery hoop, thread, and needle and asked to make 10 stitches. The other receives a demonstration of how to stitch and is then given the identical task. The embroidery hoops created by both groups are

---

NEVER ATTENDS (wiggles, distracts others, wanders away).

SELDOM ATTENDS (eyes wander, never follows fingerplays or songs, occasionally watches leader).

SOMETIMES ATTENDS (can be seen imitating hand gestures, appears to be watching leader about half the time, watches others imitating leader).

USUALLY ATTENDS (often follows leader, rarely leaves group, rarely needs redirection, occasionally volunteers, usually follows leader's gestures and imitations).

ALWAYS ATTENDS (regularly volunteers, enthusiastically enters into each activity, eagerly imitates leader, almost always tries new songs).

FIGURE 6.12 A rating scale measuring attention at group times requires data in terms of frequency, adding depth to the observation.

Child's Name _Jeff_

Time	Setting (where)	Behavior/Response (what and how)
9:00	Arrives—cubby, removes wraps, etc.	"I can put on my own nametag" (enthusiastically). Uses thumb to push sharp end of pin; grins widely. Goes to teacher, "Did you see what I did?"
9:15	Blocks	Precise, elaborate work with small cubes on top of block structure which he built with James. "Those are the dead ones," pointing to the purple cubes outside the structure. Cries and hits Kate when her elbow accidentally knocks tower off.
9:30	Wandering around room	Semidistant, slow pace. Stops at table where children are preparing snack. Does not make eye contact with teacher when invited to sit; Ali grabs J.'s shirt and tugs at it. "The teacher is talking to you!" J. blinks, then sits and asks to help make snack. Stays 10 minutes.

FIGURE 6.13 A shadow study will profile an individual child in the class. This method is especially useful for children who seem to be having trouble in school.

then compared. Some previously agreed-upon criteria are used to quantify the fine-motor skill demonstrated by the two groups' work. The major criteria for a scientific experiment may be applied to this procedure as follows:

1. The experimenters can control all relevant aspects of the behavior. (In this case, the materials can be controlled, although previous experience with embroidering cannot.)

2. Usually, only one variable at a time should be measured. (Only fine-motor skill as it relates to embroidery is observed, not other skills such as language or information processing, or even fine-motor proficiency in printing or drawing.)

3. Children are assigned to the two groups in a random manner. (In other words, the groups are not divided by sex, age, or any other predetermined characteristics.)

Few teachers working directly with children will use the stringent criteria needed to undertake a true scientific experiment. However, it is useful to understand this process because much basic research conducted to investigate how children think, perceive, and behave utilizes these techniques.

Clinical Method

The clinical method is another information-gathering technique that involves the adult directly with the child. This method is used in psychotherapy and in counseling settings, as the therapist asks probing questions. The master of **le methode clinique** with children was Piaget, who would observe and question a child about a situation as described in Chapter 4. Two examples of this method are:

Three-month-old Jenna is lying in a crib looking at a mobile. Her hands are waving in the air. The adult wonders whether Jenna will reach out and grasp the mobile if it is moved close to her hands. Or will she bat at the toy? Move her hands away? The adult then tries it to see what will happen.

A group of preschoolers are gathered around a water table. The teacher notices two cups, one deep and narrow, the other broad and shallow, and asks, "I wonder which one holds more, or if they are the same?" The children say what they think and why. Then, one of the children takes the two cups and pours the liquid from one into the other.

In both examples, the adult does more than simply observe and record what happens. With the infant, the adult questions what Jenna's responses might be and then watches for the answer. The preschool teacher intervenes in the children's natural play to explore a question systematically with them, then listens for and observes the answers. The clinical method is not strictly an observational method, but it is an informative technique that, when used carefully, can reveal much about children's abilities and knowledge.

All these observation techniques help adults watch closely to see what is going on. Figure 6.13 summarizes these systems. It is safe to say that whenever a teacher encounters a problem—be it a child's behavior, a period of the day, a set of materials, or a puzzling series of events—the first step toward a solution is systematic observation.

HOW TO OBSERVE AND RECORD

Learning how to observe is a serious activity and requires a great deal of concentration. Some preparations can be made beforehand so that full attention is focused on the observation. Thinking through some of the possible problems helps the teacher get the most out of the experience.

Observing While Teaching

To make observing workable at school, it is important to keep in mind that there is no one right way to observe and record. Some teachers find certain times of the day easier than others. Many prefer to watch during free play, while others find it easier to watch individual children during directed teaching times. While some teachers keep a pencil and paper handy to write their observations throughout the day, others choose to record what they see after school is over for the day. The professional team that is committed to observation will find ways to support its implementation.

Finding an opportunity for regular observations is difficult. Centers are rarely staffed so well that one teacher can be free from classroom responsibilities for long periods of time. Some schools ask for parent volunteers to take over an activity while a teacher observes. In one center the snack was set up ahead of time to free up one teacher to observe during group time. The environment can be arranged with activities that require little supervision when a teacher is interested in making some observations.

Some question the reliability of the data collected when children know they are being observed. Initially, children may feel self-conscious, asking pointed questions of the observer and changing their behavior as if they were on stage. However, when effective observation strategies are used (see the section in this chapter entitled How to Observe Effectively) and regular observations are done by familiar adults, children will soon ignore the observer and resume normal activity.

Teachers practice observations and recording techniques outside the classroom. Staff meetings take on an added dimension when teachers role play, devise word games, and draw up observation forms together. At home, observation strategies are used to compare notes on a segment of a television program.

The teacher who makes notes during class time has other considerations. The need to be inconspicuous while note taking is important when trying to teach and record simultaneously. Wear clothing with at least one good pocket. This ensures the paper and pencil are available when needed and the children's privacy is protected. Take care not to leave notes out on tables, shelves, or in cupboards for others to see. They should be kept confidential until added to the children's records.

Respect the privacy of the children and their families at all times. Any information gathered as part of an observation is treated with strict confidentiality. Teachers and students are careful not to use children's names in casual conversation. They do not talk about children in front of other children or themselves. It is the role of the adults to see that children's privacy is maintained. Carrying tales out of school is tempting, but unprofessional.

Method	Observational Interval	Recording Techniques	Advantages	Disadvantages
1. Narratives Diary description	Day to day	Using notebook and pencil; can itemize activity or other ongoing behavior; can see growth patterns	Rich in detail; maintains sequence of events; describes behavior as it occurs	Open to observer bias; time-consuming
Specimen descriptions/ running record	Continuous sequences	Same	Less structured	Sometimes need follow-up
Journal	Regular, preferred daily/ weekly	Log, usually with space for each child; often a summary of child's behavior		Lack detail; need to be filled in at later time; can detract from teaching responsibilities
"On-the-Hoof" Anecdotes	Sporadic	Ongoing during class time; using notepad and paper in hand	Quick and easy to take; short-capture pertinent events/details	
2. Time Sampling	Short and uniform time intervals	On-the-spot as time passes; prearranged recording sheets	Easy to record; easy to analyze; relatively bias free	Limited behaviors; loss of detail; loss of sequence and ecology of event
3. Event Sampling	For the duration of the event	Same as time sampling	Easy to record; easy to analyze; can maintain flow of class activity easily	Limited behaviors; loss of detail; must wait for behavior to occur
4. Modifications Checklists	Regular or intermittent	Using prepared recording sheets; can be both during or after class	Easy to develop and use	Lack of detail; tells little of the cause of behaviors
Rating scales	Continuous behavior	Same as for checklists	Easy to develop and use; can use for wide range of behaviors	Ambiguity of terms; high observer bias
Shadow study	Continuous behavior	Narrative-type recording; uses prepared recording sheets	Rich in detail; focuses in depth on individual	Bias problem; can take away too much of a teacher's time and attention
5. Experimental procedures	Short and uniform	May be checklists, prearranged recording sheets, audio or video tape	Simple, clear, pure study, relatively bias free	Difficult, hard to isolate in the classroom
6. Clinical method	Any time	Usually notebook or tape recorder	Relevant data, can be spontaneous, easy	Adult has changed naturally occurring behavior

FIGURE 6.14 A summary chart of the major observational techniques that the early childhood professional can use to record children's behavior. (Adapted from Irwin, D.M., and Bushnell, M.M., *Observational Strategies for Child Study*. New York: Holt, Rinehart and Winston, 1980.)

FIGURE 6.15   Observation skills are honed when teachers have opportunities to work with a few children at a time.

Beginning to Observe

In some schools, observers are a normal part of the school routine. In colleges where there are laboratory facilities on campus, visitors and student observers are familiar figures. They have only to follow established guidelines for making an observation.

Many times students are responsible for finding their own places to observe children. If so, the student calls ahead and schedules a time to observe that is convenient. Be specific about observation needs, the assignment, the ages of children desired, the amount of time needed, and the purpose of the observation.

If you are planning to observe in your own class, several steps are necessary for a professional observation and a believable recording. First, plan the observation. Have a specific *goal* in mind, and even put that at the top of your recording sheet. Goals can be general ("Let's see what activities Ajit chooses today.") or specific ("Watch for in-

stances of quarreling in the sand area."). Second, *observe and record.* To be objective, be as specific and detailed as possible. Write only the behavior—the "raw data"—and save the analysis and your interpretation for later. After class, re-read your notes (transcribing them into something legible if anyone else might need to read them) and make some conclusions. Your observation was *what* happened; the *interpretation* is the place for your opinions and ideas of *why* it happened. For instance, you may have found that three of the four quarrels were over holding the hose; this gives you a clear reason for the quarrels. The final step is implementing your solutions; plan what you will do next, and then *follow through* with your ideas. In our example, a five-pronged hose outlet could be purchased, a waiting list started for the "hose-holder job," or the teacher could be in charge of the hose.

Wherever an observation is planned, it is critical to maintain **professional confidentiality.** If observing at another site, call ahead for an ap-

FIGURE 6.16 Learning to observe and record effectively takes time and practice. Remaining unobtrusive and recording quietly allow children to continue their natural behavior without distraction.

pointment. Talk about the purpose and format of your observation with both director and teacher. Finally, in *any* discussion of the observation, change the children's names and school to protect those involved.

How to Observe Effectively

The success of the observation depends on how inconspicuous the observer can be. Children are more natural if the observer blends into the scenery. By sitting back, one can observe the whole scene and record what is seen and heard, undisturbed and uninfluenced. This distancing sets up a climate for recording that aids the observer in concentrating on the children.

There are two main reasons for an observer to be **unobtrusive.** First, it allows for a more accurate recording of the children's activities. Second, it does not interfere with the smooth functioning of the classroom, the children, or the teachers. In the case of teachers observing their own programs, you must plan ahead with co-teachers and have materials at hand that can be set aside quickly if necessary. Figure 6.16 shows an effective distance for unobtrusive observing. The following suggestions help effective observing:

- Enter and leave the area quietly. Ask the teacher where to sit. Keep in the background as much as possible. The good observer is so skilled at this that both children and teachers forget the presence of a stranger.

- Sit down in a low chair in an out-of-the-way place. Sit where the activity of the children is unobstructed. By keeping low, observers call less attention to themselves. Take care to sit outside traffic patterns so children will be able to carry on with play without interference or interruption.

- Sit at the edge of an activity rather than right in the middle of it. Against a wall or around the perimeter of the room are good vantage points for sitting. Outside, if no chair is available, blend against a wall, a fence, or a tree.

- Sometimes it may be necessary to follow children as they move from place to place. When that happens, be as inconspicuous as possible and be prepared for times when, for good reasons, the teacher might object.

- Children may occasionally ask, "What is your name? What are you doing? Why did you come here?" If asked a direct question, answer in a truthful, friendly manner, but be as brief as possible. A good response is, "I'm working." Avoid initiating conversations with children. Be as natural as possible if a child talks to you, but appear to be busy writing and observing.

- It is difficult to be in a busy classroom with children without being amused by them. Avoid a degree of response that will attract the children's attention. Laughing at them, smiling, talking, meeting their eyes, distracts them from play. It also makes the observer the center of their attention rather than their work or playmates.

- Avoid talking to other adults while observing. Sitting apart from others draws less attention to the tasks and lessens the temptation to chat. Request a brief conference before leaving to check accuracy.

- There is one time when it might be necessary to get involved with the children. If a child is in obvious danger and no one else is around, the observer should step in. Call for a teacher only if there is time. A child running out the gate toward the street or in the way of a swing needs immediate help. Two children fighting over a truck might need a teacher but are not in immediate danger.

SUMMARY

Systematic observation and recording of children's behavior is a fundamental tool in understanding children. What children do and say and how they think and feel are revealed as they play and work. By learning to observe children's behavior, teachers become more aware of the children's skills, needs, and concerns.

The ability to observe is a skill in itself; teachers examine their own lives and attitudes in order to achieve a measure of objectivity. Recording the observations is another skill, one that requires facility with the written word and an understanding of the purpose for observing. For an observation to be successful, teachers first decide what it is they want to find out about the child(ren).

Key ingredients to successful observations include clear definitions of the behaviors to be observed and techniques for observing and recording them. These provide the tools for gaining a deeper understanding of individual children and the group. They also enhance knowledge about the interrelationships of developmental areas. Too, one gains insight into the dynamics of child behavior and what influences are brought to bear on it. Finally, observing children can give insight and greater understanding of self.

The general types of observational techniques explored in this chapter include narratives, time sampling, event sampling, and modified child study techniques, such as checklists, rating scales, and shadow studies. Additional information-gathering techniques include experimental procedures and the clinical method.

As teachers observe and record the behavior of young children, they are aware of professional guidelines that protect children. The guidelines help ensure accurate observation and help the observer respect the privacy of the individual or group.

R E V I E W   Q U E S T I O N S

1. List four observational methods. Describe the advantages and disadvantages of each. Which would you prefer? Why? Which one(s) might best suit a beginning teacher? A parent? An experienced teacher? The director of the school?

2. Observe a child for 10 minutes. Using language as your paintbrush, make a written picture of that child's physical appearance and movements. Include a comparison of the child's size, body build, facial features, and energy level to those of other children in the class. Record as many of the body movements as you can, noting seemingly useless movements, failures, partial successes, as well as final achievements.

3. Perceptions of a person's character are in the eyes of the beholder. These perceptions affect how teachers behave with children. What color are your glasses tinted? Divide a piece of paper in half, lengthwise. On one side, list some words to describe your feelings about childhood, school, teachers, children, authority, making friends, losing friends, hitting, playing. On the other side, describe how these feelings may have influenced your teaching and helped create your own biases.

4. Teachers have noticed that several children consistently interrupt at storytime with seemingly irrelevant questions and constantly grab onto children seated nearby. What's happening—and why? What observational tools would you use to find out? What clues from individual behavior would you look for? How would you look at the group as a whole? What other information would you need?

5. What do you consider to be the three most important guidelines to follow when observing young children? Why?

L E A R N I N G   A C T I V I T I E S

1. Observe a children's quarrel. What was happening for you when you watched? What does this tell you about your own influences in childhood? How did the teaching staff intervene? How would you? Why?

2. Try a time sample of children's play in your classroom. Observe 10 children for one minute each during free play times, and record the type(s) of social behavior they show. Using Parten's categories, your chart would look like this one. Compare your results with the impressions of the other teachers with whom you work. Did you come to any conclusions on how children develop socially?

Child/Age	Unoccupied	Solitary	Onlooker	Parallel	Associative	Cooperative
1.						
2.						
3.						
4.						
5.						
6.						
7.						
8.						
9.						
10.						

Totals

3. Observe one child in your class and jot down a brief description of her language skills. Are they typical of her age level? How could you tell? Compare your notes with the perceptions of your supervising teacher.

4. Choose two children, one you think is doing well and one who is having trouble. Observe the adult-child interactions of each. What are the differences from the *children's* point of view in the quantity and quality of those relationships? What generalizations about the importance of such relationships in the early years can you make?

5. If you can, try a shadow study on a child in your class. Choose a child you don't know much about, you have trouble working with, or who is exhibiting inappropriate behaviors. How did this study help you to see the class and school from that child's point of view?

6. Observe a group of children for 10 minutes engaged in block play. Record your observations in running record form. Now, go back over that running record and make a list of things you want to know about the children's thinking and behavior. How could you construct this list, using the clinical method, to obtain the information you need? Would you intervene nonverbally? What questions could you ask the children directly?

B I B L I O G R A P H Y

Beaty, Janice. *Observing Development of the Young Child*. Columbus, Oh.: Merrill, 1990 (2nd Ed.).

Bentzen, Matthew. *Seeing Young Children*. Albany, NY: Delmar Publishers, 1993 (2nd Ed.).

Brophy, Jere E. "Using Observation to Improve Your Teaching." *Young Children*, April/May, 1979.

Cartwright and Cartwright. *Developing Observation Skills*. 2nd ed. New York: Mc-Graw-Hill Book Company, 1984.

Cohen, D.H., and Stern, V. *Observing and Recording the Behavior of Young Children*. New York: Teachers College Press, 1978.

Dowley, Edith M. *Cues for Observing Children's Behavior*. Unpublished paper.

Irwin, D.M., and Bushnell, M.M. *Observational Strategies for Child Study*. New York: Holt, Rinehart and Winston, 1980.

Jones, Elizabeth J., and Carter, Margie. "The Teacher as Observer—Part 1," and "Teacher as Scribe and Broadcaster: Using Observation to Communicate—Part 2." In *Child Care Information Exchange*, January/February, 1991.

Robinson, Violet B. "Wonder Why and Solve a Problem—The Teacher as Researcher." In *CAEYC Connections*, Winter, 1990.

Stallings, J. *Learning to Look*. Belmont, Calif.: Wadsworth, 1977.

QUESTIONS FOR THOUGHT

Why do children behave the way they do?

What are some ways in which the classroom environment affects children's behavior?

What do teachers need to know about themselves so they can guide children with control and concern?

What is the difference between discipline and punishment?

Are behavior goals the same for all children? Why?

What are some common problem behaviors found in young children?

What are some effective ways to deal with behavior problems?

Why is spanking harmful to children?

What is the relationship between guidance and culture?

CHAPTER 7

Understanding and Guiding Behavior

UNDERSTANDING BEHAVIOR

In the toddler class, two-year-olds Shawnsey and Kim are playing in the dress-up area. Kim grabs at one of the many necklaces Shawnsey has draped around her neck. Startled, Shawnsey lets out a cry, grabs Kim's arm and bites her.

Malcolm, a 5-year-old, enters the school room in a rush, throws his jacket in the bottom of his cubby, and walks quickly to the block area. For just a moment, he stands and watches Lorraine balancing blocks on top of one another in a tall column. With a swift wave of his arm, Malcolm topples the structure.

Mac, a three-and-one-half-year-old, is busy with a puzzle. When a teacher stops at the table to tell the children it is nearly time to clean up for snacks, Mac throws the puzzle pieces on the floor and runs over to the art table.

(See Figures 7.12 and 7.15 for discussing solutions to these situations).

These are typical scenes in any early childhood center. No matter how plentiful the materials, how many or well-trained the adults, or how preplanned the program, conflicts are sure to occur. In this chapter, students will look at ways to recognize and handle such situations; how to understand and guide children's behavior in ways that will help them deal more effectively with their feelings. Helping children learn how to cope with their anger, their fears, their frustrations, and their desires is one of the most challenging jobs for a teacher.[1]

To teach children to respect themselves and each other is a complex and difficult task. It takes experience, skill, and love and is a critical part of caring for children. Look at the examples again. What do they say about children in general? What do they say about Shawnsey, Malcolm, and Mac? How should teachers respond to these children, and how does that response influence future behavior?

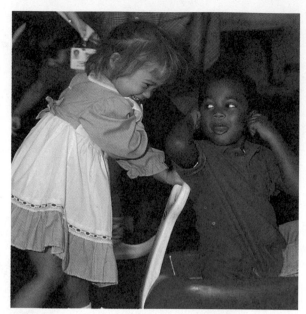

FIGURE 7.1 For guidance to be successful, a teacher must first understand children's behavior.

Theories

To guide children's behavior, a teacher must first understand it. This requires a solid background in child development, skills in observing, and understanding about *why* children behave and misbehave.

There are several ways of explaining what people do and why. One idea is that people's behavior is mainly a result of heredity (nature). Another is that experience and environment shape behavior (nurture). A third theory suggests that children go through "stages" at certain times of their lives regardless of their genes or home background.

Both sides have valid arguments in the nature/nurture debate. It is useful to remember that both heredity and experience affect behavior. Age and stage theory is also familiar. People speak of the "terrible two's" or say that all four-year-old girls are silly. There may be some truth to those generalities, but that does not excuse the inappropriate behavior of the various developmental

 OUR DIVERSE WORLD OUR DIVERSE WORLD OUR DIVERSE WORLD OUR DIVERSE WORLD OUR DIVERSE WORLD

[1]Different cultures have different ways of dealing with emotions. The educator needs an awareness of how s/he deals with particular emotions, as well as how the child's particular family culture deals with emotions.

stages. Teachers and parents cannot ignore misbe-havior just because children are the "right" age or because of their home situations. That attitude implies adults are powerless to help children form new behavior patterns. Not true!

Adults can do something about children's behavior if they understand what is happening to the child. Where does appropriate behavior come from? Why do children misbehave?

Factors That Affect Behavior

Knowing what affects children's behavior and feelings helps adults understand and manage the misbehaving child. Teachers can anticipate problems instead of waiting for them to occur; preventive guidance measures are part of guiding children's behavior.

At least five factors affect behavior: developmental factors, environmental factors, individual or personal styles, social and emotional needs, and cultural influences. These factors combine aspects of both nature and nurture theories, as well as the theories of ages and stages of development. The three vignettes at the beginning of the chapter provide examples of all five factors.

Developmental Factors

Children's growth is constant if not always smooth. Adults who work with children should be aware of developmental theory in order to know what type of behavior to expect of children at various ages.

The facts are that Shawnsey, Kim, Malcolm and Mac have been in a group setting for more than three hours and it is nearly snack time. Teachers know that preschoolers cannot be expected to be in control of themselves over extended periods of time. Conflicts and disagreements happen in any group of children. Hungry children are often ineffective problem solvers; Mac might not be as **volatile** after snack. It is also clear to the teacher that the toddlers do not have the language or social development skills to talk problems out with other children as does Malcom, a five-year-old.

Developmental theory helps teachers anticipate what children will do and how they might behave. To see behavior as predictable and develop-

ON SPANKING

. . . Physical punishment such as hitting or spanking will mean two things: one, that you are bigger than she and you can get away with it, and two, that you believe in aggression. . . . Spanking is no good. . . . It says that you believe in settling things by force—and I don't believe in that.   Brazelton (1992)

. . . I think that the uneasiness after spanking a child is most telling . . . subconsciously, we know that it is wrong, that it is not effective. Spanking does not accomplish the purpose for which it is intended. It teaches children to operate from fear rather than reason, and it breeds anger. The research evidence is also clear that physical force creates more resistance and much less cooperation.   Galinksy and David (1988)

FIGURE 7.2 Spanking children is a controversial issue. Two early childhood experts state their views. Do you agree or disagree with them? Why?

mentally appropriate is to understand it more completely. This understanding guides teachers in solving behavioral problems.

Developmental guidelines also help teachers maintain reasonable expectations. When adults are aware of which behaviors are simply beyond the capabilities of children, they can help avert situations that will lead to conflicts. Asking a group of toddlers, for example, to sit quietly together for a 20-minute story is to invite misbehavior—wriggling, talking aloud, pushing, interrupting, walking away. Yet all of these are completely normal behaviors for a two-year-old in that situation. The adult's insistence on a prolonged story time is asking these children to perform beyond their current physical, social, and cognitive abilities.

Environmental Factors

Environment for the young child is primarily home, school, or child care settings. The term environment has three distinct parts: the physical, the **temporal** (timing and scheduling), and the interpersonal. Each has an impact on children's behavior.

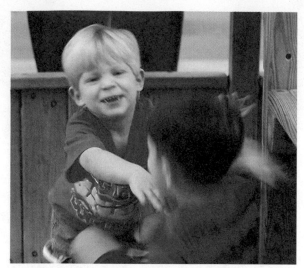

FIGURE 7.3   "I'm the boss here!"

The physical environment is a powerful tool in controlling children's behavior. Teachers can achieve a number of behavior goals through the physical facilities of the early childhood program. Child-size furniture that fits the preschool body encourages sitting and working behavior. Room arrangements that have no long, open spaces children could use as runways encourage children to walk from place to place. Low, open shelves create an expectation that children are to help themselves in taking out and putting away the materials and equipment.

Chapter 9, Creating Environments, contains a detailed discussion of many factors that should be considered when designing spaces for young children. Many of these environmental considerations directly influence children's behavior. See also the Classroom Checklist (Figure 7.9).

Materials. In addition to arrangement of room or yard, materials affect how children behave, whether in a family day care home or an after-school sports program. The materials provided can challenge children, overwhelm them, or bore them. If materials and equipment are suitable, children will feel more at ease with themselves and be more willing to accept adults' limits and controls. The materials and equipment allow appropriate outlets for children's natural tendencies; they capture interest and attention, and this helps prevent many opportunities for misbehavior. When children are occupied with stimulating, age-appropriate materials, the amount of conflict and disruption lessens. Adding materials and equipment can help prevent fights over a favorite toy, create new interests and challenges in alternative activities, and extend children's play ideas and themes. Shawnsey and Kim's teacher will want to add more necklaces to the dress-up area if there aren't enough to outfit several children. Changing the environment when needed can help avert behavior problems. Removing attractive but breakable items reduces tears and conflicts. Some materials may prove to be too stimulating and may need to be removed for a while. Some activities may need to be limited to specific locations to control the level of activity and behavior.

Time. The temporal structure, that is, the timing and scheduling of daily events, describes the sequence of a program. When there are blocks of time to choose activities, children can proceed at their own pace without feeling pushed or hurried. They feel free to work, move, and play and are able to accept the teacher's control when it is necessary. Mac, for instance, had just settled in at the puzzle table when the teacher told him that it was time to clean up. The physical needs of eating, sleeping, and toileting are met by careful scheduling so that children are able to play without concern for the necessities of life. Schedules that do not allow enough time for cleanup, for instance, produce a frantic climate. It is when children are rushed and hurried by adults that arguments, accidents, and tears ensue. Uncooperative behavior is sometimes related to time pressures.

A consistent daily plan helps promote a feeling that the world is predictable and understandable. Children need time to work out their own problems. Hurrying and wondering what happens next create tension that results in behavior problems.

Relationships. These need special consideration because they determine how learning takes place. The interpersonal environment refers to all the "people" factors. An atmosphere of trust and support helps to create a sound learning environment. In early childhood centers the significant relationships are those between teacher and child, children and other children, teacher and parents, and

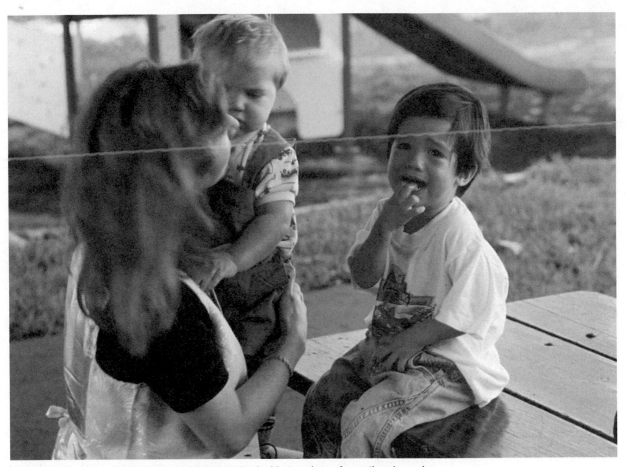

FIGURE 7.4 Teachers are called upon to deal with a variety of emotional needs.

teacher and other teachers. Each type of relationship affects and influences children's behavior. When children sense a feeling of mutual support and acceptance, their play reflects that tone. Tension among adults is quickly transmitted to children, and their behavior patterns adjust to the negative influence. The teacher will want to support and comfort Kim at the same time she lets Shawnsey know that biting will not be tolerated. It is important to maintain a level of trust with Shawnsey so that she can help her learn better ways to communicate her needs.

Other influences affect behavior. Weather seems to affect children. Wild, windy, gray, rainy days seem to stimulate children into high and excitable behavior. Bright, sunny days also seem to influence a child's mood and temperament. Problems that upset adults can make an impression on a child. A family crisis, a new baby, or a recent divorce have impact. Sharing a room, visits from relatives, illness, television and movie shows, brothers and sisters, nutrition and health cause children to behave in many different ways. The longer teachers work with children, the more adept they become at seeing how these various factors shape the behavior of the individual children in their class.

Individual Styles

People seem to come equipped with a style all their own. Pregnant women can describe a child's personality while the baby is still in the womb. Mothers know of the special way infants behave that sets them apart. Parents often comment on the differences among their own children. Raised by the same parents in the same house and neighborhood, each child is a singular and original being.

Each child in a classroom is also unique, an individual like no other. All have a personal style that needs to be acknowledged and valued.[1] Children who are not accepted for themselves may learn to hate themselves or not to trust their own instincts. A broken or timid spirit creates a timid or rebellious person.

Teachers of young children soon learn the temperamental characteristics of each child in the class.[2] Hondi works and plays with great intensity; Norman is easily distracted. Tawana fears any change while Enrique thrives on challenges. The consistent patterns of temperament that emerge help define each child's individual style.

Research by Thomas and Chess has identified three types of temperament in babies: the easy child, the difficult child, and the slow-to-warm-up child. The traits used to classify these children were:

- The child's activity level—the amount of movement or inactivity

- The regularity and rhythm of bodily routines such as sleep, digestion, and elimination

- The ability to adapt to change

- Initial reaction to something new

- Physical sensitivity to the total environment—light, heat, noise

- Intensity of reaction and strength of response

- Ease of distraction

- Overall negative or positive mood

- Persistence and length of attention span

These differences were observed in very young infants and seem to remain consistent as the child grows.

The implications for teachers in these findings are several. First and foremost, the research supports the concept of individual differences that are present from birth and the importance of acknowledging those differences. If parents and teachers come to know the nature of a child's temperament, they can accept that as part of the wholeness of that particular child. Discipline and guidance measures can be tailored to meet the unique needs of a slow-to-warm-up child, for instance, or a difficult child. Those strategies will need to be different from techniques used to discipline the easy child. Recognition of traits enables teachers and parents to deal with quirks of personality. It is also useful to compare your own temperament with that of the children you teach.

Children's temperament also affects the way people deal with them. An easy child is easy to respond to; a slow-to-warm-up child may be harder to reach. Difficult children may tend to be blamed for things they did not do. Identifying traits can be useful so long as adults are careful not to label children unfairly or prematurely.

Malcolm is enthusiastic and plunges into activities spontaneously, sometimes without looking ahead or surveying the wreckage he leaves behind. His teacher is aware that he can be personable and cooperative if he is given options and a chance to make decisions. As they talk together about Lorraine's blocks, the teacher offers Malcolm a choice: to talk with Lorraine to see if she would like to have him help rebuild the same structure or start a new one. Both find satisfaction in working together in ways that acknowledge and respect Malcolm's personal style.

Emotional and Social Needs

Some behavior problems stem from the child's attempt to express social and emotional needs. These include the need to feel loved and cared for, the need to be included, the desire to be considered important and valued, the desire to have friends, and the need to feel safe from harm. Young children are still working out ways to express these needs and feelings. Typically, since they are only just learning language and communication skills, it is often through nonverbal or indirect actions that children let us know what is bothering them. Therefore, it is also important to provide children with models of language for resolving

OUR DIVERSE WORLD OUR DIVERSE WORLD OUR DIVERSE WORLD OUR DIVERSE WORLD OUR DIVERSE WORLD

[1] and [2]Children's individual temperaments are an important consideration in developing an understanding of OUR DIVERSE WORLD. Differences in temperament may be less immediately obvious than differences in gender or race; but no less significant.

Dreikurs Four Goals Of Misbehavior	
Attention	Children seek attention, believing they are worthwhile only when someone notices them. Their need causes them to gain attention in either positive or negative ways.
Power	Children who believe they are important only when they are "the boss" seek power and control over others.
Revenge	Children who believe they are unlovable and unimportant are hurt and try to hurt back. They seek revenge by hurting others so they may feel important.
Inadequacy	Children who feel they cannot succeed will rarely try anything new or persist in an activity when frustrated. They do not want others to expect anything from them for fear of failing.

FIGURE 7.5 Since children seem to gain something from each type of behavior, psychiatrist Rudolph Dreikurs calls the behaviors goals. Each goal fulfills a particular social or emotional need for the child. (From Dreikurs, R., and Stolz, V.: *Children: The Challenge.* New York: Hawthorne Books, 1964.)

these conflicts. It is important to let children know that we recognize they can be angry, jealous, or hurt. The supportive adult will help children find satisfying ways to cope with their social and emotional feelings.[1]

Figure 7.5 describes four categories of misbehavior that seem to stem from the child's social or emotional needs. Since children have something to gain from each type of misbehavior, Dreikurs labels the behaviors goals. These goals can apply to the child's interactions with adults or with other children. More than one goal may be involved, and the particular reason for misbehavior may not be obvious. What do you think were the goals of Shawnsey, Malcolm, and Mac and what role do their social and emotional histories play in their behavior?

The facts are Shawnsey is an only child of much older parents and has little opportunity outside of school to interact with others her age. Malcolm comes from a big, boisterous family where taking care of one's own desires and needs is instilled early on. Mac's parents have just been divorced and he is now living with his grandmother while his mother looks for work in another town. Their teachers understand their bids for attention and weigh each child's social and emotional histo-

ry as they guide them toward positive behavior.

In Chapter 14, Planning for the Heart and Soul, the young child's social and emotional growth is further explored.

Cultural Influences

By the end of this century, classrooms will be filled with children who are growing up in a country of unparalleled diversity. Many different cultures are converging and creating "the first multicultural society" in the United States (America's Immigrant Challenge, 1993). Children and their teachers are living in a world of contiual cross-cultural interactions. The ability to communicate across cultures is a critical skill to have when guiding children's behavior. (See also discussions in Chapters 2, 5, 8, and 15.) A review of Erikson's and Vygotsky's theories in Chapter 4 and Bronfenbrenners in Chapter 15 underscores the connection between culture and behavior.

Discipline and guidance are deeply embedded within the values and beliefs of the family. The family's culture shapes how they raise their children, and each family is unique in the way it interprets its cultural values. The messages children re-

OUR DIVERSE WORLD OUR DIVERSE WORLD OUR DIVERSE WORLD OUR DIVERSE WORLD OUR DIVERSE WORLD

[1]The educator is mindful of cultural differences in dealing with negative emotions and may need to work with individual children and families in coming to terms with how home and school may be different in dealing with particular emotions.

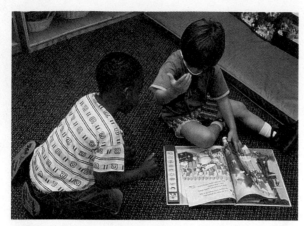

FIGURE 7.6 Children are often able to work out their own solutions to conflict.

ceive about their behavior should be consistent between school and home. Yet conflict may be inevitable since culturally influenced child-rearing practices of the family may be at odds with a teacher's ideas and expectations (Gordon and Browne, 1996). Kim (who was playing with Shawnsey) has a family culture which views the teacher as a respected authority figure and one who must be obeyed. This placed Kim in an uncomfortable position if her teacher does not understand why Kim does not make activity choices easily and prefers to have the teacher tell her where to play and work each day. What could seem like resistance to the teacher's suggestions is, in fact, appropriate behavior in Kim's family culture. As teachers become familiar with the customs and beliefs of the families in the program, they will gain insights into children's behavior and understand the reasons for the way a child responds. Each child must be valued as part of a family system, no matter the origin or definition, and the teacher's role is to support the child's sense of security and identity within the family. Unconditional respect creates a climate in which positive behavior can thrive (Gordon and Browne, 1996).

As noted, children bring their unique individuality to the classroom. They are also bearers of the context in which they are being raised: their family, culture, ethnicity, religion, socioeconomic status, neighborhood, and so on. When we are aware of these influences we are better able to match who the child is with the most effective guidance approach (Gordon and Browne, 1996).

In some families, a sense of community is valued over individualism, a concept that can create difficulty in the early childhood classroom unless it is understood and appreciated. Early childhood educators, for the most part, do not force children to share personal possessions before they seem ready to, and they encourage children to become autonomous at an early age. This is at odds with families in which cooperation and sharing is a valued concept, as is dependency on other family members. Teachers of children of the twenty-first century will need to become culturally sensitive to some of the long-held assumptions of teaching young children.

Schools must be inviting and safe places in which families from all cultures can express their perceptions, concerns, and expectations about their children. Teachers will need to be flexible and nonjudgmental as they work with the cultural implications of children's behavior. Parents are the teacher's obvious resource and partner: they can say what is respectful and appropriate for their particular culture and work with the teacher for the most compatible resolution to any differences.

The sections on "Self-Awareness" and "Attitudes and Biases" in Chapter 5 suggest ways in which teachers can address stereotypes and prejudices.

GUIDING BEHAVIOR

A Guidance Approach

The behavior of Shawnsey, Malcolm, and Mac is typical of children their age. The children we meet in early childhood programs are just learning how strong their emotions can be and what impact they have on their own behavior and on others. Behavior is the unspoken language through which children act out feelings and thoughts. Until they learn to express themselves vocally, they employ a variety of behaviors to communicate such feelings as distress, anger, anxiety, fear, hurt, and jealousy. They don't yet know what kinds of behaviors are and are not acceptable and what adults expect of them. Using words (for instance, a resounding "No!" when someone takes a toy away) is slowly replacing biting, hitting, crying, and tantrums as a way to respond to frustration.

Discipline	Punishment
Emphasizes what the child should *do*	Emphasizes what the child should *not* do
Is an ongoing process	Is a one-time occurrence
Sets an example to follow	Insists on obedience
Leads to self-control	Undermines independence
Helps children change	Is an adult release
Is positive	Is negative
Accepts child's need to assert self	*Makes* children behave
Fosters child's ability to think	Thinks *for* the child
Bolsters self-esteem	Defeats self-esteem
Shapes behavior	Condemns misbehavior

FIGURE 7.7 A guidance approach to discipline encourages children's interaction and involvement; punishment is usually something that is done to a child.

Caring adults can help young children learn to behave responsibly and be respectful of others as they explore alternative behaviors, develop social skills, and learn to problem solve.

Since it is daily experiences that children use to construct their moral and social world, adults must look carefully at the guidance approach they take. The concept of guide is an important one (Gordon and Browne, 1996). A guide is one who leads, explains, and supports. A guide points out directions, answers questions, and helps you get where you want to go. This is what teachers do as they guide children. Implicit, too, is a sense of joint commitment of teaching and learning together. Relying on punishment as a guidance tool excludes the opportunity for teaching and learning to take place. A guidance approach to discipline requires the active participation of both child and adult in order to be successful.

A large part of an early childhood educator's role is to guide and direct children in learning the inner controls necessary for them to build positive relationships with others. Guidance and discipline are common concerns of parents and teachers and can be the basis for a strong partnership as they learn together why Dominick whines or Carrie dawdles or Cleo disrupts group time. Yet there is often confusion and uncertainty about guidance and discipline and what it really means.

What is Guidance and Discipline

Many people associate **discipline** with the word **punishment**. Discipline is generally thought of in negative terms to some, the words *discipline* and *punishment* are synonymous.

Figure 7.7 shows how these terms mean very different things. Discuss these differences in class and plan intervention strategies for teachers to use with Shawnsey, Malcolm, and Mac in the situations described in the section Understanding Behavior found in this chapter. Match the proposed solutions with the developmentally appropriate expectations found in the Word Pictures in Chapter 3.

The word *discipline* stems from disciple: a pupil, a follower, a learner. This suggests an important concept, that of following an example versus following rules. Children try to be like the adults they see; adults serve as models for children. How children see adults behave tends to become part of their own behavior. Adults help children learn appropriate behavior by setting good examples.

Guiding and directing children toward acceptable behavior includes everything parents and teachers do, everything they say, in an attempt to influence the child. The guidance process is something you do with children; it is an interaction, not something adults do *to* children. In caring and understanding ways, the effective teacher helps children gain control over their own behavior. To accomplish this, teachers maintain that delicate balance between children's attempts to be independent and their need for outer controls.

It is not so much the word *discipline* that is significant as it is the form it takes. Children are

---

ABOUT CHOICES

–Give children choices whenever possible. This allows some control over themselves so they do not feel continually dominated by adults and helps them practice self-reliance, self-direction, and self-discipline. "Looks like there is plenty of room at the easels or at the lotto games, Seth. Where would you like to play?"

–Only give choices when you mean for the children to have a choice. Be prepared to accept their answer when a choice is offered. Make sure you present choices to children only when they really have one. "Some of the children are going inside for music now. Would you like to join them?" Do not ask, "Would you like to go home now? Clean up?" when it is not an option.

–Suggest two choices when there is the possibility of resistance. Let children know you expect them to comply with your request, but allow some decision on their part. Do not box them into a corner. "It's time to go home now. Would you like to get your artwork before or after you put on your jacket?"

–Make the choice real and valid. Acknowledge children's growing ability to deal with responsibility and help them practice making reasonable choices. "There are several kinds of nails, Stacey. Try them out to see which ones work best for you."

---

robbed of their self-respect when they are treated harshly and made to feel they have no ability to control themselves. Shame, disgrace, and embarrassment have no part in good disciplinary procedures.

One of the goals of a good guidance process is to help children achieve self-discipline. This happens only if adults lead in ways that support children's developing ability to control themselves. Teachers who are sensitive to this will decrease the amount of control they exercise. By gradually handing over to children the opportunity to govern their own actions, adults communicate trust. For young children, with their urge to prove themselves, their drive toward initiative, this is an important step to take. With added responsibility and trust comes an added dimension of self-respect and self-confidence. Such children feel capable and worthwhile.

Along with self-respect, the child must taste the freedom that comes with a lessening of adult controls. Children do not learn to handle freedom by being told what to do all the time. Only when they have an opportunity to test themselves, make some decisions on their own, will they know their capabilities. Young children must learn this in safe places, with adults who allow them as much freedom as they can responsibly handle.

Developmentally Appropriate Guidance

Children's growth follows certain patterns (see Chapters 3 and 4). Each developmental stage has shared characteristics, modified, of course, by a child's individual rate of growth. It is as typical, for instance, for 4-year-olds to test limits as it is for toddlers to have a strong sense of ownership about their possessions. To have a developmentally appropriate guidance approach, teachers take this knowledge and understanding of child development principles into consideration as they contemplate how best to respond to a child's behavior.

It is useful to identify the behaviors typical to a specific age group, for it provides a context in which to understand the child. Behavior then can be seen as normal and predictable and can be responded to accordingly. Guidance based on a developmental approach would, for instance, help a teacher to know that first and second graders have an ability to consider others' points of view, and so they would choose problem-solving methods that would ask children to think of how their behavior affected others. A developmentally appropriate approach also requires that the teacher take into consideration what is known about the individual child as well as what is typical for the age group.

BEING POSITIVE

—Tell children what it is you want them to do. Make directions and suggestions in positive statements, not in negative forms. "Walk around the edge of the grass, Hilla, so you won't get hit by the swing," instead of, "Don't get hit!"

—Reinforce what children do right, what you like, and what you want to see repeated. This helps build the relationship on positive grounds. "Good job, Sammy. You worked hard on that puzzle."

—Give indirect suggestions or reminders, emphasizing what you want children to do. Help them refocus on the task without nagging or confrontation. "I know you are excited about the field trip, Mickey. Looks like you are almost finished putting on your jacket so we can go," instead of "Hurry and button that jacket so we can go."

—Use positive redirection whenever possible. (See page 228)

—Use encouragement appropriately, focusing on helping children achieve success and understanding what it is you want them to learn: "Harry, I notice you are being careful about where you put your feet as you climb that tree. It looks to me like you are finding good places to stand," communicates a supportive attitude and tells the child what he is doing well. Global praise, such as "Great climbing, Harry. Good for you!" may leave children wondering what exactly it is they have been praised for and omits the learning they can derive from the experience.

—Give reasons for your request. Let children know in simple, straight forward statements the reasons behind your request. Children are more likely to cooperate when they can understand the reason why. "Tom, if you move those chairs, then you and Dee will have more room to dance," instead of "Move the chairs, Tom."

This ensures that the guidance techniques will match the capabilities of the child and that adult expectations will remain reasonable.

The Language of Guidance and Discipline

Guidance has a language all its own.[1] As beginning teachers gain experience in handling problem behaviors, they learn to use that language. The result, in most cases, is a startling **interdependence**: the more practiced teachers become in the language of guidance, the more comfortable they become in developing their own approach to disciplinary problems. And the more comfortable they are in that approach, the more effectively they use language to solve behavior problems.

The language and communication techniques in guidance are both spoken and unspoken. Teach-

ers discover how potent the voice can be; what words will work best and when. They become aware of facial expressions and what a touch or a look will convey to children. How they use their body reflects a distinct attitude and approach to discipline. New teachers should know how to use these tools in ways that will work best for them and the children.

Voice. Some adults feel that when they are speaking to children they must assume a different voice from the one they normally use. This "teacher voice" often occurs when disciplinary issues are at stake. The teacher's voice becomes tight, high-pitched, the tone increasingly strained. Teaching requires no more than a normal speaking voice. Talk to children in the same way you talk to other people. Learn to control the volume and use good speech patterns for children to imitate. In order to be heard, get close enough to speak in a normal

[1]The language of discipline may differ from culture to culture. The educator needs to be mindful of this (i.e. what one culture means by "getting a beating" can be very different than what another culture means by the exact same expression).

FIGURE 7.8 Body height and position are important. Getting down to the child's eye level provides for greater impact and involvement.

tone; get down to the child's level. Often, lowering volume and pitch is effective.

Words. Children have torrents of words rained upon them in the course of a school day. Teachers fall into the trap of overusing words. Where behavior is concerned and anger or frustration aroused, some adults seem to gain release from a string of words. This works against good guidance practices. Children tend to turn off people who are excessively verbal with them. Their eyes glaze over, they become fidgety or even frightened, and the incident loses significance.

The fewer the words, the better. Simple, clear statements, spoken once, will have more impact. The child will be able to focus on the real issues involved. A brief description of what happened, a word or two about what behavior is acceptable and what isn't, and a suggestion for possible solutions are all that is necessary.

Choose words carefully. They should convey to the child exactly what is expected. "Richy, move the block closer to the truck. Then Sarah won't bump into it again," tells Richy in a positive, concrete way what he can do to protect his block building. If he had been told, "Richy, watch where you are building," he would not know what action to take to solve the problem.

Body Expressions. When working with small children, it is important to be aware of body height and position. Show children that respect for their size by speaking with them face to face. Sit, squat, or kneel—but get down to their level. It is difficult to communicate warmth, caring, and concern from two or three feet above a child's head.

Guidance is founded on a loving, caring relationship between child and adult. In order to help children gain control over their impulses and monitor their own behavior, teachers must establish a sense of trust and well-being with children. The way teachers use their bodies invites or rejects close relationship and familiarity. A child will find teachers more approachable if they are seated low, with arms available, rather than standing, with arms folded.

By making full use of the senses, the impact of words can be softened. A firm grip on the hand of a child who is hitting out, a gentle touch on the shoulder, tells children the adult is there to protect them from themselves and others. Eye contact is essential. Teachers learn to communicate the seriousness of a situation through eye and facial expressions. They also show reassurance, concern, sadness, and affection this way.

Physical presence should convey to the child a message that the teacher is there, available, and interested.

Attitude. This is part of the unspoken language of guiding children. Attitudes are derived from experience. Most adults who take care of children reflect how their own parents treated them and how they were disciplined. Some people react against the way they were raised; others tend to follow the model their parents established. Teachers find it useful to look at the way they were disciplined as youngsters and acknowledge their feelings about it. As they begin to inhibit the behavior of the children in their classes, teachers should be aware of their own attitudes. The following questions may help that process:

● Do you accept the fact that all children will have problems, misbehave, and will make mistakes?

● Do you believe children are capable of solving their own problems, and do you involve them in the process?

● Do you accept the child's right to independence and actively encourage self-reliance?

> **PLAN AHEAD**
> –Allow plenty of time for children to respond. Give them an opportunity to decide their course of action.
> –Review limits and rules periodically. Modify them as children's growth and maturation indicate. Change them as circumstances change; be flexible.
> –Encourage children to talk things over. Be open to their point of view even if you cannot accept it. Let them know you are willing to listen to all sides of the conflict.
> –Become aware of the climate in the room or yard. Anticipate the need for a change of pace or a different activity BEFORE children become bored or troublesome.
> –Remember, it takes time and numerous opportunities for changes in behavior to occur. By using consistent guidance techniques, you will help children practice new behavior repeatedly.

● Do you think children misbehave deliberately, to bother the teacher?

● Do you help children accept the responsibility for their own actions without blaming them?

● Are you optimistic that problems can be solved and that you and the child can work it out together?

Guidance Practices

Children's behavior is influenced by more than just their own impulses, needs, or reactions. Factors beyond the scope of childhood can cause misbehavior. There are several areas over which adults have control that may cause problems for children. Three of the most common are the classroom environment, setting limits on children's behavior, and the teacher's role in guidance.

Since the classroom promotes or detracts from positive interactions and appropriate behavior, it is the first place to look for ways to improve guidance and disciplinary techniques. The goals for positive behavior should be reflected in the classroom setting. Too often, good intentions are defeated by the physical environment. The physical setting should tell children clearly and directly how to act in that space. That makes it easier for them to know what is expected and how they should behave.

Through the intentional use of the environment, the teacher indirectly influences behavior in the classroom. The schedule allows for enough time to play and clean up; there are adequate and interesting materials to use; there is a sense of order and adults are skilled in guidance techniques that work. Use the classroom checklist in Figure 7.9 to evaluate how the environment relates to your guidance philosophy and to the behavior of children.

Consider the Limits

To provide a safe and caring environment in which children can play and learn, teachers set limits on certain behavior. Limits are the boundaries set up to help children know what will or will not be tolerated. Teachers generally have two reasons for setting limits: (1) to prevent children from injuring themselves or others; and (2) to prevent the destruction of property, materials, or equipment.

Limits are a necessary part of any group or society. Every group has its bottom-line rules—rules that must be kept to ensure order and living in accord. The early childhood classroom is no exception; teachers make it clear to children what rules determine the conduct within that group. Teachers plan curriculum, arrange rooms, and follow good guidance practices so that a great number of rules are not necessary. Frequent exclamations of "Don't do this . . ." or "Don't do that . . ." need not be a part of the early childhood classroom when one understands the nature of setting limits.

Limits are like fences; they are protective structures that help children feel secure. Fences and limits are erected and maintained to help people know how far they can go. Fences—or limits—

TIME

_____ Does the daily schedule provide enough time for unhurried play?

_____ Are those periods that create tension—transitions from one activity to another—given enough time?

_____ Is cleanup a leisurely process built in at the end of each activity, with children participating?

PROGRAM PLANNING AND CURRICULUM

_____ Is there enough to do so that children have choices and alternatives for play?

_____ Is the curriculum challenging enough to avoid boredom and restlessness?

_____ Is the curriculum age appropriate for the children in the class?

_____ Are there activities to help children release tension? Do the activities allow for body movement, exploration, and manipulation of materials?

_____ Are children included in developing the rules and setting guidelines? How is this demonstrated?

ORGANIZATION AND ORDER

_____ If children are expected to put things away after use, are the cabinets low, open, and marked in some way?

_____ Are the materials within easy reach of the children, promoting self-selection and independence?

_____ Are there enough materials so that sharing does not become a problem?

_____ Are the areas in which activities take place clearly defined so that children know what happens there?

_____ Does the room arrangement avoid runways and areas with no exits?

_____ Do children have their own private space?

_____ Are children able to use all visible and accessible materials? Are there materials about which children are told, "Don't touch?"

PERSONNEL

_____ Are there enough teachers to give adequate attention to the number of children in the class?

_____ Is the group size and makeup balanced so that children have a variety of playmates?

_____ Are the teachers experienced, and do they seem comfortable in setting limits and guiding children's behavior?

_____ Do teachers use their attention to encourage behavior they want, and do they ignore what they want to discourage?

_____ Do all adults enforce the same rules?

FIGURE 7.9 Classroom checklist. By anticipating children's needs and growth patterns, teachers set up classrooms that foster constructive and purposeful behavior.

ALWAYS AVOID
- Methods that will shame, frighten, or humiliate children.
- Physical abuse.
- Comparisons among the children. This fosters competitiveness and affects self-esteem.
- Carry-overs from the incident. Once it is over, leave it behind; do not keep reminding children about it.
- Consequences that are too long, too punitive, or postponed. Children benefit most from immediate, short consequences.
- Lots of rules. Set only enough to ensure a safe environment for all children.
- Making promises you cannot keep.
- Being overly helpful. Let children do as much as they can by themselves, including solving their own conflicts.
- Threatening children with the loss of your affection.

set up a framework in which everyone knows the rules. When children know where fences are, what limits, what rules apply, they do not have to continually try to find out *if* fences are there and *where* they are. Inside the fences, children are free—and safe—to try out many behaviors.

A natural part of growing up is to stretch those limits and push those fences aside. The womb first holds and protects the growing fetus; the infant is protected in the confines of the crib. The toddler has safe space defined in a playpen. The preschool child plays first in small, protected yards before moving on to the large, open playground in elementary school. Physical limits expand as the child is able to handle more freedom, more space, more responsibility. It is the same with behavioral limits.

Children may not like fences; they may resist attempts to limit their behavior. The beginning teacher must learn to set and maintain limits with confidence and authority. Children respond to how limits are set as much as to the limits themselves. Be sure children help determine limits. Keep in mind that a good guidance process involves children as active participants; this fosters self-discipline. Children also seem less resistant to following rules when they are a part of the limit-setting procedure. Figure 7.10 illustrates positive ways to set limits when working with young children.

For the child, limits are self-protective. Young children have not yet learned the skills to control themselves in all situations. Their behavior easily goes out-of-bounds. Children are just beginning to exert that inner pressure (self-control) that will

help them monitor their own actions. Until then, they need adults to help them learn when and how to apply self-restraint. Limits keep them from going too far. Children can frighten themselves and others with anger, frustration, fear. They need adults who care to stop them from doing physical or emotional harm to themselves. Well-considered limits give the child freedom to try out, test, and explore avenues of self-expression in ways that will promote growth and protect budding autonomy. Children feel more secure with adults who will stop them from going too far and who help them learn to gain control.

Consider the Teacher's Role

A teacher has direct and indirect influence on children's behavior. Some of the ways teachers deal directly with discipline is by what they say and what they do. Indirectly, a teacher's influence is felt just as strongly. Room arrangements and time schedules, attitudes and behavior can work for or against good guidance practices.

Teachers who are well grounded in the developmental process know that problem behaviors are normal and occur in every early childhood setting. They realize that growing children must have a safe, secure place in which to test themselves against the world.

The teacher as a behavior model is an important element in guidance. Children pattern their responses after adult behaviors. They are aware of how teachers respond to anger, frustration, and aggression; how they solve problems and conflicts.

When Setting Limits	For Example
1. Make sure that the limit is appropriate to the situation.	"Andrew, I want you to get down from the table. You may finish your snack by sitting in your chair or standing next to me. You may not stand on the table."
2. Fit the limits to the individual child's age, history, and emotional framework.	"Sheila, you've interrupted the story too many times today. Find a place at the puzzle table until we are finished. Remember, I told you earlier that you wouldn't be able to hear the end of the story if you yelled again." "Jamal, I know it's your first day back since you broke your arm, but it is time to listen to the story now. You and Sascha can talk together in a few minutes."
3. See that the limits are consistently applied by all adults.	"I know you want to ride the red bike now but both teachers have said you already had a long turn today."
4. Reinforce the same rules consistently.	"Judy, remember everyone *walks* inside. You can run out-side."
5. Follow through; support your words with actions.	"I can't let you tear the books. Since this is the second page this morning, you'll need to make another choice instead of the book corner." If child does not leave, begin to pick up books. Lead child firmly to another activity.
6. Use simple statements; be clear and state limits pos-itively.	"Roger, use a gentle voice indoors. When your voice is too loud, people can't hear one another. You may use your big loud voice outside."
7. Respect the child's feelings and acknowledge them when you can.	"I know you want your mom to stay. She has to go to her job now. I'll stay with you while you feel sad and I'll take care of you until she comes back."
8. Act with authority; be sure of your purpose and be confident.	"I can't let you hurt other people. Put the block down," instead of "I wish you wouldn't do that."
9. Be ready to accept the consequences; have a plan for the next step, if needed. Maintain the limit. Don't avoid the situation or give in if the child threatens to fall apart or create a scene.	"I'm sorry, Sarah, but you missed your ride to school. When you play with your food it keeps you from getting dressed on time. Remember, Mrs. Allen said she wouldn't wait one more time. Screaming and kicking won't get her to turn the car around. Let's go feed the cat and think about what you might do at home today."
10. Have children help in defining limits.	"We'll be taking a bus to the museum next week. What are some of the rules we should follow so that we can enjoy the trip? Wally, do you have an idea?"

FIGURE 7.10   Guidelines for setting limits. Children feel safe when appropriate limits are set on their behavior.

Adults must be sure to model the desired behavior around the children they teach. To be successful models, teachers should be aware of their emotions and feelings; they do not want to compound a problem by their own reaction.

Being consistent is one of the key elements in good guidance practices. If adults want to develop mutual trust, the rules must be clear, fair, and en-forced consistently and regularly. At the same time, children need to know what will happen if rules are not followed. This, too, should be consistent.

An emerging issue, as our population be-comes more and more diverse, has to do with cul-tural values and discipline. Teachers may be con-fronted by parents with disciplinary practices that are contrary to the school's philosophy.[1] Pressure

OUR DIVERSE WORLD OUR DIVERSE WORLD OUR DIVERSE WORLD OUR DIVERSE WORLD OUR DIVERSE WORLD

[1]Working with diverse cultures with differing disciplinary practices can be viewed as a predicament or as an opportunity. It can pro-vide an opportunity to consider how ethnocentric discipline might be, educate oneself, and then consider what is in the child's best interest (i.e. "there is more than one way to skin a cat").

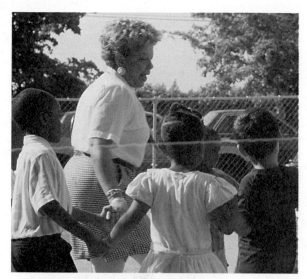

"I get to be first because I'm the biggest."

"I want my mommy."

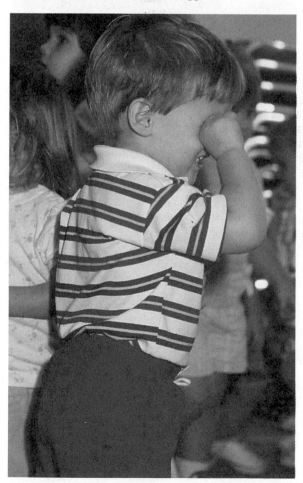

"But I don't want to help."

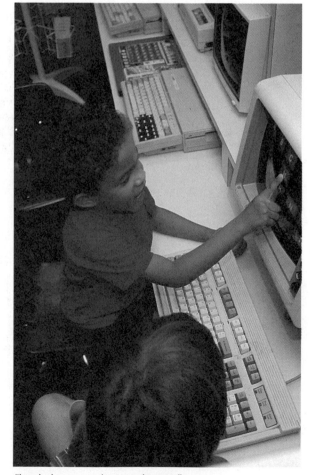

"Look, I won again, you dummy."

FIGURE 7.11 Good discipline practices involve children as active participants. How would you set limits in these situations?

may be exerted on teachers to apply some of those same techniques at school that parents use at home. Teachers want to maintain the school's as well as their own standards *without* communicating to the family that their values are wrong. They do not want to tell children, "At school we do it this way" or have children feel that something about their home and family is diminished in the teacher's eyes. Ethical issues such as these are discussed in Chapter 5. The anti-bias curriculum, as described in Chapters 5 and 9, suggests some strategies as well. Also see Child Development and Cultural Diversity in Chapter 4.

Children have a right to express negative feelings and air their grievances, but what are the considerations if a teacher shows anger? Children are very sensitive to adult emotions. It is better to acknowledge the feeling, label it, and then discuss it together. Once it is identified, it becomes more manageable for both. Adults who express negative feelings to children must proceed carefully, stating their position clearly, honestly, and objectively, and in a low, calm voice.

> It bothers me when you call Roberto a dummy.
>
> You don't need to yell at me. I can hear you from right here. Tell me again in a quieter voice.
>
> I'm serious about this . . . no biting.
>
> Sometimes I get mad when children try to hurt each other.
>
> It makes me sad to see all that food going to waste. Please put just enough on your plate so that you will eat it all.

Remember that children are frightened by strong feelings; do not overwhelm them by your own behavior.

Sometimes teachers have unrealistic expectations for children, either too high or too low. They presume children have abilities and skills they do not yet possess. This may cause children to respond in inappropriate ways. It can be helpful to rehearse with children how they are expected to act. Practice sessions are especially useful when introducing a new topic or plan. One teacher rehearsed the children for their first bus ride. They practiced singing, looking out the windows, having snacks, talking with friends. A large outline of a bus was drawn with chalk on the patio floor. The children pretended to board the bus, walk down the narrow aisle, find a seat, and remember to take big steps getting up and down the steps. When the field trip day arrived, children knew several appropriate ways of behaving while on the long bus trip.

Many times children are asked to do jobs that are too complicated for them. The young child who is just learning to put on jackets and pants or to make a bed is a good example. Children may not be able to accomplish the entire job at first; it is helpful to them if the task is broken down into smaller steps. Straighten the sheet and blanket for Gordon, then let him pull the spread up over the pillow. Little by little have Gordon assume more of the bed-making job as he becomes capable.

Preventing opportunities for children to misbehave is another part of the teacher's role. Good discipline practices call for teachers to be alert to potential problems and situations *before* they result in children's inappropriate behavior. Even then, unpredictable situations occur: A child becomes tired in the middle of snack time, one of the teachers is called out of the room with a sick child, rain forces an activity to move indoors, or a scheduled event gets postponed. At these trying and typical times, a teacher's full range of abilities is called into play. Ways to help children maintain good behavior patterns in these situations include:

● *Recognizing and labeling the problem or situation.* Acknowledge the difficulties it presents to the children. Example: "You seem tired, Gus, and I know you had to wait a long time for your snack. When you have finished your juice and cracker, put your head down on the table and rest for a minute."

● *Asking children for their help.* Get them involved in working out the solutions. Example: "Mr. Gallo had to leave for a while. How can we continue with this cooking project when I need to watch the block area too? Who has an idea? What do you think would work, Henry?"

● *Assigning a job or a task to the children who are most likely to react to the crisis.* Example: "Lorraine and Paul, will you carry the special drums inside, please, while I help the toddlers put the wagons away?"

If This Is The Behavior	Try This	For Example
Whining	Ignoring	Do and say nothing while whining persists. Pay attention to child when whining stops.
Playing cooperatively	Positive reinforcement	"You two are sure working hard on this garden! What a good team you make."
Refusing to cooperate	Provide a choice	"Reva, do you want to pick up the Legos off the floor or help Charlie empty the water table?"
Restlessness, inattentiveness	Change the activity	"This story seems long today; we'll finish it later. Let's play some music and dance now."
Daydreaming	Indirect suggestion	"As soon as you get your coat, Winona, we'll all be ready to go outside."
Arguing over the ownership of a toy	Active listening	"You really wanted to be the first one to play with the blue truck today, didn't you, Lief?"
Dawdling, late for snacks	Natural consequences	"Sorry, Nate, the snacks have been put away. Maybe tomorrow you'll remember to come inside when the other children leave the yard."
Pushing, crowding, running inside	Change room arrangement	Create larger, more open spaces so children have greater freedom of movement and do not feel crowded together.
Unable to take turns, to wait	Review daily schedule, equipment	Buy duplicates of popular equipment. Allow enough time for free play so children won't feel anxious about getting a turn.
Boisterous play	Positive redirection	"You and Sergio seem to want to wrestle. Let's go set the mats out in the other room. If you wrestle here you disturb the children who are playing quietly."

FIGURE 7.12 Varieties of guidance techniques. The astute teacher selects from the options available and individualizes the responses.

● *Always being prepared with a story to tell, songs to sing, guessing games to play, or exercises to do.* Help children pass the time in an appropriate way modeled by the teacher. Give a new focus. Example: "Oh, dear. The fire truck hasn't arrived at school yet; we'll have to wait another five minutes. While we are waiting to go and see it, show me how firefighters climb ladders and slide down poles."

● *Saying what you would like to have happen.* Admit what you wish you could do to correct the situation. Example: "Oh, little Riko, I wish I could

bring your mommy back right now but I can't. She has to go to work, but I will hold you until your crying stops."

These disciplinary practices apply equally to infants and toddlers, but there are some special considerations that teachers should remember. Infants cry—sometimes a great deal. It is their only means of communication. When they cry they should not be ignored or chastised, but comforted. It is helpful to talk to the baby, no matter how young, and begin to identify the steps you will take to ease the distress. "Oh, Fernando, you are crying and I don't know what's wrong. Let's take a look at your diaper; maybe a change will make you more comfortable. Perhaps you are teething; I know that can hurt. Maybe you are hungry; is it time for your bottle yet?" Those soothing words as a teacher changes diapers, rubs the baby's back, cuddles and rocks, ease this time of stress. Toddlers, too, need adults to use words to express problem situations, and the preceding examples readily apply to working with this active and lively age group. One word of caution, however. Removing infants and toddlers from the group as a means of discipline or confining them to a playpen or crib is not appropriate. Very young children do not understand that kind of isolation. Guidance, to be effective, should be helpful, not punitive.

Teachers can learn a great deal about the cause and effect of their discipline and guidance techniques if they are active observers in their own classrooms. When teachers observe, they can time intervention; they do not want to interfere too soon. Observations can be used to show children their actions and the consequences they have for others.

Guidance Techniques

There are a number of guidance and discipline approaches woven throughout the chapter. They have many similar components and fall under the definition of *inductive guidance*. The most effective guidance methods require children to think and reflect on their feelings and their actions and actively involve them in the process of solving the problem. This is accomplished by providing choices (see *About Choices*, p. 206), asking open-ended questions ("What would happen if you took her book?" "How do you think he would feel if you did that?"), and communicating trust and confidence in children to solve problems and control their own behavior. These are key elements in the use of inductive guidance, as are the following:

● Guidance is an interactive process and involves children as much as it does adults

● Children are increasingly held responsible for

their actions as they come to understand the impact of their behavior on others

● Teaching thinking and reasoning skills helps children achieve self-control and the development of a conscience.

These principles are based on the theories of Erikson and Piaget but owe particular credit to Vygotsky as well. Vygotsky placed the child as a learner in the context of social interactions. The concept of the *zone of proximal distance* (see Chapter 4), for instance, reinforces the reciprocal relationship between adult and child implied in most inductive guidance techniques. Too, Thomas and Chess' *goodness of fit* (1977), where the adult works with the child's unique temperament to determine the best guidance approach to take, is reflected in the following material. Family context as well continues to be a priority when selecting appropriate guidance methods.

At the other end of the guidance spectrum are *power assertive* methods, which are harsh and punitive and rely on children's fear of punishment rather than the use of reason and understanding. Spanking, hitting, calling children names, and otherwise demeaning punishments exclude the opportunity for teaching and learning to take place or to promote problem-solving.

Each of the inductive guidance methods is a valuable tool for teachers. These approaches influence children to change their behavior because they place the responsibility where it belongs: with the child. The adult informs the children of the results of their actions and trusts in their willingness and abilities to cooperate in a solution. The child's self-respect is left intact because no one has placed blame. By integrating these methods into a discipline approach, teachers enlarge the child's capacity to become increasingly self-directed and self-reliant.

One thing that becomes apparent when using many of the guidance methods which follow is the awareness that it is often the adult's behavior which must change as well, if the child is to achieve some measure of self-control. Look at the various strategies and note how many of them require the adult to alter a response or attitude before the child can be expected to alter behavior.

Tantrums as a Teaching Tool
Ways to Help Children Learn
Elizabeth Crary

Marie doesn't want Stephanie to go home.

Josh wants the truck that Eli is playing with—
Right now!

David doesn't want his diaper changed, even though it stinks.

One of your jobs as a parent or teacher is to help children understand and deal with their feelings. There are several things you can do. During the tantrum you can acknowledge children's feelings and help them distinguish between feelings and behavior. *Before* the next tantrum you can begin to teach children ways to deal with their feelings and the situation.

1. Acknowledge children's feelings. You can help do that by helping children develop a feeling vocabulary and by validating their feelings.

● Label children's feelings: *"You're disappointed we can't go to the park today."*

● Share your feelings: *"I feel frustrated when I spill coffee on the floor."*

● Read books that discuss feelings, like the **Let's Talk About Feelings** series.

● Observe another's feelings: *"I'll bet he's proud of the tower he built."*

Validate children's feelings. Many people have been trained to ignore or suppress their feelings. Girls are often taught that being mad is unfeminine or not nice. Boys are taught not to cry. You can validate feelings by listening to the child and reflecting the feelings you hear. Listen without judging. Remain separate. Remember, a child's feelings belong to her or him. When you reflect the feeling (*"You are mad that Stephanie has to go home now"*), you are not attempting to solve the problem. Accepting the feeling is the first step towards dealing with it.

2. Help children distinguish between feelings and actions. All feelings are okay. Actions may or may not be okay depending on the situation. For example, hitting a baseball is fine. Hitting a person in not acceptable. You can clarify the difference by saying, *"It's okay to be mad, and I cannot let you hit Eli."* You can also *model* the difference between feelings and action. You might say, *"This morning someone cut me off on the road. I was so mad I wanted to crash into them. Instead I . . ."*

3. Teach children several ways to calm themselves down. If telling children to *"Use your words"* worked for most kids, grown-ups would have little trouble with children's feelings. Children need a variety of ways to respond—auditory, physical, visual, creative, and self-nurturing. First children need to practice different responses when they are calm. Then when children are familiar with different ways to respond, you may ask them which they would like to try when they are upset.

For example: *"You're real angry. Do you want to feel mad right now or do you want to calm down?"* If your child wants to change her feelings, you could say, *"What could you do? Let's see, you could dance a mad dance, make a card to give to Stephanie, talk about this feeling, or look at your favorite book."* After you've generated ideas, let the child choose what works for her.

4. Offer tools to resolve situations that are hard for them. If Josh wants the truck Eli has, teach him to ask, wait, or trade for it. If Sonja gets frustrated putting puzzles together, teach her how to take breaks or breathe deeply so she does not get upset. You can use the books like *I Want It, I Can't Wait* or *I Want to Play* to introduce options. Research has found the more alternatives a child has the better their social behavior.

Elizabeth Crary is a parent educator and author of many books and articles on guidance. She wrote "Without Spanking or Spoiling" and "Kids Can Cooperate."

FIGURE 7.13 "They won't let me play with them." A sensitive teacher will move in and help redirect a child's behavior before it becomes a problem. What would you do in this situation?

Active Listening and "I" Messages

Parents and teachers can learn the art of *active listening* in order to respond to a child's feelings as well as words. The technique encourages sensitive, atuned hearing—checking on the accuracy of what is being said. To do this, teachers or parents listen carefully, trying to understand what the child is saying beyond the words being used. Then they reflect back in their own words what it is they think the child has said. The child has an opportunity to correct any misinterpretations. Further dialogue helps to clarify what it was the child meant. An example is:

Rita: I hate school!

Teacher: Sounds like you are really disappointed you didn't get a turn cooking today.

Rita: I *really* wanted to help make pancakes.

"I" messages are an adult's way of reflecting back to children how their actions have affected others.

Parent: When you scream indoors, it really hurts my ears.

Parent: I feel sad when you tell me you don't like me.

"I" messages are honest, nonjudgmental statements that place no blame on the child, but which state an observation of the behavior and its results. They avoid accusing statements, such as "You made me . . ." and call for a framework that allows adults to state their feelings to that child (Gordon, 1970).

Natural and Logical Consequences

These enhance children's ability to take responsibility for themselves. As implied, this approach lets children experience the *natural consequences* of their actions. This approach, designed by Rudolf Dreikurs, emphasizes the opportunity children have to learn from the way their environment functions:

If Libby does not eat her dinner, she can expect to be hungry later.

If Kara puts her hand on a hot stove, she is likely to get burned.

If Tony grabs the book away from Ben, Ben may hit him.

This method allows adults to define the situation for children without making judgments, and lets children know what to expect. The consequences are a natural result of the child's own actions. *Logical* consequences, on the other hand, are a function of what adults impose. A logical consequence of disrupting group time is removal from the group. For the adult, this means a commitment to follow through; consequences, once stated, must be enforced. It is important to give children an opportunity to choose a course of action for themselves once they have some understanding of what is likely to happen.

Behavior Modification

This is an organized approach based on the premise that behavior is learned through **positive and negative reinforcement** or rewards. The belief is that children will tend to repeat behavior

FIGURE 7.14 Young children should not be isolated for misbehavior in ways that damage their self-esteem.

for which they get the desired results (positive reinforcement) and are likely to avoid doing things which have undesirable consequences (negative reinforcement). Positive reinforcement is used to teach new and different behaviors to a child, and help the child maintain the change. Negative reinforcement may simply involve ignoring or withdrawing attention when the child acts inappropriately. Initially, the reinforcement (or reward) must be swift and consistently applied, as often as the behavior occurs. If the desired behavior, for instance, is for Janie to always hang her coat on the hook, praise and appreciate the effort each time Janie hangs up her wraps. Once this is a well-established routine, the reinforcement (praise) becomes less intense.

Reinforcers, or rewards, must be individualized to meet the needs of the child and the situation. Social reinforcers, such as smiling, interest and attention, hugging, touching, and talking, are powerful tools with young children. Food, tokens, and money are also used as reinforcers in home and school settings. The goal is that inner satisfaction will become its own reward, no matter the type of reinforcer one might use initially.

To succeed, the adult will focus on only one behavior change at a time. If parents want to use behavior modification methods to help their children arrive at the dinner table on time, then Dad does not nag about homework or Mom about a messy room. The behavior that is targeted for change becomes the primary concern until it is successfully altered.

Parents and teachers often take for granted the positive, desirable behavior in children and may forget to acknowledge these behaviors frequently. Behavior modification helps to correct that oversight. Whenever adults focus on a negative aspect of a child's behavior and make an attempt to change it, they also look at the positive qualities the child possesses and reinforce them. This keeps a balanced perspective while working on a problem.

Behavior modification enables adults to invite children to be part of the process, giving them an active part in monitoring their own behavior. Children are capable of keeping a chart of how many times they finished their plate, made the bed, or fed the dog. This chart serves as a natural reinforcer.

Ignoring Behavior

When misbehavior is of a less serious nature—for instance, when a child whines constantly—it may be best to ignore it. This kind of behavior, while mildly annoying, is not harmful. To use the technique successfully, the adult chooses not to respond to the child in any way and may even become occupied elsewhere while the behavior persists. This method is based on the learning theory that negative reinforcement (the adult ignoring the child) will eventually cause the child to stop the undesirable behavior. At first there might be an increase in the misbehavior as the child tests to see whether or not the adult will truly ignore the action. Once the child sees there is nothing to gain, the behavior disappears.

Redirecting the Activity

Sometimes the adult will want to change the activity in which the child is engaged to one that is more acceptable. For example, if Paco and Elena are throwing books off the reading loft, the teacher will want to redirect them and may suggest throwing soft foam balls into a makeshift basket. This technique calls for the adult to make an accurate assessment of what the children really want to do. In this case, it appears they enjoy throwing from a height. Now the teacher can consider alternatives that permit the desired activity while changing the expression or form it takes: "It looks like you two are enjoying dropping things from up there. Let's figure out a way you can do that so that books won't be damaged."

The substitute activity must be a valid one, acceptable to the adults and fulfilling to the children. In most cases children are not being deliberately malicious or destructive. More than likely they are expressing curiosity, imagination, and the need to explore. Positive redirection satisfies these needs in a way that enhances children's self-concept and self-control.

Distraction

When the adult helps focus the child's attention elsewhere, some problems may be avoided. Very young children, especially infants and toddlers, can easily be distracted from undesirable actions. Consider the example at the beginning of the chapter in which Kim grabs at one of the necklaces Shawnsey has. A fast-thinking teacher could present Kim with another attractive one. This method calls for well-timed intervention.

Time Out

Removing a child from the play area is particularly appropriate when, owing to anger, hurt, or frustration, the child is out of control. Taking children away from the scene of intensity and emotion to allow them time to cool off and settle down is sometimes the only way to help them. The teacher is firm and consistent as the child is quietly removed from play. It is important that this discipline technique be used with a positive attitude and approach, not as punishment for misbehavior.

The time-out period is very much like that used in athletic events: a brief respite and a chance to stop all activity and regroup. The teacher's role is to help the child talk about the incident—the feelings involved as well as the need for self-control—and to give the child an opportunity to gain self-control before resuming play. Children can monitor themselves and choose when they are ready to return to classroom activity. Noah, who persists in knocking down other children's block structures, might be told, "You may come back to the block area when you think you are ready to play without knocking over other children's work." Noah can then assume some responsibility for how he will behave and when he is ready to return to play.

Use this technique lightly; it can be misused too easily by adults who leave the child with a sense of rejection. As with other good disciplinary techniques, it should be appropriate to the misbehavior and should help the child toward self-discipline.

Active Problem Solving

The principle here is to actively engage children in confronting their differences and working together to solve their problems. The adult has a sensitive role to play: that of guiding children toward solutions but not solving problems for them.

The Six-Step Approach to Problem Solving

SCENARIO: Two children run outdoors to get the available wagon. They reach it simultaneously and start pulling on the handle, yelling "Mine!" One child starts shoving the other child out of the way.

Step 1: Approach (Initiate Mediation):
  —Approach the conflict, signalling your awareness and availability.
  —Get close enough to intervene if necessary; stop aggressive behavior or neutralize the object of conflict by holding it yourself.

Step 2: Make a Statement:
  —*Describe the scene.*
  —Reflect what the children have said.
  —*Offer no judgments, values, solutions*
  "It looks like you both want the wagon."
  "I see you are yelling at each other."

Step 3: Ask Questions (Gather Data, Define the Problem):
  —Don't direct questions toward pinpointing blame.
  —Draw out details; define problems.
  —Help kids communicate versus slugging it out.
  "How did this happen?"
  "What do you want to tell her?"
  "How could you solve this problem?"
  "How could you use it without fighting?"

Step 4: Generate Alternative Solutions
  —Give children the job of thinking and figuring it out.
  —Suggestions may be offered by disputants or observers.
  —Ask questions: "Who has an idea of how we could solve. . . ?"
          "You could take turns."
          "You could both use it together."
          "You could both do something else."
          "No one could use it."
  —Common mistake: rushing this stage; give it the time it deserves.

Step 5: Agree on Solution
  —When both children accept a solution, rephrase it ("So, you both say that she will be the driver?").
  —If any solution seems unsafe or grossly unfair, you must tell the children ("It is too dangerous for you both to stand up and ride downhill together. What is another way you can agree?").

Step 6: Follow-Through
  —Monitor to make sure agreement is going according to plan: If the decision is turn-taking, you may need to be a clock-watcher.
  —Tell the players and the group:
  "Looks like you solved your problem!"
  —Use the power of language to:
    • Reinforce the solvability of the problem
    • Note the ability of the players to do so
    • Point out the positive environment to be successful

FIGURE 7.15 Using these guidelines to help children solve problems, teachers listen more than talk, allow children the time to make mistakes and figure out solutions, and point out that diversity of viewpoints is natural, normal, and workable.

Posing open-ended questions helps the adult stay focused:

"What could you do —————"
"How might she feel when —————"
"What might happen if —————"
"How can you —————"

The point is to encourage children to come up with alternative solutions. This requires an accepting attitude on the part of the teacher; all of the children's suggestions must be acknowledged seriously, even if they seem unreasonable. Young children are likely to start the discussion by suggesting extreme solutions. In the case of Malcolm, for instance, (see the second example in the section Understanding Behavior found previously in this chapter), they might initially suggest a radical alternative: "Don't let Malcolm come to this school anymore." These suggestions will become tempered as other children respond; fair and reasonable solutions will eventually emerge: "Anyone who knocks over somebody else's blocks has to help them build it back up again."

Rather than assessing blame, teachers help children think through a number of alternatives, including the consequences of what they suggest: "If we close the block area, what will happen when you want to play with your favorite trucks this afternoon?" By assisting them in anticipating the results of what they suggest, teachers can help children understand how their behavior influences and affects others. This is an early lesson in a lifelong quest to become responsible for one's own behavior.

Conflict resolution should become part of the child's daily life. Teachers can help children solve disagreements nonviolently and explore alternative ways to reach their goals. Figure 7.15 outlines a process for active problem-solving and conflict resolution. It is useful for resolving differences through group discussion, as noted above, or when one or more children become embroiled in conflict. By following such a process, children learn to respect others' opinions, to express their own feelings in appropriate ways, and to learn tolerance for doing things in a different way. The process also suggests an important principle in guidance and discipline: the adult role is to intervene as little as possible, allowing children the opportunity to come up with an acceptable solution.

When children help create a solution, they come away with a sense of commitment to it. This process also gives children a sense of power and control, a sense of independence, and a feeling of self-worth.

Figure 7.12 illustrates how these disciplinary techniques may be used to best advantage. See Figure 7.15 for six steps to social problem solving.

S U M M A R Y

The early childhood educator provides opportunities for children to express their feelings in appropriate ways and to solve their social problems constructively. Children are incapable of controlling their own impulses all the time, so caring adults are needed to guide them toward self-control. Teachers base their methods and guidance principles on an understanding of why children misbehave and what factors influence behavior.

Most guidance techniques begin by accepting the feelings the child expresses and verbalizing them. Then the adult sets limits on what form the behavior may take, guiding the action as needed and following through to conclusion.

The most effective methods of guidance are clear, consistent, and fair rules that are enforced in consistent, humane ways. Children should be aware of the consequences if the rules are broken.

Good guidance practices emphasize the positive aspects of a child's behavior, not just the problem behaviors. Guidance measures have greater meaning to children if they are encouraged to take responsibility for their own actions and are part of the problem-solving process.

R E V I E W   Q U E S T I O N S

1. What are some of the goals of children's misbehavior? What techniques can adults use to deal with children who exhibit these goals?

2. What developmental factors affect children's behavior? What environmental factors? How does a child's individual style affect behavior? What do developmental and learning theories (Chapter 4) add to the discussion?

3. Why is it important to understand the child's family culture as you guide and direct behavior?

4. What is your own definition of discipline?

5. Why do teachers have to set limits on children's behavior? How does it help the child?

6. Describe ways children differ in temperament.

7. Discuss in small groups the appropriate uses of Time Out. Describe those ways in which this technique can be harmful to young children.

L E A R N I N G   A C T I V I T I E S

1. Your three-year-old daughter always interrupts when you talk on the telephone. She cries for you to play with her, hits her brothers, and crawls into cupboards. What is she doing and why? What is your reaction? How will you solve the problem?

2. List activities that channel agressive feelings into acceptable ways to play. After each, note the emotion or feeling the specific activity might release. *Example:* Clay—anger, frustration

3. Finish this sentence: "When I was four years old, the *worst* thing I ever did was..." How did the adults around you react? What would you do if you were the adult in charge? Discuss and compare responses with a classmate.

4. Children's literature helps us focus on disciplinary and behavior problems. Select a book from the following list. Define the problem behavior and the person creating the problem. Do you agree with the author's way of handling the situation? Suggest alternatives. When and with whom might you use this story?

   Suggested books: *Peter's Chair*/Ezra Jack Keats
   Annie and the Old One/Miska Miles
   Jamaica's Find/ Juanita Havill
   Momma, Do You Love Me?/Barbara M. Joosse
   Tree of Cranes/Allen Say
   Shy Charles/Rosemary Wells

Bread and Jam for Frances/Russell and Lillian
Hoban
Where the Wild Things Are/Maurice Sendak

5. Observe a group of young children during play. See whether you can identify an example of a child who might be described as an easy child, a difficult child, and a slow-to-warm-up child. What disciplinary techniques do the teachers use with each child? Are they the same? If they are different, describe the differences. How successful are the disciplinary techniques that are being used? What might you do differently?

6. How do you feel about spanking children? Were you spanked when you were a child? If so, what precipitated the spankings? Could you think of any other forms of behavior control that might have worked instead of spanking? Compare your thoughts and insights with those of another member of this class.

7. What can you find out about a technique known as "Assertive Discipline" and why do some early childhood educators consider it inappropriate for young children? Report your findings back to this class.

B I B L I O G R A P H Y

Berk, Laura E. *Infants and Children*. Boston: Allyn and Bacon, 1994.

Brazelton, T. Berry. *Touchpoints: Your Child's Emotional and Behavioral Development*. Reading, Mass.: Addison-Wesley, 1992.

Galinsky, Ellen, and David, Judy. *The Preschool Years*. New York: Times Books, 1988.

Gordon, Ann, and Browne, Kathryn Williams. *Guiding Young Children in a Diverse Society*. Boston: Allyn and Bacon, 1996.

Gordon, Dr. Thomas. *Parent Effectiveness Training*. New York: Peter H. Wyden, 1970.

Likona, Thomas. *Educating for Character*. New York: Bantam Books, 1991.

Nelson, Jane, and Glenn, H. Stephen. *Time Out: Abuses and Effective Uses*. Fair Oaks, Calif.: Sunrise Press, 1992.

Nelson, Jane, Erwin, Cheryl, and Duffy, Roslyn. *Positive Discipline for Preschoolers*. Rocklin, Calif.: Prima Publishing, 1995.

Thomas, A., and Chess, S. *Temperament and Development*. New York: Brunner/Mazel, 1977.

"America's Immigrant Challenge." *Time*, special issue, Fall, 1993.

Wichert, Susanne. *Keeping the Peace*. Philadelphia, PA: New Society Publishers, 1989.

QUESTIONS FOR THOUGHT

Why is it important to have good working relationships with parents?

What are teachers expected to share with parents?

What will parents share with teachers?

How do parents get interested and involved in the classroom?

What are the ingredients for a good parent program?

What are the ingredients for a successful parent-teacher conference?

What is the teacher's role in providing a supportive atmosphere for parents?

What are some major concerns of parents?

How do parents affect children's growth?

CHAPTER 8

Parents and Teachers: Partners in Education

HISTORICAL PERSPECTIVE

Working with parents can be one of the teacher's most satisfying responsibilities, or it can be one of the most frustrating. It is usually both.[1] The potential is clearly present for a dynamic partnership between the most important adults in a child's life. The common goal is obvious: the welfare of the child. Each has knowledge, skills, and a sense of caring to bring to that relationship. Each has a need for the other. Partnerships usually begin with such a need. So, parents and teachers become coworkers, colleagues in a joint effort to help the child develop fully.

There is a historical **precedent** for the partnership between parents and teachers. Pestalozzi and Froebel, early eighteenth-century educators, detailed many of their procedures for home use. The involvement of the mother in the education of the child was considered important even then. When kindergartens were organized in this country, classes for parents and mothers' clubs were also started. The National Congress of Mothers evolved from that movement. Today it is the National Congress of Parents and Teachers (Spodek, 1972). This well-known organization is an integral part of most school systems and continues to promote a union between home and school, teachers and parents.

There was a period of time during the 1930s when parental involvement in education was actively discouraged. Teachers were seen as experts who wanted to be left alone to do their job. In many cases, teachers felt they did little but remedy parental mistakes. Parents in or near the classroom were barely tolerated. That trend ended in the 1940s when the need for parent support and encouragement was recognized. Closer relationships between teachers and parents were established. This view of a need for closer ties between teacher and parents, now over 50 years old, stands today as a commonly accepted principle.

Teacher training curricula began to reflect the change. Teachers were exposed to courses that would help them appreciate and utilize parents as coworkers in the child's development. By the 1960s, Head Start programs required parental involvement and set about developing parent education and parent training programs. Their commitment to children included a commitment to the parents of those children.

At no other level of education is the responsiveness to the needs of parents so high. Yet, in the last decade of this century, there is a renewed effort to extend the role of parents in their child's educational process. There is a broader emphasis from serving only children to serving children and their families. Also, there is a move from parents' role as volunteers to one of family support and a deepening of parent involvement. There is general agreement among early childhood teachers that at no other age is such a relationship more important than in the early years of a child's schooling, for children's needs are so interwoven with those of their parents. Strong parent-school relationships have always been a part of the early childhood educators' portfolio in ways that have not been understood or developed by teachers of other age groups.

Parent involvement and education was largely ignored in the education reform movement of the 1980s and the typical parent education prevalent in early childhood programs is also being reassessed. That omission is now being addressed in elementary, middle, and high schools throughout the country, a fact that reinforces the need for parents and teachers of preschool children to become full and equal partners and set the stage for future relationships. Further discussion of the parent support movement follows.

Note: Throughout this chapter, the terms "parents" and "parenthood" are meant to include mothers and fathers as well as other extended family members who have the responsibility for raising a child.[2]

---

[1]Ellen Galinsky coined the word "parentist." The way in which educators must heighten their awareness of their sexist and racist bias, one must also be aware of individual bias toward particular "types" of parents.

[2]As one works in OUR DIVERSE WORLD it is important to be mindful that many children are being parented by people other than their biological or adaptive parents (i.e. grandparents, or foster parents, or aunts and uncles, or legal guardians, or an adult living with the parent, etc.).

PARTNERSHIP IN EDUCATION

What Parents Contribute

Parents have a unique contribution to make in the child's schooling. They have different knowledge about the child from what the teacher has. They know the child's history: physical, medical, social, and intellectual. They know the child as a member of a family, and the role that child plays in the total family group. Through parents, teachers learn about the home life of the children in their classes: who they live with, in what kind of family situation, and what their life style is like. Parents bring with them a sense of continuity about the child: they provide the context with which the teacher can view the whole child. As the teacher will soon learn, the parents already know what makes their child happy or sad, or how they react to changes in routines. Thus, parents have a wealth of intimate knowledge about their child that the teacher is only just beginning to discover.

What Teachers Contribute

Teachers bring to the partnership another perspective. As child development professionals, they see the child in relation to what they know are normal milestones and appropriate behaviors. They notice how each child plays with other children in the group, what seems to challenge Elizabeth and when Patrick is likely to fall apart. Unlike parents, teachers see individual children from a perspective that is balanced by the numerous other children they have taught. They observe how the child behaves with a variety of adults, sensing children's ability to trust other adults through interactions with them at school. When parents need help for themselves or for their child, teachers become resources. They may work with the parents to find psychologists, hearing and speech specialists, or other educational programs, if warranted.

A true partnership begins with recognizing the strengths that each party brings and must be a basic premise in parent-teacher relationships. By pooling their knowledge of a child, both parents and teachers gain a more complete picture of the whole child. By becoming aware of the role each plays in the life of the child, teachers and parents grow in their understanding of one another. They can respect each other's unique contribution. As they recognize their need to share their strengths, they can learn from one another.

The Value of Working Together

The very first contact between parents and teachers is likely to take place within the early childhood education setting. If parents feel welcome and important, the stage is set for ongoing involvement in their child's education. By working closely with parents, teachers establish a pattern that can be repeated as the child grows. Parents should be involved in the school life of their child at all grade levels. Their introduction to this world of schools and teachers, then, is important.

The majority of parents today want to learn the best way to raise their children and want to improve their child-rearing skills. There are numerous opportunities for the early childhood teacher to work with parents. Figure 8.2 cites a multitude of ways to begin to fulfill these needs.

What Parents Gain

One of the greatest values of a strong parent program is the opportunity for parents to meet each other. They find that they share similar problems and frustrations, and that they can support one another in finding solutions. Friendships blossom based on mutual interests and concerns about their children.

Through close home-school relationships, parents can find ways to become more effective as parents and as teachers of their children. They can observe modeling techniques that teachers find successful in dealing with children and can learn what behaviors are appropriate at certain ages. By observing how their children relate to other adults and children, parents can come to know them better as social beings. They may become more aware of school and community resources that are available to them and, in the person of the teacher, they now have access to a consultant who knows and understands their child and can help them when they need it.

FIGURE 8.1   A true partnership happens when parents and teachers share their strengths with one another for the benefit of the children they care for and love.

Parents are the child's teachers too. They teach by word, by example, and by all they say and do. Through closer home-school relationships, parents can be helped to see that their everyday experiences with their children provide teachable moments, opportunities for educating their children. Teachers can support parents in their roles as teachers of their children by keeping them informed about each stage of the child's development, by showing them how to encourage language and thinking skills, by educating them to children's social needs at any given age, by providing lists of books and toys that encourage children's thinking and creative abilities as they provide the joy of reading. Teachers should make sure parents have copies of children's favorite songs, recipes that are popular at school, and information, in a bilingual format as needed, on how to teach health and safety habits at home.[1] Parents need not teach a curriculum; they do need to use common household routines and experiences to encourage children's total growth. The teaching staff has a strong role to play in helping parents

learn how to do this. In Figure 8.3 a noted author and family counselor lists some of the most important things parents can teach their children.

A family-centered approach to parent-school relationships supports the growth of the family as well as the child. When parents have a meaningful partnership with their children's teachers, it raises their sense of importance and diminishes some of the isolation and anxiety of child-rearing. By empowering parents in a critical area of their children's lives, allowing them to participate in decisions affecting their children's education, parents can see themselves as part of the solution.

What Teachers and The School Gain

Active parent involvement benefits the teacher and school, too. Parents are an untapped resource in most schools. The skills and talents in a group of parents multiply the people resources available to children.[2] Some parents will want to work directly in the classroom with children; others may volunteer to help in the office, the schoolyard,

[1]It is important to remember that fewer than half of the children under the age of five are being brought up in two parent, middle class, English speaking, stay-at-home mom, households. Do parent-teacher policies reflect this reality?

[2]Parents are an excellent resource for bringing experiences of diversity into a classroom (i.e. a dad cooking an ethnic favorite with children).

A Checklist for Making Your School Parent-Friendly

☐ Hold an orientation for parents
☐ Provide a place for parents to gather
☐ Create a parent bulletin board
☐ Give annual parent awards for involvement
☐ Create a parent advisory committee
☐ Allow parents to help develop school policies and procedures
☐ Schedule events on evenings, weekends
☐ Provide child care for meetings
☐ Establish a book/toy lending library
☐ Provide transportation for parents who need it
☐ Provide translators for parents who need them
☐ Send duplicate mailings to noncustodial parents
☐ Survey parents for issues of interest and need
☐ Develop links to health, social support services
☐ Provide resource and referral lists
☐ Publish school newsletter on regular basis
☐ Provide multilingual written communications as needed
☐ Hire teachers with strong commitment to supporting families/parents
☐ Provide in-service training for teachers in working with parents
☐ Hire teachers who are respectful of social, ethnic, and religious backgrounds of parents
☐ Hire staff reflective of the cultural background of students/parents
☐ Encourage regularly scheduled conferences between parents and teachers
☐ Offer variety of family support programs
☐ Provide many opportunities for parents to volunteer
☐ Provide frequent opportunities for parents to air their concerns
☐ Encourage parents to ask questions, to visit, to call
☐ Encourage parents to know what goes on in the classroom
☐ Encourage parents to report back on what works well
☐ Encourage parents to attend social events
☐ Encourage teachers to make home visits

FIGURE 8.2   A checklist for a family-centered approach to meet children's needs.[1]

 OUR DIVERSE WORLD OUR DIVERSE WORLD OUR DIVERSE WORLD OUR DIVERSE WORLD OUR DIVERSE WORLD

[1]Many of the items on this list demonstrate an awareness of life in OUR DIVERSE WORLD. Can you think of others to add to make your school parent-friendly in a diverse world?

The Ten Most Important Things Parents Can Teach Their Children

1. To love themselves
2. To read behavior
3. To communicate with words
4. To understand the difference between thoughts and actions
5. To wonder and ask why
6. To understand that complicated questions do not have simple answers
7. To risk failure as a necessary part of growing up
8. To trust grownups
9. To have a mind of their own
10. To know when to lean on adults

FIGURE 8.3 A list of important basics that children can learn at home. (Adapted from Eda LeShan. *When Your Child Drives You Crazy*. New York: St. Martin's Press, 1985.)

or the kitchen. Parents can sometimes arrange to take some time off from their jobs to accompany a class on a field trip. There are parents who are willing to work at home, either sewing, typing, mending, building, or painting; others are available for a variety of fund-raising activities. In an equal partnership, however, the parent level of involvement must go beyond volunteer participation in school activities to parent participation in decision-making roles, such as serving on school boards, parent advisory committees, and other groups that advocate for children's educational needs.

Some parents may be unable to participate because of work schedules, small children to care for at home, lack of transportation, or inability to speak English.[1] If a school is serious about strengthening the family, these issues must be addressed and solutions must be found to involve all parents.

What Children Gain

The children whose parents choose to take an active part in the school reap the rewards of such involvement. Decades of research show the positive effects on achievement when children's parents are involved in their education. The family is the primary source from which the child develops and grows. It is needed to reinforce the learning, the attitudes, and the motivation if children are to succeed. Parent visibility is especially important for low income and minority children; their parent's presence can heighten a sense of belonging. Children gain and parent impact is increased when parents are able to monitor their children's progress and reinforce the mission of the school at home.

Guidelines for Working with Parents

Supporting and encouraging parents in their role is part of a teacher's responsibility. Good teachers are sensitive to parent concerns and understand their needs, similar to those expressed in the Focus Box on p. 231, written by a parent to her child's caregiver. To insure good parent-teacher relationships, review the following guidelines:

Prepare parents for what they can expect from their child's school experience. School policies and a yearly calendar should be clearly stated and thoroughly reviewed with parents as the child enters school. Then parents will know what their responsibilities are, where the school can be of assistance to them, and what expectations the school has of the parents.

Protect the parent-child relationship. Enhance the pride children naturally feel about their mothers and fathers. Tell Maggie her eyes are just like her Dad's or mention to Kevin that his Mom will be pleased to hear he slid down the big slide. Reinforce that unique place families have in children's lives. This is particularly critical for children who spend long hours in child care centers away from their parents. Parents need teachers to support them in raising their children and they like to hear when they have done well. They take pride in doing their best and appreciate teachers who acknowledge this.

OUR DIVERSE WORLD OUR DIVERSE WORLD OUR DIVERSE WORLD OUR DIVERSE WORLD OUR DIVERSE WORLD

[1] It is important to remember that fewer than half of the children under the age of five are being brought up in two parent, middle class, English speaking, stay-at-home mom, households. Do parent-teacher policies reflect this reality?

How You Can Help—
From A Parent Perspective

Yvonne Ricketts

Dear Caregiver:

I bravely smile as I reluctantly allow you to take my infant into your arms. I know in my mind that I can trust you, as I quickly go over all of your carefully chosen qualities. I know that I am doing the right thing by returning to work. But I also know that if I linger much longer my tears will take over and I will grab my baby, run to Tasmania, and go into hiding. All of my early childhood education training and experience didn't prepare me for this first separation. So, as a parent experiencing the intensity of a parent-child bond, I would like to offer some suggestions for helping to ease the separation transition:

1. Take the time to visit with me in advance of my child's first day. Show me around, let me see where my child will eat, sleep, play, and keep his belongings. Find out what our daily routine is and share yours with me.

2. Encourage me to visit with my child before his first day.

3. Help me feel relaxed and comfortable. Be empathetic and listen to me. If I am uncomfortable, my child will be, too.

4. Reassure me of how you will help my child cope while I am gone. Will he be stimulated with developmentally appropriate activities? Will he have a special "buddy" looking out for him, helping him learn the new routine? If he cries, how will you handle this?

5. When we arrive, greet me with a smile, and a hug/touch for my child on his level. Ask about his night. Help him get settled, put away his belongings.

6. If I am lingering too long, help me leave. I may feel awkward and uncomfortable and need your firm but reassuring push out the door.

7. If I am rushing out the door, remind me to say goodbye to my child, and tell him when I will return in concrete ways he can understand (e.g. "after snack").

8. If my child is having a hard time allowing me to leave, let me see you comfort him and help him with your kind words and reassuring touch.

9. Acknowledge that my child may miss me and that I may miss him. Let my child wave goodbye to me.

10. Allow me to call or visit my child during the day during convenient times for you and me.

11. When I pick up my child, tell me something specific about his day—something positive.

Try not to take it personally if I seem nontrusting, overly concerned and ask a lot of questions. Remember, I'm a new parent and I'm leaving someone precious in my life with you. I need your reassurance just as you need my trust. Helping me positively separate will help my child. Together we are creating great beginnings for my child.

Thank You!

Yvonne Ricketts is a former children's center director who is now a child advocate and the parent of Casey, seven, and Delaney, four.

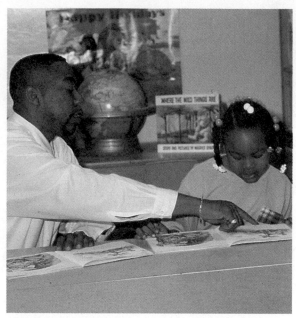

FIGURE 8.4 When a parent participates in his child's school life, it can heighten a child's sense of belonging.

Contact parents frequently and on a regular basis. Keep the lines of communication open and flowing between school and home. Be sure to know the parents by name. Take advantage of the daily contact as they bring their child to and from school. It may be brief and breezy, but it is a good way to stay in touch. Be sure to find ways to touch base with those parents who do not come to school every day, by telephone, note, or home visit.

Respect parents for the difficult job they have, the role they play, and the persons they are. Respect their religious, cultural, social, and ethnic backgrounds and heritage.[1] Respect their privacy. Do not allow one parent to seek information about another. Respect the right of the parent to disagree. Above all, respect the unparalleled part they play in the growth and development of their child.

Listen to parents. Hear them out. They, too, have accumulated experiences to share, and their views are valid. Learn to listen to them with a degree of understanding; try to hear it from their point of view. Listen to parents without judging

them or jumping to conclusions; this is the basis for open communication.

Becoming Full and Equal Partners

Families and schools are natural allies; together they claim the primary responsibility in educating and socializing children. They can and should be equal partners in that effort.

Family-Support Movement

Early childhood educators have long recognized the importance of providing parents with child-rearing information and support. Today, the task of raising children has become increasingly difficult and the type of parent education and participation is changing to meet current parent's needs. What is termed a "family-support" or "parent-support" movement is evolving where the primary goal is to strengthen families to meet the challenges of parenting in the nineties.

Parent education has often been achieved through lectures on discipline and guidance or age-appropriate characteristics. Parent participation in school activities has been through fundraising, volunteering to help out in the classroom, and driving on field trips. Resource and referrals for children's special needs has defined parent support. These are certainly important aspects of building good relationships between parents and schools, but are no longer enough for today's parents.

"Children influence and are influenced by a social network: family, school, and community" (Kagan, 1991). Many programs today offer a more comprehensive approach to the parent-school partnership out of a growing recognition of the "ecology of the family" (see Chapter 15 for further discussion). Programs with a strong family orientation create parent centers which offer counseling, cultural events, support groups, weekend family activities, and links to health and social service agencies. Factors that increase the need of a more family-centered approach are: increase in the divorce rate, the growing number of single parent families and families where both parents work,

[1]This says it all!

and increasing numbers of immigrant families. (See the following section on Today's Parent and Chapter 15 for examples and discussion). School perception of what constitutes a "family" may no longer correspond to the reality of today's definition of a family. Family support takes on new meaning when the differences in family styles are acknowledged and supported.[1]

Government Recognition

A growing awareness of the need for a family-centered approach to parent education has been recognized by several government agencies. From its beginning in 1965, Head Start mandated parent involvement as necessary for the health and welfare of many young children. More recently, the Education of the Handicapped Amendments (PL 99-457) in 1986, required early intervention services aimed at the family, not just the child. PL 99-457 includes parents as members of a team of professionals who develop an individualized plan related to the child and family's needs. Two states, Minnesota and Missouri, have developed comprehensive, family-centered early childhood programs funded through local school districts.

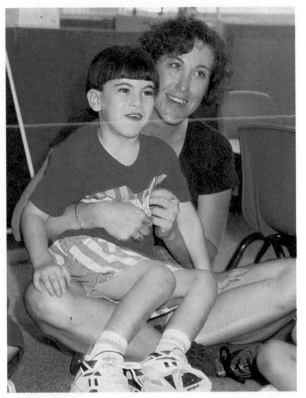

FIGURE 8.5   Visits and participation in classroom activities are opportunities for parents and teachers to support a family-centered view of the child.

Developing a Strong Partnership

Powell (1989) has defined four components of a high-quality parent program that promote the family's contribution to their children's education and growth as well as a more equal and meaningful partnership.

1. **Parents and teacher collaborate** to ensure that parent program goals, methods, and content are responsive to parents needs. The needs, concerns, and interests of parents will vary according to the population the school serves. Parents have many needs in common, but they do not all have the same needs at the same time. A good program for parent involvement reflects those needs in the number, type, and kinds of

opportunities it provides. An assessment of parent needs is critical, as is parent involvement and planning the program.

2. At the same time the **parents' social services and community support networks are strengthened,** care must be taken not to overshadow the needs of the child. The interconnectedness of the child, the family, and the community must be recognized without disturbing the balance between meeting children's needs and parents' needs. Teachers have a dual role of caring for and educating children while being sensitive and responsive to their parents. As parents and teachers develop a partnership, they should keep in mind that the children's

OUR DIVERSE WORLD OUR DIVERSE WORLD OUR DIVERSE WORLD OUR DIVERSE WORLD OUR DIVERSE WORLD

[1]The more information the school has about the families of the children enrolled (preferred language, work schedules, particular challenges and areas of expertise, etc.) the higher the likelihood of successful home-school relationships. Only plan family support services based on the two parent family described in the footnote on p. 228 if that best describes the majority of families being served.

best interests are the common goal of a good parent program.

3. **Programs must be tailored to the needs and characteristics of the specific parent population,** responding to cultural characteristics and values of ethnic populations. In order to build on the family's strength and promote the family's contribution to their children's education, some programs will serve a targeted audience. Support groups for teenage parents, non-English speaking parents, and parents who are working on their high school equivalency tests may be developed alongside the usual parenting classes and workshops.[1]

4. **Frequent discussion groups** where parents are free to share their experiences and insights with one another are critical to parent-teacher growth in the partnership. Parents will grow in self-confidence and security only if teachers will respect their native intelligence and instincts about their own children. A good parent program is based on mutual respect where parents have the freedom to accept what is useful, and where they can reject what they cannot in good conscience adopt for themselves.

Two qualifications must be added to Powell's list to strengthen and reinforce the role of the family as the most important influence in the child's life. First, teachers must be trained to work with parents from many ethnic, religious, and cultural backgrounds. They must be willing to listen to and respect parents as well as demonstrate their commitment to an equal partnership.[2]

Secondly, high-quality parent programs show they are serious about the partnership when they give parents a greater say in school decision making. Parent involvement will be limited unless there are decisions parents can make that have meaning for their children (Levin, 1990). Empowering parents to be change agents in their children's educational process results in greater parent commitment and involvement.

Reggio Emilia: An Exemplary Partnership

One of the best examples of school/parent partnerships which bears witness to Powell's criteria for high-quality programs is the schools of Reggio Emilia. A fundamental principle is an assumption of strong and active parent involvement at every level of school functioning. This is not surprising, since the schools were originally founded as parent cooperatives; part of the guiding philosophy continues to uphold a model of equal and extended partnership. Malaguzzi (1993) refers to this balanced responsibility of teachers, parents, and children as a "triad at the center of education;" who, in turn, count on the rest of the community to provide a cultural context for children's learning.

School-based management fosters meaningful participation of parents. All of the discussions and decisions are made by the teachers and parents within each school setting, including cooks and other adults who work within that particular school as well. No area seems the exclusive property of either parents or teachers. Curriculum planning, for instance, depends upon the family's involvement, interest, and contribution. Parents are the core of the individual school boards, and their numbers are well represented on the city-wide school board; they are an integral part of the decision-making process that determines their children's education. Frequent parent meetings are held to inform parents of the school's program and to bring them up to date on what their children are doing. Other meetings may be focused on a topic of interest or an opportunity for parents to explore and debate, or an expert may lecture on a topic regarding their child's development. Smaller groups of parents meet throughout the year with the teachers to talk about their children and the program; individual parent/teacher conferences, which either can request, are held to deal with specific concerns.

There are opportunities as well to be actively involved in the daily life of the school. Parents,

---

OUR DIVERSE WORLD OUR DIVERSE WORLD OUR DIVERSE WORLD OUR DIVERSE WORLD OUR DIVERSE WORLD

[1]See footnote on page 233.

[2]Many early childhood educators choose the profession because of their interest in children; only to realize that a large focus of their work needs to be on adult development as it relates to families in a multicultural world.

SIX STAGES OF PARENTHOOD

Stage	Parent Task	Age of Child(ren)
1. Image-making stage	Parents draw on their memories and fantasies of what kind of parent they want to be, prepare for changes in themselves and with other important adults.	Occurs during gestation
2. Nurturing stage	Parents confront the demands of attachment, compare their images with their actual experiences.	From birth until child says "No," around 18 to 24 months
3. Authority stage	Parents define the rules of the family system and their roles in it; they decide what kind of authority to be.	From 18 months to five years of age
4. Interpretive stage	Parents decide how to interpret the world to their child, are concerned with how they interpret themselves to their children, how they are developing the children's self-concepts; and what kind of values, knowledge, and skills to promote.	From late preschool years until the beginning of adolescence
5. Interdependent stage	Parents renegotiate the rules with their teenagers; issues of stage 3 (authority) reappear; parents form a new relationship with their almost-grown children.	The teenage years
6. Departure stage	Parents evaluate their sense of success or failure—whether they have achieved the parent-child relationship they want—and redefine these new relationships.	When children leave home

FIGURE 8.6 The role of a parent changes in various ways as parent and child grow older together. (Adapted from Ellen Galinsky. *Between Generations.* Reading, Mass.: Addison-Wesley, 1987.)

teachers, and town residents build furnishings and maintain materials for the classrooms and the school yard and rearrange the space to accommodate program needs. In sessions with teachers and *pedagogistas*, parents learn various educational techniques necessary to the program, such as photography and puppet-making, and utilize these new skills in the classroom with their children. Using the whole town as a backdrop, parents participate in many of the field trips to city landmarks, or as small groups visiting a child's home. Recording and transcribing children's activities and projects are often a parent's responsibility (see Chapter 11).

The meaning of family is communicated to the children of Reggio Emilia throughout their school environment. In classroom dramatic play areas and in the school's own kitchen there are displays of foods, materials, and utensils common to the region and found in the children's homes. Children are encouraged to bring special objects from home, and these are accorded special and

beautifully arranged display space. Photographs of children and families abound. These elements are the vehicles used to ensure a rich flow of communication between the school and the homes of the children of Reggio Emilia.

The schools of Reggio Emilia seem to have a unique reciprocal relationship with the families they serve. Parents have influence and help effect change; in turn, the schools influence and change parents. Each becomes a stronger voice for what is in the best interest of the child, whose needs are foremost.

TODAY'S PARENT

There is little preparation for the job of being a parent and most mothers and fathers feel inadequate in their role. Parents are pretty much alone as they strike out in unfamiliar territory. Due to our increasingly mobile society, most couples do not live around the corner from grandparents or

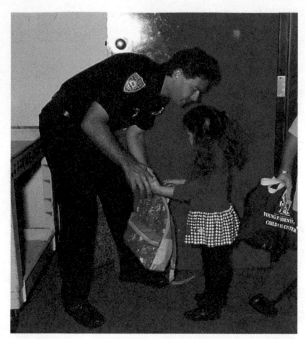

FIGURE 8.7 Since half of the women with children younger than age six work outside the home, fathers often bring children to child care.

other family members. There is no extended family to teach new mothers and fathers some of the traditional, time-honored child-rearing skills. There is no one with whom parents can share their worries, frustrations, and concerns. So the **pediatrician's** phone number is etched in their minds, and they proceed to become the best parents they can.

More recently, an important change has taken place within young families. Raising children as a shared experience is becoming a commonly accepted way of life. Young men, influenced by changing values and attitudes toward traditional sex roles, are taking an active part in raising their families. Fathers seem aware of the critical role they play in the child's life and are making appropriate changes to see that they have the time to be with their children. Child rearing is no longer just the mother's responsibility, according to a new generation of fathers.

Stages of Parent Development

The role of parent is not a static one; parents grow and change as their children do. The cycle of stages parents experience is only recently being recognized and studied. Identifiable stages of parental growth are described in a manner similar to the stages of growth that occur as all humans develop and as teachers develop (Galinsky, 1987).

According to Galinsky, there are six stages of parenthood. Because parents may have children of different ages, they may be going through several stages at once. Growth can occur at any time and during any stage. The tasks and issues at each stage vary (see Figure 8.7).

The advent of the first baby brings with it life-altering changes and implications. For many parents who were raised to believe that having children is fun, that children will keep a marriage together, or that every married couple must have children, the myths do not match the reality of the experience.

As they gain confidence in themselves, as more children are added to the family, and as each family member matures in age, parents continually change. The issues they face with only one child are altered considerably when a second or third baby is born. As each of the children grows, develops, and progresses through stages, parents are required to adapt. As parents modify their own myths about child-rearing to the realities they experience, they grow as parents. Changing their own behavior is a sign of growth. In other words, parents do not have a consistent or permanent pattern of child-rearing over the years (Bee, 1989).

Patterns of Child-Rearing

One notable study of how parents behave with preschool children was published by Baumrind in 1972. Of the three types of parental styles identified (authoritative, authoritarian, and permissive), authoritative parents were associated with the highest levels of self-esteem, self-reliance, independence, and curiosity in children. *Authoritative* parents provided a warm, loving atmosphere with clear limits and high expectations. In a follow-up study done when the children were eight or nine, Baumrind's findings persisted.

In contrast, *authoritarian* child-rearing patterns reflect high control and maturity demands combined with relatively low communication and nurturance. Authoritarian parents are dictatorial;

they expect and demand obedience yet lack warmth and affection. *Permissive* patterns are essentially the reverse of authoritarian child-rearing styles. There is a high level of warmth and affection but little control. Clear standards and rules are not set, nor are they reinforced consistently.

This research points out clearly how children are affected by the way their parents treat them. The role of the teacher becomes clear also—to help parents learn appropriate and effective ways to raise their children.

Incidentally, it has been noted that in lists defining characteristics of unusually effective schools, the qualities cited sound similar to those of the authoritative child-rearing style. The effective parent and the effective school each establish "clear goals and rules, good control, good communication, and high nurturance" (Bee, 1989).

The Changing American Family

As changes in parent development styles have been recorded about individual family systems, the American family as a whole is experiencing significant alterations. Statistics gathered 30 years apart show a dramatic picture of the changing family:

	1960	1990
Percentage of children in the U.S.	36%	26%
Number of persons per household	3.3	2.6
Number of divorced persons (per 100 married persons)	35	142
18-year-olds living with one parent	12%	25%
Families of married couples with children under 18	52%	26%
Children living in poverty in female-headed households	24%	57%
Married women with children under 6 who work outside the home	2.5%	58.9%

(U.S. Department of Education, 1991, and U.S. Census Bureau, 1991)

For the early childhood educator the implications are clear. The critical issues facing children and their families today are adequate and affordable child care, raising children alone, raising only children, becoming first-time parents at an older age, and raising children in a dominant culture not their own. The challenge for the teacher is to be prepared to understand families in their various forms, and to be part of a family support system.[1]

Parents With Special Needs

Parents are parents the world over and have mutual problems and pleasures as they go about bringing up their young. Their shared experiences create an automatic bond whenever parents meet. Today, there are some parents, however, who face additional challenges in child rearing, and who may need added teacher support. These are:

● parents of children with handicaps, developmental delays, and disabilities

● single parents

● parents who both work outside the home

● divorced parents

● gay/lesbian parents

● homeless parents

● teenage parents

● parents who are raising their children in a culture not their own

● parents who do not speak English and whose child is in a setting where English is the predominant language

● older first-time parents

Many of these family characteristics place parents in situations where they do not have access to an extended family support system. Any one or combination of these situations can create complex challenges for parents. A teacher should become aware of the forces at work within these fam-

OUR DIVERSE WORLD OUR DIVERSE WORLD OUR DIVERSE WORLD OUR DIVERSE WORLD OUR DIVERSE WORLD

[1]See the footnote on page 233 "Many early childhood educators choose the profession because of their interest in children; only to realize that a large focus of their work needs to be on adult development as it relates to families in a multicultural world."

ilies and be sensitive to their needs. Teachers should treat these parents as they do any other. It is not necessary to single them out and, indeed, such an effort may be resented.[1] For the most part, teachers can help these parents by focusing on the many interests and concerns they share with all other parents. In some cases, additional support for these parents is needed.

- Help parents locate community resources to assist them.

- Put them in touch with other parents who have similar parenting circumstances.

- Assist them in exploring school settings for the future.

- See that they are included in all school functions.

- Learn about their special needs.

- Seek their help and advice.

- Help them establish contact with other parents who may be willing to assist in translating, transporting, babysitting, and sharing friendship.

Needs of Single Parents

In their eagerness to do right by their child, parents grab for help whenever and however it is offered: how-to books, television talk shows, magazine articles. They seem willing to listen to anyone, to try anything. That is surely some measure of how lonely and frightened parents must feel at times.

These feelings may be particularly acute for single parents—men and women who are raising children without a partner. One in every four or five children today lives in a single-parent household. If current trends continue, 60 percent of all children will live in a single-parent household sometime in their lives (Wanat, 1991).

Faced with the economic necessity to work, single parents must cope not only with raising chil-

dren alone, but with child care arrangements and costs. Particularly hard-hit are women who head single-parent households. They are more likely than men to live below the poverty level, to never have married, not to have finished high school, and to be members of a minority population.

Single parents need the early childhood professional to be part of a support system for them and their children. To best serve the interests of children, educators must be sensitive to the unique aspects of raising children alone. This means reexamining school policies and attitudes that ignore the needs of single parents.[2] Overburdened child care professionals need to be flexible in exploring new avenues of home-school collaboration. They need to ask:

- What kind of involvement in a child's classroom is *possible* for a working single parent?

- How can teachers help parents feel connected even if they are unable to be at the center?

- What is appropriate support for single parents?

- How do teachers maintain the role of the professional, offering support, without getting involved with inappropriate friendships?

- How judgmental are teachers about single parents? Single women?

- How do teachers help parents and children deal with the absent parent?

- What are some of the best strategies for helping children cope with the transitions when visiting one parent or the other?

These and other similar questions must become an agenda of staff meetings, in-service for teachers, and parent-group meetings.

Needs of Immigrant Parents

The 1990 census highlights the extensive changes in immigration during the 1980s. The number of Asian-Americans and the number of

OUR DIVERSE WORLD OUR DIVERSE WORLD OUR DIVERSE WORLD OUR DIVERSE WORLD OUR DIVERSE WORLD

[1]Many of the challenges and joys of parenting young children are universal—crossing the lines of the child's family structure, culture, ability, social class, etc.

[2]School policies should be based on the two parent family described in the footnote on p. 239 only if that best describes the majority of families being served.

Hispanics more than doubled with high levels of immigration from Latin America, Southeast Asia, the Philippines, China, and India (Armstrong, 1991). These data, added to existing ethnic populations already present in the United States, challenge the early childhood teacher to a multicultural sensitivity not yet realized. A willingness to learn various cultural norms and a knowledge of languages will be helpful for teachers to communicate with children and parents whose primary language is not English. Since some studies suggest that teacher's stereotypes of racial subgroups influence their perception of parenting, teachers will want to examine their own biases (Powell, 1989). See the appropriate sections in Chapters 5, 9, and 11 for discussion of teacher bias, anti-bias curriculum, and anti-bias environments.

Miscommunication may be a problem when teaching a classroom of diverse children. When cultural perspectives of the family and the school differ markedly, teachers can easily misread a child's attitude and abilities because of different styles of languages and behaviors. Also, teachers may employ instructional strategies that are at odds with a child's cultural norms. How adults and children interact with children, their teaching language, and the strategies they use to guide children's behavior are areas in which immigrant parents can help teachers learn the cultural differences that cause difficulties for children.

The Teacher's Role

The child care specialist is often one of the first people, outside the home, to whom parents turn for help. Parents come to the center looking for teachers who know about children and who will work with them. They arrive at school confused and discouraged; being a mommy or daddy is not at all like they thought it was going to be. Helping parents with their child-rearing problems is part of a teacher's role. The way in which teachers define that role and their response to parental concerns should be carefully thought through. The following are guidelines to consider in establishing a supportive atmosphere for parents:

Do not confuse the role of teacher and parent. While committed to meeting the needs of the individual children in the class, remember that teachers are not and cannot be **surrogate** mothers. Allow parents to do their part of the job to the best of their ability, and teachers their part without infringing on that relationship.

Support all parents, even those with differing opinions. Find ways to acknowledge them and what they are trying to do even though you may be at odds with some of their child-rearing philosophies. There is a greater chance to discuss differences and affect change if there are areas where teachers and parents find agreement.[1] Children are sensitive to adult feelings, whether they are spoken or not. A teacher should not overtly disagree with a child's parents. Differences of opinions should be discussed out of the child's hearing, but teachers should also do nothing that would undermine that parent in the eyes of his or her child.

Respect the values of families. Social, cultural, and religious differences and a variety of life styles, child-rearing methods, and educational philosophies are reflected in every class. It is important that parents feel accepted. Focus on the similarities among parents and develop an anti-bias approach to teaching.

Be friendly with parents, but do not be their friends. Keep a professional distance. The temptation to move into a social relationship with some families in your class is one that every teacher faces. When a teacher develops close relationships with one family or another, this can complicate the teacher role. It makes a teacher feel good to know that friendship is desired, but it can be confusing to parents and children. The teacher maintains a more realistic, objective picture of the child if there is some detachment. The child and the family will probably benefit most if a close relationship is postponed until the child moves on to another class.

Ask parents instead of telling them. A teacher-tell approach should be used sparingly. Teachers are most helpful when they begin with the parents' concerns. Suggestions will be received more favor-

OUR DIVERSE WORLD OUR DIVERSE WORLD OUR DIVERSE WORLD OUR DIVERSE WORLD OUR DIVERSE WORLD

[1]Many of the challenges and joys of parenting young children are universal—crossing the lines of the child's family structure, culture, ability, social class, etc.

ably if teachers avoid telling parents what to do. A teacher's role is one of helping parents clarify their own goals for their children and identifying the trouble spots. Teachers then encourage and support parents as they work together to solve the problem. Parents will feel overwhelmed and inadequate if they think they must change their whole child-rearing style. The sensitive teacher will observe parents and move toward reasonable solutions.

A little support goes a long way. Everyone likes to be reinforced for doing a good job. Parents respond positively to a comment, a phone call, or any brief acknowledgment of their efforts. As Alex's parents enter or leave school, the teacher could mention how Alex has relaxed since they began to insist on a reasonable bedtime. A quick note, sent home with Juanita, that commends her parents for getting her to school on time would be appreciated.

Help parents support each other. Any group of parents represents a multitude of resources. Each parent has accumulated experiences that might prove helpful to someone else. Parents have common concerns and a lot to share with one another. The teacher can provide an arena in which sharing happens. Introduce two families to each other by suggesting that their children play together outside of school. Parent meetings, work parties, and potluck dinners are methods for getting parents involved with each other. The teacher's role can be one of providing the setting, encouraging introductions, and then letting it happen.

Enhance parents' perception of their child. Parents want teachers who know their child, enjoy their child, and are an advocate for their child. That means acknowledging the child's strengths and those personality traits that are particularly pleasing. Help parents to recognize the joys of parenthood, rather than focusing on the burdens.

Focus on the parent-child relationship. Help parents learn the "how to's" of their relationship with their child rather than the "how-to's" of developing academic skills. Concentrate on the nature of the parent-child interaction—how they get along with each other and how they interact as a family. A major concern of parents may be how to get Rhoda to stop biting her nails; how to set limits that Joel will keep; how to stop Richard and Monica from fighting at the dinner table; how to get

Timmy to stop wetting his bed; how to get Allie to take care of the puppy; or how to get Frannie to clean up her room. These issues are the heart and soul of parent-child relationships. Teachers have a role to play in enhancing the quality of those relationships by helping parents focus on the real "how to's."

Accept parents for what they are. Their feelings get aroused by teachers, schools, children's behavior, being judged, being criticized, feeling inadequate, and being told what to do. Meantime, teachers have to face their feelings about parents. The important thing to keep in mind is that parents just want to be accepted for who and what they are. As teachers accept the individuality of each child, they must accept each parent as a unique combination of traits, personalities, strengths, problems, and concerns. Parents and teachers seem frightened of one another. This is especially true of inexperienced teachers and first-time parents. Each has anxieties about what the other does—or does not do. They must work at putting the other at ease and come to some understanding and respect. Teachers who have a clear understanding of that role can help parents relax and set aside some of their fears.

TEACHER-PARENT INTERACTIONS

The Separation Process

When parents leave a child at school, it is a time of stress for all concerned. Each time this process occurs, the child, parents, and teachers are entering into a new and unpredictable relationship.

The Child's Perspective

Each year, as school begins, a child enters a classroom and says good-bye to a parent. Each year this is, in some ways, a new experience for that child, no matter how long he or she might have been enrolled in school. Children returning to the same classroom will find some changes with which they must cope. There may be new teachers and new children together with some familiar faces. The room arrangement might be different enough to cause some anxiety. For most, school is a new and alien place. Each child will react differently to the situation, and it is difficult to predict how a child will respond. Some children will have had previous group experience to draw on; others will never have been a part of a group of children before.

Here are some scenes of children entering school for the first time:

Paul, clinging to his Dad's trouser legs, hides his face from view. All efforts to talk with him are met with further withdrawal behind his father.

Sherry bounces in, runs from her mother over to the blocks area and begins to play there. Her mother is left standing alone, just inside the classroom.

Taryn clutches a stuffed animal as she enters school with her grandmother. She smiles when the teacher addresses her by name and looks surprised when the teacher asks to meet the rabbit she is holding. Taryn lets go of her grandmother's hand and moves forward to show the teacher her favorite toy. After a few moments, the grandmother tells Taryn good-bye, leaving her in conversation with the teacher.

The wide range of behavior these children exhibit is normal, predictable, and age-appropriate. Each child has a natural way of dealing with the anxieties of coming to school. Their behavior will be as varied as they are themselves.[1]

The Teacher's Perspective

The separation process is one instance in which the teacher's role is to help the parents as much as the child. Parents and teachers must be especially clear with one another during this time. It is helpful to have written school policies and procedures so the teacher can go over the process step by step, on an individual basis, as each child enrolls, or at a general parent meeting held prior to the opening of school.

In some schools, teachers arrange to make a home visit to each child enrolled in the class before school begins. This helps the teacher know more about students before they enter school and gives

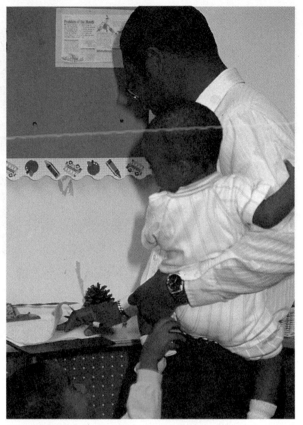

FIGURE 8.8 Good communication is enhanced when parents and teachers leave notes for one another about important changes in the child's daily routine.

children a chance to become acquainted with a teacher on their home ground.

The Parent's Perspective

Most parents want their children to make a smooth transition from home to school. Adjustment is a gradual process; parents need encouragement and guidance as their child moves toward independence. When parents are reassured their child is acting normally, and their own anxieties are common, they relax and begin to help the child feel more comfortable.

Parents encourage their child's participation in the program by asking questions and talking together about school activities. They communicate

 OUR DIVERSE WORLD OUR DIVERSE WORLD OUR DIVERSE WORLD OUR DIVERSE WORLD OUR DIVERSE WORLD

[1]Early childhood educators are reminded regularly that there is not one right way, rather many right ways.

FIGURE 8.9 Parents like to know that they make a difference.

their interest in ways to help their child meet the challenge with a minimum of stress and a maximum of enjoyment.

The Partnership

In giving support and encouragement to both the parent and the child, the teacher helps them achieve independence from one another. Together, parents and teachers make a plan, going over the guidelines and ground rules. The teacher takes the lead, encouraging the child to move out from the parent. The teacher is there to make the decisions regarding the time of actual separation. The parent and teacher prepare children and tell them when it is time. The teacher supports the parents' exit and stands by the child, ready to give comfort, if needed. This is a time when a teacher needs to act with conviction. Parents appreciate firmness and confidence at a time when their own feelings may be *ambiguous*. Children are reassured by teachers whose attitudes express a belief in what they are doing.

Some parent-child relationships are difficult to assess, and it is not always easy or obvious for the teacher to know what to do. Figure 4.12 on p. 123 may be helpful as a reminder of how patterns of attachment affect the separation process. For most children, the separation process is a struggle between their natural desire to explore the world and their equally natural resistance to leaving what is "safe." It is during these years that children are learning to move about under their own power and to trust themselves. Coming to school can provide each child with the opportunity to grow, starting with the separation from parents. Through careful planning, close communication, and sensitivity to one another, parents and teachers will assure the child mastery of this task.

Parent Education and Involvement

Almost any contact between the teacher and the parent can be perceived as parent education. Teachers interpret children's behavior to their parents, suggest alternative ways for dealing with problems, show them toys and games that are appropriate, hold workshops on parenting skills, mention books and articles of interest to parents, and reinforce parent interest and attention to their children's education. All of these activities are considered parent education. Some is planned, some is spontaneous. Parent education happens frequently, whether in a class on positive discipline or in an informal chat about car seat safety.

Parental involvement in children's education has a wide variety of options, as discussed earlier in this chapter. The concept of parent education/involvement in early childhood programs is broadening to include any number of family support programs based on the needs of parents and their children. Parent education and involvement are at the core of the family-school relationship and go a long way to promote a true partnership between parents and teachers.

Communicating with Parents

There are many ways for parents and teachers to increase their communication with one another. In doing so, teachers demonstrate that they value the role parents play in their children's lives. Parents are made aware of what their children are doing in school. Five of the most common ways teachers can involve and inform parents are:

1. *Newsletters from the classroom.* They give a general idea of what the children are doing and any special events taking place in class, personal information about new babies, vacations, or other important events in the lives of the children. Be sure the newsletter is written in the language of the parents in this class.

2. *Bulletin boards.* Posted where parents can see them, these boards contain notices about parent meetings, guest speakers, community resources, child care, babysitting, clothing and furniture exchanges, and library story hours. Information regarding health programs, automobile and toy safety, and immunization clinics are also publicized. Post information on cultural events appropriate to the ethnic makeup of the parent body.

3. *A place for parents.* An area or room at the school set aside for parent use can be an important step in letting parents know they are wanted and needed. Some schools provide space for a parent lounge, complete with a library of resource books on child rearing. If there is no available space, set up a coffee bar in the office

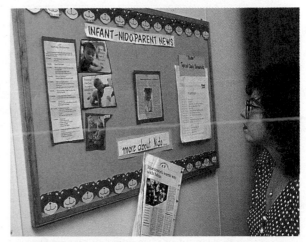

FIGURE 8.10   There are many avenues for parent-teacher communication. This bulletin board, located just outside the classroom door, holds newsletters, notices, and even children's art.

or hall. The smallest amount of space—even a countertop with magazines—is a start.

4. *Informal contacts are the easiest and most useful lines of communication with parents.* All it takes is a phone call, a brief note, or a brief talk on a daily basis. For parents who have difficulty attending meetings or who do not accompany their child to and from school, teachers can send home a note along with a sample of artwork, or a story the child has dictated, or a photograph of the child with friends.

5. *Home visits.* Depending on its purpose, a home visit can be used to enhance communications. The visit might be set up to focus only on the relationship between the teacher and the child. Or, the visit might have a purely social function—a way for teachers to meet the whole family and for them to get acquainted with the teachers. In any event, the teacher can use this as a bridge to build a pleasant, casual beginning with this family.

Parent-Teacher Conferences

Parent conferences are the backbone of any good parent-teacher relationship. They provide a way of coming together to focus on the needs of the individual child. Conferencing can be a mutu-

1. *Schedule conferences on a regular basis.* Parents and teachers should share some of the positive aspects of child growth and development and not meet only in crisis. This promotes better feelings about one another, not to mention the child, if meetings are at times other than when a problem occurs.

2. *Be prepared.* Discuss with the staff ahead of time any points they want to include. Gather together any materials, notes, and samples of the child's work that might illustrate a point.

3. *Select a quiet place, free from interruption.* If necessary, sign up for use of a conference room. Make sure that someone is available to intercept phone calls and other appointments.

4. *Have a clear purpose.* Use a written format as a guide to keep focused on the intent of the conference. This gives a brief reminder of points to be covered and serves to keep parents on the track.

5. *Put parents at ease right away.* Offer them a cup of coffee or share an amusing anecdote that just took place in the classroom. Acknowledge the important part they played in the school fair. These light, positive comments will help relax both teacher and parent.

6. *Use up-to-date information and data.* Cite examples, from teacher's observations, that occurred that morning or a few days ago. Include examples of situations that occurred when they were present. "Timmy is very empathetic for a three-year-old, isn't he? That was so clear from the way you two were talking as you came through the door today."

7. *Give them a place to shine.* Tell them what they do well—their success with car-pool crowds or in mediating fights in the yard. If they have a special talent they have shared with the class, comment on its impact on the children.

8. *Ask—don't tell.* Get them talking by asking open-ended questions. "How is that new bedtime arrangement working?" "Tell me more about Katie's eating habits." Teachers will relate these to their own knowledge and experiences with the child and then share what has worked in school, but acknowledge the difference between school and home, teacher and parent. Learn how to listen. Concentrate on what the parents are saying. Don't listen with half an ear while planning an appropriate response or comment.

9. *Avoid blaming parents.* Keep the conversation based on mutual concerns and how to help each other. Look at some alternatives together and make a plan of action. Discuss ways to check in with each other or provide for follow-through at school or home. This way the parent will have a feeling of working together rather than of being blamed.

10. *Know where and how to secure community resources and referrals.* Many parents do not know where to get a child's speech tested, or what an I.Q. test is, or where to secure family therapy. They may be unaware of play groups, gymnastic schools, library story hours, or children's museums. Be sure the school can provide this information for parents who need it.

11. *Take time to write a brief report after the conference.* Make special note of who attended and who requested the conference, what important issues were raised by either the parents or the teacher, what solutions and strategies were discussed, and what time was agreed upon for checking in with each other regarding progress.

12. *Find a good role model.* Ask experienced teachers to share their ingredients for success. When possible, attend a parent conference with one of them. Observe what works for them and learn from their experience. Ask them to critique your own performance after a conference.

FIGURE 8.11 One of the most important responsibilities of the teacher is the parent conference. A good parent-teacher conference is focused and strengthens the relationship between home and school. (See Chapter 10.)

ally supportive link established between the adults who are most concerned about an individual child, with the purpose of helping the child reach the fullest potential possible.

Conferences between parents and teachers are held for many reasons. The initial conference, when the child first enrolls in school, may focus on the family. Important information to share includes a brief overview of the child's development, daily habits, and interests, as well as the parents' view of the child and what the parents expect of the school. The teacher will want to assure parents that they are free to call at any time if they have questions about the school or their child. Farther into the school year, both parents and teachers will want an up-to-date assessment of the child's progress, noting especially the strengths of the child and areas where improvement is needed. Several formats to help focus the discussion are cited in Chapter 10.

A conference may be called at any time by either a parent or a teacher if there are concerns to discuss. A written outline listing the goals of the conference will help guide the discussion and direct it to problem areas. Every occasion when parents and teachers get together to talk about a child is a step toward building trusting relationships between home and school.

Too often, teachers are left to figure out for themselves how to have a conference that is satisfying and productive to both parties. Experience is the best teacher is an old saying that certainly has merit. The more new teachers work with parents and hold regular conferences, the more effective they become. The chart in Figure 8.11 might help the beginning teacher hold fulfilling parent conferences.

Maintaining Privacy and Confidentiality

The more involved parents are in the workings of the school, the more important it is to establish guidelines for protecting the privacy of all the families enrolled. Parents who volunteer in the office, the classroom, or on a field trip must understand they cannot carry tales out of school about any of the children, the teachers, the administration, or other parents. The school must be clear

FIGURE 8.12 A good information program about a variety of issues related to children can inform parents of the need for greater child advocacy.

about its expectations for ensuring such privacy and communicate policies to parents. Parents who work on advisory boards, planning committees, or other activities that allow them access to the school office should be sensitive to the confidentiality issue and respect the privacy of every family enrolled in the school. Parents who are involved in working at the school should not discuss the children and their families or the staff outside of school, nor should they be expected to handle files that contain sensitive information.

S U M M A R Y

The partnership in education between parent and teacher has a long and varied history, with each partner recognizing the unique part they play in the child's life. The value of sharing the information they have about the child highlights their separate but important functions.

In current practice, there is a movement to integrate parent education and parent participation toward a more highly developed family-centered approach. An equal partnership, based on mutual respect for the strengths that both parents and teachers bring to the relationship, requires a deepening of parent involvement, particularly in the decision-making process.

One of the first and most intensive ways parents and teacher work together is through the separation process that takes place when the child enters school. There are other basic skills teachers must have to work successfully with parents. Frequent communication and many levels of parent education are but two. Parent conferencing is a critical part of any parent effort, and the new teacher can be helped by guidelines that will ensure a good beginning.

R E V I E W   Q U E S T I O N S

1. What do you consider to be the most important reasons for teachers and parents to have good relationships? Why should parents be involved in their child's schooling? How would you balance this involvement with your career and/or family responsibilities?

2. Describe three ways you would encourage parents to participate in your classroom. Cite the advantages for the (a) children, (b) parents, and (c) teacher. Are there any disadvantages?

3. What are some of your own "Myths About Parenthood"? Make two lists, one headed "Myths Teachers Have About Parents" and another headed "Myths Parents Have About Teachers." Compare the two and then discuss them with both a parent and a teacher.

4. What are some of the key elements in a successful parent-child separation? What is the role of the teacher?

5. What would you do to help immigrant families feel welcome in your classroom? What are the difficulties you might have to overcome? What are the benefits to the class? To the family?

6. Describe the critical components of a high-quality parent education program. Give examples.

7. What is the value of a family-centered parent education program?

8. Outline what you would do in a parent conference that was (1) a routine get-together to discuss the child's progress; (2) to inform parents of recently observed behavioral problems; and (3) to recommend further assessment of a child's developmental delays in motor development.

L E A R N I N G   A C T I V I T I E S

1. Discuss the following in small groups, then share your responses with the rest of your classmates. Finish the sentences:

   a) "For me, the most difficult part of being a parent today would be . . ."

   b) "When I have children, I plan to (work/stay at home/do both) because . . ."

   c) "If I were a single parent, I would..."

   d) "When I have children, I will raise them (just like my parents raised me/the opposite of the way I was raised) because . . ."

2. Look at the five "Guidelines for Working With Parents." Give an example of how you would apply each of the five principles in your classroom. Do you see any examples of ways these guidelines are not being met? What would you do to change that?

3. Are there ethnic minorities in your school setting? How are these parents supported or not supported by school practices and policies? What changes would you make?

4. The twelfth step in "Successful Parent-Teacher Conferences" suggests that you find a good role model. Look around at the teachers you know and select one. Go through the steps suggested in number 12 and write up your response.

5. Interview a parent or parents of (1) a six-month-old baby, (2) two or more children, and (3) children with a wide age range. Using the Six Stages of Parenthood, identify where each of the parents are. Discuss.

6. Interview several single parents, both men and women. What do you see as the most critical issue they face? How do you see their children's schools supporting them? Where is there a need for improvement? What are the implications in your life regarding single parenthood?

B I B L I O G R A P Y

Armstrong, Liz Schevtchuk. "Census Confirms Remarkable Shifts in Ethnic Makeup." *Education Week*, March 20, 1991.

Balaban, Nancy. *Starting School: From Separation to Independence*. New York City: Teachers College Press, 1985.

Baumrind, D. "Socialization and Instrumental Competence in Young Children." In *The Young Child: Review of Research (Vol. 2)*, ed. W.W. Hartup. Washington, D.C.: National Association for the Education of Young Children, 1972.

Bee, Helen. *The Developing Child*. Cambridge, Mass.: Harper Collins, 1995.

Delpit, Lisa. *Other People's Children: Cultural Conflict in the Classroom*. The New Press, 1995.

Edwards, Carolyn, Gandini, Lella, and Forman, George. *The Hundred Languages of Children: The Reggio Emilia Approach to Early Childhood Education*. Norwood, N.J.: Ablex, 1993.

Galinsky, Ellen. *Between Generations*. Reading, Mass.: Addison-Wesley, 1987.

Igoa, Christina. *The Inner World of the Immigrant Child*. New York: St. Martin's Press, 1995.

Kagan, Sharon L. "Family-Support Programs and the Schools." *Education Week*, January 18, 1989.

LeShan, Eda. *When Your Child Drives You Crazy*. New York: St. Martin's Press, 1985.

Levin, Henry M. As quoted in Jennings, Lisa. "Parents as Partners." *Education Week*, August 1, 1990.

Powell, Douglas R. *Families and Early Childhood Programs*. Washington, D.C. National Association for the Education of Young Children, 1989.

Spodek, Bernardo. *Teaching in the Early Years*. Englewood Cliffs, N.J.: Prentice-Hall, 1972.

United States Bureau of the Census. *Marital Status and Living Arrangements, March 1990*. Current Population Reports. Series P-20, No. 450. Washington, D.C.: U.S. Government Printing Office, 1991.

——————. *Household and Family Characteristics: March 1990 and 1989*. Washington, D.C.: U.S. Government Printing Office, 1991.

United States Department of Education, Office of Educational Research and Improvement. *Youth Indicators 1991*. Washington, D.C.: U.S. Government Printing Office, 1991.

Wanat, Carol L. "Of Schools, Single Parents, and Surrogates." *Education Week*, May 8, 1991.

GUEST EDITORIAL

Places for Childhoods

Jim Greenman

Children and the Environment

Children and adults inhabit different worlds. Adults dwell far more in the world of mind and function. Children respond to the sensory and motor message of the space, while adults are more utilitarian. "Is it clean?" "Safe?" "What is it for?" We are not drawn to the hot sunny spot on the floor attractive to cats and children, or the mud, or to chipping away and enlarging the hole in the plaster. We do not view the world as puddle-rich, or full of tight angular spaces to squeeze ourselves into. Except perhaps responding to an atavistic urge to shout in tunnels or trail our fingers along a picket fence, we rarely allow space to command our bodies. Corridors do not impel us to run, nor does a trellis or stack of chairs say "climb."

A Place Not A Space

It is important to think as children's centers as "places," with character, rather than mere stage settings where the character and charm all have to come from the people and activities. Many of us spend much of our time in spaces that never become places. Places are spaces charged with meaning. We attach to places through endearing objects and people, but also the sensibility of the place: the sounds, smells, lighting, texture, and the actions that the space invites.

Quality in early education and care is an accumulation of small transactions, between child and adult, child and child, child and the objects and the physical environment. It is in the laps and conversations, the side by side work and play, and the shared bouts of silliness and sadness that a child learns that he or she is somebody important. It is the bursts of energetic noises and the interludes of silence that punctuate reflection. The sunlight, and breezes and frost on the window and the shadows descending on a corner of the room give daily life its fullness and sensuality. The three Rs are present as well in the exuberant exploration of the world, if the awareness of the value of language and number infuse every experience. The sifting, kneading, and mixing on the table, and the digging and splashing are necessary precursors to laboratories of beakers and archeological expeditions.

The rhythm of the rain and the pendulum of the swing are both mathematical and musical experiences. Gazing at the crack on the ceiling that had the habit of looking like a rabbit, the row of dandelions at attention like an army of golden soldiers, and the flashing color from the angelfish or the canary enrich our sensibilities and inform our artistic vision.

A Good Place to Be

Security: a safe, warm place that fits me; that I understand, and own.

Competence: a place scaled for me so I can feel competent and in control of my daily needs.

Different places to be: places that look, sound, smell, and feel different. Remember your childhood places, under the piano, behind the couch, on the stairs, beside the tree.

Seclusion and privacy: "places to pause" when the world moves too fast or I'm out of sorts or need to concentrate.

Autonomy: children invent the spaces they need, if we let them.

Room to grow: ample space is essential for mobility, learning centers, privacy, and social life.

A Good Place to Learn

Children don't learn in a predictable, linear fashion. They swallow experience in sips and gulps as well as measured doses. Their investigations often do not fit into tidy spaces and neat time slots. Movement is as necessary to learning as air and light and their sounds and silences punctuate discoveries. They are generous and selfish and social and solitary at will.

Young children are active, messy scientists: exploring with their senses and bodies. A child seeking a good learning environment might ask (if he or she could):

Can I be messy? Can I be noisy?
Can I be alone? Can I get some quiet?
Can I move? Can I be still?
Who can I talk to? Who will listen?
Can I spread out over space and time?

Where's the stuff, the loose parts: the raw material of discovery?

A developmentally appropriate learning environment is designed for INDIVIDUAL children to be messy, noisy and quiet, alone and social, and active and quiet. It is designed to accommodate much STUFF—loose parts: the raw material of discovery by active hands and minds. Therefore, it is designed for individual, independent learning and easy set up and "take down" so that the teacher can really focus on the children.

Jim Greenman is the author of Caring Spaces, Learning Places: Children's Environments That Work *(Exchange Press). Material for this editorial originated in his columns in the* Child Care Information Exchange.

QUESTIONS FOR THOUGHT

What does the term <u>environment</u> mean?

What criteria are used in planning the optimum environment?

How should the environment mirror program goals?

How do teachers create a self-help, anti-bias environment?

What are adults' needs in a children's environment?

What are basic materials for a classroom, and how are they selected?

In planning a daily schedule, what should teachers keep in mind?

What health and safety measures must be considered when planning the total environment?

How does the interpersonal tone affect learning?

How can the environment guide children's behavior and highlight learning goals?

CHAPTER 9

Creating Environments

WHAT IS THE ENVIRONMENT?

What does it mean to create an environment appropriate for young children? What makes up the environment? The environment is the stage on which children play out the themes of childhood: their interests, triumphs, problems, and concerns. An environment for children, therefore, includes all of the conditions that affect their surroundings and the people in it.

Each environment is unique. There is no such thing as a single model or ideal setting for all children. Each school has goals that reflect the values of its own program. When the goals and the setting mesh, the individual atmosphere of the school is created.

But just what does **environment** mean? What do teachers mean when they say they want to create:

- environments for learning?
- optimal growth environments?
- positive learning environments?
- child-centered environments?
- favorable classroom environments?

Definition

The *environment* is the sum total of the physical and human qualities that combine to create a space in which children and adults work and play together. Environment is the *content* teachers arrange; it is an *atmosphere* they create; it is a *feeling* they communicate. Environment is the total picture—from the traffic flow to the daily schedule, from the numbers of chairs at a table to the placement of the guinea pig cage. It is a means to an

FIGURE 9.1 Each environment is unique, and children respond to whatever is offered. Does this equipment challenge the physical skills of young children? Is it safe for youngsters? Can it be properly supervised? For what age range would the playground be most appropriate?

end. The choices teachers make concerning the *physical* setting (the equipment and materials, the room arrangement, the playground and the facilities available), the **temporal** setting (timing for transitions, routines, activities), and the **interpersonal** setting (number and nature of teachers, ages and numbers of children, types and style of interactions among them), combine to support the program goals. The environments adults create for children have a powerful effect on their behavior. Research shows that children's play is strongly influenced by settings and materials (Phyfe-Perkins & Shoemaker, 1986). Individual cubbies and children's art on the walls say "You belong here"; materials on low shelves tell children "You can do things on your own." Social interaction, independence, or imaginary play may all be fostered—or discouraged—by the ways the indoor and outdoor spaces are designed and used. The environments teachers create should be safe, effective, challenging, and in concert with the theoretical framework of the early childhood program. Figure 9.2 illustrates this.

CRITERIA FOR CREATING ENVIRONMENTS

All settings for the care and education of young children have the same basic environmental components and the same basic goals—meeting the needs of children—despite the fact that programs vary widely in the size of the group, age of children, length of day, program focus, and number of staff. Although there are endless variations in planning for children, certain common elements must be considered: (1) the physical plant, (2) available resources, and (3) program goals.

Physical Plant

Before creating an environment for children, the early childhood teacher must analyze the physical plant. The building that is inviting and beautiful beckons children to enter; a space with color and light encourages children to play with both. Many settings use space designed for other purposes, such as a church basement or an empty elementary school classroom. The size and shape of

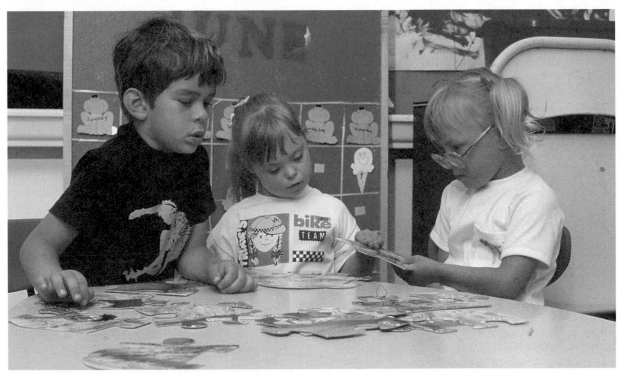

FIGURE 9.2 The environment includes not only physical space and materials but also aspects of time and interpersonal relationships.

the designated space determine how to plan for safe and appropriate use. To rescale the space, teachers shift from an adult perspective to a child's scale. Getting on one's knees provides a glimpse of the environment from the child's point of view; child space is measured from the floor and playground up. A child's stature determines what is available to and noticed by that child. For crawling infants, space consists primarily of the floor, while school-aged children can use and learn from the space up to about five feet, roughly their own height. It is this perspective that teachers must remember as they plan the physical space for children (see Planning section in this chapter for details).

Resources

In planning the environment, it is essential to know what kinds of resources are available. Rarely do teachers have unlimited dollars: "This year we can only afford . . ." determines many of the decisions made about the environment. Priority is usually given to teacher salaries and benefits, equipment and materials for the school, and other related services (maintenance, office help, bus service). Despite budget constraints, teachers must beware of operating on too low a materials budget. Lack of necessary materials can create increasingly passive, angry, and unhappy children out of sheer boredom. Only by knowing the extent of the fiscal boundaries and budget limits can a teacher plan a complete environment.

There are ways to stretch that budget, however. Good environmental principles are not dependent upon numerous or expensive equipment, materials, or buildings. A creative child-centered environment can happen in any setting, regardless of the lack of financial resources. Some equipment can be made, borrowed, or purchased second-hand. In church-based schools, annual rummage sales at the church provide a wealth of dress-up clothes, books, toys, and some appliances. Resource books are filled with ideas for recycling materials into usable equipment for young children. Parents and others can provide computer paper, wood scraps, or office supplies for dramatic play kits. Community sources, such as the public-library storyteller or a senior citizens group, may be available for extended experiences for the children. Effective fund raising provides an added source of revenue in many schools and centers.

The human resources must also be identified. Adults do their best with children when their abilities, experience, and availability are matched with what is expected of them. Volunteers, for instance, will feel satisfied if their time is organized and spent in ways meaningful to them. A first-year teacher's resources are best expended in the classroom rather than on administrative projects. A master teacher is ready to be challenged in other ways, such as orienting parents or evaluating curriculum materials. When the entire community values its children, as in the case of Reggio Emilia, the school is a showcase, sending a strong message of how important children are in the life of its citizens. Just as we try to match children's developing skills to the tasks at hand, so, too, should we consider individual people as part of an environment's resources.

Program Goals

The program must be defined in relationship to the physical space, since the goals and objectives of the program are expressed directly in the arrangement of the environment. Teachers of young children ask themselves: What sorts of goals should there be for children and families in their care? Harms (1989) names three general goals in designing environments: to plan soft and responsive settings that avoid behavior problems, to set up predictable environments that encourage independence, and to create a stimulating space for active learning. The physical space and materials should tell the children exactly what is going to happen and how they are to go about their work. In every program, consideration of what children are to accomplish puts goals and environments together.

The goals of an early childhood program will vary widely because early childhood settings contain such a wide range of age and experience. Some programs are housed in large centers, others in homes; children may attend all day or for part of the day and for educational, recreational, or even custodial reasons. The important point is that good environments for children must reflect clear and reasonable program goals. Once we know what we wish to do, and why we want to do it, we can create space, timing, and an atmosphere in which to meet those goals.

Reflecting Goals in the Environment

In creating an environment, teachers plan a program directed toward their goals:

1. They take care to arrange the daily schedule in ways that provide the time blocks needed to teach content when and how they want to teach it.

2. The room and yard are arranged to give maximum exposure to the materials and equipment they want children to use.

3. They see that a warm relationship exists among the teachers and in their interactions with children.

It is essential that teachers have a clear idea of their program goals before they begin to arrange the environment for children. When they invite children in to work, play, and learn, teachers must be sure that the way they have expressed goals through room arrangements, daily schedules, and personal styles, matches what they believe. Blending all the factors that create an environment for children uses the environment to its fullest and demonstrates a belief in how and what children need for learning to take place.

If a goal of the program is to have children practice cognitive and fine-motor skills, games using prereading and writing materials should be prominent. Puzzles and table toys should have a central place in the classroom. Enough tables and chairs should be provided to accommodate all the children. Larger amounts of time should be made available for children to work on these activities every day, and teachers should be available to reinforce and encourage children as they play. Research on children's behavior in preschool settings (Moore, 1983; Rubin, 1977) indicates that social participation and child involvement in activities can be influenced by equipment and materials placement, as well as the teacher's interactive style.

When children walk into a classroom, the environment should communicate how they are to live and work in that setting. Children should receive clear messages about what they can and cannot do there as well as cues that tell them:

- Where they are free to move to and where they cannot go.

- How they will be treated.

- Who will be there with them.

- What material and equipment they can use.

- How long they have to play.

- That they are safe there.

- What is expected of them.

Teachers communicate these messages in many ways. Figure 9.3 describes how teachers use the environment to tell children what is important there. For instance, when it is time to go outside, the doors are opened. If children need to stay off a piece of equipment, it is marked by dividers or a flag, and a teacher stationed nearby explains the instruction. Children know that they matter when they are welcomed each day, and they know their time is valued when teachers tell them how long they have to complete a project or play sequence and when that time is nearly up.

The teacher is the key element in making a creative environment. It is not the facility itself that counts as much as the teacher's understanding of the use of all the environmental factors and how they relate to one another. The indicators of quality in a program, such as the adult-child ratio, the stability, education, and experience of the caregiver, and group size all contribute to an environment that meets its goals for children. Chapter 2 details these indicators and Chapter 10 describes their place in program and teacher evaluation.

A room is just a room and a yard is just a yard until a teacher makes them environments for learning. The teachers themselves are the most responsive part of the environment; it is they who converse, hug, appreciate, give information, and see the individuality of each child. They are the ones who create the space, the time, and the atmosphere that will engage children's curiosity and involvement. Figure 9.3 summarizes these environmental goals.

The Self-Help Environment

There is one common goal in most early education programs which can be demonstrated

Children Need to . . .	So the Environment Should . . .
Have an opportunity to make choices and participate in independent learning.	Be arranged to encourage free exploration and a clear view of what is available. Offer a variety of activity centers so children can explore, manipulate, probe. Allow large blocks of time for child-initiated free play so children can make more than one choice. Provide an adequate number of trained teachers to support self-discovery.
Be treated as individuals, with unique strengths and developmental goals.	Ensure that the teacher-child ratio supports one-to-one interactions. Provide private as well as public spaces so children can experience group and solitary play. Ensure that children have ready access to teachers and materials. Be staffed by teachers who will set goals for each child based on observation and assessment. Be equipped with materials that will match the developmental level of the group. Provide a balance of quiet and active times.
Learn to be part of a group.	Be set up for group play with three to five chairs around the tables, easels adjacent to one another, more than one telephone, carriage, wagon. Facilitate regular scheduling of small and large group times, which children are encouraged to attend and participate in. Include trained staff who select developmentally appropriate group activities for the group. Allow children to use each other as resources. Provide activities that will stress cooperation and social interaction.
Become responsible for the setting and take care of the equipment and materials.	Schedule cleanup times as part of the daily routine. Include teachers and children working together to restore order. Allow time for children to be instructed in the proper use of materials and be made aware of their general care.
Be aware of the behavioral limits of the school setting.	Ensure that the teachers and the daily schedule reflect the important rules of behavior. Include teachers who deal with behavior problems in a fair and consistent way. Allow plenty of time during transitions so that children can move from one activity to another without stress. Be arranged to avoid runways and dead ends created by furniture.
Be with adults who will supervise and facilitate play, and encourage learning throughout the day.	Be set up before children arrive so teachers are free to greet them. Encourage teacher-child interactions through the use of small groups, and a time schedule that allows for in-depth interactions.

FIGURE 9.3   The environment mirrors the goals of the program.

through the careful use of environmental factors. Promoting self-help and independent behavior in children is a widespread practice. In planning the environments, teachers attempt to create situations and settings where this is likely to happen.

A self-help environment has as one of its fundamental goals the development of children's own skills—fostering their mastery of basic abilities that will allow them to become responsible for their own personal care, their own learning, their own emotional controls, their own problem solving, and their own choices and decisions. A self-help environment gives children the feeling that they are capable, competent, and successful. It allows children to do for themselves, to meet the challenge of growing up. A self-help environment reflects the belief that autonomy and independence are the birthright of every child.

Nothing renders people more helpless than not being able to maintain their own needs or to take care of themselves in basic ways. Children are still in the process of learning about what they can and cannot do. They need many different kinds of experiences to help them learn the extent of their capabilities. Most of all, they need adults who understand their tremendous drive to become self-reliant, adults who will not only encourage their abilities and provide the time for them to practice skills, but adults who understand that it is the nature of the child to develop this way.

Self-concept is based on what we know about ourselves, which includes the ability to take care of one's own needs. To care for oneself, to feel capable of learning, to solve problems, are all related to feelings of self-esteem. Self-esteem is the value we place upon ourselves; how much we like or dislike who we are. Helping children achieve a positive self-concept and self-esteem is the most important part of teaching. The development of a strong sense of self-esteem is a lifelong process; its origins are in the early years.

For all of these reasons, teachers establish settings that promote self-help. They want children to feel good about themselves and they want to foster that growing sense of self-esteem. This happens in classrooms which allow children to do what they are capable of doing. For the teacher, the reward comes from each child who says, "I can do it all by myself."

Planning an environment designed to promote self-help skills is the teachers' responsibility. Every aspect of the environment, from the room arrangement to the attitudes of the teachers, supports children in doing all they can for themselves. Each activity is designed to foster self-reliance, thereby building self-esteem. The supermarket is a good example of an environment created for maximum self-reliance. Shelves are accessible and the products are clearly marked and attractively displayed. It takes that kind of thoughtful preparation to create space that says to children, "Do me. Master me. You are capable." Teachers want to communicate to children that they value self-help skills as much as they appreciate an art project or science experiment. The ultimate goal is for children to see self-reliance as valuable. If Claudia feels that learning to tie her shoes is worth doing just because of the pleasure it gives her to manipulate the

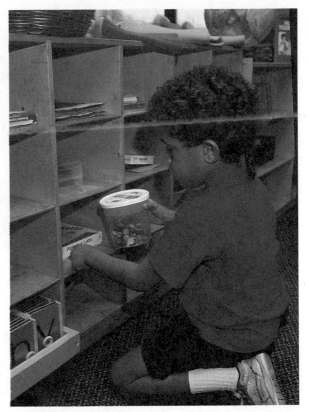

FIGURE 9.4 "I can do this myself!" Through self-help environments, children become independent.

strings, weave them through the holes, and bring them together in a knot, then that becomes her reward. She becomes capable of reinforcing herself and leaves the way open for adults to praise her for other important learnings.

The Anti-Bias Environment

Among the core values (see NAEYC Code of Ethical Conduct, Appendix C, and Professional Ethics, Chapter 5) in any good early childhood program is the recognition of each child as unique, as deserving of respect, and as a part of a family. Each child has the right to achieve full potential and to develop a positive self-esteem. Each family deserves support for the unique role it plays. Part of the commitment of the early childhood teacher is to help children learn to value one another's uniqueness, the differences as well as the similarities. Teachers do this, in part, by expressing such inclusive attitudes.

FIGURE 9.5 The anti-bias environment encourages girls and boys to play together, respecting differences and including others in new ways.

The **anti-bias curriculum,** developed at Pacific Oaks College, encourages children and adults

1. To explore the differences and similarities that make up our individual and group identities, and

2. To develop skills for identifying and countering the hurtful impact of bias on themselves and their peers (Derman-Sparks, 1987).

The physical and interpersonal environment can be used to help children see that culture consists of the various ways people do similar activities. This approach is different from the "tourist curriculum," which provides only superficial information that is often detached from the child's own life. It is also different from an approach that is based only on the interests of the class and gender, racial, and cultural groups represented therein. The anti-bias environment incorporates the positive aspects of multicultural curriculum and uses some of the activities that highlight other cultures, but provides a more inclusive, on-going approach that avoids patronizing or making trivial isolated, exotic differences (Derman-Sparks, 1989). There is an inherent feeling of fairness to self and others in the anti-bias approach, as children explore the many ways people do the basic human tasks of everyday life. Think of the diverse cultures expressed in how babies and things are carried from place to place in different parts of the world. How many ways do people eat? Cook? Shop for food?

A value common to all early childhood programs is expressed in this aniti-bias curriculum: that every person is valuable and so diversity is valuable, and peaceful and just cooperation among all is possible. The key here is the belief that "unity is the completed puzzle, diversity the pieces of the puzzle" (Hernandez, 1991). In this curriculum, the environment and the activities are derived from three sources: the children and their behavior, the teachers' awareness of the developmental needs and learning styles of the group, and societal events. Teachers, of course, make general selections of what children are to learn and arrange the environment for learning to begin. Then, the environment, which includes the children themselves, begins to change. If children are especially interested in making things, perhaps the theme "All people live in homes" emerges, with activities that focus on how people build things, what they use the buildings for, and how they work to get something built

Lessons about children's identity and budding attitudes concerning race, gender, disability, and age are learned early in life. With the prevalence of stereotyping in society, and the impact of bias on children's development (Cross, 1985; Gutierrez, 1982; Kutner, 1985), early childhood educators have a responsibility to find ways to prevent, even counter, the damage done by such stereotyping. Teachers do this by arranging an anti-bias physical environment, as well as creating an atmosphere of problem-solving and learning in the day-to-day conflicts and interactions that arise naturally. Think about how teachers provide the materials and encourage an atmosphere of trust and time for conflict resolution in these examples:

> A kindergarten teacher shows the children a magazine picture entitled "Brides of America." All of the women pictured are Caucasian. She asks, "What do you think of this picture?" Sophia responds, "That's a silly picture. My mom was a bride, and she's Mexican." (Derman-Sparks, 1989)

> A toddler teacher sets up the water play table for washing babies. Choosing dolls that represent several racial and ethnic groups, she invites the children to soap and rinse them. One 2-year-old begins to wash the teacher's arm, then scrubs it hard. "Do you wonder if my color will wash off?" the teacher asks. The child nods, and several others look up. "Does it? Go ahead and try. . . . See, a person's color is her own and stays with her. Try yours, too. That's one way people look different: we all have skin, and yet we each have our own color." (Gutierrez, 1987)

The anti-bias approach to creating environments has its roots in the theories of Maslow and Erikson (see Chapter 4). Research data reveals that children begin to notice and construct classifications and evaluative categories very early; indeed, two-year-olds begin to notice gender and racial differences and may even notice physical disabilities (Froschl & Sprung, 1983; Honig, 1983; Katz, 1982). Early childhood programs must develop a child's basic sense of trust and mastery so that children can learn to understand themselves and become tolerant and compassionate towards others. The anti-bias approach to a classroom goes hand in hand with self-help principles:

- *Positive self-concept.* Curiosity and creativity stem from being able to affect the environment and what is in it. When Jamal says his baby's hair is fuzzy like his, his smile tells how good he feels about it.

- *Awareness.* All people have interests and feelings, both about themselves and about others. Yoko notices that her classmate Julie runs and throws her arms around her dad, while she prefers a less demonstrative greeting.

- *Respect for diversity.* This stems from the ability to classify similarities and differences and then to appreciate both. For example, when the children create self-portraits for their class books, some choose different colors of paper for drawing faces, but all of them use the same markers to draw in their features.

- *Skills in communication and problem solving.* Learning how to express thoughts and feelings includes being able to hear others and finding peaceful ways to resolve conflicts. Jim and LaNell are quick to tell Eben he can't play, but they find out that telling him he is "too little" does not work. He does not accept that simply being three years old is enough reason to leave him out, and they must either try to include him or make a claim for privacy.

Both the self-help approach and the anti-bias curriculum differ from traditional educational practices often seen in classrooms for older children in that the self-help, anti-bias environment is pluralistic and developmental. As Elizabeth Jones (1984) stated:

> The pluralistic view assumes that (1) people are different from each other and (2) differences are valuable; they add to the richness of everyone's experiences. The task of the worker with children, then, is to acknowledge and appreciate differences. The developmental view assumes that growth and learning are spontaneously motivated. The task of the teach-

FIGURE 9.6 Children develop a sense of self when they have their own space, labeled with a photo or other visual clue so that they can easily identify it as their own.

er is to provide a supportive environment that frees each individual to grow and learn—to empower children so that they will assert their needs and develop thoughtful strategies for meeting them.

Principles of Successful Environments

● *Give children ways to identify their own space.* Label their cubbies with their names, a photo, or a familiar picture so that they can see where to put up their wraps, artwork, and other personal belongings.

● *Give children an opportunity to make choices.* Both indoors and out, children should be given an abundance of materials and a range of activities from which to choose so that they will decide how they spend their time. Choosing to play with the hamster rather than in the block corner helps children practice self-direction. Children should also be able to decide with whom they would like to play and with which teachers they would like to establish close relationships.

● *See that children are responsible for caring for the equipment and materials.* Establish a cleanup time in the daily schedule and allow children time to help restore the room and yard. Label shelves

and cupboards with pictures or symbols of what is stored there so that children can readily find where things belong. Outlining block cabinets with the specific shape of the blocks that are stored on each shelf will encourage children's self-help skills. Outdoor areas, clearly marked for wheel toys, help children function independently. A drying rack with large clothespins that is accessible to children tells children that they are expected to care for their own artwork.

● *Involve children in the process of planning and setting up the environment.* Let the children help decide what they want to learn by developing areas and units around what they bring into class. For instance, if a child's pet has babies, encourage a visit and then send a newsletter asking for other pets, arranging a field trip to a pet store, and organizing a dramatic-play corner as a pet hospital or pet shop. When furniture or outdoor equipment needs moving, include the children in planning what the changes will be and then assist them in moving the pieces themselves. Make the yard more interesting by encouraging the children to rearrange climbing boards. Let them choose what game from the shed will be used that day. And the class feast is made more exciting when the children themselves move all the tables together.

● *Provide children with enough time.* One of the ways children learn is to repeat an activity over and over again. They explore, manipulate, experiment, and come to master an 18-piece puzzle, a lump of clay, or how to brush their teeth. Large blocks of time in the daily schedule—especially for routines—let children proceed to learn at an unhurried pace.

● *Allow children to solve their own problems without adult interference whenever possible.* See how far a child can go in discovering how to manipulate a pin so that it will close, or work out with another child who will use the red paint first. In solving social or mechanical problems, young children can begin to find out for themselves what is or is not successful. One mark of a good teacher is a person who can let a child struggle sufficiently with a problem before stepping in to help.

● *Accept children's efforts.* To support children in their quest for independence, the adult must be satisfied with children's efforts, and be ready to accept the way Tom made his sandwich or Shelley's boots on the wrong feet.

- *Communicate expectations.* Let children know what they are expected to do. Tell them in both verbal and nonverbal ways. "You don't have to hurry; we have plenty of time for cleanup" lets children know they can do a job without pressure. Prompt children by giving them clues that indicate how to proceed: "If you pull up your underpants first, it will be easier to get your trousers up," can be said to Raymond who is waiting for an adult to dress him. Give him feedback on what is working. "Good. You've got the back up. Now reach around the front." Focus on how Raymond is succeeding and communicate your confidence in his ability to finish the task.

- *Be sure staff expectations are consistent.* The teaching team should set common goals for each child and reinforce them consistently. Janice will become confused if one teacher tells her to get her cot ready for nap and another teacher does it for her.

- *Consider the developmental level of the child.* Recognize that there are many things young children will not be able to do for themselves, but allow them the chance to do all they can. Be developmentally aware—know what children in the class are capable of, where they are now in their development, and what the next step should be. Perhaps three-year-old Sophie can only zip her jacket now. Soon she will be able to put the zipper in the housing by herself. Recognize her readiness for taking the next step.

- *Make it safe to make a mistake.* Children learn from their own actions and their own experiences. Let them know it is perfectly acceptable, indeed inevitable, that they will at times make mistakes. Children need to be accepted for who and what they are, and this includes when they are in error. Help them deal with the consequences of their mistakes. Adults in the preschool can provide models for children in coping with unexpected results and how to bring forth a positive resolution. When Chelo spills her juice, she is encouraged to find a sponge and clean up the table. The teacher reinforces

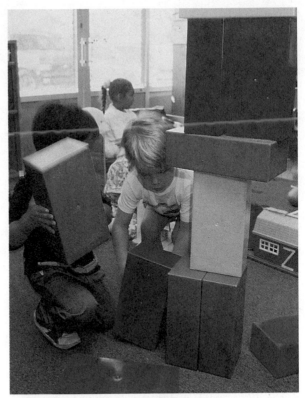

FIGURE 9.7 Allowing children to solve their own problems without interference is one principle of successful educational environments.

Chelo's efforts and comments on her scrubbing ability or her swift action in preventing the juice from going on the floor.

- *Give credit where it is due.* Provide feedback so that children will know when they have been successful. Compliment Chaz on the length of time he took sorting through the nails to find the one he wanted. Tell Ellen she worked hard at opening her own thermos bottle. Let children take some credit for their own accomplishments.

- *Be sure children have access to enough toys and materials.* Help children imagine and live in alternative worlds, in communities and homes where things are different. Show children respect by giving them the option to take care of themselves. Make sure that supplies are stored in such a way that adults do not have to hand them to children each time they will be used. Equipment placed at a child's height on open, low shelving permits children to proceed at

The Role of the Environment in Reggio Emilia

Rebecca S. New

Historians have long noted that one index of the value of children is the extent to which they are visible and differentiated in the physical elements of a society. School environments can also reveal much about the values, beliefs, and goals of the adults who are responsible for children's education. Yet traditional images of schools often fail to make children visible. School environments themselves are often nothing more than containers for educational enterprises and convey little of the actual pursuits of the adults and children who spend their days in school.

In contrast, early childhood educators in Reggio Emilia assign significant credit to the role of the environment in their work with young children. Their discussions of its critical importance remind me of anthropological interpretations of sociocultural contexts within which young children learn and develop. In Reggio Emilia, the school environment not only reflects what it is that children are learning; it plays an active role in nurturing and stimulating that learning and development. Such an interpretation of the environment includes not only the physical elements associated with schooling—tables, books, paints, blocks, paper—but the social, intellectual, and ideological elements as well.

Thus, teachers in Reggio Emilia arrange the environment to promote children's relationships—with one another as well as with adults. The drilling of small peepholes in the divider between the blocks and the dramatic play area, the installation of real telephones between classrooms, the visibility of the kitchen and the accessibility of the central "piazza"—all are designed to contribute to the aim of schooling based on relationships.

Reggio Emilia teachers' interpretation of their own roles as *provocateurs* in children's learning is extended to the environment as well. Classrooms and hallways are designed with the intent to surprise, inform and inspire. Children reflect on their images and their actions in the many mirrored surfaces to be found on the floors and walls. Play areas modified with the addition of draped fabric invite children to reconceptualize old patterns of play. Juxtapositions of children's work in various media highlight the common themes in their experiences, as well as the rich possibilities inherent in diverse forms of self-expression.

Perhaps most importantly, the environments in Reggio Emilia convey an image of children who are "rich in potential, strong, powerful, competent, and most of all, connected to adults and other children" (Malaguzzi, Young Children, Nov. 1993, p. 10). Documentation panels portray children's knowledge—of shadows, the rain—as well as their need to grapple with profound concerns in contemporary society—gender, war, friendship.

When Reggio Emilia teachers describe the environment as a "third teacher," they are acknowledging a professional role that goes far beyond that of providing a safe and stimulating setting for children's learning. In Reggio Emilia, the environment serves an advocacy role on behalf of young children, inspiring adults—parents and community members as well as teachers—to work together to realize the potentials of children. The effectiveness of such advocacy is apparent in the quality of care and commitment on behalf of young children that has characterized Reggio Emilia's efforts over the past three decades.

Rebecca S. New is an Assistant Professor, Department of Education, University of New Hampshire, Durham, N.H. She has studied extensively in Reggio Emilia and has led numerous study tours to the Reggio Emilia schools.

their own pace and select materials without depending upon adults to serve them.

● *Let children teach one another.* Encourage children to share the skills they have mastered with their peers. Actively seek out each child's way of doing things; support a diversity of approaches. Those who can tie shoes enjoy helping their friends with stubborn laces or slippery knots. Whether reading or telling stories to one another, or showing a friend a fast way to put on a jacket, children benefit from helping each other.

Adults who work with children should remember to interact with children in ways that will help them grow toward independence. To perceive children as helpless is to rob them of the satisfaction of achievement. A well-planned environment opens up infinite possibilities for children to achieve a feeling of self-satisfaction while they explore the boundaries of their own beings. Chapters 1 and 5 expand on educational ethics that serve as guidelines in working with children; Chapter 10 gives suggestions for how to evaluate children, teachers, and programs to check that these goals are met.

PLANNING FOR THE ENVIRONMENT

Who Is in the Environment?

Many people live and work in the early childhood environment. Cooks, bus drivers, office personnel, yard and building maintenance people are but a few. Each of these persons has special demands on the environment in order to do the job they are hired to do.

Teachers, parents, and children have the greatest influence on the early childhood environment; their needs are outlined below.

Children

Children's needs are met through the environment. The physical, social, emotional, and intellectual requirements of children suggest the type of building, the size of the furniture, the choice of equipment, the size and age range of the group, the number of teachers who lead and su-

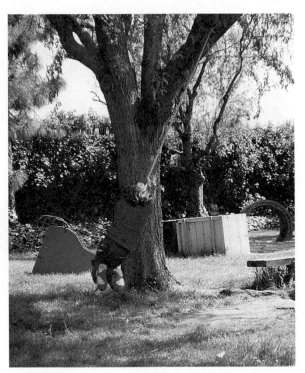

FIGURE 9.8   Children learn through play, and the outdoor play environment stimulates motor development, thinking skills, and social interaction.

pervise, and the budget allocations. Guided by child development principles, teachers match the setting to the children who will learn and play there. The individuality of a particular group of children, a school, and its philosophy is expressed by the arrangement of the environmental factors. First and foremost, though, is the question: Who are the children who will use this space? What are their needs? How can those needs be met in this particular setting?

Routines. What is meant by a **routine?** Routines are the framework of programs for young children. A routine is a constant; each day, certain events are repeated, providing continuity and a sense of order to the schedule. Routines are the pegs on which to hang the daily calendar. When should children eat? Sleep? Play? Be alone? Be together? These questions are answered by the placement of routines. The rest of the curriculum—art activities, field trips, woodworking—works around them. Routines in an early childhood environment setting include:

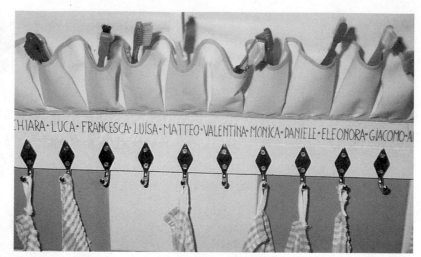

FIGURE 9.9 Self-help is an international goal. Toothbrushes and towels are accessible so that children in the Reggio Emilia centers in Italy can help themselves. (Courtesy of the city of Reggio Emilia, Italy.)

- Self-care (eating, rest/sleeping, dressing, toileting)
- Transitions between activities
- Group times
- Beginning and ending the day/session
- Making choices
- Task completion
- Room cleanup/yard restoration

Most routines are very personal and individual rituals in children's daily lives. Children bring to school a history firmly established around routines, one that is deeply embedded in their family and culture. Routines are reassuring to children, and they take pride in mastering them; they are also a highly emotional issue for some.

The self-care tasks—eating, sleeping, dressing, and toileting—can be difficult issues between adult and child, virtually from the moment of birth. Everyone can recall vivid memories associated with at least one routine. They seem to become battlegrounds on which children and adults often struggle. Many times this is where children choose to take their first stand on the road to independence.

The early childhood teacher must be able to deal with the issue of self-care routines in sensitive and understanding ways. Children adjust to routines when they are regularly scheduled in the daily program and when there are clear expectations.

Routines are an integral part of creating a good environment for children. All three environmental factors are influenced by routines:

1. *Physical:* Child-sized bathroom and eating facilities; storage of cots, blankets, and sleeping accessories; equipment for food storage and preparation.

2. *Temporal:* Amount of time in daily schedule for eating, resting, toileting, cleanup.

3. *Interpersonal:* Attitudes toward body functions; willingness to plan for self-care tasks, interactions during activities and transitions, expectations of staff, parents, and children.

As teachers plan for children's basic needs, they are aware of the learning potential of ordinary, everyday routines. Figure 9.10 illustrates how self-care routines teach the young child important skills and habits. In the four curriculum chapters of the next section ("What Is Being Taught?," Chapters 12–14), there is specific planning for routines, transitions, and group times. It is these times that provide a sense of security for children. Beyond the planning for indoor and outdoor activities, careful teachers realize that helping children with the routines of daily living provides a solid underpinning so other learning can take place.

Teachers

What about the needs of the teachers who work in the setting? Do they have an office? A teachers' room? A place to hold conferences? Where do they keep their personal belongings—or the materials they bring to use at school? Do they have a place to park? All teachers need room to create curriculum materials, or evaluate their programs, to review other educational materials, to meet with their peers. Recent research (Howes, 1988) indicates that the working environment of caregivers (including the general context of the setting, opportunities for professional development, status, and wages) are important predictors of the quality of care children receive. How well teachers are provided for helps to determine the atmosphere they will establish in their classrooms for children.

Parents

The needs of parents will differ, depending upon whom the program serves. Parents who bring their children to child care or school need adequate and safe parking facilities. In settings where parents are free to stay, a reading room, resource library, or a comfortable place to talk with other parents is desirable. Parents who participate in the class are welcomed by a teacher, shown a place to put their belongings, and given a name tag and task card.

There are many reasons parents may need to contact the school or center. Are there ways for parents to reach teachers and children in emergencies? How welcoming is the environment to parents as they enter the building? The office? The classroom? What does the environment say about parent involvement and interest?

To meet parents' needs, the school environment can be made accessible and welcoming in several ways. Posting telephone numbers at which school authorities and teachers can be reached when the school is closed assures parents that teachers are available whenever needed. A bulletin board for community notices and for parent use can be put up along with mail pockets. Written communication can go between parents and teachers and among families. Working with parents is vital to creating both an anti-bias and self-

help focus in children's education and care. Teaching from these perspectives is more likely to create positive changes in children's lives when parents are included in the process. The classroom that offers both the teacher and other resources helps parents feel that their children and families are important.

Health and Safety in the Environment

Regardless of how many children are in the setting and for how long, the first priority is to provide for their health and safety. Health, safety, and nutrition are closely related because the quality of one affects the quality of others (Marotz, Rush & Cross, 1993). Therefore, programs for children must establish policies that provide for the protection, service, and education of child health and safety at all times. Government regulations vary, but all establish some kind of standards to ensure good health and safety practices.

Keeping Children Healthy

Sanitation. When groups of people live in close quarters, proper sanitary conditions are imperative to prevent the spread of disease. For an early childhood center, the physical plant must have adequate washing and toileting facilities for both children and adults. The number and size of toilets and wash basins are usually prescribed by local health or other regulatory agencies. Children don't realize their role in spreading germs, especially as their moist and warm hands touch and handle everything. Through gentle reminders and role-modeling, teachers help children learn the *habit* of washing their hands at important times such as before snack and mealtimes.

The classrooms require daily cleaning, and equipment that is used regularly should be sanitized on a periodic basis. Nontoxic paint must be used in all circumstances, including on outdoor equipment, cribs, and for art activities with children. Classroom dress-up clothing, pillows, nap blankets, and cuddle toys all need regular laundering, either at school or at home.

Temperature, Ventilation, and Lighting. Heating and ventilation should be comfortable for

Eating Teaches Health:
> Introduction to new and different foods, good nutritional habits

Eating Teaches Social Skills:
> How to manage oneself in a group eating situation, focusing on eating *and* conversing; acceptable meal-time behavior and manners

Eating Teaches Fine-Motor Skills:
> Pouring; handling spoons, forks; serving self; drinking, eating without spilling

Eating Teaches Independence Skills:
> Finding and setting one's place, serving self, making choices, cleaning up at snack and lunch times

Eating Teaches Individual Differences:
> Likes/dislikes; choices of food; fast/slow pace of eating

Resting/Sleeping Teaches Health:
> Personal care skills; relaxation habits; internal balance and change of pace; alternating activity to allow body to rest

Resting/Sleeping Teaches Independence Skills:
> Preparing own rest place; selecting book/toy; clearing bed things after rest

Dressing Teaches Independence Skills:
> Self-awareness: size of clothes, comparisons between clothes for girls and boys, younger and older, larger and smaller children, and children in and out of diapers or training pants
>
> Self-esteem: caring for one's own body; choosing one's own clothes

Dressing Teaches Fine-Motor Skills:
> How to manage snaps, buttons, zippers; handling all garments; maneuvering in and out of a snowsuit or jacket, matching hands and feet with mittens and boots or shoes

Toileting Teaches Emotional Skills:
> Self-awareness: body functions, comparisons between boys and girls, learning the names and physical sensations that go with body functions
>
> Self-identity: what girls/boys do
>
> Self-esteem: caring for one's own body without guilt, fear, shame
>
> Human sexuality: in a natural setting, promotes healthy attitudes toward the body and its functions; that adults can be accepting, open, and reassuring about the body and its care

FIGURE 9.10 Every routine can be used as a vehicle for learning within the environment.

the activity level of the children and should change when weather conditions do. Adequate, nonglare lighting is a necessity. Studies indicate that uniform, fluorescent lighting may not be the best environment for children; therefore, a mixture of lighting such as is in homes is preferable (Ott, 1990; Greenman, 1987). Rooms should have some means of controlling light (shades, blinds). Cross-ventilation is necessary in all rooms where children eat, sleep, or play. Proper heating and insulation are important.

Communicable Disease. This is an important issue when dealing with young children in group care. Some people question the advisability of early group care on the grounds that it exposes children to too much illness. Others claim that such exposure at an early age helps children build up resistance and that they are actually stronger and healthier by the time they enter primary grades. In the largest U.S. study to date on children's health, the Center for Disease Control concluded that, while infants and toddlers face a higher risk of colds and viruses, day care was not seen as increasing children's illnesses at older ages and not a risk overall (Education Week, 1991).

Parents should be notified when normal childhood diseases (such as chicken pox) or common problems (such as head lice) occur in the classroom. Infections of special concern to adults include chicken pox, hepatitis A, and cytomegalovirus (CMV). A description of the symptoms and the dates of exposure and incubation period may be helpful to parents. They can then assist the school in controlling the spread of the disease in question.

In group care, children can contract a fair number of colds and viruses, especially when they are eating and sleeping in close proximity. The school and its staff have a responsibility to ensure that good health standards are instituted and maintained to keep illness to a minimum.

Health Assessment and School Policies. Every early childhood center should establish clear health policies and make them known to parents. A daily inspection of each child will help adults spot nasal discharge, inflamed eyes, and throat and skin conditions of a questionable nature. This daily check will screen out more serious cases of chil-

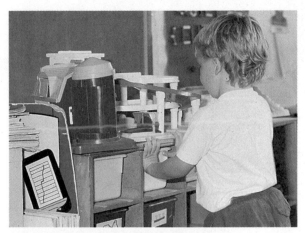

FIGURE 9.11 Cleanup time. How can this routine be made interesting and appealing to children?

dren too ill to remain at school, and may be done by a teacher, nurse, or administrator. Educating parents about the warning signs of illness will encourage sick children to be cared for at home.

It is very important for the school to inform parents about what happens when children are refused admittance or become ill during the school day. Every school should provide a place for sick children where they can be isolated from others, kept under supervision, and be made comfortable until they are picked up. For their part, parents must arrange to have sick children cared for elsewhere if they are unable to take them home. School policies on these issues must be *explicit* and upheld consistently and compassionately, for the sake of all the children.

Teachers must be sensitive to parents' feelings and situations when sending a sick child home. This situation often produces guilt feelings in parents and work-related stress. Working parents may need school assistance in locating alternatives for care of a sick child.

Most schools require, under state or local laws, a doctor's examination and permission to participate in an early childhood education program before a child can enter the program. This includes a record of immunizations and the child's general health. Parents, too, should submit a history of the child, highlighting eating, sleeping, and elimination habits. It is critical to note any dietary restrictions or allergies and then post them in the classrooms for a reminder.

FIGURE 9.12 Children need clothing in which they can be active, playful, and messy!

Nutrition. What children eat is also important for proper health. Places where food is prepared and stored must be kept especially clean. The child who has regular, nutritious meals and snacks will likely be healthier and less susceptible to disease. Many children do not have the benefits of healthy meals and snacks. Some do not receive adequate food at home; others are used to sugar-laden treats and "fast foods." Education about nutrition becomes the responsibility of a school that is concerned with children's health and physical development. The need for educating parents regarding child nutrition exists in virtually all early childhood programs, regardless of social or economic status. Some centers establish food regulations in an attempt to ensure that nutritionally sound meals are served to children. Most schools attempt to provide a relaxed atmosphere at meal and snack time. Children are asked to sit and eat, sharing conversation as well as food. Since life-long eating patterns are established early in life, teachers of young children have a responsibility to understand the critical role nutrition plays in the child's total development.

Clothing. The health and safety of children is affected by the clothing they wear. A simple way to be sure children stay healthy is to encourage them to dress properly for play and for varying weather conditions. Children need clothing in which they can be active—clothing that is not binding, and is easy to remove and easy to clean. To promote a self-help environment, children need clothes they can manage themselves (elastic waistbands, velcro ties, large zippers). Pants are a good choice for both boys and girls; long dresses can become a hazard when climbing, running, or going up and down stairs. The safest shoes for active play should have composition or rubber soles. Whenever possible, it helps to keep changes of clothes at school.

Health of the Staff. A responsible early childhood center is one that supports and maintains a healthy staff. Teachers should be in good physical and mental health to be at their best with children. It is wise to check the health regulations and benefits of the individual school when employed there. Many states require annual chest X rays as a condition of employment. Sick leave policies should be clearly stated in print.

Early childhood education is an intense job involving close interpersonal contact. Most teachers work long hours, often with low wages and few health benefits, and with clients in various stages of health. Such working conditions produce fatigue and stress, which can lead to illness or other stress-related problems.

Guarding Children's Safety

Beyond the continual supervision of indoor and outdoor space, everything is planned with the children's safety in mind. Creating a hazard-free environment for children takes careful observation and attention to detail. A quick walk around the room and yard will reveal potential problems:

- Are there any sharp corners at children's height?
- Are rug edges snagged or loose?
- Are absorbent surfaces used wherever there is water? Are mops and towels available for spillage?
- Is hot water out of the reach of children?
- Are children allowed to run inside?
- Are there rules governing the children's use of scissors, hammers, and knives?
- Are safety rules explained to children and upheld by adults?

- Are electrical outlets covered when not in use?

- Do open stairwells have gates?

- Do adults monitor the use of extension cords and appliances?

- Is broken equipment removed promptly?

- Are fences high enough to protect and safe to touch?

- Are there areas where wheel toys can move freely without fear of collision?

- Are swings placed away from traffic areas and set apart by bushes or fences?

- Can a child's foot or ankle be caught on equipment; under a chain-link fence?

- Does traffic flow easily?

- Are the toys safe for children's use?

Additionally, with an estimated 12 to 15 million children participating in organized sports each year (Nelson and Raymond, 1989), safety issues are paramount for school-aged children. The adults serve as the link between children and sports and are the chief means of prevention of injuries and accidents.

Figure 9.14 is a safety checklist for the indoor areas, while Figure 12.9 shows how to make playgrounds safe.

FIGURE 9.13 Be sure that swings are placed away from the traffic area and set apart so that other children can keep at a safe distance.

First Aid. Every school should establish procedures for dealing with children who are injured on the property. First aid instructions should be required of all teachers and made available as part of their in-service training. Teachers should know how to treat bumps and bruises, minor cuts and abrasions, bleeding, splinters, bites and stings, seizures, sprains, broken bones, and minor burns.[1] Each classroom should be equipped with two first aid kits. One is for use in the classroom and yard, the other should be suitable for taking on field trips. The kit should be readily available to adults, but out of children's reach, and supplies should be replenished regularly.

Emergency numbers to be posted near the telephone in each room include those of the ambulance squad, fire department, police, health department, nearest hospital, and a consulting physician (if any). All families enrolled at the school should be aware of school policy regarding injuries at school and provide the school with emergency information for each child: the name of their physician, how to locate the parents, and who else might be responsible for the injured child if the parents cannot be reached. The school in turn must make sure they notify parents of any injuries the child has incurred during the school day.

Fire Safety. Most local fire regulations require that fire extinguishers be in working order and placed in all classrooms and the kitchen area. Fire exits, fire alarms, and fire escapes should be well

OUR DIVERSE WORLD OUR DIVERSE WORLD OUR DIVERSE WORLD OUR DIVERSE WORLD OUR DIVERSE WORLD

[1]All teachers should receive training in using universal health precautions with all children. Teachers should not make assumptions about who is at risk and who is not for the HIV virus or hepatitis.

SAFETY LIST FOR INDOOR ENVIRONMENTS

_____ Person monitoring children (at entrances, indoors, outdoors)

_____ First aid and emergency:
    _____ Materials readily available to adults, out of children's reach, and regularly stocked and updated
    _____ Adults trained in First Aid/CPR regularly and familiar with emergency routines

_____ Safety plugs on all outlets

_____ Cords:
    _____ Electric cords out of children's reach; avoid using extension cords
    _____ Curtain/window cords, window pulls and poles out of children's reach

_____ Floormat/carpet tacked down to avoid slippage

_____ Doors:
    _____ Made to open and close slowly
    _____ All clear access, marked exits, and not blocked

_____ Cubbies and storage cabinets
    _____ Bolted to walls (or back-to-back togehter)
    _____ Cabinets equipped with child-proof latches
    _____ Any dangerous materials in locked area

_____ Toys:
    _____ In good repair; no splinters or sharp, broken edges
    _____ Check for size with younger children (purchase safety sizing gadget or estimate to keep at the size of a child's fist)
    _____ Check for peeling paint

_____ Plants and animals:
    _____ Nonpoisonous plants _only_
    _____ Check animal cages regularly
    _____ Supervise animal handling carefully
    _____ Store animal food away from children's reach

_____ Adult materials:
    _____ Keep adult purses, bags, and so on, away from children
    _____ Avoid having hot beverages around children
    _____ No smoking in children's areas

_____ Kitchen and Storage:
    _____ Children allowed in _only_ with adult supervision
    _____ Poisonous or hazardous materials are stored in a locked area

FIGURE 9.14 Children's safety is of primary importance to teachers and caregivers. Careful evaluations and regular safety checks eliminate dangerous materials and conditions in children's spaces.

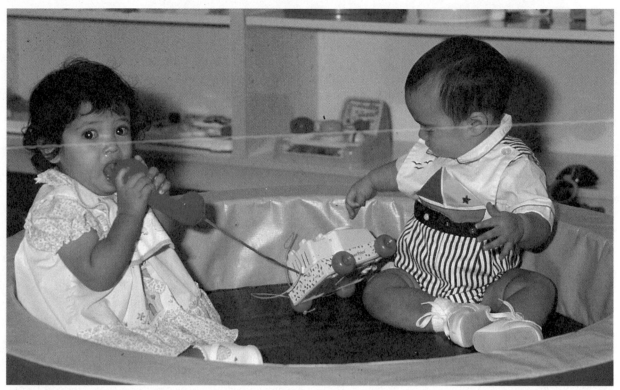

FIGURE 9.15   When planning for infants and toddlers, toys must be checked carefully, as children explore them with all their senses.

marked and functioning properly. Children and teachers should participate in fire drills regularly and, in some areas of the country, earthquake and tornado drills. These experiences can reinforce in parents the need for establishing similar procedures at home.

Automobile Safety. Automobile safety is a related concern when considering potential hazards for preschool children. The use of approved car seats and restraints for children riding in automobiles has received national attention in recent years. Some states have passed legislation requiring the use of specific devices to ensure safer travel for young children. Whether or not they walk to school, children should also be aware of basic rules for crossing streets. The school parking lot can be a source of danger unless the school articulates policies to parents regarding the safety needs of chil-

dren. There are potential risks when cars and children occupy the same space. Children should not be left unattended in parking lots.

Maintaining Children's Well-Being

The overall environment for children takes into consideration many factors. In order to provide for children's *health and safety*, teachers look at the physical environment carefully–its materials, the equipment, and their arrangement and presentation (see Figure 9.14). Another factor in children's care and education is their *well-being*. Young children are growing up in a world threatened by violence abroad and at home, drug abuse, unresolved conflicts among adults, and constant bombardment of television and the media. This chapter, as well as those on the curriculum, demonstrate the importance of teachers addressing issues of rac-

 OUR DIVERSE WORLD OUR DIVERSE WORLD OUR DIVERSE WORLD OUR DIVERSE WORLD OUR DIVERSE WORLD

[1]The skilled early childhood educator is well informed in a wide area of topics challenging our society as we enter the next century.

ism, sexism, and handicappism as well as helping children cope with growing up in a nuclear/war and television age[1] (Carlsson-Paige and Levin, 1990; Derman-Sparks, 1989; Smith, 1989).

The health, safety, and nutritional needs of the children are of primary and fundamental importance. The National Academy of Early Childhood Programs has established explicit guidelines for health, safety, nutrition, and food service (NAEYC, 1984). When the basic needs of children are protected, the foundation for sound development has been laid.

CREATING THE ENVIRONMENT

The Physical Environment

Every school setting is organized fundamentally around physical space. This means teachers work with the size and limitations of the facility, both inside and out-of-doors. The building itself may be new and designed specifically for young children. In Reggio Emilia, for example, it is the environment that creates an atmosphere of discovery. As founder Louis Malaguzzi explains (Edwards, et al., 1993):

> There is an entrance hall, which informs and documents, and which anticipates the form and organization of the school. This leads into the dining hall, with the kitchen well in view. The entrance hall leads into the central space, or *piazza*, the place of encounters, friendships, games, and other activities that complete those of the classrooms. The classrooms and utility rooms are placed at a distance from but connected with the center area. Each classroom is divided into two contiguous rooms . . . to allow children either to be with teachers or stay alone. . . . In addition to the classrooms, we have established the *atelier*, the school studio and laboratory, as a place for manipulating or experimenting.

More than likely, however, the space is a converted house or store, a church basement, a parish hall, or an elementary classroom. Sometimes a program will share space with another group so that mobile furniture is moved daily or weekly. There may be a large yard or none at all. Some playgrounds are on the roof of the building, or a park across the street may serve as the only available playground. (See Playgrounds in Chapter 12.)

Restraints also come in the form of weather conditions. Outside play—and therefore large-muscle equipment—may be unavailable during the winter months. This may suggest that room for active, vigorous play is needed inside during that time. Hot summer months can make some types of play difficult if there is little or no shade outdoors. Weather conditions must be taken into consideration when planning programs for children.

Early childhood programs have specific needs that must be met by the buildings they occupy. Although the choice of building is generally determined by what is available, at a minimum the setting should provide facilities for:

playing/working	food preparation
eating	storage
washing/toileting	office/teacher work space
sleeping/resting	clothing and wraps

Ideally, the setting should have enough space to house these various activities separately. In practice, however, rooms are multipurpose and more than one event takes place in the same space. A play room doubles as an eating area, since both require the use of tables and chairs. When a school room serves many functions (playing, eating, sleeping), convenient and adequate storage space is a necessity. Harms (1989) lists as important environmental supports for each of these areas:

1. personal care routines

2. appropriate furnishings and display space

3. language and reasoning experiences

4. fine- and gross-motor activities

5. creative activities

6. social development experiences

7. personal and professional needs of the adults in the program

The amount of teacher time needed to prepare the room for each change of activity is worth consideration when planning the daily schedule.

General Requirements

Ground floor classrooms are preferable for young children to ensure that they can enter and

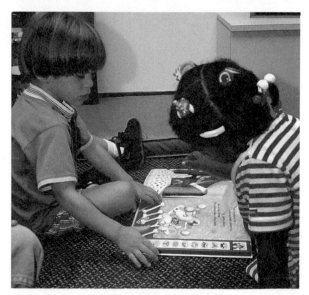

FIGURE 9.16 Early childhood programs provide for children's playing and working alone and together, with friends and teachers, indoors and out.

FIGURE 9.17 Even the hallways serve a function in the Reggio Emilia Schools in Italy. (Courtesy of the city of Reggio Emilia, Italy.)

leave with relative ease and safety. For noise reduction, the walls and ceilings should be soundproofed. Carpeting, draperies, and other fireproof fabrics in the room will help absorb sound. Floors must be durable, sanitary, and easily cleaned. They should be free from drafts. Rugs should be vacuumed each day. Room size should be sufficient to allow for freedom of movement and the opportunity to play without interference. Some licensing agencies may suggest minimum room and yard size standards.

Many local and state agencies have regulations regarding the use of space for children in group care settings. The fire marshall, health department, and similar agencies must be consulted and their regulations observed. It is wise to consider their requirements when arranging space.

The National Academy of Early Childhood Programs has developed guidelines for indoor and outdoor facilities that promote optimal growth. Besides floor and play space (minimum 35 square feet indoors and 75 square feet outdoors), the guidelines suggest how to arrange activity areas to accommodate children and what kinds of activities and materials are safe, clean, and attractive. Harms and Clifford (1980) have developed environmental rating scales that are used widely. The sections on Materials and Equipment and on Organizing Space in this chapter draw on these two exemplary works, which are cited in the chapter bibliography.

Bathrooms

These should be adjacent to the play and sleeping areas and easily reached from outdoors. Child-sized toilets and wash basins are preferable, but if unavailable, a step or platform may be built. In most early childhood settings, the bathrooms are without doors, for ease of supervision. Toileting facilities for children should be light, airy, attractive, and large enough to serve several children at a time. An exhaust fan is desirable. Paper towel holders should be at child height and waste baskets placed nearby.

If diapering is part of the program, areas for this purpose should be clearly defined and close to handwashing facilities. Handwashing regulations for the staff should be posted, and an area should be provided for recording children's toileting and elimination patterns. Closed cans and germicidal spray must be used, and diapering materials should be plentiful and handy.

Room to Rest

Schools that provide nap and sleeping facilities require adequate storage space for cots and bedding. Movable screens, low enough for teacher supervision, allow for privacy and help reduce the noise level.

Cots or cribs should be labeled with children's names and washed regularly. They should be placed consistently and in such a way that children feel familiar, cozy, and private—not in the center of the room or in rows. Teachers can develop a "nap map" that places children so they can get the rest or sleep they need while still feeling part of the group.

Out of Doors

The traditional playgrounds—typically on a flat, barren area with steel structures such as swings, climbers, a slide, perhaps a merry-go-round or seesaws, fixed in concrete and arranged in one row—are poor places for children's play from both safety and developmental perspectives (Frost, 1986). Children as young as toddlers and through the primary years much prefer the adventure or creative playground, spaces that have a variety of fixed and movable equipment (Campbell and Frost, 1985; Winter, 1983). Raw materials, such as sand, water, tires, spools, sawhorses,

FIGURE 9.18 Every routine—eating, resting, handwashing, sleeping, and diapering—has a place in the early childhood classroom.

FIGURE 9.19 No matter what age the child is, snacks are a favorite part of the day.

bowls, or pans, in combination with larger superstructures or open-air "houses" with some flexible parts, stimulate a wide variety of both social and cognitive play (including constructive, dramatic, and games play).

A wide porch or covered patio is ideal for rainy days or days when the sun is too severe. Many activities can be extended to the outside area with this type of protection. The physical plant should include adequate playground space adjacent to the building. A variety of playground surfaces makes for more interesting play and provides suitable covering for outdoor activities. Tanbark can be used in the swing area, cement for wheel toys, and grass for under climbers. Sand is used for play in a large area and also in a sensory table. No matter what the surface, the yard should be constructed with a good drainage system. Trees, bushes, and other plantings will allow for both sunshine and shade. Fences are *mandatory*. They must be durable, an appropriate height, with no opportunity for a child to gain a foothold.

Since there are no mandatory standards for the manufacture of play equipment, adults who work with children must assume responsibility for playground design. Teachers can familiarize themselves with the literature, visit high-quality playgrounds, and consult with child development specialists when selecting equipment. Given the importance to the outdoors that young children demonstrate, teachers are well-advised to concentrate their efforts in a similar fashion.

Food Service

All schools for young children serve some sort of refreshment during the daily session. In an infant program, formula and milk storage is a necessity. Whether involved in a light snack or full meal program, the center must adhere to the most rigid standards of health protection and safety provisions. Every precaution must be taken to ensure maximum hygienic food service. Daily cleaning of equipment, counters, floors, and appliances is a necessity. Proper disinfecting of highchairs and tables requires half a cup of bleach to one gallon of water; bottles of this solution can be stored away from children's reach yet handy for teachers.

Local school districts, Coordinated Community Child Care (4Cs), or affiliates of the National Association for the Education of Young Children may be consulted for guidelines on serving nutritional foods and may even offer financial subsidies. For infant/toddler programs and in many full-day programs, space for recording feeding information must be designated, and enough highchairs or low tables must be provided to prevent an unreasonable wait for eating. Each age has its unique food service needs.[1] Infants will need to be held or seated near an adult. Toddlers should not be fed popcorn, nuts, or raw carrots because of the hazard of choking. All children must be served food on disposable dishes or on dishes cleaned in a dishwasher with a sanitation cycle. Lunches brought from home by school-age and full-day children must be checked for spoilage. Information about eating patterns, proportions, and nutritional needs should be regularly shared with parents.

Materials and Equipment

Selection of materials and equipment is based on a number of criteria. Out of necessity, most

[1]Food, as well as toys and materials, need to reflect the values of the culture at large.

school budgets limit the amount of dollars available for such purchases. To make every dollar count, teachers select materials that:

- Are age and developmentally appropriate.
- Relate to the school's philosophy and curriculum.
- Reflect quality design and workmanship.
- Are durable.
- Offer flexibility and versatility in their uses.
- Have safety features (for instance, nontoxic paints, rounded corners).
- Are aesthetically attractive and appealing to children (and adults).
- Are easy to maintain and repair.
- Reflect the cultural makeup of the group and the diversity of the culture overall.
- Are nonsexist, nonstereotypical, and anti-bias.

Materials should be appropriate for a wide range of skills since children within the same age group develop at individual rates. Many of the materials can be open-ended, that is, they can be used in their most basic form or they can be developed in a variety of ways. Unit blocks, clay, and Lego® are examples of materials that children can use in a simple fashion; as skills develop these materials can be manipulated in a more complex manner.

Toys and materials need to reflect the values of the class, the families, and community.[1] From a self-help viewpoint, dressing frames and plenty of workable doll clothes will help children learn those self-care tasks. Children's books that demonstrate social values and attitudes that expand gender roles and family lifestyles show a value for an anti-bias environment. Classroom practices that encourage sociodramatic play involving interaction (restaurant, grocery store, and so on) help children learn about peaceful means to negotiate and solve problems, demonstrating a peace education perspective.

Recall the Walfdorf Schools discussed in Chapter 1. Since Steiner believed the classroom is an extension of the family experience and was to be as free as possible from the intrusions of the "modern world," a Waldorf kindergarten might look like this (Waldorf, 1995):

> The feeling of warmth and security is largely created by using only natural materials: woods, cotton, wool in the construction of the decor and toys. The curtains transmit a warm glow in the room. Ideally, the walls and floor of the room are of natural wood. In this warm environment are placed toys which the children can use to imitate and transform the activities that belong to everyday adult life. In one corner stands a wooden scale and baskets for children to pretend they are grocery shopping; a pile of timber stands ready to be constructed into a playhouse, a boat, or a train; a rocking horse invites a child to become a rider; homemade dolls lie in wooden cradles surrounded by wooden frames and cloths the children can use to create a pretend family and play house. Pinecones and flowers are artistically dispersed. Lovely watercolors adorn the walls. The effect of this beautiful arrangement of decorations and toys is the feeling of stepping out of the business and clutter of modern life into a sanctuary where one can breathe easily, relax, and play according to the impulses of one's heart.

Children are active learners, and their materials should provide them with ways to explore, manipulate, and become involved. Teachers encourage the use of fine- and gross-motor skills by providing equipment that involves their use. Children learn through all their senses, so the materials should be appealing to many of the senses. Children need opportunities for quiet, private time and space as well; particularly for children in care for long hours or in large group sizes, a cozy corner is essential.

Organizing Space

There are many different ways to arrange and organize the living space in an early childhood setting; the final result expresses the diversity of the program. Most early childhood centers are arranged by interest areas, learning centers, or activity areas. Dodge and Colker's *Creative Cur-*

[1]Food, as well as toys and materials, need to reflect the values of the culture at large.

Basic Materials in an Early Childhood Classroom

Art Supplies
Easels, paints, watercolors
Plastic dough, clay
Pens, pencils, brushes
Scissors, holepunches
Glue, paste
Collage materials
Assorted paper

Infants/toddlers: Limit materials.
Use open shelves with few choices.

School age: Have self-help table and
teacher-guided projects.

Blocks and Manipulatives
Unit blocks
Block accessories: people, animals,
vehicles
Puzzles
Construction toys: Lego®, Tinkertoys®
Stringing beads, dressing frames

Infants/toddlers: Push-pull toys, nesting
toys, soft blocks

School age: Diversify accessories,
increase complexity, add math
materials.

Discovery and Science
Nature materials
Textured materials
Water/sensory table and materials
Magnifying glasses, mirrors
Scales
Small pets

Infants/toddlers: Simplify, watch for
safety. Aquarium.

School age: Display to read, computer.

Language and Books
Books
Flannel board, accessories
Photos
Lotto games
Records, tapes
Writing center: typewriter, pads, and
pencils

Infants/toddlers: Cardboard books; use
others with adults only.

School age: Readers, listening post.

Dramatic Play
Furniture: child-sized, versatile
Clothing: variety, nonstereotyped
Dolls: variety, and accessories
Cooking utensils
Food items
Purses, suitcases, briefcases,
backpacks

Infants/toddlers: Limit the choice, add
hats or dolls that can get wet.

School age: Varied units such as
prehistoric cave, moonscape

Outdoors
Large building blocks
Sand/water toys
Wheel toys
Dramatic-play props
Balls and game materials
Workbench materials
Dancing materials

Infants/toddlers: Omit workbench;
simplify choices.

School age: Team-games equipment.
Sequence projects, such as building
bird feeders, piñatas.

FIGURE 9.20 A sample materials and equipment list for an early childhood program.
While not comprehensive, the list helps organize the environment for a variety of play.
Note the adjustments that must be made to accommodate different ages.

riculum (1992) outlines six environmental areas as being art, blocks, table toys, house corner, library, and outdoors; we elaborate on them to give you a broader view: These will most likely include:

Indoors	Outdoors
Blocks	Sand
Manipulatives/table toys	Water play/sensory play
Art	Woodworking
Discovery: Science/ nature/Cooking	Wheel toys
Music	Climbers
Math	Swings
Dramatic play	Balls/Games
Books/Language/Listening	Art
Quiet/Private place	
Water play/sensory play	Science/nature
Housekeeping	Dramatic play

Figure 9.21 shows an environmental plan for optimizing learning and interaction for three- and four-year-olds; Figure 9.22 shows indoor alternatives for toddlers and school-age children.

The room arrangement and the choice of activity centers show what is being emphasized in the program. The amount of space devoted to any one activity says a great deal about its value to the staff. A housekeeping area with plenty of space encourages active use by a number of children. Social play is promoted when two or more items are available. Four telephones, three doll buggies, or two easels can be tools for social interaction. At the same time, the environment must be flexible to respond to the developing needs and interests of the children. For instance, one class may have great interest in block-building, and thus need to expand that area for several weeks. As interests change, so does the room and yard—someone brings in a

FIGURE 9.21 Layout for a preschool child-care environment, ages three to five. For a group of 18 to 20 children, teachers plan an indoor/outdoor environment that is challenging and uncrowded.

hamster, and the discovery area blossoms, or family camping brings out tents around the grassy outdoor area.

Since the physial environment is such a powerful influence on children, it is worthwhile to consider several key dimensions which impact their experiences. Prescott (1994) names five:

1. **Softness/Hardness**
   Soft: rugs, pillows, playdough, finger paints, grass, sand, swings
   Hard: tile floor, wooden furniture, asphalt, cement

2. **Open/Closed**
   Open (no one right way to use it): sand and water, dress-up, collage materials, painting
   Closed (only manipulated one way to come out right): puzzles, many board games, most Montessori equipment
   In-between: many manipulatives such as Legos®, TinkerToys®, blocks, balls

3. **Simple/Complex**

"Play equipment can differ in its holding power; i.e., the capacity to sustain attention. . . . A simple unit has one manipulable aspect, a complex unit has two different kinds of materials combined, and a super unit has three different kinds of materials that go together."

   Simple: swings, climbers, sand pile with no toys
   Complex: dramatic play with only a kitchen
   Super: Climbers with slides and ropes; playhouse with kitchen, dress-up clothes, dolls, and/or playdough; Sand area with equipment and/or water

As you add more features to a unit, you increase its complexity and the children's interest in it. To simple playdough, add cookie cutters, then add toothpicks or a garlic press and it becomes a super unit.

4. **Intrusion/Seclusion**
   Intrusion: places where children can enter or go through easily; blocks, housekeeping, often the entire environment are often highly intrusive areas
   Seclusion: places where children can be alone or

FIGURE 9.22 Room layouts for school-age and toddler groups differ according to the developmental needs of the groups. These plans accommodate up to 20 school-age children and 12 toddlers.

with only one child or adult; cubbies, a fort, or under a table become secret places

5. **High mobility/Low mobility**

High: whole body places and activities; outdoors, climbers, trike lanes, gym mats

Low: sitting still places and activities; puzzles and games, story and group times, naptime

In-between: dramatic play, block corner, woodworking

The placement of the interest centers is important. Balance the number of noisy and quiet activities, both indoors and out. Some activities are noisier than others, so place the noisier centers together and cluster the quieter ones together. Quieter activities, such as puzzles, language games, story telling, take place in areas away from blocks, water play, or dramatic play, since the last three tend to kindle animated, active, and sometimes noisy behavior.

When arranging environments, there must be enough play spaces for the number of children in the group. Kritchevsky and Prescott (1969) analyzed the number of play opportunities in school settings, both indoors and out. Areas and activities were assigned a value. A simple area (swings, climbers) counts as one play space, a complex area (housekeeping/dramatic play) counts as four play spaces, and a super area (sand and water play combined) counts as eight play spaces. The value assigned an area generally coincides with the number of children who might be accommodated in that space. When the total for the space is figured, it is matched against the actual number of children in the group to see if there is a place for everyone to play.

Adult needs also should be met through proper organization of classroom and yard. How can the teachers supervise all areas while ensuring cozy spots for children's privacy? Are the teachers deployed evenly throughout all the space? Is storage integrated so that equipment is located near the place where it will be used? Is the space arranged for cooperation and communication among the adults as well as the children? In other words, is this a workplace that is accepting, inviting, and challenging to all?

Clearly defined boundaries and obvious pathways make it easy for children to live and work in the space. There should be enough space for larger groups to gather together as well as small groups.

A good environment for children reflects the teachers' knowledge of how children play, what skills they possess, what they know, and what they need to learn. The settings are arranged to promote those aspects of child growth and development. They also reflect the teachers' values. A self-help perspective will have spaces and materials arranged for the children's access and use without undue teacher permission or help; Figures 9.3, 9.21, and 9.24 demonstrate such environments. With an anti-bias viewpoint, the environment would reflect images in abundance of all the children, families, and staff of that program as well as of the major racial/ethnic groups of the community and nation, with a balance of men and women as well as the elderly and disabled doing many jobs typical of daily life.[1] With peace education in mind, children use materials to expand their concepts, including those of similarity and difference, develop a strong sense of self, and cooperate and resolve conflicts peaceably.

One place in particular reflects the community's value of creativity and self-expression. Upon entering one of the community preschools in Reggio Emilia, one sees (New, 1990):

> . . . the work of children (drawings, paintings, sculptures) and their teachers (photographs and displays of projects in progress), often with the dramatic use of graphics. . . . Everywhere you turn, there is something else to ponder. Art supplies, including paints and clay as well as recycled or naturally found materials (leaves, bottle caps, fabric scraps) are pleasingly arranged, often by color, on shelves within children's reach. Groupings of found objects, including flower petals and plastic bags filled with "memories" from field trips, are carefully displayed so as to acknowledge the importance children attribute to the objects as well as the aesthetic qualities (shape, color, texture) of the objects themselves.

In summary, the physical environment should be organized for children according to these criteria:

● *Availability:* open, low shelving with visual cues for placement of toys, equipment—aids in cleanup and room setup

[1]Missing footnote copy.

- *Consistency in organization:* neat, systematic, in logical order

- *Compatibility:* noisy activities are grouped away from quiet ones; art needs natural light when possible; water play near a bathroom or kitchen; messy projects on washable floors

- *Definition:* clearly defined boundaries indicating available space and what is to take place; obvious pathways outlined in class and yard; ways to get in and out of an area without disrupting activity in progress; no dead ends or runways

- *Spacing:* interest areas with enough space to hold the children who will play there; one-third to one-half of the surface should remain uncovered (Kritchevsky and Prescott, 1969); materials stored near space where they are used; storage and activity space has visual cues

- *Communicability:* tells children what to do instead of relying on adult to monitor activities; communicates to children what behavior is expected; arrangement suggests numbers of children, levels of activity.

The Temporal Environment

Daily Schedule: Time to Learn

The daily schedule defines the structure of each program. It creates the format for how children will experience the events of the day—in what order and for what length of time.

No two schedules are alike, since each reflects the program it represents. The amount of time devoted to specific activities communicates clearly what value the school places on them. The amount of time given to certain aspects of the curriculum, the variety of events, and the flexibility tell children and adults what is important in this particular setting. Figure 9.23 and Chapter 11 expand on this issue of time.

In developing a schedule by which to function on a daily basis, teachers first decide what is important for children to learn, how that learning should take place, and how much time to allow in the daily program. If small-group work and individual attention are program goals, enough time will have to be set aside to ensure its success. More time is needed to allow children a number of curriculum choices than if they only had one or two activities from which to select. Three-year-olds need more time for toileting activities than do five-year-olds, who are considerably more self-sufficient.

The golden rule for child care is to treat children as we want them to treat us. Australian educator Anne Stonehouse (1990) notes that the children in child care today are the adults of tomorrow who will be taking care of us in our old age. Remembering that, it helps to think of how often children are asked to do and finish their tasks on others' schedules, to ask permission to do what they wish, to be required to participate in activities of someone else's choice. A children's program must be *for* children, on *their* timetable as much as possible. Stonehouse's recommendations for a program's schedule reflect this respect:

1. Suitable choices are built in as much of the time as possible, avoiding the expectation that everyone should do the same thing at the same time. Flexibility . . . makes for a more human environment.

2. The need for a sensitive and flexible settling in period is taken into account. This starts with respect for the client and the client's family and the recognition that different people cope with change and new experiences in different ways.

3. Meaningless and sometimes mindless activities that simply "fill up the day," "help pass the time," or that have no intrinsic value are avoided.

4. A healthy balance between individual's need for autonomy, freedom, and independence, on the one hand, and the need for rules that help get along together, on the other, is strived for.

5. Staff balance the need for a routine, for the comfort and reassurance of the familiar, with the need for variety and novelty for change.

The physical plant itself may dictate a portion of the daily schedule. If toilet facilities are not located adjacent to the classroom, then more time must be scheduled to travel to and from the bathrooms. If the building or space is shared with other groups, some portion of the program may be modified. Many schools housed in church buildings schedule field trips during the annual church rummage sale in order to free up the space for the church's use.

The daily schedule is important for everyone in the setting. When the time sequence is clear to all, then everyone can go about the business of learning and teaching. Children are more secure in a place that has a consistent schedule; they can begin to anticipate the regularity of what comes next and count on it. In that way they are then free to move, explore, and learn without hesitation. Children can freely involve themselves without fear of being interrupted. Adults, too, enjoy the predictability of a daily schedule. By knowing the sequence of events, they are then free to flex the timing when unforeseen circumstances arise.

Developmentally Appropriate Schedules

Just as the arrangement of space should reflect the group of children within, so does the daily schedule allow for appropriate growth at the developmental level of the group. There are common factors to consider for all children in the early years, as well as some developmental distinctions at the various ages.

There are common elements in all schedules, whether they are designed for toddler groups or five-year-olds, all-day programs or half-day nurseries. Sound child development principles provide the framework on which the daily schedule is structured. The individual schools then adapt these requirements to their own philosophy as they work out their individual daily schedule. All schedules must:

- Include time for routines (to eat, rest, wash, toilet) as well as time for transitions (what happens when there is a change from one activity to another) and group times (circle time to begin the day, songtime for announcements, or storytime as closure).

- Alternate quiet and active play and work to help children pace themselves.

- Provide opportunities for both inside and outside play.

- Allow children to participate in structured activities as well as those of their own choosing.

- Make it possible for children to work individually, in small groups, or in larger ones.

- Gear the time to the age and developmental levels of the group.

- Provide for flexibility so that children's interests can be maintained and emergencies met.

- Have a beginning and an end. Some provisions must be made for children to be met and greeted when they enter. The day is brought to closure with a review of the day's activities and a daily class anticipation of what will come tomorrow. Allow time for dismissal or transition to extended care.

- Involve the adults in daily planning and review; include a regular meeting time for more substantial discussion of children, long-range planning, and evaluation.

- Include time for cleanup and room restoration.

- Incorporate the teachers' roles and assignments so that they will know their area of responsibility.

- Be posted in an obvious place in the classroom for all to see.

All schedules have a great deal in common, but certain age-related differences can be seen. Figure 9.23 outlines three typical daily schedules for a half-day toddler class, a full day for preschoolers, and a kindergarten. (See also Figures 2.1 and 2.3.) There are several important differences in schedules for the various age groups:

- More *choices* are available to children as they grow.

  Example: Two-year-olds could be overstimulated by the selection of materials that is appropriate for school-aged children.

- *Transitions* can be handled differently in the various age groups.

  Example: Older children can move through some transitions as a group, such as changing from one activity area to another or going out with a specialist in pairs or even in a single file. This is difficult for younger children, who would push or wander away. For them, the door to the yard opens quietly, allowing children to go out slowly.

Half-Day Toddler Program

9:00-9:30   Greet Children
Inside Activities
- playdough and art/easel
- home living
- blocks and manipulatives
- books

9:30   Door to outdoors opens

9:45-10:20   Outdoor Play
- large motor
- social play

10:20   Music/movement outdoors

10:30   Snack/"Here We Are Together" song
- washing hands
- eating/pouring/cleanup

10:45-11:45   Outside

11:15   "Time to Put Our Toys Away" song
- all encouraged to participate in cleanup

11:20   Closure (indoors)
- parent-child together
- story or flannelboard

Full-Day Program for Preschoolers

7:00   Arrival, breakfast

7:30   Inside free play
- arts/easels
- table toys/games/blocks
- dramatic play center; house, grocery store, etc.

9:00   Cleanup

9:15   Group time: Songs/fingerplays and small-group choices

9:30   Choice Time/small groups
- discovery/math lab/science activity
- cooking for morning or afternoon snack
- language art/prereading choice

10:00   Snack (at outside tables/cloths on warm days) or snack center during free play

10:15   Outside free play
- climbing, swinging; sand and water, wheel toys, group games

12:00   Handwash and lunch

12:45   Get ready: toileting, handwashing, toothbrushing, prepare beds

1:15   Bedtime story

1:30   **Rest time**

2:30   Outdoors for those awake

3:30   Cleanup outdoors and singing time

4:00   Snacktime

4:15   **Learning centers; some outdoor/indoor choices, field trips, story teller**

5:30   Cleanup and read books until going home

Half-Day Kindergarten Plan

8:15-8:30   Arrival:
Getting ready to start
- checking in library books, lunch money, etc.

8:30   Newstelling
- "anything you want to tell for news"
- newsletter written weekly

9:00   Work assignment
- write a story about your news *or*
- make a page in your book (topic assigned) *or*
- work in math lab

9:30-10:15   Choice of indoors (paints, blocks, computer, table toys) *or*
second grade tutors read books to children
- when finished, play in loft *or* read books until recess

10:15   Snack

10:30   Recess

10:45   Language: chapter in novel read *or* other language activity

11:15   Dance *or* game *or* visitor and snack

11:45   Ending: Getting ready to leave
- check out library books
- gather art and other projects

12:00-1:30   for part of group each day:
Lunch, then:
- field trips
- writing lesson
- math or science lab

FIGURE 9.23   Daily schedules reflect the children's needs and ages while meeting the program's goals. The time and timing of the school day show what is valued in the program.

TRANSITION TIMES MADE EASIER

Questions for Planning

* Who is involved in the transition time (child, parents, teachers, other children, visitors, etc.)?
* What kind of activity has preceded the transition time and what will follow?
* What will the children be asked to *do* during transition?
* What will the teachers be doing *during* transition?
* How will the children be told or find out what to do during the transition?
* What do you know about child development and this particular child(ren) that can help with these questions?

Teaching Strategies

Arrival

* Greet each child with a smile and welcome child and parent with what activities are available.
* Make name cards and/or an attendance sheet that child and parent can participate in as a starting point.
* Plan with parents, and alert the child, a simple and clear way for them to say goodbye and for the parents to leave (see chapter 8 for details).

Cleanup Materials

* Give the children a five-minute "warning" to alert them to upcoming changes.
* Have a consistent and calm signal to start putting away toys.
* Use music as background and/or sing during cleanup.
* Consider having necklaces or cards of specific areas for children, or make teams.
* Construct the environment so that it is clear where things go and children can do the majority of it themselves.
* Occasionally thank the children publicly for cleaning up, noting individual efforts and specific chores done well.

Preparing Children to Attend

* Make a chart that shows the choices available.
* Sing a song or familiar fingerplay to get everyone's attention and participation.
* Ask the children to put on "elephant ears," (rabbit, etc.) or lock their lips and put the key in their pockets.

Ready to Rest/Naptime

* Prepare the environment ahead of time to be restful–darkened room, soft blanket/cuddlies nearby, quiet music, teachers whispering and available to walk children to their places and stay with them.
* Read a story to the group in one place before they are to lie quietly, or split larger groups into small subgroups with a teacher reading to each.

Moving to Another Place/Building

* Gather the group and tell them exactly what will be happening.
* Ask for ideas of how to behave ("What will we need to remember? How can we stay safe and have fun together?", and reinforce with a few concrete rules.
* Have the children be a train, with an adult as the engine and caboose, or a dragon with head and tail.
* Have the children choose a partner to stay with/hold hands.
* Ask preschoolers and early primary children to remember the "B" words ("beside or behind") in staying near adults.

Waiting for Others to Finish

* Prepare a part of the room for children to move to, such as a book corner or listening post, having an adult in that space with more than two children.
* Make an apron or hanging with several pockets filled with activity cards or small manipulatives for children to use alone.
* Plan a special table with folders or large envelopes with activities.
* Have a "waiting box" with special small items for these times only.

FIGURE 9.24   Transitions are a regular part of children's routines and should be learning times that are as well planned as other parts of the day.

Example: A child care class of 3- and 4-year-olds is dismissed from song time to snack by the color of people's shirts, or the first letter of their names, rather than as one whole group. Figure 9.24 gives examples of handling transitions for all ages.

● The *structure* of the day changes with age.

Example: The balance of free-play and teacher-directed activities shifts from relatively few directed activities for younger children to some more for the nursery school and child care ages. The kindergarten schedule provides more structure both in individual work projects and teacher-focused time. A first-grade schedule with some whole-group teacher instruction times is developmentally appropriate for those older children.

● The *content of group activities* changes with age.

Example: In the toddler class, group times are simple: a short fingerplay, story with a flannelboard or puppets, and a song to dismiss is adequate. Preschool group times include several songs, a dramatization of a favorite fingerplay, and a short story. By kindergarten, groups can last 15–20 minutes, with announcement and weather board, children's "newstelling," longer dramas, and even chapter stories.

The temporal environment thus mirrors the children's age and individual interests. In this regard it is useful to note that many programs divide the day into relatively small segments of time. This is done because adults believe that young children, particularly preschoolers, have such short attention spans that they cannot remain at an activity for long. However, we know that children can stay focused for long periods of time on activities of their choice or interest. While they may last only a short time in teacher-planned, structured activities, children need and thrive with more time to get their own creative juices flowing. Children can spend hours with blocks, Legos®, sand, water, and dramatic play. Consult Figure 9.23 to see how the temporal environment allots time for such endeavors.

The Interpersonal Environment

A child responds to everything in school: the color of the room, the way the furniture is arranged, how much time there is to play, and how people treat one another. To the child, everything is a stimulus. The *feeling* in a room is as real as the blocks or the books. Thus, the interpersonal or social aspects of an early childhood setting are powerful components of the environment.

Children are the most important people in the setting; they should feel safe and comfortable. A warm, interpersonal environment invites children to participate and to learn. When children feel secure with one another and with the setting, they will be able to engage more fully in the total program.

Parents are an important part of school, especially in the early years. The interpersonal connection between parent and teacher can bolster what happens to the child within the classroom and can offer the child a smooth transition between school and home. Learning is enhanced when parents and teachers come to communicate in supportive, nonthreatening ways.

Since it is understood that the single most important factor in determining the quality of a program is the teacher (see Chapter 5), it follows that teachers will be the key ingredient in determining the interpersonal "flavor" of a class. The first component of the National Academy's criteria for high-quality early childhood programs is the interactions among the staff and children (see Chapter 10). The human component, the connections among the people in a center or home, makes all the difference to young children, for they are the barometers of interpersonal tension or openness and freedom.

Young children develop best through close, affectionate relationships with people, particularly adults. In a human and humane environment, people are respected, and the focus of the staff is on children's strengths and capabilities; limitations are seen as needs rather than liabilities.[1] Teachers observe and engage children in interactions that include smiling, touching, listening, ask-

OUR DIVERSE WORLD OUR DIVERSE WORLD OUR DIVERSE WORLD OUR DIVERSE WORLD OUR DIVERSE WORLD

[1]The first challenge is recognize biases; the next is to restructure and expand perceptions; and the greatest challenge is the part that children are most likely to notice—how one speaks, truly feels, and behaves.

ing questions, and speaking on eye level. The language and tone of voice used is respectful and friendly, with children treated equally across lines of race, culture, language, ability, and sex.[1] Staff use positive guidance rather than punitive discipline techniques (see Chapter 7), and develop warm relationships with parents (see Chapter 8). What teachers do—and how they do it—determines what learning takes place in the class, and how each child and family will respond.

The attitudes and behaviors of teachers affect children's behaviors. Questions teachers can ask themselves as they evaluate the quality of the environment are:

● Is there a feeling of mutual respect between children and adults?

● Do teachers pick up on nonverbal/verbal expressions of both girls and boys? Of children with varying abilities? Of children of color?

● How do children treat one another?

● Do teachers model cooperative behavior with other adults and children? Do they show by example how to work through a disagreement or problem?

● Does the physical setup allow the teacher to focus on the children?

● Do housekeeping details keep teachers disconnected from children?

● Do teachers encourage children to use one another as resources?

● Do teachers take time to show children how to accomplish a task by themselves?

● Are girls complimented only on appearance and boys just for achievement? Are all children helped to appreciate similarities and differences?

● Do teachers use reasoning and follow-through?

● How and when do teachers interact with children?

● What is the teacher's posture and facial expression when involved in a problem situation?

● If I were a child, would I like to come to school here?

The answers to these questions provide teachers with a barometer of how well they are maintaining an atmosphere of positive social interaction. The most important thing to remember is that the way people feel about each other and how they express it has an impact on children.[2] Teachers must focus as much attention on the interpersonal part of the environment as they do on buying equipment or arranging the room. Chapter 11, on play, and Chapter 14, on social and emotional skills, will emphasize the interpersonal aspects of the environment further.

The Inclusive Environment. Consider Andrew (Rogers, 1994), who, at 5 years of age had a motor/muscle disability with some speech difficulties. His cognitive skills were very strong and his social skills very weak. Andrew's mother talked to everyone during class about Andrew's needs and fears. If he fell down, he had a hard time righting himself. He needed help sitting and standing. He was afraid of getting bumped because he couldn't catch himself before falling very hard and then could not get up. The children all agreed to be careful about roughhousing around him. *The setting for success was being created.*

Since Andrew did not have much control of his fine motor skills, we provided him with painting and playdough. We kept up the crafts table; soon he was gluing pictures on paper, with or without order, and was very proud of his accomplishments. He even started using scissors on simple patterns. *The physical environment was responding to his needs.*

He was a wonderful puzzle builder, and the other children asked for his help often when they were stuck. It was wonderful to watch how they included him in many things. They accepted his differences right from the beginning and treated him

---

OUR DIVERSE WORLD OUR DIVERSE WORLD OUR DIVERSE WORLD OUR DIVERSE WORLD OUR DIVERSE WORLD

[1]The first challenge is recognize biases; the next is to restructure and expand perceptions; and the greatest challenge is the part that children are most likely to notice—how one speaks, truly feels, and behaves.

[2]See footnote on page 299.

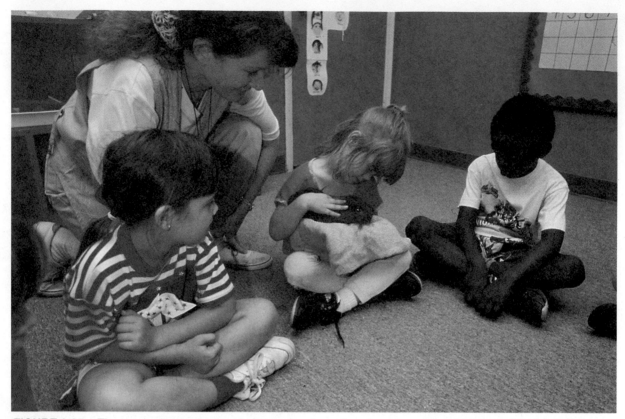

FIGURE 9.25 The teacher's posture and facial expressions show her respect for children and their learning pace and style.

just like all the rest—except they were careful when running and playing around him. His fear was apparent, and they respected it. *Thus the interpersonal environment was emerging.*

We had a regular P.E. time each day in the big room. We jumped rope, played "Simon Says," played "Red Light, Green Light," and ran obstacle courses. At first Andrew sat on the sidelines and watched. He cheered and looked interested, so I started asking him if he'd be my partner because I was a little afraid. At first he refused and told me to use someone else. I kept asking but would drop it as soon as he gave me his answer; then one day he said, "OK." We ran and jumped over the snake (rope), and all the kids laughed. We hugged, and that was the beginning. *When given the time that is needed (the temporal environment), the child triumphs.*

S U M M A R Y

A good environment for young children is a combination of many factors. Teachers must take into consideration the needs of the children, teachers, and parents as well as the program goals and objectives.

The physical environment includes the buildings and yard, the equipment and materials, and the way the space is organized and used. The setting is organized to support the program's goals and must meet necessary health and safety standards.

The daily schedule outlines the timetable of events. Time blocks are arranged around the daily routines of food, rest, and toileting. The temporal environment is balanced so that children alternate indoor and outdoor play, quiet and active play, and self-selected activities with teacher-directed learning. Good interactions between children and staff are characterized by warmth, personal respect, and responsiveness. It is the interpersonal relationships that set the tone in each environment. The size of the group, the number of teachers per child, and the quality of relationships affect the interpersonal environment.

It is essential to have a clear idea of program goals before arranging the environment. The environment mirrors those goals in the way the room is arranged, teachers are deployed, and the time schedule is framed. In early childhood settings where children's independence and self-reliance is valued, the environment is created to enhance the child's budding sense of autonomy. Anti-bias environments value individual differences in race, ethnicity, ability, and sex, and increase awareness of attitudes and institutions to help children develop positive identities. A peace education framework encourages children to learn to cooperate and resolve conflicts peaceably, as well as increase an understanding of war and peace. All environments reflect the goals through careful application of many factors.

Creating good environments for young children does not require great sums of money or newly designed buildings. In most settings, teachers can adapt general principles of environments to create challenging, safe, and effective group settings for children.

R E V I E W   Q U E S T I O N S

1. Why is there no standard or ideal environment for early childhood schools? How would you describe a good environment for one-year-olds? For three-year-olds? For six-year-olds? Why?

2. What are the three aspects of environments to consider when planning programs for children? What do you think of first and why?

3. Why is self-help a common goal in most early childhood settings? How can teachers support self-help in infants? In toddlers? In nursery schoolers? In school-aged children?

4. Discuss three school health and safety policies that help keep illness and injury to a minimum. Include how you would explain these guidelines to parents, and how you would handle a problem.

5. Why might educators want to create an anti-bias environment? How might that look in a multi-ethnic community? in a homogeneous setting?

6. Look at the daily schedule of an early childhood program. What transitions occur in the daily schedule, and how are they handled?

L E A R N I N G   A C T I V I T I E S

1. Hunch down on your knees and look at a classroom from the child's perspective. Describe what you see in terms of the principles of successful environments.

2. Examine a daily schedule from an early childhood center. What do you think are the program goals of the school? How can you tell? Compare this to a daily schedule of a family day care home. How are they alike? How are they different?

3. Below are listed some common problems that can be remedied by changing the environment. List at least one solution for each problem.

   a. Too many children crowding into one area

   b. Overcrowded shelves

   c. Grabbing or arguments over the same toy

   d. Hoarding of materials

   e. Lack of cooperation during cleanup

   f. Wheel toy collisions

   g. Children crying when others' parents leave

4. Visit a toddler program, a four-year program, and a kindergarten. How are the learning centers defined? Name the centers of interest and indicate which of them are for quiet play and which are for active play and work.

5. What are appropriate activities in a preschool for helping children understand violence? What might you do differently with first graders?

B I B L I O G R A P H Y

Aronson, Susan, M.D. "Health Concerns for Caregivers—Infectious Diseases and Job Stresses." *Exchange*, March, 1987.

Baker, B.R. "Transition Time: Make It a Time of Learning for Children." *Day Care and Early Education*, Summer, 1986.

Carlsson-Paige, Nancy, and Levin, Diane. *Peace, War, and the Nuclear Threat*. Washington, D.C.: National Association for the Education of Young Children, 1990 (3rd printing).

Cross, W.E. "Black Identity: Rediscovering the distinctions between personal identity and reference group orientations." In Spencer, Brookins, and Allen, *Beginnings: the Social and Affective Development of Black Children*. Hillsdale, NJ: Erlbaum, 1985.

Derman-Sparks, Louise, and the ABC Task Force. *Anti-bias Curriculum: Tools for Empowering Young Children*. Washington, D.C.: National Association for the Education of Young Children, 1989.

Dodge, Diane T., and Colker, Laura J. *The Creative Curriculum*. Washington, D.C.: Teaching Strategies, 1992 (3rd Ed.).

Early Years. "CDC Report." *Education Week*, January 16, 1991.

Edwards, Carolyn , Gandini, Leila, and Forman, George. *The Hundred Languages of Children*. Norwood, N.J.: Ablex Press, 1993.

Froschl, M., Rubin, E., and Sprung, B. *Including All of Us: An Early Childhood Curriculum about Disabilities*. New York: Educational Equity Concepts, 1984.

Frost, Joe L. "Children's Playgrounds: Research and Practice." In Fein and Rivkin (Eds.), *The Young Child at Play: Review of Research, Volume 4*. Washington, D.C.: National Association for the Education of Young Children, 1986.

Greenman, Jim. *Caring Spaces, Learning Places*. Redmond, Wash.: Exchange Press, 1988.

Gutierrez, M.E. *Chicano parents' perceptions of their children's racial/cultural awareness*. Unpublished master's thesis, Pacific Oaks College, Pasadena, CA, 1982.

—————. *Personal Communication*, 1987.

Harms, Thelma, and Clifford, R.M. *Early Childhood Environmental Rating Scale.* New York: Teachers College, 1980.

Honig, A.S. "Sex role socialization in early childhood," *Young Children*, 38 (6), pp. 57–90.

Howes, Carolee. *Keeping Current in Child Care Research: An Annotated Bibliography*. Washington, D.C.: National Association for the Education of Young Children, 1988.

Jones, Elizabeth. Personal notes, 1984, 1990, 1991.

Katz, Phyllis, "Development of children's racial awareness and intergroups attitudes." In L.G. Katz (ed.), *Current Topics in Early Childhood Education*. Norwood, NJ: Ablex, 1982.

Kendall, Frances. *Diversity in the Classroom*. New York: Teachers College Press, 1983.

Kutner, B. "Patterns of Mental Functioning Associated with Prejudice in Children." *Psychological Monographs*. 72 (406), pp. 1–48.

Malaguzzi, Loris. For An Education Based On Relationships. *Young Children*, Nov. 1993, pp. 9–12.

Marotz, Lynn, Rush, J.M., and Cross, M.Z. *Health, Safety, and Nutrition for the Young Child*. Albany, NY: Delmar Publishers, Inc., 1993 (3rd Edition).

Moore, G.T. *The Role of the Socio-physical Environment in Cognitive Development*. Milwaukee, WI: University of Wisconsin, 1983.

National Association for the Education of Young Children. *Accreditation Criteria and Procedures of The National Academy of Early Childhood Programs*. Washington, D.C.: National Association for the Education of Young Children.

Nelson, Dr. Michael A., and Raymond, Barbara. "Sports, Kids, Fun, & Safety" *Good Housekeeping*, September, 1989. (p. 4, and p. 52).

New, Rebecca. "Excellent Early Education: A City in Italy Has It." *Young Children*, September, 1990.

Ott, John N. "Design: Keep the Kids in Mind." In *Center Management*, September/October, 1990.

Phyfe-Perkins, E., and Shoemaker, J. "Indoor Play Environments: Research and Design Implications. "In G. Fein and M. Rivkin (Eds.), *The Young Child at Play; Reviews of Research, Volume 4*. Washington, D.C.: National Association for the Education of Young Children, 1986.

Prescott, Elizabeth. "The Physical Environment—a Powerful Regulator of Experience." *Exchange Magazine*, November, 1994.

Rogers, Cynthia. "Mainstreaming: Special Needs—Special Experiences." Unpublished paper, Spring, 1994.

Rubin, Kenneth H. "Play Behaviors of Young Children." *Young Children*, 32, 1977.

Sprung, Barbara. *Non-Sexist Education for Young Children*. New York: Citation Press, 1975.

Stonehouse, Anne. "The Golden Rule for Child Care." *Exchange*, November/December, 1990.

Waldorf School (author unknown). "What is a Waldorf Kindergarten?" Los Altos, Calif., January, 1995.

Winter, S. *Toddler Play in an Outdoor Play Environment*. Unpublished doctoral dissertation, University of Texas at Austin, 1983.

CHAPTER
10

Evaluating for
Effectiveness

QUESTIONS FOR THOUGHT

What is evaluation?

Why is evaluation important?

What are the components of good evaluations? What are some common problems

What is important to know about standardized testing and developmental/readiness screening?

How can children be assessed?

What are critical issues in teacher evaluation?

How can evaluating programs help children and teachers?

578

292

INTRODUCTION

Evaluations are a part of everyday life. We look out the window and assess the weather situation, then decide if we want to carry an umbrella. Before making a purchase, we read the label on the box of crackers. We size up a person we have just met. We check the newspapers to find out where our favorite football team is ranked.

We are constantly evaluating, judging, and rating. In education, we evaluate:

● *Curriculum.* Will this language game help develop the listening skills of three-year-olds?

● *Materials and equipment.* If we order the terrarium, will there be enough money for the math lab?

● *The environment.* Should the children begin school with free play or a group time? Where can we store the nap cots? Do the cubbies create a hazard out in the hallway?

● *Children's behavior.* Evan and Francie interrupt each other too much. Should they be placed in separate work groups?

● *Teacher effectiveness.* Sandra has a knack for making parents comfortable in her classroom. Audrey finds leading large groups difficult. Karl supervises student teachers with great skill. How can each be challenged supportively? How can each learn from the other?

What Is Evaluation?

Definition

Evaluation is a process. It is at once a definition, an assessment, and a plan. Defining the kind of weather outside helps a person evaluate what to wear. Assessing a person's manner and style determines whether or not to talk with that person at a party. Planning a meal involves evaluating who will be eating and what their food preferences may be. Evaluation involves making decisions, choices, and selections.

In its simplest form, evaluation is a process of appraisal. Think of the first time you ate at a new restaurant. What did you look for—the service, setting, range of menu, or costs? Were the portions related to the price? Were the clerks helpful or friendly? Would you go back or recommend it to a friend? We evaluate things on a daily basis, in order to understand and assess our lives and experiences. Making priorities about the relative importance of the menu or atmosphere of a restaurant is similar to planning how much space in the classroom will be given to blocks and art, or how long a period will be devoted to free play or group times. Deciding whether or not to revisit a restaurant is akin to deciding if a certain activity is worth repeating with a classroom of children, or whether a teacher candidate is asked for a second interview.

In educational circles, evaluations involve materials, people, and processes. Programs may be evaluated by taking an inventory of a school's curriculum and educational materials. Classroom organization may require mapping the environment,

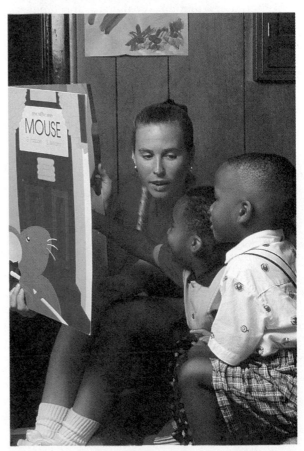

FIGURE 10.1 Evaluations are part of everday life in an early childhood setting. How are these children learning to listen? To relate to the teacher?

counting the number of play spaces in a room or yard, and evaluating the daily schedule. Observing and recording children's behavior could effectively evaluate behavior management techniques. Assessing teacher effectiveness requires gathering information about what teachers do and how they work. Feedback about performance is based on specific information concerning teacher behavior. Program evaluation might involve analyzing children, teachers, parents, and administration, and how they all work together to meet the goals of the program.

Premises

All evaluation procedures are based on three important premises:

1. *Evaluation must be part of the goal-setting process.* Without evaluation, goals are meaningless. Evaluation helps shape a goal into a meaningful plan of action. For instance, a family who wants to go weekend camping will have to decide what they need in order to pack their suitcases. In the classroom, teachers decide what they want their children to learn before ordering equipment for the program.

2. *Goals are based on expectations.* Everyone has standards for themselves and others. Standards are used to anticipate performance and behavior. Should the office buy a block of tickets to the upcoming soccer match? Many people would consider the team ranking and likelihood of a victory before making the decision. Teachers think about how two-year-olds will use puppets or what use the four-year-olds will make of wheel toys before purchasing equipment.

   In every early childhood setting, more than one set of expectations is at work. The director has job expectations of all the teachers. Teachers have standards of performance for themselves, the children, and parents. Parents have some expectations about what their children will do in school and about the role of the teachers. Children develop expectations regarding themselves, their parents, teachers, and the school.

3. *Evaluations determine the degree to which expectations are met.* By evaluating, people check to see if their goals have been realized. This can be as

simple as listening for the doorbell after hearing a car stop outside. It can be as complex as changing the curriculum to match the group as its needs and interests emerge during a school year, or as complex as analyzing questionnaires returned by parents. A good evaluation tool outlines clearly and specifically how expectations have been met. Evaluation is a system of mutual accountability. It is a way of stating expectations and defining how they are being met.

Why Evaluate?

In early childhood education, evaluations are used for several reasons. Teachers are aware that **evaluation** and *education* must be linked when creating good programs for children. To evaluate is to test the quality of the educational endeavor. Teachers are becoming more sophisticated in informal and formal assessments, in combining their daily observations with high-quality instruments that give a rich and full picture of each child or of the class as a whole. *Evaluation monitors growth, progress, and planning.*

Evaluation is a way to look at where and how improvements can be made; to challenge methods, assumptions, and purposes. Teachers and children are rated for their level of development and areas of growth. Environments are assessed to see if they foster behavior and learning according to their stated goals. Total programs are evaluated to see if they accomplish their objectives. In fact, *evaluations provide information* by which to rate performance, define areas of difficulty, and look for possible solutions.

Setting goals is a third reason for evaluating. In order to be useful, an evaluation must include suggestions for improving the performance or behavior. The assessment tool that only describes a situation is an unfinished evaluation; goals for improvement must be established.

Components of a Good Evaluation

Certain elements are common to all evaluations. The following criteria serve as a guideline to good evaluations:

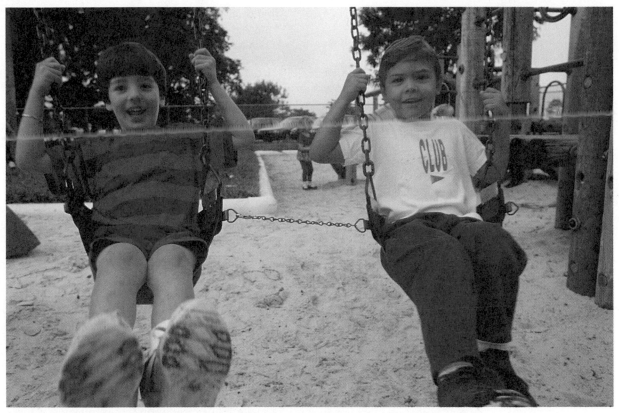

FIGURE 10.2   Know the reasons for making an evaluation. Evaluations should avoid unfair comparisons, acknowledge individual differences and uniqueness, and not look at children in a competitive manner.

1. *Select who or what will be evaluated.* Decide how often and under what circumstances the evaluation will take place.

2. *Have a clear purpose or motive.* Know the reasons you are making an evaluation and consider who or what will benefit from the process. State what you expect to gain from it.

3. *Decide how the data will be collected.* Have a good understanding of the process or format that will be used. For a report, discover what tools you might need and what is available to you. Outline who will collect the data and make the report. If more than one person is reporting, check for consistency among the evaluators. Sample tools for data collection may be found in Chapter 6 as well as later in this chapter.

4. *Know what use will be made of the evaluation.* Be aware of what decisions will be made from the results. Know who receives this information and how they will interpret it.

5. *State goals clearly.* Make sure goals and objectives are outlined in ways that can be measured and observed easily. State behavioral goals in terms of what the person will do.

6. *Make a plan.* Be prepared to act. Use the results to motivate people to put into action what they learned from the evaluation. Set new goals. Continue the process for another stated period of time. Set up a timetable to check progress on a regular basis.

Evaluations are deliberate and systematic ways to judge effectiveness. Since they are based on goals and expectations, all evaluations need some kind of **feedback loop** to recycle what is perceived (Steps 1–4) into action for improvement (Steps 5 and 6). Figure 10.21 illustrates how a feedback loop works for teacher evaluation. The important point to remember is that evaluation should be a continuous process, for without follow-through, long-lasting improvement is unlikely to occur.

Concerns

Of all the functions performed by teachers, probably none calls for more energy, time, and skill than evaluation. Be it of children, teaching, or the overall program, evaluation is challenging, sometimes one of the more difficult tasks teachers must perform. Anyone involved in evaluation should avoid:[1]

1. *Unfair comparisons.* Evaluations should be used to identify and understand the person or program involved, not to compare one to another in a competitive manner.

2. *Typecasting.* Evaluations can label unfairly or prematurely the very people they are intended to help. Insufficient data and overemphasis on the results are two areas that need close monitoring.

3. *Overemphasis on norms.* Most evaluation tools imply some level of normal behavior or performance, acceptable levels of interaction, or quantities of materials and space. People involved in an evaluation must remember to individualize the process, rather than try to fit a person or program into the mold created by the assessment tool.

4. *Interpretation.* There is sometimes a tendency to overinterpret or misinterpret results. Whether the evaluation assesses a child's skill, a teacher's performance, or an educational program, it must be clear *what* is being evaluated and *how* the information will be used. It is particularly important to be sensitive to the feelings of those being evaluated when communicating the results of the assessment. Parents and teachers need to interpret evaluations clearly and carefully if they are to understand the findings and feel comfortable with them.

5. *Too narrow a perspective.* An evaluation tool may focus too much on one area and not enough on others. Moreover, no single occasion or instrument will tell teachers all they need to know about a child's abilities, a teacher's performance, or a program's effectiveness. It is essen-

tial that information be gathered in many ways and on several occasions. Using a single yardstick to assess program effectiveness, for example, would ignore the comprehensive nature of the goals that most early childhood programs are designed to attain. These goals may encompass all areas of development while providing services for children and their parents that affect the health and well-being of the whole family. Sampling only children's skills as the single measure would lead to conclusions that were neither reliable nor valid. An imbalanced assessment gives an incomplete picture.

6. *Too wide a range.* An evaluation should be designed for a single level or age group and not cover too wide a range. It is appropriate to measure a child's ability to print at age six but not at age two. A teacher's aide should not be evaluated with the same method used to rate head or supervising teachers. The expectations of the person or task should be taken into account and the evaluation method modified accordingly.

7. *Too little or too much time.* The amount of time necessary to complete an evaluation must be weighed. The evaluation that is too lengthy loses its effectiveness in the time it takes. Time for interpretation and reflection must be included in the overall process.

For evaluations to be most productive, teachers must use caution in selecting an assessment method. Often, they will rework a common technique to meet their needs better. For instance, a testing tool could be used to describe children's skills, but the averages that accompany the test could be discarded. In this way, teachers would avoid overemphasizing norms (Caution 3), making unfair comparisons (Caution 1), or typecasting the children according to the results (Caution 2).

Sometimes a staff or administrator will design an instrument, rather than using one already devised. Individualizing the evaluation process can thus balance an assessment, giving a perspective that is more in tune with the individual or program in a particular setting (Caution 5). Periodic evaluation checks give more than one set of re-

[1]Numbers 1–6 directly relate to working in our diverse world.

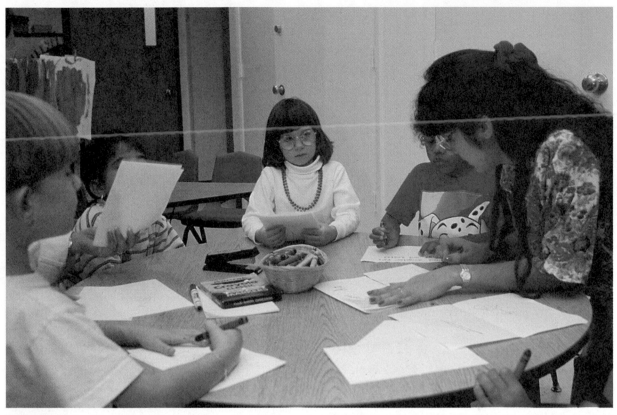

FIGURE 10.3 Evaluations in programs with a wide age range may need to be individualized to adequately record children's skills.

sults, so that early childhood personnel are less likely to misinterpret or overemphasize the data (Caution 4). A comprehensive evaluation done semiannually is more time efficient than a lengthy, detailed one done only once every year or so (Caution 7). In all evaluations, it is important to keep in mind that children and teachers are at various stages of development and skill; an assessment that is individualized or one in which a range of scores is acceptable allows for these variations (Caution 6).

Evaluations in the Early Childhood Setting

In the educational setting, the process of evaluation is separate from the teaching or instructing process (Spodek, 1978). Judging an activity, a child's growth, or a teacher's performance is something "extra," apart from the everyday routine of the class. Yet it need not always be so. Teaching and evaluating are closely integrated. As teachers examine how they work, they also look at the effect this has on the children, the curriculum, parent relationships, and themselves.

Evaluation is a very broad concept, often confused with testing and measurement. Formal testing or separated assessment is only one way of measurement. To be truly accurate, evaluations of children, teachers, and programs must be done in a multitude of ways, with a combination of informal and formal methods.

The teacher plays a critical role in the evaluation process. Through evaluation, teachers link specific goals to larger, more encompassing objectives, such as those illustrated in Figure 10.4. These goals focus on the relationship between teaching in the classroom and the overriding educational objectives. The teacher sees the broad picture and keeps a perspective on education that includes the children, the program, and the teaching staff.

Educational Aims	Behavioral Goals
To achieve independence and autonomy.	Children separate from their parents successfully; can manage their own clothing needs; initiate own activities.
To become a functional part of a larger society.	Children participate actively in small and large groups.
To learn to live effectively with others.	Children develop social skills with peers and adults, show tolerance of differences.
To learn basic tools for acquiring knowledge.	Children show signs of curiosity, memory, and symbol recognition.

FIGURE 10.4   Teachers relate what happens in the classroom (behavioral goals) to traditional educational goals.

The three areas of evaluations we will discuss in this chapter are: (1) evaluating children; (2) evaluating teachers; and (3) evaluating programs. The purposes underlying each type of evaluation will be examined, followed by specific techniques for effective evaluations.

EVALUATING CHILDREN

How do we evaluate children? What do we look for? How do we document growth and difficulties? How do we communicate our findings to parents? These questions focus our attention on children's issues and the evaluation process.

Why Evaluate?

Children are evaluated because teachers and parents want to know what the children are learning. Evaluations set the tone for a child's overall educational experience. Highlighting children's strengths builds a foundation from which to address their limitations or needs. The process of evaluating children attempts to answer several questions: Are children gaining appropriate skills and behaviors? In what activities does learning take place? What part of the program supports specific learning? Is the school philosophy being met? Are educational goals being met?

In evaluating children, teachers first decide *what it is they want to know about each child, and why.* With an understanding of children in general, teachers then concentrate on individual children and their unique development. Goals for children

stem from program objectives. For instance, if the school philosophy is, "Our program is designed to help children grow toward increasing physical, social, and intellectual competencies," an evaluation will measure children's progress in those three areas. One that claims to teach specific language skills will want to assess how speaking and listening is being accomplished.

Evaluations provide teachers with an opportunity to distance themselves from the daily contact with children and look at them in a more detached, professional way. Teachers can use the results to share their opinions and concerns about children with each other and with parents. For instance, an infant-toddler center might schedule parent conferences around a sequence of child evaluations: the first, a few weeks after the registration of the child; the second, 6 months after the child's admission into the program; and the third, just before the move up to an older age group (such as moving from the infant to the toddler class), which would include the parents and two teachers, the current and the receiving one (La Guardia, 1992). This concentrated effort expands everyone's vision of who and what the child can be, highlights patterns of the child's behavior, and helps in understanding the meaning of that behavior. It gives teachers the chance to chart growth and acknowledge progress and, in doing so, sets the child apart as an individual and unique human being. Evaluations are a reminder to all that they work with individuals and not just a group.

Of course, evaluations contain varying degrees of subjectivity and opinion. To be reliable and valid, multiple sources of information should be used. Chapter 6 contains specific tools for direct observation of children, and Chapter 8 discusses parent interviews, both of which are useful in assessing children (Cryan, 1986; Meisels, 1989, NAEYC, 1987). A proper evaluation of a child documents a child's growth over time (for instance, keeping a portfolio of the child's creations, dictations, teacher observations—anecdotes of behavior or snips of conversations overheard). The Focus Box by Gayle Mindes offers some key ideas about child assessment.

In general, evaluations are made to:

1. Establish a baseline of information about each child by which to judge future progress.

2. Monitor the growth of individual children.

3. Have a systematic plan for intervention and guidance.

4. Plan curriculum.

5. Provide parents with updated information on their child.

6. Provide information for making administrative decisions.

To Establish a Baseline

One purpose of evaluating children is to establish a starting point of their skills and behavior. This is the beginning of a collection over a period of time of important information on each child. Through this cumulative record, teachers learn a great deal about the children: whom they play with, how they spend their time, how they handle problems, what fears and stress they show. In other words, they learn a lot about how children live their lives.

A baseline is a picture of the status of each child; an overview of individual development. It shows where the child is in relation to the school's objectives since the child is being measured according to program expectations. Baseline data give a realistic picture of a child at that moment in time, but there is a presumption that the picture will change.

A Baseline Tool. The beginning of the school term is an obvious time to start collecting information. Records of a child are established in the con-

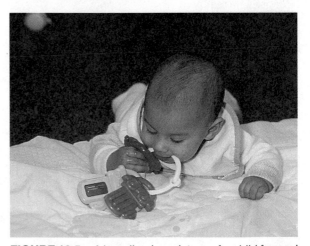

FIGURE 10.5 A baseline is a picture of a child framed at a particular moment. Infants' use of materials, fine-muscle control, and task persistence can all be seen in these assessments.

The Three R's of Assessment

Gayle Mindes

Early childhood teachers assess young children for a variety of purposes:

- to plan what, when and how to teach children

- to describe developmental progress and process

- to screen young children who may have special needs

- to document classroom progress and achievement

● to prove accountability

Each of these assessment activities requires careful matching of purpose to method, to assessment, to interpretation and to decision. Teachers must be *responsible* for the decisions that they make, *responsive* to the children they teach and *realistic* in their assessment schedule.

Responsible teachers

- know methods of assessment: observation, interviews, performance tasks, portfolios, tests

- choose the method appropriate for the necessary assessment decision

- know the limitations of each method

● understand the measurement concepts associated with performance tasks and tests

- consider the social/cultural contexts that impact assessment practices

● recognize the time limited nature of assessment results in the lives of young children

Responsive teachers

● link observation to action in the classroom

● guide children in assessing themselves and assuming responsibility for their own learning

● involve parents in the assessment process

● help the public understand the ways young children learn and appropriate documentation of this learning

Realistic teachers

● schedule routinely for assessment activities

● involve children, parents, administrators in the process

● identify ways to collect multi-purpose material for diverse assessment questions

● collect enough information to accurately and fairly answer assessment questions

● limit the volume of stored information in portfolios and elsewhere

Assessment is part of teaching: choose philosophy and goals, choose strategies for groups and individuals, teach, check that the strategies work, modify the teaching, monitor progress, report the results. Assessment must be purposeful, accurate, easy to use, appropriate for child, parent, teacher, community involvement. Assessment is a continuous sifting of information for decision making. Practiced this way, teachers are *responsible, responsive* and *realistic* in assessment activities.

Gayle Mindes, Ed.D. is a Professor of Education at DePaul University in Chicago, and author of Assessing Young Children, Delmar Publishers, 1996.

ENTRY-LEVEL ASSESSMENT

1. Child's name _____ Teacher _____
   Age _____ Sex _____ Class _____
   Major language _____ Fluency in English?_____
   Any previous school experiences? _____
   Siblings/others in household _____
   Family situation (one/two parents, other adults, etc.) _____
2. Separation from parent:
   Smooth _____ Some anxiety _____ Mild difficulty _____ Unable to separate _____
   Did parent have trouble separating? _____
   Comments: _____
3. How does child come to and leave from school?
   Parent _____Carpool _____Babysitter _____Bus _____
4. Physical appearance:
   General health _____
   Expression _____
   Dress _____
   Body posture _____
5. Self-care:
   Dressing: Alone _____ Needs assistance _____
   Toileting: By self _____ Needs help _____
   Eating: _____
   Toothbrushing: _____
   Sleeping/resting: _____
   Allergies/other health-related problems: _____
6. Child's Interests:
   Indoors:
   Clay _____ Books _____ Puzzles _____ Water play _____ Easels _____ Language _____
   Table/rug toys _____ Sensory choices _____ Art _____ Science _____ Blocks _____
   Outdoors:
   Swings _____ Climbers _____ Sandbox _____ Water play _____
   Wheel toys _____ Animals _____ Group games _____ Woodworking _____
   Group times (level of participation): _____
7. Social-emotional development:
   a. Initiates activities _____ Plays alone _____ Seems happy _____ Has to be invited _____
      Brings security object _____ Seems tense _____
   b. Plays mostly with children of: Same age _____ Younger _____ Older _____
   c. Moves into environment: Easily _____ Hesitantly _____ Not at all _____ Wanders _____
   d. Special friends: _____
   e. Does the child follow teachers? _____ Anyone in particular? _____
8. Cognitive development:
   Use of language: Follows directions _____ Clear pronunciation _____ Memory _____
   Curiosity _____ Holds conversations _____ Words/Phrases _____
9. Physical development
   Climbs safely _____ Uses scissors _____ Hand preference _____ Runs smoothly _____
   Uses pens, brushes _____ Foot preference _____ Handles body well _____
10. Goals/Points to remember: _____
   _____
   _____
   _____

FIGURE 10.6 Entry level assessments collect baseline information. Once teachers and children have had some time together, these first impressions can be documented.

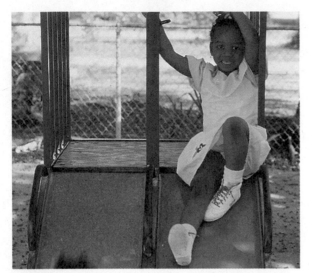

FIGURE 10.7 On her own! An evaluation can capture children's development in all skill areas, including self-concept.

text of the child's history and family background. Parents frequently submit this information with an application to the school. Teachers can gather the data by visiting the child at home or holding a parent conference and speaking directly with the parents about the child's development.

An *entry-level assessment* made during the first few weeks of school can be informative, particularly when added to the child's family history. The evaluation itself should be done informally, with teachers collecting information as children engage naturally with materials and each other. A few notes jotted during the first month of school can serve as a beginning collection of pertinent data about the child. Or the format can be more structured, such as in Figure 10.6.

Application. Teachers then use this information to understand children and their various levels of development. They can see children's strengths and weaknesses and where future growth is likely to occur. When the information is shared with parents, they feel more relaxed about their child and even laugh when they recall those first few days of school. One must remember, however, that the entry assessment is only a first impression. Care must be taken to avoid creating a self-fulfilling prophesy by labeling children so that they become shaped into those beginning patterns. Again,

teachers must be mindful of the cautions associated with all assessments as they document children's early behaviors. Still, so much happens in that short period of time; the rich information we gain from documenting this growth is invaluable.

Goals and Plans. Teachers use baseline data to set realistic goals for individual children. They tailor the curriculum to the needs and interests they have observed. An entry-level assessment is a vehicle for watching children's growth throughout the year. For instance, after setting a baseline of Mariko's language ability in English, teachers plan activities to increase her understanding and use of language. Then, they make periodic checks on her increased vocabulary as the school year progresses.

To Monitor Children's Progress

Teachers use evaluations to document children's growth. Data collected provide evidence of children's growth or lack of progress. A careful evaluation of each child furnishes the teaching staff with the necessary foundation from which they can plan the next steps.

Hita has mastered the brushes at the easel. Now we can encourage her to try the smaller brushes in table painting.

Enrico has been asking how to spell simple words. Let's see that he gets some time away from the blocks to work with him.

All the children seem able to separate from their parents and say goodbye comfortably. How can we celebrate this progress with the group?

A Progress Tool. Figure 10.8 is a sample *midyear evaluation*. Criteria for each area of development are included to build a profile of the whole child. Teachers note the intervention and guidance steps they plan, where appropriate. While a general form is outlined here, early education teachers individualize their assessments to specify the skills of their group; an infant/toddler group would have different age-appropriate skills than those of a preschool or primary-age class. Such a revised form should include what the child will do to show a suitable level of behavior in each developmental level.

A TOOL FOR MONITORING CHILDREN'S PROGRESS

Check one of the evaluations below for each skill area; for those that need work, document with specific examples.

Developmental Area	Age Appropriate	Highly Skilled	Needs Work
Self-Management Personal care Making choices Following routines	*Can feed, dress, toilet self well* *Prefers indoors to outside* *Does fine in routines*		

Physical/Motor
1. Fine Motor
   Art materials
   Woodworking tools
   Manipulatives
	Uses easels—brushes good grasp, pens also
	Likes blocks, table toys
	Hasn't chosen woodworking, but watches often		

2. Gross Motor
   Ball handling
   Balancing
   Jump/hop/skip
			Very cautious, seems fearful
			Won't swing, slide, use climber
			Wanders outdoors, sometimes does music
			Runs away when wheel toys are rolled down hill

Communication and Language Vocabulary Articulation Comprehension English as a second language Converses with children Converses with adults Listens Expresses self (needs, ideas, feelings)		*Exceptionally strong* *Converses with adults daily* *Responds to children but rarely initiates talk* *Outstanding at grouptime——lots of ideas* *Talks around fears, but fears seem to keep him from trying*	

Cognitive Development
Sees cause and effect
Processes and uses information
Solves problems with:
  objects
  peers
  adults
Premath (sequencing, measuring, numbers)
Prereading concepts (size, colors, shapes, letters, position)
		Dylan has so much information to share, and lots of interest in problem-solving with indoor materals and interactions with teachers.
		We wish he could extend these skills into work with children and open up a bit more.	

Social-Emotional Independence/initiative Positive self-concept Recognizes/accepts own feelings Deals with frustration Flexibility Leadership Initiates social contacts Prosocial behaviors (friendly, sharing, inclusive, cooperative, empathetic) Child-child interactions Child-adult interactions	*Does well on own, gets around* *Is comfortable and confident around adults*		*Seems hesitant/fearful outdoors* *Is more solitary or onlooker; is this self-esteem or just fear?* *Don't know about leadership yet; have seen little because of lack of interaction with children*

OVERALL STRENGTHS: GOALS:

FIGURE 10.8   A midyear evaluation is a more detailed description of the child. It highlights areas of concern and progress. (Developed by Bing Nursery School, Stanford University, 1975 to 1990.)

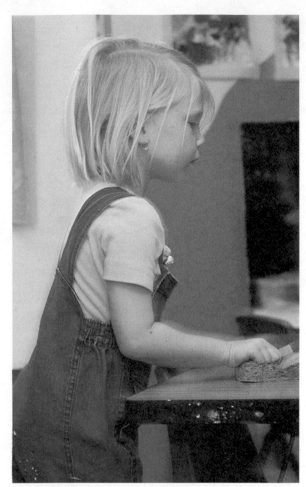

FIGURE 10.9 What do children need from a program? Evaluation assesses each individual's needs for guidance or help, such as learning the new self-help skill of cleaning a table.

Application. Information about a child will be used to assess growth and change. How often this happens can vary. Although many changes occur in rapid succession in these early years, it takes time for a child to integrate life experiences and for teachers to see them expressed as a permanent part of behavior. Evaluating too frequently does not reveal sufficient change to make it worthwhile and places an added burden on the teaching staff as well.

Once the initial baseline data has been gathered, a progress evaluation approximately every three months seems reasonable. In a normal school year, this would mean establishing a baseline in the fall and checking progress in the winter and the spring. For centers operating on a year-round basis, a brief summer report would be in order. These need not be time consuming. Many evaluations take the form of a checklist and can be accomplished while the class is in session.

Goals and Plans. Goals are established for children as a result of an assessment. These goals are changed as growth takes place. A good assessment tool monitors progress in each developmental area so that plans can be made to challenge the child physically, socially, emotionally, creatively, and intellectually.

At the same time, theory reminds us that the child develops as a whole, with each area of growth influencing and being influenced by what changes take place in other areas. Evaluations that document growth include information so that all teachers see the interrelationships among areas of development. By assessing growth in individual areas, teachers relate that development to the child's collective abilities, as in this example:

> Dylan's midyear report shows that he lacks dexterity in running and climbing, and that he is exceptionally strong in verbal and listening skills. This influences his development in the following areas:
>
> *Emotionally.* He appears to lack self-confidence, and his self-esteem deteriorates the longer he feels inept at physical skills. He may even be afraid to master the art of climbing and running for fear he will fail.
>
> *Socially.* Children tease Dylan because he often cannot keep up with them while playing outside. He often ends up playing alone or watching the other children in more active pursuits.
>
> *Intellectually.* There is a lack of risk taking in Dylan's whole approach to play. Because of his slow physical development, he seems unlikely to challenge himself in other ways.
>
> Dylan's progress report thus sets a primary goal in physical/motor skills, with the knowledge that such growth can positively affect learning in other areas. Teachers also plan the strategy of helping him talk about what he likes and dislikes about the outdoors and collecting some stories that depict characters persisting to master difficulties (such as *The Little Engine That Could*), using his strength as a springboard for growth.

CHILD GUIDANCE FORM

Presentation of Problems (In behavioral terms)

What behaviors are causing the staff concern? Be specific. Limit to three problems or concerns.

1.
2.
3.

Family History (Information from family, medical info if needed)

School History (Child's relations to adults, children, materials, activities)

Intervention (What procedures have and have not worked? What strengths does the child bring to this issue?)

Future Plans (What is going to happen as a result?)

1. In classroom

2. With parents

3. Date for reviewing results

FIGURE 10.10   One purpose of evaluating children is to plan for behavior management. A good evaluation form will include how to follow through on the plans made for intervention. (Adapted from K. McLaughlin and S. Sugarman.)

To Plan for Guidance and Intervention

A third purpose for evaluation is to help teachers determine guidance procedures. These are based on insights and perceptions brought into focus through the evaluation. This process serves as a primary tool on which guidance and planning are based. When teachers see a problem behavior or are concerned about a child, they plan for further assessment. If a developmental screening is done to assess if a child has a learning problem or needs special services, teachers will either refer the family to a proper specialist or agency or administer the screening themselves. Developmental screening tests will be discussed further in this chapter.

A Guidance Tool. Evaluations help in behavior management. Once a need has been pinpointed,

the teaching staff decides how to proceed. Individual problems are highlighted when teachers make a point of concentrating on the child's behavior. Figure 10.10 illustrates a form used to determine intervention. Used at a team meeting, this form demonstrates what steps are to be taken in addressing the concern directly. It also helps teachers clarify how to talk to parents in a concerned and supportive manner.

Application. The following case studies demonstrate how information from evaluations are used for guidance and intervention:

Elizabeth's recent evaluation revealed an increase in the number of toilet accidents she has had. The staff noted a higher incidence during midmorning snacks, but came to no conclusion as to the cause. They agree to continue to treat her behavior in a relaxed manner, and have one teacher remind Eliza-

Summary of Development/Fall Progress Reports (see forms for details)
Developmental Area: + = fine; − = needs work; ? = don't know

Child	Physical	Language	Cognitive	Social	Emotional	Creative
Greg	−	+	+	+	−	?
Anwar	?	−	+	−	−	+
San-Joo	+	?	?	−	+	+
Reva	+	+	+	+	+	+
Katy	−	+	?	?	?	−

Group Goals for Winter:
- Emphasize social and emotional areas of curriculum.
- Plan physical games (indoor games because of weather).

Individual Goals for Winter:

Greg: Encourage some creative arts, games. Observe creativity in intellectual activities.

Anwar: Needs to be helped to feel confident and express himself; don't push too hard on physical risks yet.

San-Joo: Need assessment of language and cognitive skills; observe use of table toys, receptive language at group time.

Reva: What is the next step? Is she ready for helping the others? Involve her with 100-piece puzzles and the computer.

Katy: Need to focus on her overall development; too many unknowns—is she getting enough individual attention?

FIGURE 10.11   A group chart. Teachers can use individual assessment tools to plan for the entire group and for each child in the class.

beth to use the toilet before she washes her hands for snack. At the same time, they make plans to contact the parents for further information and insights. They will confer again afterwards and agree upon an approach.

Trevor's parents report that he says he has no friends at school. At their staff meeting, the teachers make plans to suggest that Trevor's parents invite Ryan and Brooke to play with Trevor at home. Teachers have seen both children approach him, but he didn't seem to know how to respond. At school, the teachers will give Trevor verbal cues when children make attempts to play with him.

Goals and Plans. An evaluation tool, such as the *child guidance form* in Figure 10.10, helps teachers set goals for children. By narrowing the focus to include only those behaviors that concern the staff, the needs of many children can be reviewed quickly.

To Plan Curriculum

Teachers plan curriculum based on children's evaluations. Translating the assessment to actual classroom practice is an important part of the teacher's role. A thorough evaluation helps teachers plan appropriate activities to meet children's needs.

Planning Tools. All three of the previous evaluation tools can be used to plan curriculum. The entry-level assessment and midyear report are often summarized in a group chart, such as in Figure 10.11. One such chart, made at the end of the first semester of a prekindergarten class, revealed this pattern:

At least one third of the class was having trouble listening at group time, as evidenced by the group chart that identified "Group Time" and "Language Listening Skills" as areas for growth for nearly half the children. The staff centered their attention on the group time content. It was concluded that a story made the group times too long; the children were restless throughout most of the reading. It was agreed to move storytime to just before nap and shorten the group time temporarily.

Evaluation also applies to daily events, such as individual projects and the day as a whole. One tool for curriculum evaluation reviews the results of a specific activity. Figure 10.12 is a sample of that

Activity _____
How many children participated? _____ Did any avoid the activity? _____
How involved did children become? Very ___ Briefly ___ Watched only ___
What were children's reactions? Describe what they said and did. _____
_____
_____
_____
_____

What did you do to attract children? To maintain their interest? _____
_____
_____
_____
_____

How would you rate the success of this activity? Poor ___
Adequate ___ Good ___ Great ___ Why? _____
What skills/abilities were needed? Did the children exhibit the skills? ____
_____
_____

What parts of the activity were most successful? Why? _____ ___
_____
_____

Describe any difficulty you encountered. Give reasons and tell how you
would handle it if it happened again. _____
_____
_____
_____

If you did this activity again, what would you change? _____

In light of your evaluation, what would you plan for a follow-up activity?
_____
_____

How did this activity compare with your goals and expectations? _____
_____

FIGURE 10.12   Evaluating daily activities lets teachers use assessment as a planning tool. Whereas every activity will not need this scrutiny on a daily basis, careful planning and evaluation create effective classrooms. (Adapted from Vassar College Nursery School.)

kind of curriculum assessment. Chapter 11 discusses the planning of curriculum in further detail.

Application. Evaluation results assist teachers in seeing more clearly the strengths and abilities of each child in the class. Curriculum activities are then planned that will continue to enhance the growth of that child. Also, areas of difficulty will be identified:

Jolene has trouble mastering even the simplest puzzle. Provide her with common shapes found in attribute blocks (small plastic shapes of varying color, thickness, size) and do some matching exercises with her.

The younger children in the class are reluctant to try the climbing structures designed by the older ones. Build an obstacle course with the youngest children, beginning with very simple challenges and involving the children in the actual planning and building as well as rehearsing climbing techniques with them.

Goals and Plans. Each of the previous case studies demonstrates how evaluation tools can be used to plan curriculum. By analyzing both group and individual skills through periodic assessment, teachers maintain a secure and challenging environment.

To Communicate with Parents

Plans for evaluating children should include the means by which parents are to be informed of the results. Once the teachers have identified a child's needs and capabilities, parents are entitled to hear the conclusions. The teaching staff has an obligation to provide a realistic overview of the child's progress and alert the parents to any possible concerns. (See Chapter 8 for details about parents and teachers working together.)

Using the Child Guidance Form (Figure 10.10), teachers define problem behavior for a child and work closely with the parents to reach a solution:

> Yum-Tong refuses to let his mother leave. The teachers agree that there are two issues: (1) Y.-T.'s screaming and crying as his mother leaves, and (2) his inability to focus on an activity while she attempts to go (though she stays as soon as he starts screaming). The family has told them that their other two children had separation problems as preschoolers. The previous school asked the parents to stay until the children stopped protesting, although the parents report that this took nearly six months and so was a hardship for them in their work places.[1]
>
> The teachers choose to intervene by asking Yum-Tong's mother to plan ahead with Y.-T., deciding before school how they will spend five minutes together each morning. After playing and helping him to settle in, she will then say good-bye and leave Y.-T. with Pete, his favorite teacher. Pete will be prepared to be with him at the departure and stay with him until he calms down. They also plan

to have a conference date after two weeks of this intervention plan to follow through and review how it is working for everyone.

A Tool with Parents. Teachers and parents need to talk together, especially when problems are revealed by the evaluation. As parents and teachers share knowledge and insights, a fuller picture of the child emerges for both. Each can then assume a role in the resolution of the problem. The role of the teacher will be defined in the context of the parents' role, and the parents will be guided by the teacher's attitudes and actions.

Evaluation tools can help parents target areas in which their child may need special help. A child guidance form (Figure 10.10) is an effective tool for parent-teacher conferences and as a method for forming intervention plans. Chapter 8 discusses the parent-teacher relationship and offers guides for effective parent-teacher conferences. The tool that works best is one that summarizes the school's concerns and solicits high parent involvement.

Application. Aside from identifying normal behavior problems, evaluations may raise questions concerning a child's physical development, hearing and visual acuity, or language problems. Potentially serious problems may emerge from the evaluation, and parents can be encouraged to seek further professional guidance.

Goals and Plans. Since evaluation is an ongoing process, reevaluation and goal-setting are done regularly. Communicating to parents both progress and new goals is critical for the *feedback loop* of an evaluation form to be effective, as shown in Figure 10.21.

To Make Administrative Decisions

Evaluation results can help a school make administrative decisions. They can lead to changes in the overall program or in the school's philosophy. For example, a child care component might be

OUR DIVERSE WORLD OUR DIVERSE WORLD OUR DIVERSE WORLD OUR DIVERSE WORLD OUR DIVERSE WORLD

[1]Teachers need to examine theories of child development and practice for ethnocentricity (i.e. in Western-European and American culture it may be seen as the sign of a secure attachment if a parent and child separate comfortably and quietly, whereas in another culture a secure attachment may be demonstrated by a passionate and emotion-laden farewell).

FIGURE 10.13   Assessing the group is one reason to evaluate children. These children are ready for more engaging and challenging group-time activities.

added to the half-day program after learning that most children are enrolled in another child care situation after nursery school. Or an evaluation might conclude that there is too little emphasis on developing gross-motor skills and coordination. To invite more active play, the administration might decide to remodel the play yard and purchase new equipment.

In the early childhood setting, both **informal** and **formal methods** are used for evaluating children. *Informal* and *homemade methods* such as those in Chapter 6 and Figures 10.6, 10.8, 10.10, 10.11, and 10.12 include observation, note taking, self-assessments, parent interviews and surveys, samples of children's work, and teacher-designed forms. More *formal* kinds of *evaluations* are used also, although somewhat less frequently in the early years. These include standardized tests and various "screening" instruments. The yearly tests taken in school, using a Number 2 pencil, are an example of such procedures. Those and other

standardized forms are examples of formal methods of evaluation. Commercially developed, these tests usually compare the individual child's performance to a predetermined norm. It is important to choose assessment tools and techniques that are appropriate for the group or the child under consideration. Informal observations can be made more systematic (see Chapter 6) or comprehensive to gain more information about a specific problem. Formal, commercially developed instruments need to be used more carefully (see Testing and Screening).

An Administrative Tool. Many kindergartens and some nursery schools use various kinds of "screening" tests, before children begin school in the fall. The usual purpose of these evaluations is to determine readiness; that is, to verify that the child will be able to cope with and succeed in school. These tools are best devised with the individual child in mind. Their purpose is positive: to highlight the skills the child has and to identify the areas in which the child may need help in the next class. Figure 10.14 shows a homemade screening evaluation that was developed for individual four-to-five-year-old preschoolers who were leaving for kindergarten. The activity employs a one-to-one, game-like approach in which a child and a favorite teacher can explore both strengths and difficulties in a safe, supportive setting.

Some teachers conclude the year with a summary report. This evaluation serves as an overview of what a child has accomplished, what areas of strength are present, and what future growth might occur. These records are useful to parents as a summary of their child's learning experiences. Teachers may use them as references should they ever be consulted by another school about the child. Again, it is critical to administer these assessments in a sensitive and accepting manner, to keep the time period as brief as possible, and to communicate the results in the same tone. If this is not done, the child's self-esteem may be damaged and the parents' trust may be lost. The disadvan-

tages of these tools parallel those of standardized tests (see next section).

Application. Making administrative decisions based on evaluation results is a sound idea. Assessments give administrators specific and verifiable information on which to base decisions.

The issue of readiness or placement of children is difficult and complex. The next section describes the potential problems and misapplications of tests in this regard. Whether or not a child is ready to succeed in a program affects parents and children personally. Having a good evaluation tool helps in making such decisions equitably and in communicating results in a clear and kind manner.

Goals and Plans. The evaluation tool that gives a specific profile of a child's skills will allow an administrator to share information with a family clearly and honestly. By carefully choosing a tool, administrators give the parents information they can use to plan for the child's development.

SKILLS INVENTORY

Child _____ Age _____ Teacher _____
Date _____

Task	Teacher Comments
Cognitive Skills	
1. Can you say the alphabet?	1. Sequence correct? Yes ___ No ___ Length:
2. Can you tell me what these letters are?	2. Number of letters correct ___ Comment:
3. Can you count for me?	3. Note how far: Sequence correct how far? ___
4. Please point to the number.	4. 3-1-6-4-8-2-9-7-5 How many correct? ___
5. Can you put these in order from smallest to biggest? Which is the largest? Smallest? First? Last?	5. Three sizes of triangles. Comments:
6. What color is this? If child cannot, then ask to "Point to the red one," etc.	6. Point to red, blue, yellow, black, green, orange, brown, purple, Comments:
7. What shapes are these? If child cannot, then ask to "Point to the circle," etc.	7. Point to circle, square, triangle, rectangle. Comments?
8. Can you find your shoulders? Elbow? Thumb? Neck? Lips?	8. Comments:

FIGURE 10.14 By creating effective tools for assessment, we are able to evaluate children's developing skills and their readiness for the next educational step. (Developed by Bing Nursery School, Stanford University, 1975 to 1990.)

Task	Teacher Comments
9. Name all the animals you can think of.	9. Comments:
10. Please put these animals into two groups. One has the animals that live in water, and the other the ones that live on the land.	10. Giraffe, deer, cat, frog, alligator, shark, goldfish
11. Here is a bear and a cube. Put the cube on top of the bear. Under the bear. Behind the bear. Beside the bear.	11. Check correct responses:
12. Here are three pictures. Can you put them in order so that they tell a story?	12. Tree with green leaves. Tree with orange/red leaves, falling. Bare tree. Comments:

Auditory-Perceptual Listening Skills

Task	Teacher Comments
1. Please repeat these numbers after I say them (Practice with 6–3–1–4): 5–3–8–2 2–7–9–3	1. Sequence correct? Numbers correct?
2. Tell me the sentence in the same order as I say. (Practice with "The dog ran to the park.") The mother pointed to the airplane in the sky.	2. Sequence correct? Words correct?
3. Listen to what I say, and then do what my words tell you. (Practice with "Put your hands on your head.") Stand up, go to the door, and walk back to me.	3. Comments:

Fine-Motor Skills

Task	Teacher Comments
1. Print your name.	1. Note grasp, hand preference.
2. Draw a circle, square, triangle, rectangle.	2. Comments:
3. Write the letters: O E P A J	3. Comments:
4. Write the numbers: 1 3 7 2 5	4. Comments:
5. Cut out a circle.	5. Note scissor grasp, hand preference.
6. Draw the best person that you can. Have you left anything out?	6. Comments:

Gross-Motor Skills

Task	Teacher Comments
1. Jump on two feet from A to B.	1. Note balance.
2. Hop on one foot from B to A.	2. Note balance.
3. Skip from A to B.	3. Comments:
4. Walk backwards from B to A.	4. Comments:
5. Stand on one foot while I count to three.	5. Note balance.
6. Walk across this balance board.	6. Note balance.
7. Can you jump over these poles with your feet together?	7. Comments:
8. How high can you climb our climber? Go up our slide?	8. Comments:
9. Now run from the climber to the fence and back to me as fast as you can!	9. Note gait and balance.
10. Please throw the ball to me. Catch it. Kick it.	10. Comments:

FIGURE 10.14 *Continued*

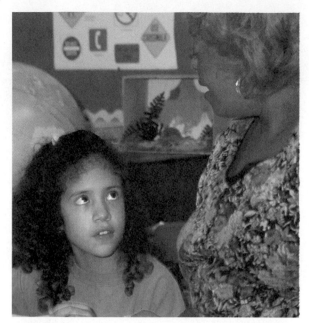

FIGURE 10.15 Fine-motor skills are one indicator of an ability to succeed in school and should be assessed as regularly as cognitive or socioemotional abilities.

Testing and Screening

The practice of testing and screening for readiness and/or retention has increased dramatically in the last decade. With the passage of Public Law 94-142 (Education for All Handicapped Children Act) and the early childhood amendment to the law (P.L. 99-457), states now have the responsibility to establish specific procedures and policies to identify, evaluate, and provide services to all children with learning problems. Moreover, testing for admittance to kindergarten or promotion to first grade has become more commonplace. The results are that more and more children are being denied entrance to a school system, being put in extra-year or pull-out programs, or being placed in kindergarten twice. Such practices raise some practical and serious philosophical issues.

● Young children do not function well in common test situations, nor do the test results necessarily reflect children's true knowledge or skills (Schultz, 1989).

● These practices (often based on inappropriate uses of readiness or screening tests) disregard the potential, documented long-term negative effects of retention on children's self-esteem and the fact that such practices disproportionately affect low-income and minority children. (NAEYC, 1988).

● While the most needed and appropriate tests (teacher-made) are the hardest to create, the standardized ones are frequently misused and misunderstood by teachers and parents (Cryan, 1986).

● Teachers are pressured into running programs that overemphasize the testing situation and test items.

● Most tests focus on cognitive and language skills; such as a narrow focus ignores other areas of development.

The practice of standardized testing has caused early childhood curriculum to become increasingly academic. Early childhood educators and parents are alarmed that:

> Many kindergartens are now structured, "watered-down" first grades, emphasizing workbooks and other paper-and-pencil activities that are inappropriate for 5-year-olds. The trend further trickles down to preschool and child care programs that feel that their mission is to get children "ready" for kindergarten. Too many school systems, expecting children to conform to an inappropriate curriculum and finding large numbers of "unready" children, react to the problem by raising the entrance age for kindergarten and/or labeling the children as failures.
>
> (NAEYC, 1988)

The implications of such testing further erode the curriculum when teachers, wanting their classes to do well on the test, alter activities to conform to what will be tested. They then begin teaching children to learn "right" answers rather than to engage in active, critical thinking. Rather than making teachers more accountable, "the overuse (and misuse) of standardized testing has led to the adoption of inappropriate teaching practices as well as admission and retention policies that are not in the best interests of individual children or the nation as a whole" (NAEYC, 1988).

Teachers and schools are beginning to respond to the overuse and inappropriate use of tests. The National Association of Elementary School

Principals now urges limited use of formal tests and retention. The Texas Board of Education has barred retention before first grade, and in New York State a coalition of groups is urging a ban on mass standardized testing of children before grade three.

Testing does have appropriate uses, such as using valid screening tests to "identify children who, because of the risk of possible learning problems or a handicapping condition, should proceed to a more intensive level of diagnostic assessment" (Meisels, 1989). The section "Evaluating Children" in this chapter demonstrates nonstandardized instruments that can be used to plan programs that respond to the individual children in them. NAEYC has adopted specific guidelines for the use of standardized testing which include using only reliable and valid instruments, and interpreting the test results accurately and cautiously to parents and others (NAEYC, 1988).

Perhaps most important is the reminder to all teachers that tests have no special magic. Evaluation is *more* than testing. A standardized test, a homemade tool (see Figure 10.14), or a screening instrument should only be one of several measures used to determine a child's skills, abilities, or readiness. Any test result should be part of a multitude of information, such as direct observation (see Chapter 6), parental report, and children's actual work. Above all, keep the testing to a minimum, thus guarding against "pulling up the plants to look at them before the roots take hold" (Cryan, 1986).

EVALUATING TEACHERS

It is understood that teachers are the *single most important* factor in determining program quality. What makes "the effective teacher" has no one simple answer. However, there are ways to evaluate teachers that guide them toward more effective teaching, in their work with children, coworkers, parents, and administrators.

Think of teachers as conductors of a symphony orchestra. They do not compose the music. They do not design or build the instruments, nor do they decide which ones will be played in the orchestra pit. They may even have limited choice of the music that will be played. Yet, it is their job to

FIGURE 10.16   Evaluating teachers can help set professional growth goals and clarify a teacher's strengths and areas of improvement.

lead a group of musicians through a medley of songs, bringing out the best in each. And all under the intense scrutiny of a critical audience. Teachers must do this with care and expertise under the watchful eyes of parents, boards, and funding agencies.

Many teachers do this well, often with little training except direct experience. As teachers' effectiveness is measured, they can learn better techniques for working with children, for planning environments and programs. The process for establishing and meeting these goals is evaluation. Teacher evaluation forms in this chapter can be adapted for use with student teachers and aides.

Why Evaluate?

Teachers are evaluated for several reasons. The end result of an assessment may be setting guidelines for what kinds of teaching are expected. Or the intent of an evaluation might be to set clear goals for job improvement. The first part of any effective evaluation procedure is a statement of purpose.

To Describe Job Responsibilities

It is essential for teachers to understand their job to do it well. A good job description outlines

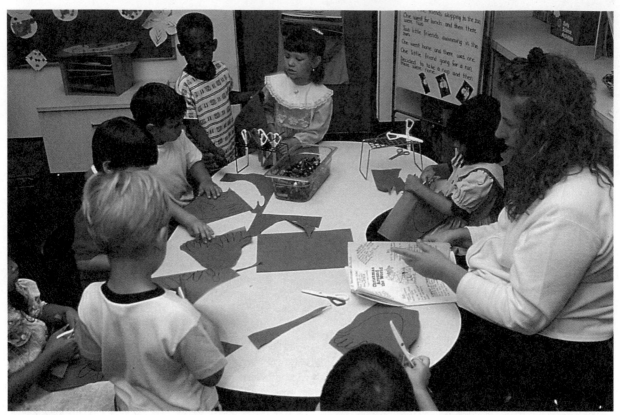

FIGURE 10.17   Teacher evaluations monitor job effectiveness as teachers work with people in several dimensions. This teacher demonstrates skill with groups as well as with individual children and adults.

what is expected. One purpose of an evaluation is to see how those expectations are being met.

In an infant/toddler center, for example, teachers try to help children learn to separate comfortably from their parents. Evaluation in this setting could focus on the exact skills needed to implement this goal. How does a teacher help a parent separate from a young child? What environmental cues does the teacher prepare? How is the child in distress comforted? What teaching strategies are important?

Evaluation for specifying job responsibilities is a part of one's professional self-definition as well as a clarification of actual duties. Studying ourselves helps us know who we are and what we do. Assessing job responsibilities aids in this process.

To Monitor Job Effectiveness

Once clear guidelines are set for teaching expectations, a method is needed to monitor actual

teaching. Most evaluation systems attempt to check teacher effectiveness. It is important to establish a process for analyzing how teachers are doing their job.

This process may vary from school to school. In some schools, teaching effectiveness is measured, in part, by child achievement, such as how children score on tests. Other centers may solicit parent opinion. A teacher's coworkers may be part of an assessment team. For the most part, an evaluation for job effectiveness will include an observation of teaching time with children.

To Clarify Strengths and Weaknesses

An evaluation procedure preferred by many teachers is one that identifies specific areas of strength and weakness. Feedback about actual teaching and other job responsibilities is helpful to all teachers, whether beginners or experienced personnel. As assessment that offers teachers information about how to perform their job better contributes to job competence and satisfaction. By recognizing strengths, teachers receive positive feedback for high-quality work. By identifying weaknesses, they can begin to set realistic goals for improvement.

To Set Professional Growth Goals

One function of teacher evaluation is to foster professional development. Teachers do not become "good" and then stay that way for life. Regardless of their stage of development, teachers need goals in order to continually improve.

Regular feedback to staff can help in setting goals for continual professional growth. Beginning teachers will need to work on skills that apply their educational training or background to the classroom and children. A professional with 15 years of experience might need to polish skills acquired a decade or more ago, or try another educational challenge, such as developing curriculum or planning a workshop.

To Determine Employment

An evaluation can also be used to decide whether teachers should be "retained, promoted, or released" (Stoops et al. *in* Hatfield, 1981). Assessment procedures are an administrator's most valuable tools in performing these tasks. With a clear and effective evaluation tool, a teacher's performance can be monitored and specific areas targeted for improvement. The administrator then has a fair and equitable way to determine promotional status of each employee.

Critical Issues in Teacher Evaluation

How to evaluate is an important issue in teacher assessment. A system for evaluating employees can be one of trust and mutual respect or of anxiety and tension. The method often determines how successful the entire evaluation will be.

Preliminary Steps

To begin with, a school follows the same guidelines for developing a teacher evaluation as

for child assessment. That is, the process includes determining a purpose, establishing who will collect the data and how, and clarifying how the evaluation will be used. When assessing teachers, the important components are: purpose (as described earlier in the chapter), evaluators, process, and follow-through.

Evaluators

Several models have been developed around the issue of who will assess teacher performance.

Self-Evaluation. This can be an effective starting point. Self-assessment is used in the Child Development Associate's evaluation system, for these reasons (Ward and CDA staff, 1976):

- The candidate is a valid source of information for use in assessment. Certain information is available only from the candidate's perspective.

- The candidate is able to clarify information on his or her performance, thereby adding to the assessment team's evidence for a valid decision.

- The candidate is better able to identify strengths and weaknesses and to receive recommendations for continued professional growth.

Figure 10.18 illustrates one type of systematic self-assessment. Another self-assessment technique, somewhat less formal, is to ask questions about yourself and your job, such as:

- What aspects of my work give me the greatest sense of satisfaction and achievement?

- What changes in my work assignment would increase my contribution to the school and my own personal satisfaction?

- What additional development activities would help me do a more effective job or prepare me for the next step on my career path?

- What would improve the effectiveness and quality of my relationship with my supervisor? (Young-Holt et al., 1983)

The answers to these few questions can provide a solid base for discussion between teacher and supervisor or assessment team.

SAMPLE SELF-EVALUATION

Rate the following items on the scale below, based on your performance in the classroom. (Note: This form allows for a yes/no response if desired. Supervisors may use this same form to rate the student following the self-evaluation.)

Superior Perf.	Acceptable Perf.	Unacceptable Perf.	Not Applicable
3	2	1	0

Relationship to Children

_____ I am able to understand and accept a child as he/she is and recognize individual needs.
_____ I use knowledge and understanding of child development principles to understand children.
_____ I use information regarding home, family, and sociocultural background to understand children.
_____ I am able to forestall situations before negative behavior occurs.
_____ I use positive suggestions and choices to redirect behavior.
_____ I use prescribed limits and follow-through.
_____ I adapt methods of guidance to the individual and adjust guidance measures to fit the situation.
_____ I avoid the use of threats.
_____ I express positive reinforcement when appropriate.
_____ I can verbalize my own feelings in an honest, open, and humane manner when interacting with children.
_____ I avoid using baby talk.
_____ I relate to individual children.
_____ I relate to children in small groups.
_____ I relate to children in large groups.

Developing the Program

_____ I permit the children to explore materials in a variety of ways.
_____ I recognize and use spontaneous happenings to help children's learning.
_____ I make use of child development principles to plan curriculum for children.
_____ I offer a wide range of experiences so children can make choices according to their interests and needs.
_____ I allow for various levels of ability among children.
_____ I utilize a variety of media when developing instructional materials.
_____ I use a note-taking system to assist in planning and evaluating experiences for children.
_____ I maintain equipment and materials in good order and consider health and safety factors.

Relating to Parents

_____ I recognize parents by name.
_____ I converse with parents at appropriate times.
_____ I incorporate the cultural backgrounds of families into the program.
_____ I facilitate a free flow of information between staff and parents.
_____ I communicate concerns to parents in both written and verbal forms.
_____ I recognize and appreciate parental values and priorities for their children.
_____ I communicate children's school experiences with parents.

Administration and Professional Development

_____ I recognize and use policies and procedures of the program.
_____ I attend and participate in staff meetings.
_____ I inform the administrative staff correctly of illness, time off, vacation, etc.
_____ I am a member of at least one professional organization in the field of early childhood.
_____ I attend meetings conducted by professional groups.

FIGURE 10.18   Self-evaluation can be an insightful and useful process. (Adapted from Young-Holt et al. [1983], and Hatfield [1981].)

_____ I make use of professional resources and contacts.
_____ I maintain professional confidentiality and discretion.

Working with Other Staff Members
_____ I show positive attitudes toward other staff members.
_____ I give directions carefully.
_____ I take directions from others.
_____ I participate as a team member.
_____ I coordinate my efforts with those of my coworkers.
_____ I share my time, interest, and resources with other staff members.
_____ I listen and hear staff feedback regarding my teaching.
_____ I act on suggestions.
_____ I communicate my perceptions of my teaching in an honest and clear manner.

FIGURE 10.18 *Continued*

One drawback of self-assessment is its subjectivity. We see ourselves too closely, too personally, to be able to be entirely objective about our teaching. Therefore, self-assessment must be accompanied by other evaluating feedback.

Supervisory Evaluation. Supervisors, or head teachers, are usually part of the evaluation process. Job performance is an administrator's responsibility; therefore, teachers can expect their supervisors to be involved in their evaluation. Supervisors often use a single form combining a teacher's self-assessment and the supervisor's evaluation. This kind of form simplifies the paperwork and assures both teacher and supervisor that both are using the same criteria for evaluation. They may, however, develop a different kind of form, such as the one in Figure 10.19.

Coevaluation. Evaluation by others associated with the teachers is a welcome addition to the evaluation process. Often a system includes more than a teacher's supervisor. Possible combinations are:

● Teacher (self-evaluation) and supervisor

● Teacher, supervisor, and parent

● Teacher, supervisor, and another team member (coteacher, aide, student teacher)

A team evaluation is a more collaborative approach. More information is collected on the teacher's performance. A team approach may be more valid and balanced, since a decision about teaching will be made by consensus and discussion rather than individual, perhaps arbitrary, methods. And the evaluation will have a wider perspective, evaluating a teacher's job performance from several viewpoints.

Coevaluation does have its disadvantages, however. It is a time-consuming process since more than one person is asked to evaluate a teacher. Feedback may be contradictory; what one evaluator sees as a strength, another may view as a shortcoming. The system can be complicated to implement. For instance, how do teachers work in a classroom and evaluate another team member at the same time? Can funds be found to bring in substitutes? Do fellow teachers have the time to devote to evaluating each other? How and when does a parent evaluate a teacher? Clearly, a school must weigh these issues carefully as evaluation systems are devised.

The Process

The evaluation tools are used determine the information gathered. Informal techniques often use information that is gathered sporadically, and conclusions may be unreliable or based on opinions. A process that is formalized and systematic has a greater chance of success. Such evaluations will be based on observable, specific information on what the teacher actually does. This is known as **performance-based assessment.** Figure 10.20 is an example of performance-based assessment in regards to a teacher's work with children. When paired with specific goals and expectations, this system is known as competency-based assessment.

Teacher Evaluation Form

Instructions: This form is designed to be used by the center director for evaluating teachers. To the left of each characteristic listed below write an **E** if the teacher's performance in this area is **excellent**, **S** if it is **satisfactory**, and **N** if it **needs improvement**. Make any explanatory notes to the right.

Name of Teacher: _____ **Classroom:** _____

___ 1. Friendly, with ability to relate positively to people.
___ 2. Enjoys the egocentricity of children.
___ 3. Speaks clearly, distinctly, and grammatically.
___ 4. Demonstrates tact, compassion, empathic concern for children and families.
___ 5. Tolerant and considerate of differences in children and adults.
___ 6. Understands humor, humorous incidents, and jokes of children.
___ 7. Displays a sense of humor with children and enjoys laughing with them.
___ 8. Smiles and shows enjoyment often.
___ 9. Is dependable and energetic.
___ 10. Makes real effort to become very involved in the program.
___ 11. Enthusiastic and excited about teaching.
___ 12. Indicates a desire to keep up in the field of ECE.
___ 13. Grows in ability to critically evaluate self.
___ 14. Can follow directions.
___ 15. Accepts and uses suggestions to improve teaching.
___ 16. Accepts share of responsibility for classroom preparation, gathering of materials, and other tasks assigned.
___ 17. Accepts individual differences.
___ 18. Uses a positive approach with all children.
___ 19. Alert to total group of children even when dealing with an individual child or small group.
___ 20. Remains controlled in *startling* or difficult situations.
___ 21. Assists children in gaining self-confidence and in becoming communicative.
___ 22. Makes an effort to joyously participate with children in small groups or 1:1 basis, indoors and outdoors.
___ 23. Displays a general positive attitude toward other adults in place of a negative, criticizing attitude.
___ 24. Responds well to adults.
___ 25. Respects the rights and teaching techniques of others in the group.
___ 26. Welcomes new ideas and demonstrates flexibility with willingness to consider new ideas.
___ 27. Realizes that situations cannot always be handled at home as they are at school.
___ 28. Evidences growth and potential for teaching young children.
___ 29. Demonstrates knowledge about growth and development of young children.
___ 30. Demonstrates knowledge about the meaning of specific activities for children.
___ 31. Is positive and supportive of parents as partners in ECE.

Signed:_____ Date:_____

FIGURE 10.19 A teacher may be evaluated by the center director or supervisor using an evaluation tool such as this form, by the late Carol Murphy of La Cresceta, Calif. (Reprinted with permission of CCIE, Issue 51, Sept. 1986, a management magazine for center directors, P.O. Box 2890, Redmond, CA 98073.)

Teacher Goal	Example
To help each child develop a positive self-concept	I greet each child daily w/a smile and a personal comment.
To help each child develop socially, emotionally, cognitively, and physically	I have goals for each child in each developmental area, Fall and Spring.
To help provide many opportunities for each child to be successful	My parent conference sheets have examples; for instance, Charlie didn't want to come to group time, so I had him pick the story and help me read it—he comes every day now!
To encourage creativity, questioning, and problem-solving	This is my weak point. I tend to talk too much and tell them what to do.
To foster enjoyment for learning in each child	I do great group times and give everyone turns.
To facilitate each child's learning through active learning opportunities that are developmentally appropriate	I went through the accreditation process and am taking an anti-bias class.

FIGURE 10.20 Performance-based assessment ties the goals of the program to a teacher's work. This example asks the teacher to do a self-assessment; a director, parent, or peer could observe and make a second assessment. (Teacher Goals from Carr and Carlin, 1991.)

Competency-based assessments outline exactly what teachers must do to demonstrate their competency, or skill, in their job assignment. Criteria are set as a teacher begins working (or a student starts a class or teacher education program). Areas are targeted that pinpoint what knowledge, skills, and behaviors the teacher must acquire.

Follow-Through

What happens after the evaluation is critical to the overall success of an evaluation system. For instance, after gathering information for an evaluation session, a supervisor and teacher might discuss and evaluate concrete examples and live performance. Together they can establish goals for changing what may be ineffective or problematic.

Follow-through is the final part of a continuous *feedback loop* in a good evaluation system. Data is collected on teacher behavior and given to the teacher in person. Goals are set to improve teaching. A follow-up check is done periodically, to see how—and if—goals are being met. Teaching improves as recommendations are put into practice. Follow-through makes the *feedback loop* complete as information about improvement is communicated. Figure 10.21 illustrates this cycle.

Evaluation takes hard work, time, and dedication to a higher quality of teaching. It is also a shared responsibility. The supervisor must be explicit about a teacher's performance and be able to identify for the teacher what is effective and what is problematic. The teacher is responsible for participating in the evaluation.

Techniques for Productive Evaluation Sessions

Teachers must value the process itself. Evaluations emphasize how valuable the work of professional teachers is, and the benefits of productive evaluation sessions are clear. They range from improved self-esteem, higher levels of job effectiveness, and less absenteeism and turnover, to assessment-related salary raises and other job benefits.

FIGURE 10.21 A feedback loop is a continuous cycle in which teacher behavior is observed for a performance evaluation. The evaluation is offered through growth goals, which are set in order to affect teacher behavior. Thus, the circle is continuous, with each part helping the next.

Teachers need to analyze and take seriously the substance of the evaluation and understand its implications for their teaching. To further their professional growth, they must use this opportunity to improve the tools of their trade.

Certain techniques help make evaluation sessions productive for teachers:

1. Become involved from the beginning as the evaluation procedure is established. Know what is expected and how you will be evaluated.

2. Set a specific meeting time for your evaluation. Ask your supervisor for a time that works for you both.

3. Set some goals for yourself before meeting with your supervisor. If you know what you want to work on, you are more likely to get help achieving your goals.

4. Develop a plan for action. Be prepared to set a timeline for when and how you will work on your goals.

5. Establish a feedback loop. Make a follow-up date and make copies of your goal sheet for both you and your supervisor.

6. Approach the meeting with a sense of trust, respect, and openness. Planning ahead promotes these attitudes.

What results from productive feedback sessions is better teaching and continued professional growth. Teacher evaluations help recognize strengths and build upon them. They identify areas where growth is needed. They individualize the process itself. No two teachers are identical; each evaluation must be interpreted in terms of the behavior and stage of development of the individual person.[1] As teachers become more effective in their work with children, the quality of the entire program is improved.

EVALUATING PROGRAMS

Why Evaluate?

To Gain an Overview

Evaluating a program gives an overview of how all the various components function together. This assessment asks the larger questions. Returning to the restaurant example earlier in the chapter, one might ask, "Would you ever go back and eat there again? Would you take a friend there?" In educational terms, the fundamental questions are, "Is this a good place for children? Would you want your child to be here? What is a high-quality program for young children?" See Chapters 2 and 9 for additional information.

Looking at children, teachers, and the total environment, a program evaluation reveals the entire environment as an integrated whole. These assessments add an awareness of how one area relates to another and how the parts mesh in a particular setting. Such evaluations, then, are the standards of quality and include:

[1]What teachers know about understanding and respecting diversity in children and families needs to be translated into working with colleagues.

- children's progress
- teacher performance
- curriculum development
- the financial structure
- the parents
- the community at large
- the governing organization of the school

In evaluating programs, each of these is assessed for how it functions alone and how each works in concert with the others.

To Establish Accountability

Besides providing an overview, a program evaluation establishes accountability. This refers to a program's being answerable to a controlling group or agency, for instance the school board or the government office. These groups want to know how their funds are being spent and how their philosophy is being expressed through the overall program. Just as a teacher's evaluation is sometimes linked to salary increases, a program evaluation may be related to future funding. This can add stress to the evaluation process since teachers and administrators must justify their worth in dollars and cents.

To Make Improvements

A third purpose of a program evaluation is to determine where and how improvements can be made. Program evaluations are an opportunity to take an objective look at how the goals of the school are being met. A good evaluation will support the strengths of the existing program and suggest where changes might improve overall effectiveness. An in-depth assessment increases the likelihood that program goals and visions will be realized. The evaluation helps determine the direction the program may take in the future.

To Acquire Accreditation

Finally, evaluations are a necessary step for some schools who wish to be approved for certification or accreditation by various organizations or government agencies. Such groups require that a school meet certain evaluation standards before the necessary permits are issued or membership is granted. Agencies such as a State Department of Social Services or Education often license family day care homes, and private schools may need to follow certain criteria be affiliated with a larger organization (such as the American Montessori Society).

To improve the quality of schools, begin with children and place them in the center of program evaluation. In seeing the children's perspective, teachers and parents must be part of program evaluation, for they are the ones closest to the children. One particular system established by early childhood professionals is noteworthy. The National Academy of Early Childhood Programs, a division of NAEYC, has established an accreditation system for improving the quality of life for young children and their families (Bredekamp, 1984, 1991).

Attempting to define a high-quality early childhood program, the accreditation system articulates what promotes the physical, social, emotional, and cognitive development of children in group care. The Academy established goals for schools around several component areas, which include curriculum goals, adult-child interactions, health, safety, and nutrition, relations between the home and program, developmental evaluation of children, and qualifications and on-going staff development of teachers.

In order for children to have positive experiences, Bredekamp (1992) identifies several *predictors of quality*:

- teachers who are specially trained in child development and early education
- enough adults to respond to individual children, adequate ratios of adults to children, reasonable group sizes
- regular communication with parents, who are welcome visitors at all times
- many, varied age-appropriate materials in a well-arranged, accessible environment both indoors and outdoors
- nutritious meals and snacks
- effective administration, including clear, written policies and procedures to facilitate com-

WHY ACCREDITATION?

The National Academy of Early Childhood Programs, a division of the National Association for the Education of Young Children (NAEYC), administers a national, voluntary accreditation system for child care centers and preschools. This system, initiated in 1985, is designed for any full-day or part-day group serving children from birth through age five and/or school-age children in before- and after-school care. One need only to refer back to Chapters 2 and 9 to recall the diversity of programs under this early childhood education umbrella.

Accredited programs include church programs, private and public programs, employer- and university-sponsored programs, Head Start and community-based programs, and prekindergarten, kindergarten and after-school programs. As this system will be implemented even more widely in the coming years, it is useful to ask the question, "Why Accreditation?"

- To improve the quality of care and education provided for young children in group programs.
- To provide additional assurance for parents about the care and education of their children.
- To enhance the professional image and status of early childhood educators.
- To provide a goal that programs can use in working toward improvement.
- To establish professional consensus regarding what constitutes a high-quality early childhood program.
- To provide tools for self-evaluation by administrators and teachers.
- To provide a mechanism for identifying programs that exceed the minimum requirements and strive toward achieving professional standards.

FIGURE 10.22 The major benefactors of accreditation are the children. Accreditation improves the quality of the care teachers provide for children.

munication, that meets the needs of adults as well as children

- systematic, ongoing evaluation of how well the program is meeting its goals for children and families

A key dimension of quality is program evaluation. The NAEYC accreditation process is the first attempt by the national early childhood profession to articulate what is meant by a "good" program for young children. As such, it is based on observing children in the United States and has some of the dominant culture's values embedded in it. Therefore, in the last decade there has been an ongoing critique of this initial model. For instance, proponents of Vygotsky argue that, since adults teach socially valued skills at a very early age, a single document could never describe practices of all subcultures in American society.

Those who are familiar with the wide diversity of cultures in America are looking with a critical eye at adapting this process. Now that a tool

has been developed, the Academy is in the process of revising this initial document. Clearly, both the Academy's accreditation and the concepts of developmentally appropriate practices will evolve as our awareness of culture and education increases.

Guidelines for Program Evaluation

Defining the Objectives

A program evaluation begins with a definition of the program's objectives. Knowing why a program is to be evaluated indicates how to tailor the procedure to the needs and characteristics of an individual school. With the objectives defined, the choice of evaluation instrument becomes clear. If, for example, a program objective is to provide a healthy environment for children, the evaluation tool used must address the issues of health, safety, and nutrition.

Choosing a Tool

Evaluation instruments vary with the purpose of the program evaluation. Moreover, a survey of various program evaluations shows that many are designed to be program-specific; that is, the evaluation itself is devised to examine one program only. Individualized assessments are difficult to generalize. However, it appears that most program evaluations assess several, if not all, of the following areas:

The Physical Environment
Are the facilities clean, comfortable, safe?
Are room arrangements orderly and attractive?
Are materials and equipment in good repair and maintained?
Is there a variety of materials, appropriate to age levels?
Are activity areas well-defined?
Is cleanup and room restoration a part of the daily schedule?
Are samples of children's work on display?
Is play space adequate, both inside and out?
Is personal space (e.g., cubby) provided for each child?

The Staff
Are there enough teachers for the number of children? How is this determined?
Are the teachers qualified? What criteria are used?
Is the staff evaluated periodically? By whom and how?
Does the school provide/encourage in-service training and continuing education?
Do the teachers encourage the children to be independent and self-sufficient?
Are the teachers genuinely interested in children?
Are teachers aware of individual abilities and limitations?
What guidance and disciplinary techniques are used?
Do teachers observe, record, and write reports on children's progress?
Are teachers skilled in working with individual children, small groups, and large groups?
Does the teaching staff give the children a feeling of stability and belonging?
Do teachers provide curriculum that is age-appropriate and challenging?
How would you describe the teachers' relationships with other adults in the setting? Who does this include, and how?
Can the teaching staff articulate good early education principles and relate them to their teaching?

Parent Relationships
How does the classroom include parents?

Are parents welcome to observe, discuss policies, make suggestions, help in the class?
Are different needs of parents taken into account?
Where and how do parents have a voice in the school?
Are parent–teacher conferences scheduled?
Does the school attempt to use community resources and social service agencies in meeting parents' needs?

The Organization and Administration
Does the school maintain and keep records?
Are there scholarships or subsidies available?
What socioeconomic, cultural, religious groups does the school serve?
What is the funding agency, and what role does it play?
Is there a school board and how is it chosen?
Does the school serve children with special needs or handicaps?
Are the classroom groups homo- or heterogeneous?
What hours is the school open?
What age range is served?
Are there both full- and part-day options?
Is after-school care available?
Does the school conduct research or train teachers?
What is the teacher-child ratio?

The Overall Program
Does the school have a written, stated educational philosophy?
Are there developmental goals for the children's physical, social, intellectual, and emotional growth?
Are the children evaluated periodically?
Is the program capable of being individualized to fit the needs of all the children?
Does the program include time for a variety of free, spontaneous activities?
Is the curriculum varied to include music, art, science, nature, math, language, social studies, motor skills, etc.?
Are there ample opportunities to learn through a variety of media and types of equipment and materials?
Is there ample outdoor activity?
Is there a daily provision for routines: eating, sleeping, toileting, play?
Is the major emphasis in activities on concrete experiences?
Are the materials and equipment capable of stimulating and sustaining interest?
Are field trips offered?
Do children have a chance to be alone? In small groups? In large groups?

Tools for program evaluation are woven together to give a more comprehensive look at the total program.

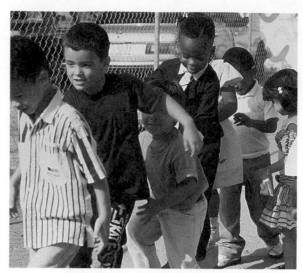

FIGURE 10.23   Program evaluations should represent the diversity of the field of early childhood education, from family day care for infants to after-school programs for primary schoolchildren.

Developmentally Appropriate Practices

Educational reform to improve the quality of programs for young children in the last several years has been spearheaded by a movement towards what is now called "developmentally appropriate practice." (Bredekamp, 1987; Elkind, 1989; NAEYC, 1984, 1991). While many readers of this text may not be engaged in philosophical debate on public policy, it is essential that all early childhood educators understand the terms and issues. Knowing what is meant by the phrase "developmentally appropriate practice" helps the dedicated teacher to be able to plan programs for children that are of high quality and integrity and to articulate what is important for children to their parents and the greater community.

Developmentally appropriate practice (DAP) describes teaching and learning from a developmental perspective—children are seen as learners with *developing abilities*, differing from one another based on their rates of growth and individual differences (i.e., temperament, family history, ethnic background, gender, and so on). Teaching content is tied to who the learners are; thus, programs change to reflect the children in them. Teachers prepare environments and ask questions that stimulate individual thinking processes. An evaluation of a developmentally appropriate program includes the environment, the quality of adult-child interaction, work with parents, and so on.

In contrast, **psychometric** philosophy is a view more commonly held in primary education. From this standpoint, children are seen as having *finite quantities of abilities*. Individual differences in performance are seen as reflecting differences in the amount of a given ability. In such classrooms, the teacher's job is to match children of similar abilities, and the curriculum will likely follow a traditional content. Such programs will be evaluated with assessments such as tests. Then, getting children to know correct information (thus high test scores) often becomes too important.

There are clear differences in these two viewpoints. Teachers of *young* children usually base their programs more on developmentally appropriate (rather than psychometric) practices, because much of the philosophy of early childhood education is based on child development theories of Piaget and Erikson, rather than the behaviorist and psychometric models (see Chapter 4). Since the theoretical underpinnings are different, early childhood programs differ from most elementary school programs. Consequently, teachers and parents find themselves with two contrasting systems of teaching and evaluation.

The debate over how to plan and evaluate programs for young children continues today, and it is useful for those who work with young children to understand the issues. NAEYC has developed an extensive list of publications that provide guidance in establishing and operating programs of quality, and that explain in detail what is meant by developmentally appropriate programs for young children. Teachers and administrators should become familiar with these documents and use them as standards for program excellence. Chapters 11 through 14 are based on materials with these guidelines.

HOW EVALUATIONS AFFECT AN EARLY CHILDHOOD SETTING

A useful assessment encourages positive change. It is easy to continue the same program, the same teaching techniques, even the same assessment techniques, year after year when a school is operating smoothly. Sometimes it is not clear what—or how—improvements could be made. A regular evaluation keeps a system alive and fresh.

Evaluations help give meaning and perspective to children, teachers, and programs. An assessment that helps clarify these processes brings renewed dedication and inspiration.

Assessments of children, teachers, and programs can blend together for positive results. Children and program evaluations often work in tandem, as program goals must be defined in terms of children and their growth. How well the children are doing is a measure of program success.

Teacher evaluations may relate to program assessment when they include an **upward evaluation,** or teacher evaluation of administrators. The program effectiveness is checked by the people who are responsible for its implementation.

A teacher's effectiveness is evaluated every day by how the children respond to the environment, the schedule, teaching techniques and relationships, and each other. No more effective test exists than the dynamics of the children at work and play in a class.

As teachers, we learn to accept evaluation as a process, rather than a series of static endpoints. In doing so, we see that there can be continuity and consistency in how evaluations of the people and programs in early childhood education work together to enhance learning and growth at all levels.

FIGURE 10.24   A program evaluation can determine how the class includes parents. The presence of parent volunteers in this kindergarten shows that the shcool welcomes parent involvement.

S U M M A R Y

Evaluation is a way of taking stock; it is an opportunity to look at how things are going. We can assess where we are now and where we want to be. A good evaluation instrument may even suggest ways to achieve our goals. A good evaluation process includes a clear purpose, knowing who and what will be evaluated, and what use will be made of the results.

Any program designed to meet the needs of children must be evaluated on a regular basis. Teachers, children, and the program must be assessed individually and then evaluated as a whole. Each supports and depends upon the other; an evaluation is a way to look at how those relationships are working. It can identify specific concerns and determine the areas of growth and potential development.

Setting goals is an important part of the evaluation process. Evaluating goals is a measure of success or lack of it. We judge whether or not we have met our goals effectively and whether or not the goals are reflective of the program.

Evaluations serve many purposes. Assessing individual children highlights their growth and potential more clearly. One method, standardized testing, is being used extensively in early childhood settings and can be misapplied and inappropriately used. Evaluation gives teachers information about their own performance and suggests ways to strengthen their teaching style. Examining the total program reveals a better picture of how all its aspects work in unison. The National Academy of Early Childhood Programs has established an accreditation system that encourages developmentally appropriate practices in settings for children from birth to eight years of age.

The process of evaluation can be positive and can encourage growth for all involved. The choice of evaluation instruments is important, as is the use made of the data collected. Programs will keep pace with their children and professional teachers if evaluation is considered an integral part of the program structure.

R E V I E W   Q U E S T I O N S

1. List three reasons for evaluation in the early childhood setting. Which do you think would be the hardest? Why?

2. What are the components of all good evaluations? What are the problems? Include some suggestions for solutions.

3. What are the reasons for assessing children's progress? How can you communicate both strengths and weaknesses to parents?

4. Describe some of the problems with testing or screening of young children. How can you address these problems if you are required to administer a standardized test to your class?

5. Who can be involved in evaluating teachers? Who would you prefer? Why?

6. How can teachers help to make their evaluation sessions productive?

7. Name three purposes of program evaluations.

8. What is the National Academy's accreditation and how does it attempt to improve program quality?

L E A R N I N G   A C T I V I T I E S

1. Does your own setting have an evaluation plan? Which of the evaluation criteria does it include?

2. Develop an informal assessment tool to evaluate children's skills in a toddler class. Discuss how this would differ from one for a preschool, and from a school-age child care program.

3. Try to establish goals for your own growth as a professional in the following areas:

	Goal	Objectives/ Implementation	Timeline
Programmatic			
Administrative			
Staff Relations			
Professional Growth			

Ask your supervisor or a colleague to help you make a realistic timeline for each goal.

4. Locate a copy of "Developmentally Appropriate Practices." Using the categories it outlines, make an informal assessment of the program in which you work. Share your results with another teacher or supervisor.

B I B L I O G R A P H Y

Boyer, Ernest L. "What Teachers Say about Children in America." *Educational Leadership*, Vol. 46, No. 8, May, 1989.

Bredekamp, Sue. *Developmentally Appropriate Practice in Early Childhood Programs Serving Children From Birth Through Age 8*, expanded edition, Washington, D.C.: National Association for the Education of Young Children, 1987, 1991.

—————. "Evaluating for Effectiveness." In *Beginnings and Beyond*, ed. Gordon and Browne, Albany, N.Y.: Delmar Publishers, 1992 (3rd Ed.).

Carr, Ann D., and Carlin, James B. "Early Childhood Education: the Important Questions." *ACEI's Focus on Early Childhood*, Vol. 3, No. 2, Winter, 1990.

Cryan, John R. "Evaluation: Plague or Promise?" *Childhood Education*, Vol. 62, No. 5, May/June, 1986.

Education Week. "Early Testing," January 16, 1991.

Elkind, David. "Developmentally Appropriate Practice: Philosophical and Practical Implications." *Phi Delta Kappan*, October, 1989.

Kamii, Constance, (ed.). *Achievement Testing in the Early Grades: the Games Grown-ups Play*. Washington, D.C.: National Association for the Education of Young Children, 1990.

La Guardia, Justina. Personal communication, 1992.

McLaughlin, Karen, and Sugarman, S. Personal communications, 1982.

Meisels, Samuel J. *Developmental Screening in Early Childhood: a Guide*, 3rd ed. Washington, D.C.: National Association for the Education of Young Children, 1989.

Murphy, Carol. "Teacher Evaluation Forms." *Child Care Information Exchange*, No. 51, September 1986.

NAEYC. "Position Statement on Standardized Testing of Young Children 3 Through 8 Years of Age." *Young Children*, Vol. 43, No. 3, March 1988.

National Academy of Early Childhood Programs. *Accreditation Criteria and Procedures.* Washington, D.C.: National Association for the Education of Young Children, July, 1991.

Schultz, Tom. "Testing and Retention of Young Children: Moving from Controversy to Reform." *Phi Delta Kappan*, October, 1989.

Ward, E.H., and CDA Staff. "The Child Development Associate Consortium's Assessment System." *Young Children*, May 1976, pp. 244–255.

Young-Holt, C.; Spitz, Gay; and Heffron, M.C. *A Model for Staff Evaluation, Validation, and Growth.* Palo Alto, Calif.: Center for the Study of Self-Esteem, 1983.

GUEST EDITORIAL

Play, the Story of Learning

Elizabeth Jones

As a developmentalist I think of human development as a history, a story in which each chapter has its own significance. There is a task to be accomplished at each stage. Babies are learning, first, to trust other people, and then to let go. Developmental tasks are cumulative; these are things we must be able to do all our lives. Very young children are learning to walk and talk, and they learn these things *so well* because we let them learn by playing.

All smart young animals (not so, the less smart) learn by playing. They play at walking, and, after awhile, they walk. They play at talking, and, after awhile, they talk all the time. If we *taught* them to speak, they'd never learn; and if you want to think about the difference, compare your first-language learning with any efforts to learn another language that you've made beyond childhood.

Young children play at writing, too, and at driving cars and at putting babies to bed and at building buildings, and, by golly, they grow up to do all these things. Play is spontaneous practice of complex skills. It is also— and this is very important— practice in *being interested* (Katz, dispositions), in choosing among possibilities, in discovering one's own identity through one's interests.

Some parents and some teachers worry, though, when children are "just playing." They worry that time is being wasted, that it's a competitive world, that children need to get ahead. I'd put it differently, but I agree that in a rapidly changing society, it's important for children to grow up smart. I don't define smart as knowing lots of facts, though; facts are useful, but they're easy to learn if you think of yourself as someone who's good at learning. Smart, for me, is being able to size up situations and solve problems. Stable societies don't need or want lots of smart children; they're a nuisance, they keep asking questions and changing the ways things are supposed to be. They make trouble. We've already got trouble, in our diverse and rapidly changing world; there are many problems to be solved and no pat solutions. Somebody—our children—is going to have to invent solutions, and I for one hope they'll be ethical solutions respectful of the diversity of human needs.

Growing up, we all lose track of possibilities; we learn the rules, the answers that our society has invented. We forget the questions. Questions come from outsiders, from the people who benefit least by the system. Children, who are too little to have much power over their lives, are full of questions—in their behavior as well as in their words: *Why* is it bedtime? Why can't I have ice cream now? Why can't I bite the baby? Why do I have to wear a seat belt?

Our style of response to all such questions helps to determine whether or not they'll grow up to be creative problem solvers, people who ask questions and are imaginative and persistent in searching for answers. I don't believe they become problem solvers—smart—by doing what they're told. Of course they often do have to do what they're told, for their safety or our sanity. But I think we should justify our teaching of facts and rules in terms of safety and adult sanity, not in terms of becoming smart. If children are asked to sit still and be quiet in school, that can't be justified as learning behavior; that's crowd control. Children who are learning are usually moving and talking, and this is true well beyond preschool.

What's play? Choosing for oneself. Children need to play in order to find out who they are, what they want, what they can do. Play is saying yes as well as no. "Hey, Alma, come be Batman with us." "No, I don't want to, I'm driving my car to the store." "Michael, gimme that block, I need it." "No, you can't have it because it goes right on my roof, see? You can use that other one over there." They need to just say NO and know why they're saying it and what they want to do instead. Children who have no idea what they want to do are fair game for advertisers, dope peddlers, and dictators when they grow up.

Dr. Elizabeth Jones is on the faculty of Pacific Oaks College, a frequent contributor to NAEYC, and the author of The Play's the Thing *and* Teaching Adults Emergent Curriculum *among many other works.*

QUESTIONS FOR THOUGHT

What is curriculum in the early childhood setting?

What is developmentally appropriate curriculum?

What is the process of developing emergent curriculum for young children?

What is the value of play?

How are play and curriculum related?

How do children learn through play?

Why is dramatic play important to the young child?

What is the role of the teacher?

How do teachers support the play process?

How is curriculum culturally sensitive?

CHAPTER 11

Planning for Play: Curriculum Basics

CURRICULUM

What Is Curriculum?

Ira, a two-year-old, is more interested in the process of pouring milk (especially what happens after the cup is filled) than in eating and conversing at snack time.

In an early childhood setting, curriculum consists of the art activity and language game; it is also the spontaneous investigation of liquids at snack time, the song that accompanies digging in the sand, and the teacher's explanation of why the hamster died. It can become, literally, everything that happens in the course of a school day.

Curriculum is the planned and the unplanned.

Kindergartners Bert and Leo become absorbed in watching a snail make its way across the sidewalk, ignoring for the moment the lesson on running relays.

Young children are like sponges; they absorb everything going on about them. Since they are young, the whole world is new and fresh. Therefore, children do not discriminate between what is prepared and structured for them to learn and whatever else happens to them at school. It is *all* learning.

Creating a good curriculum for young children is not simply a matter of practicing curriculum planning. It is a matter of understanding the process: how children interact with people and materials to learn. It is the sum of a teacher's knowledge about children's needs, materials, and equipment, and what happens when they meet.

Curriculum is the process of translating theories of education into practice. It is spontaneous, yet organized; it is planned, yet it emerges; it is based on the children's interests tempered by adult awareness of children's needs. Four areas of focus taken from Guidelines for Appropriate Curriculum Content & Assessment in Programs Serving Children Ages 3 Through 8, 1991 are:

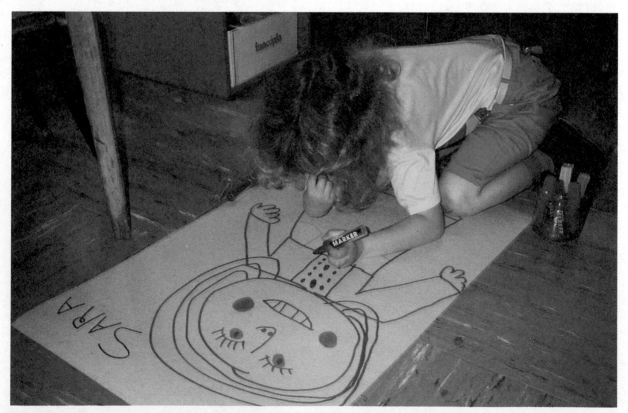

FIGURE 11.1 Curriculum happens when child meets materials. (Courtesy of Centro Infantil & de Reabilitacao de A-Da-Beja, Lisbon, Portugal.)

- The content is *what* is being taught—the subject matter or the theme—and stems primarily from children's interests. Teacher and parent observations and evaluations will ensure that the content reflects the interests, needs, and experiences of the child as well as addresses what children should learn.

- The process is *how* and *when* learning takes place, the choice of activities or projects and how they are integrated with one another, and the time frame within the daily schedule or yearly calendar. The process enhances children's involvement in their own learning through a hands-on, exploratory approach with a variety of open-ended materials. Play is the medium for the process.

- The teacher is the person *who* creates curriculum, planning and providing for activities and materials in relation to the age range of the group, and observing and evaluating children's growth. Teachers are grounded in child development theory, with an understanding of how children learn, and are aware of the need to individualize in order to meet children's special needs.

- The context is *why* certain projects and activities are chosen, based on the program's philosophy and goals, the cultural backgrounds of the children, and their family and community values and influences. To provide meaningful learning experiences, curriculum should mirror the life of the local community.

The relevance of curriculum is important to note.[1]

Head Start classes on Indian reservations in the Southwest will develop curriculum that utilizes the history and traditions of the various Native American tribes the students represent. Relevant curriculum for a suburban preschool in Seattle will include field trips to the Pike Street Market to see the recent salmon catch, while a transportation unit for inner city Chicago preschoolers will include subway and train rides. One of the factors most critical to the success of the schools of Reggio Emilia, as noted in earlier chapters, is the overlay of the child's cultural history in the curriculum. The theories of Erikson and Vygotsky are evident in this approach to curriculum, especially Vygotsky's belief in the influences of family and culture on the child's learning.

Curriculum is both *integrated* and *individualized*. Individualized curriculum is tailored to meet the needs and interests of a single child rather than those of a group. Teachers individualize curriculum to help foster specific skills and knowledge in a particular child, such as learning to cut with scissors or how to find playmates. *Integrated curriculum* coordinates many subject areas and utilizes a wholistic approach to learning. See Figure 11.4 for an example.

Open Education Revisited

The characteristics of curriculum just described may bring to mind the open schools (see Chapters 1 and 2) of the British infant school model. The emphasis in an open classroom is on the integration of the total curriculum, rather than on the separate subject matter. Academic skills—reading, writing, number concepts—comprise a natural part of all learning. Music can include math and counting; science discussions develop language arts; and dramatic play can spur writing. The stress is on the learning process—what happens when child and materials meet. Their play encourages children to explore, manipulate, and construct; classroom space encourages this. Activity areas, or centers of interest, are set up throughout the room. Children self-select where and with whom they want to spend their time, be it with clay, at woodworking, or at one of the table games. The relationship between an open school curriculum and children's learning is also discussed in Chapter 4 in the section regarding the application of cognitive theory.

Teachers facilitate, or guide, setting up the environment to promote independence and self-sufficiency so that they are free to interact with children. Team teaching is ideal for the open classroom; several teachers can provide the amount of supervision, organization, and planning necessary for success.

[1]Skilled teachers strike a balance between basing curriculum planning on the individual members of the class and the surrounding community, while exposing children to experiences from the culture beyond the immediate area.

Lesson Plan For A Week in February

AREA	GOALS OF ACTIVITY	LEARNING OPPORTUNITY	EMERGENT CURRICULUM	NOTES
INSIDE blocks	to use structure for play to build cooperatively to use different cuts for different purposes	unit blocks; scissors, paper, tape for embellishment	Tues.—add batteries, switches, light bulbs to illuminate structures	
dramatic play	to sustain play in groups of 3+ to play a variety of roles	post office; envelopes, mail boxes, individual mail boxes, stamps, bags for letter carrying	Wed.—add walking trip to post office for a tour	
writing table	to write some upper and lower case letters to dictate compositions for transcription	markers, pencils, blank books, paper, class dictionary		work with Nora on writing name indep.
sensory	to use site for exploration to explore physical properties of sand to construct knowledge of conservation	sand table; funnels, scoops, graduated measures		
manipulatives	to strengthen fine motor control to sort and classify over two variables	mosaic boards; colored pegs-cylinders, rectangles, triangles	Thur.—add pattern cards	make available materials to copy own patterns onto cards
cooking	to wait to take turns to follow a sequence to explore physical properties	fruit shakes; bananas, strawberries, yogurt, honey, butter knives, blender, cups, straws, recipe cards		vary fruit
book rug	to follow sequence of a story read aloud to relate story in own words after hearing	books about the beach, cooking, post office, mail, letters		include books of diversity—non-gender specific roles, ethnicity
OUTSIDE climbing	to climb w/alternating feet and hands to develop upper body strength	boards and boxes, play scape, tree house		
riding	to pedal, steer with skill to use for dramatic play	tricycles—traditional and low slung styles		help Miguel with steering tricycle
sensory	to use site for exploration to use site for constructing replicas of environment	sand box; scoops, buckets, trucks, cardboard piping	Tues.—add water	
dramatic play	to role play with 3+ children to incorporate many elements into play to make own props	play houses; scarves, wraps, housekeeping props, wagons	Wed.—add doll carriages	Petero's new baby to visit

FIGURE 11.2 This plan, created by Kelly Welch, a teacher at the Connecticut College Children's School, is built on the interests and abilities of the group as well as the individual needs of the children. It is a good example of emergent curriculum in a written format.

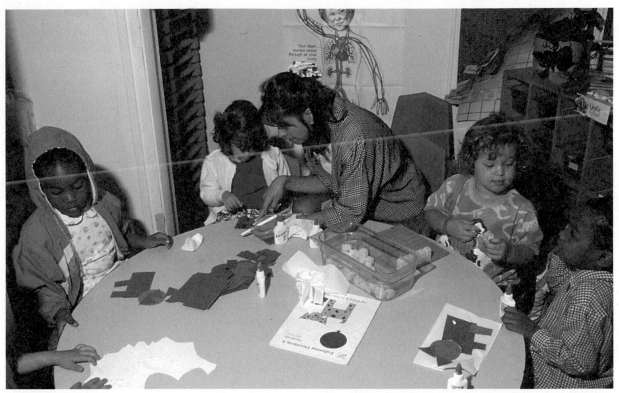

FIGURE 11.3   Children enjoy and get involved with developmentally appropriate materials. Making a collage is fun and a popular sensory experience.

While loosely structured classrooms may prove challenging and stimulating to some children, others may find the lack of structure difficult. More traditional programs offer clear goals that are measured by evaluation and testing. The open school's approach includes the children in the planning and evaluation of some of the learning that takes place. If the experiences in an open classroom are not integrated into the total curriculum and the learnings not related in some meaningful way, they remain merely good—but isolated—experiences for the child. "Done well," says Elkind, "open education can be a model of truly humanistic education; done poorly, it can be a disaster" (Elkind, 1993).

Emergent Curriculum

There are many ways to plan curriculum. One of the most common in early childhood settings is based on the premise that curriculum is everything that happens throughout the course of a day; it is all of the children's experiences as they interact with people and materials. The emphasis is on children's interests and involvement in their learning and in their ability to make constructive choices. Teachers set up the room and the yard, sometimes planning one or two activities each day that will invite children to participate. For the most part, teachers respond by watching and evaluating what children do and support what use children make of their experience. This is a process-oriented approach; curriculum content is apparent, but an end product or result is not the major focus. It is known as *emergent curriculum*. (Jones and Nimmo, 1994).

High/Scope and Reggio Emilia schools are programs which seem to typify the rationale for emergent curriculum. Based on the principles of Erikson, Piaget, and Vygotsky, they epitomize a philosophy that says that children are active, curious, powerful learners, capable of taking the initiative and constructing their knowledge through experience. Children are encouraged to use whatever style of learning (Gardner, 1983) is most natural to them, making use of the variety of materials in their

In music: Singing "Five Little Pumpkins"
In routines: Waiting for a turn because "too many" are brushing teeth already
In books: *Inch by Inch* by Lionni, *Millions of Cats* by Gag
In block play: Observing and using the fractions and wholes that make up a set of unit blocks
In physical development: Playing hopscotch
In cooking: Measuring and counting items in the recipe
In dramatic play: Noting there are only four hoses but five firefighters
In science: Counting number of rainy/sunny/snowy days; recording temperatures (thermometers); time (clocks and calendars); and seasons (charts)
In art: Numbers: learning one-to-one correspondence by counting brushes, crayons, magic markers, and colors

FIGURE 11.4 Young children learn best from an integrated approach to curriculum. Mathematical concepts are reflected throughout the classroom in a variety of activities.

own way. A materials-rich environment where play is valued forms the setting for such programs.

Emergent curriculum is a process approach to curriculum which calls for collaboration on the part of teachers with children and with other adults. The accent is on mutual learning for both children and adults. Teachers and children think, plan, and critique together. Curriculum emerges from dialogue and reflection among the teaching staff (Jones and Nimmo, 1994), as much as it draws from the interactions between children and teachers. In the Reggio Emilia schools, teachers are seen as collaborators and guides who create curriculum as they take their cues from children's interests and assist them in serious investigation of a topic (see "The Project Approach" on p. 346; the topic of "Webbing" under Planning Curriculum on p. 339 for an example of how teachers' collaboration evolves into curriculum.) Emergent curriculum seems to capture the spontaneous nature of children's play and blend it with the necessary planning and organization.

A number of sources feed into emergent curriculum: children's interests, teachers' interests, developmental tasks of the age group, the physical environment, the natural environment, people, curriculum resource books, unexpected events, everyday life experiences and routines, and the values expressed by the school, the parents, and the community (Jones and Nimmo, 1994). As teachers observe, discuss, and plan, the focus is always on the child, not the activity. Figure 11.2 is an example of curriculum planning based on the emergent curriculum approach.

Developmentally Appropriate Curriculum

Appropriate early childhood curriculum is based on the theory, research, and experience of knowing how young children develop and learn. An infant curriculum meets the basic needs of young babies; a toddler curriculum takes into consideration the emerging independence and mobility of toddlers. Four-year-olds require different materials and teaching techniques, as do five- or eight-year-olds. Each age level deserves special consideration when curriculum is being planned.

What is meant by appropriate programs, curricula, or practices has been defined by The National Association for the Education of Young Children (NAEYC) as follows:

● *Appropriateness:* Programs and practices are based on knowledge of normal development within a given age span.

● *Individual appropriateness:* Programs and practices are based on respect for the individual child, the individual rate of growth, and the unique learning style.

Developmentally appropriate curriculum takes into account a knowledge of child development theory, research and practice, including various related disciplines; cultural values; parental desires and concerns; community context; individual children; teachers' knowledge and experience; and is related to overall program goals.[1] This implies a theoretical framework about how, when,

[1]There is no one "recipe" for Developmentally Appropriate Practice; rather, sound practice is related to the individual children, families, and the community in which one teaches.

GUIDELINES FOR DEVELOPMENTALLY APPROPRIATE CURRICULUM

NAEYC and the National Association of Early Childhood Specialists in State Departments of Education jointly developed guidelines to insure developmentally appropriate curriculum. Each of the guidelines is in the form of a question to which teachers developing curriculum for young children should be able to answer "yes."

1. Does it promote interactive learning and encourage the child's construction of knowledge?
2. Does it help achieve social, emotional, physical, and cognitive goals?
3. Does it encourage development of positive feelings and dispositions toward learning while leading to acquisition of knowledge and skills?
4. Is it meaningful for these children? Is it relevant to the children's lives? Can it be made more relevant by relating it to a personal experience children have had or can they easily gain direct experience with it?
5. Are the expectations realistic and attainable at this time or could the children more easily and efficiently acquire the knowledge or skills later on?
6. Is it of interest to children and to the teacher?
7. Is it sensitive to and respectful of cultural and linguistic diversity? Does it expect, allow, and appreciate individual differences? Does it promote positive relationships with families?
8. Does it build on and elaborate children's current knowledge and abilities?
9. Does it lead to conceptual understanding by helping children construct their own understanding in meaningful contexts?
10. Does it facilitate integration of content across traditional subject matter areas?
11. Is the information presented accurate and credible according to the recognized standards of the relevant discipline?
12. Is this content worth knowing? Can it be learned by these children efficiently and effectively now?
13. Does it encourage active learning and allow children to make meaningful choices?
14. Does it foster children's exploration and inquiry, rather than focusing on "right" answers or "right" ways to complete a task?
15. Does it promote the development of higher order abilities such as thinking, reasoning, problem solving, and decision making?
16. Does it promote and encourage social interaction among children and adults?
17. Does it respect children's physiological needs for activity, sensory stimulation, fresh air, rest, and nourishment/elimination?
18. Does it promote feelings of psychological safety, security, and belonging?
19. Does it provide experiences that promote feelings of success, competence, and enjoyment of learning?
20. Does it permit flexibility for children and teachers?

FIGURE 11.5 (Adapted from *Guidelines for Appropriate Curriculum Content and Assessment in Programs Serving Children Ages 3 Through 8*. A position statement of the National Association for the Education of Young Children and the National Association of Early Childhood Specialists in State Departments of Education. *Young Children*, March 1991, pp. 21–38.)

PLANNING AN ACTIVITY

Purpose of Activity: Think about how children will learn
    Concepts
    To discriminate
    Vocabulary
    Social skills
    Motor skills
    Feelings of competence and confidence
    Method or process of the activity

Presentation: Think about
    What antecedents are necessary for this activity?
    To whom will you present it—individual, group—and what ages?
    Where are you going to present it—in/outdoors? What area?
    Materials/props you will need—how will you use them?
    What words will you use to introduce and carry through the activity?
    What are the cleanup provisions? Will children be involved? How?

Results: Ask yourself
    What was the children's response to the activity?
    Did you achieve what you wanted?
    What are the implications for other activities?
    Were there any problems and how did you solve them?

FIGURE 11.6 Good planning takes time and thought. These questions can help the teacher focus on the important aspects of planning an activity for young children.

and what children learn. The foundation for developmentally appropriate practices and curriculum content is historically rooted in John Dewey's vision that schools prepare students to think and reason in order to participate in a democratic society (see Chapter 1). Figure 11.5 lists twenty guidelines jointly endorsed by the National Association for the Education of Young Children and the National Association of Early Childhood Specialists in State Departments of Education to ensure developmentally appropriate curriculum. It can be used as a checklist as you move through the next three chapters, which focus on curriculum.

Developmentally appropriate curriculum is integrated curriculum; that is, it is woven across many subject areas. Figure 11.4 shows how mathematical principles are fostered as an integral part of the child's day. Other illustrations in this and the following three chapters that demonstrate an integrated curriculum are Figures 11.2, 11.4, 11.7, 11.10, 11.16, 11.17, 11.18, 11.19, 12.15, 12.16, 13.5, 13.6, 13.7, 13.9, 13.10, 13.15, 13.16, 13.19, 13.20, 13.23, 14.2, 14.9, 14.11, 14.21, 14.22, and 14.29.

The NAEYC's recent position statements and guidelines on appropriate program practices and curriculum for early childhood settings can be used as a basis for sound curriculum planning. These materials cover the age span of birth through age eight; developmental characteristics unique to each age group (infants, toddlers, preschoolers, and primary ages) form the basis for determining appropriate practices. A resource of this kind should be consulted before curriculum plans are developed.

Planning Curriculum

Written Plans

When developing curriculum, written plans are helpful, especially for the beginning teacher. A written plan is an organized agenda, an outline to follow, a framework for the curriculum. It may include a list of activities, goals for children's learning experiences, the process or method of instruction, the teacher's responsibilities, the time of day, and other special notations. A curriculum may be developed for a day, a week, a month, or for a specific unit or theme. The questions in Figure 11.6 should be asked when planning a curriculum activity for young children. Figure 11.3 illustrates a weekly curriculum and Figure 11.18 does the same for toddlers. This and the next three chapters contain many different examples of written lesson plans.

Planning by Objectives

Another approach to curriculum development requires more formal, organized planning. Comprehensive lesson plans are developed, sometimes for the whole year, and usually include *objectives*, the stated concepts that children will learn through this experience. These are commonly called *behavioral objectives*. The lesson plans include specific, stated, observable behaviors that children will be able to demonstrate to show that the teaching objective has been met. In other words, a behavioral objective states clearly what children will actually *do* (be able to hold scissors properly; grasp a pencil between thumb and first two fingers). If the behavioral objective is to improve fine-motor skills, the lesson plan includes activities and events that foster children's use of their fine-motor skills. Several objectives may apply to a given activity. It is then important to order the objectives so that the purposes of the lesson remains in focus. To plan successfully, the teacher needs to know developmental and behavioral theory (Chapter 4), to have good observational strategies (Chapter 6), and to possess tools to assess whether or not the objective was accomplished (Chapter 10).

Figure 11.9 reflects the planning approach with the use of behavioral objectives. A more developed plan found in early childhood classrooms would include activities for the full range of curriculum areas, such as art, motor activities, dramatic play, for each of the objectives.

Too much attention can be focused on an isolated skill (Elkin 1987) where the objectives and goal become the curriculum itself. Too little planning can result in a curriculum free-for-all where integration of learning never takes place. A balance must be achieved between excess planning and go-with-the-flow curriculum to insure that children's needs and interests are being met and to guarantee children a sense of organization and intentionality about what they learn.

Two important factors in developing curriculum objectives are (1) how much knowledge and understanding children have, and (2) what children are interested in. The most effective curriculum grows out of the child's interests and experiences. As they play, children reveal their levels of experience and information as well as their misconceptions and confusions, providing the clues from which teachers can develop curriculum that is meaningful.

Webbing

According to Katz and Chard (1989), webbing is the process through which teachers develop a diagram based on a particular topic or theme, highlighting key ideas and concepts. Ideas generated from brainstorming sessions flesh out the topic with many subheadings and lists of curriculum possibilities. Figure 11.7 illustrates a curriculum or topic web.

Webbing is a planning tool which provides depth to a topic and creates a map of possible activities and projects. A web may be organized around a theme (water), into curriculum areas (language arts, music), or around program goals (problem solving, cooperation). By their very nature, webs foster an integrated curriculum approach and help teachers extend children's learning and experiences.

Creating a web can be fun, allowing teachers to use their imaginations and calling into play their knowledge, resources, and experience. Katz and Chard (1989) suggest the following process to develop a web, using examples from Figure 11.7:

1. *Brainstorming.* Using small slips of paper, teachers write down theme or topic ideas—each idea on a separate piece of paper. For the topic "Things that happen in fall and winter," for instance, the slips would contain ideas such as "cut jack-o-lanterns" or "rake leaves."

2. *Grouping.* The slips of paper are organized into groups of similar ideas, and, using a colored piece of paper, a heading is given to each group.

"Canning and preserving" and "seasonal recipes" fall under the heading of "Cooking." Smaller subgroups can be created, if necessary.

3. *Sharing.* Teachers can share their ideas with one another, rearranging the headings and subheadings as they share skills, resources, and information with one another.

4. *Drawing.* The ideas can be transferred to a piece of paper, placing the topic or theme in the center and drawing lines radiating out to the headings (group time, manipulatives, dramatic play). This creates a visual record of the relationships between and among the ideas and becomes what Workman and Anziano (1993) call "a living, growing resource."

Jones and Nimmo (1994) echo the organic nature of a web. First created as a response to children's ideas, it creates a picture in which ideas emerge and connect in any number of ways. It is, of course, a tentative plan, for what happens next depends on the children's responses. The web creates a flexible plan which can be altered and adapted as teachers observe children and evaluate their interest.

Advantages of Written Plans

Setting lesson plans to paper has many advantages. Doing so:

● Helps teachers focus on the nature of the children they teach—their interests, their needs, their capabilities, their potential.

● Encourages thorough, in-depth planning of curriculum in a logical progression; provides a direction.

● Helps teachers clarify thoughts and articulate a rationale for what they do.

● Stimulates teamwork when teachers plan together, sharing their ideas and resources.

● Allows everyone to know what is happening; in case of absences, a substitute teacher can carry out the plans.

● Gives a foundation from which changes can be made; allows for flexibility, adaptation, and on-the-spot decisions.

● Allows for time to prepare materials, to see what is needed and what resources to gather or contact.

● Provides a concrete format from which evaluation and assessment can be made.

● Serves as a communication tool for the teaching staff, for parents, and for the governing agency.

● Teachers see how much they have offered children, and the program's worth is communicated to others.

Written plans may or may not include all of the other activities normally available in the interest centers all week. Blocks, manipulatives, and dramatic play, as well as science, math, and language materials remain available for children to choose, but some teachers include only planned learning experiences and teacher-directed activities in their written plans. Certain activities are part of the everyday routine. The more focused (and probably written) planned learning experiences are integrated with them to provide challenge and variety.

Teacher Considerations

The aim of curriculum is to help children acquire the skills and behaviors that will promote their optimal growth physically, socially, emotionally, and intellectually. Teachers consider a number of factors in developing a curriculum to provide maximum learning opportunities.

Among these are the educational philosophy and goals of the program. A family day care provider plans activities for a few children in an intimate setting while the kindergarten teacher arranges small working groups so that the large group will not seem overwhelming. The activities should support the goals of the program and result in the goals being accomplished.

Probably the single most important determinant the teacher must consider is the children themselves. Their ages, developmental levels, individuality, and learning styles are barometers of what will be successful and stimulating curriculum. The number of children in the class will affect the teacher's planning, as will their ethnic and cultural backgrounds. Teachers like to plan curriculum experiences that draw on children's prior

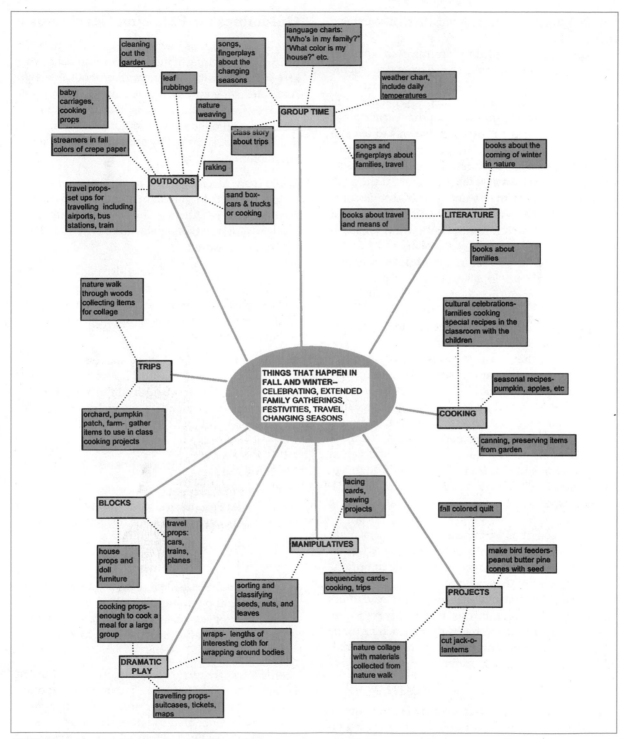

FIGURE 11.7 Using a theme bassed on children's interests and ideas, the web provides an avenue to foster relationships between ideas and events and helps extend children's knowledge and experience. (Thanks to Kelly Welch of Connecticut College Children's School for this example.)

knowledge and experience, but which also extend their thinking.

Effective curriculum planning stems from a knowledge of young children. Teachers ask themselves what concepts children should learn and how they will teach those concepts. What does the child already know, and how can the teacher build on that? What is the most effective way to teach a particular concept to this group of children—through sensory exploration or large-muscle practice? In many ways, teachers start at the end: they look at what they want the child to accomplish or to learn as a result of this experience and then plan the curriculum to lead toward those results.

Planning for a broad range of developmental skills and interests is a key factor in creating a classroom curriculum. Because the abilities of children even of the same age vary, activities must be open-ended and flexible enough to be used by a number of children with varieties of skills. Remember, too, that some children may not be interested in formal or organized art projects or science experiences. These children may learn more easily through self-selected play: by wearing a space helmet and fantasizing a trip to the moon, by building with blocks for long periods, or by running and climbing out of doors. The developmental Word Pictures of children from birth through age eight found in Chapter 3 can be useful in determining what kinds of activities appeal to young children.

All activities—especially those that are planned and formal—should be conducted in an atmosphere of play that offers the children options in choosing what they need to learn.

A **prerequisite** for planning is the availability of people and material resources and ways to use them. What are the strengths of the teaching staff? Are there enough supplies and equipment available? Are there enough adults to supervise the activities?

The amount of time available in the daily schedule and the amount of space in the room or yard affect a teacher's planning. Fingerpainting requires time for children to get involved, a proximity to water for cleanup, and an area in which to store wet paintings. All of these elements must be considered when teachers plan to include fingerpainting in the curriculum.

Guidelines for Planning Curriculum

The process of developing curriculum is the process of teaching children who and what they are. It begins with understanding what goals are set for learning and then choosing the most pressing ones for attention. Using available resources, teachers plan effective curriculum for young children. The five steps below are guidelines to sound curriculum planning.

1. *Set goals.* Decide what it is you want children to learn. What do you want them to know about themselves? Others? The world? State goals clearly, preferably in behavioral terms so results can be measured.

2. *Establish priorities.* Make a list of three to five goals or objectives you consider most important. State the reasons for your choices; your own values and educational priorities will emerge more clearly.

3. *Know the resources.* A rich, successful, and creative curriculum relies on a vast number of resources. To create a health clinic in the dramatic play area, for instance, you might need the following resources:

   ● *Materials:* Props, such as stethoscopes, X rays, tongue depressors, band aids, medical gowns, and masks.

   ● *People:* Parents and/or community people in the health care professions to visit the class.

   ● *Community:* Field trips to nearby clinics, hospitals, dentist's office.

4. *Plan ahead.* Set aside a regular time to meet for curriculum planning. This may be on a weekly, monthly, or seasonal basis. Discuss the curriculum activities as well as the daily routines in order to integrate the two.

5. *Evaluate.* Reflect on the outcome of your planning. Consider what worked and what did not, why it was successful or not. Look at the part of the experience that did not work as well as you would have liked. How can it be improved? What can you change about it? An evaluation should be immediate, precise, and supportive. Teachers need feedback about their planning and implementing skills. By refining and im-

proving the curriculum, the needs of children are better served.

Curriculum Focus

Curriculum, as defined here, is all-encompassing. Teachers select from all the possibilities that afford the potential for learning and focus on projects and activities in a balanced, integrated way. Three common approaches are to look at (1) the activity or learning centers in the classroom; (2) the skills of the children; and (3) themes.

Classroom Activity Centers

The activity centers in most early childhood programs consist of:

Indoors	*Outdoors*
Creative arts	Climbing equipment
Blocks	Swings
Table toys/manipulatives	Sand/mud/water
Science/discovery	Wheel toys
Dramatic play	Woodworking
Language arts/books	Hollow blocks
Math	Music
Music	Nature/science

All of these centers offer activities and materials for children to choose from during free play time—the greatest portion of their school day. Paints are in the easel trays, puzzles on the tables, dress-up clothes and props in the housekeeping/dramatic play center, blocks and accessories in the block corner, and books and tapes in the language area. Teachers plan the resources and materials and place them so that children readily see the alternatives available to them. Some of these activities might be teacher-directed on occasion: cooking snacks in the housekeeping area, fingerpainting in art, creating castles with blocks. For the most part, however, these activities will be self-initiating and child-directed. At all times, the emphasis will be on providing a child-centered curriculum.

FIGURE 11.8 Teachers of toddlers encourage touching and feeling, simple problem-solving, and choosing play materials. They remain patient as children explore the environment.

Whatever the area, it needs attention and planning. Wherever children are present, learning and playing will take place. Since each play space will make a contribution to children's experiences, teachers should develop appropriate curriculum for that learning area. Figure 11.7 demonstrates curriculum potential, both indoors and out.

Go back and review what Chapter 9 offers as some of the important principles in creating environments that reflect curriculum goals.

Children's Skills

Just as curriculum can be developed by focusing on the activity or learning centers, so, too, can an early childhood program be planned around the skill levels of the children in the class.

The first decision teachers must make concerns what particular skill they wish to help children develop. The skill can be in the area of physical, cognitive, language, creative, social, or emotional development. The nature of the individual class and the program philosophy will help teachers establish priorities for these skills. Teachers then select the activities and materials that will enhance the development of any one or more of those particular skills. Figure 11.10 shows how the cognitive skill of classification can be implemented in the classroom, making it the focus of the entire curriculum.

PLANNING BY OBJECTIVES

Activity	Teaching Objectives	Behavioral Objectives/Child Will
Painting with corn cobs	Tactile stimulation; awareness of textural design; fine-motor coordination; observational skills	Describe how it feels and looks; grasp, manipulate and examine cob; use thumb and forefinger to hold cob while painting; compare with other textures
Outdoor Obstacle	Spatial awareness; balance; gross-motor development; building confidence	Walk across 6' board at 2" and 4" heights; crawl through tunnel; jump from height of 2-1/2' without assistance; call for others to watch; repeat the course on own

FIGURE 11.9 Learning objectives define the goals and describe the desired behavior or outcome. (For guidelines in observation, see Chapter 6.)

Themes

A common method of developing curriculum is to focus on themes also known as units. While used interchangeably, themes are generally a smaller part of a unit allowing for a more specific focus. For example, a unit on the body may have "What I can do with my hands" as one theme. This mode of planning is used in many early childhood and elementary settings; it is often a way to emphasize holidays. Focusing on themes, however, can and should be much more than that.

Themes that are of great interest to young children are those that directly concern themselves. The body as a theme suggests many avenues for development; body parts may be emphasized; exploration using the senses may be stressed; measuring and weighing children may be used to demonstrate growth of the body. Another subject to which children readily respond is that of home and family. Animals, especially pets, are appealing to young children and can lead into further curriculum areas of wild animals, prehistoric animals, and so on.

The more in touch with children the teachers are, the more their classroom themes should reflect the children's interests and abilities. Children who live in Silicon Valley in California, in Houston, Texas, or in Central Florida will have a local interest in space shuttles and computers. The urban child of New York, Detroit, or Washington, D.C., will relate more readily to themes about subways, taxis, and tall buildings. Children's interests often focus on, but are not necessarily limited to, what they have experienced. By choosing themes that coincide with children's daily lives, teachers promote connected and relevant learning.

Television, travel, and older brothers and sisters enlarge a child's vision so that the themes a teacher chooses do not have to reflect only the world in which the child lives. With appropriate visual aids and manipulative materials, a child in the sunbelt can experience snow and ice vicariously or enjoy learning a song and dance from Spain.

Some themes in an early childhood setting can address children's own issues. All young children share similar fears and curiosity about the world they do not know but imagine so vividly. The cues children give, particularly about their concerns, suggest to the observant teacher some important themes of childhood. During Halloween, for example, it can be helpful and reassuring to children if the theme of masks is developed. Select some masks that have a function, such as hospital masks, ski masks, safety glasses, sun glasses, snorkel masks, or wrestling and football helmets. Children can try them on and become comfortable with the way their appearance changes. They can laugh with friends as they look in the mirror to see how a mask changes the appearance but does not change the person.

Prehistoric animals are another theme that calls attention to the natural world and deals with

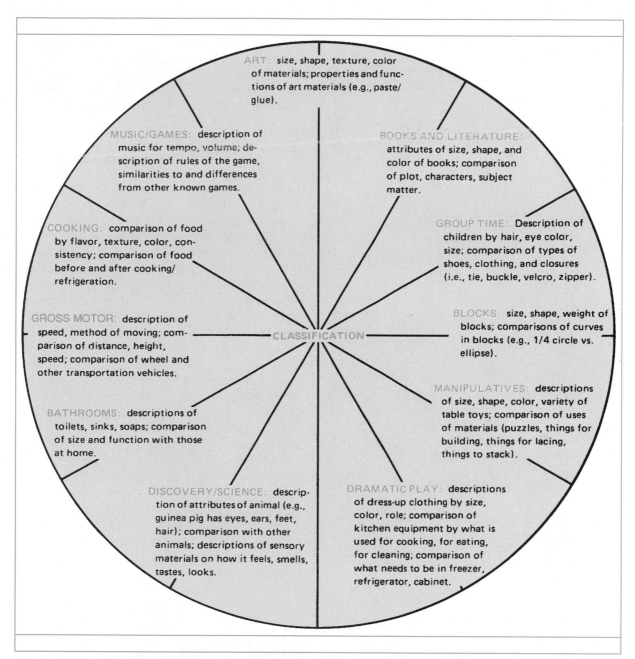

ART: size, shape, texture, color of materials; properties and functions of art materials (e.g., paste/glue).

MUSIC/GAMES: description of music for tempo, volume; description of rules of the game, similarities to and differences from other known games.

COOKING: comparison of food by flavor, texture, color, consistency; comparison of food before and after cooking/refrigeration.

GROSS MOTOR: description of speed, method of moving; comparison of distance, height, speed; comparison of wheel and other transportation vehicles.

BATHROOMS: descriptions of toilets, sinks, soaps; comparison of size and function with those at home.

DISCOVERY/SCIENCE: description of attributes of animal (e.g., guinea pig has eyes, ears, feet, hair); comparison with other animals; descriptions of sensory materials on how it feels, smells, tastes, looks.

BOOKS AND LITERATURE: attributes of size, shape, and color of books; comparison of plot, characters, subject matter.

GROUP TIME: Description of children by hair, eye color, size; comparison of types of shoes, clothing, and closures (i.e., tie, buckle, velcro, zipper).

BLOCKS: size, shape, weight of blocks; comparisons of curves in blocks (e.g., 1/4 circle vs. ellipse).

MANIPULATIVES: descriptions of size, shape, color, variety of table toys; comparison of uses of materials (puzzles, things for building, things for lacing, things to stack).

DRAMATIC PLAY: descriptions of dress-up clothing by size, color, role; comparison of kitchen equipment by what is used for cooking, for eating, for cleaning; comparison of what needs to be in freezer, refrigerator, cabinet.

CLASSIFICATION

FIGURE 11.10 Curriculum can be developed with a focus on a particular skill. Classification skills can be enhanced throughout the curriculum and in activity centers. NOTE: This a graphic way to demonstrate an integrated curriculum, not an example of a format on how to write curriculum plans.

FIGURE 11.11 A project emerged from the need for a new table. Children in Reggio Emilio, Italy, used their feet as a measuring device and drew up plans for the carpenter. Active exploration of the problem and art as a natural medium for children of all ages gives the project approach meaning.

issues of monsters, both real and imaginary. Learning about sea animals and the ocean can give young children an opportunity to talk about the wild and noisy waves, sharks, and just getting their faces wet in salty water.

Through holiday themes, teachers can reinforce the multicultural nature of the curriculum.

Ethnic, national, and religious holidays from all over the world help children celebrate the differences and similarities in people and their heritage. Themes relating to children's cultural and ethnic backgrounds and their neighborhood environments also provide rich curriculum potential.[1]

The Project Approach

A recent revival of a curriculum approach used in progressive schools (see Dewey, Chapter 1) is worth noting here. In *Engaging Children's Minds: A Project Approach* (1989), authors Katz and Chard describe how to go beyond themes and units for an in-depth study of a particular topic by one or more children. Based on the belief that "children's minds should be engaged in ways that deepen their understanding of their own experiences and environment" (Katz and Chard, 1989), the *project approach* consists of exploring a theme or topic (such as babies, dinosaurs, riding the school bus) over a period of days or weeks. Investigations of the theme and preplanning by the children and teachers is the first step: they observe, question, estimate, experiment, and research items and events related to the topic. Together they make dramatic play and display materials they need. When fully engaged, dramatic play becomes the primary vehicle by which children enact the roles related to the project theme. Children work in small groups throughout the process and have the opportunity to make numerous choices about their level of participation. Project work has different levels of complexity so it meets the needs of children of different ages and abilities.

In the small town of Reggio Emilia in northern Italy, a similar approach to curriculum has received world-wide attention. The project approach is utilized in even greater depth as it permeates the entire curriculum and school environment.

Four key elements create the unique curriculum of Reggio Emilia and enhance the project approach to learning: (1) teachers believe that children learn best when they actively explore

[1]Some programs choose not to celebrate holidays at all, questioning whether or not it is DAP, and how to adequately understand and explain the many holidays observed by people in the US. Other programs invite members of the community to educate them about their particular observances.

What is critical in ODW is to remember if holidays are celebrated, celebrations beyond the dominant culture should be included.

problems; (2) the art media, as a natural form of expression and exploration, provides the vehicle by which children can express themselves, their understanding of the world, and their learning; (3) the entire community is a resource—from a statue in a park to an observatory outside of town to senior citizens; and (4) the teachers understand their teaching role as a co-constructors with the children.

Projects emerge from children's own interests, teacher observations of children's needs and interests, and parents' suggestions. The topics reflect the local culture of the children.[1]

Art supplies range from fabrics and natural materials to pieces of wire and plastics and are artfully arranged and accessible to children. A special room in each school, the *atelier*, is used by every class for long-term projects. Sculptures, drawings, collages, and paintings throughout the school serve as reminders of numerous projects.

To achieve outstanding results, children work in small groups so they are able to discuss and analyze problems and negotiate solutions. The teacher records the activity on tape and with photographs.

The planning process is crucial to the success of the project approach as is the underlying philosophy that children can be co-constructors of their own education. This approach has much in common with both Dewey and Summerhill (see Chapter 1). The teacher helps children explore what they already know about the topic, what they might need to know, and how they can represent that knowledge through various media, reinforcing Vygotsky's theory that interaction and direct teaching are important aspects of intellectual development. Teachers pose questions for children that lead them to suggest a hypothesis: What might happen if you do that? What do you think you could do to make that work? Children are encouraged to evaluate their own work and learn to defend and explain their creations to others.

A project approach has the potential to "provide a context in which all aspects of children's minds can be engaged, challenged, and enriched" (Katz and Chard, 1989).

FIGURE 11.12 Planning for physical skills is part of good curriculum development, especially in urban areas where space is at a minimum.

CURRICULUM EXPRESSED THROUGH PLAY

What Is Play?

Play! What a wonderful word! It calls up images from the past, those childhood years when playing was the focus of our waking hours. "Will you play with me?" is one of the most expressive, expectant questions known. It carries with it hope and anticipation about a world of fun and make-believe, a world of adventure and exploration, a world of the young child.

City streets, parks and fields, tenements, huts, empty rooms, and backyards are all settings for

[1]The project approach provides the opportunity to avoid a "tourist approach" and provides children and teachers with an in-depth understanding of a particular culture and its traditions.

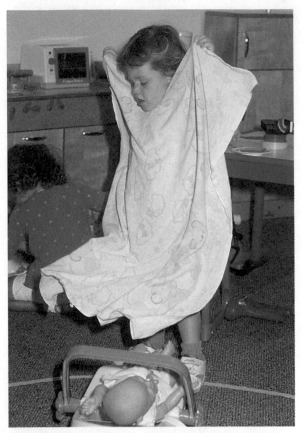

FIGURE 11.13 Play: the essence of childhood.

play. Play is a way of life for children; it is their natural response. It is what children *do* and it is serious business to them. Any activity children choose to engage in is play; it is neverending.

Play is the essence of creativity in children throughout the world. Play is universal and knows "no national or cultural boundaries" (Frost, 1985).[1] Educators and psychologists have called play a reflection of the child's growth, the essence of the child's life, a window into the child's world. It is a self-satisfying activity through which children gain control and come to understand life. Play teaches children about themselves; they learn how tall—or short—they are, what words to use to get a turn on the swing, and where to put their hands when climbing a ladder. Through play, children learn about the world: what the color purple is, how to make matzoh balls, and how

to be a friend. Play helps children define who they are.

Play takes many forms. Children play when they sing, dig in the mud, build a block tower, or dress up. Play can be purely physical (running, climbing, ball throwing) or highly intellectual (solving an intricate puzzle, remembering the words to a song). Play is creative when crayons, clay, and fingerpaint are used. Its emotional form is expressed when children pretend to be mommies, daddies, or babies. Skipping rope with a friend, playing jacks, and sharing a book are examples of the social side of play.

Types of Play

There is a general sequence to the development of social play. Babies and toddlers have a clearly defined social self. Infant play begins with patterns established at birth: babies gaze, smile, and make sociable sounds in response to the quality and frequency of attention from a parent or caregiver. Socialization of infants occurs through interaction. By the end of their first year, infants smile at and touch one another and vocalize in a sociable effort (Berk, 1994). Toddlers play well on their own (*solitary play*) or with adults. They begin solitary pretend play around one year of age. During the toddler years, as children become more aware of one another, they begin to play side by side, without interacting (*parallel play*). They are aware of and pleased about the other person, but are not directly involved with them. It is during this second year that toddlers begin some form of *coordinated play*, doing something with another child. This is similar to the preschooler's *associative play*. The preschool years bring many changes for children in relation to social development. The number and quality of relationships outside the home increase as does the ability to play with other children. At first, this is accomplished just by a child's presence in a group: playing at the water table with four other children or joining a circle for fingerplays (*associative play*). When children join forces with one another in an active way, when they verbalize, plan, and carry out play, *cooperative*

 OUR DIVERSE WORLD OUR DIVERSE WORLD OUR DIVERSE WORLD OUR DIVERSE WORLD OUR DIVERSE WORLD

[1]Play allows the early childhood educator to focus on universal characteristics which are the same for children the world over.

Solitary play.

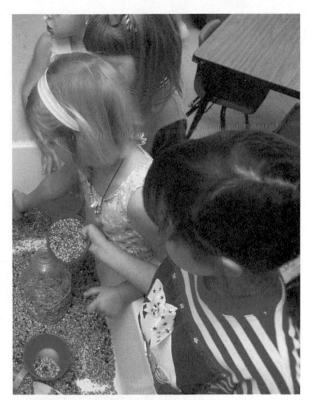

Associative play—fun to do together.

Parallel play—side by side.

Joining forces in cooperative play.

FIGURE 11.14   A timeline of social play.

FIGURE 11.15 With encouragement, boys can learn to enjoy activities, such as drawing and sewing, which are often associated with girls. (Courtesy of Centro Infantil & de Reabilitacao de A-Da-Beja, Lisbon, Portugal.)

play is established. This is the most common type of peer interaction during these preschool years. Figure 11.14 shows a timeline of social play development.

Most play is unstructured and happens naturally when the curriculum is designed for play. **Spontaneous play** is the unplanned, self-selected activity in which children freely participate. Children's natural inclinations are toward play materials and experiences that are developmentally appropriate. Therefore, when they are allowed to make choices in a free play situation, children will choose activities that express their individual interests, needs, and readiness levels.

Dramatic play—or imaginative or pretend play—is a common form of spontaneous play. Three- and four-year-olds are at the peak of their interest in this type of activity. In dramatic play, children assume the roles of different characters, both animate and inanimate. Children identify themselves with another person or thing, playing out situations that interest or frighten them. Dramatic play reveals children's attitudes and concepts toward people and things in their environment. Much of the play is wishful thinking, pretending great strength and deeds. This is the way children cope with their smallness or lack of strength. Superhero play is appealing, since it so readily addresses a child's sense of helplessness and inferiority. Pretending to be Wonder Woman makes it easier to understand and accept the limitations of the real world. Dramatic play provides the means for children to work out their difficulties by themselves. By doing so, they become free to pursue other tasks and more formal learning. For all these reasons, play is invaluable for young children.

Sociodramatic play happens when at least two children cooperate in dramatic play. Both types of play involve two basic elements: imitation and make-believe (Smilansky, 1990). Sociodramatic play is, according to Frost (1992), "the most highly developed form of symbolic play" and its importance to social and intellectual development cannot be exaggerated.

Vygotsky takes that one step further, according to Berk (1994), by naming play as "the preeminent educational activity of early childhood." His view of pretend play is that the *zone of proximal development* (see Chapters 4 and 7) allows children

Water play promotes:	*By teaching children:*
Emotional growth	The soothing effect of water; the pleasure of playing with a messy, sometimes forbidden medium; sensory pleasure in splashing, trickling, swirling water through fingers, hands, and feet.
Language development	Play with words of alliteration (swish, swirl, splish, splash); new words: funnel, eyedropper, siphon, float.
Creativity	New ways to store, move, and pour water.
Social growth	To share space at a water table as well as to share some of the equipment; to be next to or across from a friend; to have fun with others; to wait for a turn.
Cognitive development	Problem solving with tubes, sieves, pipes; experimenting with measurement, float and sink properties, volume, quantity, fractions, weight, comparisons, numbers, temperature.
Physical coordination	**Eye-hand coordination; fine-motor control in learning to pour, squeeze, balance.**

FIGURE 11.16   Water play is fun and promotes learning.

to raise themselves to higher levels of behavior. Play assists the child in creating imaginary situations which are governed by rules. Pretending to be a firefighter, Sherry grabs a piece of rope and runs toward the playhouse, saying "shhshhshshsh-shsh" while pretending to squirt water on the fire. She shouts to her playmates, "Over here! Come over here! The fire is on this side."

Sherry's make-believe scenario and her ability to follow the rules of behavior common to firefighters (grabbing hoses, imitating water noises) are the two critical factors from Vygotsky's point of view. That firefighting scene supports his theory that cognitive skills develop through social interactions. Sherry examplifies a child moving from concrete to abstract thought, since she did not require realistic objects (a hose and water) but imagined them with a rope and her ability to create the sound of water. This ability to separate thoughts from actions and objects will stand Sherry in good stead when she studies math concepts. Rules that

children follow in make-believe play teach them to make choices, to think and plan about what they will do, and to show a willingness toward self-restraint, as children learn to follow the social rules of pretend play. This is important preparation for real-life situations. Vygotsky, more than anyone else, has made that critical connection between social and intellectual development.

Edgar Klugman's Focus Box on p. 352 and Laura Berk's Focus Box in Chapter 4 illuminate Vygotsky's principles in differing but complementary ways.

Gender Differences

Teachers and parents have observed that boys and girls seem to show distinct differences in their play choices, play behavior, and toy selection from an early age. In fact, gender differences are first noticeable in children around one year of age and quite obvious by the later preschool years.

FOCUS

Play: The Curriculum of the Child

Edgar Klugman

Have you ever thought about the importance of play in the lives of young children? Think back to your own early experiences in school. When young children move from preschool to "real" school (kindergarten or first grade), in many classrooms the emphasis on play seems to evaporate. Yet we know that play continues to be a very important part of children's healthy development.

When a child enters first grade, much of the expected work has become symbolic and abstract. Playtime, as remembered by many, has often been relegated to "recess." One can think about the levels of abstraction with which an ordinary six- or seven-year-old must cope. There is the imaginary trip to the desert (social studies or science), computing the total of five plus seven (arithmetic), dictating or writing a story about a prince and princess (language arts). What is common to all of these examples is that they require children to imagine something that they may never have actually experienced or perhaps even thought about before. The imagining that children must do in adding two numbers or picturing the desert or creating a story can be done more easily and skillfully if the child has had previous experience in "make-believe." Having played out the roles of "mommy and daddy" and developed sequences in dramatic and sociodramatic play helps youngsters, at a later age, to become more expert players at the curriculum in schools and better players of the life-game. It seems clear that as adults (teachers, parents, grandparents, etc.) we need to value children's play, nurture it, and be sure not to lose sight of play as the core of high-quality early childhood curriculum.

Edgar Klugman is Professor of Early Childhood Education at Wheelock College in Boston, MA.

While biology certainly plays a part, it would seem that parents and society exert powerful influences[1] (Frost, 1992). The toys parents and teachers choose (dolls for girls, trucks for boys), the predominance of females in early childhood settings, television shows and advertising, and toy store displays combine to communicate a very strong reinforcement of traditional sex-role expectations.

Values of Play

For the first half of this century, interest in children's play focused on emotional causes and effects (Bowman, 1990). The main theme was the emotional release play provided children. Play is a suitable outlet for expressing negative feelings, hostility, and aggression. Clay can be pounded, balls can be kicked and thrown, dolls can be spanked. Young children give free expression to a wide range of emotions, playing them out and releasing tension.

But play is more than an avenue for emotional release. Rubin, Fein, and Vandenberg (1983) cite three common factors that emerge from the many definitions of play: (1) children's feelings and motivations, (2) how children behave when they play, and (3) the environment that supports play and where play occurs. The early childhood curriculum is developed with all three aspects of play in mind.

Why do children play? Why is play so universal to childhood experiences? One answer may be that play is intrinsically motivated; that is, it is naturally satisfying to children. Rubin and associates suggest other reasons as well:

- Play is relatively free of rules except for what children will impose themselves.

- Play is controlled and dominated by the children.

- Play is carried out as if the activity were real life.

- Play focuses on the activity—the doing—rather than on the end result or product.

- Play requires the interaction and involvement of the children.

Play promotes learning for the whole child as well. A wide range of learning opportunities is inherent in any single play activity. Water play is a popular activity in most early childhood settings. Figure 11.16 highlights some of the learning that is likely to occur as children play with water. All play activity holds this potential for growth and learning. Blocks, easel painting, woodworking, and clay could also be analyzed for how they contribute to the development of the child as a whole. Figure 11.17 demonstrates further the learning possibilities in all play activity.

Play as a Cornerstone of Learning

Outside of child development circles, there has been little appreciation in the United States culture for the value and importance of play for young children (Frost, 1992). Early childhood educators continually search for ways to answer, "Don't they do anything but play?" In many settings, parental pressure and teacher uncertainty have led to curriculums with more table tasks and less active play periods in the daily schedule.

Jones (Gordon and Browne, 1989) states the case aptly: "But if children are just playing, how will they learn? Each child learns by asking his or her own next questions and trying out the answers. Often both the questions and the answers take the form of actions rather than words. Children learn by doing." In summing up, Jones adds, "In play, children are autonomous; they're independent. They make decisions, solve the problems, deal with the consequences."

Early childhood specialists must become adept at speaking out on the value of play and its relationship to what children learn. Figure 11.17 highlights this relationship.

Play, Work and Learning

For some years, theorists have stated that play is the child's work. This statement is confusing, for

 OUR DIVERSE WORLD OUR DIVERSE WORLD OUR DIVERSE WORLD OUR DIVERSE WORLD OUR DIVERSE WORLD

[1]Early childhood educators need to be constantly vigilant in noticing their personal gender biases, along with staying current with research in gender differences.

as any adult knows, work is work even though it may sometimes have some characteristics of play. This theory has fostered the misconception that all young children do in an early childhood setting is play. By extension, their teachers are erroneously thought of as simply babysitters who watch children play all day. To reclaim play as a special activity crucial to children's development and growth, play and work should be seen as equally important developmentally appropriate activities for young children (Frost, 1992).

Play is the cornerstone of learning, the foundation from which children venture forth to investigate, to test out. Curriculum takes on expression through play; teachers plan curriculum that uses play as the medium for learning. As they mature, children integrate and assimilate their play experiences. What started out as play—the sheer fun of it—is transformed into learning experiences. Curiosity about magnets at age five nourishes a scientific attitude for the later years, as well as a foundation for studying gravity, planetary movements, and the like. Feeling free to sing out at group time at age three can prepare a child to be an active participant in the kindergarten classroom at age six.

Teachers want children to learn about *themselves*, to learn about the *world around them*, and to learn how to *solve problems*. A childhood filled with play opportunities should culminate in these three types of learning.

1. *Learning about themselves* includes developing a positive self-image and a sense of competence. Children should know and feel good about themselves as learners. They should develop a sense of independence, a measure of self-discipline, and knowledge based on full use of their sensory skills.

2. *To learn about others and the world around them* means developing an awareness of other people. Teachers want children to perfect their communication and social skills so that they will be more sensitive participants in the world in which they live. This means that children learn and appreciate some of the values of their parents, the community, and society at large. When

children become aware of the demands of living in today's society, it can help them become more responsible citizens. The emphasis on social interaction and group relationships in the early childhood setting underscores this goal.

3. *To learn to solve problems*, children need to be accomplished in observation and investigation. When exploring a puzzle, for example, children need to know how to manipulate it, take it apart, and put it back together, to see how other people solve puzzles, and to know how to get help when the pieces just do not seem to fit together. They should know how to predict and experiment. What will happen, wonders a kindergartener, when a glass is placed over a glowing candle? How will that change if the glass is large or small? What is the effect if the glass is left over the candle for a long time or for a second? Young children also need to learn how to negotiate, discuss, compromise, and stand their ground, particularly when they encounter and solve problems socially. "I want the red cart and someone already has it," thinks the preschooler. "Now what? How can I get it? What if the other person says no? Will the plan that works with my best friend work with someone else? When do I ask for help? Will crying make a difference?" In order to be effective problem-solvers, children must know and experience themselves and others.

Teacher Considerations

Play is a window to the child's world and the adult who knows the value of play is committed to learning about children while they play. The vast knowledge of human development and behavior comes from researchers who spent countless hours observing and recording children playing. Classroom teachers continue to learn about children by listening to and observing spontaneous play activity and planning curriculum that encourages play. They discover each child's individual personality, learning style, and preferred mode of play.[1]

OUR DIVERSE WORLD OUR DIVERSE WORLD OUR DIVERSE WORLD OUR DIVERSE WORLD OUR DIVERSE WORLD

[1]Observing children while at play supports a teacher at understanding how each child is unique *and* how each child is the same in OUR DIVERSE WORLD.

COGNITIVE/LANGUAGE

Distinguishes between reality and fantasy
Encourages creative thought and curiosity
Allows for problem solving
Encourages thinking, planning
Develops memory, perceptual skills, and concept
    formation
Learns to try on other roles
Acquires knowledge and integrates learning
Learns communication skills
Develops listening and oral language skills

CREATIVE

Fosters use of imagination and make-believe
Encourages flexible thinking and problem solving
Provides opportunity to act upon original ideas
Supports taking risks
Learns to use senses to explore
Recreates images in buildings and art media
Sharpens observational skills
Provides variety of experiences
Learns to express self in art, music, and dance
Develops abilities to create images and use
    symbols
Acquires other perspectives

SOCIAL

Tries on other personalities, roles
Learns cooperation and taking turns
Learns to lead, follow
Builds a repertoire of social language
Learns to verbalize needs
Reflects own culture, heritage, values
Learns society's rules and group responsibility
Shows respect for other's property, rights
Teaches an awareness of others
Learns how to join a group
Builds awareness of self as member of a group
Gives sense of identification
Promotes self-image, self-esteem
Experiences joy, fun

FIGURE 11.17   Play is the cornerstone of learning.

PHYSICAL

Releases energy
Builds fine and gross motor skills
Gains control over body
Provides challenges
Requires active use of body
Allows for repetition and practice
Refines eye–hand coordination
Develops self-awareness
Encourages health and fitness

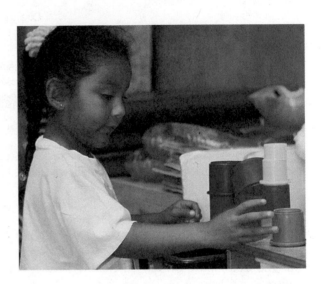

EMOTIONAL

Develops self-confidence and self-esteem
Learns to take a different viewpoint
Resolves inner fears, conflicts
Builds trust in self and others
Reveals child's personality
Encourages autonomy
Learns to take risks
Acts out anger, hostility, frustration, joy
Gains self-control
Becomes competent in several areas
Takes initiative

Curriculum Through Play for the 1½-Year-Old

Sensory Stimulation

Objective: To help toddlers begin to explore and understand the five senses

	Activity	Small-Group Focus	Optional Activities
Monday	Soap painting	Guessing game: textures. Distinguish soft/hard from familiar objects	Play hide-and-seek with two or three.
Tuesday	Water table play	Guessing game: smells. Identify familiar scents in jars.	Blow bubbles.
Wednesday	Fingerpainting	Guessing game: weights. Distinguish heavy/not heavy using familiar objects such as book or doll.	Take walk to collect collage materials of different textures.
Thursday	Making collages of textures collected day before	Guessing game: shapes. Use puzzles of shapes and shape-sorting boxes.	Have a parade of sounds from many musical instruments.
Friday	Playdough	Food fest of finger foods: Try different textures, sizes, shapes, and flavors.	Make foot or hand prints on large mural paper.

FIGURE 11.18   Example of teacher-directed activities to help toddlers explore their sensory skills.

Genuine interest is one way teachers show their approval of the play process. Creating a safe environment where children feel physically and emotionally secure is another. To establish play as an important part of the curriculum, teachers must:

● *Understand*, appreciate, and value play experiences for young children.

● *Focus* on the process of learning rather than on the process of teaching.

● *Reflect* on their observations in order to know what activities, concepts, or learning should be encouraged or extended.

Frost (1992) reminds us of the excellent advice from one of the most able contributors to the field of human development:

> . . . Erikson advises that play has a very personal meaning for each individual. Perhaps the best thing that we as adults can do to discover this meaning is to go out and play; to reflect upon our own childhood play; to once again look at play through the eyes of the child.

The two major roles of teachers in promoting spontaneous play environments are (1) as facilitators or supervisors of play, and (2) by setting the stage and creating an atmosphere for play.

The Teacher as Facilitator

One of the most difficult tasks teachers face is knowing when to join children at play and when to remain outside the activity. They must ask themselves whether their presence will support what is happening or whether it will *inhibit* the play. Sometimes teachers are tempted to correct children's misconceptions during play. Abby and Salina, deeply involved in their grocery store drama, are making change incorrectly. A teacher must judge whether or not to explain the difference between nickels and quarters at that time or create an opportunity at a later date. Teachers must be aware of what happens if they interrupt the flow of play and how they influence the direction it takes. If Abby and Salina begin to talk about their coins, showing an interest in learning how to compute their change, the teacher can move into the discussion without seeming to interfere.

Many adults enjoy playing with the children in their class. Others feel more comfortable as active observers but every teaching situation will demand the teacher's involvement at some level. The hesitant child may need help entering a play situation; children may become too embroiled in an argument to settle it alone; play may become inappropriate, exploitative, or dominated by a particular child.

Vygotsky gives us other reasons to be involved with children as they play, particularly in relation to the interpersonal nature of teaching (see Chapter 4). The belief that learning is interpersonal and collaborative is exemplified by the teachers of Reggio Emilia (see Chapters 2 and 5), who guide and support children's learning by engaging in play and knowing what strategy will best help an individual child reach the next level of skill (zone of proximal development). The Reggio Emilia approach to curriculum finds an appropriate and appealing blend of Vygotsky's concern for individual exploration and assisted discovery. The teacher's role is a balance between facilitating children's development and taking advantage of those teachable moments in which further learning is enhanced.

The following guidelines are ways teachers facilitate play. A good teacher:

● Guides the play, but does not direct or dominate the situation or overwhelm children by participation.

● Capitalizes on the children's thoughts and ideas; does not enforce a point of view on them.

● Models play when necessary. Shows children how a specific character might act, how to ask for a turn, how to hold a hammer when hammering. Models ways to solve problems that involve children interacting on their own behalf.

● Asks questions; clarifies with children what is happening.

● Helps children start, end, and begin again. Gives them verbal cues to enable them to follow through on an idea.

● Focuses the children's attention on one another. Encourages them to interact with each other.

● Interprets children's behavior aloud, when necessary; helps them verbalize their feelings as they work through conflicts.

● Expands the play potential by making statements and asking questions that lead to discovery and exploration.

Creating the Environment for Play

To structure the environment for play, teachers include uninterrupted time blocks in the daily schedule (at least forty-five minutes to an hour) for free-play time. This allows children to explore many avenues of the curriculum free from time restraints. It is frustrating to young children to have their play cut off just as they are getting deeply involved.

A variety of activity areas and learning centers set up with specific play and learning materials provides children with choices for play. There should be enough to do so that each child has a choice between at least two play options. Established routines in the schedule add to the framework of a day planned for play. The raw materials of play—toys, games, equipment—are changed periodically so that new ones may be introduced for further challenge.

In choosing materials, teachers select dress-up clothes and accessories that appeal to all children's needs, interests, and emotions. Props are required for a variety of roles:[1] men, women, babies, doctors, nurses, grocers, mail carriers, teachers, and fire fighters. Hats for many occupations help a child establish the role of an airline pilot, tractor driver, construction worker, police officer, or baseball player. Large purses are used for carrying mail and babies' diapers; they also double as a briefcase or luggage. Simple jackets or capes transform a child for many roles. Things that represent aspects of the child's daily life are important; children need many opportunities to act out their life stories.

For younger children, teachers make sure there are duplicates of popular materials. Group

OUR DIVERSE WORLD OUR DIVERSE WORLD OUR DIVERSE WORLD OUR DIVERSE WORLD OUR DIVERSE WORLD

[1]Choosing materials to place in a classroom should be done with an awareness of exposing children to images of diversity (i.e. male nurses, female construction workers, African-American physicians, etc.) rather than fostering and reinforcing exisiting stereotypes.

Play Materials to Enhance Cultural Diversity and Inclusivity

Curriculum Areas	Materials and Equipment
Music	Rainstick (Chile), marimba (Zulu), balaphon (West Africa), ankle bells (Native American), maracas (Latin America), Den-den (Japanese), Shakeree (Nigeria), drums (many cultures), ocarina (Peru), songs of many cultures
Literature	Books on family life of many cultures, stories of children from far and near, legends and folktales from many countries, stories with common childhood themes from many lands, favorite books in several languages, wordless books, sign language, Braille books
Blocks and Accessories	Variety of accessories depicting many ethnic people, aging people, community workers of both sexes in nonstereotyped roles and with various disabilities; Russian nesting dolls, Pueblo storytellers; animals from around the world
Art	Paints, crayons, markers, and construction paper in variety of skin tone colors, child-size mirrors
Dramatic Play	Anatomically correct dolls representing many ethnic groups, doll accessories, including glasses, wheelchairs, crutches, walkers, leg braces, and hearing aids; doll clothes, including cultural costumes and dress-up clothing from many cultures, cooking utensils, such as a wok, tortilla press, cutlery, chopsticks
Games	Language lotto, dreidle game, lotto of faces of people from around the world, black history playing cards, world globe
Outdoors	Elevated sand and water tables and ramps for wheelchair access, lowered basketball hoops, sensory-rich materials.
Classrooms	Carp banners (Japan), paper cuttings from Mexico and China, photographs and magazine pictures of daily life from many cultures, artwork by artists from a variety of ethnic backgrounds

FIGURE 11.19 A child's family and culture can be brought into the classroom through a variety of curriculum materials; so, too, can children with disabilities feel included.

play is more likely to occur with three telephones, four carriages, eight hats, and five wagons. Social interaction is enhanced when three space shuttle drivers can be at the controls.

Play is further enlarged by materials that are **open-ended**. These are materials that will expand the children's learning opportunities because they can be used in more than one way. Blocks, a staple of the early childhood curriculum, are a case in point. Children explore and manipulate blocks in many ways. The youngest children carry and stack blocks and also enjoy wheeling them around in wagons or trucks. They also enjoy the repetitious action of making small columns of blocks. As children learn to make enclosures, they add animals, people, and transportation toys to their block play. Older preschoolers build multistoried structures as part of their dramatic play—offices, firehouses, garages, and the like.

Cultural Diversity and Inclusivity

Throughout this text the rationale for multicultural education is underscored, from demographics to anti-bias. Vygotsky's sociocultural theory adds further endorsement. If meaningful learning is derived from a social and cultural context, then multiculturalism must permeate the environment and become totally integrated into the curriculum. Creating a truly multicultural classroom calls into question the familiar ways of doing things and provides new insights and ways of thinking about culture.

Positive attitudes towards others emerge when children know they are valued for their individuality and appreciated as members of a family and a culture. The school environment can reflect this in a number of ways. Figure 11.19 lists ways in which an early childhood program can use culturally diverse materials in activities and learning

A budding mathematician

A future architect or builder

A future doctor scrubbing up

A future artist

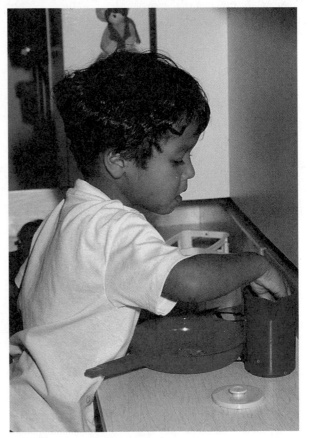
An inspired chef

FIGURE 11.20   As they play, children learn. They may even be practicing for the future.

centers on a daily basis to foster the relationship between home culture and school.

Children with special needs are often able to use most of the curriculum materials typically found in early childhood classrooms. They, too, need their life mirrored in the school setting with dolls, books, and play accessories that signify acceptance and belonging. Figure 11.19 has a number of suggestions for inclusive materials for children with special needs.

CURRICULUM PERSPECTIVES CONTINUE

A sound curriculum is the *linchpin* of a quality program for children. Curriculum planning and development is a creative act, one that is rewarding for teachers. In the next three chapters, curriculum implementations will be explored from another perspective, that of the major areas of development in the child's growth. In Chapter 12, the focus will be on how curriculum affects the growing body. Chapter 13 will emphasize the curricular role in developing the mind, and Chapter 14 will explore the curricular issues surrounding social and emotional growth.

S U M M A R Y

Curriculum encompasses the planned and unplanned events children experience in group settings. Curriculum can include whatever happens to a child while in school or day care, or it can be a syllabus with detailed lesson plans.

Developing curriculum includes setting goals, establishing priorities, knowing what resources are available, planning ahead, and then evaluating the process. As teachers develop their curriculum plans, they may focus on the classroom activity or learning centers, the skills of the children, or a particular theme. All three lend themselves to a basis for curriculum planning, and all are important vehicles for creative and effective curriculum for young children.

Play is the way curriculum is expressed in the early childhood setting. The function of play in the life of a young child is more than sheer enjoyment. Play provides an avenue for growth in social, emotional, intellectual, and physical development. Teachers, aware of play as a foundation for learning, provide an atmosphere that supports the play process. They provide a setting in which play is recognized as the curriculum of the child, the primary process through which children learn. Curriculum comes alive as children discover and take pleasure in learning.

R E V I E W   Q U E S T I O N S

1. Define developmentally appropriate curriculum for early childhood programs. What two principles determine whether or not curriculum is "appropriate"? Describe the difference between infant/toddler and preschool curriculum.

2. Name five guidelines for developing curriculum for young children.

3. What is emergent curriculum and why is it appropriate for early childhood teachers?

4. How is play beneficial to the child's development?

5. Define the common stages of play and describe at what chronological age each is likely to appear.

6. What learning occurs when children play (a) in the sand area; (b) easel paint; (c) on the climbers; (d) engage in dramatic play?

7. Describe the project approach to curriculum development, including how it can be incorporated into the curriculum. Be sure to show how it can affect every major curriculum area.

L E A R N I N G   A C T I V I T I E S

1. Create a curriculum web with several classmates following the process described on page 341.

2. Develop a curriculum for a week-long celebration: (a) for three-year-olds in a half-day nursery school; (b) for six-year-olds in an after-school extended day program; (c) for a family day care home. Use a non-holiday theme.

3. What do you think of superhero play in the preschool years? Research recent articles on the subject and prepare to present an argument for or against this type of play. Ask a classmate to prepare an opposing viewpoint.

4. Observe teachers as children play. What is the difference in the play when (1) a teacher interacts with children in their play and (2) a teacher intervenes? What happens to the play immediately after teacher contact is made? How long does the play last? What is your conclusion?

5. Develop a dramatic play kit for your school. Select a theme and collect appropriate props and accessories. Describe why you chose this theme and what you expect children to gain from this experience.

6. Write a defense of play as a hallmark of early childhood philosophy and curriculum. How would you adapt the paper for parents? For a student of early childhood education? For teachers?

7. Research festivals (other than Christmas and Hanukkah) that some cultures use to celebrate childhood. How would you integrate these into a curriculum? Why did you choose each of the specific festivals? How do your choices relate to the children in your classroom?

B I B L I O G R A P H Y

Berk, Laura E. *Infants and Children*. Boston: Allyn and Bacon, 1994.

——————. "Vygotsky's Theory: The Importance of Make-Believe," *Young Children*, November, 1994, pp. 30–39.

Bowman, Barbara. "Play in Teacher Education: The United States Perspective." In *Children's Play and Learning*, ed. Edgar Klugman and Sara Smilansky. New York: Teachers College Press, 1990.

Bredekamp, Sue (ed.). *Developmentally Appropriate Practice in Early Childhood Programs Serving Children From Birth Through Age 8*, expanded edition. Washington, D.C., National Association for the Education of Young Children, 1987.

Bowman, Barbara. "Play in Teacher Education: The United States Perspecive." In *Children's Play and Learning*, ed. Edgar Klugman and Sara Smilansky. New York: Teachers College Press, 1990.

Derman-Sparks, Louise, and the A. B. C. Task Force. *Anti-Bias Curriculum: Tools for Empowering Young Children*. Washington, D.C.: National Association for the Education of Young Children, 1989.

Edwards, Carolyn, Gandini, Lella, and Forman, George. *The Hundred Languages of Children*. Norwood, N.J.: Ablex Publishing, 1993.

Elkind, David. *Images of the Young Child*. Washington, D.C.: National Association for the Education of Young Children, 1993.

Elkind, David. *Miseducation: Preschoolers at Risk*. New York: Alfred A. Knopf, Inc., 1987.

Frost, Joe L. *Play and Playscapes*. Albany, NY: Delmar Publishers, 1992.

Frost, J.L., and Sunderlin, S. (eds.). *When Children Play*. Wheaton, Md.: Association for Childhood Education International, 1985.

Gardner, Howard. *Frames of Mind: The Theory of Multiple Intelligences*. New York: Basic Books, 1983.

Guidelines for Appropriate Curriculum Content and Assessment in Programs Serving Children Ages 3 Through 8. A position statement of the National Association for the Education of Young Children and the National Association of Early Childhood Specialists in State Departments of Education. *Young Children*, March 1991, pp. 21–38.

Jones, Elizabeth, and Nimmo, John. *Emergent Curriculum*. Washington, D.C.: National Association for the Education of Young Children, 1994.

Jones, Elizabeth, and Reynolds, Gretchen. *The Play's the Thing*. New York: Teachers College Press, 1992.

Jones, Elizabeth. "What's The Point of Play?" In *Beginnings and Beyond: Foundations in Early Childhood Education*. ed. Ann Gordon and Kathryn Williams Browne. Albany, N.Y.: Delmar, 1989 (2nd ed.).

Katz, Lilian and Chard, Sylvia. *Engaging Children's Minds: The Project Approach*. Norwood, NJ: Ablex Publishing Corp., 1989.

Klugman, Edgar, and Smilansky, Sara (eds.). *Children's Play and Learning*. New York: Teacher's College Press, 1990.

Malaguzzi, Loris. *The Hundred Languages of Children*. Department of Education, Reggio Emilia, Italy, 1987.

Neugebauer, Bonnie (ed.) *Alike and Different: Exploring Our Humanity With Young Children.* Washington, D.C.: National Association for the Education of Young Children, 1992.

Rubin, K.H.; Fein, G.G.; and Vandenberg, B. "Play." In E.M. Heatherington (ed.), *Handbook of Child Psychology*, vol. 4. Socialization, Personality and Social Development. New York: Wiley, 1983.

Smilansky, Sara. "Sociodramatic Play: Its Relevance to Behavior and Achievement in School." In *Children's Play and Learning*, ed. Edgar Klugman and Sara Smilansky. New York: Teachers College Press, 1990.

Vygotsky, L.S. *Mind In Society: The Development of Higher Psychological Processes.* Cambridge: Harvard University Press, 1978.

——————. *Thinking and Speech.* (N. Minick, transl.) New York: Plenum, 1987.

Workman, Susan, and Anziano, Michael C. "Curriculum Webs: Weaving Connections From Children to Teachers," *Young Children*, January, 1993, pp. 4–9.

ADDITIONAL CURRICULUM RESOURCE BOOKS

Croft, Dorene, J. *An Activities Handbook for Teachers of Young Children.* Boston: Houghton Mifflin, 1990.

Dodge, Diane Trister, and Colker, L.J. *The Creative Curriculum for Early Childhood.* Washington, D.C.: Teaching Strategies, 1992.

Dolinar, Kathleen, Boser, Candace, and Holm, Eleanor. *Learning Through Play: Curriculum and Activities for the Inclusive Classroom.* Albany, N.Y.: Delmar, 1994.

Eliason, Claudia, and Jenkins, Loa. *A Practical Guide to Early Childhood Curriculum.* New York: Merrill, 1990.

Fleming, Bonnie, Hamilton, Darlene, and Hicks, JoAnne. *Resources for Creative Teaching In Early Childhood Education.* New York: Harcourt, Brace, Jovanovich, 1992.

Mitchell, Anne, and David, Judy (eds.). *Explorations with Young Children: A Curriculum Guide from The Bank Street College of Education.* Mt. Rainier, Md.: Gryphon House, 1992.

York, Stacey. *Roots and Wings: Affirming Culture in Early Childhood Programs.* St. Paul, Minn.: Redleaf Press, 1991.

CHAPTER 12

Planning for the Body: Physical/Motor Development

QUESTIONS FOR THOUGHT

What is physical/motor development?

Does physical growth differ from motor development in young children?

What are the physical and motor skills children learn in an early childhood setting?

How can teachers encourage physical development?

What should the teacher of young children consider when planning for physical/motor development?

In what ways can physical/motor curriculum be developed?

Why is outdoor and playground play important?

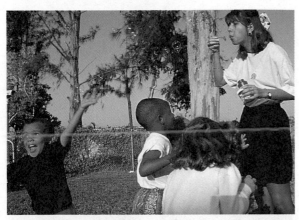

FIGURE 12.1 Children are the picture of movement, spending the greatest portion of their day in physical activity.

INTRODUCTION

Teachers often characterize children through their movements. Movements are one of the most notable features of young children's behavior. Pregnant mothers are aware of fetal motions and often assign personality traits to their children by these movements. What is striking about newborns is the extent of their full-bodied, random movements when they cry, roll over, follow, and reach for a crib mobile. Learning to walk is a major milestone in a child's development. Holding a pencil, cutting with scissors, tying a shoe are further illustrations of how motor development signifies growth. Motor skills are a good indication of how the child is progressing.

Basic motor skills develop in the early childhood years. As in other areas of development, by six or seven years of age, most motor skill development has been accomplished. These years form the foundation for movement and motor proficiency. Though skills will improve throughout a lifetime, it is generally believed that after the early years, no new basic skills will be added to children's movement repertoire (Malina, 1982).

Learning Through Movement

Motor abilities affect other areas of development. Recent research reinforces this notion. Malina (1982) claims that motor development greatly affects "the child's cognitive development, the

child's own self-discovery, and the child's ability to communicate." There is evidence of such interrelationships in children.

> Tim is reluctant to climb outside. He is easily frightened when he—or anyone else—is up in a tree or on any climber. Because he cannot risk using his body in space, he stops himself from playing with anyone who invites him to try these activities. Thus, Tim's lack of gross-motor development is affecting his social skills.

> Samantha loves to draw and cut. She chooses the art area every day she attends the two-year-old class. Not only are her fine-motor skills well developed for her age, she takes great pride in her creations. Her motor skills enhance her self-confidence in school. In turn, she receives praise and attention from others as she communicates with both adults and children through her work.

The greatest portion of the young child's day is spent in physical activity. Quality early childhood programs recognize this, providing for a full range of physical and motor experiences. Indoors, children use puzzles, scissors, and dressing frames as they practice fine-motor skills. They dance with scarves and streamers to music. **Perceptual-motor development,** as with body awareness, occurs when children learn songs and games ("Head and Shoulders, Knees and Toes" or "Mother May I Take Two Giant Steps?") or while fingerpainting. Outdoors, gross-motor skills are refined by the use of climbers, swings, hopscotch, and ring-toss.

Throughout the program, physical/motor development is emphasized as an important part of children's learning. Children will need time as well as equipment and activities to practice their skills. The value teachers place on physical/motor development is directly related to the time allotted in the daily schedule for children to pursue them.

For years, early childhood programs have made an outdoor environment available to children, assuming a great need for physical activity and that children will find ways to fill that need themselves. However, many school outdoor areas contain few challenges, perhaps only a blacktop for bouncing balls and a small, metal climber for hanging and climbing. Moreover, American children are exposed to a value system in which physical/motor fitness is not always a high priority. Children live with adults whose primary sport is as spectator only, and they are often encouraged toward *sedentary* activities themselves at an early age, such as watching TV and using computers.

Physical/motor development is the central focus of the needs and interests of young children; it should play a central role in planning the curriculum. Teachers must recognize that children have different needs from adults; they are growing, developing, emerging beings with a set of physical needs and interests that are quite different. Too often, adults try to develop miniathletes without first developing the child's fundamental movement activities.

PHYSICAL GROWTH/MOTOR DEVELOPMENT

Physical Growth

According to Bee (1989), an understanding of physical development is important to teachers and parents for a number of reasons. For example:

- New behavior is made possible through physical change: a toddler can be toilet-trained once anal sphincter muscles develop.

- Growth determines the child's experiences: observe the new vistas that open up to the brand new walker.

- Growth changes the way people respond to the child: the mobility of crawlers and toddlers leads to more restrictions from parents.

- Self-concepts are profoundly related to physical development: an obese kindergartener avoids the running and chasing games during recess.

Early childhood is the time of most rapid growth, though development does not take place at an even pace, but in starts and spurts. A child will tend to grow rapidly in infancy and as a toddler, with the growth rate beginning to taper off during preschool and middle childhood years. While there are individual differences in the rate of maturation among children, growth follows a sequential pattern.

FIGURE 12.2 Growth follows a predictable pattern: large muscles develop before smaller ones.

Development seems to follow a directional pattern as well. Large muscles develop before smaller ones—one reason why most preschoolers are more proficient at running than at cutting with scissors. Growth also starts at the center of the body and moves outward. Watch a toddler walk using whole-leg action and compare that with a five-year-old whose knees and ankles are involved in a more developed response. Children also tend to develop in a head-to-toe pattern. Infants move their eyes, head, and hands long before they learn to creep or crawl.

It is important to remember, however, that while growth is sequential and directional, it does not occur in a smooth and unbroken pattern.

Tremendous growth takes place just within the first two years of life, tapers off through the preschool and elementary-school years, and increases rapidly again during the adolescent growth spurt. Figure 12.3 shows an overview of these dramatic changes for children up to age eight.

Growth is influenced by a variety of factors. Genetic makeup, disease, and injury all play a part in how children grow. Environmental influences, such as nutrition and experience, have their greatest effect during the early years.[1]

OUR DIVERSE WORLD OUR DIVERSE WORLD OUR DIVERSE WORLD OUR DIVERSE WORLD OUR DIVERSE WORLD

[1]Early childhood educators need to be aware of each child's early experiences, experiences before coming to the program. Early experiences vary and have a direct impact on who the child is.

Age	Weight	Height	Proportion	Teeth
Newborn	7 pounds	20 inches	Head = ¼ of length	None
Infancy (up to 18 mos.)	Gains 15 pounds (now 20–25 lbs.)	Adds 8 inches (now 28–29″)	About the same	6
Toddler (18 mos. to 2½ yrs.)	Gains 5 pounds (now 28–30 lbs.)	Adds another inch or two (now 29–33″)	Legs = 34% of body	20
Preschool (2½ to 5 yrs.)	About 5 pounds/yr. (now 30–40 lbs.)	Adds 14–15 inches from birth; at age 2 = ½ of adult height (now 35–40″)	Head growth slows; legs at age 5 = 44% of body	20
Early–middle childhood (5–8 yrs.)	Doubles before adolescence; (age 6 = 45–50 lbs.)	Adds 9–10 inches (age 6 = 44–48″)	Continues to move slowly towards adult proportions	Begins to lose baby teeth; replaced by permanent teeth (age 6 = 20–24)

FIGURE 12.3   An overview of growth shows how rapid physical growth is in childhood.

Gender and Cultural Differences

There are gender differences as well. Boys have a larger proportion of muscle tissue than girls, and, from the beginning, girls have more fat tissue than boys. Each of these differences becomes more obvious at adolescence. In regard to physical development, girls mature earlier than boys and their growth is more regular and predictable. In motor skills, preschool girls exhibit greater skill than boys in jumping, hopping, and balancing. Elementary-school boys excel in running, jumping, and throwing. Before the onset of puberty, girls and boys have fairly equal physical strength, speed, and endurance; after puberty, boys excel in all three areas. (Berk, 1994).

There is some indication that physical development differs according to racial groups. African American infants and toddlers seem to walk earlier and are taller than white children. Asian children also seem to develop physically earlier than white babies but are smaller and shorter overall (Bee, 1992).

Always, while looking at general growth patterns of children, parents and teachers must keep in mind the wide individual differences in the rates at which children grow and in the timing of each change. As a general rule, the pattern within individuals is consistent; that is, a child who is early, average, or late in one aspect of physical development will be so in all aspects. There are sex differences as well in rate and patterns of physical growth. The most obvious of these is that girls generally begin puberty two years ahead of boys (Bee, 1992). Bee also found that as a group, poor children grow more slowly and are shorter than middle-class children, a finding attributed to diet. Even though the *rate* of physical development may differ, however, the *sequence* of development remains the same. This holds true even for children who are physically or mentally handicapped.[1]

Motor Development

Motor development "is the process of change in motor behavior brought about by interaction between heredity and environment" (Gallahue, 1989). It is a lifelong process of continuous change based on the interaction of (1) *maturation* (i.e., the genetically controlled rate of growth); (2) *prior experiences*; and (3) *new motor activities*. Like physical growth, motor development is a sequence of stages that is universal but still allows for individual differences.[2] Each stage is different from, yet grows out of, the preceding level. Figure 12.4 charts motor development through the early years.

Gross-Motor Development

Gross-motor activity involves movements of the entire body, or large parts of the body. Using various large muscle groups, children try to creep, crawl, roll, bounce, throw, or hop. Activities that include balance, agility, coordination, flexibility, strength, speed, and endurance foster gross-motor development.

Fine-Motor Development

Fine-motor activity uses the small muscles of the body and its extremities (the hands and feet). Such movement requires dexterity, precision, and manipulative skill. Grasping, reaching, holding, banging, pushing, spinning, and turning are all activities that refine these skills.

Perceptual-Motor Development

Perceptual-motor development is a process in which the child develops the skill and ability to take in and interpret information from the environment and respond to it with movement. Children obtain data/impressions primarily through their senses. How often have you seen babies, for instance, mimic a parent's or caregiver's mouth movements—taking in visually the various expressions, then physically responding in kind.

In a sense, every movement is perceptual-motor activity, since the body and mind must work together to complete all motor tasks. The perceptual task is to process information; the motor response activates what is received in a physical way al-

though perceptual and motor abilities do not necessarily develop at the same time or the same rate (Gallahue, 1989). The complex nature of perceptual-motor development can be seen when examining three basic categories of spatial, temporal, and sensory awareness, which also include perceptual-motor concepts of body, directional, visual, and auditory awareness.

Spatial Awareness. For children, spatial awareness means a sense of body awareness and the body's relationship to space, as well as a knowledge of what the body parts can do. For the toddler, concepts of spatial relationships are developed through motor activity: dropping objects from a high chair or forcing a large stuffed animal into a small box. Their definition of space is related to the action and movement involved in specific activities. A sense of relationship to less immediate things and places (knowing a specific route to school and home, making simple maps) develops in the preschool years. Not until ages six to eight do children develop the more abstract spatial ability of distinguishing left from right on their own bodies and others'. Specifically, directional awareness refers to left and right, up and down, front and behind, over and under. To illustrate, let us look at 2-1/2-year-old Tamara. She demonstrates her awareness of spatial relationships as she moves herself up to a table (without bumping into it), reaches to her left to pick up a ball of clay, and turns around behind her to choose a rolling pin.

Temporal Awareness. Temporal awareness is the child's inner clock, a time structure that lets the child coordinate body parts. Dancing to a rhythmic beat speeding up and slowing down, develops this kind of skill. It is also a force that helps children predict time. For instance, seven-year-old Luis and Aref ask if it is time to clean up as they finish their game of soccer. The after-school center has sports time for about an hour before getting ready for snack; the children have an inner sense of time that parallels their knowledge of the daily schedule.

OUR DIVERSE WORLD OUR DIVERSE WORLD OUR DIVERSE WORLD OUR DIVERSE WORLD OUR DIVERSE WORLD

1 and 2One is reminded of the definition of Developmentally Appropriate Practice—there are characteristics of development that are universal and sequential and there are characteristics that are highly individual.

- roller-skate/bicycling (5–8 years)
- running faster (5 years and up)
- skipping (5–6 years)
- hopping on one foot (3–5 years)
- up/downstairs with continuous movement (4 years)
- jumping on two feet (3–5 years)
- running (2–3 years)
- walks up/downstairs alone (3 years)
- toddling (18–24 months)
- standing/walking alone (12–15 months)
- climbing stairs (13 months)
- walking when led (11–12 months)
- creeping/crawling (8–10 months)
- standing holding onto something/someone (8–10 months)
- sitting and supporting self (6–8 months)
- infant on belly, with chest up (2 months)

FIGURE 12.4   Motor development follows a developmental sequence. (Adapted from Allen and Marotz, 1994.)

FIGURE 12.5   Gross-motor activity uses the various large-muscle groups so that children can move their entire bodies.

FIGURE 12.6   Fine-motor activity requires using the small muscles of the body with dexterity and precision. (Courtesy of Centro Infantile & de Reabilitacao de A-Da-Beja, Lisbon, Portugal.)

Sensory Awareness. Sensory awareness refers to use of the senses. It is another way the body gives the mind information. Vision is the dominant sense for young children. *Visual awareness* is the ability to mimic demonstrated movements, and to discriminate faces, emotions, sizes, shapes, and colors. It is the ability in three-month-old babies to recognize their mothers. *Auditory awareness* includes the ability to understand and carry out verbal directions and to discriminate between a vari-

ety of sounds ("Is this loud? fast? soft?" "Is that Josie or Dominick called you?"). Auditory skills help children process information about language. From infancy, children seem to be able to combine visual and auditory awareness. Further sensory awareness develops through touch. Babies seem to put everything in their mouths to learn. When four-year-old Stephanie picks up each object at the display table, she is using her sense of touch to discover size, shape, and volume.

PHYSICAL/MOTOR SKILLS IN EARLY CHILDHOOD

Types of Movement

Physical/motor skills involve three basic types of movement: *locomotor*, *nonlocomotor*, and *manipulative*.

● Locomotor abilities involve a change of location of the body (Gallahue, 1989) and include the skills of walking, running, leaping, jumping, climbing, hopping, skipping, galloping, sliding, and tricycling.

● Nonlocomotor abilities (sometimes referred to as balancing or stabilizing) are any movements that require some degree of balancing (Gallahue, 1989). These skills are turning, twisting, pushing, bending, stretching, pulling, swinging, rolling, dodging, and balancing.

● Manipulative abilities include the operation and control of limited and precise movements of the small muscles, especially those in the hands and feet. Manipulative skills include throwing, catching, reaching, bouncing, striking, kicking (gross-motor manipulation), and holding, grasping, cutting, sewing, (fine-motor manipulation).

These three basic movements are necessarily combined when children are active in physical play:

With Doll Buggy:	Holding onto buggy—Manipulative
	Pushing buggy—Nonlocomotor
	Walking with buggy—Locomotor
Playing Ball:	Bending down for the ball—Non-locomotor
	Throwing the ball—Manipulative
	Running to base—Locomotor
Jumping Rope:	Holding and turning the rope—Manipulative
	Jumping—Locomotor
	Balancing self after jump—Non-locomotor
Breaking a Pinata:	Holding the bat—Manipulative
	Swinging the bat—Nonlocomotor
	Running to get the prize—Loco-motor

FIGURE 12.7 To learn a motor skill, children must combine memory with experience, taking advantage of opportunities to try something new and to practice what has already been learned.

Figure 12.15 shows age-appropriate toys and games that foster the development of the three types of basic motor skills.

Learning Motor Skills

Children must use their bodies in order to learn motor skills. They acquire these skills by making comparisons between their past experience and new actions. Such comparisons use memory and experience.

Memory and Experience

Memory plays an important part in learning motor movements, since children need to recall what they just did in order to make corrections or

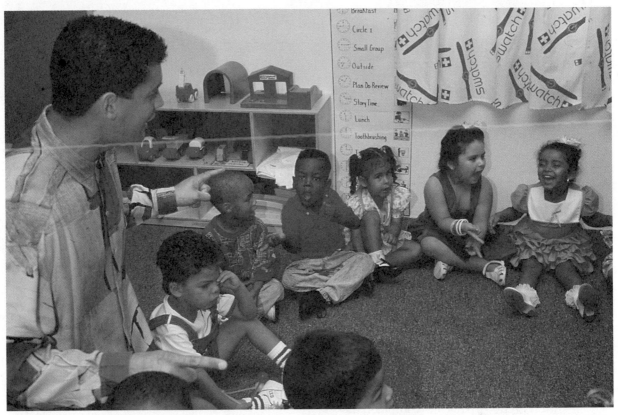

FIGURE 12.8 Teachers provide many opportunities to practice motor skills through finger play, games, and songs.

refinements. In the short term, the ball that does not reach the basket is tossed further on the next shot. To get the puzzle piece to fit, a child remembers other ways to manipulate the pieces. A long-term memory of movement is one that may go unrehearsed for longer periods of time. The experience of swimming, for example, may be recalled only in the summer. Whether using short-term or long-term memory, children learn motor skills by remembering what they have already learned and by practice.

The experiences children have and the ability to recall those experiences are necessary to the process of gaining motor skill. Rehearsal is as important to the young child as it is to the actors in a play. "Overt practice, repeating a specific movement over and over again, provides a motor rehearsal young children display everyday" (Clark *in* Ridenour, 1978). Practice, encouragement, and instruction play a key role in motor development (Gallahue, 1989).

Practicing Basic Skills

A child's typical day, at home or at school, provides numerous opportunities to practice motor skills. Through *play*, the child can practice fine-motor skills such as:

- holding a paintbrush, scissors, or rattle
- tiptoeing to music
- grasping a bottle, a hand, a toy
- threading a bead, a wide needle, a sewing board

and such gross-motor skills as:

- pumping on a swing
- climbing a tree
- digging a garden
- balancing on a board, on one foot

Through *self-help activities* the child can practice fine-motor skills such as:

● buttoning a coat or dolls' clothes

● brushing teeth, hair

● turning a faucet handle or doorknob

● feeding self with utensils

Gross-motor practice includes:

● moving a nap cot or table

● kicking covers off

● walking, holding onto furniture

● climbing into crib, bed

Children learning motor skills need experience in basic skills; they must learn simple skills before combining them into complex activities. To gain mastery over a skill, there must be an opportunity for practice. Children must have time to try, refine, and try again.

Feedback

Children modify and improve their motor skills as they receive information about their movements, both **intrinsic** (the paintbrush makes marks when it is pushed across the paper) and **extrinsic** ("I notice that your legs are very far apart as you try to somersault; how about holding them together as you roll next time?").

A Range of Developmental Levels

Any group of young children will have various levels of motor growth and physical development. An individual child may have different abilities and skills in gross-, fine-, and perceptual-motor areas; activities should, therefore, be offered on several developmental levels. Play materials and equipment, such as balls, climbers, and ladders, should accommodate a variety of skills levels, particularly if children with physical disabilities are in the class. Climbing boards put on several levels and puzzles ranging from six to sixty pieces are two examples of how teachers can meet the need for success and challenge.[1]

ROLE OF THE TEACHER

Considerations

As teachers plan programs for physical/motor development, they reflect on several important issues. One often overlooked area is that of gross-motor development as an everyday occurrence. Teachers sometimes take for granted children's progress as they walk up and down stairs, climb on and off platforms and benches, and dance with abandon. Favorite rainy-day activities such as moving around like *Tyrannosaurus rex* or spinning like a top are exercises in physical/motor development using gross-motor skills. Remember that the normal classroom setting can promote physical development every day through established routines and curriculum.

Sex-Role Stereotyping

Is motor behavior different for boys and girls? If so, why? Research indicates that there are differences between girls and boys in these areas. For example, behavioral differences in motor development are apparent in early life: one-year-old girls already spend more time in fine-motor tasks, while baby boys are more engaged in gross-motor activity. Preschool boys, on the average, are better in activities requiring speed or strength, while girls excel in jumping, hopping, and balancing. Yet by five or six, boys have begun to do better in most gross-motor tasks (Grossman and Grossman, 1994).

Why does this happen? Probably some sex differences are the result of genetics. At the same time, sex role expectations profoundly affect the motor and physical development of young children. This is the crucial issue for teachers, for their attitudes can either encourage or discourage children from developing to their fullest potential.[2] Teachers must acknowledge the differences that exist, and then ask themselves:

● What messages do I give children about physical activity? Do I value it for myself? For children? Do I value physical expression for girls as well as boys?

OUR DIVERSE WORLD OUR DIVERSE WORLD OUR DIVERSE WORLD OUR DIVERSE WORLD OUR DIVERSE WORLD

1 and 2 When planning the environment, curriculum , activities, teachers need to be ever mindful of OUR DIVERSE WORLD.

- Do I emphasize sports as a way to have fun? A way to be healthy? Do I only praise the "winner"?

- Can I provide male and female role models for physical activities using parents, grandparents, older siblings, staff, visitors, and guests?

- Do I encourage children to wear clothing that allows them the freedom to run, climb, tumble? What do I do when girls arrive in long dresses and party shoes? What should I wear?

- Are all physical/motor activities made equally available and attractive to boys and girls? What happens if some children dominate these activities, while others never choose them?

- How do I actively engage all children in every form of physical activity? Do I let them know I think it is important?

A Safe and Challenging Environment

First and foremost, teachers ensure the safety of the children. To maintain a safe physical environment, they see to it that materials and equipment are in usable condition, and that overall traffic patterns are hazard-free. For example, to make a gymnastic activity safe, teachers would provide mats and make sure that only one child is tumbling at a time.

Psychological safety requires an even finer sensitivity on the part of the teaching staff. Fear is a learned response and teachers must be careful not to discourage children from using their full range of abilities, creating overly anxious and fearful children. The new teacher is often concerned about children's safety, particularly when they are climbing. It helps to remember that children generally climb to heights that are comfortable for them; in other words, they set their own limits.

The practice of picking children up and placing them on equipment, often at their own request, is questionable. If teachers comply with children's wishes to be lifted and set somewhere high, they are placing those children in situations outside of their natural limits. The children may see this as saying, "You are incapable of climbing up there yourself," or "It is too dangerous for you to try that alone." Also, this does not allow children to gain experience in basic skills first, but

puts them in a situation that calls for skills more complex than they have at the time. This denies the child the opportunity to practice those skills. Children learn their capabilities by being held responsible for what they do. When they must seek solutions to getting up, out, in, or down, they learn to handle realistically their current level of physical and motor development. Teachers lend encouragement and confidence to children by saying, "I can't put you up there, but I will help you try." Making playgrounds safe (see Figure 12.9) is a good way to promote physical growth and sets the stage for learning through motor development.

Playground Enrichment

The playground is the natural arena for optimal physical development and the ideal environment to promote physical fitness. On the playground, all motor skills are called into play.

> Carmen *grabs* a scarf and begins to dance, *twirling* and *whirling*, *hopping* and *bending* in time to the music. Following the teacher's lead, Carmen *balances* on his toes and *waves* his scarf high over his head.

> Tina *walks* to the climber, *grasps* the highest rung she can *reach*, *pulls* herself up by *lifting* one leg and then the other until she *stretches* vertically full-length along the climber bars. Satisfied, she *pushes* off with her feet and *jumps* backward to the ground. She *bends* her knees as she lands, *balances* herself to an upright position, and *runs* off.

> Ramon *toddles* over to *pick* up the large red ball. Momentarily overwhelmed by its size, he *falls* backward to *sit* on the grass. As a teacher approaches him, he *rolls* the ball toward her. She *throws* it back to him and Ramon imitates her movements. Soon they are involved in *kicking* and *tossing* the ball to each other.

Using both small and large muscles, children gain control over their bodies as they run and play. The playground provides open space where full-bodied action takes place, providing many opportunities to develop balance and coordination.

Physical skills, however, are not the only benefit of outdoor play. Social and cognitive skills are enhanced as well. On the playground, children must negotiate turns with the wagons, ask for a push on the swing, and wait in line going up the

---

MAKING PLAYGROUNDS SAFE

Safety in the yard means:

- Enough room for the number and age of children who will use it
- Adequate empty space
- Availability of both hard and soft surfaces
- Absorbent surfaces under any equipment from which a child might fall
- Shady areas alternating with sunny spots
- No standing water—good drainage
- No poisonous or thorny plants
- Areas of play clearly defined and differentiated from one another
- Sand area protected at night from animals
- Fences high enough and in good repair
- Gates secure with latches out of children's reach

Equipment is:

- Well maintained—no exposed nails, screws, sharp edges, chipped paint
- Chosen with children's ages in mind in regard to height and complexity
- Stable and securely anchored
- Repaired immediately or removed if damaged
- Varied to allow for wide range of skills
- Not crowded
- Smooth where children's hands are likely to be placed
- Checked frequently
- Placed appropriately: slides facing north, swings away from other structures and busy areas
- Scaled to age level: steps and other openings are four inches or less apart *or* eight to ten inches apart
- Modified for age levels: swings have soft seats

Teachers:

- Reinforce safe practices
- Wear appropriate outdoor clothing
- Check frequently *where* children are playing
- Involve children in safety checks of yard, equipment, and grounds
- Provide continual, adequate supervision
- Avoid congregating to talk
- Get involved with children
- Provide enough activities and challenges
- Watch for sun exposure, especially with toddlers
- Assist children when they want to rearrange movable equipment

---

FIGURE 12.9 Before children are allowed to use a playground, teachers should use a checklist such as this to ensure that safety standards are met. A safe playground stimulates physical development, social interaction, and full exploration of the materials and environment.

FIGURE 12.9 *Continued*

slide. Some of the most intricate and involved dramatic play takes place outdoors. Problems get solved when two trikes collide. Science experiences are all around—finding a bird's nest or planting a garden. According to Frost, "good playgrounds increase the intensity of play and the range of play behavior" (McKee, 1986).

On the playground no one says "Be quiet!" or "Quit wriggling!" It is a place of motion and space, filled with the special sensations found only outdoors.

When creating and maintaining a challenging environment, teachers consider both variety and level of challenge. A choice of surfaces encourages a variety of movements. Cement may be appropriate for transportation toys, but climbing/hanging/dropping are more likely to occur with tanbark or rubber mats. Varying the equipment also stimulates motor activity. Equipment that is mobile allows for greater range of uses, and allows children to manipulate their own environment. By creating

their own physical challenges with wooden crates, children make platforms, caves, and houses to crawl in, over, and through. Another way to provide variety is to focus on the less-developed skills, such as catching and throwing, rolling, latching, snapping, or zipping. When children are encouraged to discover their own physical potential, they learn to solve problems of movement defined by the limits of their own abilities rather than by performance. This kind of learning encourages self-confidence as children find success through their own challenges.

The importance of playgrounds and outdoor play is underscored by Paula Carreiro's Focus Box on page 376.

A Child's Self-Concept

The image of physical self is an important part of self-concept. How people feel about themselves is rooted in the way they feel about their

Child's Play—Outdoors

Paula J. Carreiro

Madeline, smiling her Cheshire cat smile, sits atop the climbing structure. Her long brown hair is blowing in the wind as she surveys the activity below.

Similarly, from a less scenic vantage point, her teacher takes stock of events beginning to unfold. As an early childhood professional, she recognizes the importance of this time for her students. Just as the indoor classroom has been carefully prepared, so, too, is the outdoor environment planned, maintained, and supervised. A quick look around the area reveals many reasons for the success of this experience for these young children.

An initial planning session led to the creation of an outdoor space, which is first and foremost safe for this age group. Careful and frequent maintenance assures that the play area will remain hazard free. The adults moving around the playground provide the same pupil/teacher ratio that exists in the indoor environment. They are carefully observing behavior and giving assistance when needed.

Today there is much to behold. The large sand play area is the site for a major dig. The young explorers are assisted by buckets, shovels, measuring containers, and water. Another area is ripe for dramatic play, with a boat containing moving parts for an authentic adventure. There is an outdoor storage area where the trikes are kept only to be rediscovered everyday by drivers who are anxious to hit the highway—a paved path around the playground. A well-designed slide moves children safely along in any kind of weather, and a huge tree stump attracts the more serious scientist in search of the ultimate insect.

In one corner of the playground the older students have planted a colonial garden that all the children help maintain. Another area has been left open as a nature center with plants, flowers, and bird feeders for the children's discoveries and exploration.

The attention given to the development of the large body muscles in the arms and legs is not limited to the climbing equipment. In addition, there are swings and other structures to aid in this development. Other important features of the playground include a hard surface for bouncing balls, a balance of sunny and shaded areas, easels for outdoor painting, an area for building with large blocks, and plenty of open ended materials such as boxes and barrels for children to use in their own creative ways.

It is little wonder that a significant portion of the day is spent here. The playground not only provides important physical development opportunities, it is here that children also experience true joy in learning.

Paula J. Carreiro is the head of Beauvoir School in Washington, D.C., which serves children from preschool through third grade.

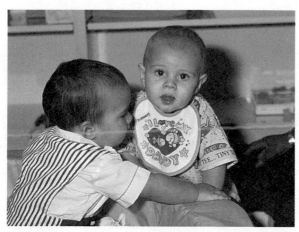

FIGURE 12.10 From early infancy, parents and teachers encourage physical play.

bodies and what they can or cannot do with them. Attitudes about the body and its abilities directly affect the types of activities children will try. Studies show that skill in games appears tied to peer-group acceptance (Gallahue, 1976). Psychologists and teachers often notice a link between learning problems and clumsiness. Children with problems seem to have motor difficulties more often than those who do well in the classroom (Cratty, 1971).[1]

Physical activity, then, contributes to a child's self-concept. With practice comes a sense of competence. Children can learn to relax as they gain experience in physical activities, and thus reduce the stress of anticipating failure. Competence breeds self-confidence, and a willingness to try greater challenges. As children try new activities, they learn more about themselves. And physical activity increases awareness of what fun it is to move—to run through a field or pump a swing just for the sheer joy of it!

Teachers support positive self-concept through physical and motor development in several ways. They let children discover their own physical limits, rather than warning or stopping them from trying out an activity for themselves. "I'm stuck!" a child shouts across the yard. Rather than rushing to lift down the child, the teacher might reply, "Where can you put your foot next? How can you find a way to get across?" To the child afraid to climb, the teacher might stand close by, responding to the fear by saying, "I'll stand close to the climbing ropes so you will feel safe." Using positive reinforcement encourages children in physical and motor endeavors. Teachers notice children who try something new: "Greg, it's good to see you cutting out the pumpkin yourself." They congratulate efforts for the achievements they really are: "Your hands reached the top this time, Shannon! I'll bet you are feeling proud of yourself." Children who stand on the sidelines observing others may need some encouragement from the teacher to take the first step in mastering the climbing frame or slide. "Here's a good place for you to put your foot, Arturo. I'll hold onto your hand until you tell me to let go."

It is often not so much what teachers say to children that influences their feelings about themselves as it is the way in which children are treated. Children value themselves to the degree they are valued by others. The way teachers show how they feel about children actually builds their self-confidence and sense of self-worth. Children create a picture of themselves from the words, attitudes, body language, and judgment of those around them.

Encouraging Physical Play

The vital role of physical activity is best fulfilled when teachers:

● Create time in the daily schedule for periods of physical activity, preferably, but not limited to, outdoors.

● Actively participate while supervising and encouraging *all* children to become involved in strenuous activity.

● Set goals for children's motor development and physical fitness.

● Use a variety of activities including science, art, and music to stimulate physical development.

● Select age-appropriate equipment and materi-

 OUR DIVERSE WORLD OUR DIVERSE WORLD OUR DIVERSE WORLD OUR DIVERSE WORLD OUR DIVERSE WORLD

[1]A skilled early childhood educator carefully observes children, documents her observations, and makes a referral if an assessment is needed for an individual child, attempting to include children with a variety of abilities in her group.

als, providing a variety of props to enhance their use.

● Give children opportunities to repeat, practice, and refine the skills they learn.

When children develop their physical and motor skills under this kind of encouragement, their confidence and sense of competence grow.

Observing children while they play outdoors allows teachers an opportunity to assess potential problems in motor development. The checklist in Figure 12.11 indicates some areas to observe.

Curriculum Planning for Physical/Motor Development

Teachers plan activities that promote physical/motor skills in the areas of gross-motor, fine-motor, and perceptual-motor development. They look at the environment, both indoors and out, to see that all three areas of physical growth are encouraged.

In the Classroom Setting

When thinking of physical/motor development in the classroom and yard, teachers tend to focus on the fine-motor (or small-muscle) tasks for the classroom, and gross-motor (or large-muscle) tasks for the outdoor play space. The indoor area lends itself more readily to activities with less movement, and the outdoor area encourages whole-body play. Yet children can have a wider variety of activities if teachers remember that both gross-motor and fine-motor projects can happen everywhere in the environment.

Indoor Areas. Indoors, the art area is stocked with pens, crayons, scissors, and hole punches that develop the fine-motor skills. Add large brushes or rollers to the easel, or plan fingerpainting, and the art area now includes gross-motor development. When children use templates to trace both inside and outside spaces, they practice perceptual-motor skill. In the science area, getting "just a pinch" of fish food is a fine-motor activity; cleaning out the turtle house requires larger muscles to move rocks and sand. Perceptual-motor development occurs as children use pitchers to fill the fish tank

Check whether child:

☐ 1. Has trouble holding or maintaining balance
☐ 2. Appears to have difficulty balancing and moves awkwardly
☐ 3. Cannot carry self well in motion
☐ 4. Appears generally awkward in activities requiring coordination
☐ 5. Has difficulty making changes in movement
☐ 6. Has difficulty performing combinations of simple movements
☐ 7. Has difficulty in gauging space with respect to own body; bumps and collides with objects and other children
☐ 8. Tends to fall often
☐ 9. Has poor eye-hand coordination
☐ 10. Has difficulty handling the simple tools of physical activity (beanbags, balls, other objects that require visual-motor coordination)

FIGURE 12.11 A checklist of possible problems in physical/motor development serves as a guideline when devising a developmentally specific profile for spotting problems.

or turtle tub and learn about water levels. At the manipulative table, when a child puts a peg into a pegboard, fine-motor skills are used. Removing puzzles from a shelf and carrying them to a table brings in gross-motor skills. Add nuts and bolts and the child's perceptual-motor skills are called into play. The block area has endless possibilities, from lifting and carrying (gross-motor), to balancing and stacking (fine-motor), to building a space so that an animal or car will fit through (perceptual-motor). The language and library areas are places for turning pages or looking at words and pictures (fine-motor). They also involve taking books off shelves and replacing them, and trying out the movements and activities read about in books. For instance, Tana Hoban's *Is It Hard? Is It Easy?* encourages children to act out the scenes pictured in the story, all gross-motor tasks. With a listening post nearby, children listen for the "beep," and coordinate what they hear (perceptual) with turning the pages (motor).

Outdoor Areas. Outdoors, children develop motor skills of all kinds. In the sand, children dig, a gross-motor activity. As they judge how big a hole is, or how much water will fill it, they are practicing and improving their perceptual-motor skills. Turn-

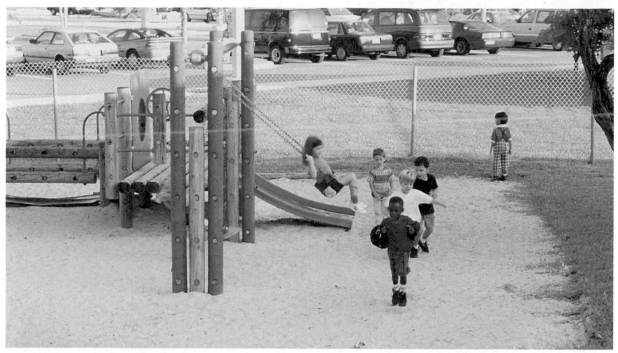

FIGURE 12.12 The outdoor area has great potential for developing gross-motor skills (climbing, bending, sliding), fine-motor skills (grasping, reaching, holding), and perceptual-motor skills (eye-hand coordination, directionality, tempo).

ing on a faucet, planting seeds, and making mudpies are for fine-motor development.

Wheel toys offer children opportunities in all motor areas. Pushing someone in a wagon develops arm and leg strength—gross-motor development. Guiding tricycles and carts on a path and around obstacles requires perceptual-motor skill. Trying to "repair" or "paint" a wheel toy with tools or with large brushes, tying wagons together, or weaving streamers through the spokes of a bicycle all use fine-motor skills. By looking at the classroom and yard with one eye to physical and motor development, teachers can plan activities that support growth in all skill areas.

Transitions and Group Times. Every part of the daily schedule can be planned to use all physical/motor skills. For instance, getting in and out of coats and snowsuits is a large-muscle activity. Children learn perceptual-motor skills as they try to get their arms in the correct sleeves. Buttoning, zipping, and tying are fine-motor activities. As children get ready for group time, often a difficult

transition, they might practice drawing faces in the air, or making their bodies into the shapes of letters, both perceptual-motor tasks.

Group times also include activities for motor development. When there are balloons, scarves, or a parachute at music time, children practice gross-motor skills. Fingerplays at group time are a fine-motor task. Activities for developing the senses of hearing and sight are two areas of sensory growth that can be utilized as content for group times.

Focus on Skills

The physical/motor skills include those that use large muscles, the smaller muscles, and the coordination of perception and motor response. Teachers planning activities for children can focus on any one of these as a basis for curriculum planning. For example, the skills of eye-hand coordination (perceptual-motor) and of walking on a balance beam (gross-motor) are elaborated below. They show how teachers can focus on a single skill and develop a rich curriculum for children.

PLANNING INCLUSIVELY FOR CHILDREN WITH SPECIAL NEEDS

(*Nathan* is a short-statured four-year-old, approximately 2/3 as tall as his peers. His legs are short in proportion to his body size and he loses his balance easily. *Ana*'s physical development is normal, but she is quite shy and prefers to watch others rather than participate in activities. A step-by-step process, which builds on children's strengths and skills, helps teachers plan meaningful activities for each child.)

1. **Ascertain child's strengths**
   Nathan—imaginative, agile, healthy, outgoing, blessed with positive self-image
   Ana—persevering, patient, compliant, methodical, aglow with each small success

2. **Ascertain child's needs**
   Nathan—to prove that he is as competent as, or more competent than, his peers, despite short stature; to improve poor balance due to disproportionately short legs
   Ana—to improve large-motor skills; to gain confidence in joining groups

3. **Set goals**
   Nathan—to gain better balance and to be offered the chance to feel tall and big
   Ana—to become a bit more adventurous, more sociable, and more comfortable with her body in space

4. **Brainstorm: What group activities are suitable?**
   Nathan—physical activities that require stretching and balancing
   Ana—noncompetitive experiences that require different kinds of motor planning and that allow her to proceed at her own pace while participating with her peers

5. **Select an activity** (e.g., an outdoor obstacle course)

6. **Plan the activity** (see "Planning an Outdoor Obstacle Course")

7. **Implement the activity** (see "Building an Obstacle Course")

8. **Evaluate the activity**
   Nathan—Was he able to stretch sufficiently to climb the rungs and reach across the empty spaces between obstacles? Did he work on his balancing skills?
   Ana—Was she willing and able to work through the course? Did she need a teacher's hand throughout? Did she interact with her peers?
   Both—Did they do the whole course or did they skip some obstacles? Did they return to a favorite spot? Did they voluntarily repeat the whole course?
   All—Did everybody have fun?

9. **Refine the activity—and try again!**

Figure 12.13 Planning inclusively for children with special needs. Adapted with permission from C.S. Kranowitz, "Obstacle Courses Are for Every Body," from *Alike and Different: Exploring Our Humanity With Young Children*, B. Neugebauer, ed. (Washington, DC: National Association for the Education of Young Children, 1992) p. 23 © by NAEYC.

Eye-Hand Coordination. Developing stitchery skills uses the perceptual-motor skill of eye-hand coordination. A series of activities can be planned to help children learn these skills. This learning begins in infancy, when the baby first begins to manipulate and examine an object, learns to grasp with thumb and forefinger *(pincer grasp)*, and shows a hand preference. Stringing large wooden beads is a first step and leads to using pieces of straw and punched paper, with somewhat smaller holes. Macaroni can be strung on shoe laces or stiff string, then onto yarn, which is softer and more challenging. Sewing cards made by punching holes in styrofoam trays can be introduced as the next activity. Large, plastic needles can be used with the lacing cards or with styrofoam trays; large embroidery needles with big eyes can be used for stitching yarn onto burlap. Children may be ready

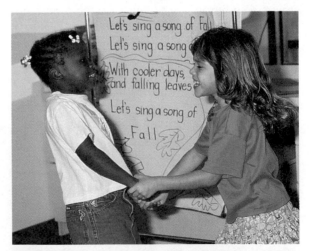

FIGURE 12.14 At an early age, children take pride in their physical accomplishments. Feeling strong or capable enhances self-confidence.

Type of Motor Skills	Infants 0-1½ years	Toddlers 1½-3 years	Preschoolers 3-5 years	Early School Years 6-8 years
Locomotor: Walking Running Jumping Hopping Skipping Leaping Climbing Galloping Sliding	Safe areas to explore body movements Balls to roll Hanging jumpseats Walkers on wheels Simple obstacle course	Walker wagons Pull/push toys Dancing Wide balance board Toddler gym—stairs and slide Ring Around the Rosey	Hippity-hop balls Sled Beginning skis Trampoline Rollerskates Jumprope Balance beam Climber Dancing	Jumprope Rollerskates Ice skates Climbing rope Tumbling mats Hopscotch
Nonlocomotor: Pushing Pulling Bending Balancing Stretching Rolling Turning Twisting	Large, safe areas for exploration Parent/caregiver play: holding, pushing arms, legs, sturdy push toys Soft obstacle course of pillows	Pounding board Simple, low rocking horse Ride-on toys Toddler-type swing Large Legos® Sturdy doll buggy Wagon Fabric tunnels Blocks Cars, trucks to push	Shopping cart/doll carriage Wheelbarrow Pedal toys, trike Rakes, shovels Slide Swing Punching bag	Scooter Two-wheel bike Sled, toboggan Exercise mat Acrobatics Diving mask for swimming Doorway gym bar
Manipulative: Grasping Throwing Catching Kicking Receiving/ moving objects Bouncing	Mobile attached to crib—kicking feet moves it Rattles, teething rings Crib activity board Soft foam blocks Snap beads Floating bath toys	Variety of balls Stacking, nesting toys Activity box—on floor Shape sorters Large, fat crayons Large pegs and board Water/sand table	Crayons, markers Clay, dough Bowling games Puzzles Woodworking tools Balls Lacing board Water/sand table	Baseball glove/bat Ring toss game Full-size balls Oversize bat Frisbee "Miss Mary Mack"

FIGURE 12.15   Toys and games help develop specific motor skills in young children.

to use embroidery hoops, with which they can make a design on burlap first and then stitch over the outlines. Buttons can be sewn on burlap or other fabric. Popcorn can be strung using a needle. A final project might be to make a group wall hanging, with squares of children's stitchery sewn together. Simple backpacks and coin purses might be made, with the children sewing most of it themselves.

Walking on a Balance Beam. Teachers might want to focus on the skill of walking on a balance beam, a gross-motor and perceptual-motor activity. Using any kind of beam requires more balance and slower movements than regular walking.

Teachers place tape on the floor and ask children to walk forward and backward on it. Use a rope on the floor and everyone can pretend to be a tightrope walker. Place a wide board flat on the floor, then substitute a narrow one (still on the floor itself) after children have mastered the first board. Next, place the wide board at a minimal height (perhaps 2 inches off the ground). Once children have successfully walked on this board, they are ready to try a narrower board at the same height. Set some boards at a slant, from the ground level up, providing a challenge that allows children to move their bodies off the ground as gradually as they wish. By planning activities for walking on wide and narrow boards of various heights, teach-

APPRECIATING CULTURAL DIVERSITY THROUGH MOTOR DEVELOPMENT

For Indoor and Outdoor Play

Activity	Motor Skill Practice	Culture
Lion or dragon dance	Gross-motor	Chinese (New Year)
Making and flying carp kites	Fine- and Gross-motor	Japanese
Chinese jump rope	Gross-motor	Chinese
Breaking the pinata	Gross-motor	Latino
Spinning like a dreidel	Gross-motor	Jewish (Hannukah)
Origami art	Fine-motor	Japanese
Weaving	Fine-motor	Native American
Make mariachi instruments	Fine-motor	Latino
Dancing to mariachi band music	Gross-motor	Latino
Make and twirl a grager	Fine-motor	Jewish (Purim)
Cooking: stir-fried rice	Fine-motor	Chinese
Making fried bread	Fine-motor	Native American
Making and beating drums	Fine-motor	Native American

FIGURE 12.16 A variety of activities that reflect many cultures can be integrated into the curriculum for motor and physical development. These activities are, at best, an approximation of traditional cultural expressions and not authentic presentations, yet they can enlarge the child's world view through physical play.

ers help children of all levels acquire the gross-motor skills necessary to master these tasks. Figure 12.15 shows age-appropriate equipment that fosters the development of motor skills.

Figure 12.14 outlines a process for developing activities to meet the needs of children with a wide variety of skills and takes into account each child's strengths and needs.

Use of Themes

When beginning teachers plan activities, they often have a theme or unit as their focus. Themes can be used to encourage physical and motor involvement. A unit of "Outerspace" involves gross-motor skills (jumping around on the moon, taking a space walk, getting in and out of the rocketship, building a spaceship with large blocks). Fine-motor skills are needed to manipulate knobs on the instrument panel, to draw maps of the stars or write out a countdown on a chalkboard. Perceptu-

al-motor skills are needed to work out how to get ready for a trip to Mars, what happens on the trip, and when and how to get back to Earth. Use the sample forms in Figures 11.4, 11.5, and 11.17 to develop an outer-space unit as well as other appropriate themes to encourage motor skills.

Once teachers realize which physical/motor skills the children possess and what the group is ready to learn, they can plan activities around a classroom unit.

Curriculum planning for motor and movement skills requires teachers to know principles of physical growth and motor development. They then can use this knowledge to plan activities that encourage children to master their own movements and to learn other skills through movement. In the early childhood setting, curriculum can be planned by concentrating on activity areas, focusing on a specific motor skill, or using a classroom theme.

S U M M A R Y

Children are in motion virtually from conception and develop their abilities to move their bodies as they grow. Young children spend most of the day in physical activity; therefore, the development of physical and motor skills must take a high priority in early childhood programs. Physical growth, that which pertains to the body, is for teachers an issue of fitness and health. They need to have an overview of growth in order to help children develop functional and flexible bodies. Motor development means learning to move with control and efficiency. Development involves maturation and experience. Teachers must know the sequence of development and what part they play in providing physical and motor experiences for the young child.

Muscular development can be categorized as gross-motor, fine-motor, and perceptual-motor. Gross-motor movements use the entire body or large parts of it, such as the legs for running or the arms and torso for throwing. Fine-motor movements, such as manipulating objects, are those that use smaller muscles and that require precision and dexterity. Perceptual-motor movements are those that combine what is perceived with a body movement. Spatial, temporal, and sensory awareness all play an important part in the development of perceptual-motor skills.

In the early childhood years, children need exposure to many motor activities. They need a chance to practice, to get feedback, and to have a broad range of experiences of variety and challenge. Since children acquire motor skills through short- and long-term memory, rehearsal plays an important role as well.

When planning curriculum, teachers must have an awareness of sex-role stereotyping and must consider safety as well as challenge. A child's self-concept is linked with the concept of physical self and skill, so teachers keep in mind which behaviors should be encouraged, and which behaviors may indicate potential problems. As they plan activities for children, teachers use classroom and yard areas, focus on a specific skill, or use a theme to develop curriculum for physical/motor skills.

R E V I E W   Q U E S T I O N S

1. How does physical growth differ from motor development in young children?

2. What factors influence motor development in young children?

3. What physical/motor skills are appropriate for young children to develop?

4. How can the teacher of young children support motor development in classroom areas?

5. How can the teacher support acquisition of specific motor skills in young children?

6. Follow (a) an infant or toddler, (b) a 3-1/2-year-old, and (c) a six- to eight-year-old during a typical play period at school or at home. Try to observe for one hour. Does the child exhibit all three basic types of movement (locomotor, nonlocomotor, and manipulative)? Describe the action of each, including any toys or materials the child uses.

7. How would you present the activities in Figure 12.13 to visually handicapped children?

8. Are there gender differences in the physical development of young children? If so, what implications are there for teachers planning motor activities?

L E A R N I N G   A C T I V I T I E S

1. Map the classroom in which you are currently working. List at least one activity in each area that develops physical motor skills. Add one more activity of your own that widens such development.

2. In what ways does a school program you know reinforce sex-role stereotyping in motor activities? What could be done to change this?

3. Try to develop the theme of "at the beach" or "camping" in your setting in such a way that physical/motor skills are used. Be sure to include gross-motor, fine-motor, and perceptual-motor activities. List at least six other themes around which you could build a similar curriculum.

B I B L I O G R A P H Y

Bee, Helen. *The Developing Child.* Cambridge, Mass.: Harper Collins, 1995.

Berk, Laura E. *Infants and Children.* Boston, Mass.: Allyn and Bacon, 1994.

Elkind, David. *A Sympathetic Understanding of the Child.* Boston, Mass.: Allyn and Bacon, 1994.

Frost, Joe L. *Play and Playscapes.* Albany, N.Y.: Delmar, 1992.

Frost, J.L., and Sunderlin, S. (eds.). *When Children Play.* Wheaton, Md.: Association for Childhood Education International, 1985.

Gallahue, David L. *Understanding Motor Development: Infants, Children, Adolescents.* Indianapolis, IN: Benchmark Press, Inc., 1989.

Grossman, Herbert, and Grossman, Suzanne H. *Gender Issues in Education.* Boston, Mass.: Allyn and Bacon, 1994.

Harris, Judith Rich, and Liebert, Robert M. *Infant and Child.* Englewood Cliffs, N.J.: Prentice Hall, 1992.

Hoyenga, Katharine Blick, and Hoyenga, Kermit T. *Gender-Related Differences.* Boston, Mass.: Allyn and Bacon, 1993.

Kranowitz, Carol Stock. "Obstacle Courses Are for Every Body." In *Alike and Different,* ed. Bonnie Neugebauer. Washington, D.C.: National Association for the Education of Young Children, 1992.

Malina, Robert M. "Motor Development in the Early Years." In Moore, Shirley G., and Cooper, Catherine R. (eds.), *The Young Child: Reviews of Research,* vol. 3. Washington, D.C.: National Association for the Education of Young Children, 1982.

Ridenour, Marcella V., ed. (Contributing Authors: Clark, Herkowitz, Roberton, Teeple) *Motor Development: Issues and Applications.* Princeton, N.J.: Princeton Book Company, 1978.

QUESTIONS FOR THOUGHT

What is the relationship between cognitive and language development?

What is meant by cognitive development?

How can the teacher support cognitive development?

What language skills are developed in an early childhood setting?

What is the teacher's role in supporting and extending language development in young children?

How does the teacher introduce and develop reading and writing in the early childhood setting?

What can children's literature offer young children?

How might computers be used with young children?

CHAPTER

13

Planning for the Mind: Cognitive and Language Development

Portions of this chapter were developed with the assistance of Gay Spitz, Salinas Adult School, Salinas, Calif.

PREFACE

What is the mind? How do children think, communicate, and then act upon the world? How does knowledge about language and thought dictate planning activities for children's development?

To begin, the relationship between language and thought must be emphasized. Thoughts are produced when people internalize what they experience. Language is what turns these experiences, such as actions and events, into thought. Language also shapes the way thoughts are produced and stored, bringing a semblance of order to the thought process. The two are intertwined: according to Bruner, language is "a logical and analytical tool in thinking" (Vygotsky, 1962).

Think of language as a tool. People are influenced by the kinds of tools they use. Farmers who work the land develop tools that till the soil, and, in turn, learn more about that soil by using those tools. Mechanics begin to see the world in terms of the nuts and bolts of the vehicles they see everyday. Tribes who are snowbound develop tools to deal with snow and ice; small wonder, then, that their language reflects more than a dozen ways to describe frozen water conditions. Language and thought are the instruments people use to make sense of and interact with the world.

For these reasons, this chapter contains curriculum planning units for both cognition and language rather than treating them in separate chapters. Inclusion in the same chapter emphasizes their close relationships. A third unit addresses the special topics of Graphic language (Reading and Writing), Children's literature, and Computers as vehicles for language and intellectual development in the young child.

INTRODUCTION

Ah, to be a child again! The world is a place of wonder and promise. There are worlds and people to discover, explore, and understand. Childhood is a time:

● Of self . . . a baby plays with his hands and feet for hours, and rolls over just for the sake of doing it.

● Of things everywhere . . . a toddler invades the kitchen cabinets to see what treasures can be found.

● Of people . . . a preschooler learns the teachers' names and then makes a first "friend."

● Of faraway places . . . a kindergartner packs for the first "sleepover."

The amount of learning that takes place in early childhood is staggering. How do children manage to absorb the sheer quantity of information and experience they accumulate in their first few years of life?

Every child accomplishes this mighty feat by *thinking*. Early theories about cognition have been based on the idea that intelligence is a general capacity or potential that can be measured by standardized tests (such as I.Q. tests) and, therefore, that cognition can be developed by a specific, rather narrow, set of teaching techniques. During the last half of this century, however, new ideas began to emerge. All of the recent theories revolve around the same fascinating question: What accounts for the remarkable changes in thinking, language, and problem-solving in young children? Jean Piaget's theories (see Chapter 4) are an important part of early childhood educational philosophy. Recent research on information-processing, plus the theories of Vygotsky (see Chapter 4) and Gardner, have broadened our notions of thinking and intelligence.

Cognition is the mental process of faculty children use to acquire knowledge. To think is to be able to acquire and apply knowledge. By using conscious thought and memory, children think about themselves, the world, and others. Educating the thinking child is a critical function of parents and teachers. Curriculum in the early years must address the thinking, or cognitive, skills.

Language is the primary form of expression through which people communicate their knowledge and thoughts. A baby does not start life with language, but always communicates. In fact, oral language begins early, as infants learn to express themselves with sounds if not words. The growing child communicates needs, thoughts, and feelings through meaningful language. Thus, language and thought are intertwined.

Yet, the two are also separate. Cognition can occur without the language to express it. For example, when the infant laughs during a game of

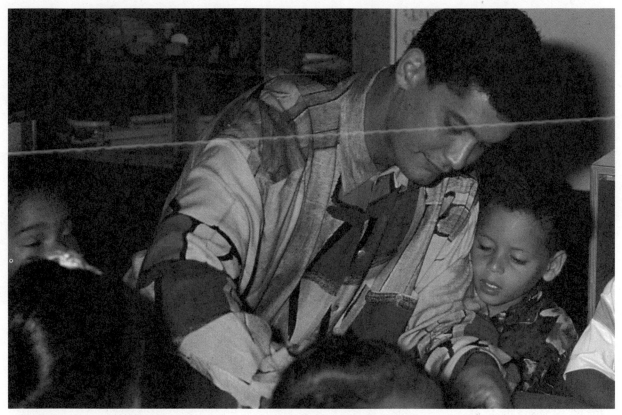

FIGURE 13.1   As children investigate the world of people and places, they ask themselves and others what they want to know.

peek-a-boo, it indicates the child's knowledge that the hidden face will reappear. Conversely, the use of language can occur without cognition (i.e., without knowing the meaning). A child counting from one to twenty (". . . 11,13,17,19,20!") is a case in point.

Cognition and language generally become more interdependent as development progresses. Children expand their knowledge base through language. They listen, question, tell. The child with good language skills can thus apply them to widen the horizons of knowledge.

Cognition and language relate not only to the developing mind, but also to all areas of the child's growth. Young thinkers are at work no matter what they are doing. For example, physical/motor development is also a cognitive process. Learning to roller-skate involves skinned knees and learning to balance (motor tasks), along with analyzing, predicting, generalizing, evaluating, and practicing

the art of locomotion on wheels (cognitive skills). When trying to enter into group play (a social task), children will think of strategies for how to get started (cognitive skill).

Children use language in developing emotionally. They listen, label, describe, elaborate, and question (language skills) as they learn to tell themselves and others how they feel (emotional tasks). And anyone who has heard a child mumbling instructions on how to get down from a tree knows that language can be of great help in using physical skills.

This chapter will explore in depth the framework for planning curriculum for the mind. For the purposes of clarity, cognition and language will be separated into units. However, teachers must remember that these work together constantly in the minds and lives of young children. Planned programs for early childhood will be more successful if that link is recognized.

● UNIT 13-1 COGNITION

THE DEVELOPMENT OF COGNITION: A PERSPECTIVE

An Eclectic Point of View

In trying to enhance cognitive development, early childhood educators draw upon developmental and learning theories and their direct experiences with children. By combining theoretical and practical viewpoints, teachers take a blended, or *eclectic,* perspective on the development of the thinking process. They work with children to encourage their ability to formulate ideas and to think rationally and logically.

Most important, the early childhood professional works toward helping children acquire skills that will lead to the development of:

Concepts: labeling or naming an idea, moving from the specific to the abstract

"What is a grape?"

Relationships: What is the association between two or more things? How are they similar or different? What are their functions, characteristics, attributes?

"How many colors of grapes are there? Do all of them have seeds? Are they different sizes? Do they taste alike?"

Generalizations: Drawing conclusions from relationships and concepts/ideas. This means grouping into classes and finding common elements.

"Are grapes a fruit or meat? How do grapes grow?"

A Piagetian Perspective

Developmental psychology, particularly through the works of Jean Piaget, has provided a deeper understanding of cognitive development. Piaget's view of cognition is twofold: First, *learning is a process of discovery,* of finding out what one needs to know to solve a particular problem. Second, *knowledge results from active thought,* from making mental connections among objects, from constructing a meaningful reality for understanding.

For Piaget, knowledge is "an interpretation of reality that the learner actively and internally constructs by interacting with it. (Labinowicz, 1980). Piaget divided knowledge into three types: physical, logical mathematical, and social. **Physical knowledge** is what children learn through external sensory experiences. Watching leaves blow in the wind, grabbing a ball, sniffing a fresh slice of bread are all instances of children learning about different physical objects and how they feel, taste, smell, move, and so on. The basic cognitive process involved in the development of physical knowledge is *discrimination*. For example, by touching magnets to paper clips, puzzles, and paper dolls, children learn first-hand about magnetism. They learn to discriminate between those objects that "stick" to the magnet and those that do not.

Logical mathematical knowledge derives from coordinating physical actions into some kind of order, or logic. This is not to be confused with formal mathematics, but rather with the mathematical kind of thinking children use in making connections about what they see, such as an infant lifting the blanket to find a hidden toy. The logic of the young child is seen in the coordinating of actions to make an **inference.** Think back to the magnets example. If a child deliberately takes a magnet to the metal drawer pulls and metal climbing bars, we can see the logical knowledge used: the child has made the inference that it is the *metal* things that "stick" on the magnet.

Social knowledge comes from our culture, the rules of the game, the right vocabulary, the moral codes. It includes learning vocabulary and being taught or told things, as well as knowledge about the social aspects of life. Value-laden and often arbitrary, it can rarely be constructed logically but is learned through life. With the aforementioned magnets, social knowledge would need to be used to decide who gets to play with the magnets, or when it is somebody else's turn.

In developing cognitive curriculum, teachers plan experiences that enhance those types of knowledge. They can teach using different forms of knowledge. **Rote knowledge** is information given with no particular meaning to the learner— that which could be learned meaningfully but is not. A teacher talking about magnets or telling children what attracts or repels gives children rote knowledge. Meaningful knowledge is what children learn gradually and within the context of what they already know and want to find out—like the example of letting the children handle the magnets themselves if they choose, and answering their questions as they arise. Both telling (rote) and asking or allowing (meaningful) can be useful; the question for the teacher is the balance between the two in everyday educational encounters.

Gardner's Frames of Mind

Research in cognition documents that children possess different *kinds of minds* and therefore understand, learn, remember, and perform in different ways (Gardner, 1991). Most experts agree that intelligence is complex and that traditional tests do not measure the entire host of skills or abilities involved. This alternative view is expressed by Howard Gardner (1983, 1991) and Robert Sternberg[1] (1986). Gardner, a Harvard University psychologist, suggests that there are seven "frames of mind":

1. linguistic (language ability)

2. musical (the earliest talent to emerge)

3. logical (ability to manipulate, order, and assess quantity and quality)

4. spatial (capacity to perceive visual world, change perceptions, recreate aspects of what one sees without its being in view)

5. body-kinesthetic (ability to control body motions and handle objects)

6. intrapersonal (understanding self, access to own feelings, and range of emotions)

7. interpersonal (social understanding)

Sternberg argues for three aspects of intelligence: componential (analytical thinking, such as measured by I.Q. tests), experiential (reactions to people and events), and contextual (sometimes called "street smarts").

Multiple intelligence theory acknowledges that people learn and use knowledge in different ways. The implications for teachers are enormous: if the ways in which children represent what they know are varied, then we are faced with which knowledge we value and how we can address all areas of intelligence in order to help each child succeed. Many of the learning centers in early childhood programs lend themselves to multi-intelligences learning. The New City School (1995) gives these suggestions for center activities for the letter "F":

- Linguistic
  Story/words—sort objects that begin with the letter F; make an "F" chant, with every word starting with "F"
  Listening—listen to "Frog Went A Courtin' "
  Computer—play "Fun on the Farm"

- Logical-Mathematical
  Manipulatives—measure by the foot
  Language—learn about feelings; talk about feeling frustrated

- Spatial
  Art—paint fancy feet or face painting
  Clay—make the letter "F" out of playdough

- Musical
  Dramatic play—listen to "Fantasia" while you play in playhouse
  Music—listen and sing in French; make rhythms with your feet

- Bodily-Kinesthetic
  Outdoors—bounce balls around a giant letter "F"
  Grouptime—draw imaginary letters ("F") on each other's back
  Sensory—use funnels

- Intrapersonal
  Manipulatives—a "one-only" game with sandpaper letters ("F")
  "Me place"—a beanbag chair for one only

- Interpersonal
  "Social table" or "help-yourself" table—"F"

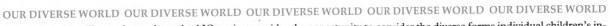

OUR DIVERSE WORLD OUR DIVERSE WORLD OUR DIVERSE WORLD OUR DIVERSE WORLD OUR DIVERSE WORLD

[1]Considering intelligence beyond standard IQ testing provides the opportunity to consider the diverse forms individual children's intelligence may take.

templates with markers and paper; "F" lacing cards

Small grouptime—partners find all the "F's" in sheet of letters

Vygotsky, Thinking, and Culture

Focusing on how our values and beliefs affect what we transmit to the next generation, Vygotsky's sociocultural theory claims that much of children's development and knowledge is culturally specific (see Chapter 4). Since children learn from more knowledgeable members of the community, they come to know those skills that are socially valued. In today's America, the most salient sources of knowledge are family members, the media, and the school. The psychological tools children need to learn higher mental functions, such as symbolic thought, memory, attention, and reasoning, need the mediation of someone who knows the tools of that particular society.

Vygotsky adds an important element to our understanding of thinking. If knowledge is connected to what a culture values, then learning must be done in a collaborative style. Teachers and parents must have some agreement about what is important in order to teach children, and the best way of teaching is a kind of assisted learning, or apprenticeship. An older child or adult serves as a guide who is responsive to what the child is ready to learn.

The implications for teaching include a strong case for mixed-age groupings so that younger children can learn from older ones. Indeed, of all the strategies used to deal with reading problems in primary grades (which has devastating effects on children), the "most effective by far for preventing early reading failure are approaches incorporating one-to-one tutoring of at-risk first graders" (Slavin, et al., 1993). Play is a valuable way for children to work with the symbols and other higher forms of thinking. With other people alongside, the child practices what is to be expected and valued in society. The teacher is both observer and participant: for instance, if a child builds with blocks, the adult might sketch the building and then encourage a joint effort to make a map or use measurement tools.

Research from cognitive-developmentalists such as Flavell (1994) and brain research (Ellison, 1990) support these alternative findings. Already preschoolers know about thinking: they can distinguish thinking from other psychological activities; three-year-olds know that thinking is not seeing or talking, and four- and five-year-olds can often tell that there is a difference between thinking and knowing. The biological evidence strongly suggests that there are sequences in children's thinking, that there are at least multiple expressions of intelligence, and that the context of learning affects what children know. These theories all attempt to describe some of the incredible diversity of human cognitive ability.

COGNITIVE SKILLS IN EARLY CHILDHOOD

The actual skills children acquire as they learn to think are considerable. A basic skill is defined by two fundamental qualities:

- A skill is basic if it is **transcurricular:** that is, if the child can use it in a variety of situations and activities throughout the school day. For example, children who can express feelings and opinions clearly—who can let adults know when they are having difficulties with a particular task or social situation—have acquired a skill that is useful anywhere.

- A skill is also basic if it has **dynamic** consequences: that is, if it leads to other worthwhile responses. For instance, children who are articulate tend to elicit more verbal responses from adults. Consequently, they are exposed to more verbal stimulation, which in turn strengthens their verbal abilities, and so on. Thus, having this skill leads to major dynamic consequences in a favorable direction, while *not* having the skill leads to dynamic consequences in an unfavorable direction (Katz, 1985).

Most skills fall into the nine categories below. The list, while long, is a comprehensive one; what children learn in the thinking realm of their development will fall into one of these categories. The teacher plans activities for all cognitive skills to ensure challenging children's thinking.

Skills of Inquiry

Young children are curious, watching the world carefully. Through exploration and examination, they increase their attention span. Inquisitive children begin to organize what they see, analyzing and identifying confusions or obstacles for themselves. The next step is communication; the child asks questions, listens, gets ideas, and makes suggestions. This includes interpreting what others communicate. Then children are ready to use resources, seeking assistance from other people and materials.

Piaget called these skills of inquiry; some of Gardner's spatial intelligence and Sternberg's experiential intelligence would also be included. Organizing and finding patterns, reasoning, and problem solving are also inquiry skills. As children examine alternatives, they choose a course of action, revising their plans as needed. Young children thrill in making educated guesses, then checking their **hypotheses** by experimenting and taking risks. In doing so, they learn to evaluate, to use the judgments and opinions, and to distinguish between fact and opinion, reality and fantasy. These basic skills of inquiry are the foundation for thinking; as such, they are far more important to develop than simple prereading or number skills.

Knowledge of the Physical World

How do children learn about the physical world? First, they use objects, spending plenty of time exploring, manipulating, choosing, using toys and natural materials. Babies search for something to suck; they begin to grasp objects and let them go. Toddlers will pick up and throw things or drop objects from a highchair to see what happens. Children observe reactions, discover relationships, and try to predict what will happen. Six-year-olds with balloons and water explore how to fill, roll, throw, and burst the balloons. This knowledge is part of Gardner's logical-mathematical intelligence and Sternberg's componential intelligence, for knowledge of the physical world is essential to making order of it. As they learn the properties of objects, children gain a better understanding of the concept of cause and effect.

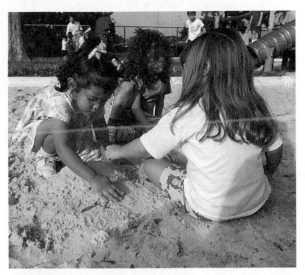

FIGURE 13.2 Being able to explore actual materials and objects encourages children to use and assimilate new knowledge.

Knowledge of the Social World

Learning about others is hard work, since the social world is not concrete and is often illogical. The child needs an awareness of self before developing an awareness of others and how to interact socially. To Gardner, this kind of knowledge requires two types of intelligence. The first is *intrapersonal*, having access to one's own feelings and a range of emotions, and the second is *interpersonal*, being able to notice others, making distinctions among individuals, particularly their moods and motivations. Infants begin by distinguishing friends from strangers. Toddlers learn to use "mine" and then to use others' names as well. The next step is to expand their knowledge of roles to include those of family, school, and the community. Four- and five-year-olds are provided with daily opportunities to cooperate, to help, and to negotiate with others about their needs and wishes. According to Vygotsky, preschoolers learn appropriate actions by playing with older children. Also, make-believe is a major means through which children extend their cognitive skills.

Children are encouraged to notice both similarities and differences in people and then are led to develop tolerance for both. Sternberg's contextual intelligence describes the ability to understand and manipulate the environment to suit one-self.[1] School-aged children seek small-group teamwork and moments of private time with a close friend. Children in the primary grades experience the development of conscience and learn rules for social living. In these ways children learn what is appropriate conduct in various situations—indoors or out, happy or sad, at the grocery store or at the dinner table.

Classification

Knowledge of the physical world teaches children to have different responses to different objects. *Classifying* this knowledge is a lengthy process. To clarify this process, consider how two-year-old Tisa learns to classify:

> What can Tisa do to the stuffed bear *and* the pet dog? What can she do with one and *not* the other? Which are her toys? Rover's? Which ones have fur? What is different about them?

Tisa learns the *attributes* of the objects by exploring, learning the class names of "toy" and "pet." Sternberg would call this a kind of componential intelligence; that is, being experimental and looking for a pattern. Tisa makes collections, sorting by similarity those that are Rover's toys and those that are her own. She uses class relationships to understand that both animals have fur, but she can tug on only one animal's ears without encountering a problem.

Seriation

How do children learn to seriate, or to arrange items according to a graduated scale? Like classification, seriation can appear confusing at first glance. To illustrate its development, look at some of the materials designed by Montessori. These toys were developed to make clear to children exactly what seriation is and how it can be learned. Many of these toys distinguish grades of intensity by size, color, weight, number. Children build pyramid towers, fit nesting blocks together, and use the counting rods. By noting differences,

often through trial and error, children learn seriation systematically. For instance, the pyramid tower is ordered from largest piece to smallest as it is built. Boxes are nested, one inside the other, by their graduated size or volume. The counting rods can be put into a staircase array, the units building on each other from one to ten. Children can arrange several things in order and fit one ordered set of objects to another. Gardner's category of musical intelligence requires seriation, as well as the skill of inquiry ("How do I make noise? Rhythm? Musical song?") and a knowledge of the social world ("How can we make music together? A real band?").

Numbers

Understanding the concept of *number* means learning about quantity; that is, understanding amount, degree, and position. Once infants develop an understanding of *object permanence* (that an object exists whether or not it can be seen), they are ready to learn about quantity as they compare objects—for example, by stacking rings on a stick. Toddlers and twos can sort by groups (large versus small, hard versus soft) and start noticing what is "more." To learn about the names of numbers, one begins with their sound. Settings for children under five have plenty of songs, chants, and fingerplays that include numbers ("One Potato, Two" or "Five Speckled Frogs"). Once children comprehend numbers, they are ready to use mathematical terms and forms of expression. For instance, after singing about the frog that jumped into the pool in the song "Five Speckled Frogs," Chantel can begin to understand that four is one less than five.

But a knowledge of number is neither complete nor meaningful unless children have direct experience with materials and objects. Learning about quantity also means comparing amounts (as when children work with table toys, blocks, sensory materials, and the like) and arranging two sets of objects in one-to-one correspondence ("Each person needs one and only one napkin for snack, Tyler"). Children can also count objects and begin computation ("Parvin, you have three

[1]Social knowledge is a critical factor in children's development, enabling them to function in OUR DIVERSE WORLD.

shovels. Here is one more; now how many do you have?"). With countless experiences such as these, children in kindergarten through third grade will be ready and excited to learn more mathematical skills.

Symbols

A symbol stands for something else; it is not what it appears to be! Young children have to think hard and long in order to symbolize. It is a task of some skill to imitate or use one object to represent something else.

Children begin by using their bodies. Infants and toddlers love to play peek-a-boo, reacting to "Boo!" with full-bodied excitement each time it is said. Preschoolers revel in playing favorite characters. Primary school children make up plays and puppet shows. Make-believe helps in the process of symbolizing, as does making sound to represent objects ("Choo-choo" is a train, for example). Using and making two- and three-dimensional models are other ways children symbolize, when they transfer what they see to the easel or to the clay table. Children are also symbolizing when they dress up in costumes and uniforms. Teachers add to the symbolizing process when they use descriptive words. Description games encourage children to do the same. For example, "It is round and red and you eat it. What is it?" (An apple!) After all these skills have been mastered, children are ready for written symbols, when they can use the written word to label, take dictation, or write notes. Using Gardner's and Vygotsky's ways of thinking, educational environments for school-age children might take the form of a discovery center, or kind of museum, where apprentice-groups with children of different ages would help children with numerical and computer skills.

Spatial Relationships

Spatial relationships develop early. Infants visually track what they see, trying to reach and grasp. As they experience one object's position in relation to another, they begin to have a mental picture of spatial relationships. Toddlers find this out as they learn to steer themselves around tables and seat themselves on the potty. The concept of

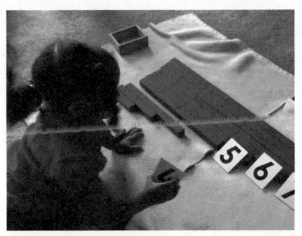

FIGURE 13.3 Cognition in action! The concepts of seriation and numbers come to life through Montessori materials. *(Courtesy of American Montessori Society.)*

"close" (the chair) and "far away" (the quesadilla cooling on the counter) give clues to length and distance ("How far do I have to reach to get one?"). As spatial skills develop, children learn to fit things together and take them apart. They rearrange and shape objects. They observe and describe things from different spatial viewpoints. This perspective is learned only through experience. The child under five needs to describe and then try out the notion that what one sees from the side of the hill is *not* what can be seen from the top.

Adults help children learn such skills by letting them locate things at home, in the classroom, in the department store. Both Piaget and Gardner would agree that body and kinesthetic knowledge are used in this type of activity. In Reggio Emilia, for instance, mirrors are placed around corners, found at the school entrance, and embedded in the floors, giving children a sense of self in space in a number of ways. They encourage children to represent such spatial relationships in their drawings, with pictures, and in photographs.

Time

Understanding time is a complicated affair, since time is composed of at least three dimensions: time as the present, time as a continuum, and time as a sequence of events. Children must learn each of these to fully understand the concept of time. In some settings children learn to stop and start an activity on a signal (when the teacher strikes a chord on the piano for cleanup time). They try to move their bodies at different speeds, indoors and out. Older children begin to observe that clocks and calendars are used to mark the passage of time. Specifically, children come to know the sequencing of events in time: which comes first, next, last? Having an order of events through a consistent daily schedule helps children learn this aspect of time. They also benefit from anticipating future events and making the appropriate preparations. Planning a course of action and completing that plan gives meaning to the idea of time.

What children learn intellectually in the early years is massive in quantity and quality. Yet young children are ready—eager, in fact—to engage themselves with the world around them in order to acquire these cognitive skills. By remaining aware of how much is to be learned, educators keep a realistic—and humble—appreciation for the "work" of children.

THE TEACHER'S ROLE

Considerations

When considering children's intellectual development, teachers should keep in mind:

FIGURE 13.4 When considering intellectual development, teachers should keep in mind that, to children, education is exploration. Let children use their imagination to use materials in new and different ways. (Courtesy of the schools of Reggio Emilio, Italy.)

● *Education is exploration.* The process of education is more than its products. Teachers enhance learning by allowing children to interact with the environment. The teacher is a source of information and support rather than one who gives answers or commands. Based on the belief that children's minds should be engaged in ways that deepen their understanding of their own experiences and environment, a project approach may be used. Consisting of exploring a theme or topic (such as shadows, houses, building a table) over a period of weeks, this approach reflects Dewey's progressive education and the British Open Schools (see Chapter 1) and is implemented regularly in the Reggio Emilia Schools. The goal is to have children ask their own questions and create their own challenges.

● *Children do not think like adults.* Children think and perceive in their own ways as Piaget believed. They think in sensory and concrete terms and come to conclusions based on what they see and touch.

● *Children's thinking is legitimate and should be valued.* Their thought processes and perceptions are as valid as adults'. Teachers support those processes by asking questions to stimulate further thought and by providing materials for exploration, as seen in Figure 13.15.

● *The language of the teacher should support cognitive development.* Throughout their interactions with children, teachers help children use words, terms, and concepts correctly:

Mariko (at water table): I need that suckup.

Teacher: The baster really does suck up water, doesn't it?

Teachers' questions are open-ended; they are not to be answered with a simple yes or no. As teachers in Reggio Emilia question children (more often than not in small groups of three or four), they explore together what the children are doing, how they are going to solve a problem, or what they would like to do next. They may even tape record the interchange so that later the child can play it back and evaluate the approach in greater depth. For example, Tony asks his kindergartners what will happen if they do not count the cups of

Skill	Teachers Can
Inquiry	• Ask questions so children make statements about their conversations. *Example:* "What do you notice about the guinea pig?" • Try to be more specific if such questions seem overwhelming or if they elicit little response. *Example:* "What sounds do you hear? What can you find out by touching her?" • Ask how children arrived at their answers. *Example:* "How did you know that the marble wouldn't roll *up* the ramp?" • Ask questions that expand the process. *Example:* "Can you tell me anything else about your doll?"

Social Knowledge	• Try not to respond to unstated needs.
	Example: "Do you want something? Can I help you?"
	• Help children define what they want or need, so that they learn how to ask for it.
	Example: Marie: I wonder who is going to tie my shoes?
	       Teacher: So do I. When you want someone to tie your shoe, you can say, "Would you tie my shoe?"
	       Marie: Would you tie my shoe?
	       Teacher: I'd be glad to.

Classification	• Ask questions that will help children focus on objects and see differences and details.
	Examples: While cooking, ask
	   Which things on the table do we put in the bowl? Which are made of plastic? Which go in the oven?
	   What on the table is used for measuring? How do you know?
	   Now look carefully—what do you see on the measuring cup?
	   What do those little red lines mean?

Spatial Relationships	• Ask for the precise location of an object the child asks for or is interested in. *Examples:* "Where did you say you saw the bird's nest?" "You can find another stapler in the cabinet underneath the fish tank."

Concept of Time	• Use accurate time sequences with children.
	Example: Teacher: Just a minute.
	       Milo: Is this a real minute, or a "wait a minute"?
	       Teacher: You're right. I'm with Phoebe now. I'll help you next.

FIGURE 13.5 Teachers' use of language affects how children develop cognitive skills. The more children are allowed and encouraged to think for themselves, the more their cognitive skills will develop.

flour while making bread. What he is really asking them to do is to predict what will happen and consider the results. The goal is to use language to help children to *think*.

Sometimes teachers use their own language skills to define a problem, help children figure out what they are doing, and decide what they need to do next. They leave the child with something to ponder.

    Teacher: I wonder why the turtle's head went back in its shell when you put your finger close by.

Teacher: If you want to play with José, how can you let him know?

Teacher: What *do* we need from the woodworking shelf to make a spaceship?

Figure 13.5 shows further how teachers' use of language helps children think and develop cognitive skills as part of their early childhood experience.

Curriculum Planning for Cognitive Development

In the Environment

Teachers can plan cognitive curriculum for their children by considering the class setting, both indoors and out, throughout the daily schedule. Each activity center can be used to encourage intellectual development with a variety of curriculum materials and methods (see High/Scope in Chapter 2). The environment and methods required to help children think include challenging situations, enriching materials, and supportive adults. Young children have special ways of thinking (see Chapter 4) that expand with age. Some children under three have a limited attention span and can be overstimulated unless the environment is kept simple. Three- to five-year-olds can absorb more and in finer detail as they have more developed motor and perceptual skills. Older preschoolers and kindergartners learn best trying to solve real problems, and the 6- to 8-year-old still benefits in discovery-oriented, "learn by doing" situations. Figure 13.6 shows how one activity (which can be done with nearly all ages) contributes to the development of children's thought processes.

Throughout the environment, teachers remember to notice and appreciate *efforts* as well as children's projects. Too often only the take-home pieces of a day, such as preschool art projects or primary written assignments are noted. Teachers can record examples of children's thinking by photographing or sketching creations made with blocks and manipulatives, and can take notes about incidences in drama and social interactions.

A specific example of their child's reasoning or problem solving tells parents of the tremendous cognitive work in children's play.

Indoor Areas. The indoor environments described in Chapter 9 include the basic ingredients of a stimulating cognitive environment. The indoor areas might have some of the following materials and activities:

Art: Include a shelf for self-chosen projects. A variety of paper, drawing implements, and tools encourages children to re-create their own reality, using representational art forms that show how children see the physical and social worlds.

Blocks: Have paper models of each block shape to help children with classification by shape and size. Accessories, such as animals and homemade trees and lakes, help children symbolize.

Discovery/Science: Rotate a display of "touch me" materials. This gives children first-hand experience with plants, seeds, animals, magnets, seashells, foods, and so on. Help children formulate questions and then experiment or observe to seek the answers. School-age children can find out which plants grow in saltwater or freshwater by setting up plants in each environment and watching daily ("Today somthing has changd!" wrote a seven-year-old. "The duckweed is not relly grren anymore. A scnd root is hanging.") If you can, have a computer available with developmentally appropriate software (see *Special Topics* section of this chapter for details).

Dramatic play: Stock this area with materials for role playing, puppet making, and acting out of adult activities. Have anatomically correct boy and girl dolls of a variety of races and with handicaps. Include clothing for all types of work, equipment for carrying things and babies, that reflect the homes of all the children in the group but also extend the play to include new ways of dressing, eating, and playing.[1] Children learn to understand the world of people as they pretend to be adults with adult occupations and responsibilities.

Language/Library: Choose books that focus on both the physical and social worlds. Children's interests in numbers, symbols, and time can also be extended by selecting literature that reflects

[1]Children's learning environments should be rich with images of diversity.

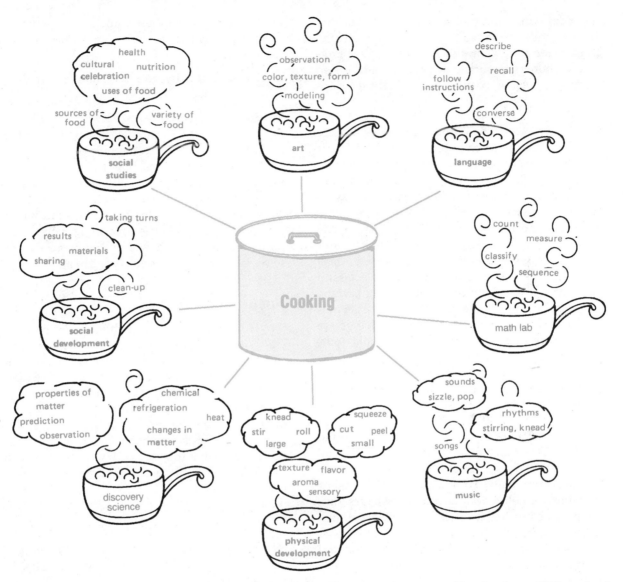

FIGURE 13.6 Each activity in the environment, such as cooking, can enhance cognitive development throughout the curriculum. A trip to the market can be an experience in classification and calculation.

their level of understanding. Look for the message in children's books and choose good stories that reflect diversity, such as *Helping Out* (Ancona), and *George the Babysitter* (Hughes). Be sure to listen to the group's interests, and make a point to place books that respond to those interests in the library. (See *Special Topic* section of this chapter.)

Manipulatives (table toys): The manipulatives area is an ideal place for materials that encourage

cognitive development; highlight this area with both favorites (Lego® or Crystal Climbers®) and new items (Construx® or sewing cards). Counting cubes aid in classification and seriation, while puzzles or nesting blocks focus on spatial relationships. Information-processing theory emphasizes the importance of experiences that develop children's working memory and familiarity. Manipulative materials (including beads, tiddley winks, and so on) and games give children hands-on experiences with counting, sorting, and organizing that is both meaningful and socially natural. Homemade lotto games or puzzles with the children's photos encourage self-esteem and group identity as well as cognitive and motor development.

Outdoor Areas. The outdoor area provides opportunities for children to plan and organize their own thoughts. Toddlers can classify what they find as they look for balls, sand buckets, and toy trucks hidden around the yard. Kindergartners playing tag need inquiry skills. Preschoolers in the sand pit predict how water will affect the sand, using their growing knowledge of the physical world. Children learn to classify water table and wheel toys; they learn seriation when they select sand buckets by size. Counting shovels to see that there are enough to go around, building with large, hollow blocks, and watching the seasons change are all cognitive skills children gain as they play outside.

Physical- and logical-mathematical activities are thus easily incorporated into the curriculum outdoors. A Piagetian approach of asking "I wonder why. . . ?" or "What would happen if. . . ?" inspires experimenting and reasoning in young children. The water table outdoors could have a large block of ice, a variety of materials such as wood, cotton balls, straws, and cardboard, or containers of colored water and eyedroppers. Balancing activities might mean hollow blocks, milk cartons, or beanbags (or all three). A hillside or long plank can become a site for predicting and trying out rolling, using different sizes of balls or even bodies.

Routines, Transitions, and Groups

Groups, transitions, and routines all play a part in developing children's knowledge base of the social world. As children learn to conduct themselves in school, they learn:

- To enter a class and start to play (transition).
- To take care of their own belongings and those of their school (routines).
- To concentrate on an activity with others around (group times).

- To interact with others while at the same time paying attention to a leader or task (group times).
- To end an activity, an interaction, a school day (transition).

Teachers plan environments, activities, and grouping of children to give the class experience in all these cognitive challenges. Look back at Figure 9.24 in Chapter 9. It describes strategies for helping children learn concrete and comfortable ways to think and live with transitions. Teachers use signs, their own words, and helpful tips that illuminate for children what is happening, what is expected of them, and how they can express themselves in all three of these daily segments.

Focus on Skills

How can teachers help children develop specific cognitive skills? After observing the children carefully, teachers identify a particular skill and then list those processes, concepts, and vocabulary involved. For instance, the skill of *inquiry* can be encouraged in every part of the curriculum by *asking questions* (see Figures 13.14 and 13.15). Teachers model curiosity by observing and asking questions about what they see and what children may be thinking. This stimulates children to look, wonder, and interact:

Teacher: I wonder which piece of wood you'll choose to glue on your board next?

Teacher: What part do you want to play in our grocery store?

Teacher: How can we find out how long your road of blocks is?

Figure 13.8 illustrates the kinds of questions teachers ask children that help children think and learn.

When children see that it is all right to ask "Why?", they feel encouraged to ask questions themselves. Brainstorming is a technique that helps children get ideas and use resources to find out how many ways there are to make a kite or build a castle.

Outdoors, inquisitive children explore their environment. Children ask questions: "Can we turn on the water? What if we bury all of the toy bears in

The Concepts:
Selecting a course of action
Making educated guesses
Making and revising a plan
Risking and evaluating the results

The Vocabulary:
Guess
Plan
Problem
Solution/solve
What? why? how?

The Process:

Activity area	Process question
Art	How many ways can you use the brush (pen, squirt bottle) to make a mark on the paper? Why is it dripping? How can you stop it when you're ready?
Bathrooms/cubbies	You found Paul's sweater . . . How can you find where it goes? Where did the water come from? How can you clean it up?
Blocks	What makes the tower of blocks fall over? How can a block be used to connect two others?
Cooking	How do we mix these ingredients together? What will happen when it is put in the oven?
Discovery/science	Why did the magnet pick up the nail and not the pen? What is the difference between the rabbit and the guinea pig? How are they alike?
Dramatic play	Who will be the dad? What happens when these other children want to play? How can you get to wear the costume you want?
Language/library	What happens next in the story? Why do you think so? Why did the child feel unhappy at first? Then what happened?
Large group	Why can't you see/hear the leader? What can you do about feeling too crowded? What can you do when your friend keeps whispering to you during story-time?
Gross-motor	How do you jump rope? What do you use to pump yourself on a swing? How will you find a ball?
Manipulatives	How do you figure out what puzzle piece fits? Do you see a pattern on the peg board? What is it?
Sensory	How do you get the water from the large pitcher to the small cup? How will you get the wet sand through the funnel?

FIGURE 13.7   Children want to know how to solve problems, such as, "How much milk will a bowl of this size hold?"

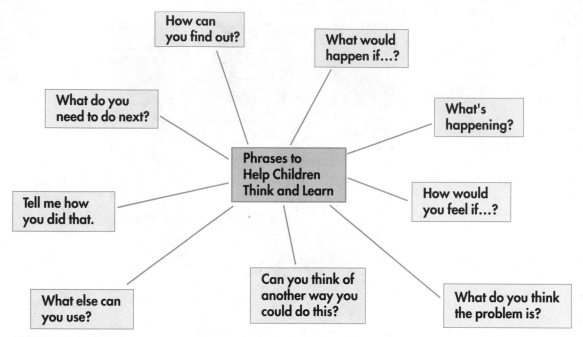

FIGURE 13.8   Teachers encourage children's thinking when they ask questions. Posted in the classroom or given to students and parents, this chart serves as a reminder that to TEACH is to ASK more often than to TELL.

the gravel?! Could we use the ladder to see over the fence? Let's all hide from the teacher?!" The way teachers handle inquiries from children about what they want to do sends a message that supports—or discourages—this cognitive skill. When there is no harm in *asking* (though the answer may be "No"), children are encouraged to develop further the skill of inquiry. Figure 13.7 illustrates exactly how the cognitive skills of reasoning and problem solving could serve as the basis for curriculum development around the entire classroom.

Use of Themes

A specific theme can be chosen for cognitive development. Units based on things in the physical world (season changes, pets, the garden), on unexpected or current events (a new load of sand, a community fair, road work nearby), or the special interests of the children (sharing the African mask or spacesuits, using the puppet stage, studying reptiles) are all appealing. Figure 13.9 illustrates a dinosaur theme.

Current events must be chosen carefully, as young children may have only passing knowledge

or interest in most of them. Meaningful events might be a space shuttle mission or a solar eclipse. More likely, the event will be a local one, such as a children's fair or someone's new baby. Units based on these happenings might be named "Space and Travel" or "Our Beginnings As Babies." Events such as the discovery of ants on the playground have a high level of interest and are worth pursuing; see Figure 13.10 for an example.

Themes can change with the seasons. Fall is the time for a unit on "Harvest Time," "Corn," or "Masks and Hats." Winter may mean a unit on "Water, Water Everywhere," since snow, sleet, hail, and rain are a regular part of most winter months in the U.S. Spring is a time for green and growing things, and a unit could focus on the physical world of growing plants from seeds, hatching chicks, visiting a farm. Summer weather on the coasts sends everyone to "The Seashore," or at least the local lake or river.

The theme of "Friendship" during Valentine's month expands children's knowledge of the social world, as they increase their awareness of others through the giving and receiving of letters and cards. Cooperation and group conflict resolution

THEME: DINOSAURS

Area	Cognitive Skill(s)	Activity
	Indoors	
Art	Organization	Papier mâché model of a dinosaur; make a "dinosaur world" mural.
Blocks	Seriation	Use blocks to compare relative sizes of dinosaurs.
Cooking	Relationships	Prepare vegetarian snack (herbivores), then meatballs for the carnivores.
Discovery	Observation	Get fossils, other skeletons.
		Collect books on how scientists learn about dinosaurs.
		Compare relationships (size, stature, etc.) of prehistoric to common animals.
		Hide bones in the sand table to dig up and role-play paleontologist.
Dramatic play	Symbols	Dinosaur puppets.
		Masks of dinosaurs.
Library	Label/recall; use of resources	Provide books about dinosaurs.
		Make dinosaur books with stamps and children's words.
Manipulatives	Reasoning; problem solving	Individual and floor dinosaur puzzles.
		Templates to trace and cut.
	Outdoors	
Sensory	Symbols	Rubber dinosaurs in pebbles; dinosaur cookie cutters in clay/play dough.
Gross-motor	Symbols	Measure children's bodies with a rope the length of various dinosaurs.
Sand	Symbols	Act out digging up dinosaur bones.
Games	Social world	"Tyrannosaurus, May I?" game, naming and taking steps of various dinosaurs.
	Groups	
Large	Label/recall; educated guessing	"Who Am I?", verbally describing dinosaur.
		Mystery Pictures, showing parts of dinosaurs and having children guess.
Music	Symbols	Acting out dinosaurs to the record, or to music of various tones.
Small	Label/communicate	Draw your favorite dinosaur; dictate what you like about it and what you know.
		Dinosaur sheet, folded in quarters, with a sentence to fill in and space to draw: The dinosaurs laid . . . / Some dinosaurs lived . . . / Dinosaurs ate . . . / Dinosaurs died because . . . /

FIGURE 13.9 Using a theme of special interest, such as dinosaurs, teachers can develop children's cognitive skills in many classroom areas.

Discovery Learning About Ants: Curriculum Planning For Primary Cognitive Development

---

The Setting:

- The playground after a rain and in the sidewalk cracks
- The classroom, especially around the wastebasket

The Discovery:

Ants everywhere!
Children: "Let's smash them!"
Teacher: "Wait. . . let's get to know them."

The Process:

Asking what you want to know about ants (RESEARCH QUESTION)

1. What do ants eat?
2. Why do they go into an anthill?
3. Do ants sleep?
4. Where do ants go when it rains?
5. What does an ant's body look like?
6. What is inside an anthill?

Finding out about these things (METHODOLOGY, PROCEDURE)

1. Consult experts (a library visit, checking at home, asking parents, looking at class copies of Ranger Rick, and so on)
2. Observe them (watch ants, collect them, put them in containers)
3. Collect information (write journals, do group stories and reports)
4. Do experiments on ants ("Do ants hear?" try blowing a trumpet; "Can ants swim?" put them in a bowl of water; "How strong are they?" give them various sizes of bread and see what they can carry)

Telling what you know (RESULTS, CONCLUSIONS, NEXT STEPS)

1. Write reports.
2. Make a drama or play and act it out.
3. Take photos or draw pictures.
4. Make a book.

FIGURE 13.10 A lesson that uses the discovery method engages the children in scientific thinking and is related directly to their own thinking. Children's innate curiosity, the foundation for scientific thinking, is thus extended into the primary years. (Special thanks to Amelia Klein. *Young Children*, July, 1991.)

expand the friendship theme. A unit can also focus on symbolizing through use of names, letters on a "post box," or the numbers and location of people's houses and apartments.

Throughout the year, teachers observe the interests of the particular group and notice what is relevant to their lives. For a group interested in the passage of time, "Watches and Calendars" could be a theme, with timepieces from hourglasses to digital watches and clanging timers and calendars from around the world. Using a calendar means involving the children in the process of construc-

tion, including events that the children look forward to (including birthdays, community events, field trips), and making it accessible so that the children can interact and "own" it.

Young children, particularly those under five, use themselves as a starting point. Working their way into the world from there, they are often interested in their bodies, and a loosely formed theme of "Our Bodies, Ourselves" allows for learning about racial, physical, and gender differences as well as differences in physical abilities.[1] Expanding this unit to family and community is a

---

Curriculum Planning for Cognitive Development with Infants and Toddlers

The Environment
- Contains soft items (such as pillows) and hard elements (such as mirrors) to see, taste, and touch.
- Has contrasts of color and design.
- Changes periodically, from the floor to strollers to swing.
- Is decorated with pictures of people's faces, animals, families.

The Skills
- Include self-help activities of eating, toileting/changing, and dressing.
- Highlight language and thinking as the adults label objects, describe events, and reflect feelings in a simplified, conversational manner.
- Encourage listening to a person, a story, a flannelboard song, a fingerplay.
- Use appropriate art media to explore and manipulate, not to produce a finished product.

The Themes
- Are loosely defined and flexible, as is the schedule.
- Are of family and belonging, of self and bodies, of babies.
- Are dictated more by children's needs than by adults'.

FIGURE 13.11 Planning for infants and toddlers involves understanding specific development and intimate knowledge of the individual child. Consistent caregiving and flexibility are as important to effective planning for children under two years of age as are the actual activities offered.

natural process that builds on a solid base. Another way to plan curriculum is to focus on the children's developmental level. Infants and toddlers have less need for theme curriculum; curriculum ideas for them concentrate on cognitive stimulation at their particular level of development such as in Figure 13.11.

● UNIT 13-1 CHECKPOINT

Cognition is the ability to learn, remember, and think abstractly. Children's cognitive development relates to learning in all other skill areas. Early childhood educators see cognitive development from an eclectic point of view and draw heavily from the works of Jean Piaget.

Cognitive skills in the early years can be put into several categories. The teacher's role is to understand how cognition develops in children and to put that knowledge to work in the classroom. While creating curriculum, teachers keep certain

attitudes and ideas in mind. Then, they set about planning for their programs.

The methods of developing children's cognitive skills are as varied and creative as the teachers—and children—can be. By focusing on the class setting, a specific skill, or a theme, teachers help children acquire and use the skills of thinking to understand themselves and the world around them.

Ask yourself:

- What perspective do early childhood teachers have on the development of cognition?

- What are nine cognitive skills of the early years?

- What should teachers consider when defining their role in cognitive development?

- How can cognitive curriculum be developed in the class setting?

- What skills could be the focus for curriculum planning?

 OUR DIVERSE WORLD OUR DIVERSE WORLD OUR DIVERSE WORLD OUR DIVERSE WORLD OUR DIVERSE WORLD

[1]What better time to deal with the potential of children's pre-prejudice attitudes and create an understanding and celebration of diversity!

● What are three themes that encourage the development of cognitive skills?

● UNIT 13-2 LANGUAGE

Alexis:	Laleña, will you help me full this pitcher up?
Laleña:	No, because my ponytail is keeping me in bothers.
Veronique:	Hey, come here! I accidentally dropped a piece of bread and the birds yummed it right up!
Abhi:	I know, that's what the tooth fairy did to my tooth.
Marty:	I'm going to keep *all* my baby teeth in a jar and the next time a baby comes along, I'll give him my baby teeth.

Language is the aspect of human behavior that involves the use of sounds in meaningful patterns. This includes the corresponding symbols that are used to form, express, and communicate thoughts and feelings. Any system of signs used for communication is language. For the developing child, language is the ability to express oneself. Language is both receptive—listening, understanding, and responding—and expressive—pronunciation, vocabulary, and grammar. In other words, as illustrated above, language has meaning.

THE DEVELOPMENT OF LANGUAGE

Language seems to be an innate characteristic of humankind. Wherever people live together, language of some form has developed. Languages worldwide vary remarkably in their sounds, words, and grammatical structure. Nonetheless, young children around the world acquire language.

What Research Tells Us

Research into language development and expression reveals several interesting characteristics. First, the language of children is different from adult language (deVilliers and Jill, 1981). Children's language deals with the present and is egocentric, taking into account only the child's own knowledge. There appears to be a lack of awareness on the child's part of language form and structure. In other words, children use language to communicate but seem to have no understanding of language as an entity itself.

Language is not learned simply by imitating adult speech (Beck, 1979). Child language is not garbled adult language, but rather unique to the child's age and linguistic level. Gardner lists language ability as one form of cognition (linguistic intelligence), and most language development theorists agree that there seems to be an innate human tendency towards language (Chomsky, 1972). Children are not just trying to imitate others and making mistakes, but are trying to come to terms with language themselves. A child will try out theories about language in attempts to understand its patterns. In language, as in so many areas of cognition, children are involved as active participants in their own learning. The use of speech is not merely imitative but productive and creative.

Moreover, language development is a process of maturation. Just as in the development of cognitive skills, there are stages of language growth that follow a specific sequence. There are also variations in timing that are important to remember.

Stages of Language Development

Children follow a six-step sequence in language development, one that seems *invariable* regardless of what language is being learned.

1. *Infant's Response to Language.* Babies begin by attending to speech, changes in sound, rhythm, and intonation. These are the precursors of speech, and young infants are especially sensitive to some sound differences. Infants need to hear speech, and plenty of it, to develop the foundations of sound.

2. *Vocalization.* By three to four months of age, infants begin cooing and babbling. Babbling increases with age and seems to peak around nine to 12 months. This is a matter of physical maturation, not just experience; deaf children do it at the same time as those whose hearing is normal. Furthermore, there are similar patterns across different languages.

3. *Word Development.* According to deVilliers and Jill (1981), the child must first separate the noises heard into speech and nonspeech. The speech noises must be further separated into words and the sounds that form them. The growing infant starts to shift from practice to playing with sounds. The end result is planned, controlled speech.

Children begin playing with sounds around 10 to 15 months of age. From this point, the development of speech is determined as much by control of motor movements as by the ability to match sounds with objects.

Most children can understand and respond to a number of words before they can produce any. Their first words include names of objects and events in their world (people, food, toys, animals). Then the child begins to overextend words, perhaps using "doggy" to refer to all animals. Finally, single words can be used as sentences: "Bye-bye" can refer to someone leaving, a meal the child thinks is finished, the child going away, a door closing.

4. *Sentences.* Children's sentences usually begin with two words, describing an action ("Me go"), a possession ("My ball"), or a location ("Baby outside"). These sentences get expanded by adding adjectives ("My big ball"), changing the verb tense ("Me jumped down"), or using negatives ("No go outside"). Children learn grammar not by being taught the rules, but as they listen to others' speech and put together the regularities they hear.

Child language, while not identical to that of adults, does draw upon language heard to build a language base. Children incorporate and imitate what they hear to refine their own language structures.

5. *Elaboration.* Vocabulary begins to increase at an amazing rate. Sentences get longer, and communication begins to work into social interaction. In the hospital corner of a nursery school, this conversation takes place:

Chip: I'm a nurse.

Brooke: I'm going to try to get some patients for you.

Megan: Do I need an operation?

Chip: Yeah, if you don't want to be sick anymore.

6. *Graphic Representation.* By five or six years of age, reading and writing emerge as children become aware of language as an entity itself and of the written word as a way of documenting what is spoken. Awareness of print and emerging literacy are the outgrowth of this last stage of development. These areas are developed in the elementary school years, yet teachers can begin this process with preschool children in an interesting and child-oriented fashion. The *Special Topic Units* on "Reading and Writing," and "Children's Literature" address the issue of language and literacy. Additionally, six professional associations who serve as advocates for literacy standards have issued a joint statement of concerns about practices in pre-first grade reading instruction. See Appendix C, Literacy Development and Pre-First Grade. Figure 13.12 is a sample of a child's developing language skills.

LANGUAGE SKILLS IN EARLY CHILDHOOD

Teachers translate language development theory into practice as they work with children. Language skills in the early childhood setting include articulation, receptive language, expressive language, graphic language, and enjoyment.

Articulation

Articulation is how children actually say the sounds and words. Children's ability to produce sound is a critical link in their connecting the sounds to form speech. Mispronunciation is common and normal, especially in children under 5 years of age. The preschool teacher can expect to hear "Thally" for Sally, "wope" for rope, and "buh-sketty" for spaghetti. As children talk, teachers listen for their ability to hear and reproduce sounds in daily conversation. Can they hear and produce sounds that differ widely, such as "sit" and "blocks"? Can they produce sounds that differ in small ways, such as in "man" and "mat"?

Stage	Age (approx.)	Sample
1. Response	0–6 months	Smiles, gazes when hearing voices
2. Vocalization	6–10 months	Babbles all types of sounds, creating babble-sentences Uses vocal signals other than crying to get help
3. Word Development	10–18 months	Mama, Dada, Doggie Bye-bye, No-no
4. Sentences	18 months–3 years	Me want chok-quit (I want chocolate) She goed in the gark (She went in the dark)
5. Elaboration	3–5 or 6 years	You're my best Mommy, you can hold my Turtle at bet-bis (breakfast). (Cough) That was just a sneeze in my mouth.
6. Graphic	5+–8 years	*(child's handwriting)*

FIGURE 13.12 Children's language skills develop with both age and experience.

Receptive Language

Receptive language is what children acquire when they learn to listen and understand. It is what they hear. With this skill children are able to understand directions, to answer a question, and to follow a sequence of events. They can understand relationships and begin to predict the outcome of their behavior and that of others. They develop some mental pictures as they listen.

Children begin early and can become experts in reacting to words, voice, emphasis, and inflection. How many times does the child understand by the *way* the words are spoken?

"You finally *finished* your lunch." (Hooray for you)

"You *finally* finished your lunch." (You slow-poke)

Children learn to listen for enjoyment, for the way the wind sounds in the trees, the rhythm of a storytelling, or the sound of the car as it brings Mom or Dad home.

Expressive Language

Expressive language in the early years includes words, grammar, and elaboration.

Words

Expressive language is the spoken word. Children's first words are of what is most important to them (Mama, Da-Da). Adults help children extend their knowledge and vocabulary by using the names of objects and words of action (walk, run, jump) and feelings (happy, sad, mad). By describing objects in greater and greater detail, teachers give children new words that increase their skills. Children are then ready to learn that some words have more than one meaning (the word "orange," for example, is both a color and a fruit) and that different words can have the same meaning (such as "ship" and "boat" as similar objects, or *muñeca* and "doll" as the same word in different languages).

Grammar

Basic grammatical structure is learned as children generalize what they hear. They listen to adult speech patterns and use these patterns to organize their own language. It helps to hear simple sentences at a young age, with the words in the correct order. Next, children can grasp past tense as well as present, plural nouns along with the singular. Finally, the use of more complex structures is understood (prepositions, comparatives, various conjugations of verbs).

Elaboration of Language

Elaboration of language takes many, many forms. It is the act of expanding the language. Through description, narration, explanation, and communication, adults elaborate their own speech to encourage children to do the same. For instance, communication for children includes talking to oneself and others. When a teacher verbalizes a process aloud, children see how language helps them work through a problem. ("I am trying to get the plant out of its pot, but when I turn it upside-down, it doesn't fall out by itself. Now I'll use this shovel to loosen the dirt from the sides of the pot, and hope that helps.") Communicating with others involves giving and following directions. ("It's time to make a choice for cleanup time. You find something to do and I'll watch you.") It means asking and answering questions. ("How do you feel when she says she won't play with you? What can you say? What can you do?") Sticking to the subject keeps communication flowing: "I know you want to play kickball, but first let's solve this problem between you and Conor about the wagon." Children are encouraged to communicate verbally with others as they see teachers using speech to get involved in play themselves. ("What a great house you have built. How do you get inside? Do you need any dishes?")

Graphic Language

"Talk written down" is the essence of graphic language. The child now learns that there is a way to record, copy, and send to another person one's thoughts. Learning to put language into a symbolic form is the gist of the reading and writing process. Children learn about print when they are read to regularly, when they see adults reading and writing, and when they are surrounded with a print-rich environment. Since words and letters are simply "lines and dots and scribbles" to young children, the teacher and parent must demonstrate how meaningful graphic language can be. Moreover, the translation of talk into print is a cognitive task (that of symbols, see previous section), so children's intellectual development as well as their language abilities are at play when learning about the printed word. This area is developed further in the *Special Topics* section of this chapter.

Enjoyment

To encourage language is to promote enjoyment in using it. Teachers converse with children, parents, and other adults, modeling for children how useful and fun language can be. Knowing the power and pleasures of language gives children the motivation for the harder work of learning to read and write. Children learn to enjoy language by participating in group discussions and being encouraged to ask questions. Reading and listening to stories and poems everyday is an essential part of any program. The program should also include children's literature and stories children dictate or write themselves.

Word play and rhyming are fun as well as educational. Group language games are useful, such as asking the question, "Did you ever see a bat with a hat? a bun having fun? a bee with. . . ?" and letting the children add the rest. Begin a song, for instance, "Do You Know the Muffin Man?", and add the children's names. Whatever contributes to the enjoyment of language supports its growth, from varying voice and tone to fit the situation (in storytelling, dramatic play, and ordinary activity periods) to spontaneous rhyming songs.

THE TEACHER'S ROLE

Considerations

When considering how to work with young children in language development, teachers should keep several things in mind.

FIGURE 13.13 Teachers and children can share intimate moments when they enjoy using language together.

Children Must Use Language to Learn It.
Adults often spend much of their time with children *talking*—to, at, for, or about them. Yet, to learn language, children must be doing the talking. Children need time, a place, and the support for practicing language. Children's conversations with each other are important in learning the basics of how to take turns and keep to one topic, and of saying what they mean, getting their ideas and themselves heard and accepted. Time with peers and adults, in both structured (group times) and nonstructured (free play) situations, allows children to practice and refine language skills.

The Most Verbal Children Tend to Monopolize Language Interactions. Research shows that teachers interact verbally with the children who are most skilled verbally (Cazden, 1979). Seek out and support language development in those with fewer skills, generally by drawing them out individually through (1) reading the unspoken (body) language that communicates their ideas, needs, and feelings, and (2) helping them express verbally those ideas, needs, and feelings.

Adults Should Know the Individual Child.
Consistency in adult-child relationships may be as important for language as for affective development during the early years. If so, teachers must have a meaningful relationship with each child. This includes knowing the parent(s) and how they communicate with their child.

Bilingualism. In early childhood terms, bilingualism is the acquisition of two languages during the first years of life. The bilingual child must learn to comprehend and produce aspects of each language and then develop two systems of communication. Bilingualism in early childhood also occurs under these general conditions:

1. Children can comprehend and produce some aspects of both languages.

2. Through natural exposure, such as in a classroom, children get experience in both languages.

3. Both languages are developed at the same time (Garcia, 1986)

With more bilingual/bicultural children in early childhood classrooms, it helps to understand how children learn a second language and how to apply this research in practical ways. Research (Diaz Soto, 1991) shows that the process of second language learning in childhood depends, in part, upon the individual child. Cognitive, social, and linguistic skills are all at work in acquiring a second language. Moreover, the child's culture, unique temperament, and learning style play a part as well. For instance, Tjarko is of Swiss-German ancestry, so it is any wonder he pronounces an English "v" like an "f," as in "Can I *haff* one of those?" Sachiko, who has moved from Japan within the year, complains, "My *neck* hurts when I drink," and disagrees that it is a sore throat, since "neck" is the word she knows.

Adults mistakenly assume that young children learn a new language quickly and easily, and that the younger the child, the more quickly a second language is acquired. Some studies (Diaz Soto, 1991) indicate the contrary: several reports favor adults in rate of language acquisition, and there appears to be no critical period for second language learning.

Putting aside those misconceptions, teachers need guidance in educating language-minority children, both in helping the child and family become part of the educational process and in supporting children's culture and language while aiding in the process of English language acquisition. Alvarado Kuster (see Chapter 5) suggests trying to become fluent in the child's first language and focusing on the family's childrearing practices, as well as learning about your own culture and personal biases. The following recommendations serve as guidelines for teachers of children who speak other languages:

1. *Accept individual differences* with regard to both the style and the time frame of language learning. Don't insist that a child speak, but do invite and try to include the child in classroom activities. Assume developmental equivalence; that is, that the children, while different, are normal. For example, Maria Elena just will not come and sit at group time. Allow her to watch from a distance and believe that she is learning, rather than be worried or irritated that she isn't with the group yet.

2. *Support children's attempts* to communicate. The learning process of a second language is not unlike that of the first; that is, encouraging children's communication bids rather than correcting them will help children try to learn. Teachers recognize developmentally equivalent patterns. For instance, Kidah may not *say* the word "car" but can *show* it to you when you ask. There are a number of equally good ways to show development, as well as teach skills.

3. *Maintain an additive philosophy* by recognizing that children are acquiring more and new language skills, not simply replacing their primary linguistic skills. Asking Giau and his family about their words, foods, customs allows teachers to use a style and content that is familiar to a Vietnamese, thus smoothing the transition and adding onto an already rich base of knowledge.

4. *Provide a stimulating, active, and diverse environment* with many opportunities for language in meaningful social interactions and responsive experiences with all children. Learning in a self-help environment with an anti-bias curriculum gives children a developmentally and linguistically appropriate education. For example, learning the origin and meaning of each person's name (*Mweli* is Swahili for "moon," and *Anna* in Hebrew means "graceful one") highlights each person's uniqueness and binds the children together as people with names.

5. *Use informal observations* to guide the planning of activities and the spontaneous interactions for speakers of other languages. A day in the life of a center or children's group has a tremendous number of "teachable moments." For instance, seeing a group of girls building a zoo with blocks, a teacher gives a basket of wild animals to Midori. Walking with her to the block corner, she offers to stock the zoo and then helps all the girls make animal signs in Japanese and English. Thus does Midori enter the play in a positive and strong way.

6. *Find out about the family*, and establish ties between home and school. "School learning is most likely to occur when family values reinforce school expectations" (Bowman, 1989). Parents and teachers do not have to do the same

Curriculum Planning for Language Development: The Teacher Talks

Description

- Use nouns for people, places, events: "We are going to visit Grandma now. That means we need to get dressed and walk to her apartment."
- Use modifiers: "That is your uncle's truck outside" or "Can you find your sister's teddy bear?"
- Use relational terms: "You are taller than the chair; the wagon is wider than the bed."
- Try more differentiated words to express differences: Instead of just "big/little," try "fat/thin" and "tall/short."

Narration

- Describe simple relationships of time: "Yesterday you stayed at home. Today is a school day. Tomorrow is Saturday, a stay-home day."
- Clarify a sequence of events: "When you come to school, first you put your things in your cubby, then you make an inside choice."
- Use words to describe repetition, continuation, and completion: "We are going to the store again, to buy food for dinner" or "I see that you and Juana are still playing together today" or "You finished building the box last time; now you are ready to paint it."

Explanation

- Point out similarities and differences: "Both Cathi and I have brown hair, but what is different about us? Yes, she has on shorts and I am wearing overalls."
- Try classifying what you see as well as asking children to do so: "I notice that all these shells have ridges on the outside; what do you see that is different about them?"

FIGURE 13.14 Several aspects of language development affect how teachers speak to children in the early years.

things, but must have a mutual understanding and respect for each other and goals for children. For example, Honwyma's parents and his teacher talk together about what of the Hopi language and culture can be brought into the classroom. Where there are differences between the Hopi patterns and those of the school, teachers deal with them directly and in an interested manner.

7. *Provide an accepting classroom climate* that values culturally and linguistically diverse young children. Teachers must come to grips with their own cultural ethnocentricity, and learn about the languages and cultures beyond their own. It is critical to value all ways of achieving developmental milestones, not just those of the teacher's culture or educational experience.

The challenge to young children and their teachers is enormous. With informed, open-minded teaching, children can learn a second language without undue stress and alienation. As of this date we can conclude that:

- Children can and do learn two languages at an early age, though the process and time varies with the individual child.

- Two languages can be learned at the same time in a parallel manner. The depth of knowledge of one language may be different from the other, or the two may develop equally.

- The acquisition of languages may mean a "mixing" of the two, as heard in children's speech when they use words or a sentence structure of both languages.

The Question: A Teaching Strategy

A 2-1/2-year-old looking at a picture of families

T: What do you see in this picture?
C: A mommy and a daddy and a baby!
T: Good for you—you see a family. Look again.
C: A baby just like me. . . more babies!
T: There is more than one child. How many children are there?
C: One-two-three. . . is that a children (pointing to a teenager)?
T: Yes, that is a child, but older—we call them teenagers.
C: I like the boy the best.
T: You like the boy—and he is just about your age, huh?

A teacher at grouptime with 3–5 year olds

T: Who has on short-sleeved shirts today?
Children (some): I do! I do!
T: Some children say they do—can you all find them and ask them to stand up?
Children (all): Johan, get up. . . .Francoise, you, too. . . Here's Patrick!
T: Now all the short-sleevers are standing. What do you notice about them?
Children (various ones): They are all different colors; two are plain, one has pictures; they all have buttons; they are different sizes.
T: Good for you, you've noticed a lot. I have written all your ideas here. If Patrick's is the smallest, whose comes next?

A 6-1/2-year-old looking at a picture of a field of flowers

T: What do you see in the photograph?
C: Flowers. . . a buncha flowers.
T: Good observation. About how many flowers would you say there are?
C: I dunno. About a hundred.
T: Do you think there are only a hundred? Look again.
C: Maybe, probably there's more.
T: Well, how many do you think?
C: About a thousand.
T: A thousand is a lot more than a hundred. That's more accurate, since there is such a difference between a hundred and a thousand.

FIGURE 13.15 Questions are the building blocks of teaching. The adept teacher asks questions that stimulate language, thinking, and interacting between a child and teacher and among children.

- Learning two languages does not hurt the acquisition of either language in the long run.

Teachers must understand the increased workload bilingualism creates, and they must keep in mind that learning another language affects cognitive and social development.

Speech and Language Disorders. Early childhood professionals should have knowledge of speech and language disorders. Disorders of both receptive and expressive language can be detected early. The perceptive teacher does a great service to children and parents by discovering potential problems. Special needs are normal and common, and Chapter 3 elaborates how these are dealt with in early childhood settings.

The Language of the Teacher. What teachers say—and how they say it—is important. Moreover, it is often what they do *not* say that communicates the most to children in their struggle to gain mastery of the language. For instance, when a child is stumbling over a word or phrase, teachers must give the child the time to work through the difficulty, rather than correcting or "helping" by finishing the sentence themselves. Teachers provide a rich environment and a high quality of interaction with the child that encourages articulation, receptive language, expressive language, and graphic language (the written word).

To *articulate* means to speak distinctly and with moderate speed. Teachers reinforce clear speech by giving frequent opportunities for children to practice speech.

Receptive language can be developed by using several strategies.

1. Give clear directions: "Please go and sit on the rug next to the chairs," instead of "Go sit over there."

2. Let children ask questions, and give them acceptable answers. For example, repeat a phrase from the child's last sentence that asks the child to try again: "You want *what*?" or "You ate *what*?". Or cast the question back to a child by changing the phrase "Where did you put it?" into "You put it *where*?".

3. Give instructions in a sequence: "Put your lunch on your desk, then wash your hands. Then you are ready to go to lunch." It often helps to ask the children what they think they are to do: "How do you get ready for lunch? What comes first? Next?"

4. Try to understand what the child means, regardless of the actual language. Look for the purpose and intent beyond what the child may have said. This is particularly important with toddlers, non-English speakers, and newcomers.

5. Ask children to state their thoughts out loud. "Tell me what you think is going to happen to the eggs in the incubator. Why do you think some might hatch and some might not?"

6. Use literature, poetry, and your own descriptions to give children an idea of how words can be used to paint verbal and mental pictures. Ask questions about children's own images and dreams. To older children read aloud from books without pictures.

Expressive language is encouraged when teachers focus on the spoken word. They use short, concise sentences to frame or highlight a word. If a child says, "Look at that!", teachers reply, "That's a butterfly," or "I see; do you think it's a butterfly or a bee?"

One way children gain a greater awareness of themselves is by describing their own actions in words. To make sure that all children experience the art of conversation, be sure to provide plenty of opportunities for them to converse with adults as well as peers to help them learn the reciprocal nature of communication. Ask them to say what they are doing. Make a statement describing the child's behavior or actions. This is particularly helpful when dealing with feelings, such as the statement "It looks like you are feeling angry" (when confronted with a frown and clenched fists).

Teachers help children by directing their attention to objects, events, and relationships.

Michelle: I have something to show you.

Teacher: Can you give us some clues?

Michelle: It's not a record and it's not a book, and you can't play with it.

Teacher: Can you hold it in your hand?

Michelle: No, silly; it's a kiss!

Give children opportunities to describe what they are going to do and what they have done. Through this, teachers discover what is meaningful to children and what they remember, and it gives them the chance to plan and review. When the class celebrates a birthday, children will want to discuss when their birthday is, what they will do, or how they feel. The answers may range from "July thirty-last" to "We're going to the moon" to "On my birthday my heart is filling me with lightening." Figures 13.14 and 13.15 demonstrate the adept teacher at work on language development.

Developing communication skills with others is particularly important for children in the early years. Encouraging active listening and repeating one child's words to another ("Bahrain, did you hear what Joanna said about the sandtruck?") give children support. Expressing thoughts and feelings in words offers a model. By telling a child what works for you ("I like it when you listen to my words"), a teacher provides a good example of how to communicate. Helping children stick to the subject shows that there is a topic at hand: "Stevie, now we're talking about our field trip to the track. You can tell us about your new dog next."

Graphic language can be developed in hundreds of ways. What is now called "emergent literacy" is a broad view of reading and writing as developing, or emerging, out of language development as a whole. Rather than a simple set of skills, early literacy involves a set of attitudes and behaviors related to written language. Teachers use their own language as a way to direct children in a variety of symbol-using activities, such as making grocery lists for a dramatic play corner or the zoo signs in the previous example of bilingual education. The *Special Topics* that follow this unit elaborate on graphic language.

Curriculum Planning for Language Development

Teachers who plan curriculum for language skills, just as for cognitive development, focus on the class setting, specific skills, and themes. They organize the environment and activities to help children acquire linguistic skills of their own.

In the Environment

Indoors. Teachers arrange space so that children will practice speaking and listening and, in programs for older children, reading and writing. Indoor areas can be arranged to enhance language development as follows:

Art

- Offer templates for tracing letters.

- Have signs and pictures that show where things are kept.

- Ask children to describe the materials they use.

Blocks

- Ask children to give each other directions for where blocks go and what they are used for.

- Label block shelves with shapes and words.

- Sketch children's structures and then write their word descriptions.

Cooking

- Label utensils.

- Describe actions (pour, measure, stir).

- Use recipe cards with both pictures and words.

Discovery/Science

- Label all materials.

- Ask questions about what is displayed.

- Encourage children's displays, with their dictated words nearby.

- Graph growth and changes of plants, animals, children, and experiments.

Language

- Label the bookshelf, record player, other equipment.

- Help children make their own books that involve description (My family is . . .), narration (It is winter when . . .), and recall (Yesterday I . . .).

- Have children "write" notes, lists, or letters, to one another, the teachers, and their families.

- Develop a writing center with a typewriter, office supplies, and so on.

Manipulatives

- Recognize this area as a place for self-communication, as children talk and sing to themselves while they work.

- Explain similarities and differences of materials and structures.

There are other ways to develop language along with cognitive and socioemotional skills. One is to build a "Talkalot Kit" (Jones, 1987). These collections of materials with something in common stimulate conversation as well as classification and dramatic play. Kits could be made of buttons, gloves, shoes, brushes, face coverings, containers: use your imagination!

Another idea for programs of older children is a "Writer's Briefcase" (Wrobleski, 1990). This is a take-home briefcase filled with stationery items such as paper, blank books, pens or crayons, envelopes, paper clips and brads, scissors and stapler, even stickers. Attached is a note to parents explaining the reading-writing connections and a little about emergent literacy and scribbling/invented spelling. Children check it out overnight and their creations can be shared at school. An alternative to this is "A Friend's Sleepover": a favorite toy, such as Curious George, takes turns going home in a bag with a journal. Parents are encouraged to take down their children's dictation of their adventures with George, to be read in school.

Outdoors. Outdoors, motor skills can be described and pointed out by teachers and children, as both use words of action and of feeling. For example, what actions does it take to get a wagon up the hill? How does a child's face feel when swinging up high? How do people sit? move? carry things?

Routines, Transitions, and Groups

Transitions and routines are more manageable if the children understand what is happening and exactly what they are to do. Teacher language helps talk children through the process so that they can internalize what they are asked to do. A teacher can write a note to "Please save" for the child who does not have time to finish a project, or they can write children's dictated notes to parents.

Group times, with fingerplays, songs, and stories, are language-intensive activities. Children's articulation skills are strengthened, as is receptive language through listening to others. Group times are also opportunities for children to express themselves. When children discuss daily news and important events, brainstorm ideas about a subject, or report on what they did earlier in the day, they gain experience in listening and speaking. Children can also dramatize familiar stories and fingerplays.

Using visual aids or name cards gives children experience in graphic language. These might include having felt letters for the song "B-I-N-G-O," numbers for the fingerplay "One, Two, Buckle My Shoe," or name cards for the activity "I'm Thinking of Someone. . . ." And children enjoy the cadence and rhythm of language spoken or chanted.

Focus on Skills

Language development involves five different skills. Teachers can plan a curriculum focusing on a single skill, be it articulation, receptive, expressive, or graphic language, or the enjoyment of language. After choosing one of the skills, they look at the environment to see how that skill can be developed.

To emphasize expressive language, teachers allow children to express themselves by practicing words and grammatical structure, and by elaborating on their own expressions. A teacher asks three-year-old Ceva to describe what she is doing with the art materials. "I'm dripping my paint," she replies. Outdoors, two-year-old Hadar describes her actions: "Teacher, look at me! I'm taller than you!" The teacher responds, "You climbed up the ladder to the top of the tunnel. Now, when you stand up, your head is above mine." At group time, the kindergarten class makes a group story about "The Mystery of Space." Then they separate into small groups with second-grade helpers to write their own books in story form, complete with illustrations.

To help children talk and learn, teachers find ways of talking that is respectful of children. Listening carefully promotes expression; writing a child's words or story encourages interest; laughing along with a joke stimulates enjoyment. At the same time, when adults speak to children they are also transmitting values and attitudes. A focus on the skills of language development sends the message that language and communication are important tools of human endeavor.

Use of Themes

How could using themes for curriculum planning be used to develop language skills? One unit with universal appeal is "Babies," charted in Figure 13.16. Other units that elicit an extensive use of language are:

● *Harvest.* Activity area: Ask preschool and kindergarten children to bring food from home for a "feast corner." Make a display of food from a harvest feast in the past—for instance, of Native Americans as well as the colonists—and then of foods today.

THEME: BABIES

Art: Limit the art materials to just what toddlers and infants can use.
Cooking: Make baby food.
Discovery/science: Display baby materials, then bring in baby animals.
Dramatic play area: "The Baby Corner" with dolls, cribs, diapers.
Manipulatives: Bring in several infant and toddler toys.
Gross-motor/games: Make a "crawling route," an obstacle course that re-
quires crawling *only*.
Field trip/guest: A parent brings a baby to school to dress, bathe, or feed.
Large group time: Sing lullabies ("Rock-a-Bye-Baby").
Small/large group: Children discuss "What can babies do?"
Joshua: Babies sleep in cribs. They wear diapers. Babies can't talk.
Becky: They sometimes suck their thumbs. Babies cry when they are
hungry.
Dennis: Babies go pee in their diapers.
Stevie: Babies sit in highchairs. Babies eat baby food that looks like
squished bananas.
Corey: Babies sleep in a basinette. Then they crawl and bite your
finger.

FIGURE 13.16 Teachers plan a unit to promote the skills they are focusing on in the class. To encourage language, a "babies" theme brings out the expert in all children.

Group time: Begin a group story using the sentence "I am thankful for . . ."

Special project: Plan a feast, with the children creating the menu and preparing both the food and the table for their families at the school.

● *Summertime.* Activity area: Toddler and preschool children bring a piece of summer clothing for a display and "try-on" corner.

Group time: Children respond to the phrase, "One summer morning..." with stories and pictures.

Special project: A trip to the beach, or a treasure hunt for buried shells in the sand area outside.

● *The Earth is Our Home.* Activity area: Kindergarten and primary children can make a large circle in a shade of blue, sketching the continents. Provide brown, green, and blue paint in pie tins and let children make a hand print on the ocean or land. Next, have the children bring from home the names of the countries of their family's ancestry. Help them locate those areas and attach their names to those parts of the world.

Group time: Sing *The Earth Is Our Home* (Greg & Steve) and *One Light, One Sun* (Raffi). Read *Just a Dream* (Van Allsburg) and *Where the Forest Meets the Sea* (J. Baker).

Special project: Help make a class recycling area or compost heap. Take a field trip to recycle the materials, or visit a garden that uses compost. Young children can learn about endangered species through Burningham's *Hey! Get Off Our Train*; older children can do research on an animal and make its natural habitat in a shoebox.

● *Favorite Foods.* Activity area: Make a salad from everyone's favorite vegetable, or follow the storyline of *Stone Soup.*

Group time: Discussion topic: "My favorite fruit is . . ." (Example: "An apple because it is crunchy and is big enough to share.")

Special project: Make recipe cards to send home. (Example: Chicken—"First you get sev-

---

Curriculum for Language Development of Infants and Toddlers

The Environment
- Is gentle and supportive, with adults who listen and respond to sounds made and who let the children initiate language.
- Is explained simply, such as what the caregiver is doing during clothing or diaper changing.
- Is responsive, as adults respond quickly to crying and redirect what the children can do and express.

The Skills
- Adults expand on the children's own words. Toddler: "The shoe." Adult: "Oh, that's your shoe you are holding."
- Adults model for children the words to say. Adult: "Elenoa, I want the puppet now."
- Children listen in small groups of two or three, on laps or next to adults, and are allowed wide variation in their participation.

The Themes
- Revolve around the children's individual interests.
- Include favorite stories presented in several ways: reading *The Three Bears*, doing a flannelboard story, singing a fingerplay, having bear puppets and stuffed animals.

FIGURE 13.17 Language experiences for infants and toddlers take into consideration the developmental milestones and the individual child's level of self-expression.

en pounds of skin. Then you get flat pieces of roast chicken. Then you put some bones in. Then you get one pound of pickle seeds and put them on the chicken. Then cook it in the oven for about five hours!")

Any theme can be developed, so long as it brings out oral and graphic language experiences.

While preschool and school-age children are challenged by specific themes, curriculum development for infants and toddlers does not always need this kind of focus. Rather, these classes look to the developmental level of the group to encourage language growth for the very young. Figure 13.17 describes curriculum ideas for language development in an infant/toddler class.

• UNIT 13-2 CHECKPOINT

Children develop language in their own ways, following patterns consistent over different cultures and countries. In the early years, language consists of several skills. The teacher's role is one of knowing how language develops and what skills to encourage in a class setting.

Then, teachers plan curriculum for language development. They organize the environment and schedule by focusing on the various areas and ac-

tivities, a specific skill, or a unit.

Ask yourself:

- What does research tell us about child language and its development?
- What are the six stages of language development?
- What are the five language skills in early childhood education?
- What are six teacher considerations in planning for language development?
- How can teachers plan a curriculum that uses language skills?
- What themes promote language skill in the classroom?

• UNIT 13-3 SPECIAL TOPICS IN COGNITION AND LANGUAGE

READING AND WRITING

As mentioned earlier in the chapter, *graphic language* is the written word. For the young child, what once looked like dots and lines become let-

When is your birthday?
- Where is your name?
- How many children have birthdays in April? February? December?
- How many children have birthdays on the 10th? the 2nd? At the end of the month?

JAN.	FEB.	MAR.	APRIL	MAY	JUNE	JULY	AUG.	SEPT.	OCT.	NOV.	DEC.
13 Ann	1 José	3 Leon	2 Mrs. K.	16 Brian	11 Katie	5 Mr. W.	2 Carrie	8 Jim	21 Chris	7 Nick	13 Keesha
19 Bill	3 Mary	7 Kirk	10 Peter	27 Adele		9 Panya		29 Danny	30 Jay		25 Carol
26 Judy	6 Sue	15 Roberto	11 Jon			12 Kevin					30 Mrs. M.
24 Tom	11 Andy		18 Jill								
	19 Sean		23 Libby								
			30 Mia								

FIGURE 13.18 A language experience chart involves children through the subject matter and the way in which information is displayed.

ters and words. How does the early childhood teacher help children in this process?

The ability to read and write does not just happen when children reach a certain age. Their readiness for graphic language must be nurtured. A child's language proficiency will determine readiness for reading. Teachers identify this readiness by knowing how well a child understands the structure and vocabulary of the language. Therefore, a program to encourage beginning reading will offer experiences in oral language. Research shows that successful readers see a relationship between spoken language and the written word. They are aware that sounds are how language is put together (Nurss, 1980). So teachers plan activities that make connections between what is said and what is written.

There is an important role for teachers of young children in the early stages of reading and writing. Teachers can influence positive attitudes toward reading and writing. Supporting children's interest in learning to read and write is a part of this role. Teachers encourage children to talk and converse with others about what they see and do; this gives them increasing experience in using and attaching experiences to words. When adults take the time to write down what children say and then read it back, it gives a sense of importance to children's language and their ability to express themselves. In these ways, teachers can help children get involved with print in natural and unpressured ways.

Children and Reading

The role of the adult is one of engaging children with print in ways that make sense to them. By creating an environment that provides rich opportunities to use the printed word, teachers help motivate children toward reading. Research tells us that children who are successful readers in elementary school are typically those who have a history of successful reading in their early years (Schickedanz, 1983).

Adults and even children often have a stereotypical concept of reading. They think the ability to read is only the literal translation of signs and symbols on a printed page (called **decoding**). In actuality, learning to read is not merely decoding the symbols. It is attaching experiences and knowledge to those words and understanding the use of the written word in their daily lives. Many parents and teachers believe that reading instruction begins in elementary school, so little is done to expand a child's simplified concept of reading before first or second grade.

Emergent Literacy

In the last several years, early childhood professionals have begun to articulate the processes involved in helping children learn graphic language. Freeman & Hatch (1989) report recent research findings that indicate:

1. Young children begin the process of literacy development before they enter [elementary] school.

2. Reading and writing develop concurrently and in an interrelated manner.

3. Literacy develops in everyday activities.

4. Children learn about literacy through interaction with their world. Furthermore, literacy development is part of the total communication process that includes listening, speaking, reading, and writing.

As Dr. Robert Calfee of Stanford University (1989) says, "We need to change our definition of reading from a *technical skill* (translating print to spoken language) to the conception of a different mode of *language use*." In the years before elementary school, this is known as **emergent literacy** Children's emergent reading skills follow stages, which overlap (Early Childhood Resources, 1995):

● *Stage One:* Children learn that print is a form of language. They find that books are filled with magic, messages, and mystery (prereading).

● *Stage Two:* Children hear stories, poems, chants,

and songs many times. They rehearse by chanting, singing, resaying, and "reading along" as we read to them (prereading).

● *Stage Three:* Children learn to recognize words. They read and know the text, and they use some phonics to discover which words say what (beginning reading).

● *Stage Four:* Children are readers. Now the task is to make them better readers (reading).

Teachers of young children will find the concepts and activities familiar, as it has been common early childhood practice for years. Figure 13.19 illustrates some of these activities.

In the early childhood setting, there is an opportunity to teach a broader concept of reading that goes beyond decoding and permeates children's lives. To do this, reading should not be taught as "basal reading," but instead should be treated as part of a child's immediate and ongoing life. This can help create positive attitudes about reading before the decoding process begins.

It is up to adults to provide children with opportunities that will enlarge their concepts of the power of the written word. Teachers and parents can wield a great deal of influence in communicating positive feelings about reading. One way to do this is by providing real and valid prereading experiences (Sawyer & Sawyer, 1994).

Children can learn to recognize, read, and write their names when given interesting ways to do it. A popular technique in many early childhood centers is to use a waiting list for highly desirable activities. By learning to read or print their names, children receive a tangible benefit: they can sign up for the activities they want and check the list to see where their names are. Some computer programs now allow children to manipulate letters for making their names, then print them (see computer section in this chapter). Through these experiential activities in reading and writing, children learn that words are useful and can be fun.

In her book *Teacher*, Sylvia Ashton-Warner describes another technique for introducing printed language to young children. A kindergarten teacher who believed strongly in children's innate creativity and curiosity, Ashton-Warner developed a system of "organic reading" in which the stu-

Reading Readiness Is	Teachers
1. Oral vocabulary	1. Encourage talking, learning new words and phrases, singing, fingerplays, remembering and reflecting verbally.
2. Curiosity about/for reading	2. Provide a separate area for books (and are available to read to children), language games (lotto), dictation from children ("If I could fly I would . . ."), notes about children that the children deliver themselves to other adults.
3. Auditory discrimination (the ability to detect sound differences)	3. Create sound discrimination boxes in the science area, a "listen-to-the-sound" walk, guessing games with musical instruments, activities that teach letter sounds by using the children's names.
4. Visual discrimination	4. Support directionality: left and right (in the "Hokey-Pokey" dance and labeled on shoes and mittens), up and down, top and bottom, likeness and differences.
5. Awareness of print	5. Help the children name and label the classroom (door, tables, book corner), with bilingual signs as appropriate. Bring children's native languages into print by asking parents for the names of common objects, numbers, and so on for use around the classroom and in song and fingerplay charts. Encourage children to help print their own names on creative works. Write group newsletters to send home. Make flannelboard letters for free play and for use in songs, such as "Bingo."

FIGURE 13.19 Children gain reading readiness skills through activities for oral vocabulary, curiosity about reading, and auditory and visual discrimination.

dents themselves build a key vocabulary of words they wish to learn to read and write. This method was effective for her classes of native Maori children in New Zealand, for whom the British basal readers held little meaning. Ashton-Warner's personal, culturally relevant teaching works well, since it flows naturally from the child's own life and interests.[1]

The child's readiness to read is related to the development of certain skills (see Figure 13.19). Readiness skills can be acquired through planned experiences in the school program that:

● Promote meaningful interaction with words.

Example: Writing children's names on their drawings; labeling cubbies with children's names and pictures.

● Are age-level appropriate.

Example: For 2-1/2-year-olds, play lotto games using pictures of familiar objects; for four-year-olds, use animal pictures; for six-year-olds, use alphabet letters.

● Are fun and enjoyable for children.

Example: Creating a class newspaper to take home.

● Take a gradual approach through the use of non-reading materials.

Example: Label toy storage boxes with pictures. Later in the year, add the words alongside the pictures.

● Acknowledge the child's ability to read the environment, to read events, to read other people.

Example: Clark, looking out the window at the darkening sky, says, "Looks like it's gonna rain." Margo "reads" her painting as she describes the vivid monster to the teacher.

● Involve the use of children's senses.

Example: Display baskets of vegetables and foods along with the book *Stone Soup.*

The school will have many activities in the area of "reading readiness." Recent research im-

OUR DIVERSE WORLD OUR DIVERSE WORLD OUR DIVERSE WORLD OUR DIVERSE WORLD OUR DIVERSE WORLD

[1]Years later, Ms. Ashton-Warner's technique is just as relevant in America.

plies that an early childhood program promotes an awareness of the graphic aspects of language by:

1. Developing children's speaking and listening proficiencies through the use of conversation, descriptive language, oral feedback, and meaningful listening comprehension activities.

2. Helping children hear phonemes (language sounds) through oral language activities such as rhyming, initial consonant substitution, and the use of alliterations in jingles and language play.

3. Providing many opportunities for children to make the connection between spoken and written language.

4. Emphasizing children's own language in beginning reading activities.

5. Filling the environment with printed words and phrases, so children become familiar with meaningful print.

6. Highlighting the language used in beginning reading instructions; for example, use the terms, "letter," "sound," "word," and "sentence."

Whole Language

The concept of "whole language" has many familiar and exciting elements from the early childhood tradition. An approach which has become popular since the early 1980s, whole language (Cruikshank, 1993)

> . . . is different in both theory and practice from the traditional basal approach. Because it is child-centered rather than teacher-dominated, curriculum activities arise from children's current interests, needs, and developmental levels. Making connections is emphasized, and it is through meaningful integrative themes that students acquire knowledge and skills. Children are also encouraged to share ideas and work with others, as socialization is valued. Evaluation focuses on the child's growth over time, and both pupil portfolios and anecdotal reporting are common assessment tools.

Goodman (1986) sets out key principles of the whole language approach which will be of interest to all teachers and a special focus for those students who teach kindergarten and primary school. Generally, whole language is a way of viewing language, learning, and people (children, teachers, parents) in a *holistic, integrated* way. All the language arts are related to each other. For instance, a teacher might read a story to the children, then ask them to make up their own endings. The class would be *listening* (to the story), *speaking* (telling their ideas), *writing* (trying their hand at spelling and handwriting), and *reading* (their creations to a friend or the class at the end of the lesson).

This integrated lesson also illustrates another principle, that of *meaningful* content. Children use language in a purposeful way, developing naturally through a need to communicate. The young child who is read stories and engaged in conversations from infancy is then led smoothly to reading and writing as another extension of language use. Since children can use language before they learn the correct form, whole language encourages this extension of *function into form*; that is, that children's own mastery of oral language and unique interests be drawn upon in teaching the "rules" of sounds, letters, and words. Figure 13.20 charts some sample "whole language" activities.

One note: critics of whole language argue that this approach leaves out teaching the decoding skills, which the traditional phonics approach emphasizes. A lengthy report by the Center for the Study of Reading (1990) recently concluded that, to learn to read, children need both specific phonics instruction and a rich background in literature (such as being read stories). Learning graphic language is a creative process that involves both an "art" (literature, rhyming songs, invented spelling) and a "science" (the nuts and bolts of decoding). It is the teacher's job to be the master craftsperson in helping children put the two together.

Children and Writing

Children learn about words in print much the same as they learn about reading and other aspects of language; that is, by seeing it used and having plenty of opportunities to use it themselves. Writing can be as natural for children as walking and talking. Children begin to write when they first take a pencil in hand and start to scribble. Later, they can write a story by drawing pictures or by dictating the words and having someone else write them down.

Whole Language in the Classroom

- Have a cozy library corner, giving children lots of time to explore and read all kinds of books.
- Make a writing corner with different kinds of supplies, using this area to develop grouptime activities (children's stories), meaningful themes (post office), and connected learning (writing and sending letters).
- Take field trips, pointing out print as they find it (street signs, store shelves, bumper stickers) and writing about it afterwards.
- Use large charts for poems, fingerplays, and songs as well as for listing choices available and for group dictation.
- Plan activities that incorporate print: read recipes for cooking projects, make menus for lunch and snack, follow directions in using a new manipulative toy, write sales tickets for dramatic play units, bring books into science displays.
- Use written notes regularly, sending a regular newspaper home that the children have written or dictated, writing notes to other team teachers that children deliver, encouraging children to send notes to each other.

FIGURE 13.20 Whole language in the primary classroom means integrating graphic language activities in a natural, meaningful way.

The early childhood classroom heightens an interest in writing through a writing center. It can be part of a language area or a self-help art center. Wherever it is located, this center will include a variety of things to write with and write on, and "writing helpers." Children write with pencils (fat and thin, with and without erasers), colored pencils, narrow and wide marking pens, and crayons. They enjoy having many kinds of paper products, including computer paper, old calendars, data-punch cards, and colored paper. Children also enjoy simple books, a few blank pages stapled together. Carbon paper, dittos, and lined paper will add variety. "Writing helpers" might be a picture dictionary, a set of alphabet letters, a print set, an alphabet chart, chalkboard, or magnetic letter board. All of these serve to help children practice writing skills.

Children's first attempts at writing will likely include drawing or scribbling. Since drawing helps children plan and organize their thoughts (and, thus, their text), teachers encourage children to tell them about their stories and can ask for a child's help in "reading" these writings. As children begin to work with words themselves, adults can help them sound out words or spell words for them. Spelling development is similar to learning to speak: adults support the efforts, not correct the mistakes, and allow children to invent their own spelling of words. Picture dictionaries and lists of

popular words help children use resources for writing. Figure 13.21 is a sample of **invented spelling** in a kindergarten.

Writing materials can be available throughout the room and yard. Paper and pencils come in handy in the dramatic play area. Menus, shopping lists, prescriptions, and money are but a few uses children will find for writing equipment. The block corner may need traffic signs; the computer, a waiting list. Outdoors, pictures can label the location of the vegetables in the garden; markers indicate where children have hidden "treasures," or where the dead bird is buried.

The "language experience" approach involves taking dictation, writing down and reading back to children their own spoken language. It is important to use the child's exact words so they can make the connection between their speech and the letters on the page. This is true for group stories, for children's self-made books, or for descriptions of their own paintings. A useful technique in taking dictation is to say the words while writing them, allowing the child to watch the letters and words being formed. When the content is read back, the child has a sense of completion. Figure 13.22 is an example of these kinds of language experiences in classrooms of three-, five-, and six-year-olds.

The early childhood setting encourages an awareness of and interest in writing by having the

I ZMTMCGO TOTHE
BECH

(I sometimes go to the beach)

I HVA BNE RABT

(I have a bunny rabbit)

TS SAPFR WAL

(This is a puffer whale)

I H V A DAL

(I have a doll)

I GOT AN YOOPEROY
GLARSIS AT ASHOPKOOLD
FOR EYES

(I got a new pair of glasses at a shop called "For Eyes.")

UAWZRPT WT HOFM
DNDS NH EH HND

(I have a wizard with a diamond in each hand)

FIGURE 13.21 Early writing usually involves children's attempts at words of their own invention. Invented spelling can be treated with respect for the efforts and as a foundation for successful writing experiences. (Courtesy of Kim Saxe.)

The Language Experience Approach

---

1. **Start with a leading sentence:**
   If I were a musical instrument. . . .
   Michelle: I would be a piano with strings and lots of sparklies on top. And you could play me even if you were blind.
   Janette: I would be a drum. I would be hit and I wouldn't be happy because they would make me hurt.
   Dennis: I would be a violin. Someone would play me with a bow and I would make a beautiful sound.

2. **Take dictation on topics and pictures of their making.**
   "On Halloween"
   Ehsan: There was a witch and skeleton and ghost in my room on Halloween night.
   Lionel: Costume night. A cow jumping over the moon. The little rabbit sleeping.
   Martine: There was a big pumpkin and a big bat and a bate and a pirate. There was a jack-o-lantern and the light glowed.
   Andrew: There was a smiley monster and Aka-Zam!

3. **Ask for stories of their own.**
   Once upon a time there's a boy named Timothy and he punched all the bad guys dead. And he was very strong and he can punch anything down. And he can do anything he likes to. And he makes all the things at winter. And he was so strong he could break out anything else. And he had to do very hard work all day long and all day night. And he had to sleep but he couldn't. And he had a very small house and cup. And then he did everything he want to all day long. The End, Tim(signed)

4. **Make a group book (including illustrations).**
   All By Myself (our version of the book by Mercer Mayer)
   "I can put on my overalls all by myself." (Stephanie)
   "I can brush my hair all by myself." (Lindsey)
   "I can make pictures all by myself." (Jessica)
   "I can buckle my jeans all by myself." (Megan)
   "I can make a drill truck with the blocks all by myself." (Lionel)
   "I can jump in the pool all by myself." (Andrew)

FIGURE 13.22   The language experience approach takes many creative forms in a classroom. (Special thanks to Gay Spitz for example 1. to Ann Zondor and Lynne Conly Hoffman and the children of the Children's Center of the Stanford Community for examples 2. to 4.)

printed word displayed regularly. Storage units are labeled with pictures and words of what belongs where (scissors, turtle food, blocks). Areas of the room are named, and stories, poems, or familiar fingerplays are hung on charts. Written signs remind children of the rules, such as "Inside Voices Here" in the book corner or "Wear an Apron" near the easels. Primary classes may add calendars and helper charts, visual cues for children to read and prepare for the next event. Story maps help children see the parts and sequencing of the writing process. Depicted as a body, the head serves as the beginning (with facial features called "topic," "characters," and "setting"), the body as the middle, and the legs as the end ("Finally . . .") A primary child can write in the various parts of the story and read it from the map or continue to elaborate with full sentences in a more traditional manner. In these ways, teachers help raise awareness of the use and enjoyment of the printed word.

CHILDREN'S LITERATURE

Children's books bring us back to ourselves, young and new in the world. "Our bones may lengthen and our skin stretch, but we are the same soul in the making. . . . Children's books are such powerful transformers because they speak, in the words of the Quakers, to one's condition, often unrecognized at the time, and remain as maps for the future. . . . In children's books we preserve the wild rose, the song of the robin, the budding leaf. In secret gardens we know the same stab of joy, at whatever age of reading, in the thorny paradise around us."

(Lundin, 1991)

Literature does indeed have an important place in the curriculum today. It is especially valuable as a vehicle for cognitive and language development. Books help to acquaint children with new words, ideas, facts, and adventures. Planned and spontaneous reading experiences are a vital part of the young child's day.

Reading books to children introduces them to the reading concept, to a different form of communication from spoken language. It is a symbol system with which they will become familiar as they learn that words and pictures have meaning.

Literature and Cognitive Development

Literature can perform several functions in aiding cognitive development. Through the use of good books, teachers can help children broaden their interests and concepts. Books that are primarily used for transmitting information expand the child's knowledge base. Thoughtful books that draw on children's everyday experiences widen their understanding of themselves and others. Through books, children can learn to see things in an endless variety of ways. Five different books will describe and illustrate behavior of cats in five different ways. Exposure to *Millions of Cats* (Gag), *Angus and the Cats* (Flack), and *The Cat in the Hat* (Dr. Seuss), as well as to the cats portrayed in *Peter Rabbit* (Potter) or *Frog Went A-Courtin'* (Langstaff), will enlarge the child's concepts of cats. Different cultures are also represented in any number of children's books, teaching a greater awareness of all of humankind.[1]

Teachers have an opportunity to encourage divergent thinking through the use of children's literature. Children gain more than facts from books; they learn all matter of things, providing they can interpret the story rather than just hear the individual words. Quizzing children about whether the dinosaur was a meat- or plant-eater will bring about responses that are predictable and pat, but comprehension does not have to be joyless. Zingy questions will provide not only thought but also interest. "Would a brontosaurus fit in your living room?" will get children to think about *Danny and the Dinosaur* (Hoff) or Kent's *There's No Such Thing as a Dragon* or Most's *If the Dinosaurs Came Back* in a new way. "Is the troll bigger or smaller than your brother?" might be a point of discussion after reading *The Three Billy Goats Gruff.* The point is not to have children feed back straight factual information, but to get them involved in the story.

Selection of books obviously plays a part in using literature to stimulate thought and conversation about what was read. The wise teacher will choose books that invite participation. Everyone can "roar a terrible roar, gnash their terrible teeth, and show their terrible claws" during a rendition of *Where the Wild Things Are* (Sendak). Meaning for children lies more in action than in words. Children will be more apt to talk about stories that have in some way touched them and stimulated their involvement.

Questions for thought and children's participation must be related to children's experiences and knowledge, yet lead them toward discovery. Books provide a pleasurable avenue for this type of intellectual growth.

Literature and Language Development

A great many language skills are learned when children are exposed to good literature in the classroom. The value lies in the use of language by the author and the use the teacher makes of the language potential.

 OUR DIVERSE WORLD OUR DIVERSE WORLD OUR DIVERSE WORLD OUR DIVERSE WORLD OUR DIVERSE WORLD

[1]Children's literature provides a window to OUR DIVERSE WORLD.

If language development is the goal, auditory appeal is one of the best reasons for choosing a book. The actual sounds of the words catch children's attention and imagination. Familiar sounds of animals or objects reinforce and provide new ways to express thoughts. "Buzz" and "humm" are playful words that have a great appeal to children. Sensory words, such as cold, soft, and slippery, capture children's attention.

Building and extending vocabulary is another function of literature in the language arts curriculum. Old familiar words take on new meaning as they reflect the content of each different story. Children love new words, especially big ones, and they do not necessarily need them defined. If used correctly in the context of the storyline, the words will be self-explanatory. Many children memorize phrases from favorite books, sometimes unaware of their meaning, but fitting the rhythm and pattern into their play.

> When Andrea was struggling to find the words to describe a large amount, Mitra began to recite: "Hundreds of cats, thousands of cats, millions and billions and trillions of cats!" (*Millions of Cats*, Gag)

> Riding home in the car after school one day, Parker chanted: "Tik-ki tik-ki tem-bo no sa rembo, chari bari ru-chi, pip peri pembo." (*Tikki Tikki Tembo*, Mosel)

> Derek and Shigeo were playing grocery store. In order to attract customers they called out: "Caps for sale! Fifty cents a cap." (*Caps for Sale*, Slobodkina)

Language—and vocabulary—come alive with such repetition, as children integrate the words into their play. This demonstrates another benefit of books and literature in language development: that of learning the skill of listening. As Trelease (1991) puts it, "If our first problem is not reading enough to children, our second problem is stopping too soon." Whether one- or ten-years-old, children need and thrive on being read aloud to regularly. Teachers could ask for no better activity to promote good listening habits than a wealth of good children's books.

Creating a Rich Literary Environment

The comics of yesterday are far outdistanced by the television and video games of today. How can teachers give children experiences in literature in the face of such competition?

The field of children's literature is rich in its variety, including both great classic stories and those of present-day situations and concerns. Fiction and informational books, children's magazines, and poetry add balance to the literary curriculum. Every classroom should contain representative works from each of these areas.

Provide plenty of time for using books and other materials. Children need time to browse, to flip through a book at their own pace, to let their thoughts wander as they reflect on the storyline. They also enjoy retelling the tale to others. Be sure to plan enough time for children to be read to every day.

Make a space that is quiet and comfortable. In addition to soft pillows or seats, locate the reading area where there is privacy. Crashing blocks and messy fingerpainting will intrude on the bookreader. A place to sprawl or cuddle up with a friend is preferable.

Have plenty of books and supporting materials. The language arts center might contain a listening post, with headsets for a record or tape player. Perhaps there is even a place where books can be created, a place supplied with paper and crayons. There may even be a typewriter, puppet stage, or flannel board nearby so that stories can be created in new ways.

Display children's literary creations. The efforts of children's stories and bookmaking should be honored by establishing a place in the room where they can be seen and read. Children then see how adults value the process of literary creation and the final product.

Teachers must model how to care for a book and keep classroom books in good repair. Children can come to realize that a book is like a good friend and should be given the same kind of care and consideration.

Fostering children's reading at home is one of the important contributions a teacher can make to the reading process. Attitudes about reading are communicated to children from the important people in their lives. Because teachers do not have a direct influence on the home environment, their route to the home is through the children. A child who is enthusiastic about books and carries them home is likely to involve parents in the quest for good books and stories. Teachers encourage this in a number of ways. Encourage parents to read good quality literature by making "book bags," large plastic ziplock bags in which the children can select a book from the classroom to read overnight and return the next day. Posting the local library hours, establishing a lending library, and providing parents with lists of favorites will reinforce the child's interest in literature.

Use books around the room. Don't confine them to just the book corner or the book shelf. Demonstrate their adaptability to all curriculum areas by displaying a variety of books in the activity centers. Ask children to help you retell or emphasize parts of a story (see Storytelling section), and ask them questions informally afterwards: "How many bowls of porridge were on the kitchen table? Which one did Goldilocks like best? How did you know?" Figure 13.23 shows how books can enhance play and learning throughout the school room.

Extending Literary Experiences

Good literature comes in many forms and can be presented in a variety of ways. A creative teacher uses books and literature to develop other curriculum materials. Translating words from a book into an activity helps a child remember them. Books and stories can be adapted to the flannel board, storytelling, dramatizations, puppets, book games, and audiovisual resources. One particularly useful resource to expand children's book experiences is *Story Stretchers* (Raines & Canady, 1989).

Storytelling

Storytelling is as old as humanity. The first time a human being returned to the cave with an adventure to tell, the story was born. Storytelling is the means by which cultural heritage is passed down from one generation to another.[1] Children's involvement with a story being told is almost instantaneous. The storyteller is the medium through which a story comes to life, adding a unique flavor through voice, choice of words, body language, and pacing.

Stories that have a few characters, plenty of repetition, and a clear sequence of events make for easy listening for young children. Fairy tales have all these elements, and contain important truths for children. These tales are fascinating, since, in a child's words, "they think about what I think about" (Howarth, 1989). Fairy tales answer basic questions such as "Who Am I? What will happen to me, and how should I act?" Moreover, these stories assure the child of a positive outcome while allowing them to experience some of the hard and scary aspects of life. Critics of fairy tales argue that many are stereotyped; others (Jung and Bettleheim, for instance) assert that the characteristics embodied in fairy tale roles are about the good and bad in us all, and that the teacher who uses fairy tales—particularly from many cultures—will find that children learn the results of kindness and evil in themselves and others.[2]

Teachers can use any familiar story, be it *The Three Little Pigs* or *Madeline*. Props can be added to draw attention to the story. Flannel board adaptations of stories are helpful; they give the storyteller a sense of security and a method for remembering the story. Children can be involved in the action by placing the characters on the felt board at the appropriate time. Puppets or an assortment of hats can be used as props. Good storytellers enjoy telling the story and communicate their enthusiasm to children.

Dramatizing Stories

Acting out characters from a favorite story has universal appeal. Young preschoolers are introduced to this activity as they act out the motions to fingerplays and songs. "The Eensy-Weensy Spider" and its accompanying motions is the precursor for dramatization. Story re-enactment helps children learn to work together, so that their *social development* is enhanced, as is the cognitive ability to engage in *collective representation*. As an extension of Steiner's theories, Waldorf kindergartens

OUR DIVERSE WORLD OUR DIVERSE WORLD OUR DIVERSE WORLD OUR DIVERSE WORLD OUR DIVERSE WORLD

[1] and [2]In many cultures, other than Western European-American culture, there is a high value placed on learning through oral story telling and rhyming and chanting; a higher value than on learning based on playing with objects.

LIVING TOGETHER: REFLECTING DIVERSITY
Knots on a Counting Rope (Martin, Jr. & Archambault)
The Legend of Bluebonnet (de Paola)
The Quilt (Jones)
The River That Gave Gifts (Humphrey)
The Big Orange Splot (Pinkwater)
Mei Li (Handforth)
Gilberto and the Wind (Ets)
Stories for Free Children (Pogrebin)

CREATING ART
Black Is Brown Is Tan (Adoff)
Start with a Dot (Roberts)
Little Blue and Little Yellow (Lionni)
My Very First Book of Colors (Carle)

DRAMATIC PLAY: ON OUR HEADS!
Martin's Hats (Blos)
Caps for Sale (Slobodnika)
Hats Hats Hats (Morris)

BUILDING BLOCKS
Changes Changes (Hutchins)
The Big Builders (Dreany)
Who Built the Bridge? (Bate)
Boxes (Craig)

FAMILIES
When You Were a Baby (Jonas)
All Kinds of Families (Simon)
Whose Mouse Are You? (Kraus)
Five Minues Peace (Murphy)

DISCOVERY SCIENCE: GROW, GROWING, GROWEST!
Growing Vegetable Soup (Ehlert)
The Carrot Seed (Krauss)
From Seed to Pear (Migutsch)
Here Are My Hands (Martin, Jr., and Archambault)
Window into an Egg (Flanagan)

MATH LAB: 1,2,3, COUNT WITH ME!
How Much Is a Million? (Schwartz)
Roll Over! A Counting Song (Peek)
Ten, Nine, Eight (Bang)
Have You Seen My Duckling? (Tafuri)
The Doorbell Rang (Hutchins)

MAKIN' MUSIC
Hush Little Baby (Aliki)
Ben's Trumpet (Isadora)
One Wide River to Cross (Emberley)
Over in the Meadow (Wadsworth)
I Know an Old Lady (Bonne)

MAKIN' FRIENDS
Friends (Heime)
George and Martha (Marshall)
Best Friends (Cohen)
Frog and Toad Are Friends (Hoban)
I'll Build My Friend a Mountain (Katz)

BOOKS FOR UNDER THREES
Goodnight Moon (Brown)
Brown Bear, Brown Bear (Martin, Jr.)
The Baby's Catalogue (Ahlberg)
Truck, Train, Boats, Airplanes (Barton)
How Do I Put It On? (Watanabe)
Spot (Hill)

BOOKS FOR EARLY PRIMARY
Charlotte's Web (White)
The Box Car Children (Warner)
Ramona (Cleary)
The Stories Julian Tells (Cameron)
Like Jake and Me (Jukes)

FIGURE 13.23 When literature is a natural part of the environment, children learn to appreciate and use it. (See also Ramirez and Ramirez, 1994.)

FIGURE 13.24 Using the computer in a classroom can help individualize a child's educational experience.

include fairy and morality tales. "Fairy tales are told to the children on successive days for up to 2 weeks, culminating in the tale as a puppet show offered to the children by the teacher or as a play with costumes acted out by the children with the teacher narrating (Waldorf, 1994). Whether the child is an observer, walk-on, mime, or actor, the learning is real in each step of the continuum.

Stories such as *Caps for Sale* (Slobodkina) and *Swimmy* (Lionni), as well as fairy tales, are popular choices for reenactment by four- and five-year-olds. They need plenty of time to rehearse, and simple props help them focus on their role. A red scarf helps Jeannada become *Little Red Riding Hood*; an old pair of sunglasses transforms Joaquin into a character from *Goggles* (Keats).

Older children may choose to write (or dictate) parts or scripts; it is appropriate for 6- to 8-year-olds to have their playmates act-out original stories. Once the "right" story has been chosen, the teacher helps the children to re-tell the story together, set the stage, and let the play begin.

Puppet Shows

Puppet shows can involve a large number of children as participants and audience. Children of all ages enjoy watching and putting on a puppet

show. Since puppets are people to young children, they become confidants and special friends. Children will confide in and protect a puppet, engaging in a dialogue with one or more puppets that is often revealing of the child's inner struggles and concerns. Teachers can support their efforts by helping them to take turns, suggesting questions and dialogue to them, and involving the audience. The project of puppet making can be quite elaborate and very engaging for older children.

Book Games

Book games are a good way to extend the literary experience. Buy two copies of an inexpensive book with readable pictures, such as *The Carrot Seed* (Krauss). Tear out the pages and cover with clear plastic. Children must then read the pictures in order to put the book into proper sequence. A book of rhymes, *Did You Ever See?* (Einsel), lends itself to rhyming games. Children can act out the rhymes from the storyline or match rhyming phrasing from cards the teacher has made.

Audiovisual Resources

Records, cassettes, and filmstrips enlarge the child's experience with books. The auditory and the visual media reinforce one another. Music brings literature alive; besides tapping into the musical aspect of intelligence, it appeals to all children to move and express themselves and thus enjoy literature and books even more. The pictures can show children new aspects of the words; sometimes the music or the voices bring the book to life. Often both happen. Hundreds of children's stories—classics and modern day—have been translated to these media.

COMPUTERS IN THE CLASSROOM

A computer can be as nonthreatening as a watercolor brush. In the hands of a child it can be a tool for experiencing the world. Early childhood classrooms are arranged so that children learn about the world directly, by piling blocks, molding sand and clay, bouncing a ball. Through these experiences, children gradually form concepts about how the world works and how they can affect it. As children touch the keys of a computer, they are challenged to explore and discover in ways never before possible.

Discovery-oriented experiences with computers enhance children's learning, especially in stimulating their cognitive thought processes. Children form new knowledge as they interact with computer-based programs to form what is described as "microworlds" (Papert, 1980). Children design and control places of their own choosing, such as building a house, the seashore, or a face. Then they create events that challenge them to think through consequences of their actions. Moreover, computer programs can be "process highlighters" for children (Haugland & Shade, 1988). That is, the program can speed up or detail hidden processes and cause:effect relationships that are more difficult to observe, such as a plant growing, a face changing expression upon command, or a dance put together with a special sequence of steps.

Developmentally Appropriate Software

Along with blocks and paints, the computer can become an expressive medium that encourages skills in a variety of ways. It is important that the computer be used in addition to other concrete experiences, not instead of them. For instance,

children need to have *real* materials on the art and manipulatives tables, and they can also manipulate *images* of those same kinds of materials at the computer table. Children need to have many experiences with *concrete* items such as paint, crayons, and markers. They are then ready to try their creative hand at computer graphics (see Haugland and Shade, 1990, and Wright and Shade, 1994, for specific suggestions for computer software for young children). More details are given in Bernadette Davis' Focus Box.

To use computers appropriately in the classroom, teachers must first be *comfortable* with the computer themselves. A computer area is in a quieter spot of the classroom (such as in or near the library/listening spot), against a wall to minimize damage to the equipment or cords. To introduce the computer, the teacher shows small groups of children the basic care and handling of the computer and disks. The computer can be one of many choices offered during free play, or can be a more limited choice with a waiting list. Interaction between children can be encouraged by including space for two or more at the computer. Sometimes the teacher will assign turns to a pair or small group of children, particularly if the computer seems to be dominated by a few. As always, the alert teacher watches to ensure that no one becomes "stuck" at the computer or any other area, helping develop children's interests and skills in many activities.

Just a few years ago, computers were seen as a wave of the future. Now computers have become firmly established in early childhood classrooms, particularly in kindergarten and primary grades but also in many preschools. This is because the *hardware*, or actual machinery, has become less expensive while being sturdy and workable for busy teachers and young children alike. The most dramatic change, however, has been in the proliferation of *software*, the computer programs themselves.

It is in the area of software that teachers of young children have a multitude of choices. These choices must be carefully made. Not every program intended for children is developmentally appropriate, and teachers must pay thoughtful attention to the program and to what they know about their own group of children. Teachers must know what to look for and how to choose programs that will be useful and appropriate for the specific age of the group. Haugland and Shade (1990) have

Software For Active Learning

Bernadette Caruso Davis

Software defines the content and quality of the computer-enriched learning experience. Whereas poor software cultivates boredom and passivity, a good piece of software can open new worlds and empower children to become active explorers.

Active learning is encouraged when children control the software. This means that the user sets the pace of the activity; rather than racing against the clock to complete a predefined task (like answering ten math problems before the volcano erupts), children should feel comfortable moving at their own pace and should have the option of escaping if the activity becomes unchallenging or frustrating.

When children control the software, they direct the session, rather than reacting passively to prompts. Using a *Colorforms Fun Set* or *Imagination Express*, a child can choose backgrounds and props to build an original scene, then use invented spelling to compose a story. Compared to drill software that requires the user to match consonant sounds or identify missing vowels, child-controlled software supports infinitely more active engagement.

As educators since Dewey have known, children are active learners when the content is pertinent to their lives. Appropriate software makes the activity relevant by allowing children to define their own goals. Providing tools and situations, but not requiring specific responses, software allows children to satisfy their own expectations. For example, graphics programs like *KidPix* or *E*A*Kids Art Center* provide all the tools necessary to create a colorful, textured picture that will be as unique as the child creating it.

Appropriate software is like a well-designed dramatic play center; available are props, costumes, and settings—everything necessary for exploring a situation—except the script. The resources are there, but what is done with them will be under the control of the children.

Bernadette Caruso Davis is the Master Teacher for the Technology In Early Childhood Habitats (TECH) Program at the University of Delaware.

developed ten criteria for evaluating computer programs. Not all software will meet all the criteria, but it is important to view the criteria as a continuum for considering computer programs for young children. Computer software should:

1. Be age appropriate.

2. Allow children to control it (children setting the pace and being active participants).

3. Include clear instructions.

4. Have expanding complexity.

5. Support independent exploration.

6. Be "process oriented" (having the software program so engaging that the product of using it is secondary).

7. Include real-world representation.

8. Have high quality technical features (colorful, uncluttered, and realistic).

9. Provide trial-and-error opportunities.

10. Have visible transformations (being able to affect the software, for example, by transposing objects).

When Child Meets Computer

Specific methods have been devised for teaching young children to work successfully with computers (Davidson, 1989). For instance, a child must be able to maneuver a joystick or mouse, find the keys on the keyboard, and insert a disk into the computer correctly. Since very young children cannot read, they will need help getting started. Teachers must be able to help children learn by setting up their classrooms with a computer positioned in a safe yet accessible place, structuring activities and the daily schedule to give children plenty of time to manipulate the machinery and programs, and choosing specific hardware and software that works with the class.

Integrating the Computer into Learning

One of the most exciting aspects of computers in the classroom is their ability to support other learning. Teachers who use the computer effective-ly as an educational tool integrate their program goals to use the computer with individual children. What happens at the keyboard matches each child's individual needs. Davidson (1989) suggests using computers to support a classroom unit on three levels:

1. Specific software can provide unit-related information. For instance, the program "Dinosaurs" can be in place while developing a theme such as in Figure 13.9.

2. Tool software—such as graphics or writing programs—can be used for creating unit-related products. For example, a program such as "Explore-a-Story" can help primary-age children write stories about their own interests and responses to whatever unit is being studied. With a younger group, the teacher could help the class make a group story to send home.

3. Computer-related activities can be designed to support the unit theme. One idea is using the program "Name-Jumping," which asks children to jump around a floor-sized keyboard. Both computer concepts and the words of a unit or theme are reinforced using children's full-body involvement.

● UNIT 13-3 CHECKPOINT

The special topics on cognition and language include reading, writing, and computers. Each offers a unique extension to children's learning in the classroom. Clearly, language and thought are learned both at home and in school and can be connected in meaningful ways.

Children and books belong together. Good literature gives insight into human behavior. Books teach children less important though exciting things such as how to play peek-a-boo or escape a hungry lion. But they also teach matters of substance and character such as how to go to sleep, make a friend, be brave. The early years should lay a foundation in literature upon which children can build throughout their lives.

> Books are no substitute for living, but they can add immeasurably to its richness. When life is absorbing, books can enhance our sense of its significance.

When life is difficult, they can give a momentary relief from trouble, afford a new insight into our problems or those of others, or provide the rest and refreshment we need. Books have always been a source of information, comfort, and pleasure for people who know how to use them. This is as true for children as for adults.

(Arbuthnot and Sutherland, 1972)

The computer is a twentieth century creation, yet is can stimulate the timeless, innate characteristics of curiosity, creativity, and discovery. A major challenge for teachers is to provide curriculum that will develop these "dispositions," or habits of the mind (Katz, 1985), so that children will be willing as well as able to develop skills. As a teacher, ask yourself:

● How do teachers help children become ready to read?

● What should a writing center in an early education classroom look like?

● How does literature support cognitive development? Language development?

● What literacy software could be used that would entice the reluctant school-aged child?

● What language activities would be appropriate with toddlers?

● What are the guidelines for creating a rich literary environment?

● What are five ways to extend literary experiences?

S U M M A R Y

People entering early childhood education as a profession are challenged to develop children's minds and language. This chapter begins with the premise that intellectual development and language are interrelated. As teachers help children learn how to think, they learn about children's thinking processes by listening to what they say, and observing how they respond to others' words, thoughts, and actions.

Much of cognitive development theory has its roots in the work of Jean Piaget. Cognitive development includes the areas of inquiry, knowledge of the physical and social worlds, classification, seriation, numbers, symbols, spatial relationships, and time. Language development, on the other hand, takes into consideration how children learn articulation, receptive and expressive language, graphic representation, and enjoyment of language.

Teachers plan curriculum to develop these skills in several ways. Many class settings offer children an opportunity to refine cognitive and language skills. At times, teachers focus on a specific skill, such as reasoning or conversation, and adapt the curriculum to emphasize those areas.

The teacher's role also requires an understanding of bilingualism and a working knowledge of speech and language disorders. Early childhood teachers use their own language abilities to stress and support the language development of their students.

Reading and writing are part of the language and thought processes. Adults in early childhood seek ways to involve children with the printed word in ways that have meaning to the here-and-now in children's lives. Books, literature, and computers further the development of reading and writing skills and provide enjoyable tools for the enhancement of cognition and language.

R E V I E W   Q U E S T I O N S

1. How are cognition and language related?

2. Match the cognitive skill with the appropriate activity:

inquiry	being aware of others
physical world	learning to locate things
social knowledge	pretending to be a puppet
classification	asking questions
seriation	sequencing events
numbers	using nesting blocks
symbols	expressing amounts
spatial relationships	sorting objects
time	manipulating materials

3. How does teacher language affect how children develop cognitive skills? Give several examples of what discourages such growth; counter that with how what a teacher says encourages skills.

4. How does the teacher help children develop speech and language skills in planning curriculum? How is this affected with children whose primary language is not English?

5. The way teachers use language is critical in encouraging children's own language. Name the four areas of language and what a teacher can say to encourage growth in those areas.

6. What are some of the criteria for evaluating computer software for early childhood? What traps are to be avoided?

7. Describe some curriculum activities for cognition and language development. Simplify them for infants/toddlers/twos and elaborate for the primary-aged youngsters.

L E A R N I N G   A C T I V I T I E S

1. Look at the program in which you now teach, or recall your own first classrooms. Find at least one example of rote knowledge, social knowledge, and meaningful knowledge.

2. Take one cognitive skill and trace how it could be developed in each curriculum area of the program.

3. Observe block play at your school. Make a chart, as in Figure 13.6, that describes the learning processes involved.

4. Choose a child in your care whose primary language is not English. How is that child processing language? What are you doing to foster the child's emerging English skills? How is that child's first language being supported in your program? What can you do to involve the family?

5. Make a list of the classroom areas. Beside each, name one activity that would foster cognitive development and one that calls for language skills.

6. One theme often used in early childhood programs is that of the changing season in the fall. How can that theme develop language and thinking skills in preschoolers?

7. Teaching reading readiness involves trying to develop oral language and listening skills. What could a teacher of toddlers plan for each? A kindergarten teacher?

8. Describe three ways children's books and literature help to develop intellectual skills and language proficiency. Through what techniques can literary experiences be extended in the curriculum?

9. Consider the use of a computer in the following classrooms:

> toddler day care program
>
> preschool half-day program
>
> kindergarten
>
> after-school primary program

Is a computer appropriate in each of them? Why and how? What guidelines, if any, would be needed in each setting? What would be the adult's role in each?

B I B L I O G R A P H Y

General

Bredekamp, Sue, (ed.) *Developmentally Appropriate Practice In Early Childhood Programs Serving Children From Birth Through Age 8* (Expanded Edition). Washington, D.C.: National Association for the Education of Young Children, 1991.

Derman-Sparks, Louise. *Anti-Bias Curriculum*, National Association for the Education of Young Children, 1989.

Gardner, Howard. *Frames of Mind*. New York: Basic Books, 1983.

Piaget, Jean. *The Language and Thought of the Child*. Cleveland: World Publishing Co., 1969.

Vygotsky, L.S. *Thought and Language*. New York: M.I.T. Press and John Wiley and Sons, 1962.

Cognition

De Vries, Rheta. "What Will Happen if . . . ? Using a Piagetian Approach to Inspire Reasoning." *Pre-K Today*, March, 1987.

Ellison, Launa. "What Does the Brain Have to Do with Learning?" *Holistic Education Review*, Fall, 1990, pages 46–51.

Flavell, John. "What Preschoolers Know about Thinking." Paper presented at Stanford University: Center for Youth and Family Studies, 1993.

Gardner, Howard. *Multiple Intelligences: Theory into Practice.* New York: Basic Books, 1985.

——————. *The Unschooled Mind.* New York: Basic Books, 1991.

Hohlmann, Mary; Banet, B.; and Weikart, D.P. *Young Children in Action.* Ypsilanti, Mich.: The High/Scope Press, 1979.

Klein, Amelia. "All About Ants: Discovery Learning in the Primary Grades." *Young Children*, Vol. 46, No. 5, July, 1991.

McCracken, Janet Brown. "Make It Math . . . Make it Fun!." *Pre-K Today*, February, 1988.

New City School Faculty. *Multiple Intelligences: Teaching for Success.* St. Louis, Mo.: The New City School, 1995.

Price, Gary Glen. "Research in Review: Mathematics in Early Childhood." *Young Children*, Vol. 44, No. 4, May, 1989.

Schickedanz, Judith A., et al. "Preschoolers and Academics: Some Thoughts." *Young Children*, Vol. 44, No. 6, November, 1990.

Simmons, Barbara, and Brewer, JoAnn. "When Parents of Kindergartners Ask 'Why?'" *Childhood Education*, pages 177–84, 1985.

Slavin, Robert E. (Ed.), Karweit, Nancy L., and Wasik, Barbara A. "Preventing Early School Failure: Research Policy and Practice." *Educational Leadership*, Vol 50, pp. 10–18, Needham Heights, MA., Allyn, 1994.

Sternberg, Robert J. Personality & Intelligence. Cambridge, MA.: Cambridge University Press, 1994.

Language

Beck, M. Susan. *Baby Talk: How Your Child Learns to Speak*, New York: New American Library, 1979.

Bowman, Barbara T. "Educating Language-Minority Children: Challenges and Opportunities," *Phi Delta Kappan*, October, 1989.

Chomsky, N. *Language and Thought.* Wakefield, R.I.: Moyer Bell, 1993.

deVilliers, Peter A., and Jill, G. *Early Language.* Washington, D.C.: National Association for the Education of Young Children, 1981.

Diaz Soto, Lourdes. "Research in Review: Understanding Bilingual/Bicultural Young Children." *Young Children*, Vol. 46, No. 2, January, 1991.

Early Childhood Resources. "Implementing Developmentally Appropriate Practice Kindergarten Through Grade 2." Corte Madera, Calif.: 1995.

Garcia, Eugene. "Bilingual Development and the Education of Bilingual Children During Early Childhood." *American Journal of Education*, Vol. 11, 1986.

Sholtys, Katherine C. "A New Language, a New Life." *Young Children*, Vol. 44, No. 3, March, 1989.

Wasserman, Selma. "The Art of the Question." *Childhood Education*, Vol. 67, No. 4, Summer, 1991.

Wolf, Dennie, (ed.) "Children's Conversations: Why They Are Important." *Beginnings*, Winter, 1984.

Wrobleski, Louise. "The Writer's Briefcase." *Young Children*, Vol. 45, No. 3, March, 1990.

Special thanks to students Sandie Goodwin, Dale Hu, and Sharon Murphy for their contributions of children's language samples.

SPECIAL TOPICS
Reading and Writing

Adams, Marilyn. *Beginning to Read: Thinking and Learning About Print.* Cambridge, MA: MIT Press, 1990.

Cruikshank, Susan. "Whole Language: a Developmentally Appropriate Alternative." In *Beginnings and Beyond*, ed. A. Gordon and K.B. Browne. Albany, N.Y.: Delmar Publishers, 1993 (3rd Ed.).

Dailey, Kathleen A. "Writing in Kindergarten: Helping Parents Understand the Process." *Childhood Education*, Vol. 67, No. 3, Spring, 1991.

Freeman, Evelyn B., and Hatch, J. Amos. "Emergent Literacy: Reconceptualizing Kindergarten Practice." *Childhood Education*, Vol. 66, No. 1, Fall, 1989.

Goodman, Ken. *What's Whole in Whole Language.* Heinmann Educational Books, 1986.

Herr, Judy, and Libby, Yvonne. *Early Childhood Writing Centers.* Fort Worth, Tex.: Harcourt & Brace, 1994.

Jones, Elizabeth (Ed.). *Reading, Writing, and Talking with Four, Five and Six Year Olds.* Pasadena, Calif.: Pacific Oaks, 1988.

Children's Literature

Arbuthnot, May Hill, and Sutherland, Zena. *Children and Books*, 4th ed. London: Scott, Foresman and Co., 1972.

Ashton-Warner, Sylvia. *Teacher.* New York: Bantam Books, 1963.

Howarth, Mary. "Rediscovering the Power of Fairy Tales." *Young Children*, Vol. 45, No. 1, November, 1989.

Ishee, Nell, and Goldhaber, Jeanne. "Story Re-enactment: Let the Play Begin." *Young Children*, Vol. 45, No. 3, March, 1990.

Jalongo, Mary Renck. *Young Children and Picture Books.* Washington, D.C.: National Association for the Education of Young Children, 1988.

Lundin, Anne. 'Secret Gardens: The Literature of Childhood." *Childhood Education*, Vol. 67, No. 4, Summer, 1991.

Raines, Shirley C., and Canady, Robert J. *Story Stretchers.* Mt. Rainier: Gryphon House, 1989.

Ramirez, Gonzalo, Jr., and Ramirez, Jan Lee. *Multiethnic Children's Literature.* Albany, N.Y.: Delmar Publishers, 1994.

Sawyer, Walter E., and Sawyer, Jean C. *Integrated Language Arts for Emerging Literacy.* Albany, N.Y.: Delmar Publishers, 1993.

Sutherland, Zena. "Literature for Children," and *The Best in Children's Books.* World Book Encyclopedia, 1991.

Trelease, Jim. *The Read-Aloud Handbook.* New York: Penguin Books, 1982.

Tubbs, Janet. "Talking with and through Puppets." *Beginnings*, Winter, 1984.

Waldorf Staff of Los Altos, CA, "Understanding the Waldorf Curriculum," pamphlet for parents, 1994.

Computers

Davidson, Jane I. *Children and Computers Together in the Early Childhood Classroom.* Albany, N.Y.: Delmar, 1989.

Haugland, Susan W., and Shade, Daniel D. "Developmentally Appropriate Software for Young Children." *Young Children*, Vol. 43, No. 4, May 1988.

—————. *Developmental Evaluations of Software for Young Children.* Albany, N.Y.: Delmar Publishers, 1990.

Scharf, P., and Chattin-McNichols, J. *Understanding the Computer Age.* Hasbrouck Heights, N.J.: Hayden, 1986.

Wright, June L., and Shade, Daniel D. (Eds.). *Young Children: Active Learners in a Technological Age.* Washington, D.C.: National Association for the Education of Young Children, 1994.

CHAPTER 14

Planning for the Heart and Soul: Emotional, Social, and Creative Growth

QUESTIONS FOR THOUGHT

What is the connection between a child's <u>well-being</u> and emotional, social, and creative development?

What are the components of self-esteem?

What is emotional growth in the early childhood years?

How do teachers handle the expression of feelings in the class setting?

What is social growth in the early childhood years?

What social skills are developed in young children?

What is creativity?

How is creativity expressed in the early years?

Portions of this chapter were developed with the assistance of Gay Spitz, Salinas Adult School, Salinas, Calif.

PREFACE

The heart and soul of any good program for young children is a commitment to help children as they struggle with (1) the reality of emotions; (2) the awareness of the need for social skills; and (3) the creative urge. The foundation must be laid in these early years for children to understand themselves and others.

Emotional, social, and creative development are related to the child's self-concept and self-esteem; the child must have an understanding of self before seeing that self in relation to others. It is primarily through emotional, social, and creative growth that children learn who they are, and they must have self-confidence to experience and learn the necessary skills.

This chapter contains three separate units. Each area—emotional, social, and creative growth—is explored individually to give a greater understanding of its importance to the developing child. An overview of development is followed by a discussion of the skills children learn in the preschool years. The crucial role of the teacher is emphasized next, followed by curriculum planning to reinforce each developmental area. At the end of each unit, a checkpoint and review serve as a short summary.

INTRODUCTION

The first thing one notices upon entering an early childhood classroom is the children at play. A quick survey of the area shows who is playing together, whether or not there is crying and fighting, and how happy or sad the children look. This overview gives an immediate sense of the emotional, social, and creative climate in that early childhood setting.

- *Emotional:* Toddler Abier giggles as she runs her hands across the water table, then cries after she splashes soap suds in her eyes and needs to be comforted.

- *Social:* Preschooler Danny wants his favorite red wagon so Pat, the student teacher, helps him negotiate a turn with Christa.

- *Creative:* Kindergartners Fabio, Erika, and Benjy work steadily to build a tall, intricate block structure. When it is finished, the three children stand back and marvel at their creation.

Together these three factors—emotional mood, social dynamics, and creative tone—define the overall atmosphere in which children play and work.

Emotional, social, and creative well-being are woven together in the developing child. Children who are sensitive to their own feelings and moods are able to begin understanding other people and thus become more socially effective and successful. Children with experience in many creative endeavors have the self-confidence that comes from having an outlet for self-expression.

These three areas are also linked to other aspects of the child's growth:

- *Creative/Physical:* Physical skills can define and limit children's creative abilities. Two-year-old Andrea, whose physical skills do not yet include balancing objects, plays with blocks by piling them on top of one another, filling her wagon with blocks, and dumping them or lugging them from place to place.

- *Social/Cognitive:* It is hard for five-year-old Karena to share her best friend Luther with other children. Her intellectual abilities do not yet allow her to consider more than one idea at a time, so she cannot understand that Luther can be her friend and Dana's at the same time.

- *Emotional/Language:* Tyler is upset with his teacher's refusal to let him go outdoors during storytime. "I hate you!" he screams, "and you aren't the boss of me!" Children learn to label and express their emotions through words.

It is difficult to observe and measure the child's growth in creative, social, and emotional areas; it is easier to determine a child's progress in physical, cognitive, and language development. After all, a child counts or doesn't count, is either 40 inches tall or not, and speaks in full sentences or short phrases. Emotional, social, and creative expressions are more subtle and subjective. A child usually gets immediate and concrete feedback when playing lotto, calling for a teacher, or riding a tricycle. That does not always happen when children express their feelings, encounter others, and

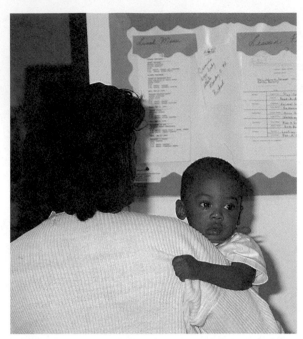

FIGURE 14.1 The emotional, social, and creative growth of children is the heart and soul of any early childhood program.

create something important. Talbot may feel rejected and sad if no one greets him as he enters the playhouse. He may mistake the children's busyness as an act of exclusion. In reality, the children did not even notice he was there. Teachers can play a critical role in helping children interpret their emotional, social, and creative interactions.

Traditionally, early childhood educators have concerned themselves with children's *well-being*, knowing that in the early years the foundations must be laid for children to understand themselves and others. Social growth, creative expression, and experience with a wide range of emotional behaviors also help children develop a strong self-concept with positive self-esteem.

What is included in children's well-being? In order to be in a good overall condition of health and happiness, children need a positive sense of themselves.

Self-esteem is an individual's sense of personal worth and an acceptance of who one is. Children's self-esteem (the way they feel about themselves) is expressed through children's behavior. They make judgments about themselves as they confront the world. To the extent that children feel worthy and capable, they are ready to succeed. If children disapprove of themselves, they may feel like failures and expect to do poorly.

Self-esteem develops as a reflection of experiences: the way people respond to you gives you some indication of your importance or value. Newborn infants have no concept of self and no past experience to judge their own worth. A young child who has positive experiences with others will more likely have a high sense of self-esteem than one who has felt unloved or unnoticed.

There appear to be four components of self-esteem (Brophy & Willis, 1981):

1. A sense of one's own identity

2. A sense of belonging (connectedness)

3. A sense of one's uniqueness

4. A sense of self (power)

Early in life, self-esteem is tied to family, friends, and other important people, such as teachers. Figure 14.2 shows how curriculum can develop each of these characteristics.

Planning for children's success builds self-esteem. It includes the following four components, which we call the "Four I's":

● *I:* When children enter the classroom, the message they receive is "I am important and this is my place." The physical environment, the daily schedule, and the curriculum are designed to give all children permission to express themselves.

● *Initiative:* Children are encouraged to initiate their own learning, to make contact with others, to take action.

● *Independence:* Self-management tasks of dressing, eating, toileting are given an important place in the curriculum. Children are assisted in taking care of their own belongings and in developing independent judgment about events and activities.

● *Interaction:* Social interaction has a high priority in the program. The room and yard are busy places with children moving about and talking among themselves and with adults. Conflicts are accepted as a natural consequence of social life. In the spirit of John Dewey (see Figure 1.6,

Emotional Skill Developed	Curriculum Activity (Use of Senses)
Self-Esteem	Use rocks of various sizes with balances, so that chil-
1. *Identity:* "Look at what I can do, the noise I can make, the weight I can pick up and move!"	dren can touch and hear when they move things around.
2. *Connectedness:* "I can make the same snakes as you, we can all make cakes."	A malleable material such as playdough can be used first alone, then with tools.
3. *Uniqueness:* "I'm pouring mine; you're dripping yours, and she is squeezing her stuff out her fin- gers!"	Make "oobleck," a mixture of cornstarch and water, in separate tubs for each child. Children can manipulate it in their own ways.
4. *Power:* "I can make this water go anywhere I want; look out for the tidal waves!"	Water play offers the child choices: pour into any of several containers, fill or empty the jug, use a funnel or a baster to squirt the water, make waves or splash hands.
Deal with Feelings	
1. *Identification* (to notice and label): "Does it feel very smooth, slippery, slidy? Is it soft and soothing?"	When fingerpainting, the teacher can describe what it appears the child is feeling. Children can identify their feelings as the teacher describes them while they use the materials.
2. *Mastery* (to accept): "She took your baker's dough and that made you angry. You can tell her you don't like it when she grabs what you are using."	Whether the sensory material is clay, cornmeal, soapy water, or fine sand, the issues of ownership and use of materials arise. Then, teachers reflect children's feel- ings and help them take responsibility for their own feelings.
3. *Expression* (to express appropriately): Child: "Tami has all the big pitchers." Teacher: "How can you let her know you want one?" Child: "And she splashed me two times!" Teacher: "If you feel too crowded, you need to tell her so."	As children begin to use the sensory materials, they need to communicate to others. Usually the issues are about wanting more material and personal space.
4. *Feelings* (to deal with others): "Whee! Yuk! Mmm! Ha!"	When children share in a sensory activity, such as a feeling walk through tubs of cornmeal, lentils, flour, and soapsuds, they have the delightful experience of enjoy- ing their own feelings with another.

FIGURE 14.2 Sensory materials offer a sensorimotor opportunity to deal with materials in a nonstructured way. Be- cause children relax with open-ended activities, they will often share their feelings as they use sensory materials in a comfortable atmosphere.

Chapter 1), democratic group living will en- courage children to interact and foster a con- sciousness of interdependence.

A positive sense of self is critical for young children in life. Research (Marshall, 1989) shows that low self-image is correlated with poor mental health, poor academic achievement, and delin- quency. In contrast, a positive self-concept relates to good mental health, academic achievement, and good behavior. These children are ready to meet the challenges of the early years. They will have the self-confidence to deal with the reality of

emotions, the changing nature of social interac- tion, and the risk of creativity.

● UNIT 14-1 EMOTIONAL GROWTH

THE DEVELOPMENT OF EMOTIONS

Emotions are the feelings a person has—joy and sorrow, love and hate, confidence and fear, loneliness and belonging, anger and contentment, frustration and satisfaction. They are responses to

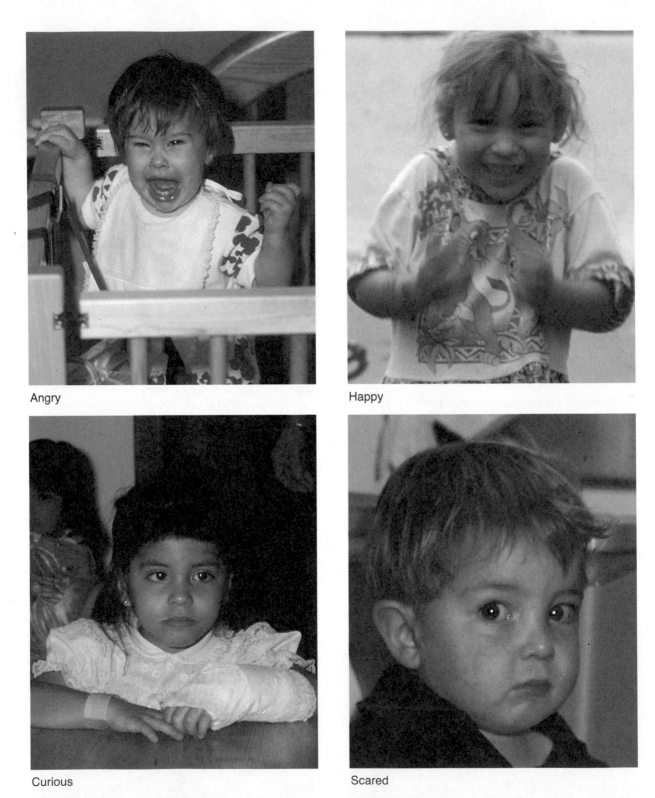

Angry

Happy

Curious

Scared

FIGURE 14.3   Young children feel their emotions strongly. Learning to read faces and body stance is essential to guiding emotional development.

events, people, and circumstances. Feelings are an outgrowth of what a person perceives is happening. Emotionally healthy people learn to give expression to their feelings in appropriate ways. They do not allow their feelings to overshadow the rest of their behavior. The optimal time to learn these skills is in the early years.

Early childhood teachers encourage children to identify and express their emotional nature so that they can learn to live with these powerful forces. When a child begins to understand and communicate feelings, the emotions are no longer in control of the child; the child is becoming the master of the emotions. Chapter 7 on Guidance and Discipline and this chapter sections on Emotional and Social Curriculum contain teacher strategies for helping children grow in these areas.

Infants respond in agitated emotion whether wet, hungry, hurt, or bored. Gradually, the expression of the emotion becomes more refined and varies with the situation. A toddler's cry of distress is different from the cry of discomfort or hunger. As children get older, their emotional expressions change as they gain control over some of their feelings and learn new ways to express them.

Strong external forces are also at work. Parents, family members, teachers, and friends are social influences, helping the young child learn socially acceptable behavior. Much of what children learn is by example, as Erikson, Bandura, Piaget, and Vygotsky would all agree. Therefore, children learn more from adult models than from simply being told how to behave (Clemes and Bean, 1980).

EMOTIONAL SKILLS IN EARLY CHILDHOOD

The emotional skills children learn in their early years are substantial. Research shows that some emotions—interest, disgust, distress, to name a few—are observable in the newborn (Sroufe, 1979) Campos and others (1983) posit that all the **basic emotions** are present within the first few weeks of life. These include happiness, interest, surprise, fear, anger, sadness, and disgust. The more **complex emotions** of shame, guilt, en-

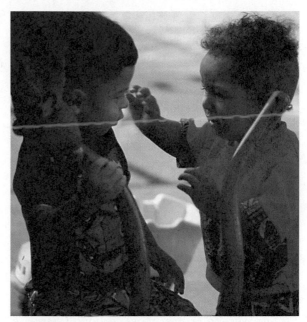

FIGURE 14.4 Children learn to appreciate and understand one another as they see each others' feelings. How can these boys learn to express hurt and comfort?

vy, and pride emerge later, once children have had the social experiences of observing these emotions in others or have been in situations that might evoke such feelings. These expressions have been observed in a wide range of cultural and ethnic groups (Eibl-Eibesfeldt, 1971).[1]

In early childhood, children learn to respond to new situations and to react and connect with a teacher, both very emotional experiences. Good teachers stimulate an emotional response to themselves and the curriculum that is a balance between interest and overwhelming fear. "Creating the 'right' emotional conditions is the path toward gaining access to the child's capacity for learning" (Fogel, 1980). Young children are not yet limited by **social mores** and standards of conduct that prevent them from sincere and truthful self-expression. Teachers observe children and learn how youngsters feel about facing their own feelings, the feelings of others, and the range of skills categorized as emotional growth.

OUR DIVERSE WORLD OUR DIVERSE WORLD OUR DIVERSE WORLD OUR DIVERSE WORLD OUR DIVERSE WORLD

[1]One is reminded of the universal qualities to be found in each of us in OUR DIVERSE WORLD. The challenge is to notice and celebrate our similarities and our differences—both are gifts.

Ability to Deal with Feelings

Dealing with feelings involves four steps. Each builds upon the other so that they follow a developmental sequence; the learning that takes place at one level affects the development of what follows. Figures 14.2 and 14.9 describe how the early childhood classroom and teacher help children deal effectively with their feelings.

To Notice and Label Feelings

This is the first step. The sobbing one- or two-year-old may have many reasons for feeling in distress. As parents recognize the cries of hunger, hurt, and fear, they name these feelings. The child will learn to notice what the feeling is and recognize it. Teachers know how to "read" children's faces and body language to give them the words for and ways to express those feelings. Chapter 6 has suggestions for becoming a skillful observer. Preschoolers are quite verbal and curious about language and ready to learn words that describe a wider range of feelings. They can learn "lonely," "scared," "silly," and "sad," and "happy." Labeling what one feels inside is a critical skill to learn. It is a healthy first-grader who can say, "I have tried to cut this string three times and the scissors aren't working. I am frustrated. I need some help!"

To Accept Feelings

Teachers recognize that children are capable of strong feelings. Children can feel overwhelmed by the very strength and intensity of a feeling, be it one of anger or of love. As children come to accept feelings, they learn how to handle the depth of the feeling and not let it overpower them. The changing nature of feelings is also part of accepting the feeling. It can be a source of comfort and relief for young children to discover that the strong emotion they experience now will pass. Adults who work with young children help them work through those feelings safely. Carlos feels sad as his mother prepares to leave. His teacher walks them to the door, then bends down and puts an arm around him as his mother waves goodbye. Acknowledging that he is sad, the teacher stays with Carlos, reminding him that his mother will return and that

the teacher will take care of him while he is at school. Since the child is allowed to feel the sadness that is natural in leave-taking, the tense feelings are over in a few minutes. The teacher smiles and encourages Carlos to find something fun to do. Once he has recovered his composure, the teacher can point this out, and Carlos can feel proud for having lived through and grown from saying goodbye. Acknowledgment of the feeling and his ability to accept it help give Carlos the confidence to move on.

To Express Feelings in an Appropriate Way

This is a two-part process. First, children must feel free to express their feelings; second, they must learn ways of expression that are suitable to their age and to the situation. Many beginning teachers are uncomfortable because children express themselves so strongly (and often aggressively). Yet the child who is passive and unable to express feelings freely should be of equal concern and should be encouraged in self-expression.

As children grow, they acquire the modes of expression that are developmentally appropriate for their age. Babies and toddlers without language cry to express their feelings; thus this type of crying calls for the same kind of immediate response given to other forms of communication in later years. Two-year-olds express their displeasure by pushes and shoves, while four-year-olds use their verbal power and argue. By six or seven, children learn to tell others—clearly and with reasons—what they are feeling. The ability to express feelings is intact, but the methods of expression change as children grow.

To Deal with the Feelings of Others

This is the culminating step in the development of emotional skills. Feelings are the spark of life in people: the flash of anger, the "ah-hah" of discovery, the thrill of accomplishment, the hug of excitement. Since recognizing and expressing emotions is closely interwoven, children who can distinguish among different emotions and have some experience in taking the perspective of others by observing their feelings develop *empathy*. To

Stage	Behavior	The Teacher Helps...
Alarm	Arousal and fear Confusion Swift mood changes	Notices when child is stressed (see changes in behavior). Listens. Offers words for child's feelings. Offers age-appropriate explanations. Is accepting of unpredictable behavior. Reassures child of teacher's constant availability. Alerts parents & others of child's state. Takes preventative actions to lessen other stressful events.
Appraisal	Attempts to understand the problem	Listens. Offers age-appropriate explanations. Helps child see situation more positively. May make a simple list of the problem. Reassures that the problem *will* be solved. Alerts other adults to the importance of the child's work.
Search	Looks for coping strategy Selects from what is at hand	Listens. Asks for the child's ideas. Helps child list possible solutions. Tells parents and others of child's solutions. Demonstrates self-control and coping skills her/himself. Encourages and enhances child's self-esteem.
Implementation	Tries out a coping strategy Applies a solution to the problem	Listens. Observes child's implementing a solution. Gives supportive feedback about relative success or failure of the plan. Helps child refine or revise strategy as needed. Encourages child's efforts.

FIGURE 14.5   Stages of and strategies for coping with stress: the teacher is observant of the child throughout, makes regular time to talk individually, and encourages the child to use art, books, and class members as supports.

respond with empathy can happen at a young age; for instance, very young children may cry or gather near the teacher when another playmate is hurt or sad, preschoolers smile at another's laughter, and kindergartners imagine themselves vividly in another's predicament during a story. Like the complex emotions discussed earlier, empathy requires cognitive abilities, such as seeing oneself as separate from other people (see the discussion of Erikson in Chapter 4) and also as connected in some way to others (see the discussion of Vygotsky in Chapter 4 and 13). Two- to five-year-olds can respond with empathy to the emotions of others. Older children, who are better able to put themselves in another's place (see the discussion of Piaget in Chapters 4 and 13) and who understand a wider range of emotions, can respond to others in distress. However, empathy is affected by early experience (Berk, 1995) and needs nurturing to grow. Helping children to tolerate and appreciate how different people express their emotions leads to understanding and cooperation.

Ability to Deal with Change

Change is inevitable. Many people fear or reject change. Children can learn that change is a constant part of their lives and to cope with the challenges changes present. Fear, insecurity, and uncertainty are some of the emotions felt when people experience changes in their lives or routines. Many times, these feelings arise from not

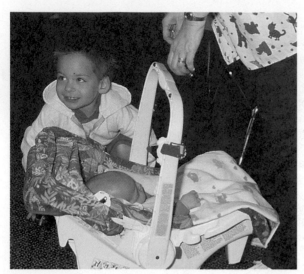

FIGURE 14.6 An awareness of their own power can bring enjoyable rewards to children. This boy enjoys kissing and saying good-bye to his baby brother as his mother drops him off at school.

knowing what to expect or how to behave or from not understanding different sets of values.

Inevitably, changes will happen in children's lives, bringing with them a measure of stress. The very act of being born is a change, marking the beginning of a life in which stress is part of the act of developmental achievement. Witness the toddler's numerous falls towards walking, the separation of parent and child at the nursery-school doorway, the concentration and frustrations of the six-year-old on roller skates. A measure of positive stress encourages a child to strive and achieve, to find out and discover.

Stress can arise from several factors, both internal (severe colic) or external (moving to a new home). Some stresses are acute in a child's life, such as a hospitalization, while others are chronic, as in an alcoholic household. Many variables are associated with different kinds of stress in children's lives. For instance, age and intellectual capacity as well as sex can influence a child's response to a stressful situation; research seems to indicate that male children are more vulnerable than female children (Honig, 1986). Housing,

poverty, and war are ecological stressors (see Chapter 15 for a discussion of violence). Family changes—the birth of a sibling, death or loss of a close family member, marriage problems and divorce—are sources of stress on a personal level.[1] Inept parenting practices that neglect or abuse children are especially troublesome as they hurt children and provide them with poor role models for learning how to cope with stress.

Yet stress and coping are part of the ability to deal with change. Much has been researched and written of stress in children's lives (Selye, 1982; Honig, 1986), and stages of dealing with stress have now been identified. Figure 14.5 lists the stages of stress and teacher strategies. Teachers help children to deal with change by supporting them in working through these stages, as they cope with changes in their lives at school, at home, and in the world at large.

For instance, teachers can help children accept change in several ways. Anticipating changes that are likely to occur and identifying the process for children is very important. "Junko, your mother will be leaving soon. We'll go looking for that favorite puzzle after you say good-bye to her." If the daily routine is altered, children should be notified. "We won't be having snacks inside today; let's use the patio table instead." When children are informed that change is anticipated, accepted, and not necessarily disrupting, they become more relaxed about handling the unpredictable. Teachers become resources for helping children cope in ways that are appropriate to the child and the situation at hand, be this by crying in sadness or fear, ignoring an unpleasant situation, finding a compromise, or accepting comfort.

Ability to Exercise Judgment

The ability to exercise judgment is an important skill, for it helps children make decisions and figure out what to do in new situations. On entering school, a child faces many decisions: Where shall I play? Who shall I play with? What if my friend wants to do something I know is wrong?

 OUR DIVERSE WORLD OUR DIVERSE WORLD OUR DIVERSE WORLD OUR DIVERSE WORLD OUR DIVERSE WORLD

[1]In working with children from potentially stress producing situations, it is important to remember and acknowledge the level of coping and resiliency so many children and their families possess.

Feeling	Behavioral Definition
1. Fear	Pale face, alert eyes, tense mouth, rigid body.
2. Surprise	Wide eyes, eyebrows uplifted, involuntary cry or scream, quick inhale of breath.
3. Anger	Red face, eyes staring, face taut, fists and jaw clenched, voice harsh or yelling, large gestures.
4. Joy	Smiling face, shining eyes, free and easy body movements, laughing.
5. Pride	Head held high, smiling face, jaunty walk or strut, tendency to announce or point out.
6. Embarrassment	Red face, glazed and downcast eyes, tight mouth, tense body, small and jerky movements, soft voice.
7. Sadness	Unsmiling face, downturned mouth, glazed and teary eyes, crying or rubbing eyes, limp body, movements are slow or small, voice is soft, trembly.
8. Anxiety	Puckered brow, pale face, tight mouth, whiny voice, jerky movements, lack of or difficulty in concentration.
9. Curiosity	Raised brow, shining eyes, perhaps tense body in absorption of the object of curiosity, often hand movements to touch and pick up object, sometimes mouth agape.

FIGURE 14.7   As we observe children's behavior, we understand how their feelings are expressed. Expressions of fear, anger, sadness, disgust, and happiness are universal, and the face can be read and understood long before children understand language.

Who will I turn to for help when I need it? Judgment is selecting what to do, when to do it, with whom to do it, and when to stop.

There is no easy way to teach children how to make decisions since each situation must be dealt with on an individual basis. The judgment a child exercises in choosing a friend to play with today may have other factors to consider tomorrow. Instead, teachers help children base their decisions on the best judgment they are capable of in each instance. One way to encourage decision-making is to provide opportunities for choice (see "Focus on Skills" on p. 453 for specific suggestions). Another aspect of judgment is a child's **self-regulation.** Recent research (Diaz, 1992) suggests that children can develop the capacity to plan and guide themselves. In contrast to self-control, in which we teach children to respond to an external rule, children's self-regulation is a combination of the cognitive and emotional realms. The teacher can encourage this process by serving as a Vygotsky-like mediator, making children participants in their own learning (thinking), and by supporting children's focus on self-competence (emotional). As they mature, children are able to sort out what judgments might be made here, what factors need to be considered there.

Enjoying One's Self and One's Power

Teachers want children to feel powerful—to know that they can master their lives and feel confident in their own abilities. This feeling of power is particularly important in the early years when so much in a child's eyes is out of reach, both literally and figuratively.

Responsibility and limits, however, go hand in hand with power. The child who is strong enough to hit someone has to learn not to use that strength unnecessarily. The child who shouts with glee also finds out that noise is unacceptable indoors. By holding children responsible for their own actions, teachers can help children enjoy their power and accept its limitations.

One kind of fantasy play most teachers encounter is that of superheroes. Common to young children as young as two, superhero play is exciting and rowdy, usually active and loud, playacting of heroic roles that give children powers they lack in everyday life. It is the embodiment of control and strength, even wisdom, and the parts to be played are clear for everyone involved.

Children's natural struggles for mastery and the attraction of rough-and-tumble play collide with teachers' concerns about fighting, aggression, and letting the play get out of hand. Kostelnik and others (1986) have described this special type of dramatic play in detail, offering suggestions for managing it:

● Help children recognize humane characteristics of superheroes.

● Discuss real heroes and heroines.

● Talk about the pretend world of acting.

● Limit the place and time for superhero play.

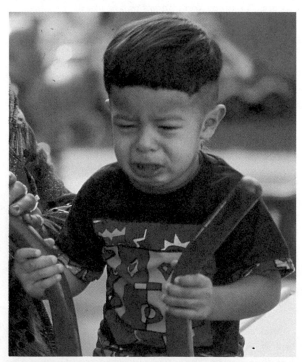

FIGURE 14.8 What causes children to become frightened? What can teachers do to handle children's emotional outbursts and crises?

● Explore related concepts.

● Help children de-escalate rough-and-tumble play.

● Make it clear that aggression is unacceptable.

● Give children control over their lives.

● Praise children's attempts at mastery.

In addition, teachers and parents are rightfully concerned with children's aggression and with their exposure to war and violence, both from the media and at home (Carlsson-Paige & Levin, 1987). Roughhousing and aggression have distinctly different patterns of behavior and should be recognized as such. Chapter 15 discusses the concerns of war play and violence in children's lives. Children need guidance to learn how to express themselves appropriately and exercise their growing powers responsibly.

Teachers can help children learn to appreciate and enjoy themselves. Each time a child is acknowledged, a teacher fosters that sense of uniqueness. "Carrie, you have a great sense of humor!" "Freddie, I love the way you sing so clearly." Saying it aloud reinforces in children the feeling that they are enjoyable to themselves and to others.

THE TEACHER'S ROLE

Considerations

The first step in helping children develop healthy emotional patterns is for adults to acquire and use a "feeling" vocabulary. Words of an emotional nature can be used to label and identify feelings as teachers talk with young children.

There are many ways to develop a list of words related to emotions. Figure 14.7 illustrates one way. Identify some of the feelings children express; then describe how the children look and act when experiencing those emotions. This helps to build a vocabulary and an understanding of children's emotional expressions.

Teachers can also become more attuned to the emotional climate in the classroom by knowing when and how feelings are expressed. To gain insights, teachers might ask themselves:

● What causes children in the class to become excited? Frightened? Calm? Loud? How does this knowledge guide curriculum planning? How can it help a teacher handle an unplanned event or change in the schedule?

● How do I anticipate children's emotional behavior? How do I follow through?

● What can teachers do to handle children's emotional outbursts and crises?

● What happens to the rest of the class when one teacher is occupied in an emotional incident with one or more children?

● What do I do when a child shows emotion? How do I feel when a child displays emotion?

● What types of emotions are most common with the young child?

In the early childhood setting, teachers help children come to grips with their strong feelings by discussing these feelings openly. They take the time to help children find names for feelings, to speak of their own feelings, and begin to be aware of the feelings of others.

When teachers perceive that children are ready to talk about their feelings, small group discussions or individual conversations can be helpful. Good books that touch upon sensitive issues (being excluded, being blamed, caring for others) offer possibilities for teachers and children to talk about feelings. Games, joking, and teasing can help children to feel relaxed and to explore feelings in an accepting way. Classroom problems (not sharing materials, pushing on the climbers) offer topics for discussion. The ability to express emotions verbally gives children the power to deal with them without resorting to inappropriate behavior.

Social referencing involves "relying on another person's emotional reaction to form one's own appraisal of an uncertain situation" (Berk, 1989). Making use of others' emotional cues can help infants to deal with stranger anxiety, toddlers to calm themselves after saying goodbye, preschoolers to avoid overreacting to a fall, and school-aged children to begin to recognize that people can feel more than one emotion at a time. Social referencing is a vital strategy in learning how to respond emotionally. The teacher who runs to the rescue after a minor spill can engender "learned helplessness" and overreaction. Conversely, the teacher who fails to respond to chil-

dren when they express emotions may give children the message that others' distress is to be ignored.

When adults show an understanding of feelings, children come to believe that adults are able to help them with their emotions, and the children become more at ease with their own feelings. When something painful happens to a child, adults can express what the child is feeling. "It really hurts to bend your knees now that you have scraped them." "You look so sad now that Gabi is playing with someone else." Children then become familiar with ways to express how they feel in a variety of emotional situations.

Adults can also help children become aware of the emotional states of others. "Look! Paul is crying. Let's go over and see if we can comfort him." Teachers can encourage children to help care for each other's hurts and needs. A child can ease the pain of a friend by sitting nearby as a wound is cleansed or by giving a hug when an achievement is made. Teachers must be sure to allow children to express their concern and to help them learn ways to respond to the emotional needs of others.

Curriculum Planning for Emotional Growth

In the Environment

Teachers set up their classrooms and yards to promote emotional growth. Materials and activities enhance self-esteem and self-expression. How activities are presented and carried out is also a factor. In looking at the class setting, it is important to remember that the "how" is as critical as the "what" in curriculum planning for emotional development. Refer to Figure 14.9 to see how curriculum can be developed to encourage emotional growth.

Indoors. Select materials that enhance self-expression. Indoors, children's inner thoughts and feelings are best expressed through:

● *The Arts.* Clay or dough lets children ventilate feelings, since it can be pounded, pinched, poked, slapped, and manipulated. Fingerpainting and painting on broad surfaces with large brushes encourage a freedom of movement that

---

Curriculum for Emotional Skill Development

Indoor Activities

Art: Reflect children's expressions and see how they are feeling.
- "You look like you are enjoying yourself."
- "Your face tells me that was funny (disappointing, etc.) to you."
  Write what children say about their work. Display it on their creations, at the bottom of a picture, alongside a sculpture.

Blocks: Be there/be aware/ask them how it feels when:
- you make a structure by yourself
- it falls down
- someone knocks it over (accidentally and on purpose)
- someone laughs

Discovery/Science:
- Use the words "curious" and "proud" to describe what children do as they explore and experiment with materials.
- Use the computer program "Choices, Choices"

Dramatic Play: Give children freedom, variety, and reflection.
- Have a full-length mirror, point it out to see themselves often.
- Provide a variety of role-play materials.
- Include wall displays with multicultural, bias-free pictures.

Language/Library:
a. Have books that reflect a variety of feelings and ways to deal with them, such as:
   Fear: *There's a Nightmare in My Closet* (Mayer); *Storm in the Night* (Stolz)
   Self-Esteem: *The Growing Story* (Krauss); *Ruby* (Glen); *Things I Like* (Browne)
   Loss: *The Maggie B* (Keats); *Amos and Boris* (Steig)
   Change: *Changes, Changes* (Hutchins); *Sam Is My Half-Brother* (Boyd)
   Friendship: *Two Is a Team* (Bemelman); *That's What Friends Are For* (Kidd); *Big Al* (Clements)
   Security: *One Step, Two* (Zolotow); *The Bundle Book* (Zolotow); *Rise and Shine, Mariko-chan* (Tomioka)
   Choice: *Best Enemies* (Leverich); *Did You Carry the Flag Today, Charly?* (Caudill)
b. Include books on themes, particularly when a child or group is dealing with an emotional issue:
   Death: *Death and Dying* (Open Family Series, by Sara Bonnet Stein); *The Dead Bird* (Brown); *Nana Upstairs, Nana Downstairs* (de Paoli)
   Divorce: *Two Places to Sleep* (Schuchman)
   Doctor/Dentist: *Curious George Goes to the Hospital* (H.A. Rey); *Your Turn, Doctor* (Robison and Perez); *My Doctor* (Harlow)
   Moving: *Mitchell Is Moving* (Sharmat); *Jamie* (Zolotow); *The Leaving Morning* (Johnson)
   New Baby: *Baby Sister for Frances* (Hoban); *I Want to Tell You About My Baby* (Banish); *Peter's Chair* (Keats)
   Nightmares: *Where the Wild Things Are* (Sendak): *In the Night Kitchen* (Sendak); *There's a Nightmare in My Closet* (Mayer)
   Spending the Night: *Ira Sleeps Over* (Waber)
c. When reading stories, stop and ask how a particular character is feeling.
d. Tie in children's lives to books. For example, have children bring a special object or toy to share. A warm cuddly can be tied into the stories of *Goodnight Moon* (Brown) or *Teddy Bear's Picnic* (Kennedy).

Outdoor Activities
Movement:
a. "How would you walk if you were glad?" (sad, mad, worried, giggly?)
b. "A Tiger Hunt" (this game is known by many names). Go on a "hunt" with children, using their bodies to describe

---

FIGURE 14.9 Whether two years old or in grade two, children learn about their feelings when teachers plan programs that encourage self-expression.

such movements as opening/shutting a gate, swishing through tall grass, climbing a tree, swimming in water, going through mud, looking in a cave, running home so that the "tiger" doesn't catch us.

Music:

a. Choose several cuts of music that differ in tone and type. Ask children how each makes them feel, then have them show you with their bodies.
b. Write songs/chants about feelings.

Routines and Transitions

1. Respect children's feelings of anticipation.
   - Have a chart of daily activities.
   - Discuss upcoming field trips or visitors ahead of time when possible.
2. When unexpected changes occur, discuss them with individuals and the group.
   - "Andy isn't here today. He has a sore throat, so he is staying home. Esther will be the teacher in his group today."
3. When possible, let the children set the stage for themselves by encouraging them to take responsibility for known sequences.
   - Use the toilet without you there constantly
   - Set their own snack table
   - Get flowers for the table
   - Help clean a place for the next child/ren
4. Provide time for self-help *without unnecessary hurry*.
   - Put on their own name tag.
   - Wash and dry their own hands.
   - Dress themselves—jacket for outdoors, shoes after nap, and so on.
   - Take care of their rest items—blanket and stuffed toy in a labelled pillowcase, books back in a basket or bookshelf...

Group Times

1. Use children's faces as a focus.
   - Practice facial expressions with mirrors, either hand mirrors for each or each pair, or a larger one up front.
   - Have them draw facial expressions on oval shapes and tell about it to the group.
   - Call out feelings, having them show you on their faces.
   - Sing "If You're Happy and You Know It,..." with a variety of feelings. Ask children what situations have them feel each.
   - Show photographs of children's faces/expressions and ask group to tell you how that person is feeling, why, and so on.
2. Try idea completions.
   - "I feel glad when..." (also mad, bad, sad, safe, excited, scared, silly)
   - "I like school when..." (also don't like; also my friend, mom, it)
   - "I wish...", "The best thing I can do..."
3. Use situations to elicit feelings.
   - "Here's a picture of a family. What are they doing? How does the child feel? The grown-ups? What happened?"
   - "I'm going to cover part of the picture of the face to see if you can guess what expression it's going to be."
   - "These are cards of situations that the teachers have seen happen in our class. Let's read them and then ask ourselves, 'How do I feel? What can I say? What can I do?'"

FIGURE 14.9   *Continued*

permits children to express themselves more fully.

● *Blocks/Manipulatives.* Vary the materials regularly to help children adjust to change and to allow them to exercise judgment about playing with different materials. A variety of props—motor vehicles, animals, people, furniture—gives children the opportunity to reenact what they see of the world.

● *Discovery/Science.* Often science projects are geared toward cognitive and language development. This need not always be so; some activities can focus on feelings. Caring for pets, for instance, brings out feelings of nurturing and protectiveness. Making "feeling clocks" can emphasize emotions. Blank clock faces are used as a base upon which children draw or paste pictures of people showing various emotional states. Display these at children's eye level so they can be changed frequently.

● *Dramatic Play.* Home-life materials give children the props they need to express how they see their own world of family, parents, siblings. Mirrors, telephones, and dress-up clothes encourage children to try out their emotional interests on themselves as well as each other.

● *Language/Library.* Stories and books in which characters and situations reflect a wide range of emotions are readily available (see Figure 13.23 and Figure 14.9 for some suggested titles). Children enjoy looking at photographs of people and guessing what the person in the photo is feeling. This encourages children to find words that label feelings; their responses can be recorded and posted nearby. Once children seem at ease in using feeling words, the discussion can continue when the teacher poses the question, "Why do you think this person is sad/happy/angry?"

● *Music/Movement.* Music of all kinds encourages self-expression and permits an endless variety of movement and feelings to be shown openly and freely. Children can be introduced to classi-cal, ethnic, jazz, or rock music while dancing with scarves or streamers or marching with rhythm sticks, as well as singing and dancing to children's recordings.[1] Since musical knowledge is the earliest of human intellectual competencies (see Chapter 13), music can be part of the curriculum for children as young as toddlers. Pounding on drums and dancing both relieve tension in a socially acceptable manner. More structured activities, such as showing children how to use musical instruments, must be balanced by plenty of freedom for individual musical expression.

Outdoors. The environment itself encourages self-expression. Whether in the sand or on a swing, children seem to open up emotionally as they relax in the physical freedom the out-of-doors fosters. Outdoor games are usually highly emotionally charged. Running, chasing, and the dramatic play of superheroes provide emotional release for children.

The outdoor area is an ideal place for large, noisy, and messy activities. It is ideal for tracing body outlines, for instance. These life-size portraits of each child reinforce self-concepts and encourage a feeling of pride in one's self. Woodworking is an outdoor activity that allows children to vent anger and tension. Nails won't be hurt no matter how hard they are pounded; there is satisfaction in sawing a piece of wood into two pieces. Music offers numerous opportunities for self-expression. Children can dance with scarves or streamers, march through the yard with drums pounding, imitate Wild Things, make a maypole around the tree, and create a Chinese dragon for a parade. A rich musical repertoire of band instruments, phonograph records, tapes, and voices can stimulate children to pretend to be elephants, tigers, and dinosaurs, as well as circus performers and ballet artists. Even a simple project such as water painting becomes an avenue for self-expression as children use paint brushes and buckets of water on trees, cement, and buildings, giving them all a fresh coat of "paint."

OUR DIVERSE WORLD OUR DIVERSE WORLD OUR DIVERSE WORLD OUR DIVERSE WORLD OUR DIVERSE WORLD

[1]Music provides the perfect way to celebrate OUR DIVERSE WORLD—all cultures have music *and* it is all different. Carefully choose tapes for group times, nap times, and for background music, with an awareness and ear for diversity.

Routines, Transitions, and Groups

These three times of the curriculum have one thing in common: changes. Since they all involve shifts from one kind of activity to another, there is a sense of uncertainty and thus they are emotionally charged. Children's behavior in these times is most likely to be unfocused. Here you will find the wandering and chasing, even oppositional or withdrawn behavior. Teachers help children best by creating an atmosphere of trust and clarity. Giving a child ideas of what to do ("Each of you can sponge a table now," or "You can sit on my lap while your Dad leaves today.") helps a child feel a sense of confidence in managing through a routine or transition. Specific suggestions for group behavior, including those generated from the class itself, inspire success. Finally, changes require teachers to be alert and flexible. As family caregiver McCormick (1993) puts it:

> Flexibility is the cornerstone of successful home child care, and an essential building block in provider/child relationships. Flexibility allows me to adapt to parents' changing schedules, children's changing sleep patterns, and even to alter the day's activities with the changing weather. By remaining flexible, especially to the children's needs, I have built a deep, personal relationship with each of the children I care for. I find ways to adapt to their schedules as much as possible instead of [always] forcing them into a [rigid] routine of the center.

Acknowledging a child's right to strong emotions and understanding a child's reactions to changes in these daily activities help children become comfortable and competent. Figure 14.9 outlines how specific materials and activities can be developed for emotional growth.

Focus on Skills

Emotional development is a lifelong process, requiring experience with one's own feelings. Each child has a unique emotional foundation, which the knowledgeable teacher assesses. Only then can teachers plan curriculum with realistic goals in mind for the children in that class. The goals teachers set for children will determine which emotional skills will be the focus as they individualize the curriculum. Maggie has difficulty with changes in the routine, Caroline never cries, no matter how she hurts, and Clyde screams when he is frustrated. To help children like these learn to *express and control their emotions*, teachers plan programs like those illustrated in Figure 14.9.

Making choices is another worthwhile skill as an emotional focus. Like any skill, it takes thought and practice. To teach children to make choices, Simon (1994) suggests examining the process you use to make your own. "Think about your choice to become a teacher. What influenced your choice? What other options did you consider? What were the pros and cons of each of your options? Did your choice turn out as you expected? Would you make the same choice today? Why or why not?" To help children make choices and decisions, focus on a step-by-step process:

1. Help children define the situation by turning it into a question. (What can we do to fix up our playground?)

2. Make a list of options or alternatives. (Plant flowers, get more bikes, add more sand toys.)

FIGURE 14.10   Teachers and children explore emotions together.

3. Ask the children to think of what might happen for each option. (Flowers would look pretty . . . but we would have to water them.)

4. Make a choice. (This is the key point!)

5. Check later to see how the choice turned out. (Look how nice the yard is! or Darn, when we forgot to water, they died.)

Figure 7.13 offers a more detailed example of this process in social problem-solving.

Use of Themes

One particular theme, that of "Who Am I?", is useful when developing curriculum for emotional growth. Figure 14.11 outlines how this theme can be incorporated in many ways, both indoors and out. A number of other units can be developed to extend the theme of "Who Am I?". Some of these are: "My Body," "The Senses," "The Community Where I Live," and so on.

● UNIT 14-1 Checkpoint

Emotional growth is a crucial part of children's development in the early years. Emotions develop as children respond to life experiences with a full range of feelings. An undifferentiated state of emotions during infancy evolves into a more refined array of feelings in childhood. Children gain control of their emotions through maturation and experience.

Emotional skills learned in the early years are: the ability to deal with feelings and with change, to be able to exercise judgment, to know and enjoy one's power. Teachers help children develop these skills by building a vocabulary of feeling words, by an awareness of the emotional climate in the classroom, by talking with children about their feelings, and by helping children sense the emotional framework of others. Self-esteem and self-concepts are enhanced by positive emotional growth.

Curriculum planning for emotional development involves an emphasis on many avenues for self-expression in the class setting, sometimes focusing on one particular emotional skill or theme that emphasizes emotional expression.

Ask yourself:

● What are the principles of emotional development? How will the 4 Is of I, independence, initiative, and interaction help in my teaching?

● What emotional skills are learned in early childhood?

● What is the role of the teacher in emotional development?

● What are three ways to plan curriculum that will enhance emotional growth?

● UNIT 14-2 SOCIAL GROWTH

THE DEVELOPMENT OF SOCIALIZATION

Social development is the process through which children learn what behavior is acceptable and expected. A set of standards is imposed on the child at birth that reflects the values of the family and the society in which the child lives.

Theorists from Freud, Piaget, and Bandura (see Chapter 4) to Gardner and Sternberg (see Chapter 13) acknowledge the relationship between social development and learning. Indeed, enhancing social intelligence "builds a set of skills that may be among the most essential for life success of many kinds" (Gardner in Coleman, 1990). How does it happen?

Social development begins in the crib. Within the first few months of life, the infant smiles, coos, and plays in response to a human voice, face, or physical contact. Young children are influenced from birth by a conscious attempt on the part of adults to guide them in ways that society expects. Parents attempt to transmit behavior patterns that are characteristic of their culture, religion, gender, educational, and ethnic backgrounds. Children imitate what they see; they adapt social expectations to their own personality.

This process—called socialization—includes learning appropriate behavior in a number of different settings (see Figure 14.12). Children learn very early to discriminate between the expectations of each environment. At school, free exploration of play materials is encouraged, but in a

THEME: WHO AM I?

1. *Art:* Body outlines
   Facial expressions pictures—variations: (a) look in a mirror, (b) have a blank face and you draw in the features, (c) have a face partly done and you complete, (d) magazine cut-outs
   Face painting
   Fingerprinting (hand and foot)
2. *Blocks:* People, furniture, structures people live in
   Pictures of same
3. *Cooking:* Share ethnic dishes (tortillas, pasta, things you like to cook at home)
4. *Discovery/science:* Height–weight charts
   Drawing around hands and feet and comparing sizes
   Doing body outlines of a large group of children, each with a different color, and comparing sizes
   Mapping—where people live, charts of phone numbers
   Put out a globe
   Weather–homes connections
5. *Dramatic play:* Lots of mirrors
   A variety of dress-up play for taking on a variety of roles and seeing how they feel
6. *Language/library:* Have children write books about themselves—variations: (a) use *Is This You?* (Krauss) as model, (b) loose-leaf binder of their own books they can add to themselves, (c) "My house is me" as title, (d) families
   Books on families of various sorts; books about other children and what they are like (Corduroy lives in an apt.)
   Where animals live
   Feelings about where children live
7. *Manipulatives:* Puzzles with body parts, with people and clothing
   Self-help skills with dressing frames
   Encourage children to build a structure that things could live in; e.g. lincoln logs.
8. *Sand and water play:* Bubble-blowing
   Using your bodies to build—digging with hands and feet, encouraging sensory exploration
   Use body parts to help you, like using your foot on the shovel.
9. *Swinging/climbing:* All these activities use body parts; teachers emphasize this when watching children at play
10. *Games:* Rolling the barrel, rolling yourself   Hide and Seek and Tag
    Mother May I?   Dramatic play games with family members
11. *Large block-building:* Making house-like structures
    Using vehicles that need your body's force to move
12. *Woodworking:* Using body parts
    Make a map board of school, neighborhood, a city
13. *Routines:* Self-help: Awareness of what you can do by yourself; by definition all "Who Am I?" tasks; teachers use verbal and musical reinforcement
14. *Transitions:* Use physical characteristics of children for transitions—"Everyone who has brown eyes . . . freckles . . . blue jeans can go outside . . . "
15. *Group times:* "Head and shoulders"
    Description games—describe someone and guess who it is as a game "I'm thinking of someone" or with song "Mary Has a Red Dress"
    "Little Tommy (Tina) Tiddlemouse," voice recognition
    "Good morning little Teddy Bear," with bear going around circle and saying names
16. *Snacktime/bedtime:* Mark places with names and pictures, such as beds or placemats
    Try to coordinate the nametag, bed, or placemat with symbol on cubby

FIGURE 14.11   A child's school experience is strongly related to how emotional events are handled.

SOCIAL DEVELOPMENT TIMELINE

Infant-Toddler	Preschooler	Primary Child
Response to Other's Distress		
Reacts emotionally by experiencing what the other seems to feel	Begins to make adjustments that reflect the realization that the other person is different and separate from themselves	Takes other's personality into account and shows concern for other's general condition
Peer Interaction		
• First encounters mutual inspection • First social contacts • (18 mos.) growth in sensitivity to peer play • (2 yr.) able to direct social acts to two children at once (beginning of social interaction)	• Adjustment in behavior to fit age/behavior of other • (3+ yr.) friendship as momentary • (3–5 yr.) beginning of friendship as constant	• Friend as someone who will do what you want • Beginning of friend as one who embodies admirable, constant characteristics
Social Roles		
• (10–20 days) imitation of adults • (3 mos.) gurgle in response to others • (6 mos.) social games based on imitation • (18 mos.) differentiation between reality and pretend play • (2 yr.) make doll do something as if it were alive	• (3 yr.) make a doll carry out several roles or activities • (4–5 yr.) act out a social role in dramatic play and integrate that role with others (mom & baby)	• (6 yr.) integrate one role with two complementary roles: doctor, nurse, & sick person • (8 yr.) growing understanding that roles can influence behavior (doctor whose daughter is a patient)

FIGURE 14.12 A timeline of social development for the ages of infancy through the primary years. (Special thanks to Gay Spitz.)

church pew it is not. Grocery stores, circuses, libraries, and Grandma's home call for a repertoire of fitting behaviors.

In general, the socialization process in a school setting revolves around a child's relationships with other people. During this time of their lives, children work out a separate set of relationships with adults other than their parents. They also establish different relationships with adults than they do with other children.

Through socialization, the customary roles that boys and girls play are also transmitted. Children come to understand how teachers, mommies, daddies, grandparents, males, and females are expected to act.[1]

Children also learn social attitudes at an early age. They learn to enjoy being with people and participating in social activities. At the same time, young children can also develop attitudes of bias, and it is in these early years that prejudicial behavior often begins (Derman-Sparks, 1989). Be honest with your feelings, for the teacher's role with negative comments, unfair acts, and exclusivity based on race, gender, or ability is crucial in combating this kind of socialization. Favorable attitudes toward people and a strong desire to be part

OUR DIVERSE WORLD OUR DIVERSE WORLD OUR DIVERSE WORLD OUR DIVERSE WORLD OUR DIVERSE WORLD

[1]Early childhood professionals need to be aware of the difference between a child developing a sexual identity and with children's sex role development. One needs to be able to communicate the difference to parents, and have an awareness of how different cultures may have differing notions about sex role development.

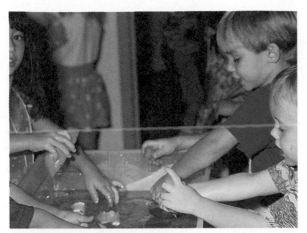

FIGURE 14.13 Through play, children learn to get along with one another.

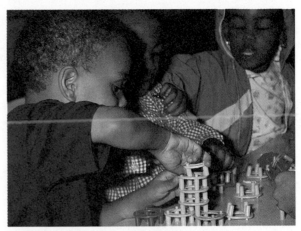

FIGURE 14.14 Socialization involves learning how to solve problems and interact with others, particularly in conflict resolution.

of the social world, to be with others, are established in the early years.

The child's social development is an integral part of the total growth process. Cognitive and social growth are related. In order to consider the consequences of one's actions, for instance, there must be a certain level of intellectual understanding. According to Smith (1982), the manner in which children define their appearance influences their attitudes toward themselves and their relationships with others. Emotional development is affected also. When children conform to the behavior expected of them, they have a greater self-acceptance and like themselves better. Language, of course, is what allows the socially developing child to communicate with others as part of the social process.

In the early years, children mature socially in discernible developmental stages. From birth to age three, children's interest in others begins with a mutual gazing and social smile in the early months (birth through eight months), continues with an exploration of others as well as some anxious behavior around strangers in the crawler and walker stages (8 to 18 months), and develops into an enjoyment of peers and adults along with an awareness of others' rights and feelings as a toddler and two-year-old (18 months to 3 years) (Lally, 1987).

In the preschool years, children learn to "control their aggressive impulses, think about others besides themselves, and resist doing what they

shouldn't" (Schickedanz, et al, 1990). This translates into four basic expectations: (1) that they will show interest in others, (2) that they will learn right from wrong, (3) that they will learn to get along with others, and (4) that they will learn a role for themselves that takes into consideration their own unique self—sex, race, ethnicity, and abilities.

Children of the primary years (five to eight years) show an increased interest in peers and social competence, and group rules become important. The development of a social conscience and of fairness rounds out the primary-grade developmental milestones (Bredekamp, 1987).

It is through play (as discussed in Chapter 11) that children learn much of their social repertoire. Dramatizations, role playing, and dramatic play provide opportunities to act out many roles and help children deal with some of the demands placed upon them. In play, the child experiments with options: finding out what it feels like to be the boss, to be the baby, to behave in ways that might otherwise be unacceptable. Carla was the oldest of three children and had many "big girl" expectations placed on her within the family setting. At school, Carla enjoyed being the baby, acting out a helpless infant role whenever she could. Under the guise of play, children, like Carla, rehearse for life without suffering the real-life consequences. Figure 14.12 traces the route of social development from infancy through the primary years.

Peer Relationships

For the young child, social development means moving away from adults toward people of one's own age. During the early years, the child learns to socialize outside the family; social contacts outside the home reinforce the enjoyment of social attitudes and prepare the child for future group activity. The intricacies of peer relationships are detailed in Cary Buzzelli's Focus Box.

Peer interactions, that is, associating with friends of the same age group, become important to the child once infancy and early toddlerhood are past. Through peer interactions, children can identify with models who are like themselves and can learn from each other's behavior. Friends provide models for imitation, for comparison, for confirmation of themselves, and are a source of support.

Playing with other children begins with solitary parallel play at around two years of age, where two or more children are in the same area with each other but do not initiate social interaction. By the ages of three and four, more interaction takes place: there is conversation as well as cooperation in playing together.

There are stages in children's friendships. In the early years, friendship first starts at an **undifferentiated** level, when children are egocentric and a friend is more of the moment. This gives way to a **unilateral** level; a good friend does what the child wants the friend to do. Toward the end of early childhood, friendship becomes more **reciprocal,** involving some give-and-take in a kind of two-way cooperation. Listen to these children trying out their friendship:

Chris: I'll be the teacher, you be the kid.

Suzanne: NO! I want to be the teacher, too.

Chris: No! No! You can't be the teacher, to cause . . . then there'd be no kids.

Suzanne: OK . . . Next time, I get to be the teacher.

Chris: Maybe! OK, everybody go wash your hands for snack time. Suzanne, you can pass out your very nutrimous snack to everybody.

Suzanne: Superfasmic, I'm the boss of snack.

A peer group is important for a number of reasons. Social development is enhanced because a child learns to conform to established social standards outside of his home setting. The expectations of the larger society are reinforced. In order to become autonomous, the child must also learn to achieve independence from the family, especially parents. Young children must also come to understand themselves as part of society. Their self-concepts are enlarged by a group of peers as they see how others respond to them and treat them.

Smith (1982) states that three trends emerge in the way children relate to each other. First, children become more sensitive to their play partners; then they begin to use language more effectively in their interactions. Finally, cooperative play increases as parallel play decreases. Rubin (1980) defines three stages of social understanding through which children pass: (1) they shift from a preoccupation with self to an awareness of the thoughts and feelings of another; (2) they shift from the observable, physical qualities of the play partner to an awareness of their friend's less obvious characteristics; and (3) they begin to perceive the friendship as long lasting.

SOCIAL SKILLS IN EARLY CHILDHOOD

Social skills are strategies children learn that enable them to behave appropriately in many environments. They help children learn to initiate or manage social interaction in a variety of settings and with a number of people.

Social cognition plays a part in the development of social skills. It is the application of thinking to personal and social behavior; it is giving meaning to social experience. Nadia used the cognitive skill of memory when she wanted to play with Paul, a very popular four-year-old. She remembered Paul's interest in the rope swing and challenged him to swing higher than she did. Bruno, on the other hand, is well known throughout the group for his inability to share materials. When Sandy wanted to play with the small fire trucks (Bruno's favorite toys), she used cognitive skills to negotiate the use of one truck. Social cognition requires children to interpret events and make decisions, to consider the impact of their behavior on others, and to consider the cause as well as the consequence of an action. Cognitive skills are necessary when we ask children to seek alternative solutions to social problems: "How else could you ask him for a turn, Pete?" These are all

Helping Children's Friendships

Cary Buzzelli

Research indicates that children who have positive relations with their peers are more successful in school and are better socially adjusted later in life. But not all children are readily accepted by their peers. Indeed, some children are actively rejected by classmates. What's a teacher to do? Can we "force" children to be included, or "muscle" a group of youngsters to let everybody else play?

Through careful observation, teachers *can* determine appropriate ways to assist rejected children in becoming more socially competent. For example, in one classroom of 4-year-olds, Carlos and Felicia were seldom asked to join in the play by other children. When Carlos approached, the children seemed to ignore him. And when Felicia came near, children often told her to get away. The teachers wondered why both children seemed to be unattractive to their peers, and so watched the two closely.

They discovered that Carlos and Felicia were being rejected for very different reasons. Carlos appeared to lack the skills needed to initiate and maintain play. Whenever anyone did approach him, he would drop his eyes or respond in a negative manner, such as frowning or turning away. Once play was started, he appeared to not know how to "keep it going", he would stand and watch, not adding to the play with his actions or ideas. Felicia, on the other hand, was very actively in-volved—too much so. She was aggressive during interactions with the other children. Either physically or verbally, she would take over the play, interrupting others with her ideas and grabbing at toys and materials.

The teachers realized that different strategies were necessary to help Carlos and Felicia. Coaching Carlos in positive ways of initiating play with other children would help, such as getting him more comfortable with someone's invitation so that he might respond with a smile instead of a frown. Also, to model how to keep the play going with ideas or additional materials could help him play cooperatively and for longer periods of time. Felicia could also use a teacher's role model, helping her to stay calm in situations that frustrate her or using her words instead of grabbing to get what she wants. Indeed, a teacher alongside Felicia might help her watch how other children "get their way" and still play together.

Not all children need or even want to be "social superstars," yet every child needs to gain the confidence and competence to engage in positive relations with peers. Being able to interact with others will greatly enhance young children's social and emotional development.

Cary Buzzelli of Indiana University is a frequent contributor to Young Children *and a long-time researcher in issues of friendship and self-esteem.*

social cognition skills, and they serve as the basis for the acquisition of other skills.

In an early childhood setting, children learn a great deal about social behavior and expectations. They develop many skills as they learn to interact with adults other than their parents and children other than their siblings. Social skills emerge as children learn to function as members of a group and as they come to understand themselves as social beings. The social skills of early childhood, then, are complex and change with the age and experience of the individual child. Broadly, the following are some of the specific skills and values young children learn.

Skills Learned with Adults

In their relationship with adults, children learn:

● They can stay at school without parents.

● They can enjoy adults other than parents and respond to new adults.

● Adults will help in times of trouble or need.

● Adults will assist in learning social protocol.

● Adults will keep children from being hurt and from hurting others.

FIGURE 14.15 Peer relationships are a source of pleasure and support. As social understanding develops, children shift from a preoccupation with themselves to an awareness of the thoughts and feelings of their friends.

● Adults will not always take a side or solve the problem.

● Adults will work with them to solve problems.

● Adults believe that every child has a right to a satisfying social experience at school.

Skills Learned with Peers

In their relationship with other children, children learn:

● There are different approaches to others; some work, some don't.

● Interactive skills, and how to sustain the relationship.

● How to solve conflicts in ways other than retreat or force.

● How to share materials, equipment, other children, friends, teachers, and ideas.

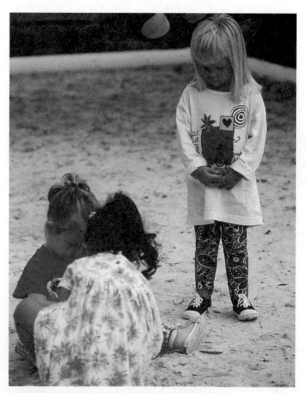

FIGURE 14.16 Rejection is a common form of social behavior in young children. In the early years children need to deal with the feelings that arise when they are told, "You can't play with us."

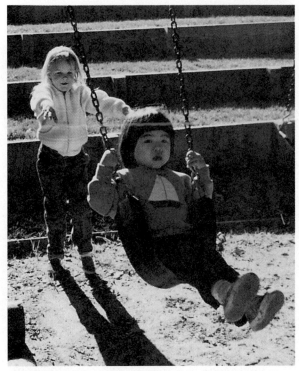

FIGURE 14.17 Cooperation: "You push me, then I'll push you!"

FIGURE 14.18 Friendship: "We can work on the painting together."

- A group identity (center room class, Mrs. T's group, four-year-old group).
- To follow a daily schedule and pattern.
- To adapt to school routines.
- School rules and expectations.
- Interaction and participatory skills: how to enter and exit from play.
- To respect the rights, feelings, and property of others.
- How to work together as a group, during clean-up time, in preparation for an event, etc.
- How to deal with delay of gratification: how to wait.

Skills Learned As an Individual

As individuals, children learn:

- To take responsibility for self-help, self-care.
- To initiate their own activities and to make choices.
- To work alone in close proximity to other children.
- To negotiate.
- To cope with rejection, hurt feelings, disappointment.
- To communicate in verbal and nonverbal ways, and when to use communication skills.
- To test limits other people set.

- How to achieve mutually satisfying play.
- Self-defense, and how to assert their rights in socially acceptable ways.
- How to take turns and how to communicate desires.
- Negotiating skills.
- How to be helpful to peers with shoelaces, information, and by modeling behavior.
- To anticipate/avoid problems.
- Realistic expectations of how other children behave and respond toward self.

Skills Learned in a Group

In groups, children learn:

- How to take part as a member and not as an individual.
- That there are activities that promote group association (stories, music).

- Their own personal style of peer interaction: degree, intensity, frequency, quality.

- To express strong feelings in socially acceptable ways.

- To manage social freedom.

Specific skills within these four areas include the social/moral aspects of nurturance, kindness, and sharing (Melson & Fogel, 1988; Krough, 1985; Smith, 1986; Pelligrini & Glickman, 1990; and Kemple, 1991). As children get older, these skills become more specific, including truth telling, taking turns or reciprocity, promise keeping, property rights, and rules (DeVries & Kohlberg, 1987).

THE TEACHER'S ROLE

Considerations

A major role for the early childhood teacher is to see that children have enjoyable social contacts and to help motivate children toward a desire to be with others. The early childhood setting affords children numerous learning opportunities for social development.

The teacher has an important role to play as children learn the give-and-take of social interaction. In the role of social organizer, the teacher creates a physical and interpersonal environment that promotes the development of children's social skills.

A first consideration is to *plan and arrange a social environment* to enhance appropriate social behaviors. To stimulate child-initiated activities, self-care, and group responsibility, the use of low, open shelves and furniture scaled to size is a necessary ingredient. Group activities, toys, materials, and placement of furniture should be structured in ways that allow children to play alone or with someone. Many areas lend themselves to group play, such as dramatic play corners or blocks. Books, puzzles, and easels, on the other hand, can be a singular experience or can generate associative play. Cooperative play is suggested in the environment when there is more than one piece of equipment. The placement of two telephones, three wagons, and eight fire fighter hats fosters child-child interactions. The teacher must also allow enough time in the daily schedule for children to get thoroughly involved in playing with one another.

A second part of the teacher's role in social development is to *help children develop trust*. Trusting in themselves, their peers, and their teachers is a part of learning about social relationships. Teachers enhance children's social knowledge as they gradually improve their sense of trust. To do this, Buzzelli and File (1989) recommend the following:

1. *Help children recognize their own needs.* Notice children who need to clarify their wishes; ask uninvolved children with whom they'd like to play; help arguing children say how they feel and what they want.

2. *Help children become aware of their social goals and the goals of others.* Teachers can aid children by helping them recognize their choices; they can also mediate so that others can express themselves.

3. *Help children develop effective social skills.* Provide a model for listening, for choosing another place to play, or for going along with another's ideas; help children find ways to stand their ground and also accommodate (see "Focus on Skills" on p. 467 for ideas about sharing).

4. *Help children recognize others' emotions.* Children become flooded with their own strong feelings and are not likely to notice someone else's emotions in the heat of the moment; teachers can help children see another's face or hear a tone of voice, thus beginning to "read" another person.

5. *Reflect with children on how their behavior affects others by pointing out what is predictable in their interactions.* Young children do not always "connect the dots" between their behavior and others' reactions. When a teacher makes a statement without disapproval, the child can then understand the effects of their behavior on others: "Wow! When you use that loud voice, I see the kids looking scared, and then they tell you not to play here."

6. *Highlight children's success by helping them learn to monitor their own behavior.* It can help children to see their successful social encounters as well as the strategies that didn't work. "When you asked them if you could play, they said, 'No!' But then you went and got shovels for everyone and that worked!"

7. *Avoid telling children who their "friends" are.* Early childhood teachers encourage children to learn about friendship; however, "legislating friendship" often backfires. Telling children "We're all friends here," or "Friends share their things with everyone" denies the distinction between positive, friendly experiences and friendship. *Classmate* and *friend* are not the same word.

The teacher's role in social development is also one of *facilitating children's interactions and interpreting their behavior.* In order to help young children understand each other and to pave the way for continued cooperation, the teacher reports and reflects on what is happening. In the classroom setting, during an active, free-play period, the teacher might:

Reflect the Action:	*Say:*
Call attention to the effect one child's behavior is having on another.	"Randy, when you scream like that, other children become frightened and afraid to play with you."
Show approval and reinforce positive social behavior.	"I like the way you carefully stepped over their block building, Dannetta."
Support a child in asserting her rights.	"Chrystal is hanging on to the doll because she isn't finished playing yet, Wilbur."
Support a child's desire to be independent.	"I know you want to help, Keyetta, but Sammy is trying to put his coat on by himself."
Acknowledge and help children establish contact with others.	"Omar would like to play, too. That's why he brought you another bucket of water. Is there a place where he can help?"
Reflect back to a child the depth of his feelings and what form those feelings might take.	"I know George made you very angry when he took your sponge, but I can't let you throw water at him. What can you tell him? What words can you use to say you didn't like what he did?"

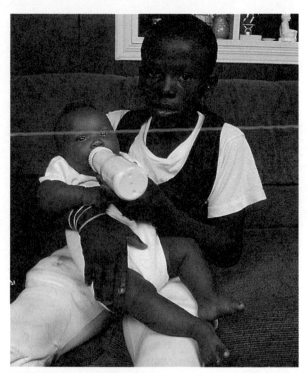

FIGURE 14.19   Helping: "Mom, I'll feed the baby, you rest."

Adult responses to children's play are particularly critical in supporting positive social development. The teacher has a powerful, emotional role in children's lives at school. As mentioned earlier, early childhood is a time when children make judgments in error, coming to conclusions about children based on race, gender, or ability. The teacher must intervene, for silence signals tacit approval. How does a teacher engage children in acting on their social environment so that they learn from one another and accept the realities and benefits of living together? In carefully observing and participating with children, the teacher must decide when and how to intervene and tap into children's own developing social skills and social/moral judgment—without taking over. This is perhaps the most dynamic and challenging part of teachers' jobs, the heart of the profession. Conflicts and their resolution illustrate the interaction between teacher and children, and the critical part teachers play in children's lives. Illustrated in Chapter 7 and Figure 7.13, the social problems in early childhood range from possession of toys, to hitting others, to keeping promises. *How* a teacher helps children identify and resolve their own conflicts is often more important than the specific problem or solution may be.

Curriculum Planning for Social Growth

In the Environment

Teaching social behavior in most classrooms usually occurs in response to spontaneous situations. The teacher's direct involvement in children's social interactions is the most frequent method used. Occasionally, teachers will approach the acquisition of social skills in a more formalized way through planned curriculum activities. The way the environment is arranged has a profound effect on social interaction among children.

Indoors. Most indoor activities are planned and set up to encourage participation by more than one child at a time.

- *The Arts.* At the art table, four or more children will share collage materials, paste, and sponges that have been placed in the center of the table. When easels are placed side by side, conversation occurs spontaneously among children. A small table, placed between the easels, on which a tray of paint cups is placed, also encourages children's interactions. If there is only one of each color, the children will have to negotiate with one another for the color they want to use.

- *Blocks/Manipulatives.* A large space for block cabinets gives children a visual cue that there is plenty of room for more than one child. Puzzle tables set with three or four puzzles also tell children that social interaction is expected. Many times children will talk, play, and plan with one another as they share a large bin full of Lego® or plastic building towers. A floor puzzle always requires a group: some to put the picture together, others to watch and make suggestions. As children build with blocks next to one another, they soon share comments about their work; many times this leads to a mutual effort on a single building.

- *Discovery/Science.* Many science projects can be arranged to involve more than one child. A display of magnets with a tray of assorted objects can become the focus of several children as they decide which ones will be attracted to the magnets. Cooking together, weighing and measuring one another, and caring for classroom pets can be times when teachers reinforce social skills.

- *Dramatic Play.* This area more than any other seems to draw children into contact with one another. Provide an assortment of family life accessories, dress-up clothes, kitchen equipment and utensils, and children have little trouble getting involved. A shoe needs to be tied, or a dress zippered up. Someone must come eat the delicious meal just cooked or put the baby to bed. A medical theme in this classroom area also enhances children's social skills. They learn to take each other's temperature, listen to heartbeats, and plan operations, all of which require one or more people.

- *Language/Library.* Children enjoy reading books and stories to one another, whether or not they know the words. Favorite books are often shared by two children who enjoy turning the pages and talking over the story together. Lotto games encourage children to become aware of one another, to look at each person's card in order to identify who has the picture to match. Name songs and games, especially early in the year, help children learn to call each other by name.

- *Music Movement.* Build in regular times for music and movement activities. The entire group can participate in familiar songs, which builds a sense of community by everyone's participation. Activities during free choice times usually involve smaller numbers, where group members can challenge one another to new ways to dance with scarves or use the tumbling mat. Finally, one-to-one experiences encourage new friendships as the intimacy of a shared musical experience brings two children or a teacher and child together.

Outdoors. The environment can be structured in ways to support group play.

- *Painting or Pasting.* Painting or pasting on murals or drawing chalk designs on the cement are art activities that promote social interaction.

- *Planning and Planting a Garden.* Planning and planting a garden is a long-range activity that involves many children. Decisions must be made by the group about what to plant, where to locate the garden, how to prepare the soil, and about the shared responsibilities of caring for the garden.

- *Gross-motor Activities.* Most gross-motor activities stimulate group interactions. Seesaws, jump ropes, and hide-and-seek require at least two people to participate. A-frames, boards, and boxes, as well as other moveable equipment, need the cooperative effort of several children in order to be rearranged. Sand play, when accompanied by water, shovels, and other accessories, draws a number of children together to create rivers, dams, and floods. Ball games and relay races also encourage social relationships.

Routines, Transitions, and Groups

Routines and Transitions are often social experiences, as they provide children with an opportunity for support and peer interaction. Teachers use these times as an opportunity to build social skills. For instance, the routine of nap-preparation can be structured with a "buddy" system so that older children are paired with the younger ones to set up the cots, choose a cuddly or books, and get tucked in. A cleanup time transition can be made fun and successful if children can wear a necklace to depict the job or area. Another way is to provide a basket of "pick-up" cards; bringing out the basket signals cleanup time and allows children to choose their chores. Children with similar cleanup cards get a sense of teamwork when putting an activity area back in order.

As a directed learning experience, small-group times afford an opportunity to focus on social skills in a more structured way. Small groups provide a setting for children and teachers to participate in more relaxed, uninterrupted dialogue. The intimacy of the small group sets the stage for many social interactions.

Group-time discussions can focus on problems that children can solve, for instance, (see Figure 14.20). Too many children crowding the water table, a child's fear of fire drills, or the noise level on a rainy day are subjects children will talk about in small groups. The most relevant situations are ones that occur naturally in the course of a program. Another curriculum idea is to make "Situation Cards" of these and other common incidents. For instance, teachers can create illustrated cards that pose situations such as:

- You tell your friends to "stop it" when they take part of the toy you are using, but they do it again.

- You open your lunch and your mom or dad has packed your favorite foods.

- You come down the slide and your teacher calls "Hooray for you!"

- You promise your friend you'll play with him at recess, but then someone else you like asks you to play with her.

The teacher then guides a discussion around the questions "How do you feel? What can you say? What can you do?" This activity can be simplified or elaborated depending on the individuals and group involved.

Solutions may emerge when the teacher supports active and involved participation. Teachers pose the problem and ask children to respond in several ways: "How does it make you and others feel when that happens? What can you and others do about it? What are some alternatives?" The problems must be real, and they must be about something that is important to children. Figure 14.20 is an example of a sequentially planned curriculum that fosters the development of social skills in small group settings.

Focus on Skills

Social development for the preschool child includes gaining an awareness of the larger community in which the child lives. The early childhood curriculum contains elements of what is often in the later grades called social studies. Visits

CURRICULUM FOR SOCIAL SKILL DEVELOPMENT

Time	Skill	Activities
Week 1	Developing a positive self-image	Do thumb print art. Make foot and hand prints. Compare children's baby pictures to current photos. Play with mirrors: make faces, emotional expressions. Dress felt dolls in clothing. Sing name songs: "Mary Wore Her Red Dress." Make a list: "What I like to do best is . . ." Post in classroom. Do a self-portrait in any art medium. Make a silhouette picture of each child.
Week 2	Becoming a member of a group	Take attendance together: Who is missing? Play picture lotto with photographs of children. Play "Farmer in the Dell." Share a favorite toy from home with other children. Tape record children's voices; guess who they are. Have a "friendly feast": each child brings favorite food from home to share.
Week 3	Forming a friendship within the group	Provide one puzzle (toy, game, book) for every two children. Take a "Buddy Walk"; return and tell a story together of what you saw. Play "Telephone Talk": pretend to invite your friend over to play. Play "copy cat": imitate your friend's laugh, walk, cry, words. Practice throwing and catching balls with one another. Form letter together with two children's bodies: A, T, C, K, etc. Play tug-of-war with your friend. Build a house out of blocks together. Make "mirror image" movements with your friend.
Week 4	Working together as a group	Play with a parachute; keep the ball bouncing. Make snacks for the rest of the class. Plan and plant a garden. Make a mural together to decorate the hallways. Play "Follow the Leader." Celebrate a holiday with a pinata. Sing a round: "Row, Row, Row Your Boat."
Week 5	Learning a group identity	Make a map of the town and have children place their house on it. Take a field trip together. Print a newspaper with articles by/about each child. Select and perform a favorite story for the rest of the class. Take a group snapshot. Make a "family tree" of photos of children in group. Learn a group folk dance. Make a mural of handprints joined in a circle.

FIGURE 14.20 Building social skills through small-group experiences, beginning with an understanding of self and moving toward an appreciation of group membership. (See Chapter 11 for specific guides to lesson and unit planning.)

LANGUAGE

Plan and perform a favorite story.
Choose a story at the listening post together.
Learn "I love you" in sign language.
Copy someone's motions, dance, block patterns.
Put on a puppet show.
Develop a "What Can I Share?" chart.
Discuss how new toys, equipment will be shared
    so everyone gets a turn.

SCIENCE

Care for classroom pets.
Have group cooking projects.
Plan and plant a garden.

MUSIC

Sing together each day.
Have a rhythm band.
Dance in groups of two or three.
Dance with a parachute.

ENVIRONMENT

Schedule cleanup daily.
Have two children share cubbies.
Bring snacks from home to share.
Set tables for two or more children.
Use large bins to store some materials; children
    will need to share contents.

COOPERATION

SOCIAL STUDIES

Make a group gift for hospital, rest home.
Create an art display for the local library.
Make cookies to sell at the school fair.
Run errands for teachers, each other.
Develop dramatic play themes of: shoe stores,
    hospital, doctors, ecology.
Collect and sort recycling materials.
Take a field trip to the town dump for recycling.

OUTDOORS

Push someone on a swing.
Pull a friend in a wagon.
Make bird feeders.
Set up bowling alley, with bowlers and pin setters.
Make an obstacle course.
Use seesaws.
Play group jump rope.
Play "Follow the Leader".

ART

Trace each other's bodies on paper.
Share paste and collage materials.
Share paints.
Make a mural.
Make litter bags.
Create a wall hanging: fabric, crayons
    and sheets; each child draws part.
Create a class quilt: each child sews a square;
    teacher puts it together.

GAMES

Play Simon Says
Play board games:
    Winnie-The-Pooh
    and Candy Land
Play Lotto
Play Bingo

FIGURE 14.21 The social skill of cooperation can be fostered throughout the curriculum. (How to plan a lesson and build a unit are discussed in Chapter 11.)

 from police officers, mail carriers, fire fighters, and other community helpers are common in many programs. Learning about children from other cultures, exploring the neighborhood around the center, and making maps are other ways children learn social studies skills.[1]

Learning to share involves using or enjoying something in common with others. While this may seem simple to adults, it is not a skill that is learned overnight, nor is it easy to orchestrate in young children. Young children understand children in different ways at different ages. As a teacher, ask yourself what sharing means to you. Does it mean giving up one's possessions when someone else wants them? Taking turns? Using a timer or the clock? Or dividing everything equally? Moreover,

OUR DIVERSE WORLD OUR DIVERSE WORLD OUR DIVERSE WORLD OUR DIVERSE WORLD OUR DIVERSE WORLD

[1]Notice these job titles are not gender specific. The titles provide an experience for children that reflects OUR DIVERSE WORLD.

does sharing mean never getting it back, or losing the thread of the play to the intruder? Toddlers and two-year-olds are rarely ready to share on their own. Grabbing what they want makes sense to them, and sharing a toy or space feels like giving it up forever. Preschoolers share more readily because of the experiences they have had in "getting it back," and because of the fuss they have seen occur when they do not share. School-age children begin to be aware that some children feel the same as they do and that others may have needs and wishes different from their own. Thus, sharing makes more sense over time. In the classroom, teachers can help by:

● *Understanding child development* and that it is normal not to want to share and to have trouble doing so

● *Explaining in simple terms what they want the child to do*

● *Making sure that children "get back" what they have shared* so that taking turns really works

● *Being an example of sharing*, since "Do as I do" is more powerful than "Do it because I told you to."

● *Letting the children experience ownership*, too, since children can't really know what it means to share until they know what it means to have something

Learning how to cooperate with others is one primary social skill in which young children need plenty of practice. Toddlers and two-year-olds can begin to see the benefits of cooperation as they become more aware of others' feelings and wishes, and as teachers help all children get what they want through taking turns, dividing materials, looking for another item when it is in demand. Three- to five-year-olds become more cooperative as they learn more self-help skills (motor development) and can express themselves (language development) as well as remember guidelines and understand reasons for prosocial behavior (cognitive development). School-age children develop an emotional sense of competence (see discussion of Erik Erikson's work in Chapter 4). They do this by acquiring knowledge and skills recognized by our culture as important (e.g., the cognitive tasks of reading and writing) and then using them with

peers. The opportunity for children to learn and rehearse these skills takes place in many areas of the classroom. Figure 14.21 illustrates this.

In preschool and primary classrooms, teachers often *involve children in "cooperative learning"* as a strategy that enhances cognitive learning through social interaction. Involving children's participation in small group learning activities, cooperative learning promotes social and academic interaction, increases enthusiasm and motivation, and rewards group participation (Lyman & Foyle, 1988). Structured activities that promote cooperation (see Figure 14.21) help children become aware of others, learning to work with and see viewpoints of those beside themselves. While most children spontaneously interact in free play periods (thus learning social skills in the process), some children need the structure of a more teacher-directed group activity to promote social development. Moreover, children's friendships can be expanded by the guided affiliation determined by a teacher and a project.

Successful implementation of cooperative learning activities in both older preschoolers and early elementary children usually needs a clear focus of project or activity (such as eating snack, writing a newsletter, building a tipi, or catching a hamster on the loose). The group size, and often members, are determined by the teacher, who also needs to make the expectations for group behavior known. The teacher then monitors the interaction, providing assistance, clarification, or problem-solving as needed. Evaluation is based on observation, and the group is rewarded for its success.

Use of Themes

A popular theme that lends itself to social growth is that of friendship. This has particular appeal during the month of February when the meaning of friendship is enhanced by the celebration of Valentine's Day. At other times, relay races and noncompetitive games (those in which everyone is a winner) promote working with friends to achieve a goal. Teachers who encourage children to help each other read, tie shoes, pour milk, fasten a smock, or sponge a table reinforce what friendship can be in the early years. Many books and

THEME: FRIENDSHIP

Concepts Children Will Learn	Activity
Everyone has a name and likes to have it used.	Friendship songs, using children's names
Each person is something special and unique.	Make a "Friend Puppet" with paper plates, tongue depressor handles. Child decorates it with felt pieces and yarn to look like a friend.
Friends are different; they do not all look the same.	Children respond to: "Tell me about your friend Alice. She . . ." (Child describes a friend as teacher writes the words.)
Having friends is fun.	Make a friendship ring: each child traces own hands on mural, making a circle.
Friends enjoy doing things together.	Go on a scavenger hunt with a friend.
Adults can be your friends.	Teacher helps child solve conflict or gives comfort when child is hurt.
Animals and pets can be your friends.	Children have an opportunity to bring small house pets to school to share with rest of class.
To have a friend is to be a friend.	Children respond to: "A Friend Is Someone Who . . ." (They describe their impressions while teacher writes down their words.)
Friends enjoy doing things for one another.	Children respond to: "Being A Friend With Someone Means . . ." (Teacher writes down children's dictation.)
Everyone can have a friend.	Teacher reads stories about friendships: *Will I Have A Friend?* (Cohen), *Corduroy* (Freeman), *Play With Me* (Ets), *Little Bear's Friend* (Minarik), *A Letter To Amy* (Keats), *Hold My Hand* (Zolotow), *Jessica* (Henkes), *Harry & Willie & Carrothead* (Caseley).
You can show someone you want to be friends.	Write a letter to a friend; invite a friend over to play.
Friends will help you.	Form a relay team and have a race.

FIGURE 14.22 A friendship unit can encourage children to express positive emotions while they use their cognitive, language, and motor skills to enhance their social development.

songs can be found that emphasize friendship. Group discussions can help children define what is a friend. Figure 14.22 illustrates how a friendship unit can be developed for an early childhood setting. Figure 14.23 shows a family unit for the early primary (K–1) level.

● UNIT 14-2 Checkpoint

Early in life children become aware of their social nature. The socialization process begins under the guidance of parents and family members. When children enter group settings, they are further exposed to behavior, social roles, and attitudes that foster social development. Much of a child's social repertoire is learned by playing with other children.

Children learn a great many social skills in these early years. They learn to enjoy and trust adults other than their parents. In their relationships with others, children learn ways to cooperate, disagree, share, communicate, and assert themselves effectively.

Children also learn how to be a member of a group—to take part in group activities, adapt to school expectations, and to respect the rights and feelings of others. The young child also learns to express feelings in appropriate ways and to begin self-care tasks.

Teachers plan and arrange the early childhood environment in ways that will promote social growth and interaction. The adults help children understand each other's actions and motivations by interpreting the behavior to children as they play.

THEME: ABOUT FAMILIES

Step 1: Establish Background Knowledge
Large Group Brainstorm: What is a family?
What are they called (Dad, Mama, Hermano, Nona, etc.)?
Individual List: Your own family and their names
A picture of your family
Small Group Discussion: Feeling words for families
Family jobs in the home
Charades depicting family jobs
Think-Pair-Share: List, then draw how families have fun together
List, then draw the tough times families have

Step 2: Decide the Theme Focus (e.g., "Family Fun")

Step 3: Review Knowledge, Make a Plan
Large Group: Review how families have fun
Pairs: Cut pictures from magazines showing family fun, make collage for classroom bulletin board
Small Group Discussion: Brainstorm then list and prioritize list of a family activity the class can do as a "family"
Large Group: Small groups present ideas, class vote (e.g., campground)

Step 4: Plan
List what is needed, vote on placement of areas, make assignments for building and map-making

Step 5: Building
Create areas in classroom (e.g., campground, forest, lake, camp store, ranger station, cave, trails, etc.)

Step 6: Play!

Step 7: Review and Conclusion
Ongoing: Teacher observes and evaluates individual participation
At the end: Group discussion on what went well and didn't work; suggestions for future projects and taking down of building

FIGURE 14.23 Cooperative learning activities involve children socially in their own academic learning. An *early primary* theme that is derived from the children and executed by them increases both learning and participation. (Thanks to Amy Buras for the kindergarten unit.)

Curriculum to develop social skills in young children can be spontaneous as well as planned. Much of the focus in an early childhood setting is on social interactions throughout the day. At other times, social growth is enhanced by group-time discussions, awareness of the community and society at large, and an emphasis on specific social skills.

Ask yourself:

● What are social expectations of infants and toddlers? Pre-schoolers? School-aged children?

● Why is peer group experience important?

● What social skills do children develop with adults? With other children? In a group? As individuals?

● How do teachers help children develop social skills?

● How are social skills fostered in the curriculum?

● UNIT 14-3 CREATIVE GROWTH

THE DEVELOPMENT OF CREATIVITY

Creativity is the ability to have new ideas, to be original and imaginative, and to make new adaptations on old ideas. Inventors, composers, and designers are creative people, as are those who paint and dance, write speeches, or create curriculum for children.[1] When people think in a different way than they usually do, when they change in how they learn or see something, that is creativity (Adams, 1987). The more teachers realize they are a part of a creative act, the more sensitive they become in helping young children develop creatively.

The roots of creativity reach into infancy, for it is every individual's unique and creative process to explore and understand the world, searching to answer larger questions such as "Who am I? What and where am I, and where am I going?" Infants' creativity is seen in their efforts to move and feed/dress themselves. Toddlers begin to scribble, build, and move for the pure physical sensation of movement. Young preschoolers create as they try for more control, such as scribbling with purpose or bobbing and jumping to music. Older preschoolers enjoy their budding mastery. Their drawings take on some basic forms and they repeat movements deliberately while making a dance. As they grow, five- to eight-year-olds communicate to the world through artistic and expressive creation. These young children have more advanced motor control and hand-eye coordination. Their drawings are representational and pictorial; dancing can include more refined movements and structured dance steps. Their dramatic play is more cohesive; their stories have imagination and form.

FIGURE 14.24 Creativity is the ability to be original and imaginative: to soar above the commonplace. (Courtesy of the schools of Reggio Emilio, Italy.)

Creativity is a process; as such, it is hard to define. As one becomes involved in creative activity, the process and the product merge.

> . . . It is probably best to think of creativity as a continual process for which the best preparation is creativity itself. . . there is real joy in discovery—which not only is its own reward, but provides the urge for continuing exploration and discovery.
>
> (Lowenfeld and Brittain, 1975)

The young child is open to experience, exploring materials with curiosity and eagerness. For young children, developing the senses is part of acquiring creative skills. Children are also quick to question, wonder, and see things that do not quite match up. These are traits of creative children.

[1]Provide a diverse range of creative adults to children—men and women from a variety of cultural backgrounds.

FIGURE 14.25 Sensitivity to one's own mental images, such as perceiving direction and movement, are part of creativity in the young child. A 5½-year-old sketched how a rat looked from below after picking it up often and watching it run on its exercise wheel.

CREATIVE SKILLS IN EARLY CHILDHOOD

There are characteristics common to creative people. For the teacher interested in fostering creative growth in children, these are the skills they should help children learn.

Flexibility and Fluency

Flexibility and fluency are dual skills that allow for creative responses. Flexibility is the capacity to shift from one idea to another; fluency is the ability to produce many ideas. "How many ways can you move from one side of the room to another?" is a question likely to produce many different ideas, one example of fluency. Children who must think of another way to share the wagons when taking turns doesn't work learn flexibility.

Sensitivity

Being creative involves a high degree of sensitivity to one's self and one's mental images. Creative people, from an early age, seem to be aware of the world around them: how things smell, feel, and taste. They are sensitive to mood, texture, and how they feel about someone or something. Seeing detail, noticing how a pine cone is attached to the branch, is a detail the creative person does not overlook.

Creative children take delight and satisfaction in making these images come to life. Their creative response is in the way they paint a picture, dance with streamers, or find a solution to a problem. Figure 14.25 shows how a 5-1/2-year-old's sensitivity to perspective and detail comes out through a drawing.

Use of Imagination

Imagination is a natural part of the creative process. Children use their imagination to develop their creativity in several ways.

Role Playing. In taking on another role, children combine their knowledge of the real world with their internal images. The child becomes a new character, and that role comes to life.

Image-Making. When children create a rainbow with a hose or with paints, they are adding something of their own to their understanding of that visual image. In dance, children use their imagination as they pretend to be objects or feelings, images brought to life.

Constructing. In building and constructing activities, children seem to be re-creating an image they have about tall buildings, garages, or farms. In the process of construction, however, children do not intend that the end product resemble the building itself. Their imagination allows them to experiment with size, shape, and relationships.

A Willingness to Take Risks

People who are willing to break the ordinary mental set and push the boundaries in defining and using ordinary objects, materials, and ideas are creative people. They take risks. Being open to thinking differently or seeing things differently is essential to creativity.

Self-esteem is a factor in risk-taking since people who are tied to what others think of them are more likely to conform rather than follow their own intuitive and creative impulses. People usually do not like to make mistakes or be ridiculed; therefore, they avoid taking risks.

A teacher concerned about creative growth in children realizes that it will surface if allowed and encouraged. When a child is relaxed and not anxious about being judged by others, creativity will more likely be expressed. With support, children can be encouraged to risk themselves.

Using Self as a Resource

Creative people who are aware of themselves and confident in their abilities draw upon their own perceptions, questions, and feelings. They know they are their own richest source of inspiration. MacKinnon found that those who excelled in creative productivity had a great deal of respect for self, that they used the self as a resource (Shallcross and Sisk, 1982).

Experience

Children need experience in order to gain skills in using materials creatively. They must learn how to hold a paint brush before they can paint a picture; once they know how to paint, they can be creative in what they paint. Teachers of young children sometimes overlook the fact that children need competence with the tools in order to be creative with them. A little sensitive, individual demonstration on proper use of a watercolor brush, sandpaper, or ink roller can expand a child's ability to create and eliminate needless frustration and disappointment. The teachers of Reggio Emilia, for instance, demonstrate how to use the tools so that the children can then make outstanding creations. Anecdotes from highly accomplished people in creative endeavors (pianists, mathematicians, Olympic swimmers) highlight the value of long-term, systematic instruction in a sort of apprenticeship with inspiring teachers as

well as parents who are committed to assist (Bloom and Sosniak, 1992). As teachers we can see how Vygotsky's theory applies in the arts and can provide the initial palette of creative activities so that children can dabble and become experienced. When the skill of the medium is mastered, the child is ready to create.

THE TEACHER'S ROLE

Considerations

The early childhood curriculum offers many rich avenues for self-expression and creativity. Beyond art and music, there is the ability to think and question, to find more than one answer to a problem. Blocks, climbing equipment, and social relationships offer risk-taking opportunities. Children use themselves as resources as they play outdoor games, experiment with science projects, and participate in dramatic play. Taruna exhibits many creative traits as she attempts to enter into play with two other children. She first asks if she can play, and when met with rejection, she demands to be one of the mommies. Taruna finally offers her doll as a prop and is accepted into the group. Her persistence is exceeded only by her creative problem solving.

Regular creative opportunities give children the necessary experience and skill to be creative. Children need frequent occasions to be creative in order to function in a highly creative manner. When children have a chance to create, their skills in perceiving the world are enhanced.

One of the teacher's most crucial considerations for supporting creative growth is that of **divergent thinking.** To diverge means to take a different line of thought or action, deviating from the normal. Finding ideas that branch out rather than converge and center on one answer is divergent thinking. Recent works suggest that creativity and problem-solving may stem from similar sources (Hitz, 1987). Real life problem-solving calls for creative thinking as well as logic and concept development. The creative arts are important if only because they tend to stress this kind of thinking. Where there are no "right" or "wrong" answers, there will undoubtedly be many solutions for problems. The curriculum section of this chapter

FIGURE 14.26 When children have a chance to create, with permission to use an abundance of materials, the results are creative. (Courtesy of the schools of Reggio Emilio, Italy.)

contains creativity questions as examples of divergent thinking.

Children and teachers can discuss issues and seek solutions to problems when divergent thinking is encouraged. In a child care center, for instance, children were fighting over the use of the two swings. The children's responses indicate their willingness to take a different line of thought:

Teacher:	How do you think we could share the swings?
David:	The kids who give me a turn can come to my birthday party.
Sabrina:	No. We will have to make a waiting list.
Xenia:	Only girls can use the swings; the boys can have all the carts.
Frederico:	Buy a new swing set.

Talking with young children about what they create—be it their artwork, table toy creations, dramatic play sequences—is an important consideration. Robert Schirrmacher (1986) offers some suggestions about talking with children about art; these hints could apply to all creative endeavors. Rather than approach children's work with compliments, judgments, or even questions:

● allow children to go about their artistic discoveries without you comparing, correcting, or projecting yourself into their art . . .

● shift from searching for representation in children's art to a focus on the abstract, design qualities . . .

● use reflective dialogue . . .

● smile, pause, and say nothing at first . . .

(Schirrmacher, 1986)

In other words, teachers allow children to take the lead in their own creative works from start to finish. Adults do not need to take over at any point, particularly at the end with questions ("What is it?") or praise ("I like it!"). If a child seems to want more response, comment on the color ("What a lot of blue you used"), texture ("I see wiggly lines all down one side") or the child's efforts ("You really worked on this painting, huh?"). Then reflect their own ideas back to the children:

Child:	The monster's gonna get you and eat you up!
Teacher:	You made a monster with the wood scraps.
Child:	Yes and it's for my daddy.
Teacher:	Let's put it on the counter so it will be dry when he picks you up.

Teacher timing and attitudes are also important in stimulating creative development in young children. The early childhood years are probably the most crucial time to encourage creative thinking. Indeed, research has found that kindergartners gave a higher proportion of original responses to creativity tasks than did second-graders (Moran, et al., 1983). "It is here that initial attitudes are established . . . and school can be a fun place where the individual's contribution is welcome and where changes can be sought and made." (Lowenfeld and Brittain, 1975)

Children need plenty of time and a relaxed atmosphere to be creative. They need encouragement and respect for the process and products of their creative nature. The teacher's attitude tells the children that what they do is important, and how they do it makes a difference. Rather than expecting a predetermined right answer, the teacher encourages creativity by valuing the answers the children give even when they appear unusual or illogical.

Curriculum Planning for Creative Growth

In The Environment

Teachers set up an environment that promotes creative expression; they choose activities and materials that can be used in many ways. These *open-ended materials* provide a continuing challenge as children use them repeatedly in new and different ways. Clay, playdough, paints, crayons and pens, blocks, water, sand and other sensory materials, and movable outdoor equipment are good examples of open-ended materials that stimulate creativity. Particularly in the area of creative art, it is important to *avoid* projects that masquerade as creative activities, such as duplicated, photocopied, or mimeographed sheets, cut-and-paste activities, tracing patterns, coloring-book pages, dot-to-dot books (Schirrmacher, 1988), and any art "project" that is based on a model for children to copy or imitate. Children are motivated to try new ways to use materials when they are flexible and challenging.

Indoors. Every classroom has a potential for creative activity.

● *The Arts.* A wide variety of materials and opportunities to choose how they will be used is the basis of the creative process. An open table with a shelf of simple, familiar materials that can be combined in many ways will lead to inventiveness. Two-year-olds like crayons, paste, and colored paper pieces; three- to five-year-olds will enjoy the addition of markers, string, hole punches and scissors, and tape. Older children can manage staplers, rulers, and protractors. Plenty of paper, such as recycled computer printouts, and cardboard round out an open-ended, self-help art shelf. More structured art activities can also be offered, particularly for the preschool child, as long as the focus is on the child's process, rather than an end product or model. As they approach the primary years, children become interested in what their creations look like, and then are ready for practical help and advise on getting started. *Creativity question: "What other ways can you think of to use the paint?"*

● *Blocks/Manipulatives.* Children use their imagi-

nation when blocks become castles, tunnels, corrals, and swamps. These areas encourage creativity when children have enough materials of one kind to "really' make something; one long block is just not enough for a road. Also, creations have a sense of permanence when they are noted and kept. Sketching or photographing a block structure, attaching signs (include taking dictation) for the day, even rethinking cleanup periodically shows how valuable these creations are. *Creativity question: "How can you use the blocks to make a forest? A stairway? Can you think of a design using the pegs?"*

● *Discovery/Science.* Building geoboards or making tangrams and cube art all blend math and art. Art activities can lead children to discover scientific principles, such as color mixing, dissolving powder paint in water, and having water available with clay. Nature materials can be used for rubbings, mobiles, and prints. Collecting materials during a "litter walk" makes interesting and informative collages. *Creativity question: What do you think will happen? Now, how can you find out why it happened that way?*

● *Dramatic Play.* The dramatic arts offer opportunities for children to express themselves. Every "unit" in the dramatic play corner brings out children's own interpretations of their world, be it a house, shoestore, farmer's market, or a campout, dinosaur cave, space shuttle. Moreover, in order to perform a familiar story, such as *Goldilocks and the Three Bears,* children can create costumes, props, a stage, and the musical accompaniment. *Creativity question: What could you use to help you pretend you are the grandpapa? How could this scarf be used in your house?*

● *Language/Library.* Besides a variety of books and children's literary experiences (see Chapter 13), the booknook can be a place for teachers to ask open-ended questions for fun and pondering. "What if you were a twin? What would you wear—eat—live?" is a social creation; "If I were a hat, I would . . ." is physical creativity; "How many ways could we make triangles with these materials on the table" challenges a child to cognitive creativity. Creative responses for language development can use a familiar storyline:

FIGURE 14.27   When children are given the materials and allowed the time, they will use their own ideas for creating masterpieces! (Courtesy of the schools of Reggio Emilio, Italy.)

for instance, the book *Did You Ever See?* (Einsel) or the song "Down By the Bay" can be used to ask children to make a rhyme to end the sentence "Did you ever see a whale . . . ("flipping its tail!")" *Creativity question: What do you think will happen next in the story?*

Outdoors. Creativity happens out-of-doors also. Large, hollow blocks can become a stairway, and wagons and carts become fire engines, buses, doll carriages, moving vans, or trucks. Dancing with ribbons, making a Chinese dragon for a parade, rearranging equipment to make a tumbling or obstacle course all combine children's motor skills with music for creative growth. The use of these activities is limited only by the creativity of the children. Sand, water, and mud provide a place for children to dig, haul, manipulate, and control in any number of ways. *Creativity questions: How many parts of your body can you use to get the ball to your friend? How many ways can you think of to cross over on the climber? I wonder how you could get the wet sand into the bucket? What is your tricycle going to be today?*

Routines, Transitions, and Groups

Teachers can apply their own creativity to many routine situations. When looking for a lost mitten, a "hunt" is organized; pretending to be vacuum cleaners, dump trucks, or robots gets the blocks picked up faster. Saying goodbye can be an exercise in creativity; the child can say "See You Later, Alligator," and the adults (parents and teacher) can make up a silly response. Another day, the child and parent can reverse roles. *Creativity question for dismissal transition: How can you use one foot and one hand in some way to go to your snack groups?*

Music is a special outlet for children's creative expression in groups. Music is a universal language that develops every aspect of affective development. It allows the expression of emotions and the opportunity to take roles as well as a delightful time to create with movement. There is a kind of developmental sequence in the creative expression of music. The very young child is receptive to music, responding by listening, singing, and making noise with instruments. Preschoolers move to rhythmic music, often singing spontaneously in play and responding to repeated songs or repetitious phrasing. Their interest in musical instruments precedes their skill, and they often need instruments to be introduced and their proper use demonstrated. Older preschoolers and school-age children are more accurate in matching their pitch and tempo to the group or played music.

Music can permeate the early childhood program. It can set the tone at naptime, signal that a clean-up task is at hand, summon children to a group, and offer cultural experiences that are meaningful and enjoyable. For instance, New Year is often a noisy time; it can be celebrated by making ankle bells and doing a Sri Lankan dance or making a West Indian Conga line. In Waldorf schools, music is quite important. Children are engaged daily in eurythmy exercises (developed by Steiner, see Chapter 1). Taught by a specialist, it is a kind of creative form which translates music and speech into movement.

Indoors or out, in structured or unstructured times children need the time and trusting atmosphere that encourages them to create. Figure 14.28 shows some ways that *art* can be the primary medium for learning, as in the community preschools of Reggio Emilia. Regardless of the material, environments and teachers encourage children's creativity.

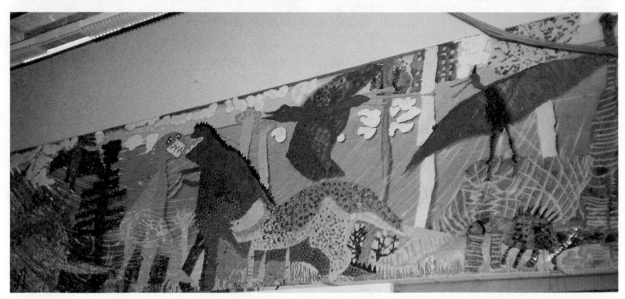

FIGURE 14.28   When a community values creativity, it puts creative skill development high as a school priority. (Courtesy of the schools of Reggio Emilio, Italy.)

THEME: GREEN AND GROWING THINGS

OUTDOOR ACTIVITIES

1. Plant a garden in a corner of the yard, in an old barrel, or in a box flat on a table. Children learn through experimentation why some things grow and others don't. Make space for a compost heap.
2. Add wheelbarrows to the transportation toys.
3. Take a field trip to a farm, at planting time if possible.
4. Add gardening tools to the sand area. With proper supervision, children can see how trowels, hand claws, rakes, and shovels can be used to create new patterns in the sand and mud.
5. Plan group games that emphasize green and growing things. Older children could run wheelbarrow races, using one child as the wheelbarrow and another as the driver.
6. Play "musical vegetables" with large cards or chalk drawings. Dance with gourds, coconut instruments, sugar cane rhythm sticks.

INDOOR ACTIVITIES

1. Leaf rubbings, printing with apples, onions, carrots, potatoes, lemons, oranges, and celery, and painting with pine boughs are ways children can create art with green and growing things, make cornhusk dolls, avocado seed porcupines.
2. Block accessories might include blue felt forms for lakes, hay for corrals and barns.
3. In the manipulative area, match a photo of familiar plants with a sample of the plant. Add sorting trays with various kinds of seeds to count, feel, mix, and match. Match pictures of eggs, bacon, milk, and cheese with the animals from which they come.
4. In the science area, grow alfalfa sprouts and mung beans. Let children mix them in salads and feed to classroom pets. As the sprouts grow, children can chart the growth. This can lead to charting their own development, comparing it to when they were infants.
5. The dramatic play center can be transformed into a grocery store to emphasize the food we buy to eat, how it helps us, and why good nutrition is important. Other dramatic play units are a florist shop or nursery, stocked with garden gloves, seed packets, peat pots, and sun hats.
6. The language area can be stocked with books about how plants, baby animals, and children grow. In small groups, children can respond to "When I plant a seed . . ." or "When I was a baby I . . . Now I . . ." to stimulate creative expression.
7. Songs and fingerplays can help focus on green and growing things, children's growth, and animals. "The Green Grass Grows All Around" can be sketched by a teacher so that children will have visual cues to each successive verse. A favorite fingerplay, "Way Up in the Apple Tree," can be adapted to a number of fruits and vegetables.

FIGURE 14.29 Creativity around the classroom. Creativity and problem-solving may stem from the same source. Real-life experiences, such as planning and building a garden, expand to provide creative thinking and logic in the classroom.

Focus on Skills

The wide range of skills necessary for creative development can be supported throughout the early childhood program. The creative thinker is one who finds many ways to solve a problem, approach a situation, use materials, and interact with others. The teacher's role is one of supporting imaginative use of equipment.

To encourage creative thinking, teachers also look at the ways they ask children questions. How can they prompt children to view the unusual and think of the exceptional? How can they encourage divergent thinking? What will encourage children to use their cognitive and language skills in creative ways? The *Creativity Questions* in the previous section demonstrate some of the ways teachers focus on children's creative skills through the use of questions.

Use of Themes

As teachers plan curriculum around a theme, they keep in mind what creative skills can be developed. Figure 14.29 charts the theme of "Green and Growing Things," and can bring out the child's creative nature.

● UNIT 14-3 Checkpoint

Young children are open to the creative process and to creative experiences. The early years are a good time to acquire the skills of flexibility, sensitivity, imagination, risk-taking, resourcefulness, and experience.

The greatest challenge for adults in nurturing children's creativity is to help children find and develop their Creativity Intersection—the area where their talents, skills, and interests overlap. (Amabile, 1989) The role of the teacher is to plan curriculum that will help develop children's creativity. An atmosphere conducive to creative work is one that supports children's divergent thinking, encourages them to take risks, and provides ways they can use themselves as resources.

Ask yourself:

● What are the creative skills learned in early childhood?

● What is the teacher's role in the development of creativity?

● What classroom area, skill, or unit promotes creative thinking?

● How can I ask children to use language to promote creative thinking?

S U M M A R Y

Emotional, social, and creative growth development are at the center of the early childhood curriculum. Planning for these areas involves an understanding of how each develops in the young child and how they are interrelated. Children learn many skills in these three areas as they interact with each other, with adults, and in the environment.

Planning curriculum for emotional, social, and creative growth calls upon teachers to play a supportive role, facilitating children's involvement with the materials and each other. Only then can children discover themselves, explore their relationships, and develop the ability to use their imagination and resources.

R E V I E W   Q U E S T I O N S

1. How do emotional, social, and creative growth relate to each other?

2. How can teachers recognize children's biased remarks or social behavior? Do they need to respond? Why?

3. What are the advantages of and problems with superhero play?

4. List some of the developmental milestones and expectations for socialization of young children.

5. How can teachers support conflict resolution and problem solving?

6. What kinds of activities masquerade as creative art?

7. Write three examples of a child's divergent thinking. How do these show the "creativity intersection"?

L E A R N I N G   A C T I V I T I E S

1. Name five people you consider creative. Match their skills with those we have identified in early childhood. Where are they similar? Different?

2. How does your center promote positive self-concept? What else could be done?

3. Observe a group of four-year-olds at play. How do they decide what roles each one takes? Are they clear in their expectations of what sex roles are appropriate for boys and girls? Is there sex-role stereotyping?

4. Taking turns and sharing equipment and materials is difficult for young children. Cite three examples you have seen where children used their social skills to negotiate a turn. Was teacher intervention necessary?

5. Make behavioral definitions of emotions you think you will see in the children you teach. Observe the children, then check the accuracy of your definitions.

6. Give three examples of children in your center trying to "break mental set." In what area of the classroom did it occur? What were the adults' responses?

7. How do teachers in your setting plan for creativity? What place does such expression take in the priority of the school philosophy?

B I B L I O G R A P H Y

General

Berk, Laura E. *Child Development.* Needham, Mass.: Allyn & Bacon, 1994.
Brophy, Jere. *Human Development and Behavior.* New York: St. Martins Press, 1981.

Marshall, Hermine H. "Research in Review: The Development of Self-Concept." *Young Children*, Vol. 44, No. 5, July, 1989.

Neugebauer, Bonnie. *Alike and Different: Exploring Our Humanity with Young Children*. Washington, D.C.: National Association for the Education of Young Children, 1992 (Revised Ed.).

York, Stacey. *Roots and Wings: Affirming Culture in Early Childhood Programs*. St. Paul, Minn.: Redleaf Press, 1991.

Emotional Growth

Berne, Patricia H., and Berne, Eve. "Nurturing Success: Positive Ways to Build Self-esteem in Your Children." *Pre-K Today*, August/September, 1988.

Briggs, Dorothy C. *Your Child's Self-Esteem*. New York: Doubleday, 1970.

Campos, J.J., Caplovitz, K.B., Goldsmith, H.H., and Stenberg, C. "Socioemotional Development." In *Handbook of Child Psychology, Vol. 2*, ed. M.M. Haith and J.J. Campos. New York: Wiley, 1983 (4th Ed.).

Diaz, Rafael. "The Development of Self-Direction in the Preschool Years." Address given to Peninsula Association of the Education of Young Children, April, 1992.

Honig, Alice S. "Stress and Coping in Children." *Young Children*, Vol. 41, Nos. 4 and 5, May and July 1986.

Kostelnik, Marjorie; Whiren, A.P.; and Stein, L.G. "Living with He-Man: Managing Superhero Fantasy Play." *Young Children*, Vol. 41, No. 4, May 1986.

McCormick, Jackie. "Family Child Care. In *Beginnings and Beyond*, ed. A. Gordon and K.B. Browne. Albany, N.Y.: Delmar Publishers, 1993 (3rd Ed.).

Selye, Hans. "History and Present Status of the Stress Concept." In L. Goldberger and S. Breznitz (eds.), *Handbook of Stress*. New York: The Free Press, 1982.

Simon, Terry. "Helping Children Make Choices." *The Creative Classroom*, September, 1994.

Sroufe, L.A. "Socioemotional Development." In *Handbook of Infant Development*, ed. J.D. Osofsky. New York: Wiley, 1979.

Social Growth

Buras, Amy. "Social Settings in the Classroom." *ACEI Focus*, Vol. 3, No. 3, Spring, 1991.

Buzzelli, Cary A., and File, Nancy. "Building Trust in Friends." *Young Children*, March, 1989.

Carllson-Paige, Nancy, and Levin Diane E. *The War Play Dilemma*. New York, Teacher's College, 1987.

Derman Sparks, *The Anti-Bias Curriculum*, Washington, D.C.: NAEYC, 1989.

Dick, Kelly. "Cooperative Learning" Mastering the Bundle of Sticks," *Childhood Education*, Vol. 67, No. 3, Spring, 1991.

Kemple, Kristen M. "Research in Review: Preschool Children's Peer Acceptance and Social Interaction." *Young Children*, Vol. 46, No. 5, July, 1991.

Lally, J. Ronald; Provence, S.; Szanton, E.; and Weissbourd, B. "Developmentally Appropriate Care for Children from Birth to Age 3." In Bredekamp, Sue (ed.), *Developmentally Appropriate Practice in Early Childhood Programs Serving Children from Birth Through Age 8*, Washington, D.C.: NAEYC, 1987.

Lyman, Lawrence, and Foyle, H.C. "Cooperative Learning Strategies and Children." Urbana, Illinois: *ERIC Digest*, 1988.

Melson, Gail, and Fogel, Alan. "Research in Review: The Development of Nurturance in Young Children." *Young Children*, Vol. 43, No. 3, March 1988.

Nurss, Sally. "Learning to Share," *Ladybug Magazine*, December, 1990.

Pelligrini, A.D. and Glickman, Carl D. "Measuring Kindergartners' Social Competence." *Young Children*, Vol. 45, No. 4, May, 1990.

Rubin, Zick. *Children's Friendships*. Cambridge, Mass.: Harvard University Press, 1980.

Scales, Barbara, et al (eds). *Play and the Social Context* (Early Childhood Education Series). New York: Teachers College, 1991.

Schickedanz, Judith A., et al. *Understanding Children*. Mountain View, CA: Mayfield, 1993 (2nd ed.).

Selman, R.L. *The Growth of Interpersonal Understanding*. New York: Academic Press, 1980.

Smith, Charles A. *Promoting the Social Development of Young Children*. Palo Alto, Calif.: Mayfield Publishing Co., 1982.

Special thanks to Chris Asaro for children's social conversations.

Creative Growth

Adams, James. *The Care and Feeding of Ideas*. Reading, Mass.: Addison-Wesley, 1987.

Amabile, Teresa M. *Growing Up Creative*. New York: Crown Publishers, Inc., 1989.

Bloom, B.S., and Sosniak, L.A. "Talent Development vs. Schooling." *Educational Leadership*, 1992, p. 39.

Cech, Maureen. *Globalchild: Multicultural Resources for Young Children*. Menlo Park, Calif.: Addison-Wesley Publishing, 1991.

Cherry, Clare. *Creative Play for the Developing Child*. Lake Publications, 1988.

Edwards, C., Gandini, L., and Forman, G. *The Hundred Languages of Children*. New Jersey: Ablex Press, 1993.

Hitz, Randy. "Creative Problem Solving Through Music Activities." *Young Children*, Vol. 42, No. 2, January 1987.

Kuschner, David. "Put Your Name on Your Painting, But . . . the Blocks Go Back on the Shelves." *Young Children*, Vol. 45, No. 1, November, 1989.

Lowenfeld, Victor, and Brittain, W.L. *Creative and Mental Growth*. New York: Macmillan, 1975.

Moran, J.D., Milgram, R.M., Sawyers, J.K., and Fu, V.R. "Original Thinking in Preschool Children." *Child Development*, pages 921–926, 1983, p. 54.

New, Rebecca. "Excellent Early Education: A City in Italy has It." *Young Children*, Vol. 45, No. 6, September, 1990.

Schirrmacher, Robert. "Talking with Young Children About Their Art." *Young Children*, Vol. 41, No. 5, July 1986.

——————. *Art and Creative Development for Young Children*. Albany, N.Y.: Delmar Publishers, 1993 (2nd ed.).

GUEST EDITORIAL

Advocates for Those Without a Voice

Jerlean Daniel

Today, in the United States of America, children are not among the country's highest priorities. Their young lives are made complex by the dynamics of such phenomena as poverty, limited access to health care, inappropriate educational programming, child abuse, hunger, racism, and classism, to name just a few. Primarily, children have long been the victims of adults' collective failure to appropriately factor children in, when social policy issues are prioritized. There appears to be a far reaching consensus, just below the conscious level, that, generally, children are resilient and will grow up to be just fine. This is overly optimistic and in many cases quite far from the truth.

Early childhood professionals are part of a broader field of human developmentalists whose range of study is the whole life span. A developmentalist's perspective indicates that all domains of the child's growth—physical, emotional, social and cognitive—are interrelated. Failure to thrive in any one area can affect all of the others. Prolonged trauma to and assault upon one or more of these growth domains, as well as failure to actively nurture them, have a devastating effect on who the child will become.

As the developmentalist partners in the care and education of America's children, early childhood professionals, based on our knowledge base, bear a particular responsibility to state unequivocally expectations for the climate of human interaction which nurtures healthy growth and development of all children. In order to do this effectively, it is important that we recognize and act upon a broader definition of advocacy that includes, but goes beyond, lobbying policy makers. Parents, the business sector, and the general public are additional audiences which need a better understanding of children's basic needs.

All of our children, without regard to social economic status, are needy because as adults we have been inattentive. The one thing all children need most from us is a consistent, nurturing attentiveness and focus, which serves to ensure a basic quality of life supportive of all of the growth domains. Children are voiceless because they have no way of participating in the prioritization of the social policy agenda. They must rely on others, specifically adults, to speak in their behalf. In a democracy we have both the opportunity and the responsibility to participate in the determination of the country's social policy agenda. If enough individuals speak up for all of our children, we can move issues impacting children up higher on that agenda and increase the likelihood of positive outcomes for all children. An informed citizenry, active on behalf of all children, is the voice currently missing from the dialogue prioritizing the national social policy agenda. All children await our focused activism.

Jerlean Daniel is an Assistant Professor of Child Development/Child Care in the School of Social Work at the University of Pennsylvania in Pittsburgh. She currently serves as President of the National Association for the Education of Young Children.

CHAPTER 15

Issues and Trends in Early Childhood Education

QUESTIONS FOR THOUGHT

What are the major issues facing early childhood educators today?

How are the major themes of early childhood education reflected in the issues facing children, families, and teachers today?

What are the issues surrounding child care and early education?

What are the challenges children and their families face, and what can we do to help them?

How are the role and structure of the family changing and how does this affect the children we teach?

What is the impact of the education reform movement on early childhood?

What is the role of television and the media in children's lives?

How do we become advocates for a quality life for children?

How does the history of the field suggest the agenda for the future?

FIGURE 15.1   How do we prepare our children to live successfully in the future?

INTRODUCTION

Early childhood education has undergone remarkable changes in the past thirty years. It has evolved from being an option for middle-class preschool children to a necessity for millions of families with children from infancy through the primary years.[1] These changes have signaled a new level of professionalism and training for teachers. Such transformations are a reflection of the economic, social, and political climate of the times. Changes in education historically have been linked to societal reform and upheaval. Issues of today and trends for tomorrow grow out of the problems and solutions in the past.

In the 1960s, social action and a war on poverty captured the American interest and spirit. Head Start programs opened around the country and were the symbols of social action of that era. The 1970s brought changes related to economic crisis. Social services were scrutinized to determine their worth and value. The family unit was affected by the job market, the end of the Vietnam War, an energy crisis, inflation, rising divorce rates, and the feminist movement. All of these factors led more women toward work in the marketplace rather than in the home. One of the expansions in public funding at this time was in the services to the handicapped and bilingual populations.

The 1980s meant further budget cuts, reduced services for children and families, and an altered state of childhood. Computers were being installed at all grade levels. Children were often in group care for most of their waking hours. They grew up with change, rather than stability, as a

 OUR DIVERSE WORLD OUR DIVERSE WORLD OUR DIVERSE WORLD OUR DIVERSE WORLD OUR DIVERSE WORLD

[1]Early childhood education and care continues to be on the forefront in dealing with the outcomes of immense social change in American society.

constant in their lives. Child abuse became a national cause for alarm. The need for early child care and educational services was well established and will be here for the next several decades. To ignore this need is to deny the reality of family life today.

The reforms in general education that began in the early 1980s brought about some rethinking in early childhood education by the early nineties. As people became aware of the shortcomings of education at higher levels, they could view the early years as a starting point for improvements. Interest in young children flourished along with reforms at other grade levels.

As the 1990s end, there is an expanded acceptance of child care for children under five, and an increasing awareness of the needs of the whole child in the early primary years. At the same time, a wide range of global and sociopolitical issues emerge that affect both the nation and the family, thus having a major impact on children and teachers.

Looking ahead to the twenty-first century, it seems especially appropriate to discuss current questions in light of the history of the early childhood profession. Take another look at Chapter 1 of this book. For all its diverse and varied past, early childhood education has had a consistent commitment to three major themes: the ethic of social reform, the importance of childhood, and transmitting values. These three themes are reflected in the major issues facing early childhood educators today and tomorrow:

● *Ethic of Social Reform*

1. What programs and services are needed for young children and families? Who will pay for and provide them?

2. What education reforms are in place that speak to the quality of life for all children? What is developmentally appropriate teaching? What else is needed to improve education for children under eight years of age?

● *Importance of Childhood*

1. What are the crises children face today, and what can be done to help them?

2. What is the value of childhood? How is the commitment to children demonstrated?

3. What is the role of family and community in children's lives?

● *Transmitting Values*

1. What is the role of television and the media in children's lives? How are concerns about media violence best addressed?

2. How do we teach children the value of peace?

3. What are the challenges of diversity in schools, neighborhoods, and families?

4. What are the basic values children should be taught in schools?

ETHIC OF SOCIAL REFORM

Every element of personal well-being, social progress, and economic development is bound inextricably to knowledge, learning, and skill.

(The National Education Study Panel on Education Indicators, National Center for Education Statistics, 1991)

The ethic of social reform, first mentioned in Chapter 1, refers to an expectation that education and schooling for young children has the potential for significant social change and improvement. There is also the clear implication that educating the mind and teaching the skills are intertwined with a person's ability to get a job and provide for one's future well-being. This is dramatically demonstrated in the discussion of the two major issues of child care and educational reform. How will young children be affected by these two forces—the need for child care and the growing call for excellence in education? The realities of cost and quality create a tension that has not yet been resolved and is only now being aggressively pursued within the early childhood field.

In this section, we will look at these two issues of child care and educational reform separately as they relate to the ethic of social reform.

Child Care

Since the mid-seventies,

● four times as many children are enrolled in three times as many child care centers;

- enrollment in regulated family day care settings increased by 53 percent;

- during that same period of time, enrollments of children under two nearly doubled, indicating a major shift toward caring for younger children outside the home (Willer et al, 1991).

Without question, the need for child care has been firmly established. The significant increase in enrollment in child care centers over the last twenty years, underscored by these demographic facts, has had a profound impact on this country: In 1990 Congress passed the first comprehensive child care legislation in nearly twenty years; a year later Head Start funding was increased significantly (see Chapter 2).

It is obvious that child care has public support. Quality child care programs have earned the respect of parents and legislators and demonstrated to society that children can thrive in good early childhood programs. (See discussion on child care in Ch. 2).

FIGURE 15.2 The quality of a child-care program is directly related to the experience and training of the teachers.

Quality and Cost

The key word, however, is *quality*—the terms "good quality" and "high quality" identify specific features in early childhood programs.

Two recent broad-based studies, one conducted in child care centers and the other in family day care settings, examined the critical relationship between quality and cost and present a disturbing picture.

Inadequate child care was found to be rampant in the first study, which was conducted in hundreds of centers in California, Colorado, Connecticut, and North Carolina (Cost, Quality and Child Outcomes Study Team, 1995). In a dramatic conclusion, the study found that most child care centers provided mediocre services and that some were of such poor quality that they threatened children's emotional and intellectual development. Infants and toddlers were most likely to be at risk for poor care in these centers; nearly half of their settings failed to meet basic health and safety needs. Yet 90 percent of the parents rated the care as "good."

The report was the first of its kind to examine the relationship between the costs of child care and

the nature of children's experiences in child care settings (quality). In centers in which researchers found high quality care, the center staffs were paid higher wages, there were more personnel, and more of them were trained in early childhood education. They were also programs which were subsidized in some way, by the government, a university, or employers of families using the services. The states which had more demanding licensing requirements had few poor quality programs. According to this report, these factors, along with teachers' salaries and administrators' prior experience are strong determinants of quality.

The results of the first major study of family day care in a decade are similarly distressing, highlighting uneven and poorly regulated conditions. Conducted by Galinsky et al (1994), the study concluded that only 9 percent of the homes they observed were of good quality and that over one-third of the providers were so indifferent in their caregiving as to be harmful to children's development. More than 40 percent of the providers planned no activities for children in their care, and only half the children showed signs of trust or attachment to the caregiver. The more a provider was paid, the better the care; the licensed or regulated providers were more likely to be warm and attentive to children, communicate with parents, and provide a safe home. Look at the ten "Indicators of Quality" as defined by NAEYC which are cited in Chapter 2 to see where there is a relationship with the findings of these two studies.[1]

Both forms of child care are equally popular. Approximately one-third of the employed families with children under 5 years choose family day care and another 30 percent choose center care. They are the programs of choice by America's working families, who, according to this research, either do not recognize what makes a quality program or who think they cannot demand it. Quality is a function of group size, low teacher:child ratios, trained and experienced staff, adequate compensation, and safe and stimulating environments (Willer, 1990, 1991). Yet these are not the first things parents look for. The family child care study found that parents rate safety as the most important factor in choosing a provider, communications with parents second, and warm attention to children as third. Adult:child ratios, professional training, and licensing rank much lower. Geographical distance and price have been cited by others as the primary criteria for choosing a child care setting (Hofferth, 1994).

To improve the quality of family child care, the reports call on government and business to increase their support in a number of ways: help parents pay for good care, establish training programs for providers, bring providers into regulation, and educate parents about high-quality care. All of the studies share a common concern that parents must be able to distinguish good from poor quality centers and demand higher quality care before the centers will increase their fees to cover the costs of providing better care.

A National Crisis

Quality care and education of young children has a cost that must be addressed. The cost of quality is directly related to the needs of the families served by the specific program. In some programs, securing the basic needs of food, housing, and health care, are an important obligation. The added cost of helping families connect with the right resources and providing the necessary comprehensive services will contribute to a higher cost for quality in that program. Fee reductions and financial aid for low-income families also add to the costs for a quality program.

Quality is significantly related to staff: how many adults there are compared to the number of children in a class; whether the salaries and benefits provide incentive for teachers to be retained for a number of years; the level of the staff's education and training; and their years of experience. These factors have created a staffing crisis of major proportion in the country today.

The crisis refers to the difficulties of recruiting and retaining qualified staff for good early childhood programs. The problems center around the costs of providing for quality teachers and staff. Salaries for early childhood employees are disgracefully low, and pension plans and health care benefits are nonexistent for many. In 1992, the annual salary of an assistant teacher (the lowest paid child care worker), was approximately $9,000 a year. The highest paid teacher, with college training in early childhood education, earned $15,500. The turnover rate that year was 26 percent, compared to businesses' rate of 9.6 percent (Child Care Employee Project, 1993). Adjusting for inflation, the salary levels of early childhood personnel have declined almost 25 percent over the past 20 years (Willer et al, 1991).

It is ironic that these cost factors result in 1) people leaving early childhood to find employment in other fields and 2) new people not being attracted to working with young children just at a time when there is an unprecedented demand for child care services. By the year 2000, it is anticipated that the country will need 56 percent more early childhood professionals than exist today (Willer & Johnson, 1989). The disappointing aspect of this seemingly good news is how to keep fees low enough to provide the necessary services of child care, yet compensate child care employees what they are worth in order to attract and retain them in the early childhood profession. The challenge is before all of us—the child care profession-

OUR DIVERSE WORLD OUR DIVERSE WORLD OUR DIVERSE WORLD OUR DIVERSE WORLD OUR DIVERSE WORLD

[1]Early childhood educators are reminded again and again of the need to have an awareness of the values, traditions, and experiences, beyond that of the dominant culture (Western European-Christian-Judaic).

als, the parents, the leaders of business and industry, and the legislators on the local, state, and national scene. A national effort called "Worthy Wage Campaign" and "Full Cost of Quality in Early Childhood Education Programs Campaign" are leading the charge in mobilizing the early childhood field to advocacy and in bringing the issues of the child care crisis to national attention.

According to Kagan (USDE, 1990), there are broader societal goals that prevent quality alone to be the focus. Equality and integrity are also needed to insure excellence in early childhood education. Equal access to good programs and the provision of services that help families break from poverty's grip are critical to the national good. Consistent standards at local and national levels for all early childhood programs ensures equality and excellence for all children. Integrity, which refers to "making whole," suggests the need for an integrated approach to the whole fabric of early childhood programs, services, and sponsors. Greater coordination among and between the various private and public systems reduces isolation of individual programs and enhances a truly systematic approach to quality early education for all children.

Education Reform

The ethic of social reform can be strongly felt in the current education reform movement. One of the primary functions of the public school system in the United States is to prepare students for productive roles in society—to produce skilled workers who will enter the job market and contribute to a healthy, competitive economy worldwide.

In the spring of 1983, the National Commission on Excellence in Education issued a report on American schools that precipitated the current reform movement. *A Nation at Risk,* as the report was called, was soon followed by a number of other significant publications which defined the educational crisis at hand and offered a variety of solutions. Early childhood education; vocational education; elementary and secondary schooling; urban schools; teacher education, preparation, and recruitment; character development; literacy; dropouts; and disadvantaged children all came under scrutiny by blue-ribbon panels.

By the late 80's, education emerged as a dominant issue in the presidential campaign. American public schools faced a crisis of quality; a national education problem was identified and a sense of urgency instilled in the public mind. In the first wave of reform, virtually every state enacted reform measures of some kind. The focus was on higher standards of student performance through the upgrading of curricula, increased requirements for homework, and firmer disciplinary methods. Reform of teacher education and restructuring of schools to strengthen the role of the teacher was included as well.

The trend in the 1990s has been toward a national agenda, as seen in America 2000, six long-range goals to improve American education by the beginning of the next century. It is the first time in history that we have had a national consensus on a vision of public education. The first goal has received widespread attention, for it is pivotal in ensuring the success of the remaining goals.

Ready to Learn

Goal number one of America 2000 states that by the year 2000, all children in America will start school ready to learn, and that the following objectives will be met:

- All disadvantaged and disabled children will have access to high-quality and developmentally appropriate preschool programs that help prepare children for school;

- Every parent in America will be a child's first teacher and devote time each day helping his or her preschool child learn; parents will have access to the training and support they need;

- Children will receive the nutrition and health care needed to arrive at school with healthy minds and bodies, then the number of low birthweight babies will be significantly reduced through enhanced prenatal health systems.

(U.S. Department of Education, 1991)

One report serves as a call to arms to ensure that children will be ready for school. The Carnegie Foundation for the Advancement of Teaching, citing a "quiet crisis" facing the nation's youngest children (Boyer, 1991), proposed a decade long

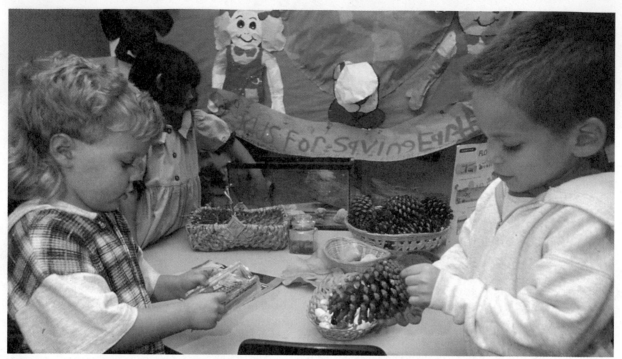

FIGURE 15.3   How do we know that all children will start school ready to learn? How can good quality early childhood programs help *America 2000* reach its first goal?

campaign on behalf of children to alter the long-established pattern of social neglect. In a report entitled, "Ready to Learn—A Mandate for the Nation," the birth- to- three-year-old age span was called the most critical period in a child's development but the most neglected by policymakers. The study surveyed over 7,000 kindergarten teachers on obstacles to readiness. The responses indicate that 35 percent of U.S. children are not ready to participate in formal learning. The most serious problem reported by over 50 percent of the teachers was language deficiencies. The report also quoted teachers voicing distress about the number of children coming to school hungry, abused, lacking attention, and with deep emotional and health problems. Some of the recommendations include comprehensive health services for infants and toddlers, improvement in child care quality, parent education programs, and family oriented workplace policies.

As education policymakers go about the task of defining the issue of readiness and discuss ways to measure it, other noteworthy reform efforts related to America 2000's first goal have emerged.

Reform Issues and Strategies

Some of the most important issues to come out of the school reform movement are:

● *Professionalization of teaching.* To place teaching on a par with other professions, such as law and medicine; looking at the ways in which teachers are educated and trained in four-year institutions.

● *School governance.* The need for more on-site autonomy, involving teachers as well as administrators.

● *Giving parents a choice.* Allowing parents to select their children's school from a range of options throughout the school district, public as well as private.

● *Teacher recruitment.* Providing professionally competitive salaries to attract good teachers; using merit pay schedules and master teacher roles to keep qualified teachers in the classroom.

● *Experimental programs.* The use of smaller

school settings, smaller classes, and magnet schools.

- *Involvement of the larger community.* To support schools in new ways; to provide more child care functions wherever necessary. Involving the private sector through business leaders promoting school improvements.

- *Equal access.* To ensure that disadvantaged students, minority students, handicapped students, and others at risk have their needs addressed and, specifically, more comprehensive programs to prepare them as adequately as middle-class students.

- *Seeing the child in context.* Taking into account the context of family, culture, and community, with respect for cultural and linguistic diversity.

Common factors in the reform agenda that early childhood educators share with other educational professionals are those related to the professionalization of teaching, parental choice, program quality, and serving all children equally.

A growing band of national organizations (led by Children's Defense Fund) calling for reforms has stressed that unless more is done to meet the early health, social, and developmental needs of young children, school reform will fail. An estimated 40 percent of America's children begin school already at risk due to poverty, family instability, substance abuse, and racial discrimination (Olson, 1991).

To meet the needs of working parents and ensure that children are ready to learn, reform strategies should be enlarged to include the following. These six reform issues predict the agenda for the early childhood profession for the remainder of this decade.

1. *Link education and child care.* The existing separation between early childhood programs is counterproductive to the reform effort. The early childhood profession includes both the caregiving and educating aspects of teaching; in recent years the distinction between the two has blurred within the profession and the two have been intentionally linked. There is a greater acknowledgment that caretaking and educational factors are involved in all programs that serve very young children. However, the general public, as well as government agencies, tend to be unaware of the critical relationships between these two factors and perpetuate the division. This dichotomy between care and education must be eliminated.

2. *Establish continuity between early childhood programs and kindergartens.* Good early childhood education is more than getting children ready to start school. It is a comprehensive vision that supports child development principles, appropriate teaching practices, active parent involvement, family support, and health services. Until there is a restructuring of the present early elementary system, many of the advantages of the preschool years and early intervention programs will be negated. To provide continuity, there must be clarity on how preschool and child care programs should differ from standard elementary school classes and how elementary school curricula can support good preschool practices. The Task Force on Early Childhood Education of the National Association of State Boards of Education calls for a restructuring of the early elementary grades to include ungraded early childhood units serving children for ages four–eight.

3. *Address children's nonacademic needs.* Unless more is done to meet the early health and social needs of children, school reform is likely to fail. The societal problems that lie outside traditional education must be met if children are to be ready to learn. Child health and nutrition services and prenatal care will help ensure that children will enter school ready to learn. Meeting the needs of poor families also includes making high-quality preschool programs available to children of all income levels and abilities. We must not choose between quality and equality (Ravitch, 1990).

4. *Promote developmental learning.* Educational policymakers must alter their perspective of readiness. When there is a mismatch between the expectations of the school and the children's abilities to meet those demands, the schools need to change. The programs must adapt to meet the developmental needs of chil-

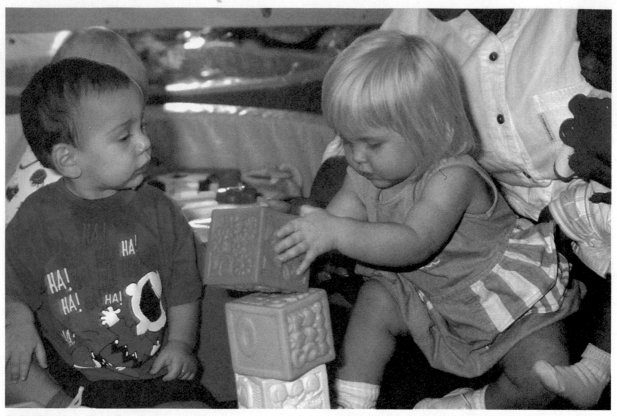

FIGURE 15.4   Good early childhood programs do not distinguish between education and care but understand that both are vital to the growing child.

dren rather than the other way around. Get *schools* ready for young children as opposed to having children be pressured and pushed to get ready for school. Ensure that schools respect the unique way children under eight learn and allow for their differing timetable of learning. Discourage the use of standardized testing for screening, tracking, and retaining young children. Avoid labeling young children or linking student readiness evaluations to school entry. Teaching practices in the elementary school years should be based on child development principles and modeled after successful preschool programs. (NASBE Task Force on Early Childhood Education, 1988)

5. *Initiate programs and policies that strengthen the family.* Develop programs that help to increase parents abilities to help their children become learners and that involve the family in the educational endeavor. Education and learning are

profoundly affected by what happens to children outside of schools (National Study Panel on Education Indicators, 1991). The family support for learning should be addressed by focusing on parental attitudes and involvement at home as well as at school and the parents' responsibility for meeting the basic care and needs of their children.

6. *Develop partnerships with the community and with businesses.* Coordinating the efforts of the many providers of child care services and collaborating with other community agencies that service young children and their families serves more children, makes better use of public funds, and improves the quality of all programs. A comprehensive system of early childhood services would include parent education and family support programs, child care, and health and social services. The effort should involve programs that are public and private, profit and

nonprofit, church and government sponsored, and home-based as well as center-based. Under such a partnership, the community as a whole could build and improve services to children and parents through joint planning and advocacy and information and resource sharing (NASBE Task Force on Early Childhood Education, 1988).

Solutions

Changes in education are historically linked to social reform. Nowhere is this more obvious than in the current reform movement. The link between poverty and school failure has been recognized and clearly demonstrated. The reform itself was spurred in part by one of the most powerful social and economic changes in this century: the employed mother.

The reforms that have been suggested cannot be solved by any single agency or institution. We must look beyond individual programs to the trend toward a diversity of services provided by an equally diverse coalition of state and federal government, business and industry, research and education. Together, a common agenda to enhance school success in the context of the child's family, community, and culture can be established, for, according to Kagan (1990) nothing less than the future direction of the field is at stake.

THE IMPORTANCE OF CHILDHOOD

Endangered Childhood

Children and childhood have changed. Gone are the days when the majority of children arrived home from school to be greeted by Mom in the kitchen, serving milk and homemade cookies. Today's child spends the bulk of time in child care centers or with a neighbor while the parent is at work. Too many arrive at empty homes and spend the next few hours alone or caring for younger siblings. As often as not, the child of today lives with just one parent at best.[1]

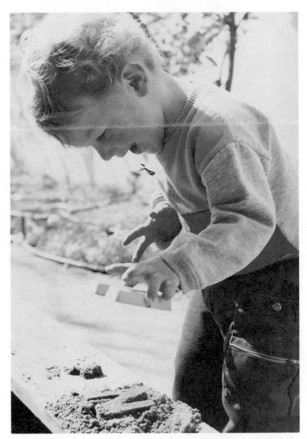

FIGURE 15.5 Every child has the right to a full and wondrous childhood.

Emphasis on Survival

A decade or two ago children seemed to be more protected than they are today; they seemed more innocent. Adults of yesteryear perceived their roles as protectors of children, keeping them at arm's length from life's stresses. Today's parents, on the other hand, are concerned that their children learn to survive, to cope with problems at an early age. They believe the best way to teach children survival skills is to expose them to adult experiences and "reality" early.

The impact of social changes in the last twenty years has been hardest felt by the children of the nation. The breakdown of the nuclear family unit, the sexual and feminist revolutions, television,

 OUR DIVERSE WORLD OUR DIVERSE WORLD OUR DIVERSE WORLD OUR DIVERSE WORLD OUR DIVERSE WORLD

[1]Do we as a society have a mindset of OUR DIVERSE WORLD, or an image/mythology based on middle-class family life of the mid 1940's- mid 1960's?

drugs, and worldwide violence have thrust children into adult situations with adult troubles. Dual-parent careers and single working parents, together with the lack of extended families, have meant that children's behavior is not as closely monitored as it once was.

Stress and Changing Parent—Child Relations

Childhood has been misplaced. The boundaries between adults and children are hazy. Adults exert pressure on children to hurry and grow up, to achieve and succeed, to perform and to please. Children respond by doing their best, all the while sensing the pressure to mature (Gordon, 1986).

People are dealing with their children differently than did their parents. They are opening up to their children, telling them of (rather than protecting them from) their own fears and anxieties. Children have been enlisted as coparents in their own upbringing, collaborating with their parents on child-rearing practices, dress codes, and behavior expectations. While this is obviously more democratic and less authoritarian, the results have been that the boundaries between children and adults have become increasingly hazy. It would appear that we are asking young children of today to assume a mantle of maturity before they are capable. We are requiring them to respond to life as adults, not as children. We no longer assure children that the adult is in charge and that their needs will be met. Instead, we ask children to share that burden with us.

Another type of parent emerged in the 1980s, the creator of the "superbaby" (Langway et al., 1983). These children began life enrolled in a series of classes by parents who hoped to give them as many stimulating experiences as they could absorb. Infant gymnastic workouts, alphabet flashcards in the nursery, and violin or acting lessons to supplement preschool signaled parental expectations for these children. These wonderkids, children of the post-World War II "baby-boom" children (who now are affluent, knowledgeable, and generally over 30), must fulfill every conceivable potential as early as possible. They were being pushed toward success by parents who themselves were more successful than their parents were. "The more, the better" sometimes seemed the motto of the day.

The focus for these parents was and is often on infant academics and superior physical achievement. This raises concerns about the welfare of the child. When the emphasis is on performance and not on unconditional acceptance or feelings, the development of the child may be focused on only one or a few areas of the child's growth. It raises questions as to whether all the basics are being met—social and emotional needs as well as creative, intellectual, and physical ones.

Today's children are expected to cope with changing family structures. Only a small percentage of U.S. households are traditional, nuclear families. Instead, children face divorce, single parenthood, sexuality issues, dual-career parents, poverty, homelessness, and other late twentieth century phenomena that produce stress. Adult coping skills are expected of two-, four-, and seven-year-olds, rather than allowing children to respond to life as children (Gordon, 1986).

For many children, the result has been a hurried childhood (Elkind, 1982). Parents push their children through the early years, urging them to grow up fast, succeed, achieve. Designer clothes are just the outward trappings these parents use to encourage adult attitudes and behaviors. The loss of childhood seems to have brought with it new problems for children. Clinicians are seeing more children with stress-related problems: headaches, abdominal pains, and even ulcers are occurring in children three and four years old.

Many common experiences that produce stress in young children are family related. Most adults would identify divorce, a move to a new home, prolonged visits from a relative, and a new sibling as classic stress situations for children. Yet there are homlier and less dramatic sources of stress, the simple everyday occurrences that children face: being told not to do something, not having a friend, being ignored by a parent, experiencing changes in the routine, not being able to read or zip a zipper or put a puzzle together (Gordon, 1986). Stress may also occur in families where both parents pursue high-powered careers and children feel the need to live up to exceptional standards in academic achievement or sports proficiency. Apathetic parents, parents who ignore their children or have no time for them, and parents who push children into frantic schedules of activity also cause stress in their children. Stress can result from happy occasions as well—holidays, vacation, or a new puppy may be overanticipated, overstructured, and overstimulating to a child.

Children respond to stress in many ways. In adults, and sometimes in older children, depression, substance abuse, underachievement, and obsession with financial success are common responses to stress. In children, signs of stress include sleeping problems (such as nightmares or sleepwalking), depression, regression to the behavior of an earlier stage, aches and pains, acting out, eating problems, and overreactions, as well as medical problems (such as headaches, upset stomach, and bleeding ulcers) (Reed, 1986).

Stress is a natural part of life and is a factor in every child's development. Review Chapter 14 for the stages of stress which children go through and for ways to help them cope with their responses.

Child Abuse and Neglect

The Crisis

In 1992, an estimated 2.9 million children were reported abused and neglected, according to the Children's Defense Fund (1994). This represents 3 times the number since 1980. Respect for children and childhood is seriously eroded when adults violate the trust of and responsibility for children through neglect and abuse. Social change over the last few decades has put many of our children at risk. The changes in the family unit, unemployment, loss of funding for programs and subsidies for families, and rising divorce rates have put parents under stress and are having a negative effect on children's well-being. When children are cared for improperly, the results are often child neglect and abuse.

A neglected child may be one whose waking hours are mostly unsupervised by adults, in front of the television or simply unconnected with—and unnoticed by—parents or an important caregiver. *Neglect* takes other, more hazardous, forms, however. When the basic needs of adequate food, clothing, shelter, and health are unmet, parents are being neglectful. Failure to exercise the care

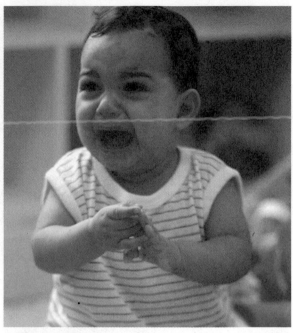

FIGURE 15.6 How do we help children cope with stress?

that children need shows an inattention to and lack of concern for children.

Child abuse is the most severe form of disrespect for children. Violence in the form of physical maltreatment and sexual abuse is an improper treatment of children, regardless of their behavior. Abusive language and harsh physical aggression are other forms of child abuse that occur in families and, unfortunately, some settings for child care.

Publicized investigations into sexual abuse of children in child care centers, preschools, and family situations have brought national attention to this hideous violence. Fewer than 5 percent of the cases reported occur outside the home and less than 1 percent involve child care or foster care settings (Lawton, 1991). Whether or not its increased incidence is due to a change in reporting practices, it is clear that the abuse of children knows no social, racial, or economic barriers. It is happening to children at all levels of the social spectrum.

Standards of Care

For child care workers, the heart of the issue lies in the regulation and licensing of early child-

FIGURE 15.7 When basic needs such as food and shelter are met, children are free to develop interests in other people and other things.

hood programs. In light of recent disclosures concerning incidents in centers, we need to take a long, hard look at who is caring for children. In what physical, emotional, and interpersonal environments are our children living? Licensing regulations for schools and teacher certification vary greatly throughout the country. Primarily they ensure only minimum health and safety standards of the physical environment. The great number of unlicensed child care facilities and the quality of children's programs are urgent issues. Governing and regulatory agencies in most states are inadequately staffed and insufficiently budgeted to handle the monitoring of child care settings.

A national call to action to increase public awareness and understanding of child abuse is underway. Standardized licensing procedures, upgrading of the certification of child care workers, and national accreditation of all preschools are some of the most frequently mentioned solutions to the problem. Helping parents identify what qualities to look for when placing their children in someone else's care is another way to prevent child abuse in centers.

Role of Teacher

Teachers have a role to play. Reporting suspected child abuse is mandated by law in *all* states. Educators must assume the responsibility to inform the proper authorities if they suspect that a child in their care is being abused by adults. Figure 15.8 lists the signs a teacher should look for if child abuse is suspected.

The mandate to report suspected child abuse applies to teachers, principals, counselors, school nurses, and staff members of child care centers and summer camps. Certain knowledge that abuse took place is not required; reports are legally required if there is reasonable cause to suspect a child has been mistreated. To protect anyone reporting abuse or neglect, the person filing the report is held immune from civil or criminal liability if the report was made in good faith.

What to Do If You Suspect Child Abuse

● Make notes of child's appearance—any bruises, marks, or behaviors that cause you concern.

● Inform the director of the program and/or your immediate supervisor; plan together who will inform the proper authorities and how to contact the parent(s).

● Discuss ways to support the staff members who make the report, the parent(s), and the child.

● Call the locally designated agency for child abuse. A written report may be required within 24 to 48 hours.

● Support the parent(s) throughout the investigation. Be available to the parent(s) and the child as they deal with the other agencies who are trained and equipped to handle this problem.

● Follow through with assistance or support if requested to do so by the child-protective services agency. Help the family by working with others who are counseling them and performing parent support services.

What to Do If a Child Tells You He or She Has Been Abused

● Believe the child; children rarely lie about sexual abuse.

● Commend the child for telling you what happened.

● Convey your support for the child. Children's greatest fear is that they are at fault and responsible for the incident. It is important to help children avoid blaming themselves.

● Temper your own reactions, recognizing that your perspective and acceptance are critical signals to the child. Do not convey your own feelings about the abuse.

Child abuse should be suspected if a child:
- Is constantly late, stays away from school for long periods of time, or arrives early and stays late, avoiding going home.
- Is withdrawn, passive, and uncommunicative or aggressive, destructive, and nervous.
- Has unexplained injuries, too many "explained" ones, or has an injury that is inadequately explained.
- Complains of numerous beatings, of someone "doing things," whether or not the parents are home.
- Goes to the bathroom with difficulty; has burns, limps, or bruises, patches of hair missing, bad teeth.
- Wears clothing that is too small, soiled, or inappropriate for the weather, or uses clothing to cover injuries.
- Is dirty, smells, is too thin or constantly tired; exhibits dehydration or malnutrition.
- Is usually fearful of other children or adults.
- Has been fed inappropriate food, drink, or drugs.

FIGURE 15.8 A child who exhibits several of these signs should be investigated as a possible victim of child abuse. (Adapted from Fraser, 1977.)

● Report the suspected abuse to the child's parent(s), the designated social service agency, and/or the police.

● Find specialized agencies that evaluate sexual abuse victims and a physician with the experience and training to detect and recognize sexual abuse.

Source of information: *Child Sexual Abuse Prevention*, Washington, D.C.: U.S. Department of Health and Human Services, 1984.

In some early childhood programs, teachers and other specialists have started programs for young children that will help them recognize and avoid abuse. Perhaps most important, teachers must stay in close touch with the parents of all their children. By knowing parents personally and being in contact with them regularly, an early childhood professional may be able to detect early signs of impending problems of both abuse and neglect. The perceptive teacher can then support parents through their difficulties, offering them help by informing them of a parental stress hotline, suggesting strategies to avoid stress and violence, and recommending professional help.

Children and AIDS

Acquired Immune Deficiency Syndrome (AIDS) is a communicable disease that breaks down the body's immune system, leaving it unable to fend off harmful bacteria, viruses, and the like. Illnesses that are not usually life-threatening to a healthy person can result in death for someone who has AIDS. When reading this section, the student is reminded that statistics and information on AIDS are constantly changing; the reader is strongly urged to consult the most recent research data.

AIDS is caused by a virus (HIV) that is primarily sexually transmitted, although it can pass from one person to another by contact with blood, blood products, or through bodily secretions that mix with a person's blood. The AIDS virus may be present in the blood even though the full AIDS syndrome does not develop. The infection, however, can be transmitted to someone else even if the person carrying it has no symptoms.

AIDS is thought to have first occurred in the 1970s, although documentation of AIDS patients did not begin until 1979. In the United States the disease is prevalent among males (90 percent of the AIDS victims are men) and occurs primarily in homosexuals, in intravenous drug users, and in hemophiliacs and other persons who receive contaminated blood transfusions.

Children, too, are AIDS victims. Those at greatest risk are:

● Infants born to mothers who have AIDS

● Infants who are breast-fed by mothers with AIDS

● Infants and children who receive blood transfusions (blood screening programs may have reduced this risk)

● Sexually abused children

The highest incidence of pediatric AIDS is found in metropolitan areas, in large cities that also have a high rate of intravenous drug use. African American children account for 52 percent of reported pediatric AIDS cases and Latino children make up 25 percent of the cases. Approximately 80 percent of the diagnosed children were infected by their mothers before or at birth. It is estimated that the number of children with HIV, who do not yet have AIDS, is twice that of those diagnosed with AIDS (Children's Defense Fund, 1991).

The greatest fears—and misconceptions—about AIDS are how contagious is the disease and how is it transmitted. "People seem to find it hard to believe that a virus which can cause such a cruel and fatal disease is not easily caught from people who are infected" (Aronson, 1987). Sexual contacts and mingling of blood are the two known routes of infection, and not one case is known to have been transmitted any other way, even to close family members of AIDS patients (Aronson, 1987). No children have caught AIDS from ordinary contact with other children. None of the cases of AIDS in the United States has been transmitted in a school or child care setting nor through hugging, sharing a glass or a plate, sharing bathrooms, or in kissing that is not mouth to mouth kissing (Aronson, 1987).

Role of the Teacher

The numbers of AIDS victims multiply rapidly. The Centers for Disease Control predict a continued increase in the heterosexual population and in babies. Early childhood professionals clearly have a role to play regarding this misunderstood disease:

● Be an informed resource to parents and other teachers. Keep abreast of current data and educate others about the *facts* of AIDS.

● Know how to answer the questions a preschooler will ask. Begin to educate children.

● Examine your own attitudes about homosexuality and drug usage.

● Keep up to date on research about AIDS; information changes rapidly and is released frequently.

● Take appropriate precautions—careful handwashing and use of plastic gloves when contact with blood may occur.

- Be prepared to counsel children and their families through long illness and death in the same way as with other fatal diseases.

- Develop school policies that reflect the current knowledge and recommendations of medical experts.

At Risk: Children in Need

Of major concern to educators for the twenty-first century is a group of Americans who are destined for limited participation in the social, political, and economic mainstream of national life. The children who are at risk of academic failure are likely to be: those who live in poverty, members of minority groups in racial isolation, children with various physical and mental disabilities, children with limited English proficiency, children from single parent families, and children attending schools with a high concentration of students who live in poverty (National Study Panel on Education Indicators, 1991).

Millions of children are poverty-bound and are at risk to repeat the cycles that keep them poor and disadvantaged. As Edelman (1993) reports,

> Young children are the poorest Americans. Almost one in four American children younger than six lived in a family with income below the poverty line in 1990, and more than one in 10 in a family with income less than one-half of the poverty line. Living in dire poverty means that children's nutrition and health care too often are traded against paying the rent or the heat; after paying the rent, a typical poor family with children has an average of $3.49 per day left to spend on all other needs.

These children and youth are undereducated, marginally literate, and lacking the necessary skills for employment. They are high risks for dropping out of school and becoming teenaged parents who will perpetuate the cycle again. In 1989, nearly 19 percent of all children and 51 percent of children in female-headed families lived in poverty. Over a 30-year period, from 1960–1990, the proportion of poor children coming from households headed by a female doubled for all children and increased 75 percent for African American children (Office of Educational Research and Improvement, 1991). The feminization of poverty is still a reality

that must be faced and amended before the next century.

There is a striking correlation between poverty and school failure. Children who start out at a disadvantage fall farther behind in academic achievement throughout their school years.

The changing school population suggests that these problems will only increase as the proportion of minority groups expands, as a larger and larger percentage of children fall below the poverty line, and as traditional patterns of child-rearing and marriage change so that fewer children will have the emotional and educational advantages of a two-parent family.

A dramatic and intensive reform effort is needed for at-risk children and a number of solutions are being considered. With one in every five children in America living in families who exist below the poverty level, commitment and action is urgent. As the National Commission on Children (1991) states:

> . . . Too many of today's children and adolescents will reach adulthood unhealthy, illiterate, unemployable, lacking moral direction and a vision of a secure future. This is a personal tragedy for the young people involved and a staggering loss for the nation as a whole. We must begin today to place children and their families at the top of the national agenda.

Families and Communities

The family of today has many shapes, sizes, and styles. A family can be:

- a dual-career family, with two parents working outside the home and children in child care;

- a single parent supporting children with little or no help—either financial or personal—from the absent parent;

- older parents raising their grandchildren;

- teen parents living with, or without, family support;

- a blended family—adults with children remarried to form a new structure, with children living full- or part-time in residence;

- an extended family (or several families) living together in a small dwelling;

● a single person living alone or with others without children.

In fact, the American family has evolved so extensively over the last few decades that, as of 1990, the Census Bureau (Edelman, 1989) reports:

● The 1990s will be the first decade to begin with a majority of mothers of young children (55 percent) in the work force, representing an increase of over 80 percent since 1970.

● The population of children under ten from single-parent households will have risen from 6 million to 8.9 million—a 48 percent increase from the 1980s.

● The population of children under six will have increased 3.3 million to 23.0 million in 1990 (and will then begin to decline).

The issue of the changing family structure affects early childhood professionals in several ways. Teachers should understand the nature of these changes, and their effects on parents and children. What new guidelines will be needed for parents in child rearing? What is the role of educators with the new American family?

Divorce and Family Structures

Perhaps no one single change has affected children as much as the *divorce* rate. The trend towards more divorce is significant. Nearly 50 percent of marriages end in divorce, and four out of ten children born in the 1990s will spend part of their growing years in a single parent home (Osborn, 1991).[1] One schoolchild in three has parents who are divorced; 30 percent of these are children in stepfamilies and the other 70 percent live with their mothers or fathers alone (Clarke-Stewart, 1989). The issues for teachers are (1) dealing with the effects of divorce on children and (2) supporting the recovery process and resumption of family life. The effects of divorce are felt for years. Getting over divorce and onto a productive life is critical for both child and parent; teachers can help.

The effects of divorce are felt by children well before the event itself. Children exhibit "predivorce family stress" by increased impulsive or aggressive behavior, and parents show the stress with headaches, fatigue, mood swings, or depression. Children's initial reaction to their parents' separation is traumatic–shock and distress (the "stage 1" responses to stress as described in Chapter 14). Even if parents are in violent conflict with each other, no child is happy about divorce (Clarke-Stewart, 1989). After divorce, many parents become overworked and overwhelmed. Children are often neglected or left with less than what both parents could provide, including emotional and financial support. Studies indicate that after a divorce women suffer a drastic drop in income; the median annual income of families with children under six is $6114 (Galinsky, 1986). Since 90 percent of children in divorced families live with their mothers, economic disaster is felt by most children of divorce.

Adjustment to divorce is difficult, but fortunately children are amazingly resilient. The age and sex of the children involved seems to have some bearing on their adjustment. Very young children recover more easily than older ones, and girls more readily than boys. The parents' ability to be caring and available makes a difference, as does the parents' relationship with each other and the quality of the children's relationship with both parents.

What can teachers do? For one, teachers should be informed about what to expect from children in the divorce cycle. They can help parents get access to outside help, such as a parent support group, community welfare services, or a parental stress hotline. Particularly with parents involved in a divorce, teachers must plan strategies for family involvement that takes into account the work demands, resources, and expertise of parents themselves. With children, teachers are open and forthcoming about the reality of different kinds of families (see "Community and School Support" section). Overall, teachers help children and parents understand and cope with the challenges and responsibilities of marriage and family life.

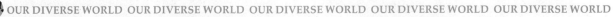

OUR DIVERSE WORLD OUR DIVERSE WORLD OUR DIVERSE WORLD OUR DIVERSE WORLD OUR DIVERSE WORLD

[1]Consider the stories read to young children. Is this reality reflected? Is this reality reflected in messages sent from program to school? scheduling parent-program meetings?

Work, Economics, and Public Policy: The Working Parent

By 1995, two-thirds of all preschool children will have mothers in the work force (Edelman, 1993), and the percentage rises when considering school-aged children as well. In fact, the Department of Labor predicted that, by the end of 1995 more than 80 percent of women between 24 and 44 years of age will be in the work force (Edelman, 1989). The trend toward more women at work affects the teacher and parents. The implications for parents are considerable. For women, the double roles of job/career and family nurturer is overwhelming, creating great conflict and the stress of chronic fatigue. Men are looking at their role in a different light; many are learning about greater involvement in child-rearing. For both parents, three issues loom large: the concern for good child care, the struggle to provide "quality time" with children and as a family unit, and the financial burden. Without parental leave, parents are forced to return to work during the critical early months of infancy or lose income and even their jobs. Edelman (1993) reports a study that found that the annual earnings of women without job-protected leave dropped 29% the first year after having a baby, compared with an 18% drop with a job-protected leave.

For educators, working families involve new issues. As more parents are fully occupied with work during the school day, they are less available for direct participation in a classroom or on a constant basis. Teachers plan *flexible* opportunities for them to become involved in their children's education. As Bettye Caldwell (1989) puts it,

> Just as societal changes have brought about the increased need for early childhood services, so will the ingenuity and creativity of professionals lead to the development of services adapted to new family realities.

In the public sector, several proposals have gained momentum in the 1990s. The most successful so far, the ABC Bill of 1990, allotted federal dollars to the states to provide support for centers, improving the quality of children's services available. The National Commission on Children, in 1990, recommended a child tax credit ($1000 per child) as part of a comprehensive blueprint for support-

ing children and families. In 1991, legislation was introduced to establish regular monies in the federal budget, a kind of "children's investment trust fund." Leading pediatrician T. Berry Brazelton's Washington-based lobby group, Parent Action, is garnering support for a family medical leave that would enable parents of newborns several months unpaid leave from their jobs to be at home and establish an attachment bond and family setting, so critical to infants' well-being and survival.

The value of children is demonstrated in the support given to parents through employment-based or household-based plans. Such support is essential for children's health and education and for their future prospects as people and workers. Most European countries fund public programs for children and support services for parents at a much higher rate than in this country. Public policy is a reflection of the attitudes and values we as a nation hold towards children and families, and the inequities are glaring. We look towards a future trend of clearer and more supportive public policies. Policies and attitudes must change to make it more attractive for adults to spend time with children, for, in the words of Colorado Representative Pat Schroeder (1991), "I have seen the future and it is wearing diapers."

Community and School Support

The relationship between schools and the community at large and the families they serve dictates the role schools play in the lives of families. Yet, as Edelman (1993) points out,

> Our communities, our work places, and our nation offer little support for parents engaged in the extraordinarily difficult task of caring for young children. Unlike virtually all of our Western European competitors, the United States has no parental leave policy (paid or unpaid) to allow parents to stay home with an infant without jeopardizing their jobs and income. Unlike those same nations, we have failed to ensure the availability of high-quality, affordable child care.

At the same time, the history of education in the United States is the story of the "progressive assumption." (Elkind, 1991) This means that the trend over time is for educational institutions to assume functions once performed by the family.

FIGURE 15.9   What responsibility does the community have to young children and their families? How do families with young children influence the community in which they reside?

There are difficulties in this progression, however, as schools are reluctant to assume some of these responsibilities and parents are wary of giving them up.

In colonial times schools were primarily private, church-based programs for boys. After the Revolution the government began forming a national public school system, based on the belief that a democracy demands literate participants. This trend continued as the "public" came to include women and people of color. In modern times, the government provides subsidies to schools to provide free or low-cost meals, medical and dental services, and physical education programs, although many of these are in jeopardy at the time of this book's printing.

In the last 25 years, schools have continued to take on more child-rearing functions. The concept of school has changed as has the concept of family. In the past, educational duties were divided into two complementary tasks, occupational (by the schools) and personal (by the parents). The reduced time available for parenting today, paired with street issues, drugs, violence, sex, and so on, calls for a renewed definition and sense of mission for schools.

Schools have a key role to play in nurturing parental involvement in education and family life. Coleman (1991) describes this role as rebuilding the "social capital" both within the family and in the community. Drawing upon an economic model, social capital refers to the richness and resources that social relationships provide for a child. The strength of these social relations help shape a child's habits, establish norms of acceptable behavior, and encourage the development of children's character, long-range goals, and even educational attainment.

One example of the school as a reflection of community life is the Reggio Emilia system, as described throughout this text (see Chapters 2, 5, 8, 9, and 11 through 14). Founder Malaguzzi understood that the child cannot be thought of in the abstract, but tightly connected to the world of relationships and experiences. Both Vygotsky (see Chapters 4 and 13) and Bronfenbrenner (see

Chapters 2 and 15) emphasize these ties, and the Reggio system implements it in several ways. Parents are elected to local school boards and thus influence (and are influenced by) a close connection with the decision-making process around educational priorities. Besides "field trips," children are expected and anticipated in public places, rather than being simply tolerated, as they are in much of America.

The issue today in America is to define a new role for schools. One that many early childhood programs already do well is to provide avenues to strengthen children's resources in the family. Some specific ways include a comprehensive approach to families, so that the early childhood program is fully integrated into the families it serves. School systems can help parents get whatever medical, dental, mental, job-related, and social services by collaborating with other agencies and individuals. Teachers who understand the powerful role of family and child-rearing styles in children's developing values will make special efforts to include parents in the "how-tos" of discipline, self-help, problem-solving, or homework (Oyemade & Washington, 1989). By offering parents meaningful and personal ways to be involved, educators promote parents' involvement with their own children. Thus children's "social capital" is rich and deep, giving children ample resources to call upon as they grow.

"It takes a village to raise a child." This old adage has new significance in today's society. But what is today's village community? John Gardner (1990) provides a stirring definition:

> It is in community that the attributes that distinguish humans as social creatures are nourished. Families and communities are the ground-level generators and preserves of values and ethical systems. . . . [Values] are generated chiefly in the family, school, church, and other intimate settings in which people deal with one another face to face. . . . We know that where community exists it confers upon its members identity, a sense of belonging, and a measure of security. . . . [F]rom the culture of their native place, the things, the customs, the honored deeds of their elders . . . humans [learn] a sense of community.

We see a future trend towards education being part of that "village," forming partnerships among parents, teachers, school boards, and community groups, working in concert so children's needs are met. As part of this effort, early childhood professionals provide the knowledge and understanding of child development, but also the ability to relate to all children, parents, and co-workers with compassion, empathy, and understanding. Early childhood programs can help articulate the *shared values* of the community and the support for *diversity* of the whole community. *Trust* and *teamwork* go together to care for community members of all ages, and to encourage *full participation* in decision making as well as services. Children depend on healthy "villages" second only to their own families to develop into members of a world community (Young-Holt, 1991).

For the Children

What, then, do children need from a family? Three areas have been identified that greatly affect children's development: role models, family values, and the "ecology" of the family.

Role Models. How people look at themselves and their roles in life is undergoing considerable transformation. Women who are heads of households and men who are serious participants in parenting are likely to deal with their children differently than did those in the traditional nuclear family. They have new ideas and habits of how parents and children treat each other, what they do and talk about together, and who is responsible for the children's upbringing. Blended families will have yet again another set of parenting issues to decide together. All these changes will affect the kinds of parents children experience. Power and custom must make way for the needs of children.

Family and Its Values. The major changes in family structure call for new ways to preserve the family and its values. To deal with the changes taking place in society, a number of possibilities must be considered, from economic issues to gender-role differentiation. Adults must question and clarify their values about children, caretaking, and child-rearing. Families with young children are increasingly dependent on agencies outside their informal social networks for emotional, informational, and material support, as demonstrated by the increasing use of information-and-referral services. Early childhood care and the education community have a central responsibility with respect to this task (Halpern, 1987). How we help the family is the issue most important to the future of our society (Freidan, 1987).

Ecology of the Family. Bronfenbrenner (1979) uses the phrase "ecology of development" to describe the system or network of family and cultural relationships that significantly influence how children develop (see also the discussion of Vygotsky in Chapters 4 and 13). Just as important, this network is one in which children themselves have a significant influence. This principle suggests looking beyond the ages and stages of child development to a larger context in which the child grows (see Anti-Bias Approach, Chapters 9 and 11–14).

It makes good sense to look at ways parents and children affect one another's growth. Galinsky (see Chapter 8) sets out stages of parent development that affect the ways parents look at themselves in the life cycle of a family. Parents are growing, changing human beings, and are influenced by their children's personalities, demands, and ages. Parents' original family and friends, society, culture, and religion all influence their thinking. In turn, parents influence their children by the way they discipline, the way they show affection or withhold it, the materials they provide, the expectations they have for their children at varying ages.

The Role of the Teacher. The role of the teacher and the school system is to accept children and families for who they are, and to invite them into the process of education and care for children. Therefore, teachers' first role is as a *resource for children*. Teachers organize space and develop materials that encourage broad participation. They clarify roles for children, and interpret others' behavior to children so that they learn to understand and are able to act for themselves in a socially responsible way. Teachers attempt to bring in children to the exciting world of learning. This is done best with choices that invite a freedom of response. Rather than offering a classroom where restrictions abound, teachers invite children (and their

parents) to share their own family customs in an atmosphere of trust. Children can bring who they are in their family into school. When teachers model curiosity and acceptance of children and their families and cultures, children feel that they belong and have a second "family," the family of their classroom.

A second and more involving role for teachers is that of a *support for parents*. Parents need sources of support outside kin networks, developing relationships with caregivers that allow parents to talk about themselves and their lives at home. Teachers are most helpful when they can be available to listen to and confer with parents about their child's behavior, but also about the parents' own hopes and dreams for themselves and their children, their feelings as parents, and getting along as adults.

Parents learn from role models, too, particularly in the changing family structures so evident today. Many experts, from Dr. Spock to Mr. Rogers, try to tell parents to trust themselves and listen to their own inner voices of what is good and healthy for themselves and their children. Early childhood professionals can help parents stay focused on what is important, to help them distinguish between the distracting noise of a busy society and the words of wisdom that do exist. The trend now, and certainly into the next century, is for the role of the teacher to become greater with families. Teachers will all come to accept the idea of teaching as a two-client job: a teacher of the child, and a resource for the parent. It is complicated work, but one with internal integrity, building relationships that will endure for the child.

TRANSMITTING VALUES

As with the other themes in early childhood education, the issue of transmitting values is not for the teacher or school alone. A deep and primary source of values is that of the family and culture. The school must work with the family to provide a sense of shared values; nonetheless, both parents and teachers must acknowledge other sources that shape children's values and behavior. Three other critical sources are television and the media, war and violence, and social diversity.

FIGURE 15.10 When both parents work outside the home, new roles for fathers emerge.

Television and the Media

In many homes, the television set has replaced the adult supervision of the past. Ninety-eight percent of the homes in the United States have televisions, and the average set is on for more than six hours each day. The average kindergarten graduate has already seen more hours of television than the time it takes to get a bachelor's degree from college (Trelease, 1989). The issue for educators revolves around the influence of television on young children.

There are four basic concerns that parents and teachers express about children's viewing of television and videos:

1. Television violence can lead to aggression and desensitization to violence;

2. Television promotes passivity, slowing intellectual development and stifling imagination;

3. Television promotes racist and sexist attitudes;

4. Television promotes materialistic consumerism.

Research from the 1960s and 1970s expanded our knowledge of the powerful effects on children of the models they see, whether they be of children, adults, or fantasy characters. Bandura's social learning theory reinforced this notion (see Chapter 4), and it is generally accepted that media images can have similar influences. Knowing this, early childhood professionals are particularly concerned as the amount of violent television programming increases dramatically (Carlsson-Paige & Levin, 1987). Many claim that children who watch violent programs become more aggressive than those who do not (David, 1988; ERIC, 1989; Solter, 1986). With television so available to children, research in this area is important. And while a direct cause-and-effect link may not be found, the effects of film-mediated aggression is important in determining the content of children's media programs.

As to the passivity argument, one need only see the enthralled look on children's faces to know that the screen images are engaging. Children do spend large amounts of time with television, but

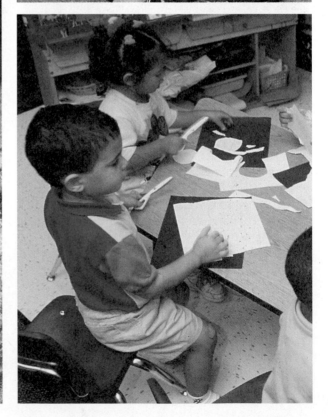

FIGURE 15.11 Antidotes to television.

the research available seems to indicate that children actually do many other activities while the set is on, and that their attention to TV is quite variable. Preschool children seem to attend to minute details of a show that interests them; most parents report very young children learning advertising jingles or details of slogans. Research about the cognitive effects of television viewing reveals that TV viewing seems to be a fairly complex cognitive activity. Still, there is little consistent evidence concerning television's influence on imagination and creativity. More research is critical, as well as an analysis of the content of the shows that children watch.

In the area of bias and stereotyping, children's television is an arena "where boys are king" (Carter, 1991). Networks generally assert that boys will not watch female-lead shows, but girls will watch shows with a male lead, and that the viewer audience is male majority (estimates are around 53 percent boys, 47 percent girls as child viewers). The pattern of "boy" dominance extends beyond the networks into public and cable broadcasting. Minority groups are also inadequately represented on TV. Thus, with children's television shows, the Euro-American and male attitudes and behaviors are reinforced.[1]

Does television promote consumerism? As Bob Keeshan, affectionately known as Captain Kangaroo, puts it, "In America, television is not a tool for nurturing. It is a tool for selling" (Minow, 1991). After the deregulation of the television industry in 1985, the amount of commercial time in children's shows increased, and the "program-length commercial" was introduced, whereby a show was developed based on a line of consumer toys and products aimed at the children's market. Proponents of deregulation had reasoned that a free market and competition would improve the quality of television. "Competition, it is said, brings out the best in products and the worst in people. In children's television, competition seems to bring out the worst in programs and the worst in children" (Minow, 1991). Therefore, in 1990 the Children's Television Act became law, requiring that stations submit an assessment of children's

television offerings when they apply for license renewal with the Federal Communications Commission. The FCC also adopted rules that encourage broadcasters to air more educational programming for children and limit the amount of advertising during children's shows.

Television and the lessons it teaches are and will be a part of children's lives. Research needs to continue about the effects of media viewing. The studies available today do indicate clear modifiers of those effects, namely, parent coviewing and teaching of critical television viewing skills. The regulation of children's television advertising is a positive step, yet parents and teachers need guidelines for family television viewing regardless of what is aired. The following list is a compilation (David, 1988; ERIC, 1989; *pre-K Today*, 1990) of such guidelines:

1. *Set limits.* Know how many hours of TV children watch, and set limits (the American Academy of Pediatrics suggests a maximum of 1–2 hours daily). Keep the TV turned off unless someone is actively viewing; TV can easily become more of a habit than a choice.

2. *Plan and participate.* Work together with children to decide what to watch. Help children choose shows with an age-appropriate viewing length, bias-free content, and peaceful action. Consider watching shows together, pointing out parts that are prosocial and asking about those parts you wonder about or disagree with. Use the "pause," "rewind," and "mute" buttons as part of the process.

3. *Resist commercials.* Children do not distinguish easily between the sales-pitch commercial and the ordinary show. Help them become "critical consumers" by pointing out the exaggerated claims. Even three-year olds can answer the question, "What are they trying to sell us?"

4. *Express your views.* Call a station that airs a show or commercial you find offensive, or write a letter to the Children's Advertising Review unit of the Better Business Bureau. Action for Children's Television in Cambridge, MA has been a

OUR DIVERSE WORLD OUR DIVERSE WORLD OUR DIVERSE WORLD OUR DIVERSE WORLD OUR DIVERSE WORLD

[1]An important task of early childhood educators is to actively counteract gender stereotypes.

leading public interest group for 20 years, and has valuable suggestions for how adults can influence children's television programming.

Violence ✳

The Situation

The trend of children's increasing exposure to violence is alarming. What is offered on television and the media, the kinds and choices of toys, and the interpersonal situations in children's homes, neighborhoods, and the world all contribute to an increased awareness of and exposure to violence. Parents report tensions in the relationships between themselves and their children. Increased violence on television along with a rising tide of war toys (abundantly advertised on television) contributes to a sense of being out of control in limiting or influencing children's behavior. Teachers see similar tensions with children in school and child care and notice changes in children's play. Many teachers report that the weapon and war play in classrooms is so single-purpose and intense that it is difficult to redirect; rule-setting and controlling overzealous play takes an inordinate amount of teachers' energy.

The increasing violence of American society has so alarmed educators and parents alike (Levin, 1994) that programs are being developed for children and for teachers. Organizations such as the Educators for Social Responsibility and National Association for Mediation Educators serve as both clearinghouses for information and material and as training institutes for teachers. Additionally, California is piloting a "Safe Start" program for teachers-in-training and those already in the field to work better with both children and families in the throes of a violent world (Eyer, 1995).

The Dilemma

Thoughtful adults find themselves in a dilemma. Should they allow this war and violence play to continue (unchecked? with limits? with intervention?)? Or ought this kind of play be altered (redirected? contained? banned?)? This dilemma illustrates children's play from two different viewpoints, a developmental one and a sociopolitical one. The *developmental viewpoint* states that play, including war play, is the primary vehicle through which children work on developmental issues. Since children need to develop a sense of how the world works, of fantasy and reality, of good and bad, war play is an extension of "superhero play (see Chapter 14) and is, therefore, a necessary part of children's play. The *sociopolitical view* assumes that children learn basic social and political behavior at an early age and, therefore, will learn militaristic concepts and values through war play. This viewpoint contends that children learn about conflict and resolution, the use of fighting, etc., and the meaning of friends and enemies in their play, and that allowing war play endorses the use of force (Carlsson-Paige, 1987).

These two ideas give teachers the basic building blocks for how to deal with the issue of developing shared values and for engaging in a dialogue with fellow teachers and parents. Every viewpoint encourages a way of understanding and explaining war and violence to and with children.

Children's Needs

What children need most is reassurance, to know they will be safe and that caring grownups will still take care of them. Constancy and predictability, in the form of a consistent routine and continued habits of behavior and tradition, will help children feel anchored in their lives. Listening carefully, answering children's questions in simple ways, asking questions to elicit their thoughts all encourage communication and a dialogue about their feelings. Most educators and counselors also remind adults to monitor children's media exposure to such war. Teachers help children find peaceful resolutions to their everyday conflicts, ensuring that in their daily school life, war will not break out and take over (see Chapters 7 and 14 for suggestions).

This last suggestion may take several paths. A family child care provider of infants and toddlers may spend extra time giving hugs and helping children share toys. One class of preschoolers may choose a cross-town child care center to exchange drawings and visits with to increase their knowledge of their city neighbors, and of ideas they could create to solve each others' problems. In a first grade class, children were so concerned that they chose to write letters to the President ("I don't like it when you make wars. My big sister says to use words when I have a problem and you should too.")

What To Do

As for the larger issues of war and violence, teachers can look at several courses of action. It is helpful to consider the options teachers have in these situations. Talk about and decide on your viewpoint and values with parents and the school board. Develop guidelines that address your values and the needs of the children. Talk with parents about toys and the role of the media in the development of children's interests and the role of parents in helping children decide and choose what and how to play. Investigate peace education. While peace is a complex issue, children know instinctively about peace and war, as they feel these contradictory emotions in themselves. By starting with what each individual child knows and feels, teachers can begin to build a foundation that emphasizes the positive steps towards peaceful negotiation, towards a balance of self and others, in terms children can understand and use.

A few general guidelines hold for children of all ages. Teachers work on their own personal feelings about war, and seek out supportive resources. A teacher must prepare for controversy; differences in opinions about war and peace will be as common as those of the daily social interactions of children in the classroom. Recognizing children's need to discuss their feelings, teachers help parents to be a source of information and support for their children (Wallinga, et al., 1991). A thorough and thoughtful approach to the issues of war and violence will help teachers and parents work together.

Diversity

Facing Reality

America as "melting pot," where all racial and cultural differences are smoothly mixed into one single blend, is a myth. Unfortunately, much of America's history can be characterized as racist,

sexist, and ethnocentric in nature by one group or another. The discrepancy between our ideals of equal opportunity and freedom and the daily reality can be altered only if we recognize the problems and then set specific goals for change.

Today's demographics point to a trend of an increasingly diverse society. In 1991 California became a "minority majority" state: that is, a majority of public school students are members of minority groups. By the year 2000, Hispanic students may be almost as numerous as whites, and other groups are expected to account for a total of 22.2 percent of all students (*Education Week*, 1991). It is predicted that 46 percent of the nation's schoolchildren will be children of color in this decade (Viadero, 1990).

The issue is that attitudes have not yet responded to reality. A recent University of Chicago survey on racial attitudes found that while support for racial equality has grown, "negative images of members of other racial and ethnic groups are widespread among whites, and most groups have at least some prejudice against all the other groups" (Armstrong, 1991). In a comprehensive study entitled *A Common Destiny: Blacks and American Society*, the National Research Council concluded that, despite gains in recent decades, "blacks still face formidable barriers on their path to educational parity with whites . . . our findings imply several negative developments for blacks in the near future, developments that in turn do not bode well for American society" (Schmidt, 1989).

Moreover, school reform efforts have done little to meet the educational needs of America's demographic profile. The Educational Leadership's Center for Demographic Policy (1989) concludes that, despite reforms, neither high school dropout rates nor poverty among the young have decreased. Standardized test scores for the lowest academic groups have not gone up, and resources have not been increased.

Not Whether, But What Kind. We know that children exhibit an awareness of racial and gender differences by age three (Katz, 1982, Derman-Sparks, 1989) and are formulating rudimentary concepts about the meaning of those differences in the preschool years. It is logical to conclude that, by the end of the early childhood years, children have consolidated their attitudes about race, ethnicity, gender, and (dis)ability, and are far along the path of attitude crystallization. Unless the social environment changes, children will recreate the prejudices of the current adult society.

What is needed is new concepts of society, one that educators translate into programs for children. Children, their teachers and parents begin by forming an awareness of difference, and learn with sensitivity the meaning of diversity.

Multicultural Education

Multicultural education is the system of teaching/learning that includes the contributions of all ethnic and racial groups. In other words, it is a curriculum that reflects more minority perspectives, providing all children with a fuller, more balanced truth about themselves, their own history, and culture. This means a responsiveness to the child's origins, habits at home, ways of self-expression.

At higher levels of education there is a great debate about how to deal with diversity. Two views dominate. One is a "separatist" education in which education is taught from a particular viewpoint, be it European, Afro-centrist, or the like. The other is a more traditional, "pluralist," approach in which education stresses the commonalities of varying peoples. Janice E. Hale (1993) offers her ideas:

> We can get our message across more effectively if we use a culturally salient vehicle. . . . [For instance], culturally appropriate pedagogy would expose African-American children to Anglo-centric and Afro-centric literature at each grade level. Exposure to Afro-centric literature would provide them with the vocabulary, history, and information about the cultural orientation of mainstream America. This exposure is essential for African-American children to be able to negotiate the mainstream. Exposure to Afro-centric literature would broaden their vocabulary, provide them with information about African-American cultural values, enhance their self-esteem, and provide motivation and inspiration . . . to educate African-American children in a culturally appropriate manner, there is a kind of dual educational process that is required.

What underlies the debate is how we see ourselves as a common culture. Our country and our

schools are struggling. When we change the metaphor of "melting pot" to one of "mixed salad," we encourage a new way of thinking that might be termed cultural pluralism—the idea that "Yes, we are all one people, but we do not necessarily divest ourselves of our ethnic origin" (Sobol in Viadero, 1990).

In early childhood education, teachers know that the basis of an authentic curriculum for children is with the individual child. Therefore, the program that responds most genuinely to diversity is one in which the child is accepted, the child's total personal diversity is respected, and the child's family and cultural traditions are part of the classroom. The last section of this segment ("In the Classroom") and Chapters 9–14 have specific suggestions. Based on developmental principles, responsive to the individual, and pro-active in its embrace of societal realities, a good early childhood program represents the best of multicultural education.

Bilingual Education

The 1980s left unresolved basic questions concerning bilingual education, and the 1990s are proving to be an explosive and exploratory time for the issues of language and learning. The goals and purposes of bilingual education remain controversial, for there are still disagreements over how to define bilingualism, how to determine who needs it, and who is to provide the services. Chapter 13 discusses bilingual education in light of language learning and curriculum development. This section will highlight the broader issues and implications.

Issues and Implications. Bilingual education has been part of the American experience since before the Revolutionary War, when school was taught in any one of the more than 18 languages that were spoken by the colonists. As early as 1870, U.S. Commissioner of Education William T. Harris argued that "national memories and aspirations, family traditions, customs and habits, moral and religious observances cannot be suddenly removed or changed without disastrously weakening the personality" of the immigrants who bear them (Castellanos, 1987).

Nonetheless, cultures have been suppressed with regularity in the United States. Both Native American and immigrant groups have categorically faced discrimination. Speaking English is only part of bilingual education: at issue are the civil and educational rights of people who speak limited English, the respect or assimilation of their culture, and their participation and acceptance in society.

Changing populations and the influx of immigrants from Asia as well as from the Hispanic nations have brought with them today new challenges of bilingual education. Bilingual programs serve primarily Spanish-speaking students. It is estimated that the number of school-age Spanish-speaking children in the country will increase by 50 percent by the year 2000 (White, 1984). How will this affect the early childhood teacher?

The School-Age Child. The questions about bilingualism for the school-age child are different from those for the young child. In elementary school, teachers and children are forced to deal with issues beyond those of receptive and expressive language. Learning graphic language (reading and writing), acquiring concepts in other subject areas through listening, and dealing with the more complex social patterns and interpersonal issues are just a few of these issues. Moreover, the age at which children should be taught a second language is highly controversial. Research shows that children *can* acquire nativelike mastery of a second language if they learn to speak the language before the age of five. Others will argue that a child should learn all the fine points of the first language before being exposed to a second one and that this exposure should not occur prior to the age of six.

Much research is centered on how children achieve second-language competence and performance. We do know that by age five, children know most of the sounds and grammatical structure of their native tongue and appear to learn a second language in a similar way. With a bilingual child, the level of competence in both languages may be low while gaining mastery in the second language.

The two pieces of legislation that have most influenced the bilingual issue in our time are the 1968 Bilingual Education Act and the 1974 *Lau* v. *Nichols* Supreme Court decision. In 1974, the Supreme Court determined that a lack of instruction in one's first language is a violation of children's civil rights.

Since 1968, Title VII programs (the Elementary and Secondary Education Act, also known as the Bilingual Education Act) addressed the needs of students with limited proficiency in English. State bilingual education laws followed, requiring special instruction for children who lack competence in English.

The result is that children are taught, in public kindergarten and elementary schools, by using both the primary language and English. For instance, children may be taught to read in their primary language first; once they have learned the reading process in their own language, they are then taught to decode in English. Yet bilingual programs are so varied that it is difficult to assess them. Some work to mainstream children into regular classrooms as quickly as possible, while others try to maintain the child's native language. A more recent program, the *dual* or *bilingual immersion method*, attempts a blending of language instruction by putting both English speakers and those with limited English into classes together, and teaching "two-way" bilingual education. By bringing together both groups for language instruction, this method also indicates respect for both languages as assets. It shows promise as a truly multicultural tool for desegregation.

Still, the controversy continues. Another political backlash is occurring in the late 1980s against non-English speakers. The U.S. Office of Education has claimed bilingual education programs have not helped children learn English. California voters declared English as the official state language, and its governor vetoed state bilingual funding in 1988. Without consensus on the effectiveness and goals of bilingual education, educators must press for continuing research and clarity.

The Young Child. In preschools and child care centers, children are still taught in regular class settings, usually with little extra instruction. This type of instruction is known as the *English immersion system*. Recent research has generated controversy about what is best for children under five. In a survey for the National Association for Bilingual Education conducted in 1990, professor of education Lily Wong Fillmore of UC Berkeley found striking differences between families who participated in English-based programs and those whose children received native-language instruction. Her data indicate that language-minority children in English-speaking schools experience a substantial erosion of their native-language ability and have difficulty communicating with their parents.

The Immigrant. Another serious challenge for schools is posed by the educational needs of immigrant children. Nationwide, there are more than 2.5 million school-age immigrants, countless children under five years of age, and thousands of other undocumented entrants. Immigrant enrollment in school can, in some places, reach more than 95 percent (Jennings, 1988).

The language barrier is the most immediate problem, followed by that of acceptance of the immigrants' native culture. Further, many newcomers arrive from countries racked with war, violence, and poverty. These children and families are under tremendous pressures and need help coping with the overwhelming stress (see Chapters 14 and 15). The way schools place and monitor these immigrant children—both their educational progress and their general well-being—challenges educators and all American citizens to clarify the responsibilities our society has toward its newcomers.

Implications for Early Education. One can conclude that, particularly for young children under five, the primary language of language-minority children should be used in schools and centers. This conclusion is not unanimous, and further research needs to be done. Nonetheless, Wong Fillmore sheds important light on our thinking about educating language-minority children. We need to take into consideration what we know of the development of cognition and primary language. Are young children vulnerable in this area? Do we disrupt their developing thinking skills as well as their sense of self and parent-child relationship to require English-language proficiency so young? While more studies in the 1990s will be needed to help answer these questions, there are several guidelines teachers can follow (Bowman, 1991, with authors' interpretations):

1. *"Teachers need to learn to recognize developmentally equivalent patterns of behavior. Before children come to school, they have all learned many of the same things, such as a primary language and communication styles."* Before judging a child as difficult or problematic, assume he or she is normal and look again. Your own vision may be clouded with "cultural myopia."

2. *"It is essential not to value some ways of achieving developmental milestones more highly than others. . . .* When children find that the way they talk is not understood or appreciated in school, they are apt to become confused or disengaged." Remember, different is not deficient.

3. *"Teachers need to begin instruction with interactive styles and content that is familiar to the children. . . . [teachers] can become more adept at planning and implementing a culturally sensitive curriculum."* You may not be able to be fluent in a child's primary language, but you can learn key words and phrases that help a child feel a sense of belonging.

4. *"School learning is most likely to occur when family values reinforce school expectations."* Parent involvement is more than just a phrase; when parents and teachers are partners in education, children are the winners.

5. *"When differences exist between the cultural patterns of the home and community and those of the school, the teacher must deal with those discrepancies directly."* Teachers ask questions and create shared understandings between themselves and children, inviting children to be interested in creating a common culture of the classroom.

Educating language-minority children can be made developmentally appropriate, by making school meaningful and welcoming of whole children, whatever languages they bring.

Equal Play and Gender Segregation

There is ample research to confirm the widespread occurrence of gender segregation in childhood (Grossman and Grossman, 1994; Hoyenga and Hoyenga, 1993; Maccoby and Jacklin, 1985). While adults may not directly contribute to biased development, teachers and parents are indirectly responsible for the inequity between the sexes in their children. For instance, in unstructured play situations, the free-play backbone of early education programs and most at-home play, children will choose playmates and play situations that are comfortable to them. They will not, typically, choose those activities with which they have had little or no experience, nor will they ordinarily choose cross-sex playmates (particularly as peer pressure increases with age). Further, boys still get more attention than girls do at most grade levels and subject areas (Sadler, 1985). Sexist treatment in the classroom encourages the formation of patterns of power and dominance that occur very early (Maccoby and Jacklin, 1985), though it is inappropriate to our current culture.

Teachers and parents must take an assertive role in recognizing this sexist bias and replacing it with more equitable experiences for all children. Summaries of wide-ranging research (Grossman and Grossman, 1994; Hoyenga and Hoyenga, 1993) indicate that both our homes and schools are "gendered environments" that spell different expectations and conduct for children based on their gender. If we are committed to an anti-bias education and environment (see Chapters 9 to 14), we must attempt to reduce gender-stereotypical behavior.

For teachers, this involves eliminating our own biased perceptions and behavior, as well as correcting children's stereotypical behavior and attitudes about gender roles. Exposing children to nonsexist roles, books, and materials is a good start. Expanding children's learning styles is helpful. Girls need more experiences with spatial exploration and gross motor coordination as well as quality attention from—without dependence on—adults. Boys in particular need experiences in flexibility, nurturance, and learning from modeling.

Eliminating stereotypical relationships is also important. Be sure that all members of a group have the opportunity to participate equally. For instance, try to reduce male dominance of females in mixed-gender situations. Keep a watchful eye in the environment to see that areas do not get labelled "off limits" by one gender, such as the blocks and trikes that become "boy places" or the house corner and art "for girls only." Encourage cross-gender interaction, and use cooperative learning

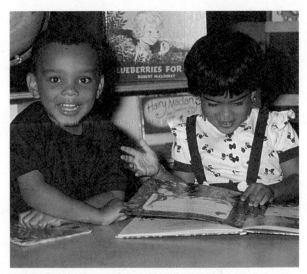

FIGURE 15.12 The program that responds to diversity is one in which the individual child is accepted and respected.

activities. Whereas there is little research about the long-term effects of these strategies, a combination of these techniques has been found effective to increase mixed-gender interactions, helping behavior and friendships (Lockheed and Klein, 1985). Additionally, strategies for all children include:

- Providing activities that all children may use, that are sex fair and sex affirmative in content.

- Developing verbal and physical interactive patterns that make all children equal participants.

- Using strategies such as teacher proximity and structured playtime to involve children in activities they may otherwise avoid (Greenberg, 1984).

Schools for Human Values

The complexities of modern life can inhibit the development of values in children. In a society so diverse, it is sometimes difficult to determine what "basic values" are. With changing family structures, shifting political and religious viewpoints, and a multitude of cultures to consider, the teacher can, understandably, feel confused and reluctant to "teach" any particular values at all.

Teaching, however, is not a "value-neutral" endeavor. Whenever something is taught, the choice of what and how to teach it implies the teacher's values. When a teacher prevents a child from hitting another, she states the value of peaceful conflict resolution. When a caregiver puts a crying child into his lap, he shows the value of responsive comforting. When children are taught reading, given free play choices, asked to sing, they are being given a sense of what is important.

Children who enter childhood without experience making decisions and paying attention to what matters, finding out what is fair or kind or "right," miss a critical part of human development. Developing moral and ethical values is an important part of growing up, giving children a basis for choice about how to behave and what conduct to follow. Teaching children our belief system is part of their education. This issue is how.

In response to growing concerns like drugs, violence, and lack of continuity through family or neighborhood, schools are beginning to respond by providing some guidance about what is right and wrong. The school of the past could be concerned with simply academic and vocational, leaving the moral and personal responsibilities to the parents. The school of the present and future can not afford that luxury.

Several states are now taking steps to encourage the teaching of values (Daley, 1990). School districts often set up councils or task forces to poll their communities about what values to teach and how to teach them. In programs for children under five, parents and teachers have historically been more involved with teaching children right and wrong. Church-related schools in particular are selected by parents because of the values, including religious values, that are taught. Discussions of discipline can go beyond technique to the values that underlie such strategies. Teachers in a center can start the dialogue about what is important to teach.

Teaching values starts with knowing your own belief system and its place in your career. Ask yourself:

● Why am I teaching? Why young children? Why children at all?

● What made me choose early childhood education as my career?

● What do I stand for? Why?

● How did I come to have my beliefs?

● Do I allow others their beliefs?

● How do I state my values to children? To parents?

● How do I keep my values and integrity while allowing myself to grow and change?

Once educators are clear about their own values, and are engaged in dialogue with parents, there remains the issue of how to generate values in young children. Sue Spayth Riley (1984) puts it this way

> When you give boys and girls the freedom to evaluate, decide, create, and re-create their world, they usually construct a happy place, a place with meaning that expresses truths and dreams that are very real to them. When children interpret those meanings and truths, and select priorities, and finally make efforts to change—freely and frequently— what does not satisfy them, they generate within themselves an inspiring force that they feel in the form of confidence and a positive attitude about their lives which any parent or teacher can see as the children work and play.

Integrity, honesty, individuality, self-confidence, responsibility can all be taught in an authentic way to young children. We prepare children to live successfully by embracing the willingness to change while at the same time holding to our beliefs of personal choice, equality, and opportunity.

Implications for Educators

Some Strategies. There are several, more global strategies about multicultural, bilingual, and values education that all educators can use. First, *education must promote minority involvement in school reform.* The 1990s mark the beginning of an awareness of including all constituencies in real decision- and policymaking. From minority businesses (Weisman, 1990) to parents (Schmidt, 1991; West, 1991) to minority policymakers (Walsh, 1991), it is critical that the populations served by education become involved.

Second, *we need an adult understanding of development.* In particular, teachers and parents must know how children develop racial, cultural, sex, and ability awareness and how children come to an understanding of what differences mean and how children develop a sense of fairness and morality. Moreover, teachers' expectations about how and when children learn skills will be influenced by their knowledge of culture (Edwards & Gandini, 1989). Adults who know child development and how attitudes are formed will be more effective in developing positive concepts and in countering stereotypes (Derman-Sparks, 1989).

Third, *teachers need more training and education about multicultural education and about various diverse cultures.* Teachers must take the time, and be supported in their efforts, to learn about both the various groups they have in their classrooms and the diversity of our culture at large. Teachers can provide an anti-bias classroom only if they are educated resources themselves (Derman-Sparks, 1989; ERIC, 1991).

Finally, *it is time educators examined their own attitudes and policies about diversity, difference, and inclusion.* Most early childhood centers want their programs to represent a pluralistic society, but how do their organizational structures stack up? Staff meetings that evaluate both the children's environments and the school as a whole are useful (Carter, 1988; Neugebauer, 1987).

In the classroom. How do we implement a multicultural, anti-bias approach to teaching? Staff and families work cooperatively to provide each child with something familiar and comfortable in the environment. Teachers base their programs on sharing of self, culture, ability, and experiences that encourages a healthy acceptance of themselves and a positive awareness and tolerance of others. Differences are noticed, discussed openly, even celebrated. At the same time, it is the fabric of custom, language, values, music, food, lifestyles, and celebrations that is shared, not a minor or dramatic detail that trivializes a group or child. Teachers can analyze their environments, plan with parents, and set goals for curriculum enhancement or change. Understanding children from other cultures (DiMartino, 1989) can be an outgrowth of this process, but the program itself begins with the children's own cultures (Head Start, 1986).

In summary, the future dictates that we equip children to live in the United States of the twenty-first century, where a diversity of races, cultures, and lifestyles will be the norm. As teachers of young children, we teach the values of a pluralistic society as well as what these diverse cultures hold in common. No one culture, religion, or child should be made to feel less valuable than another. We must be certain that we respect and celebrate the uniqueness of each child and the values of others.

TEACHING FOR THE TWENTY-FIRST CENTURY

Every day, teachers and caregivers open their doors to young children by the thousands. As they do so, they are influencing the course of our nation in the next century. If this seems exaggerated, consider this: the child born in 1992 will be a fourth grader in the twenty-first century. We are teaching the children of the future.

Issues

Early childhood education is a broad field that encompasses children, parents, communities, and a staggering variety of programs. The issues of the day have changed over the last thirty years. A review of these gives teachers a perspective on what has been and may become important in our profession:

- *The 1960s:* How important are the early years for the field of formal education? Can education in those years compensate for inadequate childhood experiences? What kind(s) of schooling makes a difference?

- *The 1970s:* What kind of early childhood program is best? Which one(s) are financially efficient?

- *The 1980s:* What are the effects of child care on children's development? What is the best match between programs and their participants? How do the family and children interact?

- *The 1990s:* How can cultural diversity be preserved while equal opportunity for all children is ensured? What will be the effect of such diversity on curriculum content? Will family-oriented policies and practices by business and government be far-reaching enough to support parents in their child-rearing roles? Can educa-

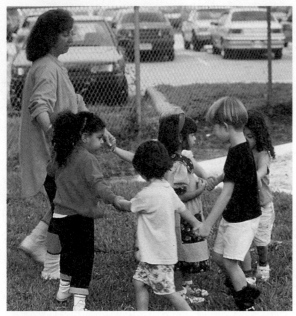

FIGURE 15.13 Young children need programs in which they can learn to trust each other as they work and play together.

tion reform be radical enough to alter the course of students who now seem destined to fail?

● *2000:* Will schools become social institutions which support academics as well as social services? How will the nation face its responsibility to see that all of its children start school ready to learn? What new partnerships will need to be created to continue public education reform? How will the role of parents continue to be underscored? Will parent demands raise the quality of child care and therefore the wage and benefit structure for early childhood professionals?

The issues of the new century are evolving out of those of previous decades. Child care and education for young children is an accepted fact: this issue is no longer "whether," but "what kind." Families, too, have changed in their outward appearance, as have the many faces of American society. How we accept such diversity and still maintain the notions of family and society is important. The nature of the job of teacher will depend, in part, upon working conditions for teachers so that they may provide a high-quality experience for children and support for families. Our challenge for the decade is before us.

Child Advocacy

Teachers are, by definition, advocates for children as they are dedicated to providing a better future for America's children.

With the issues of money and educational reform of such immediate concern, teachers need to understand the forces that affect how these issues are resolved. Teachers will have to educate themselves about the political process. They will need to know the rules and regulations regarding public funding sources. It is important to know how monies are allocated and who to work with in order to affect the decisions regarding education. By being acquainted with legislation, teachers can rally support for bills that will help children, families, and schools.

Teachers have long kept out of the political process, not unlike many minorities. But they have not been immune from its effects. As teachers, we must become informed in order to increase our power in the political and financial arenas of daily life. Just as we encourage children to help themselves, we must support each other in taking the initiative for our own profession's well-being. It was just such a coalition and coordinated effort among many people in child advocacy that secured the passage of the Child Care and Development Block Grants in 1990, the first such legislation to pass Congress in twenty years. Large-scale cooperation increased significantly the political success of that bill on behalf of all children.

Every teacher can become a child advocate. By working for children and children's services, teachers advocate for themselves as well. Effective legislative involvement proceeds through these steps:

1. Make a personal commitment.

2. Keep informed.

3. Know the process.

4. Express your views.

5. Let others know.

6. Be visible.

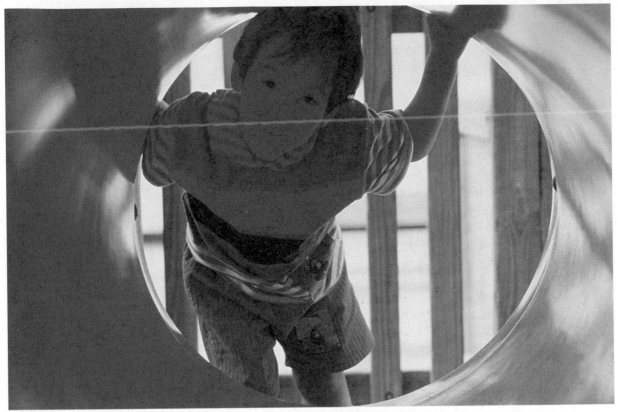

FIGURE 15.14   How do adults become advocates to ensure a fulfilling life for children in the next century?

7. Show appreciation.

8. Watch the implementation.

9. Build rapport and trust.

10. Educate your legislators (Pearce, 1983).

The teacher who works to ensure high-quality programs and services for children and their families also increases the likelihood of achieving the improved working conditions, professional opportunities, and public recognition that the field of early childhood education so richly deserves.

The Past Suggests the Future

History suggests how we might approach the future as we move from one century to another. By reflecting on our past, we are reminded of several important factors that illuminate today's issues:

1. We remind ourselves of what the pioneers of early education did to bring about reform. We look at their successes for inspiration, models, and ideas; we examine their failures in order to avoid the same mistakes.

2. Out of the past, we create a vision for the future. A backward glance along the timeline shows us that today we have a living, viable organism: a growing comprehensive vision of the field of early childhood; a growing definition of what early childhood means; a growing collaboration of early childhood professionals from all walks of life; a growing involvement in the education reform movement; a growing system of early childhood programs to serve the families of the twenty-first century; and a growing sense of our own effectiveness as advocates.

3. The ultimate goal seems timeless but bears fre-

FIGURE 15.15   What is our vision of the future for these children?

quent repetition. Our aim is to help all children learn so they can live full and satisfying lives, develop their talents and capabilities, so they are prepared for the challenges and responsibilities of adult life. For today's children, this will happen in a new century and in a different economic and technical age.

There is one unique aspect of the present that, when blended with the past, defines the future even more directly. The growing cultural diversity that makes up America at the turn of a century provides a richness of resources from which to learn. The history of other cultures presents a variety of options and insights on which we may draw as we create an agenda for future children and their families.

S U M M A R Y

Early childhood educators are facing issues today that challenge the very definition of childhood. How society handles these issues will help determine where we are headed—as teachers, children, families, a nation.

Some of the issues presented here may seem somewhat personal and even political. This is deliberate: as caretakers of the future—our children—we have serious and far-reaching questions that we must ask ourselves *now*. This book is dedicated to the quest for knowledge and action concerning a most important endeavor of the twentieth and twenty-first centuries: teaching young children. We can hardly do anything less than address those topics that are critical to the success of this task and of our profession.

T O P I C S   F O R   D I S C U S S I O N

1. Why do you think child care workers have low salaries? How can you work to change these conditions?

2. Is it possible for child care centers to provide quality programs at the same time they pay fair wages and work benefits? How?

3. What can you say to parents who ask what you teach their child? How can you respond to their insistence on teaching children to read and print before kindergarten?

4. What would you do if you suspected a child in your center was being seriously neglected or abused?

5. What can you say to help children handle separation and divorce? How will you deal with *both* parents?

6. What does the phrase "It takes a village to raise a child" mean in your program? How could that adage be applied in your community?

7. How can you provide for and deal with diversity in the classroom? What can you do to support both cultural pluralism and a sense of togetherness and mutual respect?

8. What do you do when children say "No boys (girls) allowed"? How will you include a new child with little English proficiency into your program?

9. How will you prepare yourself for the twenty-first century?

10. How do you see the education reform movement affecting your community? An early childhood program you know or work in?

11. Research changes in AIDS statistics since this text was published.

12. Select one of the pioneers and describe how that person had an impact on the reform movements of the times; compare the issue and its resolution with today's reform movement. What issues do you see repeated over time?

B I B L I O G R A P H Y

ETHIC OF SOCIAL REFORM AND CHILD CARE

Child Care Employee Project, Okland, Calif., 1993.

Compensation Guidelines for Early Childhood Professionals. Washington, D.C.: National Association for the Eduction of Young Children, 1993.

Cost, Quality and Child Outcomes Study Team. *Cost, Quality and Child Outcomes in Child Care Centers, Executive Summary.* Denver: Economics Department, University of Colorado at Denver, 1995.

Galinsky, Ellen, Howes, Carolee, Cantos, Susan, and Schinn, Marybeth. *The Study of Children in Family Child Care and Relative Care: Highlights of Findings.* New York: Families and Work Institute, 1994.

Hofferth, Sandra. Bringing Parents and Employers Back In: *The Implications of New Findings for Child Care Policy.* Urban Institute, Washington, D.C. 1994.

Kagan, Sharon L. *Excellence in Early Childhood Education: Defining Characteristics and Next-Decade Strategies.* Washington, D.C.: United States Department of Education Policy Perspectives, 1990.

National Study Panel on Education Indicators. *Education Counts.* Washington, D.C.: National Center for Education Statistics, United States Department of Education, 1991.

Whitebrook, M.; Howest, C.; and Phillips, D. *National Child Care Staffing Study.* Oakland, CA: Child Care Employee Project, 1989.

Willer, Barbara, et al. *The Demand and Supply of Child Care in 1990.* Washington, D.C.: National Association for the Education of Young Children, 1991.

Willer, Barbara, ed. *Reaching the Full Cost of Quality.* Washington, D.C.: National Association for the Education of Young Children, 1990.

Willer, Barbara A., and Johnson, Lynn C. *The Crisis is Real: Demographics on the Problems of Recruiting and Retaining Early Childhood Staff.* Washington, D.C.: National Association for the Education of Young Children.

Education Reform

Boyer, Ernest L. *Ready to Learn—A Mandate for the Nation.* Princeton, N.J.: The Carnegie Foundation for the Advancement of Teaching, 1991.

Kagan, Sharon L. *Excellence in Early Childhood Education: Defining Characteristics and Next-Decade Strategies.* United States Department of Education Policy Perspective. Washington, D.C.: 1990.

National Association of State Boards of Education. *Right From the Start.* Alexandria, VA: The Report of the NASBE Task Force on Early Childhood Education, 1988.

National Study Panel on Education Indicators. *Education Counts.* Washington, D.C.: National Center for Education Statistics, United States Department of Education, 1991.

Olson, Lynn. "Social Woes Pose Threat to Reform, C.E.D. Maintains." *Education Week,* March 6, 1991, p. 1.

Ravitch, Diane. "Education in the 1980s: A Concern for Quality." *Education Week,* January 10, 1990, p. 48.

United States Department of Education. *America 2000 An Education Strategy,* Washington, D.C.: 1991.

United States Department of Labor, Bureau of Labor Statistics. *Occupational Outlook Handbook,* 1990–91 edition. Washington, D.C.: U.S. Government Printing Office, 1990.

THE IMPORTANCE OF CHILDHOOD

Aronson, M.D., Susan S. "AIDS and Child Care Programs." *Child Care Information Exchange,* November 1987, pp. 35–39.

Children's Defense Fund. *The State of America's Children 1994.* Washington, D.C.: 1991.

Edelman, Marian Wright. "Young Children and School Readiness." In *Beginnings and Beyond,* ed. A. Gordon and K.B. Browne. Albany, N.Y.: Delmar Publishers, 1993 (3rd Ed.).

Elkind, David. *The Hurried Child: Growing Up Too Fast Too Soon.* Reading, Mass.: Addison Wesley, 1988.

Engelhardt, Tom. "Saturday Morning Fever—The Hard Sell Takeover of Kids' TV." *Mother Jones*, September 1986, pp. 39–54.

"Excerpts from the C.E.D.'s New Report, 'Children in Need.'" *Education Week*, September 9, 1987, p. 42.

Galtney, Liz. "Mothers on the Run." *U.S. News and World Report*, June 13, 1988, pp. 22–33.

Golden, Nancy. "Children and AIDS." *Newsletter* of the Peninsula Chapter of the Association for the Education of Young Children, June 1987, pp. 1–2.

Gordon, Ann Miles. "Ministries to Childhood." *National Association of Episcopal Schools Journal*, Winter 1986, pp. 22–26.

Jennings, Lisa. "More Abuse Found at Home than in Day Care." *Education Week*, March 30, 1988, p. 7.

Langway, Lynn, et al. "Bringing Up Superbaby." *Newsweek*, March 28, 1983, pp. 62–63.

Lawton, Millicent. "Child-Abuse Reports up 31 percent in Five Years, Studies Find." *Education Week*, April 24, 1991.

Murphy, Cullen. "Kids Today." *Wilson Quarterly*, Autumn 1982, pp. 61–82.

National Commission on Children. *Beyond Rhetoric–A New American Agenda for Children and Families*. Washington, D.C.: 1991.

National Committee for Prevention of Child Abuse. *The Challenge Continues. . . .* Chicago, IL: 1991.

National Study Panel on Education Indicators. *Education Counts*. Washington, D.C.: National Center for Education Statistics, United States Department of Education, 1991.

Reed, Mary S. "Stress at an Early Age." *San Francisco Chronicle and Examiner*, Sunday supplement *This World*, March 2, 1986, p. 13.

Trelease, Jim. *The Read-Aloud Handbook*. New York: Penguin Books, 1984.

United States Department of Education. *Youth Indicators 1991*. Washington, D.C.: Office of Educational Research and Improvement, 1991.

United States Department of Health and Human Services. *Child Sexual Abuse Prevention—Tips to Parents*. Washington, D.C.: 1984.

Van de Kamp, John. *Child Abuse Prevention Handbook*. Sacramento, Calif: Child Prevention Center, 1983.

Waters, H.F. "What TV Does for Kids." *Newsweek*, February 21, 1977, pp. 62–70.

Winn, Marie. *Children Without Childhood*. New York: Penguin Books, 1984.

———. *The Plug-In Drug: TV, Children, and the Family*. New York: Viking-Penguin, 1985.

Families and Communities

Divorce and Family Structures

Clarke-Stewart, K. Alison. "Single-Parent Families: How Bad for the Children?," *NEA Today*, January, 1989.

Edelman, Marian, W. "Economic Issues Related to Child Care and Early Childhood Education." *Teachers College Record*, Vol. 90, No. 3, Spring, 1989.

Francke, Linda B. *Growing Up Divorced*. NY: Linden Press/Simon & Schuster, 1983.

Galinsky, Ellen. *Investing in Quality Child Care*. AT&T Report, November, 1986.

Osborn, D. Keith. *Early Childhood Education in Historical Perspective* (3rd ed.). Athens, GA: Daye Press, 1991.

Rice, Sharon J., and McKenry., Patrick C. *Divorce*. Sage Publications, 1988.

Work, Economics, and Public Policy: The Working Parent

Brazelton, T. Berry. "Working Parents." *Newsweek*, February 13, 1989.

Cohen, Deborah. "Proposals to Ease Families' Tax Burden." *Education Week*, July 31, 1991.

Fuchs, Victor, and Diane Reklis. "Children, Economics, and Public Policy." Unpublished report, October, 1990.

Rockefeller, John D. IV. "Common Ground for America's Children." *Childcare Monthly*, San Jose, CA, October, 1991.

Schroeder, Pat. "Children in America Today." Address to California Association for the Education of Young Children, Los Angeles, CA, March, 1991.

Community and School Support

Coleman, James S. "Parental Involvement in Education." Washington, D.C.: Office of Educational Research and Improvement, U.S. Department of Education, 1991.

Elkind, David. "The family and education in the postmodern world." *Momentum*, September, 1991.

Gardner, John W. "Community." Graduate School of Business, Stanford University, January, 1991.

Hostetler, Lana. "It Takes a Village to Raise a Child." *Young Children*, November, 1990.

Oyemade, Ura J., and Washington, Valora. "Drug Abuse Prevention Begins in Early Childhood." *Young Children*, July, 1989.

Van Deusen, Jennifer. "Community Schools: A Vision of Equity and Excellence for Young Children." *Young Children*, July, 1991.

Young-Holt, Carol. "Creating a Healthy 'Community'," personal communication, 1991.

TRANSMITTING VALUES
Television and the Media

Anderson, Daniel R., and Collins, Patricia A. *The Impact of Children's Television: Television's Influence on Cognitive Development.* Washington, D.C.: Office of Educational Research and Improvement, April, 1988.

Anonymous. "Watching Videos with Kids—Choosing and Using Videotapes with Preschoolers." *Scholastic Pre-K Today*, March, 1990.

Carter, Bill. "Children's TV, Where Boys Are King." *New York Times*, May 1, 1991.

David, Judy. "When to Turn It On—and Off." *Good Housekeeping*, September, 1988.

ERIC Clearinghouse on Elementary and Early Childhood Education. *Guidelines for Family Television Viewing.* Vol. 2, No. 2, Fall, 1990.

Minow, Newton. "Worth Noting." Address to commemorate 30th anniversary of his "vast wasteland" speech. *Education Week*, June 19, 1991.

NAEYC. "Media Violence and Children. "Washington, D.C.: National Association for the Education of Young Children, 1990.

Solter, Aletha. "Television and Children." *Mothering*, Fall, 1986.

Walsh, Mark. "New Federal Rules for Children's TV Draws Fire." *Education Week*, November 1990.

——————. "FCC Adopts Final Rule on Children's Television." *Education Week*, April, 1991.

——————. "Children's TV Advocates Launch Campaign to Put 'Teeth' into 1990 Broadcasting Law." *Education Week*, May, 1991.

War and Violence

Carlsson-Paige, Nancy, and Levin, Dianne. *Helping Children Understand Peace, War, and the Nuclear Threat.* Washington, D.C.: National Association for the Education of Young Children, 1990 (3rd printing).

——————. *The War Play Dilemma.* New York: Teachers College, 1987.

Educators for Social Responsibility, 23 Garden Street, Cambridge, Mass.

Eyer, Dianne W. "Safe Start in California." Personal communications, 1995.

Golden, Nancy. "Our Children and the War." *Peninsula Chapter AEYC Newsletter*, Vol. 11, No. 6, March, 1991.

Hopkins, Susan (chair). "Bibliography I and Bibliography II for Peace Issues." California Association for the Education of Young Children Peace Committee, Sacramento, CA, 1990 and 1991.

Johnson, Bonnie. "Peaceful Resources." In *Exchange*, January/February, 1991.

Levin, Diane. *Teaching Young Children in Violent Times.* Cambridge, Mass.: Educators for Social Responsibility, 1994.

National Association for Mediation Education.

Wallinga, Charlotte, Boyd, Brenda, Skeen, Patty, and Paguio. Ligaya. "Children and Nuclear War." In *Childhood Education*, Reviews of Research, Summer, 1991.

Diversity

Multicultural Education

Armstrong, Liz S. "Racial Ethnic Prejudice Still Prevalent, Survey Finds." *Education Week*, January 16, 1991.

Carter, Margie. "Honoring Diversity: Problems and Possibilities for Staff and Organization." *Exchange*, January, 1988.

Center for Demographic Policy. *The Same Client: The Demographics of Education and Service Delivery System.* Washington, D.C.: Institute for Educational Leadership, 1989.

Derman-Sparks, Louise. *Anti-Bias Curriculum.* Washington, D.C.: National Association for the Education of Young Children, 1989.

DiMartino, Emily C. "Understanding Children from Other Cultures." *Childhood Education*, Vol. 66, No. 1, Fall, 1989.

Education Week. "Dimensions: In California, Nation's First Minority Majority." *Education Week*, November 14, 1990.

Edwards, Carolyn P., and Gandini, Lella. "Teachers' Expectations About the Timing of Developmental Skills: a Cross Cultural Study." Washington, D.C.: *Young Children*, May, 1989.

ERIC/EECE Resource List. *Multicultural Education for Children*, 1991.

Hale, Janice E. "Culturally Appropriate Pedagogy and the African American Child." In *Beginnings and Beyond*, ed. A. Gordon and K.B. Browne. Albany, N.Y.: Delmar Publishers, 1993 (3rd Ed.).

Head Start. "Bringing Our World Together." In *Pre-K Today*, November/December, 1986. From Head Start manual: *Multi-Cultural Education for Head Start Children: An Introduction for Parents and Teachers."*

Neugebauer, Bonnie. "Evaluating Program Resources for Attitudes About Diversity." *Exchange*, March, 1987.

Schmidt, Peter. "Outlook Is Bleak for Many Blacks." *Education Week*, August 2, 1989.

——————. "Asian-Americans Are Starting to Exert Influence on Education-Policy Issues." *Education Week*, February 27, 1991.

Shapiro, Walter. "Unfinished Business." *Time*, August 7, 1989.

Viadero, Debra. "Battle over Multicultural Education Rises in Intensity." *Education Week*, November 28, 1990.

Walsh, Mark. "Black Private Schools Are Championed as an Alternative to the Public System." *Education Week*, March 13, 1991.

West, Peter. "Native Americans Said to Lack Clout to Improve Their Children's Schools." *Education Week*, February 27, 1991.

Bilingual Education

Bowman, Barbara T. "Educating Language-Minority Children." ERIC Digest, University of Illinois, 1991.

Fillmore, Lily W. "A Question for Early-Childhood Programs: English First or Families First?" *Education Week*, June 19, 1991.

Schmidt, Peter. "Three Types of Bilingual Education Effective." *Education Week*, February 20, 1991.

——————. "Report Faults Preschool English for Language-Minority Children." *Education Week*, May 1, 1991.

Equal Play and Gender Segregation

Greenberg, Selma. "Recommendations for Creating the Five *E*s: Educational Equity in Early Educational Environments." In Klein, S. (ed.). *Achieving Sex Equity Through Education*. Johns Hopkins Press, 1985.

Grossman, Herbert, and Grossman, Suzanne H. *Gender Issues in Education*. Boston, Mass.: Allyn & Bacon, 1994.

Hoyenga, Katherine B., and Hoyenga, Kermit T. *Gender-Related Differences*. Boston: Allyn & Bacon, 1993.

Lockheed, M., and Klein, S. "Sex Equity in Classroom Organization and Climate." In Klein, S. (ed.). *Handbook for Achieving Sex Equity Through Education*. Johns Hopkins Press, 1985.

Maccoby, Eleanor, and Jacklin, Carol N. "Gender Segregation in Nursery School: Predictors and Outcomes." Paper presented to the National Convention of the Society for Research in Child Development, Toronto, April 1985.

APPENDIX A
TIMELINE FOR EARLY CHILDHOOD EDUCATION

Authors' Note: *A debt of gratitude is owed to D. Keith Osborn for his outstanding historical research and to James L. Hymes, Jr., for his generous time and perspective.*

5th/3rd Centuries B.C. to 1400s A.D. Few records exist concerning child-rearing practices; the development of cities gives rise to schooling on a larger scale.

1423 & 1439 The invention of printing and movable type allows knowledge to spread rapidly; ideas and techniques become available to large numbers of people; printing is credited with bringing about the end of the Middle Ages and the beginning of the Renaissance.

1592–1670 Johann Amos Comenius

1657 *Orbis Pictus*, by Comenius, is the first children's book with pictures.

1632–1714 John Locke
English philosopher, considered the founder of educational philosophy, who postulated that children are born with a *tabula rasa*, or clean slate, upon which all experiences are written.

1712–1788 Jean Jacques Rousseau

1762 *Emile*, by Rousseau, proclaims the child's natural goodness.

1746–1826 Johann Heinrich Pestalozzi

1801 *How Gertrude Teaches Her Children*, by Pestalozzi, emphasizes home education.

1740–1860s Sabbath Schools and Clandestine Schools are established as facilities to educate African Americans in the United States.

1782–1852 Friedrich Wilhelm Froebel

1826 *Education of Man*, by Froebel, describes the first system of kindergarten education as a "child's garden," with activities known as "gifts from God."

1837 Froebel opens the first kindergarten in Blankenburgh, Germany.

1861 Robert Owen sets up infant school in New Lanark, England, as an instrument of social reform for children of parent workers in his mills.

1873 The Butler School at Hampton Institute is opened as a free school for black children, including kindergarten curriculum for five-year-olds.

1837 Horace Mann, known as the "Father of the Common Schools" because of his contributions in setting up the U.S. elementary school system, becomes Secretary of Massachusetts State Board of Education.

1856 Margarethe Schurz opens the first American kindergarten, a German-speaking class in her home in Watertown, Wisconsin.

1804–1894 Elizabeth Peabody

1860 Elizabeth Peabody opens the first English-speaking kindergarten in Boston.

1843–1916 Susan Blow

1873 First public school kindergarten, supported by Superintendent William Harris, is directed by Susan Blow in St. Louis, Missouri, who becomes the leading proponent of Froebel in America. The first public kindergarten in North America opens in 1871 in Ontario, Canada.

1856–1939 Sigmund Freud (see Chapter 4)

1892 Freud cites the importance of early experiences to later mental illness, ushering in the beginning of psychoanalysis and the emphasis on the importance of the first five years.

1858–1952 John Dewey

1896 John Dewey establishes a laboratory school at the University of Chicago, and develops a pragmatic approach to education, becoming the father of the Progressive Movement in American education.

1897 *My Pedagogic Creed* is published, detailing the opposition to rote learning and the philosophy of educating "the whole child."

1860–1931 Margaret McMillan

1911 Deptford School, an open-air school in the slums of London, is opened by Margaret McMillan. The school emphasizes health and play, thus coining the phrase "nursery school."

1868–1946 Patty Smith Hill

1893 Patty Smith Hill becomes director of the Louisville Free Kindergarten Society, augmenting her original Froebelian training with her work in scientific psychology (G. Stanley Hall) and progressive education (John Dewey). She goes on to found the National Association of Nursery Education (now known as NAEYC) in 1926.

1870–1952 Maria Montessori (see Chapters 1 and 2)

525

1907   Casa dei Bambini (Children's House) is opened by Maria Montessori in a slum district in Rome, Italy. She later develops an educational philosophy and program to guide children's growth through the senses and practical life experiences.

1874–1949   Edward Thorndike, behavioral psychologist (see Chapter 4)

1878–1958   John B. Watson, behavioral psychologist (see Chapter 4)

1878–1967   Lucy Sprague Mitchell

1916   The Bureau of Educational Experiments, which becomes Bank Street College of Education (and laboratory school) in 1922, is founded by L.S. Mitchell, who is a leading proponent of progressive education at the early childhood level.

1879   The first psychological laboratory is established in Germany to train psychologists in the systematic study of human beings.

1880   First teacher-training program for kindergartners, Oshkosh Normal School, Pennsylvania.

1880–1961   Arnold Gesell (see Chapter 4)

1923   Gesell, originally a student of G. Stanley Hall, publishes *The Preschool Child*, which emphasizes the importance of the early years.

1926   Gesell establishes the Clinic of Child Development at Yale University and studies norms of child growth and behavior, founding the maturation theory of development (see Chapters 1 and 4).

1885–1948   Susan Isaacs

1929   Susan Isaacs publishes *The Nursery Years*, which contradicts the more scientific psychological view of behavior shaping and emphasizes the child's viewpoint and the value of play.

1892–1992   Abigail Eliot

1922   Dr. Eliot opens Ruggles Street Nursery School and Training Center.

1892   International Kindergarten Union founded.

1895   G. Stanley Hall runs a child development seminar with kindergarten teachers, explaining the "scientific/new psychology" approach to education. While most leave, Anny Bryan and Patty Smith Hill go on to incorporate such techniques and to see early childhood education as a more multidisciplinary effort.

1896–1980   Jean Jacques Piaget (see Chapter 4)

1926   *The Language and Thought of the Child*, one of a multitude of writings on the development of children's thought, is published by Jean Piaget, who becomes one of the largest forces in child development in the twentieth century.

1952   Piaget's *Origins of Intelligence* in children is published in English.

1896–1934   Lev Vygotsky (see Chapter 4). 1978 *Mind in Society: the Development of Higher Psychological Processes*, the seminal work of Vygotsky's sociocultural theory, is first published in English.

1897–1905   Alfred Binet develops a test for the French government to determine feeblemindedness in children. Known as the Binet-Simon test (and tested by Jean Piaget, among others), it is now known as the Stanford-Binet I.Q. test.

1902–1994   Erik Erikson (see Chapter 4)

1950   *Childhood and Society*, which details Erikson's Eight Stages of Man, is published, thus adding a psychoanalytic influence to early childhood education.

1903–   Benjamin Spock

1946   Dr. Spock's *Baby and Child Care* is published. It advocates a more permissive attitude towards children's behavior, and encourages exploratory behavior.

1903   The Committee of Nineteen, a splinter group of the International Kindergarten Union, forms to report various philosophical concepts. Members include Patty Smith Hill, Lucy Wheelock, and Susan Blow.

1904–1988   B.F. Skinner (see Chapter 4)

1938   *The Behavior of Organisms*, by B.F. Skinner, is published, advocating the concepts of "radical behaviorism" in psychology.

1906   Josephine Yates publishes an article in the Colored American Magazine, which advocates play in the kindergarten and helps translate Froebel's concepts into Black kindergartens of the day.

1908–1984   Sylvia Ashton Warner

1963   *Teacher*, published by this New Zealand kindergarten teacher, develops the concepts of "organic vocabulary" and "key vocabulary."

1909   First White House Conference on Children by Theodore Roosevelt, is held, leading to the establishment of the Children's Bureau in 1912.

1915   First U.S. Montessori school opens in New York City.

1916   First Cooperative Nursery School opens at the University of Chicago.

1918   First public nursery schools are opened in England.

1918–   T. Berry Brazelton

1969   *Infants and Mothers*, along with several other books and numerous articles, is published by this pediatrician, advocating a sensible and intimate relationship between parents and children.

1980s   Dr. Brazelton is one of the founders of "Parent

Action," a federal lobby to advocate for the needs of parents and children, particularly for a national policy granting parental leave from work to care for newborns or newly adopted children.

1919 Harriet Johnson starts the Nursery School of the Bureau of Educational Experiments, which later becomes Bank Street School.

1920–1994 Loris Malaguzzi theorizes about good programs and relationships for children, emphasizing the child's individual creative expression; starts school of Reggio Emilia, Italy, in 1946.

1921 Patty Smith Hill opens Columbia Teacher's College Laboratory School.

1921 A.S. Neill founds Summerhill school in England, which becomes a model for the "free school" movement (the book entitled *Summerhill* is published in 1960).

1922 Edna Noble White directs the Merrill-Palmer School of Motherhood and Home Training, which later becomes the Merrill-Palmer Institute Nursery School.

1925–26 The National Committee on Nursery Schools is founded by Patty Smith Hill; it becomes NANE and eventually NAEYC.

1925– Albert Bandura, psychologist in social learning theory (see Chapter 4)

1926 Bertrand Russell publishes *On Education*, urging teachers to renounce the memorization of facts and concentrate on personality development.

1926–27 Research facilities are founded at several American universities and colleges (e.g., Smith College, Vassar College, Yale University, Mills College).

1927 Dorothy Howard establishes the first Black Nursery School in Washington, D.C., and operates it for over 50 years.

1928 John B. Watson publishes *Psychological Care of Infant and Child*, applying his theories of conditioning to child-rearing (see Chapter 4).

1929 Lois Meeks Stolz (1891–1984) becomes the first President of the National Association for Nursery Education (later to become National Association for the Education of Young Children) and joins the Teachers College (Columbia University) faculty to start the laboratory school and Child Development Institute. Stolz later becomes the Director of the Kaiser Child Service Centers during World War II.

1929–31 Hampton Institute, Spellman College, and Bennett College open Black laboratory nursery schools, emphasizing child development principles as in other lab schools and serving as training centers.

1930 International Kindergarten Union, founded in 1892, becomes the Association for Childhood Education, increasing its scope to include elementary education.

1933 WPA (Works Projects Association) opens emergency nurseries for Depression relief of unemployed teachers. Enrolling over 4000 teachers in 3000 schools, they also help children of unemployed parents, and operate under the guidance of people such as Edna Noble White, Abigail Eliot, and Lois Meek Stolz until World War II.

1935 First toy lending library, Toy Loan, begins in Los Angeles.

1936 The first commercial telecast is shown in New York City, starring Felix the Cat. The pervasiveness of television sets and children's viewing habits become a source of concern for educators and parents in the latter half of the twentieth century.

1943–45 Kaiser Shipyard Child Care Center, run by Lois Meek Stolz, James Hymes, and Edith Dowley, operates 24-hour care in Portland, Oregon.

1944 *Young Children* is first published.

1946 Stanford University laboratory school is founded by Edith Dowley.

1948 OMEP, the World Organization for Early Childhood Education, is founded to promote the education of children internationally, and begins to consult with UNICEF and UNESCO in the United Nations. It starts publishing a journal, *The International Journal of Early Childhood*, in 1969.

1956 *La Leche League* is established to provide mothers with information on breast-feeding, childbirth, infants, and child care.

1957 Sputnik, a Soviet satellite, is successfully launched, sparking a renewed interest in—and criticism of—American education.

1960 Katherine Whiteside Taylor founds the American Council of Parent Cooperatives, which later becomes the Parent Cooperative Preschools International.

1960 Nancy McCormick Rambusch (1927–1994) founds the American Montessori movement, splitting from her European counterparts to try to shape Montessori education as a viable American public school alternative and to establish teacher taining programs at both early childhood and elementary levels.

1962 Perry Preschool Project, directed by David Weikart, opens in Ypsilanti, Michigan, and conducts longitudinal study to measure the effects of preschool education on later school and life (see Chapter 2).

1963 & 1966 Lawrence Kohlberg publishes child development works on the development of gender and sex roles, and moral development (see Chapter 4).

1964–65 The Economic Opportunity Act of 1964 passes, becoming the foundation of Head Start Programs in the United States, as part of a federal "War on Poverty."

1966 The Bureau of Education for the Handicapped is established.

1966 NANE becomes National Association for the Education of Young Children (NAEYC).

1967 Plowden Report from England details the British Infant School system.

The Follow Through Program extends Head Start into the primary grades of the elementary system.

1969 John Bowlby publishes the first of his major works on *Attachment* (see Chapter 4).

The Ford Foundation, Carnegie Corporation, and Department of Health, Education, and Welfare subsidize the Children's Television Workshop, which develops *Sesame Street*.

1971 Stride-Rite Corporation of Boston opens a children's program on site, becoming a vanguard for employer-supported child care.

1972 The Child Development Associate Consortium, headed by Dr. Edward Ziegler, is established to develop a professional training program. Now known as CDA, its administration moves to NAEYC in 1985.

1974 Eleanor Maccoby publishes *The Development of Sex Differences* (see Chapter 4).

1975 P.L. 94-142, the Education for All Handicapped Children bill, passes, mandating appropriate education for special needs children in the "least restrictive environment" possible, thus defining the concept of "mainstreaming."

1975 Mary Ainsworth publishes developmental research on mother-child interaction, and follows up with work on patterns of attachment (see Chapter 4).

1979 Nancy Eisenberg publishes the theory of the development of prosocial development in children (see Chapter 4).

The United Nations declares an International Year of the Child.

1980 The Department of Health, Education, and Welfare is changed to that of Health and Human Services, and a separate Department of Education is established.

1982 Carol Gilligan publishes *In a Different Voice*, challenging accepted psychological theory on moral development (see Chapter 4).

1982– Marion Wright Edelman establishes the Children's Defense Fund, a Washington-based lobby on behalf of children, and particularly children of poverty and color.

1984 NAEYC publishes a report entitled "Developmentally Appropriate Practices," which outlines what is meant by "quality" work with young children from infancy through age eight.

1985 NAEYC establishes a National Academy and a voluntary accreditation system for centers, in an effort to improve the quality of children's lives.

1986 U.S. Department of Education declares the Year of the Elementary School.

P.L. 99-457, amending 94-142, establishes a national policy on early intervention for children as young as infants.

1988–90 The Alliance for Better Child Care, a coalition of groups advocating on behalf of young children, sponsors the ABC bill in an effort to get federal support for children and families. While it fails to be signed in 1989, it is passed in 1990.

1991 "Ready to Learn/America 2000" Part of the U.S. government's educational strategy for reforming American public schools.

APPENDIX B
STATEMENT OF COMMITMENT

As an individual who works with young children, I commit myself to furthering the values of early childhood education as they are reflected in the NAEYC Code of Ethical Conduct. To the best of my ability I will

● Ensure that programs for young children are based on current knowledge of child development and early childhood education.

● Respect and support families in their task of nurturing children.

● Respect colleagues in early childhood education and support them in maintaining the NAEYC Code of Ethical Conduct.

● Serve as an advocate for children, their families, and their teachers in community and society.

● Maintain high standards of professional conduct.

● Recognize how personal values, opinions, and biases can affect professional judgment.

● Be open to new ideas and be willing to learn from the suggestions of others.

● Continue to learn, grow, and contribute as a professional.

● Honor the ideals and principles of the NAEYC Code of Ethical Conduct.

The Statement of Commitment expresses those basic personal commitments that individuals must make in order to align themselves with the profession's responsibilities as set forth in the NAEYC Code of Ethical Conduct.

APPENDIX C
LITERACY DEVELOPMENT AND PRE-FIRST GRADE

A Joint Statement of Concerns about Present Practices in Pre-First Grade Reading Instruction and Recommendations for Improvement

● Association for Childhood Education International

● Association for Supervision and Curriculum Development

● International Reading Association

● National Association for the Education of Young Children

● National Association of Elementary School Principals

● National Council of Teachers of English

Objectives For A Pre-First Grade Reading Program

Literacy learning begins in infancy. Reading and writing experiences at school should permit children to build upon their already existing knowledge of oral and written language. Learning should take place in a supportive environment where children can build a positive attitude toward themselves and toward language and literacy. For optimal learning, teachers should involve children actively in many meaningful, functional language experiences, including *speaking, listening, writing,* and *reading*. Teachers of young children should be prepared in ways that acknowledge differences in language and cultural backgrounds and emphasize reading as an integral part of the language arts as well as of the total curriculum.

What Young Children Know About Oral and Written Language Before They Come To School

1. Children have had many experiences from which they are building their ideas about the functions and uses of oral language and written language.
2. Children have a command of language, have internalized many of its rules, and have conceptualized processes for learning and using language.
3. Many children can differentiate between drawing and writing.
4. Many children are reading environmental print, such as road signs, grocery labels, and fast food signs.
5. Many children associate books with reading.
6. Children's knowledge about language and communication systems is influenced by their social and cultural backgrounds.
7. Many children expect that reading and writing will be sense-making activities.

Concerns

1. Many pre-first grade children are subjected to rigid, formal pre-reading programs with inappropriate expectations and experiences for their levels of development.
2. Little attention is given to individual development or individual learning styles.
3. The pressures of accelerated programs do not allow children to be risk-takers as they experiment with language and internalize concepts about how language operates.
4. Too much attention is focused upon isolated skill development or abstract parts of the reading process, rather than upon the integration of oral language, writing, and listening with reading.
5. Too little attention is placed upon reading for pleasure; therefore, children often do not associate reading with enjoyment.

6. Decisions related to reading programs are often based on political and economic considerations rather than on knowledge of how young children learn.
7. The pressure to achieve high scores on standardized tests that frequently are not appropriate for the kindergarten child has resulted in changes in the content of programs. Program content often does not attend to the child's social, emotional, and intellectual development. Consequently, inappropriate activities that deny curiosity, critical thinking, and creative expression occur all too frequently. Such activities foster negative attitudes toward communication skill activities.
8. As a result of declining enrollments and reduction in staff, individuals who have little or no knowledge of early childhood education are sometimes assigned to teach young children. Such teachers often select inappropriate methodologies.
9. Teachers of pre-first graders who are conducting individualized programs without depending upon commercial readers and workbooks need to articulate for parents and other members of the public what they are doing and why.

Recommendations

1. Build instruction on what the child already knows about oral language, reading, and writing. Focus on meaningful experiences and meaningful language rather than merely on isolated skill development.
2. Respect the language the child brings to school, and use it as a base for language and literacy activities.
3. Ensure feelings of success for all children, helping them see themselves as people who can enjoy exploring oral and written language.
4. Provide reading experiences as an integrated part of the broader communication process, which includes speaking, listening, and writing, as well as other communication systems such as art, math, and music.
5. Encourage children's first attempts at writing without concern for the proper formation of letters or correct conventional spelling.

6. Encourage risk-taking in first attempts at reading and writing and accept what appear to be errors as part of children's natural patterns of growth and development.

7. Use materials for instruction that are familiar, such as well-known stories, because they provide the child with a sense of control and confidence.

8. Present a model for students to emulate. In the classroom, teachers should use language appropriately, listen and respond to children's talk, and engage in their own reading and writing.

9. Take time regularly to read to children from a wide variety of poetry, fiction, and nonfiction.

10. Provide time regularly for children's independent reading and writing.

11. Foster children's affective and cognitive development by providing opportunities to communicate what they know, think, and feel.

12. Use evaluative procedures that are developmentally and culturally appropriate for the children being assessed. The selection of evaluative measures should be based on the objectives of the instructional program and should consider each child's total development and its effect on reading performance.

13. Make parents aware of the reasons for a total language program at school and provide them with ideas for activities to carry out at home.

14. Alert parents to the limitations of formal assessments and standardized tests for pre-first graders' reading and writing skills.

15. Encourage children to be active participants in the learning process rather than passive recipients of knowledge, by using activities that allow for experimentation with talking, listening, writing, and reading.

Prepared by the Early Childhood and Literacy Development Committee of the International Reading Association, December 1985. Reprinted with permission of the Association.

APPENDIX D

NAEYC POSITION STATEMENT ON SCHOOL READINESS
Adopted July 1990

PREAMBLE

State and local efforts for educational reform and improved accountability have prompted considerable concern regarding children's "readiness" to enter kindergarten and first grade. The issue gained national prominence when the President and the nation's governors adopted it as a national education goal, vowing that "by the year 2000, all children will start school ready to learn." The construct of school readiness is based on the assumption that there is a predetermined set of capabilities that all children need before entering school. Therefore, any discussions of school readiness must consider at least three critical factors:

1. *the diversity and inequity of children's early life experiences;*

2. *the wide range of variation in young children's development and learning; and*

3. *the degree to which school expectations of children entering kindergarten are reasonable, appropriate, and supportive of individual differences.*

POSITION

The National Association for the Education of Young Children (NAEYC) believes that those who are committed to promoting universal school readiness must also be committed to

1. addressing the inequities in early life experience so that all children have access to the opportunities which promote school success;

2. recognizing and supporting individual differences among children; and

3. establishing reasonable and appropriate expectations of children's capabilities upon school entry.

The current construct of readiness unduly places the burden of proof on the child. Until the inequities of life experience are addressed, the use of readiness criteria for determining school entry or placement blames children for their lack of opportunity. Furthermore, many of the criteria now used as readiness measures are based on inappropriate expectations of children's abilities and fail to recognize normal individual variation in the rate and nature of development and learning. NAEYC believes it is the responsibility of schools *to meet the needs of children as they enter* and to provide whatever services are needed *in the least restrictive environment* to help each child reach his or her fullest potential.

Every child, except in the most severe instances of abuse, neglect, or disability, enters school ready to learn. However, all children do not succeed in school. A lack of basic health care and economic security places many children at risk for academic failure before they enter school. Families who lack emotional resources and support are likewise not always capable of preparing their children to meet school expectations.

It is a public responsibility to ensure that all families have access to the services and support needed to provide the strong relationships and rich experiences that prepare children to succeed in school. At a minimum such services include basic health care, including prenatal care and childhood immunizations; economic security; basic nutrition; adequate housing; family support services; and high-quality early childhood programs.

Supporting families' childrearing efforts is critically important for ensuring that more young children enter school ready to succeed. But, such efforts address only half of the problem. Attention must also be given to ensuring that the expectations used to determine readiness are legitimate and reasonable.

Expectations of the skills and abilities that young children will bring to school must be based on knowledge of child development and how children learn. A basic principle of child development

is that there is *tremendous normal variability* both among children of the same chronological age and within an individual child. Children's social skills, physical development, intellectual abilities, and emotional adjustment are equally important areas of development, and each contributes to how well a child does in school. Within any group of children, it is likely that one child will possess exceptional language and social skills, but be average in physical development and emotionally less mature than is typical of the age group. Another child may have excellent skills in large and small muscle control but be less advanced in language abilities. Other children will present still different configurations of development. When readiness expectations are based on a narrow checklist focusing on only one or two dimensions of development, the complexity of growth is ignored and completely normal children may be judged inadequate.

Wide variability also exists in the rate of children's growth. The precise timing of when a child will achieve a certain level of development or acquire a specific skill cannot be predicted, nor does development and learning occur in a uniform, incremental fashion. Raising the legal entry age or holding an individual child out of school a year are misdirected efforts to impose a rigid schedule on children's growth in spite of normal differences.

A prevalent, fundamental misconception is that children's learning occurs in a sequential, hierarchical process and that certain basic skills must exist before later learning can occur. This misconception is the basis for requiring acquisition of such isolated skills as recognizing upper and lower case letters, counting to 20, or coloring within the lines prior to school entry. In fact, children's acquisition of higher order thinking processes and problem-solving abilities occurs in tandem with and may outpace acquisition of basic skills. For example, children are able to comprehend and compose far more complex stories than they can read or write. To focus only on sounding out letters or forming letters properly on the lines ignores children's complex language capabilities and often squelches their burgeoning interest in reading and writing. This does not mean that the acquisition of basic skills is unimportant; rather, focusing solely on isolated skills deprives children of the meaningful context that promotes effective learning.

Because learning does not occur in a rigid sequence of skill acquisition and because wide variability is perfectly normal, it is inappropriate to determine school entry on the basis of the acquisition of certain skills and abilities. Schools may reasonably expect that children entering kindergarten will be active, curious, and eager to learn. They will know about themselves, and will be interested in making new friends and sharing experiences with them. Although gaining in self-control, kindergarten children's enthusiasm will sometimes overwhelm them, as, for example, they call out an answer before the teacher calls on them. First graders, unless they have had extremely negative experiences in kindergarten, will also bring enthusiasm and curiosity to their work. Typical six-year-olds are gaining fine-motor control, but for many, writing within narrow lines can still be difficult. Likewise, six-year-olds are gaining in their ability to move beyond their firsthand experiences to more abstract thought, but the here and now remains the most meaningful.

It is often assumed that tests exist to reliably determine which children are "ready" to enter school. Because of the nature of child development and how children learn, it is extremely difficult to develop reliable and valid measures of young children's abilities. When tests are used to make decisions which have such considerable impact on children's lives as denial of entry or assignment to a special class, they must offer the highest assurance of reliability and validity. No existing readiness measure meets these criteria. *Therefore, the only legally and ethically defensible criterion for determining school entry is whether the child has reached the legal chronological age of school entry.* While arbitrary, this criterion is also fair.

The nature of children's development and learning also dictates two important school responsibilities. Schools must be able to respond to a diverse range of abilities within any group of children, and the curriculum in the early grades must provide meaningful contexts for children's learning rather than focusing primarily on isolated skill acquisition.

Today not only do many kindergartens and primary grades focus on skill acquisition in the absence of meaningful context, but the expectations that are placed on children are often not age-appropriate. Whether the result of parental pressures

or the push to improve student performance on standardized tests, the curriculum has shifted. Children entering kindergarten are now typically expected to be ready for what previously constituted the first grade curriculum. As a result, more children are struggling and failing.

Even those children who have received every advantage prior to school entry find the inappropriate demands difficult to meet, often experiencing great stress and having their confidence as successful learners undermined. The potentially greatest danger lies in the lowered expectations of parents who see their children struggle or fail, since parental expectations are the most powerful predictor of children's later school success.

STRATEGIES FOR SCHOOLS TO SUCCEED WITH EVERY CHILD

Providing a Foundation for Later Learning

Children who come to school with a history of rich experiences—being read to frequently, going to the store with their own grocery list, dictating or writing letters to grandma, taking trips to the park or the zoo, and so on—have a rich background of firsthand experience upon which later learning can be based. These experiences depend on families having the time, energy, financial, and emotional resources. Given the growing numbers of young children who spend major portions of their day outside their home in early care and education settings, it is equally critical that all early childhood programs offer these types of rich experiences as well.

Early intervention services have been successfully devised to provide families with an array of comprehensive support services to help them provide the rich environment so critical for early learning. The federally funded Head Start program is the best known example of this type of program; a number of states and communities offer variations on the theme with considerable success. Successful intervention efforts have several key elements:

1. they provide comprehensive services to ensure that a wide range of individual needs are met;
2. they strengthen parents' roles as first teachers;

3. they provide a wide array of firsthand experiences and learning activities either directly to children or through parent education.

Intervention efforts which include these critical elements are most likely to result in lasting improvements in children's achievement. Less successful are the too frequent remedial efforts in which children are drilled on isolated skills. Often, emphasis on drill and practice only causes these children to lag further behind their counterparts, because learning devoid of context is much more difficult to attain and to apply to new situations. Decontextualized learning activities lack any real meaning or challenge for the learner. Moreover, children whose background and experiences are not congruent with school expectations cannot call upon their own experiences to provide the needed context.

Making Schools Responsive to Individual Needs

Providing comprehensive services and family support to children prior to school entry will better prepare many children to succeed in school. Because of individual differences in development, however, there will always be variation in the skills and abilities of any group of children entering school. Schools and teachers must be able to respond to such variation by individualizing their curriculum and teaching practices.

Making schools more responsive to the needs of individual learners will require ensuring that teachers and administrators understand child development and how children learn. They must know how to plan and implement a developmentally appropriate curriculum that emphasizes child-initiated learning experiences as opposed to teacher lectures, small group as opposed to whole-group activities, integrated lessons as opposed to strict demarcations between subject areas, and active hands-on learning with a variety of materials and activities as opposed to drill and practice of repetitive seatwork. Rather than imposing rigid, lock-step distinctions between grades, schools must be able to offer continuous progress for children through the primary grades, recognizing that children's developmental timetables do not conform to the yearly calendar.

Making the necessary changes will require new resources and understanding. In addition to ensuring that teachers of young children have specialized training in child development and early education, class size should be reduced and additional adults available to ensure individualized instruction. Investments in classroom equipment and materials are also needed so that children have access to a wide array of materials and activities for hands-on learning.

The investment and commitment needed to ensure that every child enters school ready to succeed and that schools are ready to ensure their success will not be small. But, it is necessary. As we enter the twenty-first century, our human resources are our most precious commodity. For too long we have reserved educational achievement for the very few. We have used labeling and sorting mechanisms as a sieve and allowed too many children to fail. This nation can no longer afford such costly errors of omission. We must provide every child with the firm foundation so critical to school success and we must ensure that schools are prepared to meet the needs of individual children as they arrive at the school door. Only then will our nation be ready to enter the twenty-first century.

SOURCES FOR ADDITIONAL INFORMATION

Bredekamp, S. & Shepard, L. (1989). How best to protect children from inappropriate school expectations, practices, and policies. *Young Children*, 44, (3), 14–24.

Bredekamp, S. (Ed.). (1987). *Developmentally appropriate practice in early childhood programs serving young children from birth through age 8 (expanded ed.)*. Washington, D.C.: NAEYC.

Kamii, C. (Ed.). (1990). *Achievement testing in the early grades: The games grown-ups play.* Washington, D.C.: NAEYC.

National Association of Elementary School Principals. (1990). *Early childhood education and the elementary school principal: Standards for quality programs for young children.* Alexandria, VA: Author.

National Association of State Boards of Education (1988). *Right from the start: The report of the NASBE Task Force on Early Childhood Education.* Alexandria, VA: Author.

Shepard, L.A. & Smith, M.E. (1989). *Flunking grades: Research and policies on retention.* Lewes, England: Falmer Press.

Willer, B. & Bredekamp, S. (1990). Public Policy report. Redefining readiness: An essential requisite for educational reform. *Young Children,* 45, (5), 22–24.

GLOSSARY

Abberant. Deviating from the usual or natural type; abnormal, atypical.

Accommodation. A concept in Piaget's cognitive theory as one of two processes people use to learn and incorporate new information; the person adjusts what is already known to "accommodate" new learning. Children usually will change their way of thinking into a "schema," once they see that their usual ways do not take new information into account; they then will add new thought patterns to handle the new knowledge.

Accountability. The quality or state of being answerable to someone or of being responsible for explaining exact conditions; schools often must give specific account of their actions to a funding agency to assure the group that the funds and operation of the school are being handled properly.

Accreditation. A system of voluntary evaluation for early childhood centers. The goal is to improve the quality of care and education provided for young children. Accreditation is administered by the National Academy, a branch of the National Association for the Education of Young Children.

Active Listening. A child guidance technique of reflecting back to the speaker what the listener thinks has been said.

Activity Centers. Similar to learning centers and interest areas; areas in a classroom or yard that are designed and arranged for various activities to take place. An early childhood setting will offer several centers, or stations, for children that are based on both children's interests and what the staff hopes for them to learn in class.

Advocate. One who maintains, defends, or pleads the cause of another; in early childhood terms, an advocate is someone who furthers the principles and issues of the field by speaking to others about such issues.

After-School Care. Programs designed to care for children after the regular academic school day.

Age-Level Characteristics. Those features of children's development and behavior that are most common among a given age group.

Androgynous. Having to do with either sex; associated with both the male and female identity, behavior, etc.

Anti-bias. A phrase describing the development of curriculum that emphasizes an inclusive look at people and problems, extending the tenets of multicultural education and pluralism.

Arbitrary. A decision based on individual judgment or on a whim.

Articulation. The manner in which sounds and words are actually spoken.

Assess. To make an evaluation or determine the importance, disposition, or state of something or someone, such as in evaluating a child's skills, a classroom environment, or a teacher's effectiveness.

Assimilation. A concept in Piaget's cognitive theory as one of two processes people use to learn and incorporate new information; the person takes new information and puts it together with what is already known in order to "assimilate" the new information intellectually, such as when a toddler shakes a toy magnet first, as with all other toys, in order to get to know this new object. Children usually first try to put new experiences into the "schema," or categories, they already know and use.

Atelerista. A person trained in the arts who acts as a resource and teaches techniques and skills to children in the schools of Reggio Emilia, Italy.

Attachment/Attachment Behaviors. The relational bond that connects a child to another important person; feelings and behaviors of devotion or positive connection.

Attitude Crystallization. To assume a definite, concrete form in one's attitudes; refers to the formation of a firm set of attitudes and behaviors about others' race, ethnicity, gender, and ability that may be prejudicial and difficult to change.

Autonomy. The state of being able to exist and operate independently, of being self-sufficient rather than dependent upon others.

Baby Biographies. One of the first methods of child study, these narratives were written accounts by parents of what their babies did and said, usually in the form of a diary or log.

Back to Basics. A movement of the 1970s and 1980s prompted by a desire for schools to return to teaching the "basic" skills usually associated with academic learning, such as reading, writing, and arithmetic.

Baseline. A picture of the status of a child, teacher, or environment that serves as the basis for evaluation and later comparison.

Basic Emotions. Those emotions that are present and observable in the newborn or within the first few months of life; they include happiness, interest, surprise, disgust, distress, fear, anger, and sadness.

Basic Needs. Conditions, described by Abraham Maslow and other humanists, that are necessary for growth; these needs, such as physiological conditions and safety and security, are critical for a person's survival.

Behavior Swings. Shifts from one behavior to another, usually by a sharp change in what one is doing; e.g., from highly active to motionless, or from gregarious to shy.

Behavior Theory. A psychological theory developed in the United States in the twentieth century, which states that all important aspects of behavior and people are learned and can be modified or changed by varying external conditions.

Bilingualism. The acquisition of two languages during the first years of life; using or being able to use two languages.

Brainstorming. The process of thinking that involves bringing up as many ideas as possible about a subject, person, event, etc.

Cephalocaudal. In the direction of head (cephalic) to toe (caudal, of the tail or hind part of the body), as in how children develop physically.

Cerebral Palsy. A disorder that is the result of damage to a certain part of the brain (motor cortex); "CP," as it is commonly called, is a nonprogressive disorder (does not get worse as the child grows older); usually movement dysfunction is paired with some intellectual and perceptual impairment.

Checklist. A modified child study technique that uses a list of items for comparison, such as a "yes/no" checklist for the demonstration of a task.

Child Abuse. Violence in the form of physical maltreatment, abusive language, and sexual harassment or misuse of children.

Child Care Center. A place for care of children for a large portion of their waking day; includes basic care-taking activities of eating, dressing, resting, toileting, as well as playing/learning time.

Child-Centered Approach. The manner of establishing educational experiences that takes into consideration children's ways of perceiving and learning; manner of organizing a classroom, schedule, and teaching methods with an eye toward the child's viewpoint.

Child Neglect. The act or situation of parents'/adults' inattention to a child's basic health needs of adequate food, clothing, shelter, and health care; child neglect may also include not noticing a child or paying enough attention in general.

Church-Related Schools. Educational programs affiliated with a church or religious organization; they may have a direct relationship with the church by including religious education, by employing church members as teachers, or by being housed in a church building and using the facilities for a fee.

Classical Conditioning. The most common and basic category of learning in behavior theory, involving an association between a stimulus and response so that a reflex response (eye-blinking, salivating, etc.) occurs *whenever* a neutral and new stimulus is activated (a bell for a light, food, etc.); conditioned-response experiments conforming to the pattern of Pavlov's experiment, sometimes known as "stimulus substitution."

Clinical Method. An information-gathering technique, derived from therapy and counseling fields, in which the adult observes and then interacts with the client (in this case, children) by asking questions and posing ideas to the person or group being observed.

Cognition. The act or process of knowing, thinking, and perceiving. Cognition involves perceptual, intellectual, and emotional skills that begin as a child makes connections among objects and people and later extends to formulating mental representations.

Cognitive Confusion. State of being unsure or forgetful about what is already known, such as becoming perplexed about things or facts already learned.

Cognitive Theory. The psychological theory developed by Jean Piaget and others; the theory focuses on thought processes and how they change with age and experience; this point of view contrasts with the stimulus-response aspects of behavior theory.

Collaborated/Assisted Learning. A type of teaching-learning experience in which a child is helped by another, usually more skilled, person; often an older child or adult, this kind of learning is highly regarded in Vygotsky's theory of child development.

Compensatory Education. Education designed to supply what is thought to be lacking or missing in children's experiences or ordinary environments.

Competency-Based Assessment. Evaluation in which a teacher is judged or rated in comparison with a predetermined set of skills, or competencies, related to the job.

Complex Emotions. Those emotions that emerge in the child after infancy; these include shame, guilt, envy, and pride.

Componential Intelligence. One part of Sternberg's theory of intelligence that deals with analytical thinking.

Comprehensive. Inclusive, covering completely, such as a program for children that concerns itself with the physical, intellectual, social, emotional, creative, and health needs of the children.

Concrete. Concerning the immediate experience of actual things or events; specific and particular rather than general or symbolic.

Connected Knowledge. That kind of knowledge and information that is connected to the child in ways that are real and relevant to that individual; also known as meaningful knowledge in Piagetian terms, it is elaborated by Gilligan (see Chapter 4), Belenky, and others.

Constructivist. A description of Piagetian theory, the notion that, rather than only passively absorbing information or responding to rein-

forcement schedules, children acquire reality by actively constructing knowledge on an ongoing basis; therefore, a child's knowledge base is dynamic, based on both innate cognitive structures and experiences.

Contextual Intelligence. One part of Sternberg's theory of intelligence that deals with thinking within a certain set of circumstances that surround a particular event or situation; also known as "street smarts."

Continuing Education. The commitment of teachers to learning new approaches and ideas and to continuing to challenge themselves to higher levels of learning and competence.

Continuum. Something that is continuous; an uninterrupted, ordered sequence.

Core Values. The basic purposes or issues a professional group acknowledges as common concerns to all its members.

Cultural Pluralism. A state or society in which members of diverse ethnic, racial, or cultural groups maintain participation in and development of their traditional culture within the common society.

Custodial. Those tasks relating to guardianship of a child's basic needs for food, clothing, and shelter; they include providing for eating, dressing, toileting, resting, and appropriate protection from physical hardships such as weather, danger, etc.

Decoding. Converting from code into ordinary language; in terms of language development, decoding is the process of making sense out of printed letters or words.

Deficiency Needs. In Maslow's theory, those needs without which a person will have insufficient resources to survive.

Demographics. The statistical graphics of a population, especially showing average age, income, etc.

Developmentally Appropriate. That which is suitable or fitting to the development of the child; refers to those teaching practices which are based on the observation and responsiveness to children as learners with developing abilities who differ from one another by rate of growth and individual differences, rather than of differing amounts of abilities.

Developmental Schedules. Arrangement of a daily plan for children that is based on both individual and group levels of development.

Developmental Tasks. Those functions or work to be done by children at a particular point in their development.

Diary Descriptions. A form of observation technique that involves making a comprehensive narrative record of behavior, in diary form.

Discipline. Ability to follow an example or to follow rules; the development of self-control or control in general, such as by imposing order on a group. In early childhood terms, discipline means everything adults do and say to influence children's behavior.

Disequilibrium. Loss of balance, or a period of change.

Divergent Thinking. The processes of thought and perception that involve taking a line of thought or action different from what is the norm or common; finding ideas that branch out rather than converge and center on one answer.

Down Syndrome. A genetic abnormality that results in mongolism, one of the most common and easily identified forms of mental retardation.

Dramatic Play. Also known as imaginative play, this is a common form of spontaneous play in which children use their imagination and fantasy as part of the setting and activity.

Dynamic. Having energy or effective action; a basic skill is one with consequences that will motivate the child, affecting development or stability.

Early Childhood Education. Education in the early years of life; the field of study that deals mainly with the learning and experiences of children from infancy through the primary years (up to approximately eight years of age).

Eclectic. Choosing what appears to be best in various doctrines, methods, styles; comprised of elements drawn from various sources.

Ecology of the Family. The concept of viewing the child in the context of his or her impact on the family and the family's impact on the child. Stresses the interrelationship of the various family members with one another.

Educaring. A concept of teaching as both educating and care giving; coined by Magda Gerber is referring to people working with infants and toddlers.

Egocentric. Self-centered; regarding the self as the center of all things; in Piaget's theory, young children think using themselves as the center of the universe, or as the entire universe.

Elaboration. The act of expanding language; developing language by building complex structures from simple ones and adding details.

Emergent Curriculum. A process for curriculum planning which draws on teachers' observations and children's interests. Plans emerge from daily life interests and issues. This approach takes advantage of children's spontaneity and teachers' planning.

Emerging Literacy. The process of building upon prereading skills in a child-centered fashion, so that the ability to read evolves from children's direct experiences.

Emotional Framework. The basic "feeling" structure of a classroom that determines the tone and underlying sensibilities that affect how people feel and behave while in class.

Employer-Sponsored Child Care. Child care supported in some way by the parents' employers. Support may be financial (as an employee benefit or subsidy) or physical (offering on-site care).

Entry Level. The level of development or behavior that a child shows upon beginning a program or group experience; usually an observation-based informal assessment after the first few weeks of school.

Environment. All those conditions that affect children's surroundings and the people in them; the physical, interpersonal, and temporal aspects of an early childhood setting.

Environmental. Forces that are not innate or hereditary aspects of development; in early childhood terms, environmental aspects of growth are all those influences of physical conditions, interpersonal relationships, and world experiences that interact with a person to change the way he or she behaves, feels, and lives.

Equilibration. To balance equally; in Piaget's theory, the thinking process by which a person "makes sense" and puts into balance new information with what is already known.

Ethics. A theory or system of moral principles and standards; what is "right and wrong"; one's values; the principles of conduct governing both an individual teacher and the teaching profession.

Ethnocentric. Having one's race as a central interest, or regarding one's race or cultural group as superior to others.

Evaluation. A study to determine or set significance or quality.

Event Sampling. An observation technique that involves defining the event to be observed and coding the event to record what is important to remember about it.

Experiential Intelligence. One part of Sternberg's theory of intelligence that refers to thinking developed through reactions to people and events.

Experimental Procedure. An observation technique that gathers information by establishing a hypothesis, controlling the variables that might influence behavior, and testing the hypothesis.

Expressive Language. Those aspects of language development and skill that deal with expression: pronunciation, vocabulary, and grammar, as well as speaking and articulation.

Extrinsic. Originating from or on the outside; external, not derived from one's essential nature.

Family Day Care. Care for children in a small, home-like setting; usually six or fewer children in a family residence.

Feedback Loop. In terms of evaluation, *feedback loop* is used to describe the process whereby an evaluator gives information to a teacher, who in turn uses this information to improve teaching skills.

Fine Motor. Having to do with the smaller muscles of the body and the extremities, such as those in the fingers, toes, and face.

Flexibility. Capable of modification or change; willing or easily moved from one idea to another.

Fluency. The ability to produce many ideas; an easy and ready flow of ideas.

Formal Tests. Evaluation instruments that are administered in a conventional, "testlike" atmosphere for use with groups of children, and may or may not be developed commercially.

Four "I"s. The four components (I, Initiative, Independence, and Interaction) of early childhood curriculum for building self-esteem.

Frames of Mind. A theory of intelligence developed by Gardner that refers to intelligence as a host of seven different skills and abilities.

Genes. The biological elements that transmit hereditary characteristics.

Gifted Children. Children who have unusually high intelligence, as characterized by: learning to read spontaneously; being able to solve problems and communicate at a level far advanced from their chronological age; excellent memory; extensive vocabulary; and unusual approaches to ideas, tasks, people.

Gross Motor. Having to do with the entire body or the large muscles of the body, such as the legs, arms, and trunk.

Growth Needs. Conditions, as described by Abraham Maslow and other humanists, that are important to a person's well being; these needs, such as love and belonging, self-esteem and respect for others, playfulness, truth, beauty, etc., while not critical to a person's survival, are necessary for growth.

Holistic. A viewpoint that takes into account several conceptions of a child or situation to form a wider, more rounded description; in early childhood terms, this view includes a child's history, present status, relationships with others, and the interrelationships of development to arrive at a picture of the child; in medicine, this view includes dealing with a person's mental and emotional state, relationships, etc., as well as body signs.

Humanist Theory. The psychological theory of Abraham Maslow and others; it involves principles of motivation and wellness, centering on people's needs, goals, and successes.

Hypothesis. A tentative theory or assumption made in order to draw inferences or test conclusions; an interpretation of a practical situation that is then taken as the ground for action.

IEP. An Individual Education Plan is a process of planning for the education of children with special needs that involves joint efforts of specialists, teachers, and parents.

Inadequacy. The state of being or feeling insufficient, of not being or having "enough"; if feeling discouraged, children will display their feelings of inadequacy by misbehaving.

Inclusion. When a child with a disability is a full-time member of a regular classroom with children who are developing normally as well as with children with special needs.

Independence. Not controlled or influenced by others; thinking for oneself and autonomous.

Individualized Curriculum. A course of study developed and tailored to meet the needs and interests of an individual, rather than those of a group without regard for the individual child.

Inductive Guidance. A guidance process through which children are held accountable for their actions and where they are called on to think about the impact of their behavior on others. Reasoning and problem-solving skills are stressed.

Inference. A conclusion reached by reasoning from evidence or after gathering information, whether direct or indirect.

Informal Assessment. Evaluation based on methods and instruments that are not administered formally, as in paper-and-pencil tests, but rather are done while the subjects are at work or play in their natural environments.

Initiative. An introductory step; in early childhood terms, the energy, capacity, and will to begin taking action.

Integrated Curriculum. A set of courses designed to form a whole; coordination of the various areas of study, making for continuous and harmonious learning.

Integrated Day. A school schedule with no prescribed time periods for subject matter, but rather an environment organized around various interest centers among which children choose in organizing their own learning experiences.

Integrated Development. Growth that occurs in a continuous, interrelated manner; a child's progress as a whole, rather than in separate areas.

Intelligence. The cluster of capabilities that involves thinking (see Chapter 13 for details).

Interaction. Acting upon one another, as in the interplay or reciprocal effect of one child upon another.

Interdependence. Dependence on one another, as in the relationship between teachers' experience in the areas of discipline and their competence at knowing and using appropriate language for discipline.

Interdisciplinary Approach. A method of teaching/learning that draws from sources in more than one field of study; e.g., a course in education that uses background from the fields of medicine, psychology, and social work as well as education itself.

Interest Areas. Similar to learning centers and activity areas; one way to design physical space in a classroom or yard, dividing the space into separate centers among which children move about, rather than assigning them desks.

Interpersonal. Relating to, or involving relationships with, other people; those parts of the environment that have to do with the people in a school setting.

Intervene. To enter into a situation between two or more persons or between a person and an object; to interpose oneself into another's affairs, such as when teachers enter into children's interactions when their behavior calls for some action on the part of an adult.

Intrinsic. Belonging to the essential nature of or originating from within a person or body, such as intrinsic motivation, whereby one needs no external reward in order to do something.

Intuition. The direct perception of a fact or truth without any reasoning process; immediate insight.

Invented Spelling. Children's first attempts at spelling words the way they sound to them, based on their current knowledge of letters and sounds. Far from "correct" ("scnd" for second, "grrn" for green, or "relly" for really), invented spelling becomes more conventional over time.

Job Burnout. Exhaustion and stress from one's job, characterized by a wearing down of body and attitude.

Kindergarten. A school or class for children four to six years old; in the United States, kindergarten is either the first year of formal, public school or the year of schooling before first grade.

Kindergartners. (1) A modern term to describe the children who are attending kindergarten programs; (2) A term used in 19th century America to describe early childhood practitioners who worked in kindergartens patterned after Froebelian models.

Laboratory Schools. Educational settings whose purposes include experimental study; schools for testing and analysis of educational and/or psychological theory and practice, with an opportunity for experimentation, observation, and practice.

Latchkey Children. Children who are left home after school unattended or supervised by an adult; children who are responsible after school for themselves and perhaps younger siblings while their parents/guardians are not at home, usually working; such children have a "latchkey" (housekey) to let themselves into an empty home. Also referred to as "self-care."

Laterality. Of or relating to the side, as in children having an awareness of what is situated on, directed toward, or coming from either side of themselves.

Learning Centers. Similar to interest areas and activity areas; hubs or areas in a classroom designed to promote learning; the classroom is arranged in discrete areas for activity, and children move from one area to another rather than stay at an assigned desk or seat.

Limits. The boundaries of acceptable behavior beyond which actions are considered misbehavior and unacceptable conduct; the absolute controls an adult puts on children's behavior.

Linchpin. Something that serves to hold together the elements of a situation.

Logical Mathematical Knowledge. One of three types of knowledge in Piagetian theory; the component of intelligence that uses thinking derived from logic.

Log/Journal. A form of observation technique that involves making a page of notes about children's behavior in a cumulative journal.

Mainstreaming. The process of integrating handicapped children into classrooms with the nonhandicapped.

Maturation. The process of growth whereby a body matures regardless of, and relatively independent of, intervention such as exercise, experience, or environment.

Maturation Theory. A set of ideas based on the notion that the sequence of behavior and the emergence of personal characteristics develop more through predetermined growth processes than through learning and interaction with the environment; the theory of growth and development proposed and supported by Dr. Arnold Gesell and associates.

Meaningful Knowledge. The form of knowing that is learned within the context of what is already known; that knowledge that has meaning because it has particular significance of value to an individual.

Merit Pay. A system for teachers that gives pay bonuses for excellent teaching.

Methode Clinique. A kind of information-gathering technique, first used extensively by Jean Piaget, that involves observing children and asking questions as the situation unfolds. The purpose of this technique is to elicit information about how children are thinking as they behave naturally.

Misbehavior. Improper behavior or conduct.

Miseducation. David Elkind's term describing the end result of contemporary parents rushing their children into formal instruction too early.

Mixed-Age Groups. The practice of placing children of several levels, generally one year apart, into the same classroom. Also referred to as family grouping, heterogeneous grouping, multi-age grouping, vertical grouping, and ungraded classes.

Modeling. A part of behavior theory, modeling is a way of learning social behavior that involves observing a model (either real, filmed, or animated) and mimicking its behavior, thus acquiring new behavior.

Multiple Intelligences. A theory of intelligence, proposed by Howard Gardner and Robert Sternberg, among others, that outlines several different kinds of intelligence, rather than the former notion of intelligence as measured by standardized testing, such as the I.Q. (see "frames of mind" for more detail).

Myelination. The forming of the myelin sheath, the material in the membrane of certain cells in the brain; the development of the myelination of the brain seems to parallel Piagetian stages of cognitive development.

Narratives. A major observation technique that involves attempting to record nearly everything that happens, in as much detail as possible, as it happens. Narratives include several subtypes such as baby biographies, specimen descriptions, diary descriptions, and logs or journals.

Nature/Nurture Controversy. The argument regarding human development that centers around two opposing viewpoints; *nature* refers to the belief that it is a person's genetic, inherent character that determines development; *nurture* applies to the notion that it is the sum total of experiences and the environment that determine development.

Negative Reinforcement. Response to a behavior that decreases the likelihood of the behavior recurring; for instance, a teacher's glare might stop a child from whispering at group time, and from then on, the anticipation of such an angry look could reinforce not whispering in the future.

Networking. Making connections with others who can further career and professional opportunities.

Nonpunitive. Methods that do not involve or aim at punishment; for instance, letting a child be hungry later when he refuses to eat at snack time is a nonpunitive method of enforcing the need to snack with the group; hunger is a natural and logical consequence of the child's behavior, rather than a punishment meted out by the teacher (such as scolding or threatening).

Norm. An average or general standard of development or achievement, usually derived from the average or median of a large group; a pattern or trait taken to be typical of the behavior, skills, or interests of a group.

Objectivity. The quality or state of being able to see what is real and realistic, as distinguished from subjective and personal opinion or bias.

Open-ended. Activities or statements that allow a variety of responses, as opposed to those that allow only one response; anything organized to allow for variation.

Open School. A style of education, developed in progressive American schools and in the British infant schools, that is organized to encourage freedom of choice and that does not use predetermined roles and structure as the basis of education; an educational setting whose ultimate goal and base for curriculum is the development of the individual child, rather than of programmed academic experiences.

Operant Conditioning. A category of learning in behavior theory that involves a relation between a stimulus and response. The response is learned, rather than reflexive, and is gradually and carefully developed through reinforcement of the desired behavior as it occurs in response to the stimulus; behavior leading to a reward.

Organic Reading. A system of learning to read, popularized by Sylvia Ashton-Warner, that lets children build their own vocabulary with the words they choose.

Parent Cooperative. An educational setting organized by parents for their young children, often with parental control and/or support in the operation of the program itself.

Pedagogista. A person trained in early childhood education who meets weekly with the teachers in the schools of Reggio Emilia, Italy.

Pediatrician. A medical specialist in pediatrics, the branch of medicine dealing with children, their development, care, and diseases.

Peer Interactions. Associations with people of the same age group or with those one considers equals.

Perceptual-Motor Development. The growth of a person's ability to move (motor) and perceive (perceptual) together; perceptual-motor activity involves the body and the mind together, to coordinate movement.

Performance-Based Assessment. Evaluation based on observable, specific information on what a teacher actually does (performance while on the job).

Philosophy. Concepts expressing one's fundamental beliefs; in early childhood educational terms, the beliefs, ideas, and attitudes of our profession.

Phobia. A strong, exaggerated, and illogical fear of an object or class of things, people, etc.; one of several reactions children often have to divorce.

Phonemes. Language sounds; the smallest units of meaningful speech; two examples of phonemes are /a/ (as in hat) and /p/ (as in sip).

Physical Knowledge. One of three types of knowledge in Piagetian theory; that knowledge that is learned through external, sensory experiences.

Pluralism. (1) A theory that holds to the notion that there is more than one kind of reality or correct way of perceiving and acting upon the world; (2) A state in which members of diverse ethnic, racial, religious, or social groups participate in their traditional cultures while still belonging to the common society.

Positive Reinforcement. A response to a behavior that increases the likelihood of the behavior being repeated or increased; for instance, if a child gets attention and praise for crawling, it is likely that the crawling will increase—thus, the attention and praise were positive reinforcement for crawling.

Positive Stress. Refers to an amount of strain or tension that encourages a person to be active and challenged, rather than overwhelmed or discouraged.

Power Assertive Discipline. Harsh, punitive discipline methods which rely on children's fear of punishment rather than the use of reason and understanding. Hitting and spanking are examples of power assertion.

Practice Teaching. The period of "internship" that students experience when working in a classroom with supervision, as opposed to having a role as a regular working staff member.

Precedent. Something done or said that serves as an example or rule to authorize or justify other acts of the same or similar kind; an earlier occurrence of something similar.

Precursor. What precedes and indicates the approach of another; predecessor or forerunner.

Prejudices. Ideas and attitudes that are already formed about other people, situations, ideas, etc., before hearing or experiencing full or sufficient information; in teaching terms, those attitudes or biases that may be based less on mature thought and reasoning than on incomplete or nonexistent personal experiences.

Prepared Environment. The physical and interpersonal surroundings of an educational setting that are planned and arranged in advance with the group of children in mind.

Prerequisite. Something necessary or essential to carrying out an objective or performing an activity; when early childhood teachers determine what skills children will need in order to successfully engage in an activity, they are clarifying the prerequisites for that activity.

Private Speech. The language children use for self-guidance and self-direction, as well as helping them think about their behavior and plan for action; once known as "egocentric speech," it is used for self-regulation.

Professional. One engaged and participating in a profession and accepting the technical and ethical standards of that profession; in early childhood terms, one who has accumulated methods, course work, and teaching experience with young children along with attitudes of competency, flexibility, and continual learning.

Professional Confidentiality. Spoken, written, or acted upon in strict privacy, such as keeping the names of children or schools in confidence when discussing observations.

Professional Organizations. Those associations developed for the purpose of extending knowledge and teaching/learning opportunities in the field of education.

Project Approach. An in-depth study of a particular subject or theme by one or more children. Exploration of themes and topics over a period of days or weeks. Working in small groups, children are able to accommodate various levels of complexity and understanding to meet the needs of all the children working on the project.

Prosocial. Behaviors that are considered positive and social in nature, such as sharing, inviting, including, offering help or friendship.

Proximal to Distal. In the direction from the center of the body (proximal) toward the outer part (distal, far from the center), as in the way children's bodies develop.

Psychodynamic Theory. The psychological theory of Dr. Sigmund Freud and others; it asserts that the individual develops a basic personality core in childhood and that responses stem from personality organization and emotional problems as a result of environmental experiences.

Psychometric. Having to do with measurement of mental traits, abilities, and processes; usually a formal assessment using a standardized test.

Psychosocial. Those psychological issues that deal with how people relate to others, and the problems that arise on a social level; a modification by Erikson of the psychodynamic theories of Freud with attention to social and environmental problems of life.

Punishment. The act of inflicting a penalty for an offense or behavior.

Racist. Attitudes, behavior, or policies that imply either a hatred or intolerance of other race(s) or involving the idea that one's own race is superior and has the right to rule or dominate others.

Rating Scale. A modified child study technique similar to a checklist that classifies behavior according to grade or rank, such as using the descriptors "always, sometimes, never" to describe the frequency of a certain behavior.

Readiness. The condition of being ready, such as being in the state or stage of development so that the child has the capacity to understand, be taught, or engage in a particular activity.

Receptive Language. Those aspects of language development and skill that deal with the ability to receive messages: listening, understanding, and responding.

Reciprocal. The stage of children's friendship in which friendship is given or felt by each toward the other; a kind of give-and-take or two-way relationship, this is the stage most often seen in the latter part of the early childhood years.

Reinforcement. A procedure, such as reward or punishment, that changes a response to a stimulus; the act of encouraging a behavior to increase in frequency.

Reinforcers. Rewards in response to a specific behavior, thus increasing the likelihood of that behavior recurring; reinforcers may be either social (praise) or nonsocial (food) in nature, and may or may not be deliberately controlled.

Rote Knowledge. A form of knowing that is learned by routine or habit and without thought of the meaning.

Roughhousing. Rough and disorderly, but playful, behavior.

Routines. Regular procedures; habitual, repeated or regular parts of the school day; in early childhood programs, routines are those parts of the program schedule that remain constant, such as indoor time followed by cleanup and snack, regardless of what activities are being offered within those time slots.

Running Record. The narrative form of recording behavior; this kind of descriptive record of one's observations involves writing down all behavior as it occurs.

Schemas. A plan, scheme, or framework that helps make an organizational pattern from which to operate; in Piaget's theory, cognitive schemas are used for thinking.

Screening. Evaluations to determine a child's readiness for a particular class, grade, or experience.

Self-Actualization. The set of principles set forth by Abraham Maslow for a person's wellness or ability to be the most that a person can be; the state of being that results from having met all the basic and growth needs.

Self-Awareness. An awareness of one's own personality or individuality; in teaching terms, an ability to understand one's self and assess personal strengths and weaknesses.

Self-Care. A current description for latchkey children. (See also Latchkey Children.)

Self-Concept. A person's view and opinion of self; in young children, the concept of self develops as they interact with the environment (objects, people, etc.); self-concept can be inferred in how children carry themselves, approach situations, use expressive materials such as art, etc.

Self-Correcting. Materials or experiences that are built or arranged so that the person using them can act automatically to correct errors, without needing another person to check or point out mistakes.

Self-Esteem. The value we place upon ourselves; how much we like or dislike who we are; self-respect.

Self-Help. The act of helping or providing for oneself without dependence upon others; in early childhood terms, activities that a child can do alone, without adult assistance.

Self-Regulation. The term used to describe a child's capacity to plan and guide he self. A disposition or part of the personality (rather than a skill or behavior like self-control), self-regulation is a way of monitoring one's own activity flexible over changing circumstances.

Sensorimotor. Relating to or functioning in both sensory and motor aspects of body activity.

Sensory. Having to do with the senses or sensation, as in an awareness of the world as it looks, sounds, feels, smells, tastes.

Separation Process. The act and procedure that occurs when parents leave a child at school.

Sequential Learning. Learning based on a method of consecutive steps; an arrangement of concepts or ideas in a succession of related steps so that what is learned results in continuous development.

Seriation. The process of sequencing from beginning to end or in a particular series or succession.

Sexist. Attitudes or behavior based on the traditional stereotype of sexual roles that includes a devaluation or discrimination based on a person's sex.

Sex-Role Stereotyping. A standardized mental picture or set of attitudes that represents an oversimplified opinion of people's abilities or behavior according to their sex; overgeneralizing a person's skills or behavior based upon an inequitable standard of sex differences.

Shadow Study. A modified child study technique that profiles an individual at a given moment in time; similar to diary description, the shadow study is a narrative recorded as the behavior happens.

Social Cognition. The application of thinking to personal and social behavior; giving meaning to social experience.

Socialization. The process of learning the skills, appropriate behaviors, and expectations of being part of a group, particularly society at large.

Social Knowledge. One of three types of knowledge in Piagetian theory; that knowledge that is learned about and from people, such as family and ethnic culture, group behavior, social mores, etc.

Social Learning. Any acquired skills or knowledge having to do with interacting with others; in Bandura's theory, social learning happens when children watch other people directly, or in books and film.

Social Mores. Standards of conduct and behavior that are determined by society, as opposed to those established by family or personal preference.

Social Referencing. The process used to gauge one's own response to a situation by relying on another person's emotional reaction, such as a child who looks to a teacher after falling down before crying or getting up.

Social Skills. Strategies children learn to enable them to respond appropriately in many environments.

Sociocultural. Aspects of theory or development that refer to the social and cultural issues; key descriptor of Vygotsky's theory of development.

Spatial. Having to do with the nature of space, as in the awareness of the space around a person's body.

Special-Needs Children. Children whose development and/or behavior require help or intervention beyond the scope of the ordinary classroom or adult interactions.

Specific Development. Area of a person's growth and maturation that can be defined distinctly, such as physical, social, emotional, intellectual, and creative growth.

Specimen Description. A form of narrative observations technique which involves taking on-the-spot notes about a child (the "specimen") to describe behavior.

Spontaneous Play. The unplanned, self-selected activity in which a child freely participates.

Standardized Testing. Formal assessment techniques whose results have been tabulated for many children and thus have predetermined standards, or norms, for evaluating the child being tested.

Stewardship. Responsibility for judicious management of resources; the obligation assumed by an individual or agency to act responsibly in the use of both personal and natural resources.

Stimulus-Response. The kind of psychological learning, first characterized in behavior theory, that makes a connection between a response and a stimulus; that is, the kind of learning that takes place when pairing something that rouses or incites an activity with the activity itself in such a way that the stimulus (such as a bell) will trigger a response (such as salivating).

Stress. The physical and emotional reactions and behaviors that come from having to cope with difficult situations beyond one's capabilities.

Superhero. Those characters who embody a higher nature and powers beyond ordinary human abilities, as in "Superman," "Wonder Woman," etc.

Support System. A network of people who support each other in their work and advancement.

Surrogate. Substitute, such as a teacher acting in the place of the parent, a school toy taking the place of a blanket from home, a thumb taking the place of a pacifier.

Tabula Rasa. A mind not affected yet by experiences, sensations, and the like. In John Locke's theory, a child was born with this "clean slate" upon which all experiences were written.

Tactile. Perceptible or able to be learned through the sense of touch.

Teaching Objectives. A set of goals teachers set for themselves as they plan activities for children; these goals remind teachers what they will do in order to help children learn.

Temporal. Having to do with time and time sequence; in the early childhood setting, refers to scheduling and how time is sequenced and spent, both at home and in school.

Theory. A group of general principles, ideas, or proposed explanations for explaining some kind of phenomena; in this case, child development.

Time Sampling. A form of observational technique that involves observing certain behavior and settings within a prescribed time frame.

Traditional Nursery School. The core of early childhood educational theory and practice;

program designed for children aged two-and-one-half to five years of age, which may be part- or all-day programs.

Transcurricular. Able to be used or applied in a variety of situations or activities.

Transitions. Changes from one state or activity to another; in early childhood terms, transitions are those times of change in the daily schedule (whether planned or not), such as from being with a parent to being alone in school, from playing with one toy to choosing another, from being outside to inside, etc.

Unconscious. Not conscious, without awareness, occurring below the level of conscious thought.

Undifferentiated. The stage of children's friendships in which children do not distinguish between "friend" and "person I'm playing with," considered the first stage, usually from infancy into the preschool years.

Unilateral. The stafe of children's friendships in which children think of friendship as involving one side only; that is, a one-way situation in that a "friend" is "someone who does what I want to do," usually spanning the preschool years and into early primary.

Unobtrusive. Being inconspicuous, as in remaining in the background while observing children.

Upward Evaluation. Assessment procedure in which employees evaluate their superiors.

Vicariously. Experienced or realized through the imagination or the participation of another, rather than from doing it oneself, as in learning vicariously about something by listening to a story.

Volatile. Easily aroused; tending to erupt into violent action or explosive speech or behavior.

Webbing. A process through which teachers create a diagram based on a topic or theme. It is a planning tool for curriculum and includes as many resources as teachers can name.

Whole Language. The area of graphic language development that refers to a particular way in which language, particularly reading and writing, is learned; whole language refers to that movement within primary education that emphasizes an integrated and literary-based approach rather than a phonics, decoding-skills approach.

Word Pictures. Descriptions of children that depict, in words, norms of development; in this text, these are age-level charts that describe common behaviors and characteristics, particularly those that have implications for teaching children (in groups, for curriculum planning, with discipline and guidance).

Zone of Proximal Development. The term in Vygotsky's sociocultural theory that defines which children can learn. Interpersonal and dynamic, the zone refers to the area a child can master (skill, information, etc.) with the assistance of another skilled person; below that, children can learn on their own; above the limit are areas beyond the child's capacity to learn, even with help.

Index

SUBJECT INDEX